Proverbs

BAKER COMMENTARY *on the* OLD TESTAMENT

WISDOM AND PSALMS

Tremper Longman III, EDITOR

Volumes now available

Proverbs, Tremper Longman III
Song of Songs, Richard S. Hess

Proverbs

Tremper Longman III

Baker Academic
Grand Rapids, Michigan

Published by Baker Academic
a division of Baker Publishing Group
P.O. Box 6287, Grand Rapids, MI 49516-6287
www.bakeracademic.com

Printed in the United States of America

Library of Congress Cataloging-in-Publication Data
Longman, Tremper.
    Proverbs / Tremper Longman III.
      p.   cm. — (Baker commentary on the Old Testament wisdom and Psalms)
    Includes bibliographical references and index.
    ISBN 10: 0-8010-2692-X (cloth)
    ISBN 978-0-8010-2692-8 (cloth)
    1. Bible. O.T. Proverbs—Commentaries. I. Title. II. Series.
  BS1465.53.L66 2006
  223'.7077—dc22   2005035242

To Gabrielle Gagnon Longman,
born to Tremper and Jill Longman
on March 17, 2005

Grandchildren are the crown of the elderly,
and the glory of children is their parents.
Proverbs 17:6

Contents

Series Preface

At the end of the book of Ecclesiastes, a wise father warns his son concerning the multiplication of books: "Furthermore, of these, my son, be warned. There is no end to the making of many books!" (12:12). The Targum to this biblical book characteristically expands the thought and takes it in a different, even contradictory, direction: "My son, take care to make many books of wisdom without end."

When applied to commentaries, both statements are true. The past twenty years have seen a significant increase in the number of commentaries available on each book of the Bible. On the other hand, for those interested in grappling seriously with the meaning of the text, such proliferation should be seen as a blessing rather than a curse. No single commentary can do it all. In the first place, commentaries reflect different theological and methodological perspectives. We can learn from others who have a different understanding of the origin and nature of the Bible, but we also want commentaries that share our fundamental beliefs about the biblical text. Second, commentaries are written with different audiences in mind. Some are addressed primarily to laypeople, others to clergy, and still others to fellow scholars. A third consideration, related to the previous two, is the subdisciplines the commentator chooses to draw from to shed light on the biblical text. The possibilities are numerous, including philology, textual criticism, genre/form criticism, redaction criticism, ancient Near Eastern background, literary conventions, and more. Finally, commentaries differ in how extensively they interact with secondary literature, that is, with what others have said about a given passage.

The Baker Commentary on the Old Testament Wisdom and Psalms has a definite audience in mind. We believe the primary users of commentaries are scholars, ministers, seminary students, and Bible study leaders. Of these groups, we have most in mind clergy and future clergy, namely, seminary students. We have tried to make the commentary accessible to nonscholars by putting most of the technical discussion and interaction with secondary literature in the footnotes. We do not mean to suggest that such information is unimportant. We simply concede that, given the present state of the church, it is the rare layperson who will read such technical material with interest and profit. We hope we are wrong in this assessment, and if we are not, that the future will see a reverse in this trend. A healthy church is a church that nourishes itself with constant attention to God's words in Scripture, in all their glorious detail.

Since not all commentaries are alike, what are the features that characterize this series? The message of the biblical book is the primary focus of each commentary, and the commentators have labored to expose God's message for his people in the book they discuss. This series also distinguishes itself by restricting its coverage to one major portion of the Hebrew Scriptures, namely, the Psalms and Wisdom books (Proverbs, Job, Ecclesiastes, and Song of Songs). These biblical books provide a distinctive contribution to the canon. Although we can no longer claim that they are neglected, their unique content makes them harder to fit into the development of redemptive history and requires more effort to hear their distinctive message.

The book of Psalms is the literary sanctuary. Like the physical sanctuary structures of the OT, it offers a textual holy place where humans share their joys and struggles with brutal honesty in God's presence. The book of Proverbs describes wisdom, which on one level is skill for living, the ability to navigate life's actual and potential pitfalls; but on another level, this wisdom presents a pervasive and deeply theological message: "The fear of Yahweh is the beginning of knowledge" (Prov. 1:7). Proverbs also raises a disturbing issue: The sages often motivate wise behavior by linking it to reward, but in reality, bad things happen to good people; the wise are not always rewarded as they expect. This raises the question of the justice of God. Both Job and Ecclesiastes struggle with the apparent disconnect between God's justice and our actual life experiences. Finally, the Song of Songs is a passionate, sensuous love poem that reminds us that God is interested in more than just our brains and our spirits; he wants us to enjoy our bodies. It reminds us that we are not merely souls encased in bodies but whole persons made in God's image.

Limiting the series to the Psalms and Wisdom books has allowed us to tailor our work to the distinctive nature of this portion of the canon. With some few exceptions in Job and Ecclesiastes, for instance, the material in these biblical books is poetic and highly literary, and so the commentators have highlighted the significant poetic conventions employed in each book. After an introduction discussing important issues that affect the interpretation of the book (title, authorship, date, language, style, text, ancient Near Eastern background, genre, canonicity, theological message, connection to the New Testament, and structure), each commentary proceeds section-by-section through the biblical text. The authors provide their own translations, with explanatory notes when necessary, followed by a substantial interpretive section (titled "Interpretation") and concluding with a section titled "Theological Implications." In the interpretation section, the emphasis is on the meaning of the text in its original historical setting. In the theological implications section, connections with other parts of the canon, both OT and NT, are sketched out along with the continuing relevance of each passage for us today. The latter section is motivated by the recognition that, while it is important to understand the individual contribution and emphasis of each book, these books now find their places in a larger collection of writings, the canon as a whole, and it is within this broader context that the books must ultimately be interpreted.

No two commentators in this series see things in exactly the same way, though we all share similar convictions about the Bible as God's Word and the belief that it must be appreciated not only as ancient literature but also as God's Word for today. It is our hope and prayer that these volumes will inform readers and, more importantly, stimulate reflection on and passion for these valuable books.

One of the benefits of editing a commentary series is the opportunity to assign myself a particular book. Having already written commentaries on Ecclesiastes (NICOT; Eerdmans, 1998) and Song of Songs (NICOT; Eerdmans, 2001), I decided to tackle the book of Proverbs. It has been a joy to work and teach on Proverbs for the past five years. It is my hope and prayer that people, particularly those who teach and preach the book, will find this commentary helpful.

Tremper Longman III
Robert H. Gundry Professor of Biblical Studies
Westmont College

Author's Preface

The academy and the church (I can't speak for the synagogue) have discovered new significance and interest in the book of Proverbs. Long pushed to the side for being nontheological and even superficial, the book has found renewed use as a source for navigating life and for imparting advice about how to live life wisely. There is even a grudging acknowledgment of Proverbs' theological contribution.

My own appreciation for the book has grown immensely over the five years that I have worked on this volume. I have come to realize, for instance, that wisdom is more than a skill for living; it has profound theological significance. After all, it begins with the fear of God (1:7). Or to put it another way, wisdom involves making Woman Wisdom an integral, intimate part of our life (9:1–6). Indeed, the New Testament proclaims that Jesus is the epitome of God's wisdom and communicates this truth in many ways, including associating him with Woman Wisdom.

Even so, it continues to be true that the wisdom of Proverbs informs the reader about how to live, how to navigate the pitfalls of life, of which there are many. In this area, we will see that the contemporary discussion of emotional intelligence is relevant. Indeed, as we read the now vast literature about emotional intelligence, we note that the ancient book of Proverbs "got it" many centuries earlier.

I have also come to see that wisdom is both something one strives for through hard study and a gift from God. Wisdom comes from God, but also from the ancient Near East, and somehow these two truths do not undermine each other.

The study of the book of Proverbs is full of challenges. Perhaps the most interesting new challenge pertains to the structure of the book. As discussed in the introduction, the field is abuzz with talk of a newly discovered deep structure of the book, particularly the proverbs in chapters 10 and following. After much thought and reflection, however, I have concluded that the various schemes for describing the previously undetected groups of proverbs are misguided. Thus, one of the traits that differentiates this commentary from some of the other excellent recent contributions on Proverbs is the belief that the traditional view, that the proverbs are relatively randomly organized, is the correct one. This conclusion has led me to write a series of topical essays at the conclusion of the commentary proper. In these essays, I synthesize the teaching on some of the major topics of the book: wealth and poverty, speech, neighbors and friends, and business ethics, to name a few.

I have written this commentary for all readers: lay, professional, and scholarly audiences. But the group I had most in mind as I wrote was the second category. By "professional," I mean ministers and future ministers (seminarians). It is my hope that this commentary can help them as they prepare sermons and Bible studies on the book of Proverbs.

I wish to thank a number of colleagues and friends for their help in writing this commentary. I want to acknowledge their contribution while also freeing them from responsibility for my interpretive conclusions. Indeed, I know that at least some of them strongly disagree with some of the more controversial conclusions I have reached (such as the relationship between wisdom and law [and covenant], views of the afterlife in Proverbs, the christological reading of the book, and conclusions about structure). Even so, they each contributed greatly to the final form of the book. First, I wish to express my deep appreciation to John Goldingay, who served as conceptual editor of this volume. He challenged me on a number of points and helped me greatly improve the commentary. I would also like to thank Jim Kinney of Baker Academic, who recruited me to edit the series and (indirectly, since I chose it myself) to write this volume. As many will testify, Jim has done a wonderful job at Baker Academic in shaping its publication agenda and encouraging a number of very helpful projects. I also wish to thank Wells Turner and his staff for their excellent work in bringing this book to press.

Over the course of the past few years, I have also benefited from teaching the book of Proverbs in intensive seminary classes at Westminster Theological Seminary in Philadelphia, Fuller Theological Seminary, Mars Hill Graduate School in Seattle, Canadian Theological Seminary in Calgary, and Reformed Theological Seminary in Washington, DC. While I cannot name all of my students, I thank them all.

Finally, I dedicate this book to the newest member of our family, Gabrielle Gagnon Longman. She is the first grandchild of my wife, Alice, and me, and the daughter of our son Tremper and his wife, Jill. Welcome to the family, Elle.

Tremper Longman III
Robert H. Gundry Professor of Biblical Studies
Westmont College

Abbreviations

Bibliographic and General

ANET	*Ancient Near Eastern Texts Relating to the Old Testament,* ed. J. B. Pritchard, 3rd ed. (Princeton: Princeton University Press, 1969)
b.	Babylonian Talmud
BHS	*Biblia Hebraica Stuttgartensia,* ed. K. Elliger and W. Rudolph (Stuttgart: Deutsche Bibelgesellschaft, 1967–77)
ca.	circa (about)
chap(s).	chapter(s)
COS	*The Context of Scripture,* ed. W. W. Hallo, 3 vols. (Leiden: Brill, 1997–2002)
CTA	*Corpus des tablettes en cunéiformes alphabétiques découvertes à Ras Shamra–Ugarit de 1929 à 1939,* ed. A. Herdner, 2 vols., Mission de Ras Shamra 10 (Paris: Imprimerie Nationale, Geuthner, 1963)
Eng./ET	English/English translation
ESV	English Standard Version
GKC	*Gesenius' Hebrew Grammar,* ed. and enl. E. Kautzsch, trans. A. E. Cowley, 2nd ed. (Oxford: Clarendon, 1910)
Heb.	Hebrew
Kethib	the word as written in the Hebrew text
lit.	literally
LXX	Septuagint
MT	Masoretic (Hebrew) Text
n(n).	note(s)
NAB	New American Bible
NASB	New American Standard Bible
NEB	New English Bible
NCV	New Century Version

NIDOTTE	*New International Dictionary of Old Testament Theology and Exegesis,* ed. W. VanGemeren, 5 vols. (Grand Rapids: Zondervan, 1997)
NIV	New International Version
NJB	New Jerusalem Bible
NJPS	New Jewish Publication Society Version
NLT	New Living Translation
NRSV	New Revised Standard Version
NT	New Testament
OT	Old Testament
Qere	the word to be read in the Hebrew text
REB	Revised English Bible
Sir.	Sirach
TNIV	Today's New International Version
v(v).	verse(s)
Waltke-O'Connor	Bruce K. Waltke and M. O'Connor, *An Introduction to Biblical Hebrew Syntax* (Winona Lake, IN: Eisenbrauns, 1990)

Old Testament

Gen.	Genesis		Song	Song of Songs
Exod.	Exodus		Isa.	Isaiah
Lev.	Leviticus		Jer.	Jeremiah
Num.	Numbers		Lam.	Lamentations
Deut.	Deuteronomy		Ezek.	Ezekiel
Josh.	Joshua		Dan.	Daniel
Judg.	Judges		Hosea	Hosea
Ruth	Ruth		Joel	Joel
1–2 Sam.	1–2 Samuel		Amos	Amos
1–2 Kings	1–2 Kings		Obad.	Obadiah
1–2 Chron.	1–2 Chronicles		Jon.	Jonah
Ezra	Ezra		Mic.	Micah
Neh.	Nehemiah		Nah.	Nahum
Esther	Esther		Hab.	Habakkuk
Job	Job		Zeph.	Zephaniah
Ps(s).	Psalm(s)		Hag.	Haggai
Prov.	Proverbs		Zech.	Zechariah
Eccles.	Ecclesiastes		Mal.	Malachi

New Testament

Matt.	Matthew	1–2 Thess.	1–2 Thessalonians
Mark	Mark	1–2 Tim.	1–2 Timothy
Luke	Luke	Titus	Titus
John	John	Philem.	Philemon
Acts	Acts	Heb.	Hebrews
Rom.	Romans	James	James
1–2 Cor.	1–2 Corinthians	1–2 Pet.	1–2 Peter
Gal.	Galatians	1–3 John	1–3 John
Eph.	Ephesians	Jude	Jude
Phil.	Philippians	Rev.	Revelation
Col.	Colossians		

Introduction

Title

English readers are familiar with the title "Proverbs" or "book of Proverbs." The title thus associates the book with its most pervasive genre, the proverb—short, pithy observations, admonitions, warnings, and prohibitions (particularly in chaps. 10–31; see "Genre" below). This name derives from the Latin Vulgate title, *Liber Proverbiorum*.

The Hebrew name of the book is *mišlê*, the first word, which is the construct plural form of *māšāl* and means "proverbs." In the Septuagint, the book is called *paroimiai*, the Greek word used to translate *māšāl* in the first verse. *Paroimiai* is close in meaning to *parabolē*, "parable," since both can stand for the Hebrew *māšāl*, both can be translated "proverb" or "parable," and both can refer to a wide variety of figurative language.[1] In sum, the title in Hebrew, Greek, and English tradition all point to the most distinctive genre of the book, the proverb.[2]

---

1. The word *paroimiai* is used in this sense in the Gospel of John, whereas the Synoptics use *parabolē*. See R. E. Brown, *The Gospel according to John*, Anchor Bible (Garden City, NY: Doubleday, 1966–70), 1:385–86.

2. G. Wilson states: "The *māšāl* seems to represent a more general category of wisdom saying than two other terms found in Proverbs 1:6: *ḥîdâ*, riddle; and *melîṣâ*, parable, figure, warning. In this most general sense, *māšāl* serves as an appropriate title for the book of Proverbs . . . although some think the title was shifted to its present position from the beginning of the proverbial collections in chapters 10–31" (*NIDOTTE* 2:1134–35).

Canonicity

In his definitive work on the canon of the OT, Roger Beckwith (*Old Testament Canon*) remarks that some rabbis stumbled over the apparent contradiction of Prov. 26:4–5:

> Don't answer fools according to their stupidity;
> otherwise you will become like them yourself.
> Answer fools according to their stupidity;
> otherwise they will become wise in their own eyes.

On the surface of it, these two verses seem to offer a blatant contradiction, and some rabbinical authorities[3] therefore concluded that, since God does not contradict himself, this book could not be the Word of God. As we will point out under "Genre," such a viewpoint represents a misunderstanding of the genre of proverb. In any case, these rabbis were in a minority. As Beckwith also points out, there is abundant attestation from Jewish (Pharisee and Essene) and Christian sources going back to the second century BC that the book was accepted as authoritative.[4]

Place in Canon

Those who use English versions of the Bible find the book of Proverbs after Psalms and before Ecclesiastes and Song of Songs. This follows the order in the Greek OT, which contains a more chronological order than the Hebrew Bible. It is likely that Proverbs, Ecclesiastes, and Song of Songs are listed together because of their common connection with Solomon.

In the Hebrew canon, Proverbs is contained in the third part of the Tanak: the Ketubim, or Writings. Proverbs is thus found in a different order of books. The Ketubim begin with Psalms, then continue with Job and then Proverbs.[5] Ruth and then the Song of Songs follow Proverbs. It is likely that Psalms precedes Job in the Ketubim so that massive and important book can introduce the third and final part of the Tanak. Job may then follow because of its ancient setting, to be followed by Proverbs.

3. Beckwith, *Old Testament Canon*, 284, cites the Talmud in *b. Šabbat* 30b.
4. As Beckwith says (ibid., 319), "The Book of Proverbs is certainly or probably treated as Scripture by Ecclesiasticus, 4 Maccabees, the Dead Sea Scrolls, Philo, the Epistle to the Romans, the Epistle of James, 1 Clement and Josephus." See also ibid., 72–76, 79–80, 98–99 (nn65, 67).
5. Though in some early manuscripts and Hebrew editions the order of Job and Proverbs is reversed. See Fox, *Proverbs 1–9*, 4.

After Proverbs come the Megillot, or Festival Scrolls, books that were important in connection with specific major Jewish celebrations: Ruth (Weeks), Song of Songs (Passover), Ecclesiastes (Tabernacles), Lamentations (the 9th of Ab), and Esther (Purim).[6] Even though the Megillot are a separate section within the Ketubim, we do well to note the sequence of Proverbs, Ruth, Song of Songs. Proverbs ends with a powerful poem on the virtuous woman (ʾēšet-ḥayîl), to be followed by Ruth, who is called a virtuous woman (Ruth 3:11). Song of Songs, which contains poems, most of which are sung by a woman, ends the sequence.

Finally, Proverbs, along with Psalms and Job, is distinct from the other books in the canon for having an accentual system that indicates the Masoretes regarded this book as poetical.[7]

Authorship and Date

As is typical with wisdom and prophetic books, Proverbs opens with a superscription, which functions something like a title page in a modern book:

The proverbs of Solomon, the son of David, king of Israel—

Standing at the head of the entire book, the superscription appears to lead to the conclusion that the book at least claims to have been produced if not authored by Solomon, the third king of Israel (ca. 970–930 BC).

Indeed, a strong tradition connects Solomon with wisdom and specifically with the proverb form. After all, the book of Kings credits Solomon with pursuing and receiving the gift of wisdom from God (1 Kings 3:1–15). Solomon's fame is associated with his great wisdom in 1 Kings 4:29–34, a wisdom that is described in an international context and includes the fact that "he composed three thousand proverbs, and his songs number a thousand and five" (4:32 NRSV). The verb that NRSV translates "composed" is actually simply "uttered" or "spoke" (from *dbr*). Further, the Kings tradition illustrates how Solomon used his wisdom in judging cases (3:16–28). It further shows how people from all over the world, like the Queen of Sheba (10:1–13), marveled at his wisdom.[8]

6. Webb, *Five Festal Garments*.
7. Kugel, *Idea of Biblical Poetry*, 114–15.
8. On the basis of this tradition, Brueggemann ("Social Significance of Solomon," 129) suggests that the reference to Solomon in the superscription of Proverbs "is not interested in historical concreteness, but in the memory that it was Solomon, for better or for worse, who opened Israel's way for such an intellectual enterprise."

Furthermore, Solomon's connection with wisdom is demonstrated by his mention in the superscriptions of Ecclesiastes and Song of Songs. Indeed, one rabbinic tradition offers a sequence for the writing of these three books during the life of Solomon. The *Midrash Rabbah* talks of Song of Songs, Proverbs, and Ecclesiastes as belonging to three phases of his life, with the explanation that "when a man is young he composes songs; when he grows older he makes sententious remarks; and when he becomes an old man he speaks of the vanity of things."

Though one's first impression might be to conclude that Solomon was the author of Proverbs, the situation is actually significantly more complex. In the first place, as we read on in Proverbs, we see that other sections of the book are marked by captions that seem to attribute authorship to people other than Solomon. For instance, 22:17 and 24:23 mention a group called simply "the wise"; 30:1 and 31:1 mention two unknown men named Agur and Lemuel respectively; 10:1 and 25:1 mention Solomon again, but the latter also ascribes some type of role to the "advisers of King Hezekiah of Judah."

As a second complicating factor in authorship, authors do not typically sit down and compose proverbs. Instead, proverbs often emerge in an oral context and eventually may find their way into a written collection like the book we know as Proverbs. What would it mean to say that Solomon composed proverbs?

A third item to keep in mind is the relationship between these biblical proverbs and those of the broader ancient Near East. As we will discuss (see "Ancient Near Eastern Background" below), a number of proverbs bear similarity to proverbs that we find in Egyptian and Aramaic collections, some of which clearly predate the Israelite book. Thus again, thinking of Solomon as original composer of the book is hard to sustain.

A fourth consideration weakens an argument based on the supposed Solomonic authorship of Ecclesiastes and Song of Songs. Close studies of those books suggest that Solomon's name there has a different purpose than establishing that Solomon authored these books as a whole.[9]

All of this leads us to ask what picture emerges from the data. Certainly, it seems reasonable and defensible to recognize Solomon's hand in the book, but it is also important to honor the other clear compositional indications. When we do so, we realize that the book of Proverbs is actually a collection or anthology that has the following form:

Preamble (1:1–7)

Extended Discourses on Wisdom (1:8–9:18)

---

9. See the position taken in Longman, *Ecclesiastes*, and idem, *Song of Songs*.

Solomonic Proverbs (10:1–22:16; 25:1–29:27)
Sayings of the Wise (22:17–24:34)
Sayings of Agur (30:1–33)
Sayings of King Lemuel (31:1–9)
Poem to the Virtuous Woman (31:10–31)

What does the text actually say about Solomon's contribution? Again, he is mentioned in superscriptions in 1:1; 10:1; and 25:1. The mention in 1:1 may simply serve the function of noting Solomon's foundational importance to the collection. It does not mean he wrote the whole book, nor does it necessitate the view that he was responsible for 1:2–9:18. If he were, then why would there be a Solomonic superscription at 10:1? Thus, the text explicitly connects Solomon to 10:1–22:16 and 25:1–29:27. For the latter collection, the book also ascribes a scribal and perhaps an editorial role to King Hezekiah's men.[10]

The other named composers/collectors are either not given personal names ("the words of the wise" [22:17; 24:23]) or have names that are otherwise unknown and are perhaps to be understood as non-Israelite (Agur [30:1] and Lemuel [31:1], the latter citing advice of his mother).

In conclusion, it seems likely that the composition of Proverbs, like the composition of the book of Psalms, took place over a long period of time before it finally came to a close and no more proverbs were added. Indeed, the considerably different structure of Septuagint Proverbs as well as a number of additions may indicate that this process continued even beyond the time that the Hebrew text tradition adopted by the Masoretes came to a close (see "Text" below).

Before concluding this discussion of authorship, we should introduce the fact of repeated proverbs throughout the book. Daniel Snell has catalogued the evidence for repeated verses according to the following categories (of which only represented examples will be placed in the brackets):[11]

1. Whole verses repeated with spelling variations (14:12/16:25; 18:8/26:22)
2. Whole verses repeated with one dissimilar word (6:10–11/24:33–34)

10. Indeed, early Jewish tradition may have ascribed authorship of the entire book to them on the basis of this verse: "Hezekiah and his company wrote the Proverbs" (b. Baba Batra 15a).

11. Snell, Twice-Told Proverbs, 34–59. Not all his categories are repeated here, but simply the four types where the verses are the most similar.

3. Whole verses repeated with two dissimilar words (10:1/15:20;
   11:1/20:23)
4. Whole verses repeated with three dissimilar words (10:2/11:4)

This evidence is best understood to indicate that proverbs were added over time. As in the Psalms (compare psalms like 14 and 53), similar and near similar psalms were perhaps added because different groups of psalms came into the collection at different times. While there would be a majority of new psalms in a new group, it may contain one or more that already existed in the collection. Even so, their presence may indicate something to us: the importance of such a theme. Repetition, resulting from whatever reason, leads to emphasis.

In any case, it does not seem possible to use this information to date when individual proverbs came into the collection. As a matter of fact, with the exception of saying that Solomon's role preceded Hezekiah's men's role (provided one takes the superscriptions seriously and also the historicity of the monarchy seriously), we cannot say anything with great confidence. However, in my view that is of no major importance; what is of interest is the final product and how the proverbs function in their present context.

In summary, we cannot say much about the identities and dates of the individual composers and editors of the book.[12] However, can we say anything about the social location of the proverbs? Are they from the upper levels of society or the lower? Are the proverbs derived from the court, the farm, the school, the temple, or some other place within ancient Israelite society?

Social Setting

The issue of the social setting of the composition and reading of Proverbs became particularly interesting after scholarship concluded that Solomon was not the sole author. However, even if Solomon is the foundational figure associated with the composition of the book, this does not settle the issue of the origin of proverbs. By their nature, proverbs are not only authored; they are also collected. Another way to approach the question of authorship is to ask whether the book of Proverbs betrays a connection with a specific sector of Israelite society.

There have been a number of different answers to this question. In his seminal *Wisdom in Israel*, von Rad argues that the proverbs in the

12. According to Snell, "Scholars generally agree that there are few indications of the absolute dates when the composers and editors worked" (*Twice-Told Proverbs*, 74).

book of Proverbs were produced by scribes employed in the service of the court. A number of lines of evidence may be used to support his idea. In the first place, the text's tradition of association with both Solomon and the "men of Hezekiah" presumes a relationship with the court. Second, it has often been argued that the analogy between the biblical books and ancient Near Eastern texts like Amenemope show a connection between the genre and the court, though Amenemope himself was a lower-level bureaucrat.

In recent days, the question of the court origin of the wisdom of Proverbs has been tied up with the issue of the existence of scribal schools that might have fed its graduates into the royal bureaucracy. It is true that the first mention of a school in Israelite literature is found in Sir. 51:23 (the *bêt hammidrāsh*) in the early intertestamental period. Of course, the first extant reference to a school does not decide the issue, but it does mean that arguments in favor of formal education in Israel become purely inferential.

One of the leading advocates for the position of the schools' existence, A. Lemaire,[13] focuses on archaeological evidence in favor of schools. He notes the discovery of a handful of extrabiblical inscriptions that look as though they come from a school setting. Tablets that contain lists of the alphabet provide a good example. However, as other scholars have pointed out,[14] while this supports the idea of literacy, it does not support the existence of schools in the biblical period. In the final analysis we need to remain agnostic about the question. While the idea may be strongly suppported by the fact that Egypt, Mesopotamia, and even Canaan provide evidence of such schools, we have nothing like a smoking gun that will prove their existence. After all, the explicit comments about education in the OT (Deut. 4:10; 5:31; 11:19) as well as the dynamics of Prov. 1–9 suggest that learning came about when a father instructed his son in a family setting.

One interesting new approach to the question has been provided by Westermann and Golka,[15] who look at modern societies that are arguably close to that of ancient Israel. In particular, they examine the use of proverbs in tribal Africa. The similarities lead them to support the idea that the biblical proverbs, at least those in chaps. 10–31, are the product of a society of small Israelite farmers.

However, close analysis of the proverbs themselves makes one wonder whether it is best to imagine multiple backgrounds to the proverbs, even those that may have been collected rather than composed by Solomon.

---

13. Lemaire, "Sage in School and Temple," 165–83. For an excellent survey of different opinions and a reasoned conclusion, see Crenshaw, "Sage in Proverbs," 205–16.

14. Golka, "Israelitische Weisheitsschule."

15. Westermann, *Wurzeln der Weisheit*; Golka, *Leopard's Spots*.

The content of some proverbs clearly makes one think that they come from a court setting. While it is true that many proverbs mentioning a king may still be relevant for those who stand some distance from the court, others, like 23:1–3, have direct relevance for someone who serves in the presence of the king:

> When you sit down to dine with a ruler,
>> carefully consider what is in front of you.
> Place a knife at your gullet
>> to control your appetite.
> Don't long for his delicacies,
>> for they are false food.

This proverb would only be directly relevant to someone who served in the court, even though one might think of applications of the principle to other situations where there is a power imbalance.

On the other hand, there are individual proverbs that are a world apart from the court and seem more at home in the type of social context that Whybray envisions. An example would be 10:5:

> An insightful son harvests in the summer;
>> a disgraceful son sleeps during harvest.

In conclusion, it seems unlikely that we can dogmatically assert a single social setting for the proverbs. The book seems to collect wise sayings from many different settings.

Text

The main issue surrounding the text of Proverbs becomes clear when the Hebrew Masoretic tradition is compared with the Greek Septuagint. The latter has been dated to 200 BC.[16] For the former we use the Leningrad Codex found in *BHS*, which has been dated to around AD 1000. Relative dating is not determinative of the quality of these texts as representations of the original.

The most noticeable indication of a problem may be seen in the structure of these two versions of Proverbs. The order of the Septuagint matches that of the Masoretic Hebrew text up through 24:22. After that the arrangement diverges in the following way:

16. Cook, "Dating of Septuagint Proverbs."

Masoretic Hebrew text	Septuagint
24:23–34 (Further Sayings of the Wise)	30:1–14 (Agur)
25:1–29:27 (Hezekiah's Men)	24:23–34 (Further Sayings of the Wise)
30:1–14 (Agur)	30:15–33 (Numerical Parallelisms)
30:15–33 (Numerical Parallelisms)	31:1–9 (Lemuel's Mother)
31:1–9 (Lemuel's Mother)	25:1–29:27 (Hezekiah's Men)
31:10–31 (Poem to the Noble Wife)	31:10–31 (Poem to the Noble Wife)

Besides a difference in order of passages in the last part of Proverbs, there are also a number of texts that we find in the Masoretic Text that are not found in the Greek (4:7; 8:33; 16:1, 3; 20:14–22) as well as many additions in the Greek text that are not in the Masoretic Text.[17]

Thus, there is a difference between the two, and the questions are, Why? What is the significance of the difference? The issue has been debated at least since the important work of P. A. de Lagarde in 1863.[18] Even today, a century and a half later, no consensus has emerged among the experts.[19] Tov, for instance, has argued that the Septuagint and Leningradensis represent two different editions of the book. However, after review, the most persuasive hypothesis based on the textual evidence is articulated by Waltke, who suggests, following Barr, that the differences between the MT and the Greek may be explained in large part by the fact that the latter is a very free translation that is heavily influenced by Stoic philosophy and Jewish midrashic thinking.[20] Such a conclusion reduces the value of the Greek as a textual witness to the original text. Even so, as the commentary will argue, there are individual verses in which the Septuagint does offer help to recover the original.

The other versions (Syriac, Vulgate, Targum) are of no additional help since they reflect either the MT or the Septuagint. The Dead Sea materials only included a minimal witness to the book of Proverbs.

Genre

Proverbs is one of a number of books known in the English tradition by a genre label (Chronicles, Psalms, Song of Songs, Lamentations, Acts,

17. See E. Tov, *Textual Criticism of the Old Testament* (Minneapolis: Fortress; Assen: Van Gorcum, 1992), 337; and idem, "Recensional Differences."

18. For an outline of the debate, see Whybray, *Book of Proverbs: A Survey*, 161–64.

19. Compare the work and conclusions of Tov (*Textual Criticism*; "Recensional Differences") with Cook, *Septuagint of Proverbs*; McKane, *Proverbs*, 33–47; and Waltke, *Proverbs*, 1:6–9.

20. Waltke, "How We Got the Hebrew Bible," 34–35. Barr, "BʾRṢ-MOLIS"; Gerleman, "Septuagint Proverbs."

Revelation). The name comes from the superscription that begins "the proverbs of Solomon" (1:1). In Hebrew, the word "proverbs" comes from the singular *māšāl* and is in the construct plural (*mišlê*).

Unfortunately, one does not get very far trying to define the genre through etymology or even through a study of the word itself since its semantic field seems rather broad. In 1:6, the term is parallel with "words of the wise," so perhaps the word *māšāl* simply refers to the fact that this literary vehicle is part of the wisdom teacher's pedagogical repertoire. The Greek equivalents are *paroimiai* and *parabolē*, which support this idea and also point to the fact that the underlying verb may be *māšal I* ("to be like"), implying a comparison or teaching by metaphor, rather than *māšal II*, a verb translated "to rule" or "to dominate." It is possible but not likely that the noun "proverb" plays on both words. If so, it would point to the fact that the proverb intends to draw comparisons so the recipient can stay in control of a situation.

But again, we are not interested in defining the genre by the etymology of its label. That would be like trying to understand the nature of an apocalyptic book, say Revelation, by the meaning of the Greek word *apokalypsis*, which broadly means "revelation."

As we look at the contents of Proverbs, we see more than one type of genre in the book. For instance, we immediately sense a difference between chaps. 1–9 and 10–31. The former is made up of discourses or speeches, while the latter are closer to what we call proverbs in English. The discourses are extended speeches from the father or Woman Wisdom to the son or sons, or perhaps in the case of Woman Wisdom to all the young men who are going by.

Fox has correctly described the components of the discourse as consisting of an exordium, a lesson, and a conclusion, though there is considerable variety in the amount of space devoted to these three elements. The exordium includes a call for the recipient to pay attention, which is accompanied by motivation to do so. The lesson is the object of teaching, and the conclusion brings the teaching to a close, sometimes by describing the consequences of listening or not listening to the lesson.[21]

Proverbs 2 is an example of a discourse that has a major emphasis on the exordium, which essentially takes up the first half of the chapter. It invokes the son ("my son," v. 1), calling on the son to pay attention. Motivations are given, notably the fact that if the son seeks wisdom, God will grant it to him. The lesson includes avoiding evil women and men (vv. 12–19), and the conclusion is stated in the last three verses (20–22).

---

21. Fox, *Proverbs 1–9*, 45–46.

In English, we typically reserve the word "proverb" to refer to the type of literature that we find in chaps. 10–31. We will describe the proverb in the light of a specific example, namely, 10:4:

A slack hand makes poverty;	ro'š 'ōśeh kap-remîyâ
a determined hand makes rich.	wĕyad ḥārûṣîm ta'ăśîr

This proverb is chosen not because it is a particularly impressive proverb, but because it is fairly typical. In the first place, note that a proverb is a brief, pointed statement. Proverbs express ideas commonly accepted as true. They do not argue for the truth of the statement or nuance it. Proverbs can state an insight, make an observation, or offer advice in the form of an admonition or prohibition. This particular proverb is an observation. Even an observation, however, can imply advice. The fact that it is hard work and not laziness that makes a person rich intends to motivate a person to get to work.

Another feature of a proverb is that it does not teach a universally valid truth. On the contrary, proverbs are true only if stated at the right time and in the right circumstance. A number of proverbs make this explicit. For one thing, a number of proverbs urge that a person must say the right thing at the right time.

> It is a joy to a person to give an answer!
> How good a word at the right time! (15:23)

This implies that the same word spoken at a different time is not good. For instance, take a cheerful greeting, which one might expect to be a good thing at all times. According to the sages, however,

> Those who bless their neighbors with a loud voice in the early
> morning—
> it will be considered a curse to them. (27:14)

Proverbs 26:4–5 is indicative of the circumstantial nature of the proverb:

> Don't answer fools according to their stupidity;
> otherwise you will become like them yourself.
> Answer fools according to their stupidity;
> otherwise they will become wise in their own eyes.

Which is it? It depends on the circumstance. One must not only know the proverbs but also be able to read the people and the circumstance to know which applies. Proverbs otherwise are useless or even dangerous:

> The legs of a lame person dangle,
> > and a proverb in the mouth of fools. (26:7)

> A thornbush in the hand of a drunk,
> > and a proverb in the mouth of fools. (26:9)

The ability to read the circumstances and people around them is crucial for the wisdom task. After all, God made everything "appropriate for its time" (see Eccles. 3:1–15).[22]

Turning our attention again to 10:4, we can easily name exceptions to the "truth" of this proverb if it is taken as a universally valid proposition. What about someone who inherits a fortune? We could name some contemporary sluggards who are fantastically wealthy. Does this disprove the proverb? Of course not. Generally speaking, for most people it is true.

The time-sensitive nature of proverbs is not unique to Hebrew wisdom; it is inherent in the proverb form. "Haste makes waste" and "the early bird catches the worm" are both true, if applied at the right time. "Too many cooks spoil the broth" is right when a person wants to cook a meal without interference, but "many hands make light work" is appropriate when it is time to do the dishes. If spoken at the right time, the proverb is unarguable. One just has to accept or reject it. Otherwise, it falls flat and can easily be ignored.

Another aspect of the time-sensitive nature of the proverb is often missed but can be illustrated by 10:1:

> A wise son makes a father glad,
> > and a foolish son is the sorrow of his mother.

This seems like a simple observation, but is it? Is it always true that a happy father indicates a wise son? What if the father is a godless abuser who takes pleasure in physically harming his children? Is this proverb a mandate not to resist his blows? Surely not. The proverb presupposes a godly parent. The reason the father is happy is that this father is godly and his joy is evoked by the godly behavior of his son.

The point is clear. The conditions for the truth of the proverb must be explored before or as it is being applied.

While all this is true and very important in the proper understanding of proverbs, we must admit that certain proverbs are always true. For instance, 11:1 states:

22. It was one of the great frustrations of Qoheleth that though he knew God made everything appropriate for its time, he could not read the time. See Longman, *Ecclesiastes*.

> Fraudulent scales are an abomination to Yahweh,
> but an accurate weight brings his favor.

If there are exceptions to this proverb, they are so rare as to be unimportant.

Another common misconception about proverbs has to do with the connection between wise behavior and reward and foolish behavior and punishment. For this aspect of the proverb, please consult the discussion under "Retribution," below. There we argue that proverbs are not promises or guarantees, but rather the rewards and punishments are (dis)incentives of certain types of behavior. The proverbs direct one toward that behavior most likely to produce beneficial results—all things being equal. Thus, it is true that a man is much less likely to get into trouble with a jealous husband if he doesn't sleep with the man's wife. However, the fact that Joseph got in trouble with Potiphar (Gen. 39) does not disprove the teaching of the book of Proverbs on the matter.[23]

Literary Style

The book of Proverbs is made up of both discourses and proverbs proper. While the former is a longer type of speech, they are both forms of poetry. Thus, to read Proverbs well, one must understand how to read poetry.

Poetry is compressed language, saying a lot with just a few words. The obvious implication of this characteristic is that poetry is to be read reflectively and not quickly. Also, poetry is inherently more ambiguous than prose, though what it lacks in precision of communication it makes up for by its vividness and its appeal to the whole person—emotions, imagination, will, and intellect. Of course, this distinction between prose and poetry is not one of kind as much as degree, especially in the Bible, where the prose is highly literary.

Poetry has three major characteristics: terseness, parallelism, and intense use of imagery. There are also a number of what might be called secondary poetical devices.[24]

Terseness

Terseness refers to the economic use of words characteristic of poetry. One notices this even in English translations of Proverbs—there is a lot

23. See Waltke, "Does Proverbs Promise Too Much?"
24. For the best presentation of biblical poetry available, consult Watson, *Classical Hebrew Poetry*.

more white space on the page than in a prose book like Genesis. Economy of words is brought about by the use of ellipsis (allowing a verb or noun in the first line to do double duty by being implied but unexpressed in the second line) and a sparing use of conjunctions. The second colon (a poetic phrase, typically in parallel with another phrase) of a poetic line is almost always shorter than the first.

Proverbs is well described as terse when compared with prose. It is composed of cola in parallel lines, not sentences in paragraphs. However, compared with other poetry, it is wordy. Proverbs 31:11 will be our example:

| Her husband entrusts his heart to her, | *bāṭaḥ bāh lēb baʿlāh* |
| and he does not lack plunder. | *wĕšālāl lōʾ yeḥsār* |

We can see how the Hebrew is terser than its English translation. Typically, English translations of Hebrew poetry will have more words than the original. The second colon is shorter than the first, even though in this case there is a conjunction, a simple *wāw* that connects the two cola. The brevity of the second colon is achieved by the subject "her husband" (*baʿlāh*) being understood and not stated in the second colon.

Parallelism

Parallelism refers to the correspondence that occurs between the phrases of a poetic line. We can hear the echo in a proverb like 16:13:

> Righteous lips draw the favor of kings;
> they love those who speak with virtue.

"Draw the favor" parallels "love"; "righteous lips" echoes "speak with virtue." The relationship is not strictly synonymous (A = B); rather, the second colon always intensifies or seconds the first.[25] Righteous lips are more specifically defined in the second colon as virtuous speech.

If we refer back to 31:11, the relationship of the two parallel cola is not highly synonymous, but we can observe that that relationship should be described as "A, and what's more, B" rather than "A = B." In other words, the second colon flows from the truth of the first colon. Because her husband trusts her, she can go out into the world and gain a profit for the benefit of her family.

25. The language comes from the groundbreaking work of Kugel, *Idea of Biblical Poetry*.

We should point out three special features of parallelism in Proverbs. There is a high frequency of antithetic parallelisms, better-than parallelisms, and number parallelisms.

Antithetical parallelisms use antonyms rather than synonyms in conjoint cola and look at the same truth from opposite perspectives.

> A wise son makes a father glad,
> and a foolish son is the sorrow of his mother. (10:1)

Antithetical proverbs are frequent in Proverbs because the book delineates two major categories, that of wisdom and that of folly.

One qualification of this idea is exposed by the presence of better-than proverbs like 19:1:

> Better to be poor and walking in innocence
> than have crooked lips and be a fool.

Better-than proverbs state relative values. Other proverbs indicate that there is nothing wrong with wealth, and it may indeed be a sign of Yahweh's blessing (10:22), but a better-than proverb recognizes that some people will have to make a choice between wealth and moral rectitude.

Third, Proverbs contains numerical proverbs. This follows an X + 1 pattern, as seen in 30:18–19:

> Three things are too wonderful for me,
> and four things I cannot figure out.
> The way of an eagle in the sky,
> the way of a snake on a rock,
> the way of a ship in the heart of the sea,
> and the way of a man with a young woman.

Such a device is a way of saying that there are a number of different examples of a given phenomenon, only a few of which are mentioned. (The phenomenon here is the mysterious movement that leaves no trace, the fourth example being an allusion to sexual intercourse.) In Proverbs, the list that follows the introduction usually has the same number of elements as the second, larger number.

Imagery

Poetry is rich in images, and Proverbs is no exception to this rule. As we will see in the description of the theology of Proverbs, "the path," which stands for one's life journey, is central particularly but not exclusively to the first nine chapters. Furthermore, the figures of Woman Wisdom and Woman Folly loom large in the critical chap. 9 of the book.

There are also more local images used, such as is found in 16:24:

> Pleasant words are liquid honey,
>> sweet to the taste and healing to the bones.

The proper interpretation of these images is to unpack them. How are pleasant words like liquid honey? This type of question will occupy us in the commentary proper.

Secondary Poetical Devices

Terseness, parallelism, and imagery are pervasive through the book of Proverbs, but we also will observe the use of other occasional poetic devices. Two examples will suffice here; others will be pointed out in the commentary.

Proverbs 31:10–31 is a poem to the noble woman. Its twenty-two verses each begin with a consecutive letter of the Hebrew alphabet. The sense of the whole, accordingly, is that we have the A to Z of the noble woman.

We will also encounter sound plays such as that found in 30:20:

This is the way of the adulterous woman:	*kēn derek ʾiššâ měnāʾāpet*
she eats and wipes her mouth,	*ʾokělâ ûmāḥătâ pîhā*
and she says, "I have done nothing wrong!"	*wěʾāmĕrâ lōʾ-pāʿaltî ʾowen*

The content of this verse focuses on the woman's mouth, and this message is underlined by the fact that a high proportion of the letters are labials, signifying sounds formed by the lips (particularly *m*'s and *p*'s).

The Structure of Proverbs

In one sense, the book of Proverbs provides its own outline by virtue of various rubrics that typically indicate authorship. The issues surrounding authorship have already been discussed above. There we observed that the following passages have superscriptions associating a section of the book with some figure:

> 1:1 Solomon, for the whole book
> 10:1 Solomon, for 10:1–22:16

22:17 the wise (see also 24:23), for 22:17–24:34
30:1 Agur, for 30:1–33
31:1 King Lemuel, for 31:1–9

Recognizing that 1:1 is a superscription for the entire book and that 1:2–7 is a preamble certainly added late in the process of collection to describe the purpose of the whole book, we find the following structure.

1:1	Superscription
1:2–7	Preamble (stating the purpose)
1:8–9:18	Extended discourses on wisdom
10:1–22:16; 25:1–29:27	Solomonic proverbs
22:17–24:34	Sayings of the wise
30:1–33	Sayings of Agur
31:1–9	Sayings of Lemuel
31:10–31	Poem to the virtuous woman

However, this is not the only way to view the structure of the book. In terms of literary form, we can clearly recognize a break between Prov. 9 and 10. In chaps. 1–9, the book contains extended discourses of two types. One type is when a father speaks to his son, and the other has Woman Wisdom publicly addressing the crowds of naive young men who are walking by her. Proverbs 10–31, for the most part, is composed of the short, pithy proverbs that give the book its name. Thus, we propose the following as a second way of understanding the structure. This structure will be relevant for our theological analysis of the book as given below.

I. Extended discourses (1:1–9:18)
1. The purpose of the book (1:1–7)
2. Avoid evil associations (1:8–19)
3. Don't resist Woman Wisdom (1:20–33)
4. The benefits of the way of wisdom (2:1–22)
5. Trust in Yahweh (3:1–12)
6. Praising wisdom (3:13–20)
7. The integrity of wisdom (3:21–35)
8. Embrace wisdom! (4:1–9)
9. Stay on the right path (4:10–19)
10. Guard your heart (4:20–27)
11. Avoid promiscuous women: Part I; love your wife (5:1–23)
12. Wisdom admonitions: Loans, laziness, lying, and other topics (6:1–19)
13. The danger of adultery (6:20–35)

14. Avoid promiscuous women: Part II (7:1–27)
15. Wisdom's autobiography (8:1–36)
16. The ultimate encounter: Wisdom or folly (9:1–6, 13–18)
17. Miscellaneous wisdom sayings (9:7–12)

II. Assorted Advice, Observations, and Warnings (10:1–31:31)

Recent work on Proverbs raises the issue of whether there is some order to the proverbs found in the latter part of the book. When one reads Prov. 10–31 for the first time, the impression is of a rather random collection of proverbs. Like the Psalms, the reader occasionally notices unannounced groupings. For instance, Prov. 15:33–16:9 contains a number of sayings that feature Yahweh, followed by sayings in 16:10–15 that feature the king; but on closer inspection even these appear unsystematic. Such occasional groupings appear indisputable.[26]

Nonetheless, the latter part of the twentieth century up to today has seen a growing consensus among interpreters that there is more here than meets the eye. The argument has been made that an intentional and subtle structure permeates large parts of 10–31. An early precursor to such a view is G. Boström's (1928),[27] but most of the studies that try to uncover deeper structures have appeared since 1980.

As illustrative of this trend, we review the recent book by K. M. Heim (2001).[28] Heim incorporates a number of other studies in his own understanding of the arrangement of proverbs. This includes earlier studies by Hermisson, Perry, Krispenz, Whybray, Meinhold, Murphy, Hildebrandt, Scoralik, and others.[29]

But we should not get the impression from this long list of names that there is much consensus here beyond the basic premise that there is some arrangement of proverbs hidden from casual reading. There are as many different nuances in the schemes suggested to unravel the

---

26. Whybray, "Yahweh-Sayings." See also the article by Goldingay ("Arrangement of Sayings in Proverbs 10–15"), which builds on Whybray by pointing out a clustering of ethical vocabulary in 10:1–11:3 that, he believes, establishes an ethical context for 10:1–22:16.

27. *Paronomasi i den äldre hebreiska maschallitteraturen.* He saw "paronomasia in aural links, such as alliteration, assonances, rhymes, etc. He was not interested in the arrangement of sayings, but nevertheless provided a list of catchword links from one saying to the next." So Heim, *Like Grapes of Gold*, 30.

28. Ibid. This critique of Heim stems from a paper I delivered as the Brownlee lecture at Claremont Graduate School in April 2002. Since that time, M. Fox has written an important review in *Hebrew Studies* 44 (2003): 267–72. My understanding and critique has been greatly enriched by his insights.

29. Hermisson, *Studien zur israelitischen Spruchweisheit*; Perry, *Structural Patterns in Proverbs 10:1–22:16*; Krispenz, *Spruchkompositionen im Buch Proverbia*; Whybray, *Composition of the Book of Proverbs*; Meinhold, *Sprüche*; Murphy, *Proverbs*; Hildebrandt, "Proverbial Pairs"; Scoralick, *Einzelspruch und Sammlung*.

mystery as there are scholars. Heim is aware of this but is not rattled or dissuaded from his search. Rather, he approvingly quotes Whybray's response to McKane's conclusion that individual proverbs have no broader context as follows: "McKane's assumption that individual proverbs have no context but occur in random order amounts to no more than an admission that modern scholars have so far not been able satisfactorily to discover what such a context, whether literary or theological, might be."[30] Heim gains further encouragement from the fact that his survey of recent commentaries discovering some form of arrangement shows that seven out of nine believe there is some form of structure relevant to interpretation.

Surveying these previous attempts, he sees that there are multiple strategies employed together to find editorial groupings: "chapter divisions, 'educational' sayings, paronomasia and catchwords, theological reinterpretations, proverbial pairs, and variant repetitions."[31] Heim says that none of these will quite do, at least individually. For instance, he shows how educational sayings appear only sporadically at the beginning of sections.[32] The use of repeated words as catchwords to form a unit is done, in his opinion, without controls. There is, after all, a rather basic wisdom vocabulary in Proverbs.

Heim ultimately argues for coherence between sayings through phonological, semantic, syntactic, and thematic repetition.[33] He believes that scholars looking for thematic or logical development within these short units have made a huge mistake. Once a unit is determined, he says, it is equally possible to read it from the beginning to the end, the end to the beginning, or from the middle outward. Nonetheless, the units do provide a context in which the proverbs should be read. The analogy that Heim invokes, associating proverbs within a unit, is from the title of his book, taken from Prov. 25:11: "The right word at the right time is [like] grapes of gold set in silver." In his own words, "The cluster forms an organic whole linked by means of small 'twiglets,' yet each grape can be consumed individually. Although the grapes contain juice from the same vine, each tastes slightly different. It doesn't matter in which sequence the grapes are consumed, but eating them together undoubtedly enhances the flavour and enriches the culinary experience."[34]

However, let me immediately register my concern about the criteria that he uses to divide these units. Unlike some before him, he gives up on the possibility of finding "boundary markers" that delineate clear

30. Whybray, *Composition*, 65.
31. Heim, *Like Grapes of Gold*, 63.
32. Ibid., 64.
33. Ibid., 106.
34. Ibid., 107.

units. Instead, he looks for repetitions of a variety of sorts, both sound and meaning, to associate a group of proverbs, and then he reads them in the light of each other. My problem is that the criteria of association are so broad and varied that different scholars will continue to come up with different units. Also, by his own admission there is no correlation between the various criteria of association or even any coherence of criteria within a proverbial unit. And once the unit is determined in this rather ad hoc way, there is of course no problem with doing a contextual reading. Creative minds can create subtle associations between proverbs in a cluster. The human mind, after all, can associate the most disparate facts.

What then are we to make of the organization and arrangement of the proverbs in chaps. 10–31? The best conclusion is that the proverbs are indeed arranged in a more or less random fashion, especially with regard to contents.[35] For example, proverbs on laziness and determination are scattered throughout the book (see "Appendix: Topical Studies"); there is no attempt to bring them all together.

A partial explanation for such randomness may be the result of the history of composition. Since, as Snell has pointed out, there are many near and completely identical proverbs in the book (see the discussion of his work under "Authorship and Date" above), it seems logical to think that proverbs were added over time either individually or in groups. In this way, the collection of proverbs is similar to that of psalms. The arrangement probably changed innumerable times before settling in its final form as we have it in the MT.

Further, the randomness of proverbial collection is also the case in most ancient Near Eastern wisdom collections. In Egyptian tradition, for instance, we get a clear arrangement along thematic lines only with the Papyrus Insinger, the copy we have being dated to the first century AD, though its composition may go back to Ptolemaic times (fourth to first centuries BC), still very late in comparison to biblical proverbs.

In fact, a systematic collection of proverbs may give the wrong impression. It would give the sense that life is systematic and that Proverbs was a "how-to" fix-it book. In other words, the random collection of Proverbs reflects the messiness of life. As McCreesh puts it, the lack of structure is "based on a refusal to see life as a neat system."[36] Of course, even this comment is pure speculation as to the conscious strategy of the redactors of the book.

35. In other words, I believe von Rad (*Wisdom in Israel*, 6) got it right when he said, "Basically each sentence, each didactic poem, stands on its own."
36. McCreesh, "Wisdom as Wife," 45.

Though I do not see a systematic structure to Proverbs, there is no doubt that proverbs of similar topic are occasionally grouped together. Proverbs 10:4–5 is a good illustration:

> A slack hand makes poverty;
> a determined hand makes rich.
> An insightful son harvests in the summer;
> a disgraceful son sleeps during harvest.

There is no question but that there is a relationship between the two verses. The first states a general principle, and the second is a specific illustration of laziness versus diligence. But the question is, What brought these together? Was it a conscious structuring device that permeates the book, as Heim and others have argued? In actuality, though, this type of clear connection between neighboring proverbs is relatively rare. The explanation may be nothing more complex than that one of the redactors at some point along the way saw a connection and placed them next to each other. In other words, one proverb acted like a magnet for the placement of the next. And this was done only occasionally, or so it appears from the end result of the process.

Even more importantly, and contra Heim, reading the proverb in context does not change our understanding of either proverb. It doesn't even enrich our understanding. And in the final analysis it appears that Heim is very concerned about the need for a context. According to W. Mieder, a proverb in a collection is dead.[37] After all, as Kirschenblatt-Gimblett[38] has pointed out, a proverb needs a context to make sense, and its original context is oral. Once placed in a literary context, if understood as isolated, then how would anyone know what it really means? Heim's view is that his "twiglet" model provides the answer.

In response, I would say that for the proverb to come alive again, it needs to be spoken orally in the right context.[39] What is the right context? That is for the wise person to sort out. In reference to the so-called contradictory 26:4–5, for instance, the wise need to determine what kind of fool they are speaking to. To make these proverbs live, one must read the fool. Understanding proverbs is not just a matter of memorization or a simple academic exercise; they must flow from a character formed by wisdom.

37. Mieder, "Essence of Literature Proverbs Study."
38. Kirschenblatt-Gimblett, "Toward a Theory of Proverb Meaning."
39. As Murphy states, "Although it has been said that a proverb in a collection is dead, presumably because the original proverb performance cannot be captured, this is not necessarily so. One can use imagination and be open to multiple applications of a saying. This is not difficult for a reader who is sensitive to the imagery and the succinctness employed in proverb-making" ("Can the Book of Proverbs Be a Player in 'Biblical Theology'?" 5).

The implication of my view of organization is that we should be suspicious of complex schemes to find under-the-surface arrangements. Instead, we should go back to interpreting the proverbs as randomly structured. Thus, for the most part, the commentary in Prov. 10–31 will proceed in a verse-by-verse manner. The theological and practical implications of the proverbs will be discussed in the appendix. There the proverbs will be grouped into their proper contexts and examined as clusters. In this I depart from other recent commentaries that I feel have imposed, rather than discovered, structuring devices on these chapters.[40]

Ancient Near Eastern Background

The Bible presents a view of faithful Israel at war with pagan religions. The worship of Baal, Asherah, and the other deities from Canaan, Mesopotamia, and Egypt exerted an unholy pull on the hearts of Israel's people and leaders alike. The question of the origins and development of Israel's monotheism has been raised with vigor in recent days,[41] but if there was henotheism (the belief that only one among many gods matter) or polytheism in Israel's past, it is only subtly detected in the present text. Most of the Bible is couched in the language of Yahweh versus the pagan gods. When most people think of the relationship between Israel's religion and the religions of the ancient Near East, one thinks of prophets like Elijah, Elisha, Jeremiah, or Isaiah. For these men there was no room for compromise, no appreciation for the opponent.

How surprising, then, when we come to wisdom literature and examine the thought of the sages. When Solomon's wisdom is praised, it is evaluated not in contrast to but in comparison to the wisdom of Egypt and other Near Eastern traditions:

> God gave Solomon very great wisdom, discernment, and breadth of understanding as vast as the sand on the seashore, so that Solomon's wisdom surpassed the wisdom of all the people of the east, and all the wisdom of Egypt. (1 Kings 4:29–30 NRSV)

Such a statement acknowledges the wisdom of the east and of Egypt. Solomon's wisdom is not of a completely different order. To praise something by saying it is better than something else is to appreciate the latter.

40. It is my understanding (through personal communication), however, that Michael Fox will dispute these recent attempts to find pervasive structure in his forthcoming commentary on Prov. 10–31 in the Anchor Bible commentary series.

41. Smith, *Early History of God*.

Indeed, as the following survey will hint at and the commentary proper will indicate, there clearly are connections between specific proverbs and other ancient Near Eastern proverb connections. In this section, we survey the texts from the broader Near East that provide a generic background to the book of Proverbs, and in the commentary we point to specific proverbs that may have been adapted from a non-Israelite background and brought into the collection.

Egyptian Instructions

As mentioned, even the Bible recognizes the wisdom of Egypt, and outside the Bible, no other ancient wisdom tradition has been so carefully studied. The primary genre of wisdom in Egypt had the native term *sbyꜣt* attached to it.[42] This word is often translated "instruction" or "teaching," though J. D. Ray suggests that "enlightenment" may be closer to its true meaning.[43] These texts appear as early as the Old Kingdom (2715–2170 BC) and down to the demotic period (seventh century BC and after). Indeed, it is one of the most popular genres in all Egyptian literature. Space will only allow us to mention the high points.

These instructions come from the upper echelons of Egyptian society (but see below for some exceptions) and in large part are composed of advice about how to get along in that society and perhaps even move upward. The form of the genre is a father who is instructing his son. In some examples the father is the king. The father is old and experienced, about to step down from his high position in society, and his son is just starting. These compositions begin with a prologue that introduces the speaker in particular as well as the addressee.

Instructions from the Old through the Middle Kingdoms: Hardjedef, Kagemni, Ptahhotep, and Merikare

Egyptologists judge that the writings of instructions began during the Old Kingdom period. Even though the earliest papyri come from

42. We should note that M. Lichtheim (*Maat in Egyptian Autobiographies*) has questioned the existence of wisdom literature in Egypt, based primarily on the lack of a word that can clearly be translated "wise/wisdom" before the Late Period. In our opinion, she bases too much on the linguistic argument. Even if she is right that there is not a word that can be translated "wise/wisdom," the concept is present. Also, she curiously divides wisdom ideas from morality and piety.

43. Ray, "Egyptian Wisdom Literature," 18. R. Williams ("Sages of Ancient Egypt," 7) reminds us that this Egyptian term is not identical with "wisdom tradition," since in Egyptian literature it is applied to a broader group of texts.

the Middle Kingdom period and the texts are often, but not always, judged as pseudonymous, the Instructions of Hardjedef, Kagemni, and Ptahhotep are thought to come from the Fifth and Sixth Dynasties of the Old Kingdom.[44]

Hardjedef is thought to be the oldest composition and has the simplest prologue. We cite it here because, in spite of its brevity, it has the basic elements of such an introduction:

> Beginning of the Instruction made by the Hereditary Prince, Count, King's Son, Hardjedef, for his son, his nursling, whose name is Au-ib-re. [He] says:[45]

This Hardjedef is known as the son of Cheops, the builder of the Great Pyramid. We have this text on nine ostraca from the New Kingdom and on an even later wooden tablet, but again, it is judged to be a product of the late Old Kingdom, though a pseudonymous work. The instructions that we have are fragmentary and brief and concern the establishment of a household and preparation for death.

We know Kagemni from the first two pages of the Papyrus Prisse, located in Paris at the Bibliotheque Nationale. In the text, an unspecified person, but presumably his father, addresses Kagemni. The composition dates itself to the reign of King Sneferu and adds that Kagemni was promoted to vizier based on the wisdom demonstrated in the text. In the text, Kagemni is instructed in proper behavior, even table manners, before the king.

The most important text for our purpose during this early period is Ptahhotep, also known to us from the Papyrus Prisse. Ptahhotep is said to be vizier under King Izezi of the Fifth Dynasty, but this text is often understood to be pseudonymous and from the Sixth Dynasty. Ptahhotep is much longer than the previous two instructions and begins with a lengthy prologue. Egyptologists inform us that this composition is composed in very difficult Egyptian, and so there is some variation between translations. The instructions themselves are divided into thirty-seven maxims and are followed by an epilogue. The maxims promote the ideal of a quiet, contented man of humility over against a heated, anxious, and striving man.

We possess an instruction from the time of transition between the First Intermediate Period and the Middle Kingdom, specifically from the Ninth or Tenth Dynasty, named after Merikare, the addressee of the instructions. One innovation here is that the speaker is a king, and thus

---

44. See the argument by Lichtheim, *Ancient Egyptian Literature*, 5–8.
45. Translations are from ibid., 58–59.

we have a royal testament. What is interesting about this text is that it is a royal instruction where the previous king lays out a political agenda for the next king.

New Kingdom and Later: Ani, Amenemope, Ankhsheshonqy, and Papyrus Insinger

Ani was a middle-level scribe in the court of Queen Nefertari, the wife of Ahmose, who along with his brother Kamose expelled the Hyksos from Egypt (Eighteenth Dynasty).[46] J. D. Ray summarizes the contents as "a collection of conventional themes: respect for motherhood and religion, avoidance of alien or unfaithful women, honesty in transactions (greatly emphasized), restraint in the face of aggression, and reticence before strangers."[47]

The Instruction of Amenemope requires special treatment because of the role it has played in the interpretation of the biblical book of Proverbs (for more, see below). E. W. Budge, the eminent Egyptologist, first discovered the main papyrus from which we know this composition in 1888, but it was not presented in translation until the same scholar did so in 1923.[48] The papyrus, now in the British Museum, has been most consistently dated to the tenth–sixth centuries BC.

The text is typical of Egyptian instructions in that it is the advice of a senior Egyptian bureaucrat, Amen-em-ope, described as the "Overseer of Grains,"[49] to his son, Hor-em-maa-kheru.[50] Similar to other instructions, the text has an introduction that gives not only lengthy descriptions of the speaker and a shorter one of his addressee but also a statement of purpose that includes "the teaching of life, the testimony for prosperity, all precepts for intercourse with elders, the rules for courtiers, to know how to return an answer to him who said it, and to direct a report to one who has sent him . . . , to rescue him from the mouth of the rabble, revered in the mouth of the people." Unique to Amenemope among the Egyptian instructions is its division of the advice section into thirty chapters.

46. The most recent edition of Ani is found in Quack, *Lehren des Ani* (1994). He dates the composition to the early Nineteenth Dynasty.

47. Ray, "Egyptian Wisdom Literature," 23.

48. Plates I–XIV in E. W. Budge, *Second Series of Facsimiles of Egyptian Hieratic Papyri in the British Museum* (London, 1923).

49. All translations of this text are from J. A. Wilson in *ANET* 421–25.

50. Nonetheless, H. C. Washington, *Wealth and Poverty in the Instruction of Amenemope and the Hebrew Proverbs* (Atlanta: Scholars Press, 1994), has recently argued that the advice given in this text is not only for the elite of society but for all of society. He persuasively argues that scribes were not as well off or elitist at this time as we might be led to believe.

The explicit setting and the advice all point to a court setting. Egyptologists have observed how this text signals a shift from previous instructions in that Amen-em-ope values more inward virtues and rewards than materialistic ones. It contrasts the "heated man" and his strivings with the humbler and more modest "silent man." We will later cite some of the more striking instructions when we compare this text with Proverbs.

Two instructions will serve as examples of the genre from late in Egyptian history. We begin with the Instruction of Ankhsheshonqy.[51] The text was first known from a very damaged papyrus discovered in 1896 and placed in the British Museum. It is written in Demotic, the late cursive form of Egyptian, and was originally dated to the first century BC. References that seem to come from this text, though, have been discovered in two papyri dated to the second century BC, and so the composition is now usually thought to be from the Ptolomaic period.

The text begins with a narrative frame that explains why Ankhsheshonqy is writing a wisdom text to his son. In a word, he is imprisoned in connection with an attempt on the pharaoh's life and so does not have the opportunity to teach his son personally. The story that led to his imprisonment is given in the prologue and goes as follows. Ankhsheshonqy, priest of the sun god, had traveled to visit an old friend, Harsiese, who had been appointed chief physician to the pharaoh. He wanted to ask his friend some advice, but when he arrived, he found him embroiled in a plot to do away with the king. The priest never joined the conspiracy, so he was spared a death sentence when the word got out, but he also knew about the plot and did not report it, thus the prison sentence.[52]

After the lengthy prologue comes a large number of proverbs and maxims. Indeed, the form of these maxims is something of an innovation in that they are brief prose sentences, making an observation or giving advice. While they are often grouped roughly by topic or form, they still have a random feel to them. However, some themes are emphasized more than others. Perhaps, given the prison setting of the advice, it is not surprising to find that one of the major themes is "the ubiquity of change and the vicissitudes that go with it, and the fact that actions have consequences."[53] The following is illustrative:[54]

> When a youth who has been taught thinks, thinking of wrong is what he does.

51. Sometimes spelled Onkhsheshonqy. The text may be found in Lichtheim, *Ancient Egyptian Literature*, 3:159–84. Translations are from this source.

52. Lichtheim (*Late Egyptian Wisdom Literature*) believes she recognizes some parallels with the Aramaic Ahiqar (see below).

53. Ray, "Egyptian Wisdom Literature," 26.

54. From Lichtheim, *Ancient Egyptian Literature*, 3:171.

. . . .
When a man smells of myrrh his wife is a cat before him.
When a man is suffering his wife is a lioness before him.
Do not be afraid to do that in which you are right.
Do not commit theft; you will be found out.
Do not let your son marry a woman from another town, lest he be taken
    from you. (15.9, 11–15)

We will look at one last Egyptian instruction, found on the lengthy
Papyrus Insinger. This text is named after the man who bought it for the
collection at the Rijksmuseum in Leiden in 1895. It is written in Demotic
and comes from the first century AD. The original composition probably
comes from an earlier time, but no earlier than the Ptolemaic period.
There are other fragments in Copenhagen and also other collections,
some of which have not yet been published. The first part of this text
is damaged, and what we have begins with proverbs and maxims. Like
Ankhsheshonqy, these texts are single-line prose sentences, but unlike
the earlier text, there is a definite thematic arrangement complete with
headings. An example is the beginning of the ninth instruction:

The Ninth Instruction: The teaching not to be a fool, so that one does
    not fail to receive you in the house.
Wrongdoing [occurs] to the heart of the fool through his love of women.
He does not think of the morrow for the sake of wronging the wife of
    another.
The fool who looks at a woman is like a fly on blood.

Furthermore, there is a close connection drawn between religion and
ethics. We can see this in the admonition, also found in the ninth instruction, to avoid an evil woman:

There is she whom I hold in contempt as an evil woman.
Fear her on account of the fear of Hathor.

Before leaving this survey of Egyptian instructions, we need to look
at a concept central to many of them, the idea of *Ma'at*. As a concept
Ma'at is important not only to the instructions but also to Egyptian
thought generally. *Ma'at* refers to the order and harmony of creation; its
associated ideas are truth and justice. A rupture in the harmony, truth,
and justice of the creation is an assault against *Ma'at*. *Ma'at* often is
presented and seems to be seen as an impersonal concept, but it also is
at times represented as a goddess. The following are excerpts from the
instructions that mention *Ma'at*.[55]

55. For more, see Lichtheim, *Maat in Egyptian Autobiographies*, as well as Assmann,
Ma'at.

47

If thou art a leader commanding the affairs of the multitude, seek out for thyself every beneficial deed, until it may be that thy (own) affairs are without wrong. Justice (*Ma'at*) is great, and its appropriateness is lasting; it has not been disturbed since the time of him who made it, (whereas) there is punishment for him who passes over its laws. It is the (right) path before him who knows nothing. Wrongdoing has never brought its undertaking into port. (It may be that) it is fraud that gains riches, (but) the strength of justice (*Ma'at*) is that it lasts, and a man may say: "It is the property of my father." (Ptahhotep 85–95 [*ANET* 412])

Do justice (*Ma'at*) whilst thou endurest upon earth. (Merikare 64 [*ANET* 415])

Ma'at determines what is right and wrong. The instruction genre as well as didactic literature generally seeks to inform a person how to live in conformity with *Ma'at*.

Sumerian Wisdom

Proverb Collections

Sumerian proverbs have been discussed for decades, but a real turning point came in 1959 with the publication of E. I. Gordon's translation of the proverb collections known at that time.[56] Just recently, this monumental work has been replaced by another written by B. Alster that brings the study up to date and publishes the twenty-eight extant proverb collections.[57] Alster shows how we now have examples of collections that extend as far back as the Early Dynastic III period (2600–2550 BC), and how they continued in use, being cited in the Sumerian language in Akkadian literature, even after Sumerian was no longer spoken. Most of the texts come from the Old Babylonian period. He also points out that some of these texts were translated into Akkadian, being found in Ashurbanipal's library in the seventh century (see mention of bilingual proverbs under "Akkadian Wisdom" below). These texts come from such Sumerian cites as Nippur and Ur (yielding by far the largest number) as well as Sippar, Susa, and Kish. Alster further provides evidence that these proverb collections were used as exercises in the scribal schools, and some bear marks of their school setting:

> A scribe who does not know Sumerian,
> what kind of scribe is he? (2.47)

56. Gordon, *Sumerian Proverbs*.
57. We cite the following proverbs from Alster, *Proverbs of Ancient Sumer*.

Alster summarizes the major topics of concern of the proverbs as "a woman's daily routine, family relationships, the good man, the liar, legal proceedings, Fate, the palace, the temple and their gods, a well as historical and ethnic allusions."

He also argues for a strong division between religion and a "secular" attitude toward life. He suggests that "these proverbs clearly testify to the contemporary existence of a completely secular attitude toward social behavior."[58] When we read some of the proverbs in an isolated fashion, we might develop the same idea:

> Something which has never occurred since time immemorial: Didn't the young girl fart in her husband's lap? (1.12)
>
> He who eats too much cannot sleep. (1.103)
>
> He didn't plow the field in the cold season.
> At the time of the harvest he applied his hand to carding. (2.20)
>
> A fox urinated into the sea.
> "All the sea is my urine," it said. (2.67)
>
> Those who live near the water look into the mountains.
> They don't look in their own direction. (2.149)

Nonetheless, it is hard to believe that the Sumerians would have kept their religion separate from their worldview and behavior standards as expressed by the proverbs. It is more likely that it was presupposed. It is true that these proverbs were almost certainly not thought to be revealed by the gods, but rather that through long observation they were getting in touch with the creation as their gods had ordered it. Occasionally, the gods are explicitly mentioned in a proverb, as in the following:

> A disorderly son, his mother should not have given birth to him. His god should not have created him. (1.157)

Instruction of Shuruppak

Besides lists of proverbs, Sumerian wisdom also attests an instruction similar to the Egyptian *sbȝt* described above, as well as to Prov. 1–9. This is the Instruction of Shuruppak, named after the father of the famous sage Ziusudra, who survived the flood. We know this text primarily through what Alster calls the "standard version," dated to 1900–1800

---

58. Ibid., xviii.

BC, but it is known from a version dated to the Early Dynastic period (specifically twenty-sixth century BC).[59] There are some later Akkadian translations of this Sumerian work.

The text contains the instructions of Shuruppak to Ziusudra his son, and it speaks to many of the subjects of wisdom instruction from other Near Eastern cultures, including Proverbs. Notably, there is material relating to sexual relationships:

> Do not laugh with a girl who is married; the slander is strong.
> My son, do not sit (alone) in a chamber with a woman who is married. (lines 33–34)

> Do not have sexual intercourse with your slave girl; she will name you with disrespect. (line 49)

> Do not buy a prostitute; she is the sharp edge of a sickle. (line 154)

Akkadian Wisdom

W. G. Lambert holds pride of place in the presentation and analysis of Akkadian wisdom texts.[60] While there are Akkadian proverbs, they are not as numerous as those in Sumerian. Indeed, it may be that the Sumerian proverbs served Akkadian speakers. Nonetheless, there are bilingual proverbs that are extant as well as a Babylonian/Akkadian composition entitled the Counsels of Wisdom, which has the form of a father giving advice to a son.[61] In addition, an Akkadian version of the Instructions of Shuruppak is also available. Lambert speculates that Akkadian literature did not preserve proverbs in abundance because the Kassites, who transmitted Akkadian literature in the mid–second millennium BC, did not respect literature with oral/popular roots.

Northwest Semitic Wisdom: Ahiqar

One of the most striking examples of a wisdom text written in Northwest Semitic is the Ahiqar text. The story was first known through the apocryphal book of Tobit as well as in Syriac, Armenian, Arabic, and other languages.[62] However, in the early part of the twentieth century,

59. See B. Alster, "Instructions of Shuruppak," in *COS* 1:569–70. Translations are from Alster.

60. Lambert, *Babylonian Wisdom Literature*.

61. See *ANET* 425–27. A more recent translation of the Counsels of Wisdom may be found in B. Foster, *Before the Muses*, 1:328–31.

62. Lindenberger, *Aramaic Proverbs*, 3–6.

an Aramaic version was recovered from Elephantine, Egypt.[63] The papyrus is from the fifth century BC but may well reflect a composition that was written soon after the text's setting, a hundred years earlier. The story is set in the sixth century during the reigns of the Assyrian kings Sennacherib (704–681 BC) and his son and successor Esarhaddon (680–669), both of whom Ahiqar is said to have served as a high-level counselor. However, there is no solid independent evidence of a historical Ahiqar, though there is a text from the Seleucid period (ca. 165 BC) that mentions a man whom the Aramaeans called Ahuqar, who was the *ummanu* (a scholar or sage), but we have no reason to accept this text as preserving an authentic historical memory.[64]

The state of the text is extremely fragmentary, and the best edition of the proverbs of the Aramaic version in English is that of Lindenberger.[65]

The following synopsis is in part based on the fragmentary Aramaic text, supplemented by the later versions.[66] Indeed, the Aramaic text preserves neither the beginning nor the end of the narrative, but only the middle. However, it does preserve a number of the proverbs and maxims that follow the narrative.

From the later versions, we learn that Ahiqar, who began his career as a counselor to Sennacherib, has no son, so he raises his nephew Nadin to be his successor. When Esarhaddon is on the throne, Nadin betrays his uncle, with the result that the king orders his officer Nabushumishkun to execute the older man. Fortunately for Ahiqar, he had earlier saved this officer's life, so he appeals to him for his life. Nabushumishkun kills a eunuch who is in his service and passes the body off as that of Ahiqar. Later, the Egyptians approach Esarhaddon to request an adviser for a large building project, and the king bemoans the fact that the brilliant Ahiqar is not available. Nabushumishkun chooses this moment as the right one to bring Ahiqar back to public attention. The king greets him warmly, and then Ahiqar beats Nadin for his traitorous activities.

This narrative is followed by a large number of wisdom sayings.[67] They are short and rather randomly organized. Examples similar to teachings found in Proverbs include these:

---

63. Parker ("Literatures of Canaan," 2400) suggests that the reason Ahiqar survived in Egypt was that Aramaic-speaking readers of the text took it with them when they migrated to Egypt. Papyrus can only survive in a very few areas, like Egypt.

64. Note the discussion of this text in Greenfield, "Wisdom of Ahiqar," 44.

65. *Aramaic Proverbs.*

66. This synopsis may be justified on the basis of general similarity between versions of the story; nevertheless, "it is now quite clear that there were different bodies of gnomic sayings attached to the figure of Ahiqar" (Greenfield, "Wisdom of Ahiqar," 50).

67. Indeed, Lindenberger lists over one hundred sayings. A translation of the extant Aramaic text by H. L. Ginsberg is in *ANET* 427–30. A more recent translation, but less

The son who is instructed and restrained, and on whose foot the bar is placed, [will prosper in life]. (saying 2)

Spare not your son from the rod; otherwise, can you save him [from wickedness]? (saying 3)

There are two things which are good,
and a third which is pleasing to Šamaš:
one who drinks wine and shares it,
one who masters wisdom [and observes it];
and one who hears a word but tells it not.
Now that is precious to Šamaš. (saying 12)

Proverbs in the Light of Ancient Near Eastern Wisdom

In the light of the above survey, we conclude that the book of Proverbs exists in the context of a widely attested genre of literature. In many ways, wisdom literature may be the most widely shared genre in the ancient Near East, as our opening quotation from 1 Kings 4 anticipated. Space does not permit a detailed comparison between the different literatures, but we conclude with some observations on relationships between the texts. As expected, we see similarities as well as differences, but studying Hebrew wisdom in the light of the broader ancient Near East gives us a much deeper understanding of Proverbs. In all traditions, wisdom is not abstract and philosophical, but rather practical, with the hope of getting on and getting ahead in life.[68]

Amenemope and Proverbs

We begin with a look at a comparison between a specific Egyptian instruction text and the book of Proverbs. We do this because it was really the publication of Amenemope that raised the issue of the relationship between biblical and ancient Near Eastern wisdom literature. In particular, it was noted that the Egyptian text had a special relationship with Prov. 22:17–24:22, the so-called sayings of the wise, as well as similarities with other parts of the biblical book.

Clear similarities include the following examples:[69]

accessible, is by Lindenberger, *Aramaic Proverbs*. The cited translations are from the latter's work.

68. Clifford, *Proverbs*, 8.

69. These examples (including the translation of Amenemope) are taken from the article by Ruffle, "Teaching of Amenemope."

Proverbs	Amenemope
Do not rob the poor because they are poor, or crush the afflicted at the gate. (22:22 NRSV)	Guard yourself from robbing the poor, from being violent to the weak. (4.4–5)
Do you see those who are skillful in their work? They will serve kings; they will not serve common people. (22:29 NRSV)	As for the scribe who is experienced in his office, He will find himself worthy to be a courtier. (17.16–17)
Do not wear yourself out to get rich; be wise enough to desist. When your eyes light upon it, it is gone; for suddenly it takes wings to itself, flying like an eagle toward heaven. (23:4–5 NRSV)	Do not strain to seek excess when your possessions are secure. If riches are brought to you by robbery, they will not stay the night in your possession. When the day dawns they are no longer in your house. Their place can be seen but they are no longer there. The earth opened its mouth to crush and swallow them and plunged them in dust. They make themselves a great hole, as large as they are. And sink themselves in the underworld. They make themselves wings like geese, And fly to heaven. (9.14–10.5)
Do not remove an ancient landmark or encroach on the fields of an orphan, for their redeemer is strong; he will plead their cause against you. (23:10–11 NRSV)	Do not remove the boundary stone on the boundaries of the cultivated land, nor throw down the boundary of the widow. (7.12)

These and other parallels have led to an intense debate over the origin of the wisdom reflected in both texts. Advocates of Egyptian priority,[70] Israelite priority,[71] and a third common source may be cited. One of the problems that make this a difficult question is the lack of certainty about when the various parts of Proverbs, or for that matter Amenemope, were written. The fact that Amenemope has thirty sayings and that a word with obvious textual problems in Prov. 22:20 can be relatively easily emended to mean "thirty" has led most modern translations (NRSV, NIV) to make that emendation with confidence.

However, as Ruffle and others have argued, the similarities between Amenemope and Proverbs, while real, are not unique.[72] In other words,

---

70. Early on by Erman, *Eine ägyptische Quelle* (1924).

71. R. O. Kevin, *The Wisdom of Amen-em-ope and Its Possible Dependence on the Book of Proverbs* (Austria: Adolf Mozhausen's Successors, 1931).

72. Ruffle, "Teaching of Amenemope"; Kitchen, "Proverbs and Wisdom Books."

the more we learn about Egyptian instruction, the more parallels we see not only with this one text but with many Egyptian instructions. Not only that, but we also see similarities of both with other cultures' wisdom, most notably the Aramaic Ahiqar. Perhaps the best conclusion is that there is not a specific relationship between Proverbs and Amenemope; rather, both texts are part of an international tradition of wisdom that shares many similarities. In the light of the similarities, the differences—particularly the role of Yahweh in the wisdom of Proverbs—stands out even more.[73]

Father-Son

Egyptian instructions are most often addressed as the advice of a father to a son. The book of Proverbs, particularly the first nine chapters, also presents admonitions of the father to the son. However, as Day points out,[74] though Egyptian instructions mention the father-son dynamic in the prologue, it does not work itself into the advice section of the text as it does in Proverbs (1:8, 10, 15; 2:1; 3:1, 11, 21; 4:1, 10, 20). In addition, he demonstrates that other Semitic practical wisdom is similar to the book of Proverbs, not to Egyptian wisdom. He cites Aramaic Ahiqar (lines 82, 96, 127, 129, 149) as well as Akkadian and Sumerian (admittedly non-Semitic) wisdom.

Even so, all the Near Eastern traditions clearly place their practical wisdom in the setting of father and son. This leads to the debate as to the exact nature of the relationship. Is it biological, or is the language a metaphor for a professional relationship, as with a teacher and an apprentice? Often the two probably coincided, with the biological son succeeding the father in his profession. Egyptian instruction seems to be the profession most consistently focused on, but even there its teaching often articulates principles that are useful for getting along in life generally. As we comment elsewhere (see "Social Setting" above), the wisdom of proverbs is a mixture of family, professional, and scribal advice. But there is no doubt that the father-son dynamic is often biological. Adding support to this viewpoint is the appearance of the mother, rare to be sure, along with the father in the instruction of their son (see Prov. 1:8; 6:20; 31:1).

Wisdom Forms

The proverb, understood broadly, is a short, pithy saying that offers advice or an observation on the world. E. I. Gordon defines it more spe-

---

73. This view is shared by Whybray, *Book of Proverbs: A Survey*, 6–17. See the counterview of Emerton, "Teaching of Amenemope," 431–52.

74. J. Day, "Foreign Semitic Influence on the Wisdom of Israel," in *Wisdom in Ancient Israel,* ed. J. Day et al., 65–66.

cifically as a "short familiar saying, expressing some well-known truth or common fact of experience," and he cites Cervantes' memorable definition that a proverb is a "short sentence founded on long experience."[75] It packs a lot of meaning into a very short statement. In Proverbs, these are usually two-part parallel lines, most often in antithetic relationship. Proverbs 15:1 is typical:

> A soft answer turns away wrath,
>> but a harsh word stirs up anger. (NRSV)

Egyptian wisdom does not know this form until the late instructions of Ankhsheshonqy and Papyrus Insinger, but other Semitic poetry as well as Sumerian proverbs attest similar forms. This is true of even subcategories of the proverb genre. For instance, the numerical proverb (such as Prov. 6:16–19) is not known in Egyptian wisdom but is found in Ahiqar and in nonproverbial contexts in Ugaritic. Proverbs 6:6–8 is an example of an animal proverb, again rare if existent in early Egyptian wisdom, but found in other Semitic texts.[76]

While there are many parallels between non-Egyptian wisdom forms and Prov. 10–31, the case is different with the first nine chapters of Proverbs. These more extended discourses find their closest formal parallels with Egyptian texts. We have also already noted that the so-called "sayings of the wise" in 22:17–24:12, which contain longer proverbs, also have some similarity to Egyptian forms of wisdom.

Wisdom Themes

One cannot help but be struck by similar interests and themes that appear between Proverbs and other ancient Near Eastern wisdom traditions. To illustrate them, we mention two themes here and leave more specific connections to be discussed in the commentary proper.

The Dangerous Woman

A quick survey of the above descriptions of the texts from Egypt, Mesopotamia, and Palestine shows a number of quotations from texts that concern the dangerous woman, a woman who can distract and seduce a man into doing crazy things and abandoning his commitments to his profession and family. Again, there is no need to suggest any kind of intentional and specific borrowing; the literature deals with a frequent temptation that the addressees, being young men, face in every culture

---

75. Gordon, *Sumerian Proverbs*, 1.
76. Day, "Foreign Semitic Influence," 64–65.

up to the present day. Since we have quoted a number of examples above, we will, for convenience' sake, add just one more, the first from the Babylonian Counsels of Wisdom, and this may be compared to what we see in Prov. 5–7:

> Don't marry a prostitute, whose husbands are legion,
> Nor a temple harlot, who is dedicated to a goddess,
> Nor a courtesan, whose intimates are numerous.
> She will not sustain you in your time of trouble,
> She will snigger at you when you are embroiled in controversy.
> She has neither respect nor obedience in her nature.
> Even if she has the run of your house, get rid of her.
> She has ears attuned for another's footfall. (2.23–30)[77]

The Wise and the Foolish

Wisdom literature, through observation and advice, seeks to guide the student to navigate life. If there is a right way to live life, then there is also a wrong way. The biblical book of Proverbs speaks of this as the way of wisdom and the way of folly. Those who take the right road are themselves wise; those who take the wrong road are fools. In Proverbs, there is a strong ethical content to wisdom and folly. Wisdom is connected to justice and righteousness. Wisdom is constructive and leads to life, while folly is destructive and ends up in death.

Theology of the Book

The theology of the book of Proverbs has often been approached more as a problem than anything else. The book's teaching majors in practical advice and observations and seems distant from the theological concerns of the bulk of the OT. We look in vain, for instance, for any connection with the events of redemptive history. Nothing is said of the patriarchs, the exodus, the establishment of the monarchy, and so on. In addition, while the term "covenant" (*běrît*) is not absent from the book (2:17) and associated words like "covenant love" (*ḥesed*) occur even more often (3:3; 14:22; 16:6; 19:22; 20:6, 28), the concept of covenant cannot be said to be a major theme of the book. Finally, references to God, though frequently made by using God's covenant name "Yahweh," occur sporadically in the text. In particular, many of the proverbs in chaps. 10–31 have no reference to God and at first glance appear relatively isolated from a broader context. No wonder the book has been described as containing

---

77. Quoted in Clifford, *Proverbs*, 12.

secular advice.[78] Some scholars have even gone so far as to say that when Yahweh's name is found in a proverb, it is a sign of a late addition to a consistently secular book.[79]

As we have stated, it is true that Proverbs has an ancient Near Eastern context unlike that of a historical book or a prophetic book. The wisdom of the broader environment receives a respect accorded no pagan prophet, for instance. Individual proverbs are arguably collected from or inspired by earlier non-Israelite sources. In the minds of some, this also minimizes the theological distinctiveness of the book of Proverbs and wisdom in general.

While all the above observations about the book are correct, the conclusion that the book is not theological is wrong. Proverbs is not rightly understood if it is taken as a book of practical advice with an occasional nod of the head to Yahweh. The book is thoroughly and pervasively theological. We intend to establish this by first looking at the expression "the fear of Yahweh," followed by an analysis of the role of Woman Wisdom.

The Fear of Yahweh

The conclusion of the preamble to the book states:

> The fear of Yahweh is the beginning of knowledge,
> but fools despise wisdom and discipline. (1:7)

The position of this verse signals that the complier intends to color our view of the teaching of the book as a whole. A more detailed exposition of the meaning of the verse may be found in the commentary proper, but the important thing to point out at this stage is that this statement claims that there is no "knowledge" (a near synonym of "wisdom," which is actually used in the formula elsewhere)[80] apart from a relationship with Yahweh that is characterized by fear.

Wisdom is not simply a matter of learning certain principles of life and applying them mechanistically. Wisdom begins with a relationship with God. That this relationship is described as characterized by fear

---

78. O. Eissfeldt says, "The basis for the commendation of wisdom and piety is . . . purely secular and rational" (*The Old Testament: An Introduction* [New York: Harper & Row, 1965], 47).

79. The view that earlier secular wisdom has been Yahwehized by later theologically minded redactors may be associated with Whybray, *Wisdom in Proverbs*, 72; McKane, *Proverbs*, 1–22. It is properly disputed by L. Boström, *God of the Sages*, 36–39.

80. For other uses, see especially 9:10, but also 1:29; 2:5; 3:7; 8:13; 9:10; 10:27; 14:2, 26, 27; 15:16, 33; 16:6; 19:23; 22:4; 23:7; 24:21; 28:14; 29:25; 31:30.

means that the sages understand their place in the universe. While fear is not to be equated with terror, it is probably more than mere respect (see 1:7).[81] After all, people are totally dependent on Yahweh, who created and sustains them. The sages understood this and therefore trembled in the presence of God.

Pagans may well stumble on some interesting and helpful truth that provides insight on how to avoid a problem or achieve a desired goal. They may even be able to formulate that bit of advice in a way that is memorable. The Israelite sages may even adapt the advice for inclusion in the book of Proverbs. However, based on 1:7, they still would not judge pagan wisdom teachers as truly and authentically wise, because they lack fear of Yahweh.

The bottom line is that there is no wisdom apart from a relationship with Yahweh. The very concept of wisdom is a theological concept, and it runs throughout the book. The pervasiveness of the theological perspective of the book is underlined by the role of Woman Wisdom, and to that subject we now turn.

Embracing Woman Wisdom

A second important entrée into the discussion of the theological richness that pervades the book of Proverbs has to do with the metaphor of Woman Wisdom.

We begin by remembering the fundamental division of the book into two major parts: the discourses (chaps. 1–9) and the proverbial sayings (chaps. 10–31). It is our contention that the latter was meant to be read in the context of the former. The discourses are mostly the address of a father to his son, but in some cases the speaker is a Woman whose name is Wisdom (1:20–33; 8:1–9:6). The following discussion presents conclusions that are argued in the commentary proper. Relevant alternative proposals are also presented there. Here we adopt the position related to our exegetical conclusions.

In the first place, Woman Wisdom represents God's wisdom. While there are debates concerning the source of the inspiration of this personification (for instance, a foreign goddess like Maʿat or Isis), most people agree that in its present context the figure represents Yahweh's wisdom. The key to the relationship between a divine figure and Woman Wisdom is the location of her house on the highest point of the city. In Israel, as throughout the ancient Near East, the only building allowed on

---

81. M. V. Van Pelt and W. C. Kaiser (*NIDOTTE* 2:527–33) argue that *yrʾ* can mean "respect" or "fear." However, it means "respect" only in a very few contexts, and according to them, it means "worship" with God as the object of the *yrʾ*.

the high place was the temple. On this basis, however, I would take the image further than most and suggest that Woman Wisdom represents not only Yahweh's wisdom but Yahweh himself.

One possible objection to this idea is the fact that some of the details of the self-description of Wisdom in chap. 8 ill fit Yahweh. What would it mean to say that Yahweh was the firstborn of creation and specifically that Woman Wisdom was formed by Yahweh (see 8:22–29)? Or that Wisdom witnessed or at best was the agency through whom Yahweh created creation rather than the Creator himself?[82] But for that matter, with regard to God's attribute of wisdom, what would it mean to press the language in detail as a literal description? Like all poetic metaphors (and personification is a type of metaphor), the language is not meant to be understood in that way. Part of the art of interpretation is the uncertain process of coming to grips with how far the comparison may be taken. The major point of these verses seems to be that creation and W(w)isdom are inextricably bound. Thus, if one wants to know how the world works and thus to successfully navigate life, one had better know this woman, which is Yahweh's wisdom and Yahweh himself.

Whether we take Woman Wisdom simply as Yahweh's wisdom or Yahweh himself, we recognize just how theological the very notion of wisdom becomes in this book. But what, then, about Folly? After all, she too has a place on the highest point of the city (9:14). Does this mean she too represents a deity? By the logic of the preceding argument, the answer must be yes. However, by virtue of her description as ignorant, she is best understood as a metaphor for all the false gods and goddesses that provided such a tremendous illicit attraction to Israelites. In a word, she represents the idols, perhaps no one specific idol, but any false god that lured the hearts of the Israelites. Among the ones that we know pulled the hearts of the Israelites are Marduk, Asherah, Anat, Ishtar, and perhaps most notoriously Baal. Thus, in the same way that personification gives wisdom a theological dimension, so also folly is more than simply a mistaken way to act or speak. They represent diametrically opposed relationships with the divine and alternative worldviews.

These women appeal to the men who are walking by their homes to join them for a meal (9:1–6, 13–18). Apparently, the path that these men are walking on goes by the high hills where the women live.

Throughout the first part of Proverbs, the path is a pervasive metaphor culminating in chap. 9. Everyone is walking on a path, or perhaps, better said, on one of two types of path, a straight path or a crooked path. "Path" (*derek* is the main Hebrew term, but there are a host of near

---

82. Whether Wisdom is a witness or the agent of creation depends at least in part on how we understand the *ʾāmôn* of 8:30 (see commentary).

synonyms) refers to one's life. Even today, it is common to refer to life as a journey. Path implies a current point of origin (where one is in life now), a destination, and key transitional moments (forks in the road or an encounter, as we are now discussing). In fact, two paths are open. One is "crooked" (2:15) and "dark" (2:13). Danger lurks on this path (1:10–15; 2:12–15). These dangers include traps and snares that can foul up one's walk on the proper path of life. The dark path represents one's behavior in this life, and it culminates not in life but in death.

On the other hand, there is the right path, the path that leads to life. This path is straight and well lit. One who stays on this path will not stumble.

The reader of Proverbs, as we have seen, is represented by the son, or in the case of 1:20–33 and 8:1–9:18 by all young men. These are the implied readers of this part of the book. However, as we have argued, the preamble broadens the audience of the book to include everyone, male and female, naive and wise (1:1–7). Thus, all actual readers must identify with young men, who are the implied readers of the book. Whether old or young, male or female, for the purpose of understanding the book, we all must use our readerly imagination to place ourselves in the position of the son.

This interpretive move is particularly important for understanding the encounter of the young men with Woman Wisdom and Woman Folly. They both issue invitations for dinner. The invitations suggest intimate, perhaps even sexual relationships. The call then is to become intimately involved with Wisdom or Folly, to make one of them an integral part of our lives.

Thus, chap. 9 at the end of the first part of Proverbs calls for a decision. With whom will we dine? Will we dine with Woman Wisdom, who represents Yahweh's wisdom, even Yahweh himself? Or will we dine with Woman Folly, who represents the false gods of the surrounding nations?

This is the background through which we should read the individual proverbs that follow. As an example, we cite 10:19:

> In an abundance of words, wickedness does not cease;
> those who restrain their lips are insightful.

Here we have a typical antithetical proverb, which contrasts the "wicked" with the "insightful." These two words are closely connected with folly and wisdom respectively. The proverb associates those who speak all the time with wicked folly, and those who watch carefully what they say with the insightful wise.

But in the light of chaps. 8 and 9, wisdom is more than good sense or proper behavior and speech. Those who speak a lot and thus commit abundant evil deeds are associated with Woman Folly: they are connected to or at least are acting like idolaters.

On the other hand, those who act with appropriate verbal restraint are insightful, thus showing they are related to Woman Wisdom; they are acting like good followers of Yahweh.

In summary, I have argued that chaps. 1–9 serve as an introduction, even a kind of hermeneutical prism, through which we should read the rest of the book. This first part of the book requires a decision of the young men, who represent the reader. With whom will one dine, with Wisdom or with Folly? This is a call for a religious decision, a decision between the true God and false gods.

Reading within the Context of Ecclesiastes and Job

Now that we have described what we believe to be the pervasive theological significance of the book of Proverbs itself, we now look at the book's connection to the rest of the canon, beginning with the OT and focusing on two other wisdom books, Ecclesiastes and Job.

Proverbs makes a very important argument in favor of the connection between certain behaviors and their outcomes. Wise actions and speech result in positive consequences, and foolish ones have negative consequences. We have discussed this (above) in connection with the issue of retribution. It is not the intention of a proverb to yield guarantees or promises but rather to point toward behaviors that, all things being equal, will normally lead to desired ends. Thus, laziness normally leads to poverty. However, all things aren't always equal, and a lazy person might be the recipient of a significant inheritance or stumble across a lost treasure. Such exceptions do not disprove the rule, however. But it does remind us that, to use a modern proverb, one "can't tell a book by its cover." One cannot immediately judge that a certain rich person is hardworking, or that a certain poor person is lazy. Indeed, we have already acknowledged that Proverbs itself shows an awareness that a person may have to decide to be wise and not wealthy. In other words, the consequence does not always follow. The biblical story of Joseph is an excellent example of this, since he does just as the proverbs urge—rejecting the advances of a promiscuous woman—but, rather than being rewarded, ends up in jail (Gen. 39). To judge by immediate consequences, the way of wisdom led to trouble rather than blessing.

However, in spite of the built-in safeguards of thinking there is an invariable connection between godly behavior and rewards, it appears that many people fell into the trap of presuming on the results of their behavior. In a word, they thought that good things should happen to good people and bad things happen to bad people. When such a connection did not exist, it threw them, at least temporarily, into a conundrum (Ps. 73).

In the books of Ecclesiastes and Job, we have a recognition and assessment of the issue. These wisdom books of the OT beg to be read in conjunction with Proverbs. Indeed, in my opinion, Ecclesiastes and Job function in part as a canonical corrective to an overreading of the book of Proverbs. They quash any presumption that one invariably and immediately receives rewards for good behavior and punishments for bad behavior.

The issue of the proper interpretation of the book of Ecclesiastes is vexed, and my reading follows the interpretive strategy presented and argued for in my earlier commentary on the book.[83] At the center of this interpretation is a recognition of two voices in the book. On the one hand, we hear Qoheleth, commonly rendered "the Teacher," speak in the first person in the body of the book (1:12–12:7). The frame (1:1–11 and 12:8–14) contains the words of a second wisdom teacher who is quoting Qoheleth and speaking of him in the third person. He is exposing his son (12:12) to the thought of Qoheleth and critically evaluating it.

The basic point Qoheleth is making in his long speech is that life is difficult and ultimately meaningless because one dies. As a wisdom teacher himself, he is particularly upset because he does not see or experience a proper connection between good deeds and good consequences. A selection of passages illustrates the point:

> In my vain life I have seen everything: there are righteous people who perish in their righteousness, and there are wicked people who prolong their life in their evil-doing. Do not be too righteous, and do not act too wise; why should you destroy yourself? Do not be too wicked, and do not be a fool; why should you die before your time? It is good that you should take hold of the one, without letting go of the other; for the one who fears God shall succeed with both. (7:15–18 NRSV)

In 8:10–13, Qoheleth seems to go back and forth between what he sees and what he knows, and then finally back to what he sees. He knows that the godly should live long and do well, but what he sees is the opposite.

And Eccles. 9 is filled with the expression of frustration at the unfair way that life works out. Illustrative of this are vv. 11–12:

83. Longman, *Ecclesiastes*.

Again I saw that under the sun the race is not to the swift, nor the battle to the strong, nor bread to the wise, nor riches to the intelligent, nor favor to the skillful; but time and chance happen to them all. For no one can anticipate the time of disaster. Like fish taken in a cruel net, and like birds caught in a snare, so mortals are snared at a time of calamity, when it suddenly falls upon them. (NRSV)

Thus, Qoheleth expresses exasperation at the fact that retribution does not work out "under the sun." When the second wise man comes to evaluate the words of Qoheleth, he acknowledges that he speaks the truth ("and he wrote words of truth plainly," 12:10 NRSV). In spite of this, however, he points his son not to the same tone of resignation as Qoheleth's carpe diem passages suggest (2:24–26, etc.), but to what we might call an above-the-sun perspective (12:13–14).

Ecclesiastes thus serves as a check against an overly optimistic view of rewards promised to the wise. It does this by showing that the principle of retribution does not always work out in under-the-sun experience. Ecclesiastes does not solve the issue as much as it urges the son to stay in relationship with God and expect the coming judgment. It belies the view that rewards always follow wise behavior.

The same may be said of the book of Job. In the person of Job himself, this book definitively does away with the idea that godliness always leads to blessing and wickedness always leads to punishment. The reader knows, beyond any doubt, that Job is "blameless and upright." Not only does the narrator inform the reader of this (1:1), but God himself also boasts of him to "Satan." In other words, we clearly have a divine affirmation of his godliness, and we know that his suffering has nothing to do with his ethical state.

The three friends, Elihu, and perhaps even Job himself operate with the contrary idea. The three friends look at Job's suffering and conclude that he is a sinner in need of repentance. Elihu essentially argues the same point, and Job himself wonders what has happened. God must have made a mistake.

The book does not offer a solution to the problem of suffering but rather again illustrates the recognition that rewards may not come in this life and that one must simply submit oneself to the power and wisdom of God.[84]

---

84. The fact that Job is blessed at the end is not a compromise of this argument. It is not asserting a belief that everyone who is godly will ultimately be rewarded in this life. The restoration is an affirmation that Job has done the right thing in the light of his inexplicable suffering; he simply submits. Read in the light of the entire canon, however, the thought may be developing toward the idea of an afterlife, a time when retribution will finally be worked out.

Reading Proverbs in the Light of the New Testament

Having discussed the place of Proverbs in the OT canon, we take a broader view that includes the NT. The hermeneutical issue of the relationship between the OT and the NT is a much-discussed and disputed question. Even among Christian scholars we can find great hesitation to recognize that the NT presents itself as a continuation and fulfillment of the OT. Part of this hesitation is out of respect for the concern of Jewish friends and colleagues that we are wresting the Hebrew Bible away from them, to whom it was most directly addressed. However, Christian scholars should listen to Jon Levenson when he encourages them to be Christian in their theology.[85] Other scholars are reluctant to read the OT from a NT perspective because it warps the distinctive contribution of the OT to the canon.[86]

I firmly believe in the importance of studying the OT/Hebrew Bible on its own terms first. I also have considerable doubt that the original authors of OT books had a conscious understanding of the future significance of their words. Perhaps they had a sense that what they were saying had eschatological implications, but certainly not to the extent that the NT authors took it. It seems that the appearance of Jesus led to a deeper understanding of the message of the OT. In the light of Jesus's death and resurrection, his followers read the OT in a new way.

While the nature of Jesus's messiahship was surprising to everyone,[87] Jesus himself was angry that they did not in essence understand what the OT was talking about. He expressed his frustration on two occasions in the days after his resurrection.

In the first, Jesus walked with two of his disciples who were utterly confused and dismayed at his recent crucifixion. They did not recognize him,[88] and as they expressed their consternation, they revealed their previous expectation when they said, "We had hoped that he was the

---

85. J. Levenson, *The Hebrew Bible, the Old Testament, and Historical Criticism: Jews and Christians in Biblical Studies* (Louisville: Westminster John Knox, 1993).

86. Three of the most articulate spokespersons for this view are W. C. Kaiser Jr., *Toward an Exegetical Theology: Biblical Exegesis for Preaching and Teaching* (Grand Rapids: Baker, 1981); idem, *Preaching and Teaching from the Old Testament: A Guide for the Church* (Grand Rapids: Baker, 2003); J. E. Goldingay, *Israel's Gospel* (Old Testament Theology; Downers Grove, IL: InterVarsity, 2003); and J. Walton, whose otherwise masterful treatment of Old Testament topics is marred by his refusal to consider New Testament connections. For an example, see most recently Walton's *Genesis* (NIV Application Commentary; Grand Rapids: Zondervan, 2002).

87. As I argue in "The Messiah: Explorations in the Law and Writings," a paper I delivered at the Bingham Colloquium at McMaster Divinity College in Hamilton, Ontario, June 2004.

88. "Their eyes were kept from recognizing him" (Luke 24:16 NRSV).

one to redeem Israel" (Luke 24:21 NRSV). Jesus replied: "Oh, how foolish you are, and how slow of heart to believe all that the prophets have declared! Was it not necessary that the Messiah should suffer these things and then enter into his glory?" These words are backed by his appeal to Scripture, when the narrator reports that "beginning with Moses and all the prophets, he interpreted to them the things about himself in all the scriptures" (24:25–26 NRSV). Soon thereafter, he appeared to a broader group of disciples, and Luke reports the event as follows:

> Then he said to them, "These are my words that I spoke to you while I was still with you—that everything written about me in the law of Moses, the prophets, and the psalms must be fulfilled." Then he opened their minds to understand the scriptures, and he said to them, "Thus it is written, that the Messiah is to suffer and to rise from the dead on the third day, and that repentance and forgiveness of sins is to be proclaimed in his name to all nations, beginning from Jerusalem. You are witnesses of these things. And see, I am sending upon you what my Father promised; so stay here in the city until you have been clothed with power from on high." (Luke 24:44–49 NRSV)

There is much about this passage that can be debated; however, certain things are clearly delineated here. First, the disciples had an expectation, though it was apparently not clearly formed or accurate. The imperfection of their expectation is implied by their confusion at the time of the crucifixion and their reaction to reports of the empty tomb. Second, Jesus was angry or at least disappointed that they did not know what to expect. After all, he taught them during his earthly ministry. Third, he gave them another lesson, a lesson in hermeneutics, which we are to assume convinced them this time in the light of the resurrection. From this point on, the disciples could not read the OT except in the light of the resurrected Jesus.

The Bible is one continuous and organic story, though told in a variety of genres and by a variety of authors, who provide different perspectives on the same truth. The Bible is composed of many books but in the end is a single book. It has many authors but ultimately is the product of a single Author. It is important to study the books of the Bible from the perspective of their distinctive contribution as well as their connection to the whole.

In terms of the latter, the Bible is like any narrative. On a first reading the story of the OT unfolds in ways not expected. However, on second and further readings of the canon, one cannot, except as an intellectual exercise, read the beginning without knowledge of the end. In terms of the study of the OT, Christian scholars should initially do their best to bracket their understanding of how the story ends in the NT. However, such a reading is an intellectual exercise. In reality, one cannot and ultimately should not read the beginning of a story the same way twice. Indeed, a second reading of the beginning of any story and in particular the story of the Christian Bible will be accompanied by recognition of how that story ends.

Of course, Proverbs is not a story as such. However, as we have observed above, the book presents a striking metaphor of God's wisdom and arguably God himself in the form of Woman Wisdom. Readers of the NT cannot help but notice the description of Jesus as, in the first place, the very epitome of God's wisdom and, second, in association with Woman Wisdom herself.

We begin by an exploration of NT passages that characterize Jesus as the apex of God's wisdom. The infancy narratives are brief, but they pay special attention to the growth in Jesus's extraordinary wisdom. Of the two Gospels that report his birth and youth, Luke shows a special interest in Jesus's wisdom. For instance, after Jesus is born, we learn twice that this young man grew physically but also "with wisdom beyond his years" (Luke 2:40 NLT; cf. also 2:52). These two notices surround a story that gives us Christ's wisdom, and it too comments on one of the few events related to us from Jesus's youth.

Like good Jewish parents, Mary and Joseph took their son every year to Jerusalem for Passover. When Jesus was twelve, they made the trip as usual, but this time as they returned to Nazareth, they panicked when they realized that Jesus was not with them. With fear in their hearts, they rushed back to Jerusalem and spent three days frantically searching for him. They finally discovered him in the temple "sitting among the religious teachers, discussing deep questions with them" (Luke 2:46 NLT). People were watching with amazement "at his understanding and his answers" (2:47 NLT). After all, he wasn't speaking with just anyone; he was in a discussion with the leading theologians of his day, and they were paying attention to what he was saying. Here was a child who reflected God's wisdom.

When Jesus began his ministry, people recognized him as a wise teacher. In Mark's first report of his teaching, we hear the people's reaction: "Jesus and his companions went to the town of Capernaum. When the Sabbath day came, he went into the synagogue and began to teach. The people were amazed at his teaching, for he taught with real authority—quite unlike the teachers of religious law" (Mark 1:21–22, cf. NIV, NLT). Later, in Nazareth, those who knew him while he was growing up also acknowledged his gifts: "Where did he get all his wisdom and the power to perform such miracles?" (Mark 6:2 NLT).

The most characteristic form of Jesus's teaching, the parable, was part of the repertoire of the wisdom teacher. Indeed, the Hebrew word (*māšāl*) was translated into the Greek word "parable" (*parabolē*). Accordingly, it is not a stretch to say that Jesus was a first-century wisdom teacher.

Jesus recognized himself as wise and condemned those who rejected his wisdom. In Luke 11:31, he tells the crowd: "The queen of Sheba will rise up against this generation on judgment day and condemn it, because she came from a distant land to hear the wisdom of Solomon. And now someone greater than Solomon is here—and you refuse to listen to him" (NLT).

While the Gospels demonstrate that Jesus was wise—indeed, wiser than Solomon—Paul asserts that Jesus is not simply wise; he is also the very incarnation of God's wisdom. Twice Paul identifies Christ with God's wisdom. First in 1 Corinthians, a passage that will occupy our attention later, he says, "God made Christ to be wisdom itself" (1 Cor. 1:30 NLT). Second, in Col. 2:3 Paul proclaims that in Christ "lie hidden all the treasures of wisdom and knowledge" (NLT). With this as background, it is not surprising that the NT subtly associates Jesus with Woman Wisdom, particularly as presented in Prov. 8.

Gospels and Epistles both attest to Jesus's wisdom being the most profound expression of God's wisdom. Moreover, the link with Woman Wisdom is explicit in several other passages that we now explore.

We begin with Matt. 11. In this passage, Jesus addresses opponents who argue that John the Baptist was an ascetic in his lifestyle, while Jesus was too celebratory. Notice the final assertion in his reply:

> For John came neither eating nor drinking, and they say, "He has a demon." The Son of Man came eating and drinking, and they say, "Here is a glutton and a drunkard, a friend of tax collectors and 'sinners.'" But wisdom is proved right by her actions. (Matt. 11:18–19 NIV)

In that last sentence, Jesus claims that his behavior represents the behavior of Woman Wisdom herself.

Elsewhere in the NT Jesus is described in language that is reminiscent of Prov. 8. We turn first to Col. 1:15–17:

> Christ is the visible image of the invisible God.
> > He existed before anything was created and is supreme over all creation,
> for through him God created everything in heaven and on earth.
> He made the things we can see
> > and the things we can't see—
> Such as thrones, kingdoms,
> > rulers, and authorities in the unseen world.
> > Everything was created through him and for him.
> He existed before anything else,
> > and he holds all creation together. (cf. NLT)

Though this text is clearly not a quotation from Proverbs, someone as well versed in the OT as Paul was would recognize it as saying that Jesus occupies the place of Wisdom. Indeed, the literal rendition of the Greek of the sentence that ends "is supreme over all creation" is "He is . . . the firstborn of all creation" (NRSV). Paul is inviting a comparison: Wisdom was firstborn in Prov. 8; Jesus is firstborn in Colossians. Wisdom is the agent of divine creation in Proverbs; Christ is the agent in Colossians. In Prov. 8 we read:

> By me kings reign,
>   and nobles issue just decrees.
> By me rulers rule,
>   and princes, all righteous judgments. (Prov. 8:15–16)

And in Col. 1:16, Christ made "kings, kingdoms, rulers, and authorities" (NLT). The message is clear: Jesus is Wisdom herself.

The author of Revelation is a further witness to the connection between Wisdom and Jesus. In the introduction to the letter to the church at Laodicea, we read, "This is the message from the one who is the Amen—the faithful and true witness, the ruler of God's [new] creation" (Rev. 3:14b NLT). The last phrase (*hē archē tēs ktiseōs tou theou*) resonates with the ideas behind Prov. 8:22–30. In particular, the phrase may represent the meaning of that difficult word in Prov. 8:30, the "architect" (*ʾamôn*) of creation. The allusion is subtle but clear: Jesus stands in the place of Woman Wisdom.

Even more subtly, we might note that the great preface to the Gospel of John echoes with language reminiscent of the poem about Woman Wisdom in Prov. 8. The Word of God (the Logos), who is God himself (John 1:1), was "in the beginning with God. He created everything there is" (NLT). Indeed, the "world was made through him" (1:10 NLT). Jesus, of course, is the Word, and the association is with language reminiscent of Woman Wisdom.[89]

Seeing the connection between Jesus and Woman Wisdom has important implications for how Christians read the book of Proverbs. We have already established the fact that the ancient Israelite would read the metaphors of Woman Wisdom and Woman Folly as a choice between Yahweh and the false gods of the nations. This decision would have little relevance to modern readers who are not trying to make a choice between God and Baal; the latter is not a live option, and the NT claims to reveal the nature of the Godhead more carefully. Thus, the NT presents Jesus as the mediator of our relationship with God. The gospel choice

89. As we observe in the commentary proper, there is a debate over whether Wisdom is the agent through whom God created creation or simply a witness to it. Of course, if the latter is the correct view, then the connection is weaker with John 1.

is a decision whether to follow Jesus. Thus, to understand the invitation of Woman Wisdom as the invitation of Christ to relationship with God makes the book contemporary to Christian readers.

As for Woman Folly, she may be taken as anything or anyone who seeks to divert our primary attention away from our relationship with Jesus. Idols today are typically more subtle than in ancient times. Rather than deities and their images, we are lured by more abstract and conceptual idols: power, wealth, relationships, status, and so forth.[90]

Other Developments of the Metaphor of Woman Wisdom

The NT was not the only or the earliest post-Hebrew Bible writing to further develop the metaphor of Woman Wisdom. The first[91] that we know of is found in the two intertestamental wisdom books, Sirach and Wisdom of Solomon.

Sirach, also known as Ecclesiasticus, is known from a Greek translation (ca. 130 BC), which is based on an earlier Hebrew composition (ca. 180 BC). It is a prominent member of the OT Apocrypha. Sirach 1 introduces the figure of Woman Wisdom:

> Wisdom was created before all other things,
>   and prudent understanding from eternity. . . .
>   It is he who created her;
>   he saw her and took her measure;
>   he poured her out upon all his works,
> upon all the living according to his gift;
>   he lavished her upon those who love him. (1:4, 9–10 NRSV)

Chapter 24 in particular develops the description of Woman Wisdom. The most notable innovation has to do with associating Wisdom with Israel and specifically with the law of Moses.[92]

> Then the Creator of all things gave me [Wisdom] a command,
>   and my Creator chose the place for my tent.

90. For an examination of modern idols in the light of the book of Ecclesiastes, see D. Allender and T. Longman, *Bold Purpose* (Wheaton: Tyndale, 1997).

91. Unless one counts the Greek translation of the LXX that arguably was done around 200 BC. According to Cook ("ʾIshâ zārâ"), Prov. 8 was rendered into Greek in a way that purposefully protected against assimilation with Hellenistic ideas of wisdom. In particular, it makes clear, clearer than in the Hebrew, that God was the sole Creator.

92. The present commentary argues (see "Wisdom and Law" below) that the connection between wisdom and law is implicit in the book of Proverbs. Sirach is making the connection explicit.

He said, "Make your dwelling in Jacob,
  and in Israel receive your inheritance." (24:8 NRSV)

Whoever obeys me [Wisdom] will not be put to shame,
  and those who work with me will not sin.
All this is the book of the covenant of the Most High God,
  the law that Moses commanded us
    as an inheritance for the congregations of Jacob. (24:22–23 NRSV;
      see also 15:1; 19:20; 33:2)

While Sirach represents one further development of the metaphor of Woman Wisdom in the direction of a Jewish particularism,[93] the Wisdom of Solomon (sometime between 50 BC and AD 100),[94] also a deuterocanonical book, uses the figure to try to assimilate Jewish with Hellenistic wisdom, in particular a Stoic and Neoplatonic mind-set:

She [Wisdom] is an exhalation from the power of God,
  a pure effluence from the glory of the Almighty;
    therefore nothing tainted insinuates itself into her.
She is an effulgence of everlasting light,
  an unblemished mirror of the active power of God,
    and an image of his goodness. (7:25–26)[95]

In the early church, Prov. 8 with its personification of wisdom provided a source of controversy regarding the arguments of a popular preacher and theologian, Arius (260–336 BC). Arius and his followers noted the connection between Jesus and Wisdom and then applied all the characteristics of Wisdom to Jesus. They pressed literally the language in the Greek version of Prov. 8 that Wisdom (Jesus) was created or brought forth as the first of creation. On that basis, they reasoned that since God is "Creator" and Wisdom, who stands for Jesus, is "created," then Jesus cannot be God.

In response, we simply point out that Prov. 8 is not a prophecy of Jesus or any kind of literal description of him. We must remember that the text is poetry and is using metaphor to make important points about the

93. As J. G. Snaith ("Ecclesiasticus: A Tract for Our Time," in *Wisdom in Ancient Israel*, ed. J. Day et al., 181) puts it, "With Hellenistic reform seemingly just around the corner in Jerusalem, Sirach wrote his book, ignoring the Jews still in Babylon, to provide a Zionist-like declaration of the values of traditional Judaism, a book treasured at Qumran and Masada, and found in the Cairo Geniza, and indeed well known to Jews and Christians throughout the world thanks to the Greek translation of a loyal grandson."

94. For a particularly helpful look at the Wisdom of Solomon, see Enns, *Exodus Retold*.

95. Translation and commentary may be found in D. Winston, *The Wisdom of Solomon*, Anchor Bible (Garden City, NY: Doubleday, 1979), 184–87.

nature of God's wisdom. Indeed, even in its OT setting, where Wisdom stands for Yahweh's wisdom, we would be wrong to press the language of creation literally, as though at some point God was not wise and only later became wise just in time to create the world.

We must remember all this when we see that Jesus associates himself with Wisdom in the NT. Woman Wisdom is not a preincarnate form of the second person of the Trinity. Jesus is not to be identified with Wisdom. The language about Jesus being the "firstborn of creation" is not to be pressed literally, as though Jesus were a created being. But—and this is crucial—the association between Jesus and Woman Wisdom in the NT is a powerful way of saying that Jesus is the embodiment of God's Wisdom.

Athanasius (ca. 296–373) led the charge against Arius. The controversy allowed the church's leaders to further reflect and define their understanding of the nature of Christ and the Trinity. The culmination of their work issued in the development of the Nicene Creed, which asserts the following about Jesus, making it clear that Arius's implications from Prov. 8 were wrongminded:

> We believe . . . in one Lord Jesus Christ, the only-begotten Son of God, and born of the Father before all ages, (God of God,) Light of Light, true God of true God, begotten not made, consubstantial with the Father, by whom all things were made.

Though the Catholic, Protestant, and Orthodox churches followed Athanasius in this regard, the teaching of Arius is not dead. Rather, it is found in groups like the Mormon Church or among Jehovah's Witnesses, who deny that Jesus is fully God as well as fully man. In their understanding Jesus is a created being, and Prov. 8 again is a proof text for them.

Proverbs 8 is the origin of another form of modern theological speculation as well. In recent decades a group of feminist scholars[96] have protested what they see as the patriarchal nature of NT religion, with

---

96. Not all feminist scholars identify with the viewpoint described here. There are a host of different feminist perspectives on the book of Proverbs. Those that proceed in the direction of treating Woman Wisdom/Sophia as a feminine alternate to the male Christ include E. A. Johnson, "Jesus, the Wisdom of God: A Biblical Basis for Non-androcentric Christology," *Ephemerides theologicae lovanienses* 61 (1985): 274–89; E. Schüssler Fiorenza, *In Memory of Her: A Feminist Theological Reconstruction of Christian Origins* (New York: Crossroad, 1983); J. M. Robinson, "Very Goddess and Very Man," in *Images of the Feminine in Gnosticism*, ed. K. L. King (Philadelphia: Fortress, 1988), 113–27. A "Re-imagining 1993" conference was held in Minneapolis and attended by church leaders, theologians, and laypeople. This conference was attempting to make the faith more palatable to modern women by presenting Sophia as an alternative mediator between God and humanity.

its masculine Savior, by worshipping God through Sophia, a female picture of God. "Sophia," of course, is the Greek word for wisdom, and not surprisingly Prov. 8 has been a place where they have sought some textual support. However, as we have already tried to establish, such a view of Prov. 8 is out of keeping with the nature of the text. It treats the description of Woman Wisdom as a literal description rather than as a poetic metaphor. In a word, it takes the metaphor too far and in a way that it contradicts other parts of Scripture.[97] Even so, the church should not simply react against this view but should examine what has driven these scholars, pastors, and laypeople to such a viewpoint. Perhaps the church has been guilty of overpatriarchalizing the gospel—but that is a subject for another study.

Selected Theological Topics

What follows includes a study of certain topics that are of special interest for the book of Proverbs. Presented in no certain order, they are a miscellany of topics that allow us to explore issues of interest in the book.

Gender and the Theology

Proverbs is composed of discourses and proverbs. The discourses of 1:8–9:18 are clearly addressed to men. Most are speeches of a father, speaking on behalf of himself and his wife and addressing his son or sons. The exceptions are 1:20–33 and 8:1–9:6, where Woman Wisdom speaks to all the young men; and 9:13–18, where Woman Folly speaks to the same group. The addressees of the proverbs that follow in chaps. 10–31 are only rarely made explicit, but when they are, the text again refers to the "son" (as in 19:27; 23:15, 19, 26; 24:13; etc.). Also, the observations are geared toward the son and not the daughter or children in general (as in 10:1, 5; 13:1; 15:20; 17:2, 25; 19:13). Furthermore, the subjects are directed toward men more than toward women, as the extensive teaching on choosing the right woman (31:10–31) and avoiding the wrong woman (chaps. 5–7) would indicate. There is no comparable teaching about avoiding the wrong man or husband or choosing the right one. In essence, 1:8–31:31 is addressed to young men.

97. For a full and devastating critique of modern feminist Sophia theology, see K. Jobes, "Sophia Christology: The Way of Wisdom?" in *The Way of Wisdom: Essays in Honor of Bruce K. Waltke*, ed. J. I. Packer and S. K. Soderlund (Grand Rapids: Zondervan, 2000), 226–50.

Indeed, to feel the full force of what is arguably the most important metaphor of the book, one must put oneself in the position of a male. The relational and erotic overtones of Woman Wisdom's and of Woman Folly's appeals to the young men to dine at their respective houses (9:1–6, 13–18) may only be fully realized if one is or imagines oneself to be a male. J. Miller (*Proverbs*) makes an important point when he says that modern gender-inclusive translations like the NLT lose something when they typically translate "son" as "child."[98]

However, there is more to the issue. Proverbs 1:1–7 functions as a kind of preamble or title page to the book as a whole. The collection of materials that follow the preamble needs to be read in its light. Among other introductory matters, the preamble names those to whom the book is addressed. We are not surprised that the "simple" and the "young" are numbered among those to whom the book is directed (1:4), but we might be surprised to see that 1:5 specifically names "the wise" as among the book's audience. Since the gender of the addressees is not specified in the preamble, it is appropriate to believe that males and females are both intended.

A further argument in support of the idea that the final form of Proverbs is meant to be read and appropriated by both genders and all ages is the mere presence of the book in the canon. The canon provides a new context for the book, and it is one that broadens the audience to include all of God's people.

When we think about it, Proverbs is no different from most other biblical books. After all, few if any books of the Bible were addressed to the whole of the people of God. The original settings had specific audiences in mind. Samuel–Kings was written for the exilic community, and Chronicles for the postexilic community. Romans was written to the Roman church, and Galatians to the church of Galatia. The mere presence of these books in the canon indicates to us that they have some continuing relevance for us today. We first of all must study the book of Galatians in its original context, struggling to know, for instance, the nature of the false teaching it resists. After doing this, we do our best to understand the significance of the book for us today. Proverbs is no different, especially if we are not young men. However, once the process of understanding is initiated, we can see that it really is not that difficult. Women may not be directly addressed by a proverb like 21:9:

> It is better to live in the corner of a roof
> than with a contentious woman in a shared house.

---

98. However, it is also true that the NLT is generally careful to preserve the awareness of the male addressee when Woman Wisdom makes her appeal to those who pass by.

But it is appropriate and not difficult for the woman to apply the proverb to her own situation:

> It is better to live in the corner of a roof
> than with a contentious *man* in a shared house.

Nor is it difficult to think of a male sexual predator rather than a female one as a woman appropriates chaps. 5–7 to her situation.

Before we leave this situation, we make a comment concerning the value and appropriateness of gender-inclusive translations of Proverbs. The fact that the book was addressed to young males in its original setting might argue for preserving the gender-specific language of "son" in our translations. Indeed, it is difficult to see how one can avoid doing so in chapters such as 5–7, where the son is warned against the wiles of the promiscuous woman. However, the preamble plus the presence of the book in the canon does seem to allow for the translation "child" for "son."

The bottom line is that there is not a right or wrong answer to this question. All translations must make compromises with the original meaning since no two languages have a one-to-one correspondence. The best solution is to have both types of translations available to the serious student. For Bible readers a gender-inclusive translation may be best so they understand that the discourses and proverbs apply to them, whether male or female. Among the most popular translations, some are gender specific (ESV, NIV, NASB) and some are gender inclusive (NLT, NCV, TNIV). Serious students will have both available as they study, particularly if they lack a knowledge of Hebrew.

The Sources of Wisdom

Where does the wisdom of the discourses and proverbs of the book of Proverbs come from? The book of Proverbs recognizes a number of ways in which a person grows wise. They include observation, instruction, learning from mistakes, and, finally and most important, revelation, recognized by those who fear the Lord.[99]

Observation and Experience. A wise person has been observant of life. While many people live unreflectively, the wise person tries to understand why certain behaviors work and others do not. Provided a person has been self-aware and self-critical, the more experience one has, the wiser one is apt to be. Since experience is important for growth in wisdom, societies have generally thought that older people tend to be wiser than

---

99. Estes, *Hear, My Son*, 87–100.

the young. While the three friends of Job show that this is not a universally valid principle, it is generally true. In Proverbs, it is always the father instructing the son, never the son instructing the father.

Occasionally, the teacher in Proverbs appeals explicitly to the process of observation in order to back up his teaching. One of the best examples comes from 6:6–8:

> Go to the ant, you lazy people!
>> See its paths and grow wise.
> That one has no military commander,
>> officer or ruler;
> it gets its food in summer,
>> gathers its provisions at harvest.

The teacher instructs his pupils about laziness by inviting them to go out and observe the diligent ant. From this experience, the teacher feels confident that the hearer will draw the lesson that follows in the text:

> How long, you lazy person, will you lie down;
>> when will you rise up from your sleep?
> "A little sleep, a little slumber,
>> a little folding of the arms to lie down"—
> and your poverty will come on you like a prowler
>> and your deprivation like a person with a shield. (6:9–11)

Later, the sage warns his son about the dangers of an immoral woman by sharing the following observation:

> When from the window of my house,
>> from behind my lattice I looked down,
> I looked for a moment,
>> and I perceived among the sons a youth who lacked heart.
> He was crossing the street at the corner,
>> and he marched on the path to her house
> at beginning of the evening of the day,
>> in the middle of night and darkness. (7:6–9)

The story continues as it tells of the woman's seduction of the young man and the horrible consequences:

> He impetuously goes after her.
>> He goes like an ox to the slaughter
>> and like a stupid person to the stocks for discipline,
> until an arrow pierces his liver,
>> like a bird hurrying to the snare,
>> not aware that it will cost him his life. (7:22–23)

75

From this observation the sage advises the son to avoid this woman (7:24–25).

Though this type of conscious reflection on the process of experience and observation is infrequent in the book, it does appear in more places than those just cited (see also 22:10, 26–27; 26:15).

Instruction Based on Tradition. Observation and experience allow the sensitive person to know how to navigate life. Strategies that succeed are repeated and taught; those that fail become the subject of warnings. The observation or experience need not be personal. We also rely on the learned analysis of others. Here, of course, we speak of the role of the father/teacher. In Prov. 4, the father instructs his son based on the tradition handed down by his father:

> Hear, sons, fatherly discipline,
>   and pay attention to the knowledge of understanding.
> For I will give you good teaching;
>   don't forsake my instruction.
> For I was a son to my father,
>   tender and the only one of my mother.
> He taught me and said to me:
>   "Let your heart hold on to my words;
>   guard my commands and live." (4:1–4)

Indeed, in this context we can also reflect back on Prov. 7. The lesson about the seductive, immoral woman was based on wisdom gleaned through the observation of the father, but it was passed on to the son by instruction. The son did not have to directly observe or experience the situation to learn from it. In other words, we may learn wisdom from the traditions of others who have gone before us.

A new section of the book of Proverbs begins in 22:17 and is introduced by the following verses:

> Incline your ear and hear the words of the wise;
>   set your heart toward my knowledge,
> for they are pleasant if you guard them in your innermost being
>   and have all of them ready on your lips.
> So your trust will be in Yahweh,
>   I will inform you, even you, today.
> Have I not written for you thirty sayings
>   with advice and knowledge?
> Their purpose is to inform you of true, reliable speeches,
>   so you can return reliable speeches to those who sent you. (22:17–21)

The thirty sayings represent a tradition passed on from father to son, down to the present time. From this instruction the son will grow wise. Indeed, this is the admonition of the following two proverbs:

> The wise of heart grasps commands,
>> but a dupe's lips are ruined. (10:8)

> Listen to advice and receive discipline,
>> so you might grow wise in your future days. (19:20)

We have seen that Israel's wisdom teachers depended not only on native Israelite tradition but also on the wisdom of the broader ancient Near East (see "Proverbs in the Light of Ancient Near Eastern Wisdom" above).

Learning from Mistakes. Part of gaining wisdom by experience and observation is learning from one's mistakes. Proverbs supposes that everyone makes bad choices along the way. The difference between the wise person and the fool is that the former learns from mistakes, but the latter simply refuses to change behavior. In this regard, the book of Proverbs uses two key words: *mûsār* and *tôkaḥat*. The first is often translated by "discipline" and the second by "correction." The two words are in the same semantic field (a group of words with related meaning) and often occur parallel to one another in the same verse.

Discipline and correction are directed toward those who wander off the right path, encouraging them to get back on. As 12:1 says:

> Those who love discipline love knowledge;
>> and those who hate correction are dullards.

And 10:17 states why it is good to love discipline and not ignore those who try to correct our mistakes:

> Those who guard discipline are on the way to life,
>> and those who abandon correction wander aimlessly.

Discipline is hard to accept; it means admitting that one made a mistake. This is a humbling experience, but a wise person is humble, not proud. Indeed, Proverbs has a lot to say about the dangers of pride. In 8:13, Woman Wisdom herself, speaking in the first person, says

> Those who fear Yahweh hate evil,
>> pride and arrogance, and the path of evil.
>> I hate a perverse mouth.

On the other hand, God loves those who are humble:

> He mocks mockers,
>> but he shows favor to the humble. (3:34)

After all, pride has very negative side effects and outcomes, while humility takes us back to the good path that leads to life.

> When insolence comes, then shame will come,
>> but wisdom with modesty. (11:2)

> The fear of Yahweh is wise discipline,
>> and humility comes before glory. (15:33)

> Pride comes before a disaster,
>> and before stumbling comes an arrogant attitude. (16:18)

So, learning from one's mistakes as well as observing the mistakes of others is an avenue to wisdom, which puts one on the road to life. Only humility, acknowledging one's weaknesses and failings, will allow this kind of instruction to work its benefits in one's life.

Revelation. According to Proverbs, observation and experience, tradition, and learning from one's mistakes—all are important sources of human wisdom. However, at the heart of wisdom is God himself. Apart from God there is no true insight into the world. God is the only source of true wisdom. Even the ability to observe and experience comes from the Lord:

> An ear to hear and an eye to see—
>> Yahweh made both of them. (20:12)

We have already seen that Proverbs establishes this from the very beginning, when it concludes its opening purpose statement with:

> The fear of Yahweh is the beginning of knowledge,
>> but fools despise wisdom and discipline. (1:7)

The theme of the fear of the Lord reverberates through the whole book. After all, if wisdom depends on understanding the world correctly, how can that be achieved if one does not acknowledge that God is the center of the cosmos? Everything must be understood in relationship to Yahweh himself. This is what leads to humility, which comes, after all, from knowing that there is a greater power in the universe:

Many plans are in people's hearts,
    but the advice of Yahweh, that is what will succeed. (19:21)

And so we look to the One greater than us to provide the instruction we need to navigate life:

To humans belong the plans of the heart,
    but from Yahweh comes a responding tongue. (16:1)

We have also looked closely at the figure of Woman Wisdom and have discovered that she ultimately stands for Yahweh. As we listen to her, we listen to God himself. Indeed, all true wisdom, knowledge, and insight—even that gained by tradition, instruction, experience, observation, and correction—comes from God himself:

For Yahweh bestows wisdom,
    from his mouth come knowledge and understanding.
He stores up resourcefulness for those with integrity—
    a shield for those who walk in innocence,
to protect the paths of justice
    guarding the way of his covenant partners. (2:6–8)

Wisdom and Creation

Though the theme is not extensively developed in Proverbs (however, see the divine speeches in Job 38:1–40:2 and 40:6–41:34), two of the most interesting texts in Proverbs show the close connection between wisdom and creation. Proverbs 3:19–20 states the matter more directly than 8:22–31, but both present the same fundamental truth: God created the cosmos through his wisdom. While chap. 3 makes this point in so many words, in chap. 8 we have the development of the complex metaphor of Woman Wisdom.[100] Through this Woman and in her presence, God created the earth and the heavens. Woman Wisdom is a personification of Yahweh's wisdom and ultimately stands for Yahweh himself. The implicit teaching of the connection is to tell the reader that the best way to know how to get on in the world is to become acquainted with the One so intimately involved in its creation. The key to successful living is wisdom.

As we saw earlier, the NT associates Woman Wisdom with Jesus in John 1 and specifically does so by using the language of creation. Just

---

100. For the many different perspectives on the origin and function of this metaphor, see the commentary. Here we make a summary statement of our own conclusions.

as God created the cosmos through Woman Wisdom according to Prov. 8, so God created the cosmos through Jesus Christ, the Word.

Wisdom and Law

It is not hard to see a connection between wisdom and law. Both make demands upon a person's life and behavior.

> Honor your father and mother. (Exod. 20:12 NRSV)

> Answer fools according to their stupidity. (Prov. 26:5)

Even the observations of Proverbs imply a mode of behavior:

> A wise son makes a father glad,
> and a foolish son is the sorrow of his mother. (Prov. 10:1)

It is also true that words associated with the law (in particular "command" [$misw\hat{a}$] and "instruction/law" [$t\bar{o}r\hat{a}$]) are used in connection with demands of the book of Proverbs.[101] These observations lead one to see a close connection or even identification between wisdom and law.

However, as noted by various scholars,[102] one must acknowledge a difference as well. The law comes with no stated or unstated exceptions. One must always honor one's parents. One may never worship other gods, make an image, take God's name in vain, commit adultery, steal, murder, bear false witness, or covet. Wisdom is another matter. Though Prov. 26:5 demands that a person answer a fool, the previous verse demands that a person not answer a fool. While this might be considered a contradiction if judged as though these verses were law, it is in the nature of the proverb to consider the circumstance (see "Genre" above). What kind of fool is one speaking to? Will answering help or just mire one in a hopeless controversy? Perhaps, then, it is best to consider the wisdom of Proverbs as good advice rather than as required stipulation. However, such a conclusion might be premature.

While not related like brothers, law and wisdom are like close cousins. Both intend to shape the behavior of the covenant community (see comments below on "Covenant and Wisdom"). In the first place, we must acknowledge the wisdom of Proverbs as a matter of take it or leave it. Some of its requirements are nonnegotiable and do not depend on the

101. For $misw\hat{a}$, see 2:1; 3:1; 4:4; 6:20, 23; 7:1, 2; 13:13; 19:16. For $t\bar{o}r\hat{a}$, see 1:8; 3:1; 6:20, 23; 7:2; 13:14; 28:4, 7, 9; 29:18; 31:26.
102. Note the debate between Zimmerli and Gemser described in connection with the occurrence of the word "command" in Prov. 2:1.

circumstance. This is true, for instance, concerning its extensive teaching on how to react to a promiscuous woman. Indeed, we should observe the connection between this teaching and the seventh commandment, not to commit adultery (Exod. 20:14). Indeed, a number of proverbs may be related to specific provisions of the Ten Commandments—not all of them, but certainly a majority, especially those concerning human-to-human relationships. The following chart is not exhaustive but does demonstrate the connection I am talking about:

Commandments (Exod. 20:12–17)	Proverbs
Fifth: Honor father and mother	1:8; 4:1, 10;[103] 10:1; 13:1
Sixth: Do not murder	1:10–12; 6:17
Seventh: Do not commit adultery	2:16–19; chap. 5; 6:20–35; chap. 7
Eighth: Do not steal	1:13–14; 11:1
Ninth: Do not bear false witness	3:30; 6:18, 19; 10:18; 12:17, 19
Tenth: Do not covet	6:18

Here again, law and wisdom are not identical. They are different genres, and it is important to bear this in mind. In a recent book on OT narrative, Gordon Wenham made an important distinction that appears relevant to our understanding of the ethical quality of Proverbs.[104] That distinction is between what he calls ethical ideals and legal requirements. The latter is connected to law and should be considered rock-bottom acceptable behavior for the covenant community. Wenham recognizes that "obedience to the rules is not a sufficient definition of OT ethics, but that much more is looked for by members of the covenant people than this."[105] That much more may be described as, among other terms, character and virtue. Though, as we have just seen, many proverbs intersect with legal requirements, wise behavior certainly extends beyond that bottom-line requirement. A good example is the extensive teaching concerning diligence and avoiding laziness. This teaching is not directly connected to the law, though some might argue that it is an extension of the Sabbath commandment and in certain situations of the law not to steal. However, the wisdom teaching is calling for something above and beyond the call of duty as defined by the law.

103. Proverbs 4:10 even connects obeying one's father to a reward of a long life, reminiscent of the commandment.

104. G. J. Wenham, *Story as Torah: Reading the Old Testament Narrative Ethically* (Grand Rapids: Baker, 2000).

105. Ibid., 79.

Covenant and Wisdom

Having discussed the relationship between law and wisdom, we are in a position to address the connection between wisdom and covenant. It is a well-known fact that wisdom has always been a difficult part of the canon to assimilate into a biblical theology that insists on a "center," and this is particularly the case when that center has been defined as redemptive history or covenant.[106] Now it is true that the word "covenant" does appear in Proverbs and words associated with covenant like *ḥesed* are also found; but even so, it has been difficult for scholars to deeply integrate Proverbs or wisdom in general with the covenant idea.

On the other hand, law fits in easily since covenant is a legal metaphor. Comparisons between the biblical idea of covenant and ancient Near Eastern treaties have made this connection even clearer since law is part and parcel of a treaty document. The law expresses the will of the sovereign king, and the king's subjects show their thanks for his gracious actions, as delineated by the historical prologue (in the case of the Bible, as narrated in the historical books). Meredith Kline has put forward the most forceful arguments in seeing Proverbs related to covenant by virtue of its association with legal requirements.[107] The covenant community listens to law and wisdom in order to live life in obedience to their covenant king.

Our above analysis of the relationship between law and wisdom would support Kline's idea in the main, but also inject a note of caution. The note of caution is connected to the fact that law and wisdom, though similar, are not identical. It is probably impossible to insist on a single center of biblical theology, whether covenant or any other topic, and do full justice to the distinctive nature and quality of a varied canon. While it is possible to relate covenant and wisdom, it is also important to reflect on a theology of wisdom, thereby treating that subject as the center of a biblical theology. In a later work I hope to return to this subject.

Retribution

In the discourses, the father and Woman Wisdom urge men/sons to wise behavior and to avoid foolish behavior. Part of their strategy involves pointing to the good things that follow from the former and the bad consequences that flow from the latter. According to the teaching of

---

106. See comments in D. G. Spriggs, *Two Old Testament Theologies* (London: SCM, 1974), 40–41, 105, with other references.

107. M. Kline, *The Structure of Biblical Authority* (Grand Rapids: Eerdmans, 1975).

the book, the ultimate outcome of wisdom is life, and the final outcome of foolish behavior is death. Proverbs 3:2 refers to the wise:

> For length of days and years of life
> and peace they will add to you.

In regard to the fool, 24:20 states:

> For there will be no future for evil;
> the lamp of the wicked will be extinguished.

But life and death are not the only rewards (and for the significance of "life" in the book, see "Afterlife" below). Other more temporal rewards are associated with wise actions and attitudes, and punishments with foolish ones. A selection of proverbs will illustrate:

> Honor Yahweh with your wealth
> and from the first of your produce.
> And your barns will be filled with plenty,
> and your vats will burst with wine. (3:9–10)

> All the haughty are an abomination to Yahweh;
> they will surely not go unpunished. (16:5)

> The lips of a fool lead to accusation;
> his mouth invites blows. (18:6)

> The violence of the wicked will sweep them away,
> for they refuse to act with justice. (21:7)

> For the righteous may fall seven times, but get up,
> but the wicked will stumble in evil. (24:16)

This is just a sample of proverbs that connect godly action with blessings and ungodly action with curses, but they are illustrative of the approach to retribution found in the book.

A number of questions are raised by the rewards and punishments of the proverbs. The first is the agency of the punishment, while a second important one is whether they are true to life.

With regard to the first question, while in Proverbs good things happen to good people and bad things happen to bad people, rarely is the agent of the blessing and punishment named. Sometimes the connection between act and consequence is just stated, with no mention of how it will happen. In the case of a text like 21:7, it seems as if the evil acts themselves will boomerang back on evildoers. They reap the consequences of their actions. In 18:6, the very words of fools will result in their pain. Interestingly, a text like 24:16 reveals that the sages understand that bad things will happen to good people; the righteous are said to stumble and more than once. However, they, as opposed to the evil, will get up again. In other words, the bad things that happen to good people are simply temporary setbacks. They are, after all, on a road that ends in life.[108]

On the other hand, a text like 16:5, though it doesn't make a direct connection, certainly leaves the impression that Yahweh has something to do with the punishment. The fact that the act is an abomination to Yahweh leads to the punishment. Finally, there are passages that do make a connection between Yahweh and reward and punishment:

> For the one whom Yahweh loves he will correct,
> even like a father who treats a son favorably. (3:12)

> The curse of Yahweh is in the house of the wicked,
> but he blesses the home of the righteous. (3:33)

> Yahweh will not let the righteous starve,
> but he will push away the desire of the wicked. (10:3)

So there are texts that lead us to think that the act of the wicked will come back to haunt them and those that imply or directly connect Yahweh to the rewards and punishments that come on people. However, the two are not really different. The former may imply that Yahweh will see that people get what they deserve. Perhaps the best way to think of it is that Yahweh built the world in such a way that punishments are inherent in bad actions and rewards in good actions. Yahweh is ultimately behind all consequences. As Boström puts it, "Our investigation . . . has led us to the conclusion that the world view of the sages was neither built upon a concept of an impersonal order nor of actions with 'automatic,' built-in consequences, but on the active participation of the Lord in the affairs of men in conjunction with man's own responsibility."[109]

However, this raises an even more troubling question: Is Proverbs' teaching on retribution true? Is it really the case that good things happen to good people and bad things happen to bad people? The question may be most pointedly stated with reference to 10:3. If Yahweh does

---

108. K. Koch ("Gibt es ein Vergeltungsdogma im Alten Testament?" *Zeitschrift für Theologie und Kirche* 52 [1955]: 1–42) famously described this as "the act-consequence relationship": an act leads inexorably to a certain consequence. Others (Boström, *God of the Sages*, 90–91) have qualified this to "the character-consequence relationship," recognizing that acts arise out of character and are more like a symptom than the reason for the consequence.

109. Boström, *God of the Sages*, 139; also argued by Waltke, *Proverbs*, 1:73–76.

not let the righteous starve and pushes away the desire of the wicked, why does it appear as if some godly people go hungry and even die of starvation while some wicked people are fat and happy?

This raises the question of whether it is correct to consider the threats of punishments and the anticipation of rewards as promises or guarantees. Is Proverbs saying that whoever acts in a wise way will definitely and without fail be wealthy, healthy, and happy? And will the one who acts foolishly always be poor, sickly, and sad?

The answer to this important question is no. It is in the nature of the proverb not to give promises but rather to indicate the best route toward reward—all things being equal. We illustrate what we mean here by an examination of a commonly abused proverb, 22:6:

> Train up youths in his [God's] path;
>   then when they age, they will not depart from it.

The commentary proper may be consulted for a full examination of the proper interpretation of this difficult question. Here we look at the connection between the admonition for action ("train up youths") and the consequence that they will not depart from it. But is this true? Are parents who train their children in God's way promised that they will be godly when they are older? And if so, may the behavior of adult children be used as a diagnostic tool to evaluate the efforts of their parents?

Due to the nature of the proverb as explained above, the answer is no. Parents are here encouraged to train their children in God's way since that will lead to their godliness—all other things being equal. It is much more likely that children will go the right way if so trained than if their spiritual education is ignored. But all things might not be equal. Perhaps the children fall in with a bad crowd who persuade them to go a different direction. Or there may be a host of other reasons for why a child rejects God's way. A single proverb does not intend to address all the nuances of a situation; it just gives a snapshot of life to motivate proper behavior.[110]

The books of Job and Ecclesiastes guard against the misunderstanding that wisdom and righteous behavior inexorably lead to good things. But even within the book of Proverbs itself, there is awareness that the wise do not always receive all the blessings immediately. As Van Leeuwen has shown, this is indicated by the better-than proverbs. We illustrate with 22:1:

> A reputation is preferable to much wealth,
>   and graciousness is better than silver and gold.

110. Waltke, "Does Proverbs Promise Too Much?"

A better-than proverb states relative values. It implies that one may need to make a choice between two things and points the reader toward the one that is preferable. Here we see that reputation and graciousness are better than material wealth. So, even though some proverbs may suggest that righteous people become wealthy, we see here that sometimes people may have to sacrifice wealth in order to gain virtues associated with wisdom.[111]

Afterlife

Christians who read Proverbs and the rest of the OT in the light of the NT cannot help but wonder how its understanding of the afterlife might relate to the issue of retribution in the OT generally and to Proverbs in particular. The issue of the OT teaching on the afterlife is difficult, and the struggle on the issue among Jewish interpreters in the first century may be seen in the divide between the Sadducees and the Pharisees.[112]

The problem of proper retribution is not limited in the OT to Proverbs. Deuteronomy and Deuteronomic thought made a strong connection between obedience to the law and blessings and between disobedience and curse. For the most part, the prophets warned the people of God of great punishments because they had disobeyed the law. Of course, such threats were not necessarily immediate. In the case of Samuel-Kings, for instance, the argument is based on what might be called delayed retribution. Finally redacted during the period of the exile, it may be making the case for why God had allowed for the destruction of Jerusalem by showing how the sins of the past generations had "come to roost."

The perspective provided by the NT is that retribution does work out in the long run. In its vision of the afterlife, it suggests that people ultimately get what they deserve. However, an important component of this is that the final assessment is based not exclusively on obedience but on relationship with God.

But does Proverbs itself demonstrate an awareness of an afterlife where people meet their final reward? Most scholars say no. They suggest that the reason earthly rewards—wealth, long life, happiness—are put forward is that there was no sense of anything beyond this life. And certainly there is no definitive argument to prove otherwise.

111. A point well made by Van Leeuwen, "Wealth and Poverty."
112. Part of the divide may also be explained by the fact that the Sadducees, who denied the afterlife, considered only the Torah as "canonical," while the Pharisees affirmed the Prophets and Writings as well. However, according to many contemporary scholars, the latter (with the possible exception of Dan. 12:1–3) did not teach a concept of the afterlife either. As will become clear, I do not share this skepticism.

Even though the word "life" does not clearly point to knowledge of the afterlife, in some contexts such a minimalist reading makes the sages seem incredibly naive. What does it mean to promise life to those who are wise and death to those who are foolish when everyone knows that all die? Of course, this is the question that Qoheleth raises, concluding that in the final analysis the wisdom enterprise is not worth it (Eccles. 2:12–17).

Even so, we cannot determine the intention of the ancient sages with certainty. When they said "life," did they simply mean to suggest that God would reward good people with a few more years, or did they have a sense of something beyond?[113] This may be the case particularly with regard to passages like the following in Proverbs:

> In the way of the righteous is life,
>   and the path of abomination leads to death. (12:28)

> For one with insight, the way of life is upward,
>   to turn aside from Sheol below. (15:24)

> Don't withhold discipline from young people.
>   If you strike them with the rod, they will not die.
> Strike them with a rod,
>   and you will extricate their lives from Sheol. (23:13–14)

However, the textual and philological difficulties of these verses make certainty impossible.[114]

Though we cannot answer this question with regard to the intention of the human composers and ancient speakers of these proverbs, those who read the same texts in the light of the fuller revelation of the NT do so with more confident teaching on the nature of the afterlife.

---

113. This is not to take the side of M. J. Dahood, who argued on the basis of Ugaritic comparisons that the Hebrew word "life" (*hay*) frequently meant "eternal life." See his *Proverbs and Northwest Semitic Philology*, 25–26. This approach has been roundly rejected. See N. J. Tromp, *Primitive Conceptions of Death and the Netherworld in the Old Testament* (Rome: Pontifical Biblical Institute, 1969), 43.

114. See discussion in Johnston, 207–9.

Part 1

Extended Discourses on Wisdom

(1:1–9:18)

The first main division of Proverbs, constituting the first nine chapters, begins with a prologue (1:1–7) containing an authorship and genre designation as well as indications of the prospective audience. The prologue continues with a lengthy statement of purpose and concludes with the theological motto of the book (1:7). The rest of the first division contains sixteen discourses (see "The Structure of Proverbs" in the introduction), most of which are lectures from a father to his son (or sons) while some (1:20–33; 8:1–9:6) are the words of Woman Wisdom to all the men who pass by her. This division ends with a third speaker, Woman Folly, who competes with Woman Wisdom for the attention of the young men.

Proverbs 1–9 functions as a hermeneutical guide to Prov. 10–31. As we will see, the reader is confronted in chap. 9 with a choice between Woman Wisdom and Woman Folly. This is a theological decision between allegiance to Yahweh and the worship of idols and serves to bring theological profundity to the use of the words *wisdom* and *folly* and their associated terms throughout the book.

Chapter 1

Translation

¹The proverbs of Solomon, the son of David, king of Israel—
²to know wisdom and discipline;
    to understand insightful sayings;ª
³to receive the teachingᵇ of insight,ᶜ
    righteousness, justice, and virtue;
⁴to give to the simple prudence,
    to the young knowledge and discretion.
⁵Let the wise hear and increase teaching;
    let those with understanding acquire guidance,
⁶so they may understand a proverb and a difficult saying,
    the words of the wise and their enigmas.
⁷The fear of Yahweh is the beginning of knowledge,
    but fools despise wisdom and discipline.

⁸Listen, my son, to the teachingᵈ of your father;
    don't neglect the instruction of your mother.
⁹It is a garland of grace around your head,
    and beads for your neck.
¹⁰My son, don't let sinners entice you;
    don't accedeᵉ ¹¹when they say:
"Come with us, and let's set up a deadly ambush;
    let's lie in wait for the innocent for fun.

a. Literally, "to understand sayings of understanding" (*lĕhābîn ʾimrê bînâ*), but this is opaque in English.

b. This word, *mûsār*, may be and typically is translated "discipline" in what follows, but "teaching" makes more sense in the present context.

c. *Haśkēl* comes from the root that we will normally translate "insight," but here we note that it is a different root from that translated "insightful" in v. 2.

d. While I typically translate *mûsār* as "discipline" (see v. 2), here I take it as "teaching," since that word works better with the verb "listen." See also 1:2.

e. An apocopated (shortened) form of the qal second-person imperfect from ʾbh, "to be willing" or "to accede."

¹²Let's swallow up the living like Sheol—
   whole, like those who go down into the pit.
¹³We'll find precious wealth;
   we'll fill our houses with plunder.
¹⁴Throw your lot in with us;
   one bag of loot will be for all of us."
¹⁵My son, don't go on the way with them;
   keep your feet from their trail,
¹⁶for their feet run toward evil,
   and they hurry to shed blood.
¹⁷For in vain is a net cast[f]
   in the sight of any bird.
¹⁸But they set up a deadly ambush;
   they lie in wait for their lives.
¹⁹Thus is the way of all who seek profits by violence;[g]
   they take the life of their owner.

²⁰Wisdom shouts in the street;
   in the public square she yells out.
²¹At the top of the noisy throng she calls out an invitation;
   at the entrances to the gates in the city she says her piece:
²²"How long, O simple, will you love simplemindedness,
   and mockers hold their mocking dear,
   and fools hate knowledge?
²³You should respond to my correction.
   I will pour forth my spirit to you;
   I will make known to you my words
²⁴Because I invited you, but you rejected me;
   I extended my hand, but you paid no attention.
²⁵You ignored all my advice,
   and my correction you did not want.
²⁶I will also laugh at your disaster;
   I will ridicule when your fear comes.
²⁷When your fear comes like a tempest,[h]
   and your disaster arrives like a storm,
   when distress and oppression come on you,
²⁸then he will call me, and I will not answer;
   he will seek me, but he will not find me.
²⁹Because they hated knowledge
   and did not choose the fear of Yahweh.

f. The verb *mĕzōrâ* is difficult. The context calls for a meaning to "spread out," and here as elsewhere (see Fox, *Proverbs 1–9*, 88) we connect it with the root *zrh*, which means "to cast," usually of seed. See discussion also in Driver, "Problems in the Hebrew Text of Proverbs," 173–74.

g. Harland ("*Bṣᶜ*," 311–12) cites this verse as a clear instance, because of the context, in which the root *bṣᶜ* implies violence.

h. Reading Qere (*šōʾâ*) rather than the Kethib (*šaʾăwâ*).

³⁰They did not want my advice,
   and they rejected all my reproof.
³¹They will eat from the fruit of their way,
   and they will be sated from their own counsels,
³²For the turning away of the simple will kill them,
   and the complacency of fools will destroy them.
³³Those who obey me will dwell securely;
   they will be untroubled from the horror of evil.

Interpretation

1:1–7. *Superscription and purpose of the book.* The book of Proverbs opens with a superscription (1:1) that introduces the book as a whole. It is also the opening line of a seven-verse extended introduction that clearly states the purpose of the book that follows. Though the book is the result of bringing together different collections of wisdom over time (see "Authorship and Date" and "The Structure of Proverbs" in the introduction), this introduction must have been one of the latest additions to the final form of the book and one of the factors that give the final compilation a feeling of organic wholeness. This unit begins with a typical superscription, proceeds through a lengthy and technical description of its purpose, and then ends with what proves to be the underlying principle of the book's teaching as a whole. This introductory passage is jam-packed with words that are important to wisdom literature and are repeated throughout the book. For this reason, we will reflect at some length on their meanings and refer back to this place when these words appear later in the book. Johnson is correct in saying that in these verses "the author first identified the material; second, he declared the objectives; third, he called the hopeful to receptivity; and fourth, he pointed up the motto of wisdom that aspiring 'sages' must never forget."[1]

Proverbs is not unique in having a prologue such as 1:1–7, though it is unique in the specific content. Most Egyptian wisdom begins with an introduction before describing observations and offering advice. We offer as an example an excerpted quote from the prologue to Amenemope, which, like Proverbs, states its intention as well as its author.

   Beginning of the teaching for life,
   The instructions for well-being,
   Every rule for relations with elders,
   For conduct toward magistrates;

1. Johnson, "Analysis of Proverbs 1:1–7."

Knowing how to answer one who speaks,
To reply to one who sends a message.
So as to direct him on the paths of life,
To make him prosper upon earth;
To let his heart enter its shrine,
Steering clear of evil;
To save him from the mouth of strangers,
To let (him) be praised in the mouth of people.
Made by the overseer of fields, experienced in his office,

. . . .

Who has a chapel at Abydos,
Amenemope, the son of Kanakht,
The justified in Ta-wer.
[For] his son, the youngest of his children,

. . . .

Hor-em-maakher is his true name. (Amenemope 1.1–13; 2.10–13; 3.4)[2]

---

¹The proverbs of Solomon, the son of David, king of Israel—

The first verse is the superscription. Superscriptions appear at the beginning of many other biblical books, most consistently with works of prophecy. The superscription is like the title page of a modern book in that it provides information about the genre, author, and occasionally the subject matter and date of a book (e.g., Isa. 1:1; Jer. 1:1; Nah. 1:1). Superscriptions are found in other wisdom contexts (Eccles. 1:1; Song 1:1), and the one closest to the opening of Proverbs is found in Eccles. 1:1: "The words of Qoheleth, son of David, king in Jerusalem." In Ecclesiastes, this is part of the frame narrator's strategy of near identity between Qoheleth and Solomon.[3]

In the case of Proverbs, the book's superscription provides the genre ("proverbs") and an authorship designation ("Solomon, son of David, king of Israel"). The date is left unexpressed, and the subject matter is explicated in the lengthy description in vv. 2–6, which is appended to the superscription. That extension also delineates the original intended recipients.

The most natural reading of the superscription in wisdom and prophetic literature is that a second, subsequent hand added it. It is not impossible that the author or speaker wrote the superscription, referring to himself in the third person, but the only reason to argue in this direction is to defend a rather mechanical view of biblical inspiration and insist that only one author stands behind a single book.

2. Translation by M. Lichtheim, in *COS* 1:116.
3. See Longman, *Ecclesiastes*, 57.

For the term "proverbs" (*mišlê*, from *māšāl*), see "Genre" in the introduction. For the significance of the reference to Solomon, son of David, king of Israel, see "Authorship and Date" in the introduction.

What we identify as the purpose statement may be divided into four parts. It begins a general statement of intention that is directed toward no specific group and therefore should probably be understood as intended for all readers. Then the next two parts are distinguished by reference to the addressee. Verse 4 addresses the "simpleminded," while vv. 5–6 speak to the wise person. Finally, the seventh verse states the motto of the book.

> ²to know wisdom and discipline;
>   to understand insightful sayings;
> ³to receive the teaching of insight,
>   righteousness, justice, and virtue;

These verses describe qualities that the teaching of Proverbs is supposed to impart to its readers. Unlike v. 4 and vv. 5–6, no specific group is named as the recipients. Two interpretations of this are possible. Perhaps these verses are specifically directed to the "simple," whose identification is delayed until v. 4. On the other hand, these verses describe some of the most fundamental concepts of the book and may outline the goal for every reader, whether "simple" (v. 4) or "wise" (v. 5). The latter view seems most reasonable.

The statement of intention begins with the verb "to know" (*ydᶜ*), related to the noun "knowledge" (*daᶜat*). Here and elsewhere in Proverbs, this verbal root has the sense of "to acknowledge" or "to recognize" (see also 3:6a). It implies more than simply intellectual assent.

This verb governs two objects. The first word is "wisdom," or *ḥokmâ*, a concept discussed in the introduction, which is the general term from which all the other terms flow. The next word also frequently occurs; indeed, it appears once each in vv. 2 and 3. We translate the term "teaching" (*mûsār*), though elsewhere we typically translate "discipline." The word is formed from the verb *ysr*, "to admonish" or "to correct" (*NIDOTTE* 2:479–82). The verb as well as the noun implies the threat of punishment if one does not obey the words of teaching. As we will see later in the book (10:13; 13:24; 19:18, 25; 20:30; 22:15; 23:13–14; 26:3; 29:15, 17, 19), corporeal punishment was very much a possibility for the reluctant learner. This word group can denote either the threat or the application of the punishment.

The parallel colon has a second verb, "to understand," from *byn*, and it governs the object, which we have translated "insightful sayings." However, note that "insightful sayings" (*ʾimrê bînâ*) is more literally rendered "sayings of understanding," the root *byn* being repeated twice in the colon. These are general terms. The verb occurs over 160 times in the Bible, many times in the wisdom literature. The noun *bînâ* as well as another noun formed from the root (*tĕbûnâ*) are often also found. According to *NIDOTTE* 1:652, this word is less relational than *yādaʿ* and "is used more to refer to the insight that comes from knowing. The verb means to perceive through the senses."

The third verse again mentions "discipline" but this time joins it with the word "insight"[4] (*haśkēl*), which we are taking as a hiphil infinitive absolute, along with Fox, who points out that "it is one of several terms for wisdom" and that it is difficult in the final analysis to determine its precise nuance in connection with the other words, including *ḥokmâ*.[5] It comes from the verbal root *śkl*, which means "to instruct" or "to act intelligently." Insight refers to the recognition of the true nature of a situation or circumstance. The word can also carry the meaning of success, and one can see how insight could result in a successful treatment of a particular situation.

The final colon of v. 3 explicitly for the first time introduces us to the ethical nature of wisdom. It is not just knowledge that the book seeks to impart but also righteousness, justice, and virtue. What constitutes righteousness, justice, and virtue is not specified or spelled out in the immediate context but will receive content as proper behaviors and attitudes are promoted in the chapters to follow. The words also raise the question of the relationship between wisdom and law, a much-debated topic. As we saw in the introduction ("Wisdom and Law"), we side with those who believe that the sages assumed a knowledge and adherence to the commandments found in the Torah. Thus, those who are righteous, just, and virtuous are those who conform to the principles both of wisdom and of law.

> ⁴to give to the simple prudence,
> to the young knowledge and discretion.

This verse is directed toward the simple or simpleminded. The simpleminded are the *pĕtāʾîm*, plural of *petî*, from the verb *pth* I, which means "to be inexperienced, be naïve" (*NIDOTTE* 3:714–15). The opposite of the simpleminded person is not the wise but the prudent person (*ʿormâ*), and this is the characteristic that the wisdom of Proverbs seeks to provide to the naive reader. The simpleminded person is in a much better place than a fool (*kĕsîl*) or a mocker (*lēṣ*). The main advantage the simpleminded

---

4. It is hard to determine whether these words should be understood in a genitive relation, as we take it here, or as "discipline and insight/success."

5. Fox, *Proverbs 1–9*, 59–60.

have over fools and the mockers is that they are teachable. The simple-minded are the ones addressed by Woman Wisdom in pivotal chap. 8. Again, there as here, Wisdom hopes to impart prudence (ʿormâ) to the simpleminded (8:5).

The word "prudence" (ʿormâ) can have a negative nuance in contexts outside of Proverbs and in those contexts is best translated "shrewd," "cunning," or "deceptive" (most notably Gen. 3:1, describing the serpent). However, in Proverbs it is used only in a positive manner, as something that is in the company of wisdom and knowledge. According to Prov. 8:12a, "I, Wisdom, live with prudence." "Prudence" describes one's ability to use reason, in context under the fear of God, to navigate the problems of life. Prudence carefully considers a situation before rushing in. It implies coolheadedness.

So, one important purpose of the book is to give prudence to the simpleminded. Parallel to this is the intention to give knowledge and discretion to the "young" (naʿar). The naʿar usually is chronologically young,[6] typically an adolescent and unmarried,[7] though in any case, another nuance of the word might also come into play in the present context, and that is "immature." The naʿar is immature and needs the knowledge and discretion that will be provided by the book of Proverbs. "Knowledge" (daʿat) is a very general term, formed from the extremely common verb "to know" (yādāʿ). The word is so general that really the only distinctive thing to remark about it is that it probably implies a relationship with the object that is known. This would explain the use of the verb to mean "to have sexual intercourse" (as in Gen. 4:1). In any case, as we have seen in the introduction and throughout the book, knowledge was never an abstract proposition in the book of Proverbs; it always implied a relationship. The word "discretion" (mĕzimmâ), however, is more specific. It is a noun formed from the verb zmm, "to think, plan, purpose, devise" (NIDOTTE 1:1112–14). It, like "prudence," can have a positive or negative meaning, depending on whether the planning is for constructive or destructive purposes. When the meaning is negative, then the translation "to plot" or "plan evil" is often appropriate. Positively, though, the noun means either "discretion" or "resourcefulness." It imparts the ability to walk the path of life in a constructive way and to avoid the lures of the evil path (Prov. 2:11).

> [5]Let the wise hear and increase teaching;
> let those with understanding acquire guidance,

6. Though it is used for a thirty-year-old in Gen. 41:12 (see also v. 46).
7. So J. Hartley, NIDOTTE 3:125.

> [6]so they may understand a proverb and a difficult saying,
> the words of the wise and their enigmas.

These two verses address the wise person (*ḥākām*). This indicates a different category than we observed in v. 4, where the simple/young person was addressed. The wise person is more mature. He already participates in the wisdom program, but the introduction reminds the reader that even such an advanced person can benefit from reflection on the instructions that follow. In this case, it is a matter of increasing (*ysp*) what is already there, building on a structure that the person already has. The introduction also refers to this person by the closely related term "understanding" (*nābôn*), a noun formed by the commonly occurring verb *byn* (see commentary on v. 2). According to Shupak, the noun almost always occurs in parallel with *ḥākām*, though it, unlike *ḥākām*, refers never to God but always to human beings.[8]

What will the wise or understanding person gain from what follows? In the first place, an increase in "teaching" (*leqaḥ*). This term occurs only nine times in the Bible, all but two (Deut. 32:2; Isa. 29:24) in Job and Proverbs (elsewhere at Prov. 4:2; 7:21; 16:21, 23). The idea seems to be that the wise person will enhance and increase his wisdom.

More difficult in meaning, however, is the word we translate "guidance" (*taḥbulôt*). This word only occurs a handful of times in the Hebrew Bible, mostly in Proverbs (see also 11:14; 12:5; 20:18; 24:6). Shupak argues against the traditional understanding of the development of the word from *hebel* (rope) to *ḥōbēl* ("sea captain," who uses ropes to guide a ship) to *taḥbulôt* (guidance). Shupak draws on an Egyptian analogy to suggest that the word does come from rope, but suggests a knot. Thus, "figuratively speaking then, *taḥbulôt* is a saying that is tightly phrased, well constructed, a pithy maxim made like a series of knots and loops. Such a saying is the work of a craftsman, only a craftsman expert in the craft of speech can understand it."[9] However, while the translation "maxim," perhaps implying a pithy saying that embodies guidance, may be a meaning of the term and indeed one that could work in this context, it seems to me that the traditional understanding makes sense and fits better into all the following contexts of the book.[10]

According to v. 6, the wise will increase their wisdom by reading the writings that follow. This has the effect (v. 7) of granting understanding of four types of wisdom sayings: the "proverb" (*māšāl*), the "difficult saying" (*mĕlîṣâ*), the "words of the wise" (*dibrê ḥăkāmîm*), and "riddles"

8. Shupak, *Where Can Wisdom Be Found?* 244.
9. See the extensive discussion by Shupak, ibid., 313–17 (quote is from 316).
10. See also *NIDOTTE* 4:285.

(*ḥîdot*). One might assume that these are forms to be encountered in the book of Proverbs itself, but it is also possible that the intention is broader and, by listing these four forms, simply indicates that the one who masters what follows will be adept at the interpretation of difficult sayings. We will look at the meaning of each of these four expressions separately, but the first observation we make is that they all seem to refer to indirect language, and therefore language difficult to understand at first glance.

We begin with *māšāl*, a term that in one sense characterizes the entire book. In Hebrew tradition, the book is entitled *Mišlê*. In one sense, then, we might say that the entire book is composed of *měšālîm*. Indeed, the term *māšāl* denotes what we recognize as many different types of writing. As Perdue points out, the *māšāl* (proverb) includes "sayings (1 Sam. 10:12; 24:14; Ezek. 12:22–23), didactic poems (Isa. 14:4–10), wisdom psalms (Ps. 49:4 [5 MT]; 78:2), and parables (Ezek. 17:2; 21:5). Among the variety of sayings are the proverb (Prov. 21:12, 25, 31), the comparison (Prov. 10:26; and 11:22), the beatitude (Prov. 8:32, 34), the better saying (Prov. 15:16, 17), the numerical saying (Prov. 30:15–16, 18–19, 21–23, 24–28, 29–31), and the abomination saying (Prov. 3:32; 6:16; 8:7; 11:1)."[11]

The verbal meaning of *māšāl* (*mšl*) means "to be like." One would expect comparison to be a constituent part of the proverb, and indeed, many of the proverbs use simile and metaphor to communicate important ideas. However, not all *měšālîm* are built on comparison, and Fox is right to point out that the word also indicates that the saying carries the "presumption or claim that they are well known and in widespread use."[12]

While *māšāl* is a broad term, "difficult saying" (*mělîṣâ*) is more restricted; at least it occurs more rarely (see only Hab. 2:6). Scholars argue for a more precise nuance based on supposed verbal roots of the noun or translations by the versions. *NIDOTTE* 2:798–800, for instance, associates the noun with the verb "to mock," which is so frequent in Proverbs, and defines it as "an enigmatic saying, a saying laden with satire, sarcasm, and innuendo." However, this would be an odd connection considering that the context demands that the *mělîṣâ* is a wisdom saying, not associated with the fool, who is a mocker. It is more likely derived from the hiphil of *lyṣ*, with the meaning of "to interpret," but this still does not lead to a very satisfying specific understanding of the word.

The second colon of v. 6 lists two more types of wisdom sayings. Again, it begins with what appears to be a broad designation ("the words of the

11. Perdue, *Proverbs*, 73.
12. Fox, *Proverbs 1–9*, 55.

wise") and then a narrower one ("enigmas"). The "words of the wise" (*dibrê ḥăkāmîm*) probably does not refer to informal sayings as much as to written wisdom collections. These wise men are the sages who teach wisdom to the young. The expression also occurs in Eccles. 12:11, where the unnamed frame narrator warns his son that the words of the wise are like goads and firmly implanted nails, things that hurt. He warns his son of them (12:12). In this verse, there is a much more positive attitude toward the words of the wise. The collections of wisdom that follow in Proverbs are easily seen as such words.

Lastly, the prologue refers to "their enigmas" (*ḥîdōtām*), the "their" being a reference to the wise. This word has generated much mystery because it is often translated "riddle," and as we read on, we see that there are no riddles in the book of Proverbs. The word can indeed include riddles and specifically does so in Judg. 14:14, referring to Samson's wedding-day riddle. However, the word probably is to be understood more broadly as an enigma or difficult speech. Many proverbs, particularly in their original Hebrew, have an element of ambiguity to them, which makes them difficult at times. This is probably the correct understanding of the word *ḥîdâ*.

> [7]The fear of Yahweh is the beginning of knowledge,
> but fools despise wisdom and discipline.

The final verse of the prologue is its climax. Indeed, this verse has been called the motto of the book. I would agree that it is its most foundational truth, and it is repeated with some variation in a number of places in the book (especially 9:10, but see also 1:29; 2:5; 3:7; 8:13; 9:10; 10:27; 14:2, 26, 27; 15:16, 33; 16:6; 19:23; 22:4; 23:17; 24:21; 28:14; 29:25; 31:30).[13]

"The fear of Yahweh is the beginning of knowledge." As a beginning, this statement claims that there is no knowledge apart from a proper attitude and relationship to Yahweh. Fear of Yahweh is foundational to knowledge, which here functions as a close synonym to wisdom. In this way, the book acknowledges the radically relational and theocentric nature of knowledge/wisdom. This is important especially in the light of the fact that the wisdom literature does not hammer away at this idea. Many of the proverbs in the latter part of the book cite experience, observation, or human reason as the grounds for their advice, and this has led some scholars to suppose that wisdom, at least in its early

13. Bartholomew (*Reading Proverbs with Integrity*, 8) suggests that the references here and in 31:30 might form an inclusio to the final form of the book. This may be the case, but with such an important and repeated idea, which also occurs in many other places in the book, it is hard to determine whether it is an intentional inclusio.

stages, is a "secular" enterprise. However, the present form of the book is thoroughly theological (see "Theology of the Book" in the introduction), so that even human observation depends on divinity in a foundational way. After all,

> An ear to hear and an eye to see—
> Yahweh made both of them. (20:12)

It is also significant that Proverbs uses the Tetragrammaton, Yahweh, to refer to God here. Yahweh (the Lord in Eng.) is God's covenant name and connects him with the Torah (Exod. 3). Much is made of the fact that Qoheleth in Ecclesiastes distances himself from the God of Israel by referring to him only with the generic *ĕlōhîm*, and we should accordingly note that Proverbs uses "Yahweh," again a reminder that the final form of Proverbs is far from secular or completely removed from the ancient traditions of Israel.

The verse demands a particular attitude in one's relationship to Israel's covenant God, and that is communicated by the noun "fear" (*yir'at*, from the verb *yr'*). The verb has a semantic range that goes from what might be called "respect" or "awe" to "utter terror." Indisputable, however, is the basic premise that to fear Yahweh is to stand in a subservient position to him, to acknowledge one's dependence upon him. In the context of knowledge, it is to recognize that there is no true knowledge without reference to him (for more on this topic, see "The Fear of Yahweh" in the introduction).

The second colon looks at the same truth from the opposite perspective. Wisdom begins with the fear of Yahweh, but fools despise wisdom and discipline. Of course, it is ridiculous to think that those who reject God have no knowledge or understanding of anything. Indeed, in ancient as well as modern times, some of the brightest people are either indifferent or even hostile toward God. As we saw in the introduction, the Bible recognizes the wisdom of foreign cultures (see "Ancient Near Eastern Background" in the introduction). However, fools do not see the big picture. One might be an expert, say, on sailing, and the Bible even calls pagan sailors wise (Ps. 107:23–32; see the use of the root *ḥkm* in v. 27), but they do not understand who made the winds and the sea and who ultimately guides one's way. True knowledge begins with an acknowledgment that everything is created and sustained by God and that he is the one who imparts knowledge not only through revelation but also through experience, observation, and reason.

This is the beginning of knowledge. The word "beginning" (*rē'šît*) has the sense not only of "first" but also of foundation or even source. It may not be stretching the concept too far to think of the beginning of wisdom functioning as a presupposition or preunderstanding. It is the first thought that makes all other thoughts fall into place. Proverbs, and the Bible as a whole, does not try to prove the existence of its God; it rather presents God's existence as a presupposition that is manifest in history and nature.

While most attention focuses on the first colon of this verse, the second colon, for the first time, states that not everyone is willing to submit themselves to Yahweh to gain knowledge and wisdom. There is a group of people who despise wisdom and therefore implicitly despise Yahweh, and they are the fools. The Hebrew word for "fool" used here (ʾĕwîl) is part of a rich vocabulary of folly. We will treat these words as they appear in the text, but we must first recognize that their semantic ranges overlap. Nonetheless, a hierarchy of fools can be roughly constructed, and the ʾĕwîl stands between the kĕsîl ("fool") and the lēṣ ("mocker"). On the basis of Prov. 27:22 ("Though you crush a fool in a mortar with a pestle along with crushed grain, yet his folly will not depart from him"), Shupak characterizes the ʾĕwîl as an "incorrigible ignoramus." Its verbal root means "to grow thick."[14] It would take such a fool to reject wisdom and discipline, which leads to such wonderful consequences, as we will see.

The expression is found outside of Proverbs in Psalms, Job, and Ecclesiastes. Psalm 111 concludes:

> The fear of the LORD is the beginning of wisdom;
>   all who follow his precepts have good understanding.
> To him belongs eternal praise. (111:10 NIV)

Perhaps here we are to see a connection between wisdom and following God's laws (something made explicit in later Israelite wisdom, as in Sir. 24). One who fears Yahweh will follow his law, which is the way of wisdom. In Job 28 such fear serves as the climax to the powerful poem about the source of wisdom. Human beings can plumb the earth for rare gems and precious metals, but only God knows the way to wisdom. The chapter ends:

> And he said to them,
> "The fear of the LORD—that is wisdom,
> and to shun evil is understanding." (28:28, cf. NIV)

Ecclesiastes presents the most difficult usage of the phrase, and a justification for the viewpoint presented here is to be found elsewhere.[15]

---

14. Shupak, *Where Can Wisdom Be Found?* 204–5.
15. See the introduction and commentary on the relevant verses in Longman, *Ecclesiastes*.

In that book we do not have the whole expression, but frequent calls to "fear God." Most of these occurrences are found in the speech of Qoheleth, the confused wise man who speaks in the body of the book (3:14; 5:7; 7:18; 8:12, 13). In the immediate context, it is clear that Qoheleth believes that God acts the way he does to frighten people into submission, not to arouse a sense of respectful awe of his power and might. However, the expression appears one last time in the epilogue in the voice of a second unnamed wise teacher who is instructing his son, using the words of Qoheleth. Here the admonition to fear God is much more likely to be in keeping with the meaning we have seen in the book of Proverbs.

Theological Implications

Proverbs is a book of wisdom firmly rooted in the ancient world, as we learned from our survey of ancient Near Eastern wisdom (see "Ancient Near Eastern Background" in the introduction). The prologue addresses the ancient reader to inform him, and here the male gender is intentional (see "Gender and the Theology" in the introduction), of the advantages of reading the book of Proverbs. Above, we inquired into the original meaning of the text; now, we want to explore how a modern reader might read the prologue.

Most modern readers of the book, lay and ministerial, read Proverbs for exactly the same reason as the ancient readers—for theological enlightenment and practical advice. Only a certain type of scholar is solely interested in the ancient meaning of the text. What does the prologue say to modern readers about what to expect in the pages that follow?

In the first place, we learn that the book is addressed to everyone who is open to its teaching. It is addressed to those we might call the mature and immature of the faith. The only category that is excluded is the fool. We will read much more about fools in the pages to come. They are on the outside, according to the last colon of this section, because they have consciously and intentionally chosen to be outside. They resist the teachings of wisdom. What the prologue makes clear is that the benefits of wisdom are available only to those who have already made a fundamental religious commitment—"the fear of Yahweh is the beginning of knowledge" (1:7) and "of wisdom" (9:10).

Even though the addressee of the book is male, and a young male at that, this should not discourage female and more mature readers from feeling addressed by the book today. After all, the books of the OT and NT were usually written with specific audiences in mind. Samuel and Kings were specifically addressing an exilic audience, while Chronicles a postexilic audience. Matthew tells the story of Jesus to a Jewish Christian audience, while Luke speaks to a Hellenistic Christian audience. Galatians was written to the Galatians. In all these cases, part of the hermeneutical task is to take these culturally specific messages and apply them to our lives and situations today. However, to do so with integrity to the original meaning, we must, as a first step, imagine ourselves in the place of the original audience and then consider how the book's message might apply to our modern situation today. The prologue of Proverbs warns that benefits are available only to those who are receptive, not to fools, who reject the book's teaching out of hand.

The benefits to readers, both ancient and modern, are described in what is essentially a foundational vocabulary of wisdom literature: wisdom, teaching, understanding, insight, prudence, knowledge, and discretion. The ethical component of wisdom is also underscored with words like "righteousness," "justice," and "virtue." In addition, the prologue reveals wisdom's interpretive power with the promise that the wise person will be able to understand maxims, proverbs, enigmas, difficult sayings, and the words of the wise. Interpretation, not only of the text but also of circumstances and people, is at the heart of wisdom activity, as we will see in numerous places in the book.

Finally, the prologue lays down the basic foundation for wisdom; it asserts that wisdom begins with the fear of Yahweh (1:7). One properly fears Yahweh because he is the most powerful being in the universe. Only fools would not be afraid of a being who has the power of life and death over them. Such persons do not understand their place in the cosmos and thus do not know how to act in the world. All other wisdom builds on this point, and there is no wisdom without it. Indeed, in the words of M. L. Barré, "Fear of Yahweh . . . is the first step—'square one'—in the quest for a meaningful existence."[16]

1:8–19. *Avoid evil associations.* We thus come to the first discourse or instruction of the father to the son. Some scholars believe that an earlier form of the book began with chap. 2 since the two discourses of chap. 1 as well as the prologue shows signs of being intentionally added to provide a link with the Torah (vv. 8–19) and the Prophets (vv. 20–33, since only here does Wisdom speak like a prophet).[17]

This first discourse follows a structure that will become familiar.[18] It begins with an exhortation for the son to listen to the message of the

16. Barré, "'Fear of God,'" 41.
17. This is the position of Harris, "Proverbs 1:8–19, 20–33," 207–31. Such a view is worth considering but cannot be proved.
18. The description of the structure of the discourses follows that of Fox, "Ideas of Wisdom," 614–15.

father (v. 8) accompanied by a motivating sentence (v. 9). Then follows the message, which concludes with a summarizing statement (v. 19). In a nutshell, the message of this particular discourse is to avoid associations with evil people, who are defined as those who seek gain at others' expense, even their lives.

We are also for the first time introduced to the metaphor of the path. The path is one's course of life. As we will see, the image will be developed in a way that entails the idea of two possible paths, one good and one evil. Here the son is being warned to stay off the path of those who are trying to make him complicit in their evil dealings.

> **8**Listen, my son, to the teaching of your father;
> don't neglect the instruction of your mother.

This first discourse begins with a call to attention. Both parents, father and mother, are mentioned as involved in the instruction of the son. We understand this to be far more than a function of parallelism, which would suggest that the mention of the father necessitates the appearance of the mother in the second colon. Indeed, the reference to a mother in the position of a teacher is very unusual in ancient wisdom literature.[19] It is true that even in the biblical book of Proverbs, the mother is only infrequently mentioned, and most of the time it is the father who speaks to the son (see 6:20 and 31:1). In any case, the son is first of all encouraged to pay attention to the teaching that follows. The son is the explicit addressee of the early discourses, and we, the actual readers, are to identify and take the position of the son as the parents, and later Wisdom herself, address the son.

The son is called upon to "listen to" (*šmᶜ*) the father. The Hebrew word denotes more than the simple act of hearing; it implies obedience. The son must act on the instruction that follows, not just learn it as brute fact. The negative is used in reference to the mother's teaching, but it implies the same thing. To not "neglect" her teaching means to act on it.

Two words are used to refer to the teaching that follows. The first "teaching" (*mūsâr*) has been discussed above in 1:3, but there with the meaning "discipline." The word implies the threat of punishment if one does not obey the words of instruction, but it is hard to convey that notion when the verb that governs it is *šmᶜ*. In any case, corporeal punishment was very much a possibility for the reluctant learner. This word can either denote the threat or the application of the punishment; here the former is clearly meant. The second word, "instruction" (*tôrâ*), is to be

---

19. An exception is found in the conclusion of Duachety's teaching for his son Pepi in the Satire of the Trades (see Lichtheim, *Ancient Egyptian Literature*, 1:191), where he exhorts his son to "praise god for your father, your mother, who set you on the path of life."

taken in the general sense of instruction and not specifically pointing to the Torah, or law or instruction of the first five books of the Bible. On the other hand, the teaching of the parents in this discourse may be an outgrowth of the Ten Commandments, specifically the commands not to kill, rob, or covet (see "Wisdom and Law" in the introduction).

> [9]It is a garland of grace around your head,
>   and beads for your neck.

The parents give their son further motivation to attend to their instructions in the form of a metaphor that implies reward. They draw a comparison between their advice and jewelry. Jewelry enhances one's beauty; it is expensive and desired. The image is apt for the further reason that wisdom is later said to result in an increase in wealth. The specific ornaments mentioned are first a head ornament of some type, most likely a "garland"[20] rather than a tiara, and then "beads" around the neck. Perhaps it is not pressing the image too far to see these images framing the head, which possesses the instruments of speech and hearing, so important to the wisdom task. It would be anachronistic to suggest that the Israelites located the center of thought with the brain, particularly when they explicitly associated it with the heart.

> [10]My son, don't let sinners entice you;
>   don't accede [11]when they say:
> "Come with us, and let's set up a deadly ambush;
>   let's lie in wait for the innocent for fun.
> [12]Let's swallow up the living like Sheol—
>   whole, like those who go down into the pit.
> [13]We'll find precious wealth;
>   we'll fill our houses with plunder.
> [14]Throw your lot in with us;
>   one bag of loot will be for all of us."

The first instruction of the parents is negative. It is a warning to stay far away from sinners. In particular, they imagine a gang who wants to enlist their son for the purposes of murder and robbery. Gang members prey on the innocent for their own advantage.

The parents warn their son to resist the enticement of their recruitment. They do so by narrating an imaginary scenario and quoting the ringleader of a gang who tries to convince their son to join them. For this imaginary scenario to have any cachet, however, it must reflect a

---

20. See also 4:9, where Wisdom will place a "garland of grace" on the head of the wise son.

real possibility in the society of the time: the existence of gangs who preyed on law-abiding members of society.

The verb "entice" (*pth*) is related to the noun "simpleminded," already encountered in the prologue (v. 4). Camp, in her wisdom reading of the Samson narrative, points out that the verb is also used by the Philistines when trying to enlist Samson's new bride in their plot to discover the meaning of his riddle (Judg. 14:15).[21] Jeremiah also uses the verb to accuse God of "enticing" or "seducing" him into his role as prophet of judgment (20:7). All these instances also carry the connotation of deception as well. The parents are warning the son, in other words, against the attraction that the violent gang represents, because under the surface the attraction is deceptive. They look like they will pillage others, but in the outcome, it is they who will be pillaged.

The parents even take on the voice of the gang as the latter tries to entice their son. Their representation of the gang's speech makes them sound particularly brutal. It is specifically the "innocent," those who do not deserve it, who will be the object of their deadly adventures. Their goal is robbery; they conspire to rob others for their own gain. Their cowardice is suggested by the fact that this will be an ambush of the innocent (v. 11). They do not even give their victims a fighting chance. The parents imply that while the gang wants the son to participate in the violence and therefore benefit from the shared bag of loot, in reality they will entangle their accomplice in guilt and ultimate retribution.

The criminals claim to operate by a kind of inner justice when they say they will share the plunder ("one bag of loot will be for all of us," v. 14). However, their injustice toward the innocent would make one wonder whether they would follow through on this claim. Their only object is to get rich at the expense of others.

Some of the language of the gang members may have mythological overtones. They speak of swallowing "up the living like Sheol" (v. 12). Sheol is the grave, but it has overtones of the underworld generally.[22] With similar language, the Ugaritic texts describe the god Mot, Death, as one who swallows his prey. Perhaps this language is a subtle way by which the parents associate the gang with the "dark side." They are those who model themselves after their master Death. However, we have to leave open the possibility that the language of death or the grave swallowing its victims had become a kind of frozen metaphor, not resonating with mythological allusion.

> [15]My son, don't go on the way with them;
> keep your feet from their trail,

21. Camp, *Wise, Strange, and Holy*, 133.
22. See the excellent work on the subject by Johnston, *Shades of Sheol*.

> ¹⁶for their feet run toward evil,
>   and they hurry to shed blood.
> ¹⁷For in vain is a net cast
>   in the sight of any bird.
> ¹⁸But they set up a deadly ambush;
>   they lie in wait for their lives.
> ¹⁹Thus is the way of all who seek profits by violence;
>   they take the life of their owner.

We return now to the words of the parents after the quotation of the gang leader. They are blunt in their advice. "Don't go on the way with them; keep your feet from their trail" (v. 15). For the first of many times, we encounter the metaphor of the path, or trail (see "Theology of the Book" in the introduction). The "way" (*derek*) is a metaphor for life. Everyone walks on a way. Proverbs also uses near synonyms like "path" (*nĕtîbâ*) with the same meaning (both terms in v. 15). According to chaps. 1–9, there are two types of way: a wise, good way and a foolish, evil way. The parents here urge their son to stay off the latter, while the gang tries to get him to join them on it.

The parents do not leave their advice unsupported. In the rest of the section, they tell their son why it is a bad idea to follow in the way of these sinners. The motivation section begins, as is typical, with the word "for" (*kî*, v. 16).

In a word, the son should avoid the way of the sinners out of self-interest. After all, the sinners are the ones who will ultimately forfeit their lives, and the parents don't want their child to be included among those who destroy themselves.

First, the parents characterize the actions of the sinners as a determined intent to do evil. They "run" on the path toward their wicked goal. They are urgent in their desire to perpetrate violence: "They hurry to shed blood."

The next verse initiates an analogy that is based on the well-used image of the fowler who casts a net to catch a bird (e.g., Ps. 91:3; 124:7; Prov. 6:5; Jer. 5:26; Hosea 9:8). For the net to work, it has to be camouflaged. No bird is going to walk into a trap that is clearly a trap. Thus, as the verse states, it is a waste of time ("vain") to set up a net where a bird can clearly see that it is a trap. Here, the metaphor is used of the punishment that will befall the evil ambushers. Here we find the idea expressed that evil people will get enmeshed in their own traps (as also in Pss. 9:15 [16 MT]; 35:7–8).

The first parental instruction ends with the lesson that such a certain and disastrous end to the plot will not discourage the gang from setting up their deadly ambush. The members of the gang are ready to ambush, but what they foolishly do not realize is that they are lying in ambush for themselves. Finally, the parents draw a general principle from their narrative. All those who seek profits will end up taking their own lives (v. 19).

But as the phrase *kol-bōṣēaʿ bāṣaʿ* (v. 19a, translated as "all who seek profits by violence") implies, these are not just any profits; they are profits sought by illegitimate means. The sages are not against the pursuit of profits through honest, hard work. Many of the proverbs that follow actually encourage hard work with the intention of gaining profits. Nothing is more foolish to the wisdom tradition of Proverbs than the lazy person (as in 6:6–11; 10:4; 15:19; 21:25; 27:23–27; 31:27).

Theological Implications

Throughout the book of Proverbs, the parents, and in particular the father, are sources of authority addressing the "son." As explained in the introduction, there are good reasons for us to understand the demands of this book to extend beyond males and include females, and beyond young men and include more mature men. We all need to listen to the voice of the parents as they instruct their son.

We must be careful, however, not to transfer the authority structure presented in the textual dynamic to our own real-life situations. At least, not too quickly. The text is not telling all children to listen without question to their parents. The parents in the book of Proverbs are not real people but an ideal couple. They are wise parents, and not everyone's parents today are wise in the sense that Proverbs describes wisdom. In short, Proverbs asks us without reservation to listen to these parents, and to our own parents as they also reflect divine wisdom, and we will do so as we proceed. After all, the rewards are great, according to the book.

Here and elsewhere, magnificent rewards are presented as motivation for following the wise way. How are we to understand the rewards in their original setting and today? As will become increasingly obvious, the good things that flow from wise behavior are neither magical nor absolutely guaranteed. These are not promises as such. However, the wise way is the best way to navigate life.

In the present case, the parents are warning their child to avoid the temptations of quick gain through violent actions. One may get rich through thievery, but it will not last. In the words of 10:2:

> The treasures of the wicked do not profit,
>   but righteousness extricates from death.

Indeed, though we will have plenty of opportunity later to observe the value Proverbs puts on wealth in its proper place, it certainly isn't worth compromising one's integrity:

> Better a little bit with righteousness
>   than a large yield without justice. (16:8)

In any case, such wealth is not worth it:

> When a wicked person dies, hope perishes;
>   yes, expectation based on money perishes. (11:7)

Trying to get rich in this way is foolish. It ends up harming the person more than helping. It is not the proper way to navigate life.

1:20–33. *Don't resist Woman Wisdom.* A new character speaks in the second discourse of the chapter. After the father speaks to the son, a woman named Wisdom addresses all the immature men who come across her path. She will not speak again until chaps. 8 and 9, but the father's speeches will refer to her as a woman whom his son should get to know—intimately. In any case, it is probably not an accident that the two voices dominating the first nine chapters, the father and Woman Wisdom, each have an introductory discourse in the first chapter.

Woman Wisdom is a complex figure, one whom we will discuss further in the contexts of chaps. 8 and 9. However, as Trible says, we immediately recognize her in this chapter as "a poet, who preaches, counsels, teaches, and prophesies."[23]

An unnamed narrator introduces Woman Wisdom's speech (vv. 20–21). Perhaps the narrator is assumed to be the father who speaks in most of the other discourses, including the one immediately preceding. When Wisdom speaks, she begins with an angry denunciation of the foolish men for ignoring and rejecting her invitation to receive advice from her (vv. 22–25). Because of their previous rejection, she will laugh at their certain disaster. Indeed, if they call her in the midst of the trouble that will result from their failure to take advice, she will spurn them, giving them some of their own medicine (vv. 26–31). Finally, the distinctive fates of the fool and the righteous are stated (vv. 32–33).

---

23. P. Trible, "Wisdom Builds a Poem: The Architecture of Proverbs 1:20–33," *Journal of Biblical Literature* 94 (1975): 509, though I do not agree that she has successfully discovered a chiasm in this chapter. Her outline on p. 518 does not demonstrate consistent symmetry, and there is also quantitative imbalance between supposedly paired members (i.e., two verses over against one). Indeed, I believe the bar for demonstrating a chiasm is much higher today than it was in the mid-1970s, when she wrote. On this passage, see also Murphy, "Wisdom's Song."

Woman Wisdom comes across in this speech as angry and unyielding. She shows no mercy to those who come to their senses in the midst of the punishment that their foolish action brings on them. However, the intention of this speech is to spur present action. She does not want them to wait till they are in the midst of their suffering, but she wants them to turn to her right away to avoid the pain.

> [20]Wisdom shouts in the street;
>   in the public square she yells out.
> [21]At the top of the noisy throng she calls out an invitation;
>   at the entrances to the gates in the city she says her piece:

With this discourse we are introduced to the most important character in the book of Proverbs, Woman Wisdom. As mentioned, we will delay our fuller discussion of her role and identity until that place in the commentary. Nonetheless, it is not premature to give the general outlines of who she is. As argued in the introduction, we know that she is the personification of Yahweh's wisdom and thus stands for God himself. When she speaks, she solicits relationship with those around her, reminding us of the words of the "motto" of the book (cf. 1:7): "The fear of Yahweh is the beginning of knowledge." There is, in other words, no wisdom outside of a relationship with this Woman. We will watch her closely as we proceed through the book. In the first nine chapters, she speaks to a young male audience, as do his parents. The parents and Woman Wisdom support each other's teaching.

She shouts her message in public areas, the street (ḥûṣ) and the public square (rĕḥōb). She brings her message to the crowds. This is no secret society; it is open for all to hear and to respond. In essence, she is a street evangelist or prophet. Like an evangelist or prophet, her audience is not there to hear her. They are going about their daily activities. She has to shout in order to get their attention, and as we will see, it appears that many of her hearers are in no mood to listen, not to speak of obeying what she has to say.

> [22]"How long, O simple, will you love simplemindedness,
>   and mockers hold their mocking dear,
>   and fools hate knowledge?
> [23]You should respond to my correction.
>   I will pour forth my spirit to you;
>   I will make known to you my words
> [24]Because I invited you, but you rejected me;
>   I extended my hand, but you paid no attention.
> [25]You ignored all my advice,
>   and my correction you did not want.

She begins with a lament. "How long?" (*ʿad-mātay*) or its equivalent may be found in laments in the Psalms and has the suggestion that the negative situation to be described has been going on far too long. The expression also communicates the desire on the part of the speaker that the negative situation would end soon. See, for instance, the beginning of Ps. 13 (with the near synonym *ʿad-ʾānâ*):

> O LORD, how long will you forget me? Forever?
>   How long will you look the other way?
> How long must I struggle with anguish in my soul,
>   and sorrow in my heart every day?
> How long will my enemy have the upper hand? (13:1–2 NLT)

In particular, Woman Wisdom addresses three classes of fools. The first we have already seen above (1:4), the simple (*pĕtāʾîm*). These are the most teachable of the three groups and may be understood also as naive or immature. The second type of fool, the "mockers" (*lēṣîm*), may be the most hardened. They hear advice and then criticize and ridicule the one who gives them the advice. Finally, she uses a word that may be the most generic of all the terms, and so we simply translate it "fools" (*kĕsîlîm*).

Her problem with these three groups of people is that they each relish their present state of ignorance. They not only tolerate it but also embrace it wholeheartedly, as communicated by the verbs "love" (*ʾhb*) and "hold dear" (*ḥmd*). The latter verb is the rarer of the two and is most notably found in the tenth commandment (Exod. 20:17). It is the idea of coveting something. Finally, in a poetic twist, the third class, the fools, are said to "hate knowledge." Indeed, in the world of Proverbs, to love folly is to hate wisdom and vice versa. There is no middle ground.

In v. 23 we hear Wisdom's invitation to these foolish people. She has appealed to them to change their injurious style of living ("my correction"). She has offered to give them "her spirit" (*rûaḥ*). This comment is interesting in the light of connections elsewhere between God's Spirit (*rûaḥ*) and wisdom (*ḥokmâ*). For instance, when Yahweh commissions Bezalel to be the chief craftsman for the building of the tabernacle, he announces, "I have filled him with the Spirit [*rûaḥ*] of God, with skill [*ḥokmâ*], ability [*tĕbûnâ*] and knowledge [*daʿat*]" (Exod. 31:3 NIV). We also notice the connection between God's Spirit and wisdom in Isa. 11:2–3a in referring to the shoot from the stump of Jesse:

> The Spirit [*rûaḥ*] of Yahweh will rest on him—
>   the Spirit of wisdom [*ḥokmâ*] and of understanding,
>   the Spirit of counsel and of power,
>   the Spirit of knowledge and of the fear of Yahweh—
> and he will delight in the fear of Yahweh. (cf. NIV)

This connection between Wisdom and spirit and God will become even clearer later when we explore the relationship between God and Wisdom in chaps. 8 and 9.

However, thus far the fools have rejected the invitation of Wisdom. Verses 24 and 25 make it clear that they have slapped the hand that has offered them such a wondrous gift. She offered to help them, and they have refused her.

> ²⁶I will also laugh at your disaster;
>   I will ridicule when your fear comes.
> ²⁷When your fear comes like a tempest,
>   and your disaster arrives like a storm,
>   when distress and oppression come on you,
> ²⁸then he will call me, and I will not answer;
>   he will seek me, but he will not find me.
> ²⁹Because they hated knowledge
>   and did not chose the fear of Yahweh.
> ³⁰They did not want my advice,
>   and they rejected all my reproof.
> ³¹They will eat from the fruit of their way,
>   and they will be sated from their own counsels,

In this section Wisdom articulates her fury at being spurned. The relationship that she has offered them is intimate (see also the language of 9:1–6), but they have turned their backs on her. Indeed, "hell hath no fury like a woman scorned." One thing is certain: Since they have rejected her advice on how to live in a way that will avoid the troubles of life, such troubles will surely come. Thus, she speaks to them of "your disaster," "your fear," "distress and oppression." These will come on them with devastating force, indeed, like a "tempest" (*šôʾâ*) or "storm" (*sûpâ*). While this horrible fate is bad enough, it is Woman Wisdom's response that sends chills down the readers' spines. She will laugh and ridicule them. This reaction reminds us of the language of Ps. 2, as God in heaven contemplates the fruitless plots of the kings of the nations:

> The One enthroned in heaven laughs;
>   the Lord scoffs at them.
> Then he rebukes them in his anger
>   and terrifies them in his wrath. (Ps. 2:4–5 NIV).

But worse yet than this, Woman Wisdom imagines that the suffering fools will then call to her. After spurning her earlier advice and offer of relationship, they now turn to her in the resultant mess they have gotten themselves into. But she will disdain them! They may look for

Wisdom, but they will not find her. Why? Because they had their chance (vv. 29–30) and rejected it. As a result, they will suffer the consequences (v. 31). They rejected her advice, so now they must experience the results of their own counsels.

> ³²For the turning away of the simple will kill them,
>   and the complacency of fools will destroy them.
> ³³Those who obey me will dwell securely;
>   they will be untroubled from the horror of evil.

The discourse ends by a generalizing conclusion that addresses the fates of both the fools who disobey and the ones who obey Wisdom. For the first, the result is death. For the second, it is secure life, far from trouble.

Theological Implications

In the first place, the discourse emphasizes the urgency of Wisdom's appeal. It is not a good idea to put off a decision to follow Wisdom. To be complacent is as bad as outright rejection (v. 32). Wisdom wants the immature, the fool, and the mocker to know the horrible consequences of not obeying her, so they will respond positively to her right away.

This appeal is made to all. The fact that Woman Wisdom is in public places and shouting loudly shows that acquiring wisdom is not hard to do. However, foolish people find it better to follow their own advice because they do not see that it will lead to negative consequences. Wisdom's harsh words serve the purpose of shaking some reality into their heads in order to preserve them from an awful fate and steer them toward a secure life.

The NT also registers a sense of urgency, calling for repentance before it is too late. Paul, for instance, says:

> Another reason for right living is that you know how late it is; time is running out. Wake up, for the coming of our salvation is nearer now than when we first believed. The night is almost gone; the day of salvation will soon be here. So don't live in darkness. (Rom. 13:11–12 NLT)

Chapter 2

Translation

¹My son, if you grasp my speech
  and store up my commands within you,
²bending your ear toward wisdom,
  extending your heart toward competence[a]—
³indeed, if you call out for understanding,
  shout for competence,
⁴if you seek it like silver
  and search for it like hidden treasure—
⁵then you will understand the fear of Yahweh,
  and you will find the knowledge of God.
⁶For Yahweh bestows wisdom,
  from his mouth[b] come knowledge and understanding.
⁷He stores up resourcefulness for those with integrity—
  a shield for those who walk in innocence,
⁸to protect the paths of justice,
  guarding the way of his covenant partners.[c]
⁹Then you will understand righteousness and justice
  and integrity,[d] every good course.

a. We expect the apodosis of the conditional statement to begin here, but it is delayed until v. 5 for rhetorical effect.

b. The LXX has "from his face" rather than "from his mouth."

c. The Hebrew of this verse is shaped in a nice chiasm. Two common verbs (protect/guard, *nṣr/šmr*) open and close the verse, and the two nouns in the middle (way/path, *ʾārḥôt/derek*) are the direct objects of these verbs and stand in construct with nouns indicating moral qualities (justice/covenant partner).

d. This verse may be a rare example of enjambment in Hebrew poetry. "Enjambment means 'straddling (e.g., of a horse),' and is present when a sentence or clause does not end

[10]For wisdom will penetrate your heart,
and knowledge will be attractive to you.[e]
[11]Discretion will guard you;
competence will protect you,
[12]extricating you from the evil path,
from the people who speak perversities,
[13]who abandon the way of integrity
to go on dark paths,
[14]who enjoy doing evil;
they rejoice in evil perversities;
[15]whose ways are twisted
and who go on the wrong courses;
[16]extricating you from the strange woman,
from the foreign woman with her flattering speech,
[17]abandoning the intimate relationship[f] of her youth,
forgetting the covenant of her God.[g]
[18]For her house sinks down[h] to death,
and her courses to the departed ancestors.[i]

---

when the colon ends but runs over into the next colon" (Watson, *Classical Hebrew Poetry*, 333). In this verse, "righteousness and justice and integrity" could be viewed as flowing together and constituting a single phrase (see 1:3). However, if "integrity" is regarded as part of the first colon, a very unusual imbalance between the first and second cola results. The MT places the *ᵓatnāḥ* (accent marking the middle of the verse) under "justice," indicating their understanding of how the lines should be divided. I follow the MT line division.

e. Here, as in v. 8, we have a chiastic structure in Hebrew. After the opening conjunction "for," verbs (penetrate/be attractive) stand on either end of the verse, and the subjects of the verbs (wisdom/knowledge) with prepositional phrases (in your heart/to you [lit., to your soul, or self]) in the middle.

f. "Intimate relationship" (*ᵓallûp*). The verbal root (*ᵓlp*) means "to learn" in the qal (Prov. 22:25) and "to teach" in the piel (Job 15:5; 33:33; 35:11). According to *NIDOTTE* 1:415–16, the noun often means "close friend," based on the idea of "one learned or known" (see Ps. 55:13 [14 MT]; Jer. 3:3–5; Mic. 7:5). The present context clearly refers to the woman's husband, the one who is supposed to be the most intimately known of all.

g. Here again, we observe a chiastic structure to the Hebrew verse. The verbs bracket the verse by appearing as the first and last words in their respective lines, while the direct objects, both construct phrases, stand in the middle.

h. Emerton ("Note on Proverbs 2:18") argues that the MT is awkward as it stands, since "house" is a masculine noun and the verb is feminine. However, the lack of gender concord is not uncommon in Hebrew. He also wonders about the metaphor of a house sinking into the underworld, but figurative language is frequently surprising. It certainly is understandable. Thus, I see no good reason to follow him by emending the verb (*šāḥā*) to the noun (*šûḥâ*, pit), yielding the translation "her house is a pit (leading) to death."

i. The term here translated "departed ancestors" is *rĕpāᵓîm*. Though the word is much discussed, there is really little agreement about its meaning. One recent article lists the following different understandings of the term: "dead kings and heroes, divinized ancestors, healers, savior, shades, a guild of (deceased) warriors, and devotees of the god *rpu*" (*NIDOTTE* 3:1174). In our present context (*rĕpāᵓîm* stands in parallel to death [*māwet*]), there is no doubt that the *rĕpāᵓîm* are deceased. Besides this passage, see these other occurrences of the term: Job 26:5; Ps. 88:10 [11 MT]; Prov. 9:18; 21:16; Isa. 14:9; 26:14, 19.

19All who go to her will not return;
    they will not reach the ways of the living.
20So you will go on the path of good people,
    and you will keep on the ways of the righteous.
21For those with integrity will dwell in the land,
    and the innocent will remain in it,
22but the wicked will be cut off from the land,
    and the faithless will be uprooted from it.

Interpretation

The benefits of the way of wisdom. The chapter is an instruction, but it is unusual in that no specific advice is given as would be typical in this literary form. The instruction is essentially an admonition to strive after wisdom, so there is a lengthy *exordium* (call to worship),[1] the first half of the chapter. The instruction is also unusual in having no imperatives.

The chapter is composed of twenty-two verses and contains twenty-two poetic bicola. According to the traditional terminology in use since the time of Lowth, these bicola show "synonymous parallelism," but more recent nomenclature has moved away from this label as misleading. The second colon of each bicolon does more than restate what is said in the first; instead, it takes it further.

Clifford argues that the chapter is an acrostic in which the first three stanzas (vv. 1–4, 5–8, 9–11) are headed by words that begin with the Hebrew letter ʾālep and the second three stanzas (vv. 12–15, 16–19, 20–22) are headed by words that begin with the letter lāmed.[2] Although Prov. 2 has twenty-two verses and the Hebrew alphabet has twenty-two letters, the two-letter pattern that appears in this chapter makes it unlikely that a Hebrew acrostic structure was intended. The only commonly accepted acrostics are so-called abecedaries, such as Ps. 119, which proceed sequentially through the entire alphabet.

This list omits occurrences in prose contexts, which raise other issues. The usual understanding of the *rephaim* as shades who dwell in the underworld seems correct, particularly in light of the Isaiah passages. For a recent, helpful discussion of the issue, see Johnston, *Shades of Sheol*, 128–42. Johnston concludes that the Hebrew and Ugaritic uses of the term *rephaim* are different; the former believe the *rephaim* are "lifeless and need rousing, they tremble before God, they are not limited to heroes or kings, they are never individually named, they do not travel, participate at banquets or play any role *vis-à-vis* the living as protectors or patrons" (p. 142).

    1. Fox, "Pedagogy of Proverbs 2," 234.

    2. Clifford, *Proverbs*, 45–46. See also Murphy, *Proverbs*, 14, who cites Skehan, *Studies*, 9–10, 16.

Proverbs 2 is one long discourse of a father to his son. Indeed, it is as if the father took a deep breath and uttered the contents of the entire chapter in one long sentence. For ease of reading, however, the translation above has broken the speech into several sentences. The chapter is a complex conditional sentence (if . . . then, ʿim . . . ʾāz) that is punctuated with lengthy motive clauses (marked by "for," kî) and purpose clauses ("to," marked by the prefix lĕ). The chapter urges the son actively to pursue wisdom, which is associated with the father's words, so he may discover the fear of God with all of its practical and ethical implications. Such wisdom will save the son from all kinds of trouble in life, including the danger represented by the strange woman. The chapter ends with the declaration that those who are upright, or innocent (presumably because they have heeded the father's words and found the fear of Yahweh), will be allowed to stay in the land, but those who do not (described as those who are wicked/faithless) will be removed from the land.

Due to the cohesive nature of the chapter as a whole, any division of the father's speech into parts is somewhat artificial. However, to aid in analysis, the following sections will be treated in turn.

2:1–8: The son is urged to listen to the father, to discover the fear of Yahweh and gain wisdom, which protects those who have it.

2:9–15: Wisdom breeds ethical sensitivity (conscience), which will keep the son from evil people.

2:16–19: Wisdom will also keep the son from falling prey to the strange woman.

2:20–22: Ultimate consequences: the upright will stay in the land; the wicked will be removed.

> ¹My son, if you grasp my speech
>   and store up my commands within you,
> ²bending your ear toward wisdom,
>   extending your heart toward competence—
> ³indeed, if you call out for understanding,
>   shout for competence,
> ⁴if you seek it like silver
>   and search for it like hidden treasure—
> ⁵then you will understand the fear of Yahweh,
>   and you will find the knowledge of God.
> ⁶For Yahweh bestows wisdom,
>   from his mouth come knowledge and understanding.
> ⁷He stores up resourcefulness for those with integrity—
>   a shield for those who walk in innocence,

⁸to protect the paths of justice,
    guarding the way of his covenant partners.

2:1–8. The father addresses his son and, through the use of a conditional sentence, urges him to listen to his teaching. Indeed, the whole chapter may be understood as an appeal to pursue wisdom. The actual content of wisdom is presented only indirectly in this chapter.

The father desires that his son do more than simply listen to him; the verbs he uses ("grasp" [see also 10:8], "store up") ask the son for a willingness to accept what the father has to say, not just for an open mind. Verse 1a uses a general term ("speech") for what the father wants his son to heed, with a more specific word ("commands") appearing in v. 1b. In other words, "commands" further specify "speech." We are left with a question, though: How are we to understand this second term? Is the word "command" referring simply to the instructions of the father, or is it referring specifically to the commands of God that are being communicated through the father? In other words, do we have here a link between wisdom and torah?

At the very least, we can say that the words the father is urging on the son come with a great deal of authority. However, the overwhelming number of occurrences of the word "command" (*miṣwâ*) in the Bible are associated with the law of God, and sometimes the word is used as a near synonym for *tôrâ* (Gen. 26:5; Exod. 16:28; 24:12; Lev. 27:34; Num. 36:13; Deut. 30:10).[3]

Verse 2 continues the protasis (the "if" clause) of the conditional sentence by encouraging the son to bend an ear and extend his heart toward wisdom and common sense. The poetic pair "ear/heart" is an interesting intensification. One hears with the ear, but the father requires more of the son than simply the act of listening. The heart represents what we would call the basic personality or character of a person. Though "heart" stands for the whole inner person, on occasion there is an emphasis on the cognitive. In any case, "ear/heart" provides an external/internal de-

---

3. This point is made by P. Enns, who also provides the list of Scripture references (see "*Miṣwâ*," *NIDOTTE* 2:1070–71). However, Enns differentiates the use of *miṣwâ* in Proverbs (see also 3:1; 6:20; 7:1–2) from the law of God and believes it points simply to "human or father instruction." In this conclusion, Enns appears to agree with Zimmerli ("Concerning the Structure of Old Testament Wisdom," 175–207), who argues that in Proverbs *miṣwâ* is parallel to *ʿēṣâ* ("advice") and thus refers to something that "stimulates reflection and independent decision" in contrast to a "command," which carries authority that "disposes without further justification" (180). However, it seems clear to me that once reflection has determined the proper mode of conduct in a situation, sound advice becomes authoritative in a dogmatic way, and in some cases (e.g., one's stance toward the "foreign woman") there is not even room for discussion. Thus, I find myself closer to the position argued by B. Gemser, "Spiritual Structure."

velopment. More than the simple act of hearing is involved in the reception of the father's teaching; one must be predisposed toward wisdom to benefit from it.[4]

One might expect v. 3 to begin the apodosis (the "then" clause) of the conditional sentence. If so, our expectations are foiled; the protasis continues, delaying resolution to the thought. Such a delay intensifies the anticipation of the resolution. The father desires the son to take the next step in the search for wisdom. The son is not only to be open to wisdom's influence as it comes to him, but he is also to pursue it actively.[5] Verse 3 urges the son to use his voice to call out to wisdom, while v. 4 encourages him to take action. Both "understanding" (*bînâ*) and "competence" (*tĕbûnâ*) in v. 3 are nouns formed from the verb "to understand." "Competence" also appears in v. 2, but "understanding" seems to be the more general term.

Verse 4 describes the type of action the father wants the son to take to gain wisdom and conveys a sense of increasing urgency. The second verb ("search," *ḥpś*) is rarer than the common and more general word for "seek" (*bqš*) that appears in the first part of the verse. Both cola contain a simile that also enhances the sense of urgency of the search. The search is for wisdom, also described by the related terms "competence" and "understanding," but the search should have the insistence of a search for silver or for hidden treasure. This conveys the idea of the importance of the search and of the value of the object being sought. Throughout the book, wisdom is often compared favorably to precious metals (e.g., 3:14–15).

Verse 5 brings us to the apodosis (the "then" clause) of the conditional sentence. If the son follows the instructions of the father in vv. 1–4, then he will understand the fear of Yahweh and find the knowledge of God. These are weighty matters (for more on the "fear of Yahweh," see 1:7). This verse reminds us that wisdom and relationship with Yahweh are integrally entwined.

Verses 6–8 then support the conditional sentence of vv. 1–5 with a lengthy motive clause. The reasoning of this section seems circular, and in a sense it is. Seek wisdom, and one will find God. Find God, and one will gain wisdom. In another way this emphasizes the deep connection between wisdom and God. Verse 6b sharpens the thought of 6a by saying that wisdom (here described by the closely related words "knowledge" and "understanding") derives specifically from Yahweh's mouth. But where do we find the words of God's mouth? In light of the authority

---

4. For "wisdom" (*ḥokmâ*) and "competence" (*tĕbûnâ*), see the discussion at 1:2–3. Fox defines "competence" as "the pragmatic, applied aspect of thought, operating in the realm of action; it aims at efficacy and accomplishment" (Fox, *Proverbs 1–9*, 37).

5. "Yet not even a desire for wisdom is sufficient, the pupil must take the initiative and actively summon—'call to'—wisdom" (ibid., 110).

with which the father's words are delivered (see 2:1), perhaps we should say that the father is Yahweh's mouthpiece and therefore, by extension, that the father's words as written in the book of Proverbs are words from Yahweh's mouth (see under "Theological Implications," below).

Verse 7 elaborates on the benefits of gaining the wisdom that brings one into relationship with God. We also see the interplay between wisdom words and ethical qualities. Here the wise are described as having "integrity" (*yēšer*) and innocence (*tōm*). These people do what is morally correct. In this context, they are the ones who heed the commands of the father and gain wisdom. It is difficult for those who have read Paul's statements on the profound and universal sinfulness of human beings (e.g., Rom. 3:9–20) to appreciate the OT concept of innocence. Perhaps the best example within the pages of the OT is Job, who is called "innocent" (*tām* in 1:1, an adjective related to *tōm*). Yet Job was not completely without sin, for he himself acknowledges that no person is completely righteous (9:1). Nevertheless, there are people whose lives are marked largely by ethical rightness and legal obedience. These are the innocent, who are closely related to the wise in the book of Proverbs.

For these people, God provides resourcefulness (*tûšîyâ*), defined by Fox as "an inner power that helps one escape a fix."[6] With this definition, we can understand why resourcefulness may be likened to a shield. It protects one from the vicissitudes of life. If a problem arises, then the recipient of God's wisdom will have the wherewithal to deal with it. Indeed, this resourcefulness provided by God is called a shield in v. 7b. It shields, or protects, those who possess it.

Verse 8 concludes the opening section of chapter 2. With its verbs of protection, it is an expansion of the shield metaphor used to describe the resourcefulness that God imparts to his followers. The metaphor of the path is invoked in this verse, a frequently occurring image. The path is the life journey (here associated with justice and the covenant), and the verse claims that God protects the life journey of his people. The word *ḥăsîd*, here translated "covenant partner," is a particularly rich term and difficult to capture in a simple English translation. It is used to describe those who possess *ḥesed*, a word best understood as "covenant love," the love that exists between covenant partners. According to the Torah and the Prophets, God has entered into a covenant with his people. There is little explicit covenant language in the book of Proverbs, but here is an exception.

> [9]Then you will understand righteousness and justice
> and integrity, every good course.

6. Ibid., 114.

> ¹⁰For wisdom will penetrate your heart,
>   and knowledge will be attractive to you.
> ¹¹Discretion will guard you;
>   competence will protect you,
> ¹²extricating you from the evil path,
>   from the people who speak perversities,
> ¹³who abandon the way of integrity
>   to go on dark paths,
> ¹⁴who enjoy doing evil;
>   they rejoice in evil perversities;
> ¹⁵whose ways are twisted
>   and who go on the wrong courses;

2:9–15. Remember that this whole chapter is a single, fairly cohesive speech, able to be translated as one very long sentence. So the divisions are somewhat artificial but helpful for the purpose of exposition. Verse 9 begins with another "then" (*ʾāz*), indicating the continuation of the apodosis ("then" clause) that began in v. 5. This second apodosis is followed in v. 10 by another motive clause that begins with "for" (*kî*).

The apodosis in v. 9 focuses on the moral sensitivity resulting from embracing the father's instruction that leads to wisdom and the knowledge of God. Wisdom brings ethical enlightenment, an understanding of "righteousness, justice, and integrity," three foundational words in the moral vocabulary of the Hebrew Bible (see comments on 1:3). The understanding of these ethical concepts seems equivalent to what we call "conscience." These characteristics are associated with the "good course," "course" (*maʿgal*) being related to the more common words "path" (*derek*) and "way" (*ʾārḥôt*). Specifically, *maʿgal* refers to a smaller course going off the main track, but here in Proverbs it seems to be used as a near synonym for *derek*.

Verse 10 offers a second motive clause (see 2:6) beginning with "for" (*kî*) and provides the reason for this new moral sensitivity. Wisdom/ knowledge will become an integral part of the son's character (for "heart," see 2:2). Verse 11 continues the motive clause and again describes the protective function ("guard . . . protect") of wisdom and its derivatives. In this case, discretion is emphasized. The Hebrew word for discretion (*mĕzimmâ*) also has a shadow side (as in 30:32), where it means something like shrewdness. In the present context, however, it denotes the positive quality of thinking through the consequences of an action and choosing the way of integrity. Fox translates the word as "shrewdness" in this context (though not with negative overtones) and describes it as a "private, unrevealed thought, often but not always used in scheming. As the ability to think for oneself and keep one's own counsel, it is especially valuable in withstanding temptation."[7] The second colon of v. 11 adds "competence" (see 2:2) to the arsenal of the wise person.

Verses 12–15 describe the people from whom the wisdom of God and its associated qualities will protect the son. The protection takes the form of extrication, removal from association with a certain type of person. Indeed, v. 12 begins with the purpose of extricating the son, and this will be paralleled below at the beginning of our next section (starting at v. 16). Already, in the first lesson of the father (1:8–19), the son has heard the warning that associating with evil people will produce calamity in life. So wisdom here promises to remove the wise son from evil associations. These people not only speak and do bad or even perverse things; they also relish them ("enjoy/rejoice," 2:14). The noun "perversity" occurs twice in this unit (vv. 12, 14), a number of other times in the book (6:14; 8:13; 10:31, 32; 16:28, 30; 23:33), but only once outside Proverbs (Deut. 32:20). The related verb means to "turn against" or "be overturned." It is often used in opposition to faithfulness and righteousness, so it may indicate the overturning of those positive qualities. To say or do something perverse would mean to say (perhaps a crudity or a blasphemy) or do something that offends righteousness and goes against the dictates of the father or of God himself.

In this unit, the path metaphor emerges again. The people from whom the father hopes the son will be extricated are those who have left the way of integrity and are now on the evil path, the dark path. Their ways are twisted, and their courses are wrong.

> 16extricating you from the strange woman,
>   from the foreign woman with her flattering speech,
> 17abandoning the intimate relationship of her youth,
>   forgetting the covenant of her God.
> 18For her house sinks down to death,
>   and her courses to the departed ancestors.
> 19All who go to her will not return;
>   they will not reach the ways of the living.

2:16–19. The above translation shows this unit beginning in the middle of a sentence. However, for clarity of interpretation, vv. 16–19 have been separated in our exposition because together these verses deal with another threat to the son: the strange woman. The subject of 2:12–15 was evil people in general, perhaps more specifically evil men. Now the father's attention turns to the strange woman.

This unit briefly introduces a topic that will dominate many of the following discourses (5:1–23; 6:24–35; 7:1–27). The warnings against the

7. Ibid., 116.

strange/foreign woman will be supplemented by admonitions to sustain a healthy and vital relationship with one's wife (cf. 5:15–20). Furthermore, the rivalry in affections between the strange/foreign woman and the virtuous wife mirrors the rivalry between Woman Wisdom and Woman Folly (see particularly chaps. 8–9). For a synthesis of the teaching on this subject, see "Theology of the Book" in the introduction.

But what makes the strange woman strange, the foreign woman foreign? The two Hebrew words "strange" (zārâ) and "foreign" (nokrîyâ) may be understood in a variety of ways. However, it is unlikely that "foreign" in parallel with "strange" would be used to indicate a non-Israelite woman. The strangeness of this woman is seen in her willingness to operate outside the bounds of moral, legal, and customary restraints—an idea developed further in the following chapters. This lack of restraint is described in v. 17 as a failure to honor her commitments to the intimate relationship (ʾallûp; see the note on v. 6 of the translation) of her youth as well as to the covenant of her God. The first colon thus accuses her of not sustaining her marriage vows, since the words "intimate relationship" refer here to her own marriage. By committing adultery, therefore, she is breaking her covenant with God.[8] The fact that she is described as having been in a covenant with God is further support for the view that this woman is an Israelite temptress, not an ethnically foreign one.[9] And a temptress she is. As we will see in all the contexts in which she is described, her primary strategy for seducing the man is through her flattering speech and then secondarily through physical attraction.

This woman seems so enticing, so right, but she is very, very dangerous for the man. The last two verses of the section (vv. 18–19) describe the consequences of entering into a relationship with such a lawless woman. It leads to death, to the place of the departed ancestors (on rĕpāʾîm, see the second translation note on v. 18). Her path ("courses") leads to death and away from the path ("ways") leading to life. Some scholars think the image of the house sinking into death, or the underworld, is strange and indicates a textual problem. I disagree, believing it provides a strong image of not only the woman careening toward death

8. Among those who affirm that this covenant is with Yahweh, there is disagreement over whether the reference is to the Sinaitic covenant (see Kidner, *Proverbs*) or to the marriage covenant that is mentioned in Mal. 2:14 (so Hugenberger, *Marriage as a Covenant*, who provides the best discussion of the matter). This distinction is not important for understanding the import of the verse; it is a serious matter to break any covenant that one has made with Yahweh.

9. G. Boström (*Proverbiastudien*, 103ff.) argues that "covenant" here refers to a covenant with a pagan deity. However, it is hard to imagine that the sages would criticize her for breaking a covenant with a false deity; they would be more likely to condemn her for being in such a covenant.

but also all that belongs to or is associated with her.[10] In any case, these statements about the consequences of evil associations provide a proper segue to the climactic section of the chapter.

> ²⁰So you will go on the path of good people,
>   and you will keep on the ways of the righteous.
> ²¹For those with integrity will dwell in the land,
>   and the innocent will remain in it,
> ²²but the wicked will be cut off from the land,
>   and the faithless will be uprooted from it.

2:20–22. The last three verses of the unit provide a climactic concluding statement. Verses 11–19 have emphasized the benefit of wisdom in keeping a person away from evil influences, from the paths of those who depart from God's way. Verse 20 returns to the idea that the acquisition of wisdom keeps people on the right path. The son will not travel this path alone; it is the path of other good and righteous people.

The final two verses state the ultimate consequences of the two paths. There are two possibilities, no gray middle ground. On the one hand, those with "integrity," the "innocent," will remain in the land (the same word pair is found and discussed in 2:7), while the wicked/faithless will be removed from the land. It is notable that Proverbs here threatens the loss of the land, presumably the land of Israel, for the land is not a major part of the explicit theology of the book (though see also 10:30). Indeed, these verses sound a lot like the covenant blessings and curses described in passages such as Deut. 27–28.[11] In fact, the verb translated "uproot" here (*nsḥ*) is attested relatively infrequently but found in Deuteronomy:

> If you do not carefully follow all the words of this law, which are written in this book, and do not revere this glorious and awesome name—the LORD your God—the LORD will send fearful plagues on you. . . . Just as it pleased the LORD to make you prosper and increase in number, so it will please him to ruin and destroy you. You will be *uprooted* from the land you are entering to possess. (Deut. 28:58–59a, 63 NIV, italics added)

In chap. 2, the father has presented a strong argument and an impassioned plea for his son to accept the wisdom that begins with the fear of Yahweh. Only in this way will he escape life's threats and move toward life and away from death.

10. Murphy and Van Leeuwen are examples of recent commentators who have difficulties here. The issue stems from the article by Emerton, "Note on Proverbs 2:18," 153–59.

11. Compare also Ps. 37:3, 9, 10–11, 22, 28–29, 34, and 35–36 (all cited by Perdue, *Proverbs*, 94), which say that those who are upright will inherit and keep the land.

Theological Implications

The chapter is an extended appeal by the father to his son to acquire wisdom. This appeal has a paradox at its center: Wisdom is something the son must strive vigorously to achieve, but it is a gift from God. Murphy states it thus: "One must strive for the goal, but also realize that wisdom remains a divine gift. Ultimately we have a picture of the acquisition of wisdom by means of human industry and divine aid and generosity."[12]

The son—and the reader who stands in the place of the son—is told to work hard to gain wisdom. Indeed, the son/reader is to seek wisdom with the same urgent passion as one might look for hidden treasure. As Van Leeuwen points out, here the son is told to cry out for Wisdom just as Wisdom was portrayed in 1:20–21 (and later, in 8:1) as crying out for young men.[13] The wisdom that the son is to bend his ear to and extend his heart toward is associated with the father's speech. The authoritative nature of the father's speech is underlined by its being called "commands" in the parallel colon in v. 1. In other words, wisdom is thus identified with tradition passed down from father to son. That this tradition may have some connection with God's law, also called "commands," was suggested above but cannot be proved.

According to v. 5, this wisdom leads to the fear of Yahweh/knowledge of God, but then, surprisingly, this knowledge of God leads to wisdom (v. 6). This is the circular paradox: Seek wisdom, find God; seek God, find wisdom. And once one does find wisdom, one is to thank God for it.

On a practical level, what does this mean for someone who wants to heed the admonition of the father and become wise? Work hard at it. Study the book of Proverbs and the rest of the Bible. However, the acknowledgment that whatever wisdom we have comes ultimately from God chastens our pride and leads to humility. It does not allow the pursuit of proverbial wisdom to lead to the pride that separates us from God. It also reminds those who are wise to be thankful for whatever wisdom they have.

There are analogies to this paradox in other parts of Scripture. One example is the theme of the divine warrior. Israel must enter the battle at the instruction and command of God and fight, but when they win, they are not to praise themselves. Rather, they are to thank God, who allowed them to win. The battle of Jericho and David's fight with the giant Goliath illustrate this principle well.

Doesn't this analogy also stand at the center of the Christian faith? Hear the words of Paul in Phil. 2:12–13: "Therefore, my dear friends,

---

12. Murphy, *Proverbs*, 16.
13. Van Leeuwen, "Proverbs," in *New Interpreter's Bible* 5:43.

as you have always obeyed—not only in my presence, but now much more in my absence—continue to work out your salvation with fear and trembling, for it is God who works in you to will and to act according to his good purpose" (NIV). We are to work hard at our salvation, but ultimately we must recognize that salvation is a gift of God's grace and thank him for it.

Chapter 3

Translation

[1]My son, don't forget my instruction,
  and let your heart protect my commands.
[2]For length of days and years of life
  and peace they will add to you.
[3]Do not let covenant love and faithfulness abandon you;
  bind them on your neck;
  write them on the tablet of your heart.
[4]Find grace and good favor[a]
  in the eyes of God and humanity.
[5]Trust in Yahweh with all your heart,
  and don't depend on your own understanding.
[6]In all your paths, know him
  and he will keep your ways straight.
[7]Don't be wise in your own eyes.
  Fear Yahweh and turn away from evil.
[8]This will bring health to your body[b]
  and refreshment[c] to your bones.
[9]Honor Yahweh with your wealth,
  and from the first of your produce.

a. As Fox points out (*Proverbs 1–9*, 147), *śēkel* concerns "perception." When it is one's own perception, the word means "insight" (10:19); when it is the other's perception, it means "favor" or "regard."

b. The word "body" (*śōr*) clearly means umbilical cord in Ezek. 16:4, and its use here is somewhat debated. We follow the meaning provided by the Greek term "body" (*tō sōmati sou*), which involves an emendation to *liš'ērekā* or *libśārekā*.

c. "Refreshment" (*šiqqûy*) is a noun formed from the verb "to drink" (*šqh*). Bone was thought to be dry, and the picture of water on dry bone suggests refreshment. The use of the term *šiqqûy* in this meaning may also be found in Hosea 2:5 [7 MT], according to R. H. O'Connell (*NIDOTTE* 4:233).

[10]And your barns will be filled with plenty,[d]
   and your vats will burst with wine.
[11]The discipline of Yahweh, my son, do not reject,
   and do not loathe his correction.
[12]For the one whom Yahweh loves he will correct,
   even like a father who treats a son favorably.

[13]Blessed are those who find Wisdom,
   and those who gain Competence.
[14]For her profit is better than that of silver,[e]
   and her yield, better than gold.
[15]Her value is more than pearls,
   and all that you want is not the equal of her.
[16]Length of days is in her right hand;
   in her left are wealth and honor.
[17]Her paths are pleasant paths,
   and all her trails are peace.
[18]She is a tree of life to those who embrace her,
   and those who hold her tight are blessed.
[19]Yahweh laid the foundations of the earth with Wisdom,
   establishing the heavens with competence.
[20]With his knowledge the deeps burst open,
   and the skies drop dew.

[21]My son, don't let them slip from your eyes;
   protect resourcefulness and discretion.
[22]Let them be life for your soul
   and an ornament for your throat.
[23]Then you will walk in safety on your path,
   and your foot will not stumble.
[24]If you lie down, you will not be terrified.
   When you lie down, your sleep will be pleasant.
[25]Don't be afraid of a sudden terror
   or the ruin that comes to the wicked.
[26]For Yahweh will be your confidence,
   and he will guard your feet from capture.
[27]Don't withhold good that belongs to him,
   when it is in your power to do it.
[28]Don't say to your neighbor, "Go and return;
   I will give it to you tomorrow," when you have it.
[29]Don't intend evil toward your neighbor,
   who lives confidently with you.
[30]Don't accuse anyone without a reason,
   when they have done nothing evil against you.

d. Rather than "plenty" (*śābāʿ*), the LXX has "lots of grain" (*plēsmonēs sitou*).
e. Literally, "For its profit is better than the profit of silver."

³¹Don't be jealous of violent people,
  and don't prefer their path.
³²For the devious are an abomination to Yahweh,
  and the virtuous are his confidantes.
³³The curse of Yahweh is in the house of the wicked,
  but he blesses the home of the righteous.
³⁴He mocks mockers,
  but he shows favor to the humble.
³⁵The wise possess glory,
  but fools exude[f] shame.

Interpretation

3:1–12. *Trust in Yahweh.* This wisdom poem contains a series of admonitions marked by imperatives as the father addresses the son (vv. 1, 3, 5–6a, 7, 9, 11). The father also offers motivation for following the imperatives by naming the positive consequences that will flow from obedience (vv. 2, 6b, 8, 10, 12). Verse 4 begins with an imperative, yet seems to be a consequence of obedience. That is, if the son obeys, he will find grace and good favor in the eyes of God and humanity. Or, perhaps to put the same thing in different words, to find grace and good favor in the eyes of God and humanity, the son must pursue obedience.

In any case, through admonitions and the promise of reward, the father urges the son to pursue a life of wisdom that entails fear of Yahweh and obedience to his commands.

Waltke makes an interesting observation: "In theological terms, the admonitions in the odd verses of 3:1–12 present the obligations of the son, the human covenant partner; the argumentation in the even verses shows the obligations of the Lord, the divine covenant partner. The human partner has the responsibility to keep ethics and piety, and the divine partner the obligation to bless his worshiper with peace, prosperity, and longevity."[1]

¹My son, don't forget my instruction,
  and let your heart protect my commands.

The passage begins with an appeal to the son to pay close regard to the father's instruction and commands.[2] We have already discussed

---

f. Literally, "exalt." The idea is that fools make their shame obvious by their actions. In today's English, "exude" fits this context well.

1. Waltke, "Does Proverbs Promise Too Much?"

2. Such an exhortation to listen is found in many places in the book (4:1–2; 5:1; 7:1–3, for example). Ruffle ("Teaching of Amenemope," 37–38) points to parallels in Egyptian wisdom literature as well, particularly Amenemope and Amennakht.

the important issue of the status of the father's "instruction" (*tôrâ*) and "commands" (from *miṣwâ*) in our commentary on 2:1. Here the "my" refers directly to the father, but what is the source of the father's commands? Are they totally distinct from laws found in the Pentateuch? It is our contention that they are not; rather, the commands and instruction the father wants his son to follow are from the parental teaching that is dependent on the pentateuchal law.[3] These laws are not to be forgotten. Not to forget is to remember, and to remember something in the OT means more than mere cognitive retention. To remember, or not to forget, means to obey. That the son's obedience is to be more than a superficial matter is specified in the second colon, where it is his heart (*lēb/lēbāb*), standing for his core personality,[4] that is to protect the commands. Again, protection means to observe the commands that are to be deeply embedded in the son.

> ²For length of days and years of life
> and peace they will add to you.

The first motivation for obedience comes in the form of reward. To obey the commands will result in a long life (length of days and years of life). The commands are in part at least guidelines for healthy living. All things being equal (see "Retribution" in the introduction), those who follow God's way of living as taught by the wise father will live longer than those who flaunt those same commands. But it is more than simple longevity that is envisioned here. A long life of suffering or strife is not something to be prized, so in colon 2, the father adds the qualification that the long life of the obedient son will be characterized by "peace." Peace means more than the absence of strife; it points to a rich and meaningful existence.

> ³Do not let covenant love and faithfulness abandon you;
> bind them on your neck;
> write them on the tablet of your heart.

The next verse reverts to admonition. Two other qualities are also said to accompany an obedient life: covenant love (*ḥesed*) and faithfulness

---

3. Clifford, *Proverbs*, 51, is an example of the view that believes it refers not to pentateuchal law in any sense but rather exclusively to the teaching found in Prov. 1–9.

4. We translate *lēb/lēbāb* as "heart" throughout, but understand that the closest English equivalent is "core personality" or what Waltke, *Proverbs 1–15*, 90–92, refers to as "the psyche's function" and "the spiritual function." Sometimes the "heart" may emphasize one aspect of the core personality, especially the mind but also emotions or will, but typically it refers to one's whole inner self.

(*ʾĕmet*). These two words are often found together (Exod. 34:6b; Ps. 86:15; 108:4 [5 MT]; 115:1; 117:2; 138:2). God's very character is described by these terms in Exod. 34:6–7:

> The Lord, the Lord,
> a God merciful and gracious,
> slow to anger,
> and abounding in steadfast love [*ḥesed*] and faithfulness [*ʾĕmet*]. (NRSV)

These words thus describe God's attitude toward his covenant partners: God stays involved and takes care of them. Our verse in Proverbs personifies these abstract qualities of Yahweh and says they will be constant companions to the one who obeys. In truth, there is a bit of an ambiguity whether the covenant love and faithfulness that persist are those of God or those of the wise son. However, it seems best to take it at least as the latter if not of both.

In the second and third cola of the verse, the father continues the demand to live a life characterized by covenant love and faithfulness. He asks that his son bind them on his neck and write them on the tablet of his heart. Grammatically and contextually, the "them" in both cases are covenant love and faithfulness.

The demand to bind something on one's neck is not found outside of Proverbs (see also 6:21; also, 7:3 admonishes the son to bind the father's commands on his fingers). However, the language reminds the reader of Deut. 6:4–9, which includes a command to bind the law on one's hands and fix it to the forehead.[5] Perhaps the neck is here mentioned because disobedience is elsewhere described as a stiffening of the neck (e.g., Jer. 7:26; 17:23). The metaphor of the heart as a tablet on which one writes the law points to an internalization of God's commands in one's life, so that not only one's actions but also one's motives are pure (see also Prov. 7:3; Jer. 31:33). The only other place in the OT that specifically mentions writing on the heart is Jer. 17:1, saying that Judah has written sin on their hearts.

> [4]Find grace and good favor
> in the eyes of God and humanity.

---

5. Overland ("Did the Sage Draw from the Shema?") lists six similarities between the Deut. 6 passage and the present one: (1) "the figurative use of 'bind' (*qāšar*)"; (2) "'bind' used in conjunction with 'write'"; (3) "'heart' (*lēb* or *lēbāb*) modified by 'all'"; (4) "the concept of personal desire correlated with *nepeš*"; (5) "the concept of material abundance correlated with *mĕʾōd*"; (6) "covenant love in the Shema and Proverbs 3:3–4." He concludes that Proverbs has summarized from Deuteronomy.

The following verse begins with an imperative like all of the admonitions in this poem; however, its content is best understood as a consequence of obedience rather than a call to obedience. In other words, the best way to understand this verse is with an implied "In this way (that is, by obedience)" before "find grace and good favor in the eyes of God and humanity."

The reward, therefore, of obedience is that God and fellow human beings will respect such a person for having grace and good favor. They will be honored and sought after for their wisdom.

> [5]Trust in Yahweh with all your heart,
>   and don't depend on your own understanding.
> [6a]In all your paths, know him

Again, the father admonishes the son to trust Yahweh. To trust Yahweh implies that one will not trust one's own resources.[6] Verse 7 will say essentially the same thing (see also 26:12; 27:1; 28:11, 26). In acknowledging one's own innate lack of resources, one becomes open to God's power and wisdom, which is a better guide to life. Verse 6a continues the admonishment but for the first time in this poem invokes the metaphor of the path. If you know (in the sense of "recognize" or "acknowledge") God in your paths, then you will certainly be on the right ones. This leads to another statement of reward in 6b.

> [6b]and he will keep your ways straight.

Flowing specifically from the path metaphor in 6a, knowing God on the paths will keep one's paths straight. The straight paths are the best, with the least obstacles. These are to be contrasted with the crooked paths, which end in death (9:18; cf. 2:15).

> [7]Don't be wise in your own eyes.
>   Fear Yahweh and turn away from evil.

The call to the son not to be wise in his own eyes is an alternative way to state that he should not depend on his own understanding (see v. 5b). If he thinks he is wise, then he will try to do things with his own resources, which will not be sufficient. The opposite of being wise in one's own eyes is to fear Yahweh. The fear of Yahweh puts one's own

6. Von Rad (*Wisdom in Israel*, 102) rightly points out in regard to this and other passages concerning people who think too highly of their own wisdom: "The acquisition of wisdom and competence was stressed by none as highly as by the teachers; but they also knew that wherever it gives a man a sense of security or where it tempts him into boasting, wisdom has already cancelled itself out."

abilities and resources in proper perspective. It also naturally leads to an aversion to evil.

The warning about being wise in one's own eyes may be found elsewhere in Proverbs (3:5; 26:12; 27:1; 28:11, 26) as, of course, is the case with the admonition to fear Yahweh (1:7; 9:10; 10:27; 14:26–27; 15:16, 33; 16:6; 19:23; 31:30) and turn away from evil.

> ⁸This will bring health to your body
> and refreshment to your bones.

If people fear Yahweh, avoid evil, and are not wise in their own eyes, then they will be healthy and refreshed. As discussed in the introduction (see "Retribution"), this is not a promise but generally true, all things being equal. It provides an incentive for doing the right thing.

> ⁹Honor Yahweh with your wealth
> and from the first of your produce.

One can show they have the proper attitude toward Yahweh, in trusting (v. 5) and fearing him (v. 7), if they are willing to give up some of their wealth. How would one honor Yahweh with one's wealth? Though it does not specify, it would seem likely that we are talking here of turning over a portion of one's wealth and produce to the temple officials who collect the tithes.

> ¹⁰And your barns will be filled with plenty,
> and your vats will burst with wine.

To obey the admonition of v. 9 leads directly to the reward of v. 10. It is a paradoxical truth, but if one is willing to give of one's wealth to honor Yahweh, then such persons will find an increase of their wealth, not a diminishing of it. The increase is described in agricultural terms. Their barns will be filled, and their vats will burst with wine. We should note that the process of such an increase is not explicated, but we are surely to recognize God behind the abundance.

> ¹¹The discipline of Yahweh, my son, do not reject,
> and do not loathe his correction.

The father ends with a final admonition not to reject Yahweh's correction. The wise want to correct their mistaken thinking and behavior; only fools reject correction (9:7–12). This correction is often mediated by the sages themselves. Here the father is the sage and communicates Yahweh's discipline.

> ¹²For the one whom Yahweh loves he will correct,
> even like a father who treats a son favorably.

God corrects out of love. He does not want his people to continue in life-damaging attitudes and behavior. The analogy that the father presents is that of a father who treats his son favorably. This is particularly poignant since the discourse is the loving admonition of a human father to his son. Correction, though painful, is thus seen as a favor, a sign of grace.

Theological Implications

In this section, the father urges the son to pursue his instruction and, once he has appropriated it, never to depart from it. Such pursuit entails trust in Yahweh and dependence on him in all things. In other words, if there is a difference between pursuing the father's commands and those from Yahweh, it is insignificant.

If the son does what his father urges him to do, then he will find great reward. That reward is spelled out in terms of health, safety, and wealth.

In this, the father's lesson is repeated elsewhere in the first nine chapters and could be understood as the major theme: "Pursue wisdom and be rewarded."

One interesting element of this particular instruction is the final admonition, which has to do with the discipline of Yahweh. The father urges his son not to reject divine discipline and likens it to the loving and concerned discipline of the father. This advice fits into the broader theme of Proverbs, to listen to correction and be ready to learn from one's mistakes (9:7–12; 10:17; 12:1; 14:9; 15:10, 12, 31, 33; 25:12; 26:11; 27:5–6; 28:13, 23). These verses are quoted in Heb. 12:5–6 in the midst of that author's argument that God's discipline, though painful, shows that he cares for his children. It is the neglectful parent who spares the rod, after all (29:15).

The difficulty is knowing when suffering is to teach us and when there is some other reason behind it. Job discusses these issues and cautions against drawing too facile a conclusion about the divine purpose of suffering. Elihu, for instance, wrongly insists that discipline for sin was the purpose behind Job's sad plight (Job 36:21). Nevertheless, as the psalmist was well aware, suffering can often bring us closer to God:

When I was prosperous I said,
    "Nothing can stop me now!"
Your favor, O LORD, made me as secure as a mountain.
    Then you turned away from me, and I was shattered.

135

I cried out to you, O LORD.
　　I begged the Lord for mercy. . . .
You have turned my mourning into joyful dancing. (Ps. 30:6–8, 11 NLT)

3:13–20. *Praising wisdom.* The poem of 3:13–20 pronounces a blessing on those who find wisdom. Wisdom is here personified as a woman (see 1:20–33 already; chap. 8; 9:1–6). The bulk of the passage is a description of the qualities and benefits of wisdom, which serves as an explanation for why the person who finds wisdom is blessed. The purpose of such a poem is to encourage those who have not yet begun their quest for wisdom to begin it.

The description of wisdom begins with a statement of its worth, which is expressed by means of comparative parallelisms proclaiming wisdom's superiority to precious metals and pearls (vv. 14–15). After this, wisdom's connection with a long and wonderful life is described (vv. 16–18). Finally, the role of wisdom in creation is narrated (vv. 19–20).

13Blessed are those who find Wisdom,
　　and those who gain Competence.

The poem's identity as a blessing, or beatitude, is revealed by the first word. It pronounces a blessing on those who find wisdom (see also 8:32, 34; 14:21; 29:18). The word "blessed" is from the Hebrew root *ʾšr*, which is not strictly synonymous with another Hebrew root also often translated "bless" (*brk*). The word used here is closer to the English term "happy," whereas *brk* "speaks more of being empowered or favored as the recipient of blessing from the Lord."[7]

Thus, the beatitude proclaims that those who find wisdom, who gain competence, are truly happy. Such a statement is intended to motivate the naive or young to pursue wisdom in order to achieve happiness.

What does it mean to find wisdom, however? The text does not specify, but from the broader context we might profitably think of wisdom in an important sense as a journey. Over time one grows in wisdom. However, in a more fundamental sense wisdom is not a content that is accumulated; it is an attitude, a state of mind. That state of mind is most pointedly captured by the phrase "fear of Yahweh." Those who fear Yahweh are those who have found wisdom, because, as we learn in various places but most dramatically in chaps. 8–9, Yahweh is the source of all wisdom.

14For her profit is better than that of silver,
　　and her yield, better than gold.

---

7. *NIDOTTE* 1:763.

> **15**Her value is more than pearls,
>   and all that you want is not the equal of her.

These verses use comparative parallelism to show the preeminent value of wisdom. Silver, gold, and pearls are all extremely precious and expensive. But the profit or value of wisdom surpasses them all. Solomon recognized this when he chose wisdom over wealth.

This type of comparison is used frequently in Proverbs (8:10, 19; 16:16) and elsewhere, but nowhere is it as fully developed as in Job 28. That text develops the idea that gold and silver are immensely valuable precisely because they are so difficult to extract from the earth. Though hard, humans can do it. However, finding wisdom is not just difficult; it also is impossible for men and women. They cannot exert their strength or intelligence to find it. Only God has it; and thus the chapter ends with an exhortation to fear Yahweh.

> **16**Length of days is in her right hand;
>   in her left are wealth and honor.
> **17**Her paths are pleasant paths,
>   and all her trails are peace.
> **18**She is a tree of life to those who embrace her,
>   and those who hold her tight are blessed.

The value of wisdom is here explained in reference to the benefits attached to its acquisition. As personified, Wisdom is said to hold gifts in her hands. In her right is long life, and in her left, honor and wealth. Long life, honor, and wealth are greatly desired by humans, and here we see that these things are Wisdom's gifts to distribute to those with whom she is in relationship. Again, this provides great motivation for the pursuit of wisdom. Wisdom is the insight into life and the way the world works, so that people avoid the pitfalls that might lead to an early death or a damaged reputation. They also allow one to have the insight that will accrue in great material wealth. In this passage the sage wants to motivate people to pursue wisdom. Other passages will grapple with the fact that some wise people are not wealthy, healthy, and powerful, while some wicked people are (Ps. 73; Job; Ecclesiastes).

Verse 18 presents a memorable metaphor that also associates Woman Wisdom with life. Invoking the memory of Eden, she is identified with the tree of life, that tree whose fruit grants life.

One's relationship with Wisdom is described in sexual terms. One obtains life if one embraces this woman and holds her tight. At this point we must remember that the primary audience of this text is young men, to whom such a metaphor would speak volumes.

Finally, it is not just quantity of life (length of days) that is promised to those who have a relationship with Wisdom, but quality as well. Wisdom's path is pleasant. The path refers to one's life, and the lives of those who are wise are not only pleasant but also characterized by peace. This reminds us of the consequences promised to those who heed the instruction/commands of the father in 3:2:

> For length of days and years of life
> and peace they will add to you.

> ¹⁹Yahweh laid the foundations of the earth with Wisdom,
>   establishing the heavens with competence.
> ²⁰With his knowledge the deeps burst open,
>   and the skies drop dew.

The poem concludes by associating wisdom with creation.[8] While this is the first time this connection is made in Proverbs, it will recur later (8:22–31) and constitutes a profound theme of the book.

The creation is ordered, not random. God established it by his wisdom. This assertion belies the thought that it might be the result of chance. Experience at times might lead to the latter conclusion (see Eccles. 9:11), but that would be a fateful mistake. No, earth and heaven were created by wisdom. The order of creation can also be learned from Gen. 1. Such a teaching would lead us to conclude that the apparent disorder observed in creation is the result of the fall, not the original creation.

Furthermore, understanding wisdom's role in creation should motivate humans to acquire wisdom. After all, if one wants to know how the world works and thus benefit from recognizing the rhythms of creation, what better way to do that than to share in the wisdom that produced the world to begin with?

Verse 20 continues the theme but specifies an aspect of creation, the waters below (depths) and the waters above (dew). The rhythms of the water cycle are also connected to wisdom. Here the synonym "knowledge" is used.

It is interesting to note the similarities between 3:19–20 and 24:3–4, where the latter is rendered:

> With wisdom a house is built;
>   with competence it is established.

---

8. We agree with those interpreters who see the transition to the theme of wisdom and creation as abrupt (see Whybray, *Proverbs*, 68), but we do not think this requires that we isolate these verses as a separate poem or consider the verses misplaced. Wisdom's relationship with creation is another benefit of acquiring wisdom, which motivates its acquisition.

> With knowledge rooms are filled
> with all precious and pleasant wealth.

Perhaps we are to think of Yahweh's construction of the cosmos as building a house. Indeed, that is the conclusion of Van Leeuwen, who also provocatively suggests further connections between 3:19–20 and other passages in the OT. He does this on the basis of the concurrence of the three words that we have translated "wisdom," "competence," and "knowledge."[9] First, he points to the use of these words in conjunction with the building of the tabernacle in Exod. 31:1–3, noting that it is now a scholarly commonplace to comment on the connection between God's cosmos building and the construction of the tabernacle. Next, he points to the use of the three words in relationship to Solomon's construction of the temple, the building that replaced the tabernacle (see 1 Kings 7:14).[10]

Theological Implications

By means of a beatitude, this discourse promotes wisdom. It is not explicit who pronounces the blessing or who receives it, but it is best imagined to be the commendation of the fatherly sage to his neophyte son. Such a blessing encourages the son to pursue the acquisition of wisdom, which is not an easy task. In other words, this discourse speaks to one side of the paradox of chap. 2. Yes, God is the one who gives wisdom, but he is not in the habit of doing so unless the person struggles to discover it.

Though the road to wisdom is not easy, it is one with great rewards. Wisdom is better than material wealth. Solomon chose wisdom over riches (1 Kings 3) but, because of his choice, also came into great wealth. As the book of Proverbs teaches again and again, wisdom, while not fail-safe, is the most certain route to legitimate and long-lasting material gain (3:15–16; 10:22). In the same way, wisdom is the road to a long and peaceful life. Living by the principles of wisdom minimizes obstacles and threats to life. Again, this is not a guarantee, but it is generally true. On the subject of life, we should also raise a question: Just how robustly did the sages think of life? It would be hard to prove it, but the metaphor of the tree of life certainly suggests something more than just long life here on the earth. As long as one embraces the tree of

9. Van Leeuwen, "Building God's House."
10. Van Leeuwen goes on to find connections in the NT, but I do not find these suggestions as persuasive as the others.

life, one lives. In order to prevent Adam and Eve from extending their lives, they had to be ejected from the Garden, with its access to that tree. Through wisdom, the sage now has contact with that tree. If it wasn't the intention of the sage author of this discourse to imply eternal life as the reward for the acquisition of wisdom, it is hard to read it any other way in light of the fuller revelation of the NT.

3:21–35. *The integrity of wisdom.* The coherence of this passage could be questioned, but in the absence of strong indications that it is composed of different discourses, we will treat it as a single unit. The poem begins (vv. 21–22) with a parental admonition to the son that he be characterized by resourcefulness and discretion, concepts closely related to wisdom. Verses 23–25 then give the motivation for doing so, highlighting safety and confidence as consequences. Verse 26 finally reveals that it is Yahweh who provides the protection.

The next section (vv. 27–31) somewhat abruptly introduces five prohibitions, describing how one should relate to others. The first three specify relationship with neighbors, while the fourth does not delineate a particular relationship, and the last one warns against envy of the violent. Unless we treat this section as a separate unit, then we should understand this teaching as providing examples of how one lives by resourcefulness and discretion.

The last four verses (vv. 32–35) are motivations for heeding the prohibitions, if not the whole section. All four contrast the negative consequences of folly (the devious, wicked, mocker, fool) and the positive reward of wisdom (virtuous, righteous, needy, wise).

> [21]My son, don't let them slip from your eyes;
>   protect resourcefulness and discretion.
> [22]Let them be life for your soul
>   and an ornament for your throat.

These verses are the opening admonition to the son to pursue resourcefulness and discretion,[11] two words that are closely connected to wisdom. He warns his son against letting his focus move away from the way of wisdom. He must be diligent in his cultivation of resourcefulness and discretion. We have already seen the word "resourcefulness" (*tušîyyâ*) before this occurrence (2:7) and have agreed with Fox that it

11. The parallelism here is interesting. The first colon does not name the qualities that the father does not want the son to let slip from his eyes, but simply uses the pronoun "them." The identification of "them" is delayed until the second colon. In this way, the poet engages the reader's curiosity. It is unnecessary to follow Whybray (*Proverbs*, 70) and others who believe that there has been a transposition of the cola in the history of transmission.

may be defined as "an inner power that helps one escape a fix."[12] In 2:7, it is likened to a shield because it protects one from the vicissitudes of life. If a problem arises, then the recipient of God's wisdom will have the wherewithal to deal with it. We have already encountered "discretion" (*mĕzimmâ*) before as well (1:4). The Hebrew word "discretion" also has a shadow side (as in 30:32), where it means something like shrewdness. In this positive context, however, it denotes thinking through the consequences of an action and choosing the most effective way. Fox defines this word (which he translates as "shrewdness" in this context, though not with negative overtones) as a "private, unrevealed thought, often but not always used in scheming. As the ability to think for oneself and keep one's own counsel, it is especially valuable in withstanding temptation."[13]

Rather than ignore these important qualities (v. 21), the father encourages the son to make resourcefulness and discretion crucial elements in life. They are to be life for the soul; indeed, they are the way to life. The metaphor of the second colon emphasizes the teaching in the first colon. Resourcefulness and discretion will be like a necklace around the neck of a person. That is, they will enhance and enrich the life of the one who possesses them.

> [23]Then you will walk in safety on your path,
>   and your foot will not stumble.
> [24]If you lie down, you will not be terrified.
>   When you lie down, your sleep will be pleasant.
> [25]Don't be afraid of a sudden terror
>   or the ruin that comes to the wicked.
> [26]For Yahweh will be your confidence,
>   and he will guard your feet from capture.

The first three verses of this section (vv. 23–25) contain the motivation to keep focused on resourcefulness and discretion, the admonition of vv. 21–22. They motivate by naming the consequences of such a decision. All three verses present variations of the same theme: wise behavior creates a safe environment, which breeds confidence. Verses 23 and 24 form a kind of pair in that the first describes the safety of daily living, and the second the confidence the wise can have as they sleep. Verse 23 describes daily life as walking on the path, a common theme of the book, particularly the first nine chapters. The son who protects resourcefulness and discretion will walk in safety, not even stumbling on the path. Verse 24 states that safety will continue even during the

---

12. Fox, *Proverbs 1–9*, 114.
13. Ibid., 116.

particularly dangerous time of sleep. When people sleep, their guard is down, and they therefore are more open to attack. Also, as one lies down to sleep, the mind can wander to all the problems of the day and anticipated threats of the future. The person who is armed with wisdom will not have to worry about such things.

Verse 25 turns from statements about safety to an admonition not to be afraid of an unexpected tragedy. Such "ruin" interrupts the life of the wicked, not the life of the righteous. Verse 26 provides a reason for the confidence that follows from a life of wisdom: the presence of Yahweh in one's life. God himself will guarantee one's protection. The presence of Yahweh is likely to be connected to the teaching explicit elsewhere in Proverbs that those who are wise are in relationship with Yahweh (1:7). It is Yahweh himself who will keep the wise person's feet from capture. It is not clear who or what will capture the person, but whether the verse refers to enemies or to traps along the path, the teaching is that God is the guarantor of safety.

> ²⁷Don't withhold good that belongs to him,
>   when it is in your power to do it.
> ²⁸Don't say to your neighbor, "Go and return;
>   I will give it to you tomorrow," when you have it.
> ²⁹Don't intend evil toward your neighbor,
>   who lives confidently with you.
> ³⁰Don't accuse anyone without a reason,
>   when they have done nothing evil against you.
> ³¹Don't be jealous of violent people,
>   and don't prefer their path.

Five prohibitions follow rather abruptly from the previous verses. All five verses are bound together by beginning with the negative ʾal plus a jussive verb (a form sometimes referred to as the vetitive, according to Waltke-O'Connor 34.2.1b). Below, we will suggest that the first two verses (27–28) are connected, thus forming four separate proverbs out of five verses.

It is possible that these four proverbs form a separate section, but there are no indications (like a separate invocation of the "son" by the father) that we should treat them as such. Perhaps we are to understand these prohibitions as examples of the type of behavior that illustrates living life with the "resourcefulness" and "discretion" described in v. 21.

Verses 27–28 form a unit dealing with the same circumstance. Indeed, not dissimilar to the relationship between the cola in 3:21, the pronominal suffix "him" in 3:27a has no antecedent. The identity of the "him" is revealed in 3:28 with the reference to the "neighbor."

The proverbial statement of these two verses prohibits withholding some "good" from one's neighbor or even delay in giving the neighbor the "good." The identity of the "good" is left unspecified because it could refer to any number of things in real life. The "good" could be money (or its equivalent), a tool that the neighbor needs, a certain type of expertise, or physical aid—the list could go on and on. The "good" is further identified as that which belongs to the person who has come to claim it. As Fox explains, the word at issue here (*ba'al*) makes it clear that the "good" or "benefit," as he translates the word, is something that belongs to the requester "by right."[14] The point of the proverb is that the wise are attentive to the needs of their community, particularly those who live near them.[15] Beardslee suggests that this proverb may stand behind Jesus's teaching about the persistent prayer in Luke 11:5–8.[16]

The second prohibition (v. 29) also concerns one's relationship with a neighbor. It warns the wise against doing something bad to a neighbor, specifically one who "lives confidently," trusting that people will behave in a forthright way. To do something "evil" will breed, not confidence, but suspicion and fear in the community.

Verse 30 does not specify action against a neighbor but still has to do with harmony in the community. The verse is a warning against false accusations against a person. The verse does not prohibit accusation across the board. If there is a reason, then an accusation is appropriate, but in the absence of a clear-cut infraction, then no accusation should be lodged. Again, accusations disrupt peaceful community living.

And finally v. 31 warns against jealousy of violent people. This proverb recognizes that there is a surface attraction to those who use power to get what they want. Psalm 73 points out that it often appears as if the violent, or godless, have all the material blessings of the present life. The sage warns against acting on this surface impression, because that path does not lead to life, as it seems to, but rather to death.

> [32]For the devious are an abomination to Yahweh,
>   and the virtuous are his confidantes.
> [33]The curse of Yahweh is in the house of the wicked,
>   but he blesses the home of the righteous.
> [34]He mocks mockers,
>   but he shows favor to the humble.
> [35]The wise possess glory,
>   but fools exude shame.

14. Ibid., 164.
15. The Greek makes it clear that it understands the verse to apply specifically to the poor, and thus it is an encouragement to charity, but this is not justified by the Hebrew.
16. Beardslee, "Uses of the Proverb," 65.

The unit ends with motivations to follow the proper mode of behavior that is described most immediately in the five verses of prohibitions that precede these verses. However, a number of scholars simply take v. 32, with the clear connection provided by the "for" (*kî*) clause, as the motivation.[17] But just as this verse motivates by distinguishing Yahweh's attitude toward the wicked (negative) and the righteous (positive), so do the following three verses.

The "devious" refers to those who go on the wrong path (niphal participle of *lûz*). In that sense they deviate from the right way. For the phrase "abomination to Yahweh" (*tô'ăbat Yhwh*), also sometimes rendered as "Yahweh detests," see commentary at 11:1 and 20:23. On the other hand, the "virtuous," those who go straight on the right path, are those who know God well. They are in his inner circle.

The next verse (v. 33) again contrasts the "wicked" with the "righteous" (using this terminology rather than "devious" and "virtuous"; all these words are closely related to one another) in terms of their relationship with Yahweh. He curses the wicked and blesses the righteous, and not just them as individuals but also their households. The behavior of individuals has repercussions for those around them, a theme we see in a number of places in the book (11:11; 14:34). Curse and blessing bring the language of the covenant to play here. However, it may be doubted that we should make a major connection, considering that covenant is rarely an explicit concept in the book, though there may be an implicit association (see "Covenant and Wisdom" in the introduction). Even so, if we reflect on similar language in places like Deut. 28 and remember the language of reward and punishment throughout Proverbs, we are likely right to think of blessing as including things like long life, health, material wealth, happiness, and curse as the opposite. Such a description, of course, is intended to push people toward righteous and away from wicked behavior.

The next verse (v. 34) also divides the wicked fools (mockers) from the righteous wise (humble). From a human perspective, one would think the mockers strong and the needy weak. Mockers feel so confident in their position in life that they can ridicule others, especially those who might be critical of them. Here, God mocks the mockers (in both cases the verb is *lûṣ*). While the Hebrew word is not exactly the same in Ps. 2:4 (there it is *lā'ag*: "ridicule" or "scoff"), the idea is the same. In response to the rebellious and uppity "kings of the earth," the psalmist proclaims:

---

17. For instance, Whybray, *Proverbs*, 69, 73; Clifford, *Proverbs*, 58–59; Murphy, *Proverbs*, 23; Fox, *Proverbs 1–9*, 166–67; but we are in agreement with Van Leeuwen, "Proverbs," in *New Interpreter's Bible*, 5:54–55.

"The one who rules in heaven laughs. The Lord scoffs at them" (NLT). Why? Because he is so much more powerful than they are.

Finally (v. 35), the sage associates the wise with glory and the fool with shame. Again, this description has as its purpose the motivation of proper behavior and the acquisition of wisdom.

Theological Implications

In this passage, the fatherly sage admonishes his son to keep his focus on wisdom, here named by two closely related terms: "resourcefulness" and "discretion." By warning his son against letting these wise qualities slip from his eyes, the father reminds us that wisdom is not something that can be achieved and forgotten about. Rather, it is something that entails a lifelong pursuit.

The father uses a strategy of positive reinforcement to encourage his son to the task. He tells the son of the benefits that come to those who protect resourcefulness and discretion. They not only give life, but they also enhance life like an ornament worn around the neck (throat). Life is less threatening for the wise person, both during his waking and also sleeping hours. The wise are not vulnerable to the sudden tragedies of life that await the wicked.

A series of prohibitions are given primarily regarding one's attitude and behavior toward others. These prohibitions express a concern for proper and peaceful community. The wise person does nothing that would upset relationships with other people.

Yahweh is explicitly and implicitly mentioned in four verses (vv. 26, 32–34). He is the guarantor of the positive things predicted for the wise persons who obey the prohibitions, and also of the negative things that will happen to those who are wicked fools, who do not obey the counsel of the father. Yahweh is clearly on the side of those who affirm wisdom.

Chapter 4

Translation

[1]Hear, sons, fatherly discipline,
 and pay attention to the knowledge of understanding.
[2]For I will give you good teaching;
 don't forsake my instruction.
[3]For I was a son to my father,
 tender and the only one of my mother.
[4]He taught me and said to me:
 "Let your heart hold on to my words;
  guard my commands and live.
[5]Acquire Wisdom;
  acquire Understanding.
 Don't forget,
  and don't divert from the speeches of my mouth.
[6]Don't abandon her, and she will guard you.
 Love her, and she will protect you.
[7]The beginning of wisdom: Acquire wisdom!
 And above all your acquisitions, acquire wisdom![a]
[8]Esteem her highly, and she will exalt you.
 She will honor you, if you embrace her.
[9]She will place on your head a garland of favor,
 she will bestow on you a crown of glory."

a. Many commentators (see Clifford, *Proverbs*, 60) argue that v. 7 is a later addition, based on the fact that it is missing from the Greek, awkward to the context, and made up of phrases found elsewhere. However, it is not so awkward as to be without possible meaning in the text, and the fact that it is missing from the Greek could have a number of different explanations, including the fact that the LXX translator did not understand it and then dropped it, as does Clifford. Fox (*Proverbs 1–9*, 175) is not convinced v. 7 is original, but does point out in its favor that it is part of a chiastic structure in the passage.

[10]Listen, my son, and receive my speech,
    and years of life will be multiplied for you.
[11]On the path I taught you;
    I led you on a straight course.
[12]When you walk, your step is not constricted.
    When you run, you do not stumble.
[13]Be determined in discipline; don't slack off.
    Protect it, for it is your life.
[14]In the way of the wicked, don't go.
    And don't walk straight onto the path of evildoers.
[15]Avoid it! Don't cross over to it!
    Turn aside from it and cross over.
[16]They do not sleep if they do not do evil.
    Their sleep is deprived if they do not cause someone to stumble.
[17]For they dine on the bread of evildoing,
    and the wine of violence, they drink.
[18]And the way of the righteous is like a shining light
    that keeps illuminating until the day is established.
[19]The path of the wicked is like deep darkness;
    they don't know where they will stumble.

[20]My son, to my words, pay attention;
    to my speech, extend your ear.
[21]Don't let your eyes slip;
    guard them in the midst of your heart.
[22]For they are life to those who find them,
    healing to their entire body.
[23]Above all you guard, protect your heart,
    For, from it, life derives.
[24]Have nothing to do with a perverse mouth;
    keep loose lips far from you.
[25]Focus your eyes straight ahead;
    keep your eyelids[b] right in front.
[26]Watch your feet on the course,
    and all your paths will be established.
[27]Don't veer off to the right or the left;
    turn your feet aside from evil.

Interpretation

4:1–9. *Embrace wisdom!* The father approaches his son and again urges him to embrace the way of wisdom. As in other discourses (Prov. 2:1–22;

b. This appears to be what ʿapʿap means, derived from ʿwp, "to fly" or "to flutter." However, meanings derived directly from this verb are a bit awkward in English translation, and perhaps Fox (*Proverbs 1–9*, 186) is correct to render the word "gaze."

147

3:21–35), the strategy is to highlight the benefits that wisdom will bring to one's life. Here all the emphasis is on the positive results of adopting wisdom, and nothing is said about the punishments of rejecting wisdom and going with folly, as is the case in many of the other related passages. However, what is truly distinctive here is the appeal to tradition. The primary dynamic of the book is a father's instruction to a son. Here we have an explicit statement to the effect that the father is simply continuing a tradition that stretches back for generations. He is speaking to his son as his own father (on behalf of himself and his mother) had earlier spoken to him. It is not only in Proverbs that we see the passing down of religious tradition, but also in the area of law (Deut. 6) and historical traditions, which themselves contain theological and ethical lessons (Ps. 78:5–8).

> ¹Hear, sons, fatherly discipline,
>   and pay attention to the knowledge of understanding.
> ²For I will give you good teaching;
>   don't forsake my instruction.

Unless there is a scribal error (replacing "my son" [*běnî*] with "sons" [*bānîm*]),¹ we have here an unusual address to plural "sons" rather than a single one. Not much significance can be made from this. It certainly does not prove or even argue strongly in favor of the idea that the father/son dynamic should be understood not biologically but rather professionally (especially since the mother is mentioned in colon 2 of v. 3). Certainly, one father can have multiple sons. It would suggest, however, that the individual discourses do not have one original setting but rather are a collection.

In any case, like most of the other discourses in this part of the book, this one begins with an exhortation on the part of the father to the son to pay attention to his teaching, a teaching that will direct the son toward a life lived with wisdom. Though the word "wisdom" (*ḥokmâ*) is not specifically used, the vocabulary that we saw as early as 1:2–7, which is very closely related to it, is piled up here: "discipline" (*mûsar*), "knowledge" (*daʿat*), "understanding" (*bînâ*), "teaching" (*leqaḥ*), and "instruction" (*tōrâ*).²

> ³For I was a son to my father,
>   tender and the only one of my mother.
> ⁴He taught me and said to me:

---

1. One might argue that the final *mēm* is not a plural ending but rather the result of dittography due to the fact that the next word is a noun starting with a mem (*mûsar*). However, the MT as it stands makes sense, though it is unusual.

2. For discussion of these words, see commentary at 1:2–8.

Here we have an introduction to the words of the father's father. The passage begins with the simple statement that the father also had a father. It is true that children sometimes forget that truth. It is hard to think of one's own father as the son of another, even though intellectually someone the age of the "son" in Proverbs would have certainly been aware of that fact. The second colon of v. 3 introduces the speaker's mother as well, and here the language grows more personal. He describes himself as "tender" and the "only one." These words are the language of affection. The mother had strong feelings toward the son, and these surely are evoked to imply motivation for the parents' instruction in wisdom. Now the father does the same for his son today. While v. 3 introduces the parents of the teaching father, v. 4a introduces the words of their teaching.

> "Let your heart hold on to my words;
>   guard my commands and live.
> ⁵Acquire Wisdom;
>   acquire Understanding.
> Don't forget,
>   and don't divert from the speeches of my mouth.
> ⁶Don't abandon her, and she will guard you.
>   Love her, and she will protect you.
> ⁷The beginning of wisdom: Acquire wisdom!
>   And above all your acquisitions, acquire wisdom!
> ⁸Esteem her highly, and she will exalt you.
>   She will honor you, if you embrace her.
> ⁹She will place on your head a garland of favor,
>   she will bestow on you a crown of glory."

The following words are from the son's grandfather, directed toward his father.[3] They serve to bolster the father's own appeal to the son. In essence, the burden of generations is placed on the shoulders of the son in order to get him to move in the right direction.

The grandfather began with an admonition that the father listen to his words, which are also described as commands.[4] When an object of instruction himself, the father was urged to internalize the words of his own father ("let your heart hold on"). Once taken in, though, the struggle

---

3. It is not exactly clear just how long the quotation of the "grandfather" extends, but in the absence of a clear indication of a change back to the words of the father, we take it as extending to the end of the unit (v. 9). In one sense it does not matter, because the idea is that the father is quoting the grandfather to buttress his own points. The generations past are united in their instruction to the present young generation.

4. For the meaning of *miṣwâ* and the controversy surrounding that word, see comments on 2:1.

was not over; they were to be guarded. Wisdom is not a once-and-for-all decision; it is a process. It is not "once wise; always wise." One could lose one's wisdom unless it was "guarded."

The simplest of the commands that was to be heeded and guarded was this: "Acquire Wisdom." It is sometimes tricky to know when Wisdom is personified and when not, but the language of v. 6 suggests that we are to think of Wisdom appearing as a female. The wise person is to love her and in return will be protected. The commands of the (grand)father to his son are also expressed negatively. Wisdom is not only to be acquired; it also is not to be forgotten. His words are not only to be heard; the "son" must also not turn away from them. She must not only be loved; she must also not be abandoned. Stating the same thing both positively and negatively adds tremendous emphasis to the command.

Verse 7 begins in a surprising way. In it the grandfather informs the father (and now the father quotes it to his son) that the beginning of wisdom is the acquisition of wisdom! What makes this surprising is that in 1:7 (and 9:10; 10:27; 14:26–27; 15:16, 33; 16:6; 19:23; 22:4; 31:30) we learn that the beginning of knowledge is the fear of Yahweh. We are not to make much of the distinction between wisdom and knowledge as if they are two completely different things; in this book, they are typically used as near synonyms. The explanation is that there are two sides to the wisdom enterprise. One must seek wisdom, but when one finds it, one realizes that it was not because of the effort, but because it was a gift of God. We have already encountered this paradox in 2:1–22. Another way of understanding the connection between the two "beginnings" or "foundations"[5] is to recognize that the acquisition of wisdom involves assuming the right stance (fear) toward Yahweh. Verse 7b then points out that there is nothing more important to acquire in life than wisdom. The youthful Solomon's example is instructive here. He could choose any gift from God, but he chose wisdom over wealth and power (1 Kings 3). This wisdom was the means to power in a way that wealth and power could not move to wisdom.

The grandfather's speech ends with a clear personification of Wisdom as a woman. The metaphor takes an erotic shape as he urges his son to "esteem" her (v. 8, with the *hapax legomenon* of the pilpel of *sll* I) and embrace her. In short, he is to become intimate with this woman, who returns the favor by exalting and honoring him. Verse 9 provides the metaphor of crowning him as indicating the kind of glory he will receive. The crowning with favor/glory suggests the fact that the wise person's reputation will be public. He will be known as someone with wisdom,

5. For the meaning of *rēʾšît*, see commentary at 1:7.

perhaps also with wealth and power, again like the young Solomon. This "crown" may be a wedding crown (see Song 3:11).

Theological Implications

One of the most interesting elements of this discourse is the fact that the father appeals to his father to bolster the authority of his message to the son. The quality of the father's advice stands on the fact that it is not new with him, but rather something that he received from his father. In this teaching, however, we do not receive content, but rather exhortation to pursue wisdom. Wisdom is personified as a Woman, and the son is encouraged to grow intimate with her. The character of this woman will be expanded upon in chaps. 8 and 9. The emphasis here is on the pursuit of Wisdom, and again, the positive consequences (glory and honor) that result from the acquisition of Wisdom is what motivates the son.

4:10–19. *Stay on the right path.* In the next discourse of father to son, the former urges the latter to stay on the right path. The assumption here is that the son has already at least initially heeded the advice of his father, and now the father gives him further encouragement to stay the course. Again, this shows that wisdom is not a once-and-for-all decision but involves a lifetime of commitment and rededication. Indeed, part of the appeal is that the son's experience on the straight path means a minimization of problems (he does not stumble on this path). A large part of the speech is a warning against going over to the dark side, the other path, which is evil. On the surface such a move might be tempting, but in actuality it leads to trouble and heartache.

> [10]Listen, my son, and receive my speech,
>   and years of life will be multiplied for you.
> [11]On the path I taught you;
>   I led you on a straight course.
> [12]When you walk, your step is not constricted.
>   When you run, you do not stumble.

As is typical, the speech begins with an appeal to the son to listen and receive the teaching of his father. If the son does so, then his life will be lengthened. Though specific content is not given here, a large part of the wisdom enterprise is to encourage a lifestyle that promotes life and avoids situations that might lead to premature death.

The father goes on to testify (v. 11) that he has already taught the son to go on the straight course, another word for "path." The straight path is liberating, not narrow and leading one frequently to stumble.

---

¹³Be determined in discipline; don't slack off.
     Protect it, for it is your life.

However, though the son is presently on the path, the father feels it necessary to admonish him to maintain his diligence. Wisdom is not gained by a onetime decision, but a decision followed by a lifetime of discipline. It is a rigorous endeavor, involving study as well as self-control, especially in light of the apparent rewards from going on the easier path of the wicked. But wisdom is worth the pursuit because it leads to life.

---

¹⁴In the way of the wicked, don't go.
     And don't walk straight onto the path of evildoers.
¹⁵Avoid it! Don't cross over to it!
     Turn aside from it and cross over.
¹⁶They do not sleep if they do not do evil.
     Their sleep is deprived if they do not cause someone to stumble.
¹⁷For they dine on the bread of evildoing,
     and the wine of violence, they drink.
¹⁸And the way of the righteous is like a shining light
     that keeps illuminating until the day is established.
¹⁹The path of the wicked is like deep darkness;
     they don't know where they will stumble.

The father recognizes that the son may well be tempted to go the route of the wicked. Through a series of prohibitions, he warns his son not to move from the straight course, the path that he himself taught his son to walk, to avoid the way of the wicked. Verses 14–15 do not give reasons for not making this move; they just bombard the son with imperatives commanding him not to do it.

Verses 16–17 add some substance to the prohibition by describing the intentions of those who are evil. They are compulsive evildoers, and they want to enmesh others into their lifestyle. In particular, they want to harm others. What gives them sleepless nights is their inability to mess up someone's life, to "cause someone to stumble." Verse 17 employs the metaphor of eating and drinking to describe just how deeply ingrained in their lives is their desire to do evil, and in particular to hurt others. Just as ingested food and drink become a part of a person, so they eat evil and drink violence. It is a part of them.

The final two verses contrast the "way of the righteous" and the "path of the wicked," using the imagery of light and darkness. The righteous live in the clarity of light. They can see where they are going and avoid obstacles.[6] They can find their way to a desired end. On the other hand, the wicked walk in darkness. As a result, their life course (the path) is filled with obstacles that cause them trouble. The comparison implicitly encourages the son to stay on the right path and avoid the wrong one.

Theological Implications

Isolated from the broader context in the book, this speech is not very theological in the narrow sense. The father does not explicitly mention God. However, by invoking the two-path theology that dominates the first part of the book, we note exactly how theological the speech is. As described in this speech, the two paths include the path on which the father has set the son, and now he urges him to persist on that track; this contrasts with the warnings he issues the son against going on the path of the wicked. By this time, we know that the father's path is the one that God protects; it is the way of God. It is the path of light, which leads to life, as opposed to the darkness of the way of wickedness. The two-path theology does not allow for a third, compromising way. One is either on the straight path or on the crooked path. The two-path theology is reminiscent of the teaching of Psalm 1, properly categorized as a wisdom psalm.

4:20–27. *Guard your heart.* As with the previous discourse, the father here encourages his son to maintain the course. He is on the straight path, and he must summon all of his resources to remain diligent and not veer off this path to go onto the other path, described as evil (v. 27). That all the son's resources need to be marshaled to the task is underlined by the many references to different body parts that must play their role: ear, eyes, eyelids, mouth, lips, feet, and above all—the heart.

> [20]My son, to my words, pay attention;
>   to my speech, extend your ear.
> [21]Don't let your eyes slip;
>   guard them in the midst of your heart.
> [22]For they are life to those who find them,
>   healing to their entire body.

Typically, this discourse begins with the father calling on the son to listen to his teaching. His ears must be attentive to the important message that follows. He then commands his son to keep his focus (eyes)

---

6. Ecclesiastes 2:12–16 makes the same point but not as enthusiastically. The lack of enthusiasm arises from the fact that, though wisdom can help in the present, it cannot avoid the fate of death, and therefore it is ultimately meaningless.

by guarding them (the father's words) in his heart. The heart is one's innermost being, one's core personality (see commentary at 3:1). The father is not interested in just a superficial response from his son, some kind of behavior modification; he desires that his child be wise at his very core. Actions and speech will flow from a wise character. Verse 22 gives motivation to the son to pay attention to his father. If he takes the message to heart, then that will lead to life and wholeness.

> 23Above all you guard, protect your heart,
>   For, from it, life derives.

In the previous verses, we have described the "heart" as equivalent to character or core personality. We are now in a position to understand the importance that the father gives to the heart in this verse. It is most important that the son preserves the integrity of his heart. It is from the heart that life derives. The father is not speaking literally. The heart can remain beating, but a person be dead in other ways. An evil heart is a dead heart.

> 24Have nothing to do with a perverse mouth;
>   keep loose lips far from you.

As part of the process of guarding his heart, the wise son must keep a perverse mouth/loose lips far from him. It is not clear whether this admonition applies to one's own speech or to what one hears, but the father would say both. Don't speak or listen to foolish speech. As to what constitutes the speech of a perverse mouth/loose lips, while not defined here, many later proverbs will help us understand. A partial list would include lips that speak gossip, spread slander, lie, or harm in some other way (10:6, 18; 12:6; 22:10; 25:18).

> 25Focus your eyes straight ahead;
>   keep your eyelids right in front.
> 26Watch your feet on the course,
>   and all your paths will be established.
> 27Don't veer off to the right or the left;
>   turn your feet aside from evil.

The remainder of this discourse utilizes the language of the two paths, to encourage the son to do the right thing. The son is to remain focused on what is ahead. The picture we see is the son walking on the straight path of wisdom, heading toward the goal of life, and he is keeping his eyes straight ahead. The son is not distracted but keeps his eyes on his feet so they do not veer but, rather, clearly follow the path. To turn off this path, whether to the right or left, is to start off on another path, which is the path of evil.

Theological Implications

The father is vitally concerned to keep his son moving on the right path in his life. In many ways, this discourse is an admonition like the previous one. It does not mention God explicitly, but by invoking the two-path theology, it does so implicitly, since the father's path is the one that is associated with God. The admonition to the son here is to focus all of his energies on staying on the right path and avoiding the evil path. Again, this underlines the idea that wisdom entails a lifetime of work and not a single decision.

Chapter 5

Translation

¹My son, to my wisdom pay attention;
    to my competence, extend your ear,
²so you might guard discretion,
    and your lips might protect knowledge.
³For the lips of a strange woman drip honey,
    and her palate is smoother than oil.
⁴But in the end[a] she is bitter as wormwood,
    sharp as a two-edged sword.
⁵Her feet go down to death;
    her step grabs on to Sheol.[b]
⁶She refuses to observe the way of life.
    Her paths wander, but she does not know it.[c]

⁷And now, sons, listen to me,
    and don't turn aside from the speeches of my mouth.
⁸Let your path be far from her;
    don't go near to the entrance to her house.
⁹Lest you give to others your vitality;
    your years to a cruel person.

a. Literally (but awkwardly in English), "in her end."
b. For Sheol, see commentary on 1:12.
c. Murphy (*Proverbs*, 30) correctly points out that the grammar can be read in more than one way. In the first colon, many simply read *pen* (lest) as equivalent to *ʾal* (not). Here I follow Fox (*Proverbs 1–9*, 193), who presents arguments for the conclusion that "*pen* itself comes to provide the negative optative." Also, we are taking the verbs as third-person feminine, though recognizing that they formally could be read as second person.

[10]Lest strange people sap your strength,
and your hard work ends up in the house of a foreigner.
[11]And you groan at your end,
when your body and your flesh are exhausted.
[12]And you say, "How I hated discipline!
How my heart despised correction!
[13]I did not listen to the voice of the one who instructed me;
I did not extend my ear to my teacher.
[14]I am on the edge of complete ruin
in the assembled community."[d]

[15]Drink water from your own well,
gushing water from your own cistern.
[16]Should your fountains burst forth outside,
streams of water in the public squares?
[17]They are yours alone
and not for strangers who are with you.
[18]May your spring be blessed;
rejoice in the wife of your youth.
[19]She is a deer of love and an ibex of grace.
Let her breasts[e] intoxicate you all the time;
be continually inebriated by her love.[f]
[20]Why, my son, should you be inebriated by a stranger
and embrace the bosom of a foreigner?

[21]For the eyes of Yahweh are on the paths of humans,
observing all their courses.
[22]The wicked will be captured by their own guilt,
grabbed by the cords of their own sin.
[23]Those without discipline will die,
inebriated by their own stupidity.

Interpretation

Avoid promiscuous women; love your wife. Chapter 5 is the first major teaching on the dangers of consorting with a woman who is not one's wife. The discourses of the first part of the book contains three large blocks of such teaching (5:1–23; 6:20–35; 7:1–27), while the proverbs of the second part also have a number of pithy sayings that support

d. Taking this phrase (along with Murphy, *Proverbs*, 30) as a hendiadys. Literally, the Hebrew has "in the assembly and community."

e. So the MT. Some emend *dad* to *dōd*, "love" or, better, the concrete activity of "lovemaking."

f. Clifford (*Proverbs*, 68–69) follows the NEB by inserting 6:22 here, on the basis of the fact that the Greek seems to have some connection to that verse. However, most versions, including the revision of the NEB (the REB), have rejected this emendation.

the teaching found there (such as 22:14; 23:27; 30:20). The dynamic of this chapter continues to be a father instructing his son, and here the fact that the child is male is vitally important since the topic is the prohibition of intimate relationships with women who are outside of a marriage relationship.

The father addresses this concern with all the rhetorical power that he can muster because the temptation is great. An intimate relationship with a woman outside the bounds of marriage promises great pleasure and satisfaction. The truth behind the appearance, however, is that such liaisons result in tremendous pain. Thus, the father warns the son not to follow one's desires, but rather to obey the instruction. If the son does not do so, he will deeply regret the ruin that he has brought into his life.

However, the father does not stop with warning about bad behavior; he also encourages the son to proper behavior in the area of intimate relationships. Using quite provocative metaphors, the father tells the son to enjoy intimacy with his wife. In this discourse, the son is married, so we are likely to think of him as a young adult. In any case, the father encourages the idea that the best defense (against committing adultery) is a strong offense (reveling in the joys of marital sex). However, in the end, he appeals to the watching eye of Yahweh to push the son to proper behavior. Obedience is what separates the righteous from the wicked, and the wicked end up dead.

> [1]My son, to my wisdom pay attention;
>   to my competence, extend your ear,
> [2]so you might guard discretion,
>   and your lips might protect knowledge.
> [3]For the lips of a strange woman drip honey,
>   and her palate is smoother than oil.
> [4]But in the end she is bitter as wormwood,
>   sharp as a two-edged sword.
> [5]Her feet go down to death;
>   her step grabs on to Sheol.
> [6]She refuses to observe the way of life.
>   Her paths wander, but she does not know it.

5:1–6. The father's admonition begins in a straightforward manner. He first of all gets the son's attention and prods him to listen to the following teaching (v. 1). This is the only time that the father refers to "wisdom" as specifically "his." What he represents as "his" is not to be differentiated from divine wisdom. In essence, he is a conduit of divine wisdom to the son.

A purpose clause follows in v. 2, suggesting that listening will lead to the preservation of discretion and knowledge (through the metaphor of guarding, expressed through the word pair "guard" [*šmr*] and "protect" (*nṣr*]). These words, of course, are associated with wisdom, and so the father is addressing the issue of his son's wise behavior. Usually one's lips are associated with speech, so on the surface it appears that the father is telling the son to act in a certain way in order to preserve his ability to speak wisely. However, as we see in the next verse, there may be a double meaning here, since lips are used not only to speak but also to kiss.

Certainly, such a double entendre is active with the reference to the lips of the "strange woman" (v. 3), which drip honey. On one level, this refers to the flattery that she employs to attract the man (6:24; 7:5, 21). But honey is a metaphor of taste. One wants to lick honey, and so the reference likely also suggests sweet kisses. The erotic nature of lips that drip honey may be seen by comparing the use of the same imagery in a more positive context in the Song of Songs (4:11; 5:1). The fact that her palate is smoother than oil also is sensuous, but admittedly not in a metaphor of taste.

But who is the "strange" woman? A fuller discussion may be located in the comments on 2:16, where our conclusion is that the woman is "strange" in regard to the legal and social customs. She is acting outside of community norms. An adulteress or a prostitute would qualify for this description.

But the father quickly says that appearances are misleading, even deadly. What looks sweet turns out to be "bitter," like "wormwood." The latter is commonly identified with *Artemisia absinthium*, and it not only has a bitter taste, but parts of it can also be deadly if ingested. So, instead of being sweet like honey, she is really bitter (and deadly), like wormwood. Further, instead of being smooth like oil, she is really sharp (and deadly), like a two-edged sword.

Verse 5 makes explicit what is implicit in the metaphors of v. 4, that a relationship with this woman will lead to death. As we have discussed elsewhere, this woman is the human reflex to Woman Folly (see "Embracing Woman Wisdom" in the introduction), and so we are not surprised to hear that to follow her leads to the underworld. Finally, this first unit in the larger poem that constitutes chap. 5 concludes with an allusion to the two-path theology rampant in this part of the book. There is a path of life, but she does not know where it is, or at least she does not acknowledge it. Rather, she wanders all over the place.

> [7]And now, sons, listen to me,
>   and don't turn aside from the speeches of my mouth.
> [8]Let your path be far from her;
>   don't go near to the entrance to her house.
> [9]Lest you give to others your vitality;
>   your years to a cruel person.

> ¹⁰Lest strange people sap your strength,
>   and your hard work ends up in the house of a foreigner.
> ¹¹And you groan at your end,
>   when your body and your flesh are exhausted.
> ¹²And you say, "How I hated discipline!
>   How my heart despised correction!
> ¹³I did not listen to the voice of the one who instructed me;
>   I did not extend my ear to my teacher.
> ¹⁴I am on the edge of complete ruin
>   in the assembled community."

5:7–14. The father's speech continues, but we have an unexpected exordium (call to listen) in v. 7, and in this case, the invocation is not just to "my son" but to "sons." This verse again admonishes the hearers to pay close attention. Verse 8 gets right to the point. Avoid temptation by not even moving close to such a woman. Again, employing the two-path theology, he tells them to keep their path far from such a woman.

The father bolsters his admonition to the son not to go near the "strange" woman by pointing out the negative consequences of such behavior (vv. 9–10, introduced by "lest" [*pen*] clauses). The first comments on the expenditure of the son's "vitality." This word (*hôd*) typically means "splendor" or "majesty" (*NIDOTTE* 1:1016–17). However, here (and perhaps also in Dan. 10:8) the word refers to a person's strength, vigor, or vitality. It may mean that the son expends his sexual energy on the strange woman. That this is a life-sapping activity is commented on in v. 9b. Verse 10 uses another word for one's life force (strength, *kōaḥ*), which is said to diminish because of this illegitimate sexual activity. Verse 10b may imply that the person's material wealth, generated by hard work, also ends up in the house of a "foreigner" (*nokrî*, a term often used in parallel to "strange" in Proverbs). Finally, v. 11 foresees a sad end, when the person's body gives out because of his behavior.

Before leaving vv. 8–11, we should comment on the move from the singular "strange woman" to the plural "strange people." To be honest, it is a bit vague as to whom is meant by the plurality of people who end up exploiting the son. The plural is masculine, so it probably doesn't point to a multitude of women. Perhaps men connected to the woman (pimps?)[1] are indicated by this reference.

At this point, the father warns that if it comes to this, the son will rue the day he rejected the advice that he is now receiving from him. What the son is now getting are words of discipline/correction. "Do not go to the house of the strange woman!" He will regret it if he ignores the ad-

---

1. Or so Whybray, *Proverbs*, 88: "Members of the woman's family who, by whatever means, take their revenge by ruining the man."

vice. And at that point it will be too late. The public shame (ruin before the assembled community) will be complete and unchangeable. No one will ever forget that the son had reached the point of being completely spent by profligate activity.

> [15]Drink water from your own well,
>   gushing water from your own cistern.
> [16]Should your fountains burst forth outside,
>   streams of water in the public squares?
> [17]They are yours alone
>   and not for strangers who are with you.
> [18]May your spring be blessed;
>   rejoice in the wife of your youth.
> [19]She is a deer of love and an ibex of grace.
>   Let her breasts intoxicate you all the time;
>   be continually inebriated by her love.
> [20]Why, my son, should you be inebriated by a stranger
>   and embrace the bosom of a foreigner?
> [21]For the eyes of Yahweh are on the paths of humans,
>   observing all their courses.
> [22]The wicked will be captured by their own guilt,
>   grabbed by the cords of their own sin.
> [23]Those without discipline will die,
>   inebriated by their own stupidity.

5:15–23. At this point, the father switches strategy. He moves from warning about wicked behavior to encouraging proper behavior in the context of sexuality. Again, the idea seems to be that the best defense against the wiles of the "strange" woman is a vital relationship with one's proper sexual partner, the wife. The OT does not discourage sexual relations for a moment; it just puts it in its proper context—heterosexual marriage.

The father uses tasteful but clear metaphors to urge his son toward a vital sexual relationship with the wife of his youth. He urges his son to drink water from his own well and gushing water from his own cistern. These highly erotic images refer to the wife.[2] As we can see from the ancient Near East as well as Song 4:10–15 and from the logic of the comparison, these are references to a woman's vagina.[3] So in v. 15 the

---

2. As recognized by many, including Kaiser, "True Marital Love."

3. See Longman, *Song of Songs,* 155; and S. Paul, "A Lover's Garden of Verse: Literal and Metaphorical Imagery in Ancient Near Eastern Love Poetry," in *Tehillah le-Moshe: Biblical and Judaic Studies in Honor of Moshe Greenberg,* ed. M. Cogan et al. (Winona Lake, IN: Eisenbrauns, 1997), 99–110; and for its use in Egyptian love poetry, see M. Fox, *The Song of Songs and the Ancient Egyptian Love Songs* (Madison: University of Wisconsin Press, 1985), 283–87.

father advises his son to find sexual fulfillment with his own wife rather than another woman.

Then in the next verse (v. 16) the father uses similar imagery to refer to male sexuality. It is true that "fountain" is used in Song 4:10–15 to refer to the woman, but the fact that a fountain (as opposed to a well) emits its waters makes it a suitable comparison with male ejaculation. The father tells the son that sexual relations are proper to the home, not to the outside world (with women outside the household). His sexual vitality should be spent on his wife, not on others (v. 17).

Verse 18 pronounces a blessing on the son's "spring" (*mĕqôr*). A spring, like a fountain and unlike a well or a cistern, suggests the emission of waters, and so might be an image of male ejaculation. On the other hand, elsewhere in the Bible "spring" metaphorically points to the female vagina.[4] Furthermore, the parallel in colon 2 is with the "wife of your youth." Though there is this ambiguity,[5] the gist of the verse is clear. It is a blessing on a proper relationship with his wife. A blessing conveys the wish for happiness and life. It would likely include the hope both for sexual pleasure and for progeny.

Verse 19 further characterizes the wife of his youth in terms that are erotic and reminiscent of the Song of Songs. In the latter, however, it is the male term "gazelle" (Song 2:9, 17; 8:14) that is used rather than the female term. However, the image conveys sleekness and smoothness, as does ibex,[6] the parallel.

The sensuous description of the wife continues with the wish that the son might be intoxicated by her breasts and inebriated by her love. The language of intoxication is suggested also in the Song of Songs, where the woman claims that the man's "love is better than wine" (4:10). Love and lovemaking make one lightheaded, similar to the effects of drinking wine.

Verse 20 makes the father's point most pointedly. In the light of the delights of one's wife, why should the son pursue sexual pleasure in the arms of another, considering all the potential dangers?

However, the father has saved his most powerful argument for last. Thus far he has warned concerning quite human dangers. He has told his son that a liaison with another woman looks good but has bitter consequences. The relationship leads to death, not life. It saps strength

---

4. Granted that it does so in reference to the flow of blood from the vagina (Lev. 12:7; 20:18), but we can easily see how it might be used in connection to the moistness of an aroused vagina.

5. Whybray (*Proverbs*, 90) seems sure that the metaphor connects to the male, while Murphy (*Proverbs*, 32) seems equally clear that it points to the female.

6. "Ibex" is chosen here to translate *yaʿălâ* rather than "mountain goat," which does not sound particularly complimentary in English.

and vitality and resources. But the ultimate motivation for not entering into an illicit relationship is because "the eyes of Yahweh are on the paths of humans, observing all their courses." God is watching, and so the punishments of vv. 22–23 (ultimately death) are not a matter of chance, but certainty; the implication is that no matter what particular form the punishment might take, God will assure that it will happen. The sin of the adulterers will come back and harm them (v. 22). If they are not inebriated by the love of their wife, then they will be inebriated by their own stupidity, and that will result in their death.

Theological Implications

This passage contains the first of three (see also 6:20–35 and 7:1–27) extended teachings of the father to the son on the subject of intimate relationships with women. The mere fact of such extensive teaching indicates the importance of the topic. The father recognizes that sex is a major temptation in the life of a young man and poses a tremendous threat to the possibility of a legitimate sexual union in the form of a marriage. However, probably more than sexual ethics is involved in the father's concern. As will be expanded upon below, the relationship between the son and the wife of his youth reflects the relationship that the father wants him to develop with Woman Wisdom. On the other hand, the father wants him to avoid the "strange" or "foreign" woman in the way he wants him to avoid Woman Folly.

The two women in this section are described as the "wife of your youth," on the one hand, and the "strange" or "foreign woman," on the other. The former is easily understood as simply a woman with whom the son has entered into a legal commitment. It is within that realm of commitment that the father encourages his son to expend his sexual energies. When marital intimacy is encouraged, the motivation that is given has to do with sensual pleasure, not progeny. It may be that the blessing of v. 18a ("may your spring be blessed") implies progeny, but even that is speculative. In teaching such as we have in this chapter (as well as in the Song of Songs), we observe the very positive attitude of the Bible toward sensuality and sexuality, when enjoyed in the context of marriage. This, we maintain, goes back to Gen. 2:23–25, which provides the foundation for marriage. When Eve is created, we hear Adam exclaim:

"This is now bone of my bones
    and flesh of my flesh;
she shall be called 'woman,'
    for she was taken out of man."

163

> For this reason a man will leave his father and mother and be united to his wife, and they will become one flesh.
> The man and his wife were both naked, and they felt no shame.
> (NIV)

Here God mandates a leaving of previous familial primary loyalties, a weaving together, culminated by a cleaving that reaches its height in the act of marital intercourse.

The threat to this relationship comes from the temptation of the "strange" woman. We have concluded that the woman is "strange" in the sense that she is outside law and custom. She is an illegitimate sexual partner because sex takes place outside of formal acts of commitment.

The extensive and consistent teaching about the evil of extramarital sexual contact leads to questions about the nature of the proverb and its relationship to legal materials. Elsewhere (see "Genre" in the introduction), we have noted that the proverb form does not inherently communicate instruction that is universally and always valid. The proverb is a time- and circumstance-sensitive form. However, the teaching on avoiding the "strange woman" is always and without exception true. There are no mitigating factors that make it acceptable behavior. One cannot imagine the father telling the son, "Don't go to the home of the 'strange' woman, unless your wife is unresponsive." In this line of teaching, the book of Proverbs is consistent, I would argue, because the Torah does not allow leeway here. Here I simply reaffirm what we have already said concerning the relationship between law and wisdom (see "Wisdom and Law" in the introduction).

Thus far, we have talked about ethics, but not theology proper. It is true that Yahweh is only mentioned one time in the chapter. He is described as ever watching human behavior in order to motivate the son to stay on the right path (v. 21). However, the relationship between the son and his wife and the "strange" or "foreign" woman, when read within the context of the whole book, reflects the relationship between the son and Woman Wisdom and Woman Folly. The exegetical argument is still forthcoming (see chaps. 8 and 9), but we will see that Woman Wisdom represents Yahweh's wisdom, and ultimately Yahweh himself, while her dark counterpart, Folly, represents the way of false gods and goddesses, and ultimately these deities themselves. Throughout the Bible, the marriage metaphor is used for relationship with God (see "Theology of the Book" in the introduction). The common point of reference is that they are the only two mutually exclusive relationships that humans enjoy. One has more than one parent and may have numerous children, friends, and so forth, but only one spouse and one God: Yahweh.

Perhaps the most difficult aspect of the book's teaching about illegitimate sexual relationships has to do with the male perspective and the description of the strange woman. In a word, the book here and elsewhere (6:20–35; 7:1–27) describes the woman as a sexual predator, on the prowl to ensnare the unwitting young man. While it would be hard to deny that such women did or do exist, most people's experience today would suggest that males are more often predatory than females. In response, we do well to remember that the book was written to males, and not just to all males but to males who were on the path leading to wisdom. It was not addressed to fools. These young men who were the recipients of the sage's teaching could move from the status of wise to fools by becoming sexual predators, but for now, in the imagination of the discourse, they were not.

Further, by virtue of the book's inclusion in the canon as well as the book's prologue (see "Canonicity" in the introduction), we suggest that women readers transform the language to suit their context. In other words, instead of a honey-lipped female seducing a male reader, they should read in terms of a sweet-talking male trying to entice them into bed.

Chapter 6

Translation

¹My son, if you make a guarantee for your neighbor,
  clasp your handsᵃ in agreement with a stranger,
²you will be trapped by the speech of your mouth;
  you will be captured by the speech of your mouth.ᵇ
³Then do this, my son, and extricate yourself.
  For you have come into the grasp of your neighbor.
  Go, humble yourself, and pressᶜ your neighbor.
⁴Don't give sleep to your eyes
  or slumber to your pupils.
⁵Extricate yourself like a gazelle from his hand,
  like a bird from the hand of a fowler.

⁶Go to the ant, you lazy people!
  See its paths and grow wise.

a. The verb *tqᶜ* means "to drive, thrust, clap one's hands, blow (the trumpet); ni[phal] put up security for something, pledge oneself" (*NIDOTTE* 4:329). Here it is in the qal, and it means to clap hands to ratify an agreement (see also Job 17:3; Prov. 11:15; 17:18; 22:26).

b. The repetition of "the speech of your mouth" in cola 1 and 2 of v. 2 seems awkward, but that is what the MT has. Some (see Murphy, *Proverbs*, 34) want to emend one of the occurrences to "lips," based on the Syriac. This seems unnecessary and in any case does not affect the sense.

c. The two verbs in this colon are rare, and their exact meaning is difficult to pinpoint. The first verb, *rps* (connected to *rpś*), typically means "befoul" (see Prov. 25:26), and here it may mean that those trying to get out of a loan should be willing to demean themselves

⁷That one has no military commander,ᵈ
   officer, or ruler;
⁸it gets its food in summer,
   gathers its provisions at harvest.ᵉ
⁹How long, you lazy person, will you lie down;
   when will you rise up from your sleep?
¹⁰"A little sleep, a little slumber,
   a little folding of the arms to lie down"—
¹¹and your poverty will come on you like a prowler,ᶠ
   and your deprivation like a person with a shield.ᵍ

¹²Worthlessʰ people are people of iniquity,
   who go around with crooked mouths.

---

to do so because the danger is so high. The second verb, *rhb*, means to "press" or "assail."
See *NIDOTTE* 3:1063.

d. Healey ("Models of Behavior") argues that Matt. 6:26//Luke 12:24 have as part of their
background the ancient versions' rendition of Prov. 6:7a. Instead of *qāṣîn* (military commander), they read *qāṣîr* (harvest), making it say that the ant had no harvest. This causes
an internal contradiction between v. 7 and v. 8, but Healey argues it offers the background
for the idea that God provides food for animals that do not harvest.

e. The LXX adds a proverb about the wisdom and strength of the bee:

> Or go to the bee,
> And learn how industrious she is,
> And how seriously she performs work,
> Whose products kings and commoners use for health.
> She is desired by all and well known.
> Though being weak physically,
> By having honored wisdom she has obtained distinction. (6:8a–c)

From the translation of Giese, "Strength through Wisdom."

f. The form is a hiphil participle of the verb *hlk*, which simply means "to walk to and
fro." However, in the context the meaning must be something like "prowler" or perhaps
"robber" (as Murphy, *Proverbs*, 36, translates it). Others understand the participle to refer
to someone who is going to and fro with the intent not to rob but rather to beg (NJB).
The parallel in 24:34 is similar but not exact. There we find the hitpael participle without
the comparison. It may be that 24:34 has a textual problem; this accounts for our variant
translation at that place.

g. A literal translation of *ʾîš māgēn*. A shielded man, of course, is a warrior (see NRSV).
Some translations take their clue from the alternate translation of colon 1, which translates
"vagrant" rather than "prowler" or "robber." Thus the NJB translates *ʾîš māgēn* as "beggar."
This interpretation is supported by Clifford, *Proverbs*, 74.

h. The difficulty of catching the precise nuance of this phrase (*bĕlîyaʿal*) in English is
captured by Murphy (*Proverbs*, 38), who says that "the phrase means more than 'worthless,' and less than 'devilish.'" Waltke (*Proverbs*, 1:342–43) helpfully surveys the use of this
word: "This term is used of troublemakers of all sorts, revolutionaries against God and his
godly people (Deut. 13:13 [14 MT]; 1 Sam. 2:12; Nah. 1:11, 15 [2:1 MT]), his anointed king
(1 Sam. 10:27; 2 Sam. 20:1; 2 Chron. 13:7; cf. 2 Sam. 16:7), justice (1 Kings 21:10 [= 13];
Prov. 19:28), community solidarity (Deut. 15:9; 1 Sam. 30:22; Ps. 101:3), social propriety
(Judg. 19:22 [= 20:13]; 1 Sam. 1:16), and even life itself (2 Sam. 22:5 [= Ps. 18:4 (5 MT)]; Ps.
41:8 [9 MT]). His inflammatory speech is quoted in Deut. 13:13 [14 MT]; Judg. 19:22 and

¹³They are those who purse their eyes, scrape their feet,
   gesture with their fingers.
¹⁴They are perverse in their hearts and determined in evil;
   they cause conflicts all the time.
¹⁵Therefore their disaster will come suddenly;
   they will be broken quickly, and there will be no healing.

¹⁶Look, there are six things Yahweh hates,
   and seven that are an abomination to his soul:
¹⁷haughty eyes, a lying tongue,
   and hands that spill the blood of the innocent,
¹⁸a heart set on iniquitous plans,
   feet hurrying to run to evil,
¹⁹a false witness who proclaims lies,
   and those who cause conflicts among brothers.

²⁰Protect, my son, the command of your father;
   don't abandon the instruction of your mother.
²¹Bind them to your heart continually;
   fasten them around your neck.
²²When you walk around, they[i] will lead you;
   when you lie down, they will protect you;
   and when you awake, they will occupy your attention.[j]
²³For the commandment is a lamp, and the instruction a light,
   and the path of life is disciplined correction[k]
²⁴to guard you from the evil woman,[l]
   from the flattering tongue of the foreign woman.
²⁵Don't desire her beauty in your heart;
   and don't let her absorb[m] you with her eyelashes.

[is] said to be like a scorching fire (Prov. 16:27). He is implacable (1 Sam. 25:17; 2 Sam. 23:6)." See also Thomas, "*Beliyaᶜal* in the Old Testament."

i. Literally, "it" or "she" and throughout as the subject of the verbs in this verse. The difficulty is that v. 21 refers to the "command/law" of the father and mother with plurals, and it is hard to explain how the shift took place. Some scholars, as early at least as Delitzsch, explain this as a reference to Woman Wisdom, but such a reference is not grounded in the text. Other scholars resort to treating v. 22 as out of order. See Fox (*Proverbs 1–9*, 226–27), who believes that vv. 22 and 23 should be reversed; and Clifford (*Proverbs*, 77–78), who places v. 22 after 5:19. See also the earlier treatment by Skehan, "Proverbs 5:15–19 and 6:20–24." He argues that 6:22 is out of its original context and should be removed from its present place and relocated between vv. 19 and 20 of chap. 5.

j. This is a difficult verb (*śyḥ*) in this context and may also mean "talk to you."

k. The phrase is literally "the correction of discipline" (*tôkĕḥôt mûsār*), but I here understand it as a hendiadys. The two words more often appear as near synonyms parallel to one another, operating as a word pair.

l. We stick with the MT (*ʾēšet rāᶜ*), and surely no one would deny that according to the sages she is an evil woman. However, other scholars (see Fox, *Proverbs 1–9*) will emend, based on the Greek term *gynaikos hypandrou* ("married woman") to *ʾēšet rēaᶜ* ("wife of a neighbor"), since it is a better parallel, or so they think, to "foreign woman."

m. Or "capture."

²⁶For a prostitute costs a loaf of bread,ⁿ
   but a married woman hunts for a man's life.
²⁷Can a man scoop fire into his lap
   and his clothes not get burned?
²⁸Or can a man walk on hot coals
   and his feet not get singed?
²⁹Thus, the person who goes to the wife of his neighbor;
   all who touch her will not go unpunished.
³⁰One does not despise a thief when he steals
   to fill his stomach if he is starving.
³¹If he is caught, he must pay sevenfold;ᵒ
   he must give all the riches of his house.
³²He who commits adultery with a married woman lacks heart;
   the one who does it destroys himself.
³³He will find affliction and shame,
   and his reproach will never be blotted out.
³⁴For passionate is the anger of a man,
   and he will not forgive on the day of vengeance.
³⁵He will not regard the repentant face,
   and he will be unwilling, though the fineᵖ is large.

Interpretation

6:1–5. *Loans.* A frequent theme in the book of Proverbs is advice pertaining to giving loans or securing debts (11:15; 17:18; 20:16; 22:26; 27:13). The teaching is consistent: don't give loans or secure debts. To understand this teaching, we need to put it in a broader context. In the first place, interest-bearing loans to fellow Israelites are forbidden (Exod. 22:25 [24 MT]). It was possible to give interest-bearing loans to foreigners, but if "stranger" implies foreigner here, then even these are discouraged. On the other hand, we need to remember that it is also the frequent teaching of the book to be generous to the poor (28:27; 29:7, 14). These are not loans, but rather outright gifts. And that seems to be the point. If people have needs, then give them what they need. The problem with loans is that often they are given in contexts where the lender cannot afford to lose the money, and the risk is just too high.

n. The Hebrew of the entire colon is difficult. Literally, it means "because for a prostitute up to a loaf of bread." We read this as a statement of price, while some believe that the expression indicates that having intercourse with a prostitute reduces someone to a loaf of bread, perhaps meaning begging for a piece of bread.

o. The law indicates that a thief pays back less than sevenfold (Exod. 22:1–4, 9 [21:37; 22:1–3, 8 MT]), but Murphy (*Proverbs*, 39) helpfully points out that this is probably a figurative use of "seven" to mean "a lot."

p. Or "bribe."

> ¹My son, if you make a guarantee for your neighbor,
> clasp your hands in agreement with a stranger,

The protasis ("if" clause) of this conditional sentence[1] addresses the son and then imagines the son as guaranteeing the credit of others. In colon 1, the other is the "neighbor." This term refers to someone nearby and on occasion can also be translated "friend." In colon 2, however, the "other" refers to a "stranger." This is the masculine form (*zār*) of the word that was also used to refer to the "strange woman" (*zārâ*) in the previous chapter and elsewhere. The use of "neighbor" in colon 1 and "stranger" in colon 2 functions as a merism,[2] essentially implying everyone. In other words, the following sentences apply to those who stand surety for anyone.

There is some uncertainty and disagreement over whether the borrower is the one referred to by the references to "neighbor" and "stranger." Fox represents the viewpoint that "neighbor" is the lender and "stranger" is the one for whom the son is standing surety.[3] His position depends on the argument that it is the "neighbor" who is badgered to let him out of the arrangement and that only the lender could let him out. On the other hand, it would be more likely that the son would be open to helping out a "neighbor" in this way rather than a "stranger." And if there is an association with the person, then the son would likely go to the person he knows in order to press him to make alternate arrangements. In the final analysis, we cannot be certain about the details of the situation envisioned, but there is no question that securing debt is in general frowned on.

> ²you will be trapped by the speech of your mouth;
> you will be captured by the speech of your mouth.

The apodosis ("then" clause, though "then" is more often implied than expressed) describes the negative consequences of making a loan. The agreement that has been accomplished by the "speech of your mouth" will become a burden. The metaphors used are from fowling and the military. The former is implicit in the word "trapped," meaning trapped

---

1. Some translations treat vv. 1–2 as a continuation of the protasis, assuming an implied "if" at the beginning of each cola or at least the first three (so REB, NIV, and NJB; contrast NRSV and NAB).

2. While Murphy (*Proverbs*, 36) may well be right that "stranger" may not imply a foreigner here, he seems wrong when he goes on to suggest that the word may simply be a synonym to "neighbor." On the surface of it, "neighbor" and "stranger" do not appear to be overlapping ideas.

3. See Fox, *Proverbs, 1–9*, 211.

like a bird in a snare. The second is military, implying captured like a prisoner of war.

> ³Then do this, my son, and extricate yourself.
>   For you have come into the grasp of your neighbor.
>   Go, humble yourself, and press your neighbor.
> ⁴Don't give sleep to your eyes
>   or slumber to your pupils.
> ⁵Extricate yourself like a gazelle from his hand,
>   like a bird from the hand of a fowler.

These verses advise the son in the possibility that he finds himself in the bind of a loan. In a phrase, the son should do whatever it takes to get out of the loan. The dangers are so severe that the son is advised to lose sleep in his efforts to get out of the loan. He should even humble himself before the person and urge him to allow him to get out of it. The final verse (v. 5) picks up on the trapped animal/bird imagery implied in v. 2a.

Theological Implications

For theological implications of this section, see the topical essay "Business Ethics" in the appendix.

6:6–11. *Laziness.* The next topic the sage tackles is laziness. Like the matter of putting up security for another in the previous section, the sage's advice concerning laziness here anticipates extensive advice in the second part of the book (see "Laziness and Hard Work" in the appendix). With the call to go and observe the activity of the industrious ant, we see here an explicit example of the importance of observation in the development and support of wisdom principles (see "The Sources of Wisdom" in the introduction).

> ⁶Go to the ant, you lazy people!
>   See its paths and grow wise.
> ⁷That one has no military commander,
>   officer, or ruler;
> ⁸it gets its food in summer,
>   gathers its provisions at harvest.

The sage directs his hearers' attention to the ant. A study of the ant's behavior (referred to as the ant's "paths") will direct the lazy person to grow wise. As we will see, in this case growth in wisdom means giving up lazy patterns of behavior and adopting a hardworking lifestyle similar to that of the ant.

Verse 7 describes the ant as not having hierarchy in its social structure. The fact that modern scientific study has uncovered hierarchy in an ant colony is beside the point. This information was not available to the ancient Near Eastern observer, so the sage is speaking from the point of view of naive observation. And without obvious social structure, these creatures cope quite well.

The amazing fact is that ants, through their seemingly ceaseless labor, gather enough food to carry them through the winter. In 30:25 ants are described as having no strength, thus their success in gathering food is based on their diligence.

Clifford rightly points out[4] that Proverbs seems especially concerned about laziness in connection with gathering food during harvest (see also 10:5), since the survival not only of the individual but also of the community depends on activity during this time.

> [9]How long, you lazy person, will you lie down;
>   when will you rise up from your sleep?
> [10]"A little sleep, a little slumber,
>   a little folding of the arms to lie down"—
> [11]and your poverty will come on you like a prowler,
>   and your deprivation like a person with a shield.

These final three verses apply the lesson of the ant to the lazy person by way of contrast. While the ant is industrious, those who are lazy are ridiculed as not getting out of bed. As is typical of the overall teaching concerning sloth in the book of Proverbs, this section uses hyperbole and satire in the attempt to motivate those who are lazy to get to work. Verse 9 contains taunting questions, while v. 10 creates an imaginary statement of a lazy person. The lazy person says they just want a "little sleep," but we suspect that little nap will become a long sleep to avoid work necessary to sustain life. Verse 11 describes the results of a lazy lifestyle, which is poverty. The onset of poverty is described by using similes. In the first place, it is likened to a prowler, and in the second colon it is likened to a man carrying a shield. In both cases, this simile describes individuals whose arrival portends harm. It also suggests the idea that poverty will sneak up on the person and arrive suddenly. Again, the function of this description is to serve as a warning, with the hope that people who have a propensity to be lazy will stir themselves into activity.

4. Clifford, *Proverbs*, 76.

Theological Implications

For the theological implications of this section, see the topical essay "Laziness and Hard Work" in the appendix.

6:12–19. *Other topics.* The third teaching of this section contains a description of the traits of worthless people, another way to refer to evil people generally, also known as fools. Clifford helpfully describes the movement of the passage as follows: They "describe the wicked person, in his essence (v. 12a), demeanor (vv. 12b–13), inner life (v. 14a), effect upon society (v. 14b), and destiny (v. 15)."[5] We would underline that v. 15 appears to be the point of the passage. It asserts a doctrine of retribution. Evil people may cause some trouble, and they may be shifty, but they will not escape their punishment. Such a saying both warns against being evil as well as comforting those who think that shifty evil people are getting away with their dastardly deeds.

Proverbs 6:16–19 is the first of several examples of number parallelism in the book of Proverbs (see other examples in 30:15–16, 18–19, 21–23, 24–28, 29–31). The device is attested also outside of the book (e.g., Amos 1–2; Mic. 5:5 [4 MT]), not to speak of an even more frequent use in Ugaritic poetry.[6] This form allows the poet to present a list under a single rubric. It causes the reader to consider each element as related to the others. Sometimes, but not always, the emphasis is on the final element (as is clearly the case in Prov. 30:18–19).

As Watson also points out, there is a sense in which the x, x+1 pattern of a numerical parallelism is demanded by the nature of parallelism. There is no synonym of a number, and to say "there are seven things Yahweh hates, and seven that are an abomination of his soul" is boring. To say "six, yea seven" gives the impression that there are a large number of items in the list, or as Watson puts it, a purpose of some numerical parallelisms is "to denote abundance." Sometimes (see examples in Amos 1–2) the numbers don't even coincide with the list, but when it does, the list always conforms to the second, larger number.

> [12]Worthless people are people of iniquity,
>   who go around with crooked mouths.
> [13]They are those who purse their eyes, scrape their feet,
>   gesture with their fingers.
> [14]They are perverse in their hearts and determined in evil;
>   they cause conflicts all the time.

---

5. Ibid.
6. See the discussion by Watson, *Classical Hebrew Poetry*, 144–49.

These verses provide a description of evil people. Verse 12a does not seem to be defining or clarifying "evil people" with "people of iniquity." More likely we are to understand these as two similar phrases that describe the same group. The description follows, starting with v. 12b and on through v. 14. The description of evil people proceeds by naming different parts of the body. In the first place, they have crooked mouths. From such mouths one would expect lies (6:19; 13:5; 14:5, 25; 25:18), rumors (18:8), slander (10:18; 20:19), and gossip (11:13; 17:4). All of these are destructive of relationships, both intimate (family) and beyond (society). In short, a perverse mouth speaks falsehoods.

Verse 13 describes gestures typical of an evil person. Their precise significance is embedded in ancient culture, and we may not understand their full significance. Indeed, these may be gestures connected to ancient practices of sorcery,[7] by which one puts a spell or hex on another. More likely they are the gestures of persons who are doing something secretive and passing along signals with their eyes, feet, and fingers. Alternatively, they could also be "understood as a restless shifting and shuffling, a sign of inner disquietude."[8]

Verse 14 then takes the description to a more profound level as it characterizes the hearts of evil people as perverse. The heart is the core of a person from which emanate all actions, motives, and speech. The heart of an evil person is bent on evil.

> [15]Therefore their disaster will come suddenly;
> they will be broken quickly, and there will be no healing.

The final verse of this section makes plain the end of evil people. They may seem as though they are getting away with their actions, but they will ultimately be ruined; that ruin will come suddenly and will not be reversible.

> [16]Look, there are six things Yahweh hates,
> and seven that are an abomination to his soul:

This particular numerical proverb tracks the "six, yea seven" pattern, followed by a listing of seven items. The topic for these items is given in this verse, and they are described first as "things Yahweh hates" and then as things that "are an abomination to his [Yahweh's] soul." Needless to say, this is very strong language. It is hard to imagine a more definitive way to express God's displeasure than with these two sayings. As strong as it is to say that God hates something, colon 2 heightens it. In the first

7. McKane, *Proverbs*, 325.
8. Fox, *Proverbs 1–9*, 221.

place, this is a rare instance of the use of *nepeš* (here translated "soul" but meaning "inner person") in connection to God. The meaning seems to be equivalent to saying that it is a hate emanating from the deepest part of his being. And then the word "abomination" is itself expressive of the most profound dislike. The phrase "abomination to Yahweh" (*tōʿăbat Yhwh*) is used a number of times in the book and is discussed at 11:1.

> ¹⁷haughty eyes, a lying tongue,
>   and hands that spill the blood of the innocent,
> ¹⁸a heart set on iniquitous plans,
>   feet hurrying to run to evil,

The first four items in the list of things God hates are all related by specifically tying them to a body part. Haughty (or lifted up) eyes denote a demeanor shaped by pride. That God hates pride and respects humility is repeated many places in the book (see "Pride/Humility" in the appendix). This theme is motivated by the fact that pride does not allow a person to be self-critical. Thus, such people perpetuate bad behavior. Second, in what again will be an important emphasis in the book, the list names a "lying tongue." Proverbs loves truth and hates those who dissimulate. Third, Yahweh hates hands that shed innocent blood. Innocent blood is specified because, after all, God commands the shedding of some blood in the context of holy war and execution as the penalty for capital crimes. Finally, the list describes feet that hurry into evil. The evil is not specified, but there is a propensity of evil people toward bad actions of many different types.

> ¹⁹a false witness who proclaims lies,
>   and those who cause conflicts among brothers.

For the last two items that Yahweh hates, the sage departs from the naming of body parts. In what almost appears to be a repetition of the second thing in the list, he talks about false witnesses and their lies. As mentioned, this is similar to the "lying tongue" but more specific. Then finally, and again this may be the emphasized element, the list concludes with those who cause conflicts among brothers. Unnecessary conflicts themselves are bad, but if those conflicts are among brothers, then it is particularly bad. Ambiguity remains whether "brother" here means simply biological or also includes broader kinship (for instance, all Israelites might consider themselves brothers). In any case, this proverb could be read in conjunction with the harmony extolled in Ps. 133 in recognizing the importance placed on brotherly harmony. Elsewhere Proverbs also teaches the importance of familial and societal relationships (see "Family Relationships" in the appendix). This proverb reminds us that it is wrongminded to think of the book as a collection of individual ethics. The community is very much in mind throughout.

Theological Implications

For the theological implications of this section, see the topical essay "Family Relationships" in the appendix.

6:20–35. *The danger of adultery.* For a second time, the father turns to his son with strong advice concerning relationships with women. The passion of the rhetoric as well as the sheer quantity of teaching devoted to this topic show that the sage is well aware of the dangers of sexual temptation. This teaching is not called "counsel" (*ʿēṣâ*), but rather "command" (*miṣwâ*) and "instruction" (*tôrâ*), conveying the father's belief that the behavior he is prohibiting carries the weight of divine law.

The passage reveals some interesting aspects of ancient Israelite culture. In the first place, it warns against two classes of dangerous women: the prostitute and the seductive but married woman. Having sexual relationships with either is wrong, but the argument of the father makes it clear that there is a difference between the two. After all, the consequences of sleeping with a married woman are much larger than sleeping with a prostitute. This difference is summed up in v. 26: "For a prostitute costs a loaf of bread, but a married woman hunts for a man's life." The point seems to be that the prostitute will sap material resources, but when one sleeps with a married woman, one must reckon with her jealous husband, who will have the support of the law behind him as he seeks revenge.

> ²⁰Protect, my son, the command of your father;
> don't abandon the instruction of your mother.
> ²¹Bind them to your heart continually;
> fasten them around your neck.
> ²²When you walk around, they will lead you;
> when you lie down, they will protect you;
> and when you awake, they will occupy your attention.

The next discourse begins in the same way as many of the discourses that preceded it: the father calls his son's attention to the teaching that follows. The verb he uses in the first colon, "protect" (*nṣr*),[9] indicates that the son may well already know and follow the commandment. Something protected or guarded is already in one's possession. Thus, the

9. Used elsewhere with the near synonym "guard" (*šmr*).

176

son is presently on the path of wisdom and is not himself functioning as a predator. This may help explain why the father's instruction takes the form of warning against female predators rather than addressing the son's active search for illegitimate relationships. If the son were doing so, then he would be addressed as a fool who rejects discipline, not as a wise person who needs to be aware of attacks that will throw him off the path of life.

As mentioned in the introduction to this section, the teaching is called a "command" (*miṣwâ*) and "instruction" (*tôrâ*). Since we have already addressed the debate surrounding the force of *miṣwâ* earlier in the commentary (see at 2:1), here we simply reassert our opinion that this word (and also *tôrâ*) carry a level of meaning that indicates great authority, whether that authority is grounded in parental teaching or directly in the law of God. In any case, when it comes to illegitimate sexual relationships, there is no question but that the father's teaching is at one with the pentateuchal law (note the seventh commandment, prohibiting adultery, in Exod. 20:14).

Up to now, we have referred to the teaching in this section as that of the father, and indeed he is the one who speaks. On the other hand, it is important to point out that he represents not only his own wisdom but also that of the son's mother as well. As the mother is mentioned elsewhere (e.g., 1:8; 31:1), we point out that this is a rarity when compared with the wisdom teaching of other, related Near Eastern texts (see "Ancient Near Eastern Background" in the introduction).

The demand to bind something on one's heart reminds the reader of Deut. 6:4–9, which includes a command to bind the law on one's hands and to fix them to the forehead.[10] Perhaps the heart is here mentioned because it is the core of one's personality. If one's heart is disobedient, then disobedience will follow soon thereafter. Note Prov. 3:3, where covenant love and faithfulness are to be bound on the wise person's neck. Also, 7:3 charges the son to bind the father's teaching on his fingers. In the present verse, the second colon insists that the son fasten them (the father's commands/law) around his neck. As in the passage in 3:3, the neck may be specified because disobedience is elsewhere described as a stiffening of the neck (e.g., Jer. 7:26; 17:23).

Verse 22 then informs the son that this teaching will bring benefits all the time, not only when the son is active (when you walk) but also continually during the sleeping hours, from the time he lies down till

---

10. Though the connection between the Proverbs and Deuteronomy texts are fairly well accepted, it is debated which text influenced the other, with Scherer (*Weise Wort*) arguing for the priority of Proverbs, and Maier ("Conflicting Attractions") taking the other side.

the time he wakes up. The same sequence of verbs to indicate "all the time" may be found in Deut. 6:7 and 11:19 as well.

> ²³For the commandment is a lamp, and the instruction a light,
>   and the path of life is disciplined correction
> ²⁴to guard you from the evil woman,
>   from the flattering tongue of the foreign woman.

As signaled by the initial "for" (*kî*), these verses provide a reason to maintain obedience to the teaching of the parents in this passage, and they do so through use of the pervasive path theology of the book. The command/instruction, not yet articulated, will illuminate that path—thus implying that the son's journey will not meet unseen obstacles. That path is called the path of life because it promotes a long and rich life experience. As in the following verses, the command/instruction warns against a behavior that might result in an early and violent death. However, to stay on that path is not easy. It involves "disciplined correction." These two words (*tôkaḥat* and *mûsār*) are also frequently used in the book and refer to the hard work, suggestive even of physical punishment, that it takes to keep doing the right thing. One's natural propensity would be to give in to the strong temptations that lead one to leave the right path, so the parents remind the son that it takes work.

Verse 24 for the first time states the place from which the danger emanates: a woman called both "evil" and "foreign." We have already encountered the latter in chap. 5 (see 5:10, 20) and have determined that "foreign" is used here not in an ethnic sense, but rather with the idea that this is a woman who operates outside of customary social mores. This is what makes her evil.

The first warning has to do not with her body or the pleasures of touch, but rather with her words. She has a "flattering tongue." The way she will seduce is through her speech. This comment shows psychological insight: the sage is aware that men falter not always for the obvious reasons of beauty but also because of an appeal to self-vanity.

> ²⁵Don't desire her beauty in your heart;
>   and don't let her absorb you with her eyelashes.
> ²⁶For a prostitute costs a loaf of bread,
>   but a married woman hunts for a man's life.
> ²⁷Can a man scoop fire into his lap
>   and his clothes not get burned?
> ²⁸Or can a man walk on hot coals
>   and his feet not get singed?

However, physical beauty also strongly appeals to men, and so the father goes on to warn the son not to desire her beauty. This comment reveals an awareness that unethical behavior begins with an internal desire. Verse 25b specifies her beauty with a reference to her eyes.[11]

The next three verses provide a colorful and interesting reason for not pursuing such a woman. Indeed, it begins by dividing the "foreign" woman into two classes: the prostitute and the married woman. Illicit relationships with either will cost the son, but the latter will be much worse than the former in terms of consequences. A prostitute will cost money, but a relationship with another man's wife may well cost the son his life, as will be specified in vv. 34–35. The wording of v. 26b, "A married woman hunts for a man's life," is likely poetic exaggeration. She is not necessarily thinking that she will lead to his demise, but that is the practical consequence of her seduction of him.

The next two verses are memorable statements to the effect that there is no escaping the consequences of this illicit act. They comment in a humorous and memorable way that it is sheer idiocy to think that one can get away unscathed. The danger of sleeping with a woman other than one's wife is comparable to scooping hot coals in one's lap. The reference to lap is surely evocative of the man's genitals, with which he engages the wrong woman. The same may be the case with the reference to singed feet, since feet are a well-known euphemism for genitalia in the Bible (Exod. 4:25; Judg. 3:24 [see NRSV note]; 1 Sam. 24:3 [see NRSV note; 4 MT]; Isa. 6:2; 7:20).

> 29Thus, the person who goes to the wife of his neighbor;
>   all who touch her will not go unpunished.
> 30One does not despise a thief when he steals
>   to fill his stomach if he is starving.
> 31If he is caught, he must pay sevenfold;
>   he must give all the riches of his house.
> 32He who commits adultery with a married woman lacks heart;
>   the one who does it destroys himself.
> 33He will find affliction and shame,
>   and his reproach will never be blotted out.
> 34For passionate is the anger of a man,
>   and he will not forgive on the day of vengeance.
> 35He will not regard the repentant face,
>   and he will be unwilling, though the fine is large.

---

11. The word here translated "eyelashes" (ʿapʿappayîm) may not be so precise, since it is used as a near synonym for the more common word for "eyes" (ʿênayîm). However, the more traditional translations like "orbs" or "pupils" are somewhat awkward in this context.

The final section of this passage focuses on the inevitability of punishment for those who have a physically intimate relationship with a woman married to another man. The previous section (vv. 25–28) acknowledged the folly of sleeping with a prostitute but also registered the increased danger of sleeping with a married woman.

One might question why this would be the case since sleeping with a prostitute also intrudes on the man's marriage with his wife. And again, it is not that sleeping with a prostitute is right, but that the other is doubly wrong. Two marriage relationships are shattered. And we must realize that the argument the parents are mounting here is very practically oriented, not purely ethical.

By saying that punishment is inevitable, v. 29 implies that one who sleeps with a married woman does wrong. The assumption of the verse is that punishment is not only inevitable but also fully deserved. The deservedness of punishment is then bolstered in vv. 30–31 by an argument moving from the minor to the major. One might understand and have compassion for those who steal because they do not have enough to eat. Faced with starvation, who might not steal something in order to survive? However, if caught, such people must repay sevenfold what they stole. Since they had nothing to begin with, that presumably would completely eradicate what remained: they must give all the riches of their house. Even in such a case, punishment is inevitable.

But there is no such pity for the person who sleeps with another man's wife. Such a person elicits no compassion: just the opposite, pure contempt. The adulterer lacks heart. The characterization of the fool as one who "lacks heart" is interesting. The heart is the core personality (see commentary at 3:1). Fools thus have nothing inside to share with others or even to sustain themselves. In this context, the expression may more specifically point to a lack of discernment or judgment. The phrase also occurs in 10:13, 21; 11:12. Verse 32b describes these people as self-destructive.

The punishment itself is cited in vv. 33–35. In the first place, the adulterer will be afflicted and shamed. Shame involves public exposure of a reprehensible act. This shame will never go away. The last two verses imply, though, that the rest of the adulterer's life likely does not last very long. The "man" in v. 34a is the offended husband. The word translated "passionate" (*qin'â*) also could be rendered "jealous," and certainly the passion of his anger should be understood as energized by jealousy, which is an emotion fueled by the desire to protect one's intimate relationship.[12] The specific word here for "man" (*geber*) is

---

12. For a study of jealousy in the Psalms, see D. B. Allender and T. Longman III, *Cry of the Soul: How Our Emotions Reveal Our Deepest Questions about God* (Colorado Springs: NavPress, 1995), 107–32.

related to the verb "to be strong, to prevail" (*gābar*). In other words, the poet chose a word for the offended husband that accentuates the power he would have over the son if the son becomes intimate with his wife.

The logic of vv. 34b–35 depends on the nicety of Hebrew law. The penalty for adultery is death for both the man and the woman (as in Deut. 22:22). However, technically, it would be possible to substitute a monetary fine in place of the death penalty. This can be gathered from Num. 35:31–32, which states that a ransom (a fine) cannot be substituted for murder. The implication is that other capital offenses can be commuted into monetary fines. Furthermore, the goring-ox law also provides for such a substitution at Exod. 21:30. It is not clear who can "demand" such a substitution, but likely the victim (in the case of adultery, the offended husband) would be involved in the decision. This implication makes sense of our present passage, which implies that the husband's jealousy would be such that he would refuse any suggestion to commute the death penalty.[13]

Theological Implications

This is the second (see also 5:1–23) of three (also, 7:1–27) sets of instructions the father gives the son concerning proper sexual relationships. Here in 6:20–35 the father's instruction builds on ideas found in chap. 5, so the theological implications there are largely relevant for this section as well, though we will not repeat all the points we made for that chapter.

An important consideration to keep in mind is the implied status of the son to whom the parents address their advice. The admonitions to protect the command of the father and not abandon the instruction of the mother indicate that the son is presently wise and that the parental purpose is to encourage their child to stay on the right path. It is our contention that this explains why the son is warned against a predator female rather than being admonished to not be predatory himself. Indeed, based on modern statistics—and we have every reason to assume ancient ones as well—it is more likely that a male would attempt to seduce a woman than vice versa. In this regard, Proverbs has been painted as a piece of sexist literature, but such a judgment does not take into account the status of the young man.

---

13. H. G. L. Peels ("Passion or Justice?") has made the case well that the "day of vengeance" refers not to a personal act of vengeance but rather to the pressing of a legal remedy.

In terms of substance, the father's argument is pragmatic and "self-regarding."[14] He warns his son by pointing out the potentially devastating effects of the decision to sleep with another woman. To sleep with a prostitute might impoverish the son, but even worse, sleeping with another man's wife might result in his death. Thus, to follow the command, the instruction of the parents is indeed a lamp that illumines the path of life.

The consequences that attend improper sexual activity, according to this passage, are "inevitable."[15] This inevitability is expressed pointedly in the rhetorical questions in vv. 27–28. Appeal to God, who would assure such punishment, is never made explicitly; instead, the text stresses the very real threat of the jealous husband.

14. Clifford, *Proverbs*, 79.
15. Fox, *Proverbs 1–9*, 237.

Chapter 7

Translation

¹My son, guard my speech,
  and my command hide within you.
²Guard my command, and live,
  and my instruction like the apple of your eye.
³Bind them on your fingers;
  write them on the tablet of your heart.
⁴Say to Wisdom, "You are my sister."
  Call Understanding "Friend,"
⁵so that she might guard you against the strange woman
  and from the foreign woman whose speech flatters you.

⁶When from the window of my house,
  from behind my lattice[a] I looked down,
⁷I looked for a moment,
  and I perceived among the sons a youth who lacked heart.
⁸He was crossing the street at the corner,
  and he marched on the path to her house
⁹at beginning of the evening of the day,
  in the middle of night and darkness.

¹⁰All of a sudden[b] a woman propositions him,
  in the attire[c] of a prostitute and with guarded heart.

a. A rare word, *ʾešnab* (lattice), appears only here and in Judg. 5:28, in parallel to *ḥallôn* (window).

b. Translating *hinnēh*, an exclamatory particle that indicates "immediacy" (*NIDOTTE* 4:1032).

c. Attire (*šît*) occurs only here and in Ps. 73:6.

183

¹¹She is boisterous and defiant;
    her feet do not rest[d] in her own house.
¹²A foot[e] in the street, a foot in the public squares,
    she lurks beside every street corner.
¹³She grabs him and she kisses him.
    Her face is brazen as she speaks to him:

¹⁴"I have fellowship offerings;
    today I pay back my vow.
¹⁵So, I have come out to meet you,
    to seek your face, and I have found you.
¹⁶I have ornamented my bed with bed coverings,
    with colored linens from Egypt.
¹⁷I have sprinkled[f] my bed with myrrh,
    aloes, and cinnamon.
¹⁸Come, let's be intoxicated with lovemaking till morning;
    let's rejoice in love.
¹⁹For the man is not in his house,
    having gone on a faraway trip.[g]
²⁰He has taken a pouch of money in his hand;
    he will arrive at his house on the day of the full moon."

²¹She seduces him with all her talk;
    she compels him with the flattery of her lips.
²²He impetuously goes after her.
    He goes like an ox to the slaughter
    and like a stupid person to the stocks for discipline,[h]
²³until an arrow pierces his liver,
    like a bird hurrying to the snare,
    not aware that it will cost him his life.

²⁴And now, sons, listen to me,
    and pay attention to the speech of my mouth.
²⁵Don't turn your heart to her paths;
    don't wander onto her trails.

d. Literally, "her feet do not lie down in her own house." There may be a sexual allusion to this awkward Hebrew clause (see commentary).

e. The Hebrew word *paʿam* can mean "foot" or "now." According to *NIDOTTE* 3:650, *paʿam* means not only "time" but also "foot" or "sole of foot." Virtually all translations and most commentaries take it as "now," but I believe that "foot" is more likely since the previous verse has said that her feet (plural of *regel*) do not remain at home.

f. The verb *nûp* II occurs only here and in Ps. 68:9 [10 MT] with the meaning "sprinkle."

g. Literally, "going on a far-flung path."

h. Colon 3 is difficult. I retain the MT, like the NJPS version and also (with some variance) the NJB. However, most versions, followed by many commentaries, emend so that there is another animal simile here. See Murphy (*Proverbs*, 41, with note on 42), who translates "like a stag (*ʾayyāl?* for *ʿekes*) springing to a trap."

²⁶For she has caused many corpses to fall,
    and abundant are all those she has killed.
²⁷Her house is a path to Sheol,
    going down to the chambers of death.ⁱ

Interpretation

Avoid promiscuous women: Part II. The chapter constitutes a separate teaching, but in theme it is closely connected to 5:1–23 and 6:20–35, since it contains a warning from the father to the son to avoid an intimate relationship with a woman other than one's wife. In many ways, the present chapter underlines aspects of the teaching of the previous two passages. The father[1] describes the strong allure of such a relationship and in particular warns the son to watch out for the woman's flattery (5:3). In addition, it describes the deception that is involved in such a relationship. And finally, and perhaps most importantly, it reminds the son of the horrible consequences that await those who give in to the temptation.

What is unique about this teaching is its appeal to observation. The sage recounts the story of a "youth who lacked heart" who gave into the temptation. The story narrates his foolish actions as well as the negative consequences that arose from them.

¹My son, guard my speech,
    and my command hide within you.
²Guard my command, and live,
    and my instruction like the apple of your eye.
³Bind them on your fingers;
    write them on the tablet of your heart.
⁴Say to Wisdom, "You are my sister."
    Call Understanding "Friend,"

i. Jones ("Wisdom's Pedagogy") argues that that *ḥeder* (chamber) here signifies the vagina. He suggests that "the term *ḥeder* likely refers simultaneously to the metaphorical entrance to the underworld, namely, her genitalia." However, this is extremely unlikely. In the first place, his argument is based on the fact that *ḥeder* later occurs in construct with *beṭen* ("belly") and means "innermost being." However, *ḥeder* does not appear in construct with *beṭen* here, and even when it does, it does not refer to genitalia.

1. Bellis ("Gender") argues that the teacher is a female voice. Along with Brenner and van Dijk-Hemmes (*On Gendering Texts*, 57–62, 113–26), she argues: "The fact that the speaker looks through a window at a scene below [is] an action that is much more frequently associated with women than men" (Bellis, "Gender," 16). That this type of scene is more typically associated with a female watcher does not preclude a male occupying the same role, as is clearly the case here. However, I agree with her view, contra Brenner and van Dijk-Hemmes, that this chapter is an attempt to control male, not female, sexuality and that monogamy was something valuable for ancient women.

⁵so that she might guard you against the strange woman
and from the foreign woman whose speech flatters you.

7:1–5. Like many of the discourses of the first part of the book, this one begins with an exhortation to pay attention to the teaching that follows. Much of the language of these verses, particularly the first three, are reminiscent of other introductions. In the first place, the father's teaching that follows is called "my speech" (see 2:1), "my command" (2:1; 3:1; 4:4; 6:20), "my/your mother's instruction" (1:8; 3:1; 6:20). We have already pursued the issue of whether it is legitimate to consider the teaching as bearing only the authority of the father or that of the legal code (see "Wisdom and Law" in the introduction). Without rehearsing the debate, at this point we simply report our conclusion that the father's authority is backed by the fact that it reflects the Sinai covenant. The father's and mother's "command/instruction," in other words, is coterminous with God's.

For the son's part, he is to "guard" (see also 2:8, 11, 20; 4:4; 5:2; and many other places) this teaching. As mentioned previously, the exhortation to guard the teaching implies that the son is presently in possession of it. He is a wise person, not naive. The father's intention is to encourage the son to stay on the right path. A new twist comes with the statement that the son should guard the instruction just like he guards the "apple"[2] (or middle) of his eye. The eye is among the most tender spots on one's body. As such, we with great passion tend to guard our eyes from physical harm. In 7:1 guarding the speech is parallel to hiding the command. The verb *spn* has the primary meaning of "hide" but can mean, and is sometimes translated as, "store up" or "treasure." In any case the point is clear. The command is to be internalized.

Furthermore, we have earlier seen the language of binding instruction and writing it on the tablet of one's heart. In terms of binding, the father urges the son to bind his commands on his neck (3:3) and heart (6:21). For the metaphor of writing on the heart and its connection to Deuteronomy, see comments on 3:3. In any case, by such an admonition, the father is instructing the son that the command must change him internally (in the heart) and externally in terms of his actions (via the fingers).

Finally, and most provocatively, the father tells the son to cultivate a relationship with Wisdom. The context makes it very clear that here

---

2. The expression is actually "the little man of the eye," which is comparable to our expression "apple of the eye." The phrase may have developed from the idea that people could see themselves reflected in miniature in the pupils of others. No matter how we might construe its etymological development, however, it is clear that the phrase refers to one's pupil.

Wisdom (and the parallel reference to Understanding) is personified (see 1:20–33; chap. 8). He is to call Wisdom his sister. In its ancient context, this language is intimate. "Sister" is here not a reference to a sibling, but rather a romantic designation similar to its use in Song 4:9. It is now well established that the use of "sister" as a term of endearment between an intimate couple was common in the Near East, particularly in Egypt.[3] The metaphor of Woman Wisdom as the object of one's romantic attention will be developed further in 9:1–6.

The purpose for developing an intimate relationship with Woman Wisdom is to block out an illicit relationship with the "strange/foreign" woman. This language refers not to an ethnically or politically foreign woman but to one who is outside social custom and law, as is argued at 2:16. It is telling that the father mentions flattery as the first characteristic of the woman that might attract the son to an illegitimate relationship (see also 6:24). It is not her beauty but her appeal to the man's vanity that is so dangerous.

> [6]When from the window of my house,
>   from behind my lattice I looked down,
> [7]I looked for a moment,
>   and I perceived among the sons a youth who lacked heart.
> [8]He was crossing the street at the corner,
>   and he marched on the path to her house
> [9]at beginning of the evening of the day,
>   in the middle of night and darkness.

7:6–9. The father now recounts a story to the son in order to make his point about the dangers of a relationship with a woman other than one's wife. Such a story demonstrates the importance of experience and observation in the acquisition of wisdom (see "The Sources of Wisdom" in the introduction). The first few verses simply set the scene. The father tells the son that he was looking into the street[4] and noted a youth whose actions soon betray that he "lacked heart."[5] However, at the moment of first sighting, he seems to be minding his own business. He is simply walking along the path and crossing the street at the corner. The language

---

3. See Longman, *Song of Songs*, 151; and J. G. Westenholz, "Love Lyrics from the Ancient Near East," in *Civilizations of the Ancient Near East*, vol. 4, ed. J. M. Sasson (New York: Scribner's Sons, 1995), 2474.

4. Specifically, from the window (*běhallôn*) of his house. O'Connell ("Proverbs VII 16–17") points out that there are seven OT episodes that include "a woman and an elevated window" (Gen. 26:8; Josh. 2:15, 18, 21; Judg. 5:28; 1 Sam. 19:12; 2 Sam. 6:16 = 1 Chron. 15:29; 2 Kings 9:30, 32; Prov. 7:6. In all these cases, there is the issue of "sexual attraction" and "deception and danger."

5. For the phrase and its meaning, see comments on 6:32.

of these verses may intimate that he is treading on dangerous ground, though it is not clear whether the narrating father wants us to think he is doing anything wrong yet.

The corner is a place where dubious women look for men. However, there is nothing inherent about a street corner necessitating that it is a seedy place. The path is described as the one to "her" house, but it does not say that he is heading to her house or even knows that her house is on the path. The father knows, but then, he is a neighbor in the story. The time is also suggestive in that it is the onset of darkness, the time when illicit actions take place. However, though the description of the scene might be a harbinger of bad things to come, we should probably not imagine the young man as purposefully seeking out an improper liaison. The next section will show the woman as the initiator, which in this story is in keeping with the teaching of the other two passages, 5:1–23 and 6:20–35.[6]

> [10]All of a sudden a woman propositions him,
>   in the attire of a prostitute and with guarded heart.
> [11]She is boisterous and defiant;
>   her feet do not rest in her own house.
> [12]A foot in the street, a foot in the public squares,
>   she lurks beside every street corner.
> [13]She grabs him and she kisses him.
>   Her face is brazen as she speaks to him:

7:10–13. The father describes the event to his son as if it were unfolding before their eyes.[7] As the naive youth walked down the path near the house of the strange/foreign woman, she suddenly comes forward and propositions him. Again, it appears that this encounter is unexpected on the part of the youth and not premeditated by him. It is almost as though she is lying in ambush for him (see 1:11). Though it could be translated as benignly as "invite" or "meet," we render the verb *qārā'* here as "proposition," since the context implies a specifically sexual invitation. She may not be a prostitute, but she is dressed like one. We are uncertain what this means in ancient society. It may mean she was

---

6. A survey of the leading commentaries reveals that most interpreters disagree, thinking that the youth is making a beeline for her house, with the intention of an illicit union (Murphy and Whybray as examples). I am gratified, though, to see that Fox shares the perspective argued here. The former position does not take seriously enough the force of the seemingly abrupt and unexpected appearance of the woman on the street.

7. As Fox (*Proverbs 1–9*, 243) points out: "This sentence, with *hinnēh* + noun clause, is the equivalent of the English historical present, used for vividness in recounting a past event."

veiled,[8] but it almost certainly means that her dress was provocative. Since she seems well-off and never asks for money, we assume she is not a professional. She refers to her husband as being away. The description of the woman points to a married woman who is transgressing legal and social boundaries to pursue an illicit relationship with the youth.

The reference to her "guarded heart" is difficult. It may point out that though her actions are outgoing, her motives are hidden. She is loud, but one does not really know what is going on inside of her since she keeps it hidden. It points out just how dangerous she is.

In terms of her actions, however, she is anything but silent, according to v. 11. In language that will echo in the description of Woman Folly (9:13), she is boisterous and defiant. The description suggests just how much she lacks self-discipline. She is not content at home, so she is out on the streets. As is well known, the "foot" is not infrequently a euphemism for genitalia (see discussion at 6:25–28). Thus, the assertion that her feet do not rest at home (v. 11b), but rather that she has a "foot" in the street and a "foot" in the public squares, may have double meaning and suggest that she has taken her sexual desire from the private sphere of marriage to the public areas. This also reminds us of the admonition of the father not to let one's sexuality manifest itself in public areas (5:15–17). The interpretation that this encounter is like an ambush is confirmed by the fact that she is said to lurk beside every street corner. She has been waiting for someone like this youth to come by.

Her approach to the youth is not simply restricted to words; she goes so far as to grab him and kiss him. As she does so, she speaks to him with a brazen face. Her brazen face is another indication that though her actions seem "out there," her motives remain hidden. She also has no apparent feelings of shame as she crosses sexual boundaries.

> [14]"I have fellowship offerings;
>   today I pay back my vow.
> [15]So, I have come out to meet you,
>   to seek your face, and I have found you.
> [16]I have ornamented my bed with bed coverings,
>   with colored linens from Egypt.
> [17]I have sprinkled my bed with myrrh,
>   aloes, and cinnamon.
> [18]Come, let's be intoxicated with lovemaking till morning;
>   let's rejoice in love.
> [19]For the man is not in his house,
>   having gone on a faraway trip.

8. See Gen. 38:14–15 and Song 1:7 and discussion of the conflicting evidence in Longman, *Song of Songs*, 100–101.

> [20]He has taken a pouch of money in his hand;
> he will arrive at his house on the day of the full moon."

7:14–20. The father then quotes the woman's invitation to him. The cultic language of the woman's proposition surprises us. She tells the youth that she has just offered fellowship offerings, and she informs him that she has just completed her vows. Because she has just done this, she has come out to find the youth.

As might be expected, there is debate concerning the significance of the woman's words and actions. Some argue that the woman thus shows that she participates in pagan ritual, and that the sex, along with the sacrifice, is a part of the vow to the deity.[9] However, this is hard to prove; she mentions that her husband has gone away, thus indicating that she is engaged in adultery, not pagan ritual. The fellowship (or peace) offering is described in Lev. 3 and 7:11–21. There we see that this sacrifice emphasizes the communion one has with God and fellow worshippers. Only a small part of the sacrifice is given to God, while the most edible parts are available to the worshippers for a meal. Leviticus 7:16–18 specifically describes the fellowship sacrifice that is offered to fulfill a vow. It says that the offered meat must be eaten on that day.[10] The woman mentions it to the man to entice him not only with sex but also with a scrumptious meal. The intended effect on readers is to apprise them of just how shameless she is. Thus, we can see that the debate concerning the ritual status of the sexual activity is really not all that important. Whether she seeks sex to fulfill a religious vow[11] or simply uses the meat for a feast to accompany adulterous sex, the act is just as bad. She is not only engaging in illicit sex; she is also blaspheming the holy things of God.

Verses 16–17 paint an even more enticing picture. Sexual enjoyment appeals to all the senses, not just touch and taste (the sacrificial meat) but also sight (colored linens) and smell (myrrh, aloes, and cinnamon). It is likely that the specification of the linens as coming from Egypt indicates their special character. The spices are familiar also in the Song of Songs in describing the woman's garden, a euphemism for her private sexual parts.[12]

---

9. So Perdue, *Wisdom and Cult*, 147–49.

10. For further on the description in Leviticus, see Longman, *Immanuel in Our Place: Seeing Christ in Israel's Worship* (Phillipsburg, NJ: P&R, 2001), 89–92.

11. Or to obtain money to pay off a religious vow; so K. van der Toorn, "Female Prostitution in Payment of Vows in Ancient Israel," *Journal of Biblical Literature* 108 (1989): 193–205.

12. See comments on Song 4:14 in Longman, *Song of Songs*, 157; as well as Yee, "'I Have Perfumed My Bed.'"

She then explicitly invites the youth to a night of lovemaking. Her husband is gone on a business trip (signified by the mention of his taking a pouch of money). He will not return till the full moon (an auspicious day [perhaps because the light of the moon makes travel safer] to return from a trip).

> ²¹She seduces him with all her talk;
>   she compels him with the flattery of her lips.
> ²²He impetuously goes after her.
>   He goes like an ox to the slaughter
>   and like a stupid person to the stocks for discipline,
> ²³until an arrow pierces his liver,
>   like a bird hurrying to the snare,
>   not aware that it will cost him his life.

7:21–23. These verses describe his capitulation to her seduction and his resultant fate. It is her talk, not her beauty, that does the trick. Her flattery appeals to his vanity, and he goes after her. His impetuous response indicates that he is not thinking with his brain, but like an ox he goes off to the slaughterhouse. The ox is happy as it goes into the house, not knowing that a violent end is at the other end of its journey. There are translation problems associated with v. 22c (see translation footnote), but in any case it speaks of a victim who unknowingly walks straight into a bad situation. Verse 23 culminates this section and says that ignorance persists till the horrible end, an end that is likened to an arrow piercing one's liver. The location of the arrow in the liver specifies a particularly painful way to die.

> ²⁴And now, sons, listen to me,
>   and pay attention to the speech of my mouth.
> ²⁵Don't turn your heart to her paths;
>   don't wander onto her trails.
> ²⁶For she has caused many corpses to fall,
>   and abundant are all those she has killed.
> ²⁷Her house is a path to Sheol,
>   going down to the chambers of death.

7:24–27. The chapter ends with a direct application to the son of the lesson learned from the anecdote just delivered by the father. The latter begins with a typical exhortation that the son pay close attention to the words that follow (see also 1:8; 2:2; 4:1). The bottom line warns the son against repeating the folly of the youth. Stay far away from such women. Her house, which on the surface looks like a place of great pleasure, is actually the gateway to Sheol, which signifies the grave and death and ultimately the underworld.[13]

Theological Implications

This discourse is the third that warns the son against illicit relationships with women (5:1–23; 6:20–35). Again, the sheer quantity of teaching devoted to this subject both demonstrates the strength of the temptation to the son as well as the dangerous consequences that result.

It is often said that the OT presents a double standard when it comes to sexual infidelity, with the woman being more harshly treated than the man. One reason the law might focus more on restricting women's sexuality is that she might bear children who are not her husband's and therefore confuse the inheritance of the land. Thus, for instance, Num. 5 presents a ritual to detect the marital infidelity of a woman, but not of a man. That concern is not so much moral as it has to do with offspring and inheritance. This may be indicated by the penalty for transgression, which is a withering of the "thigh," clearly a euphemism for the womb.

In any case, Prov. 7 (as well as 5 and 6) shows that men are not viewed with impunity when it comes to illegitimate sexual activity. The consequences are clear and simple: death. To be sure, the grounds given to the son to avoid this behavior are practical and involve an appeal to his own self-interest. Also, the woman is seen as the aggressor/predator, which is not always or even typically the case in such matters. However, as we have already suggested on the basis of hints within the text, the son addressed is on the path of wisdom and therefore at the point when the advice is given is by definition not a predator.

Also of theological interest in the present chapter is the blatant grounding of the advice in observation. Though I do think there is a subtle appeal to the law (in the words "command" and "instruction" in vv. 1–2), this is not the substance of the father's argument. He does not say: "Son, don't have sex with the strange woman because God tells you not to do it." Rather, his argument is, "Son, don't have sex with the strange woman because you will ruin your life and perhaps end it, and here is a story to illustrate what I am telling you."

The story itself is based on the father's observation and therefore also encourages attention to circumstances as part of the wisdom process. Wisdom involves looking at the rhythms of life, seeing what works and what doesn't work (see "The Sources of Wisdom" in the introduction).

13. See the extensive discussion in Johnston, *Shades of Sheol.*

This chapter also reiterates what we saw in chap. 5, namely, that in matters of sexual fidelity the best defense is a strong offense. In other words, to avoid consorting with the wrong woman, the son should cultivate a loving relationship with another woman. Whereas in chap. 5 the other woman was the wife, here the proper woman is Woman Wisdom (vv. 4–5).

Finally, we point out that Proverbs is not the only or even the first wisdom text in the ancient Near East that warns the son to avoid dubious women. We should consider the following examples from Egypt and Mesopotamia:

> Beware of a woman who is a stranger,
> One not known in her town;
> Don't stare at her when she goes by.
> Do not know her carnally.
> A deep water whose course is unknown,
> Such is a woman away from her husband.
> "I am pretty," she tells you daily,
> when she has no witnesses;
> She is ready to ensnare you,
> A great deadly crime when it is heard.
> (The Egyptian Instruction of Ani 3.13ff.)[14]

> Don't marry a prostitute, whose husbands are legion,
> Nor a temple harlot, who is dedicated to a goddess,
> Nor a courtesan, whose intimates are numerous.
> She will not sustain you in your time of trouble;
> She will snigger at you when you are embroiled in controversy.
> She has neither respect nor obedience in her nature.
> Even if she had the run of your house, get rid of her.
> She has ears attuned for another's footfall.
> (The Babylonian Counsels of Wisdom 2.23–30)[15]

14. Translation by M. Lichtheim, in *COS* 1:111.
15. Translation taken from Clifford, *Proverbs*, 12.

Chapter 8

Translation

[1]Does not Wisdom cry out,
   and Understanding give forth her voice?
[2]At the top of the high places on the path,
   at the crossroads she takes her stand.
[3]By the gate before the city,
   at the entrances she shouts.

[4]I cry out to you, O men;
   my voice goes out to the sons of humanity.
[5]Understand prudence, you who are simpleminded;
   you fools, take this to heart.
[6]Listen, for I speak noble things,
   opening virtuous lips.[a]
[7]For my mouth[b] utters the truth,
   and my lips despise wickedness.[c]
[8]All the speeches of my mouth are righteous.[d]
   Nothing in them is twisted or perverse.
[9]All of them are straightforward to those who understand
   and virtuous for those who seek knowledge.
[10]Take discipline and not silver,
   and knowledge more than choice gold.

a. Literally, "the opening of my lips is virtuous."
b. The Hebrew has the more specific "palette" (ḥēk), though that seems a bit too precise a translation for this context.
c. Literally, "the abomination to my lips is wickedness."
d. Literally, "in righteousness: all the speeches of my mouth."

¹¹For Wisdom is better than pearls,
    and nothing is more delightful than she.

¹²I, Wisdom, dwell with prudence.
    I have found knowledge and discretion.
¹³Those who fear Yahweh hate evil,
    pride and arrogance, and the path of evil.
    I hate a perverse mouth.
¹⁴Advice and resourcefulness belong to me,
    as do understanding and strength.
¹⁵By me kings reign,
    and nobles issue just decrees.
¹⁶By me rulers rule,
    and princes, all righteous judgments.
¹⁷I love those who love me,
    and those who seek me will find me.
¹⁸Wealth and honor are with me,
    enduring riches^e and righteousness.
¹⁹My fruit is better than gold, even fine gold,
    my yield than choice silver.
²⁰I walk on the way of righteousness,
    in the midst of the trials of justice,
²¹to cause those who love me to inherit substance,^f
    and I will fill their treasuries.

²²Yahweh begot me at the beginning of his paths,
    before his works of antiquity.
²³From of old I was formed,
    from the beginning, from before the earth.
²⁴When there were no deeps, I was brought forth,
    when there were no springs, heavy with water.
²⁵Before the mountains were settled,
    before the hills, I was brought forth.
²⁶At that time the earth and the open country were not made,
    and the beginning of the clods of the world,
²⁷when he established the heavens, I was there,
    when he decreed the horizon on the face of the deep,
²⁸when he strengthened the clouds above;
    when he intensified the fountains of the deep,

e. Or perhaps "negotiable wealth," according to Hurowitz, "Two Terms for Wealth," 252–54. If so, it refers to wealth that can be transported during a trip, perhaps for business purposes. In either case, Woman Wisdom claims to be able to make a person rich.

f. The word *yēš* is unique as a noun in Hebrew. It typically has the sense of a copula "there is" or "there was." Hurowitz ("Two Terms") argues that it is related to the Akkadian *busu*, which also developed from the verb "there is" and means "valuables, goods, moveable property." Hence my translation "substance."

²⁹when he set for the sea its decree,
  wherein the water could not pass where he said.ᵍ
³⁰I was beside him as a craftsman.ʰ
  I was playing daily,
  laughing before him all the time.
³¹Laughing with the inhabitants of his earth
  and playing with the human race.

³²And now, sons, listen to me;
  happy are those who guard my path!
³³Listen to discipline, and be wise,
  and don't avoid it.
³⁴Happy are those who listen to me,
  watching daily at my doors,
  guarding my doorposts.
³⁵For those who find me find life,
  and they gain favor from Yahweh.
³⁶Those who offend me do violence to their lives;
  all those who hate me love death.

g. "Where he said" is literally "his mouth."

h. The translation of this difficult yet important word is much discussed, and relevant bibliography will be cited here. The consonantal text of the Hebrew is ʾ-m-w-n, and the Masoretes vocalized the word as ʾāmôn, which means "craftsman" or "master crafts-man." (For Dahood's defense of the translation "Master Architect," see "Proverbs 8,22–31," 518–19.) However, many readers find this difficult for two reasons. First, Wisdom is never said actually to participate in the acts of creation in this chapter. Second, many people, including me, would find it troubling if the text presented the picture of a second, separate creator who, along with Yahweh, brought the cosmos into existence. It appears that for these reasons, particularly the second, some scholars, going back at least to Aquila and his Greek translation, repoint the word with a *u*-vowel, thus ʾamûn, and understand the word as "nursling" or "child." I will briefly mention yet another approach, that of Scott ("Wisdom in Creation"), who revocalizes the text as ʾōmen ("binding together"): thus, "I was at his side a living link."

Most scholars agree that the word could produce either meaning, provided one is open to vocalic emendation. However, it appears that the only real reasons for moving away from the MT "craftsman" are theologically motivated. This is usually not satisfactory, but it is true that we should try to understand this text in the context of orthodox Yahwism. Rogers ("Meaning and Significance") tries to solve the problem by appealing to grammar. He says that we should take the word as appositional to the pronominal suffix "him," thus "I [Wisdom] was beside him [Yahweh], who is a craftsman."

My own view is as follows. I agree with Rogers that the word ʾāmôn refers to Yahweh, but, contra Rogers, I also believe it refers to Woman Wisdom. How so? The answer to that question rests on the exegesis of Prov. 9:1–6. Anticipating discussion thereon, I believe that Woman Wisdom is a poetic personification of Yahweh's wisdom; indeed, as indicated by her house's location on the high point of the city, Wisdom ultimately represents Yahweh himself.

Fox ("ʾĀmôn Again") suggests reading ʾāmôn as an infinitive with the meaning "being raised" or "growing up." The colon would thereby refer to Wisdom's growing up in the presence of God.

196

Interpretation

Wisdom's autobiography. Chapter 8 is the most difficult and profound chapter in the book. The grammar and meaning of the Hebrew is not the problem, but the description of Woman Wisdom and her place in the developing canon have provided the vehicle for much discussion and controversy. Full discussion of these issues will follow the exegesis, in the theological implications sections.

For now we simply introduce the chapter to set it up for the section-by-section exegesis that will follow.

This chapter is devoted to Woman Wisdom and to her speech delivered to the men who are within the sound of her voice. The men are the implied readers[1] of the text, but the rhetorical intention is for actual readers of the book to identify with these "men" and consider how her words apply to them. Woman Wisdom has spoken once before, in 1:20–32, a passage that has some overlap with our present chapter.

The passage (chap. 8) begins with a third-person voice that introduces Woman Wisdom (vv. 1–3). In the context of the book, we should probably understand the narrator to be the sage, the father, who has been speaking throughout the book, though this identification is not crucial for our understanding of the text. He calls attention to the Woman's speech and provides some interesting geographical locators that have significance for our understanding of the metaphor (see commentary below).

In v. 4 we have a transition from third-person speech about Wisdom to first-person speech by her. She speaks directly to the men, who, from v. 4 all the way to the end of the chapter, are further specified as "fools" and "simpleminded." However, we can identify three subunits within this large passage.

The first subunit comprises vv. 4–11 and is an exordium (foreword) that encourages the men to listen and take Wisdom's message to heart. This is communicated by imperatives and also by the positive description that she gives to her message. Wisdom speaks of noble things with virtuous lips. She speaks the truth, and her words are righteous. They lead to understanding and knowledge. Finally in this section, she adopts a frequent trope in the book (see also 3:14–15; 8:19; 16:16) and favorably compares her speech with precious metals and jewels.

Although first-person speech begins in v. 4, a formal autobiographical introduction is found in v. 12, where the first-person speaker identifies

---

1. For "implied reader" and its relationship to the "actual reader," see S. Chatman, *Story and Discourse* (Ithaca, NY: Cornell University Press, 1978), 149–50; and T. Longman III, *Literary Approaches to Biblical Interpretation* (Grand Rapids: Zondervan, 1987), 84–85.

herself as Wisdom and then proceeds to characterize herself. She does so first by talking about those qualities (and these may also be personified characteristics) with which she is associated—prudence, knowledge, and discretion—and then those from which she distances herself: evil, pride, arrogance, a perverse mouth.

She is the quality that makes for good rule, provides material benefits, and bestows a good reputation. Her way is the ethical ("righteous") way.

The autobiography takes a tantalizing turn in v. 22. In vv. 22–31 Wisdom describes her relationship with Yahweh particularly in connection with the act of creation. In this subunit in particular, establishing the exact nature of Wisdom is most intriguing and problematic, and we will have to pay special attention to the alternatives of translation and understanding in this subunit, though we will reserve our synthesis until the theological implications section.

The third subunit of the autobiography (vv. 32–36) takes explicit note of the audience again. This time the "men" are referred to as "sons," which is more typical in the first nine chapters. And again the message is to pay attention to what this Woman has to say. The final two verses give the most serious consequences of obedience or lack thereof. Listening to the message of Wisdom brings life, while turning a deaf ear means violence and death.

> [1]Does not Wisdom cry out,
>   and Understanding give forth her voice?
> [2]At the top of the high places on the path,
>   at the crossroads she takes her stand.
> [3]By the gate before the city,
>   at the entrances she shouts.

8:1–3. In the first few verses of the chapter, we hear a voice talking about wisdom in a manner soon making it obvious that this abstract concept is personified; thus we capitalize the English translation. The voice that speaks about wisdom is never identified, but perhaps there is an implicit identification with the father/sage whose presence dominates the first nine chapters as he speaks to the son.

In any case, the speaker begins with a rhetorical question presented in poetic parallelism. This question clearly assumes a positive answer. Its first statement is, "Does not Wisdom cry out?" We know that she does because, as the chapter continues, we will hear what she cries out. Already we have heard her speak in 1:20–33. The second colon of v. 1 is quite similar to the first. It does not technically say the same thing as colon 1 for a second time. It uses a different name for the woman: "Understanding." There may be a difference of nuance between these two Hebrew words, the first being *ḥōkmâ* and the second *tĕbûnâ*, but if there is a difference, they are used so often that it is hard for us to catch any differing specificity after so many centuries. However, the general picture is clear. Wisdom, also called Understanding, is shouting out loudly. We must wait to find out her audience and her message. Beginning with such a rhetorical sentence grabs the attention and interest of readers, so we press on to find the answers to these questions. Indeed, at this point we really don't know much about this mysterious speaker.

Verse 2 now tells us the location of Wisdom as she shouts out. First, we note that she is associated with the path. Up to this point in the book, the path has been a frequent metaphor. It stands for a life journey, and the reader, who is identified with the implied reader, the son, is walking on the path. By mentioning the path in this way, the sage informs us that as people live their lives, they will encounter this woman. But further than this, we hear that she is at the "top of the high places." Here and elsewhere (9:3), we see that Wisdom is associated with heights. We await our exegesis of 9:1–6 to develop the significance of this aspect of her location, but it is critical to fully understand the personification. On a superficial level, the fact that she is shouting from the high point near a path means that she is going to be heard by those who pass by. Verse 1b now tells us another facet of her location: she is by the crossroads. The crossroads are a place where many people will travel. We envision a mass audience for Wisdom as she delivers her message. The fact that prostitutes stand at crossroads soliciting men to engage them in sexual intimacies (see Gen. 38:14) may presage an erotic component to Woman Wisdom's solicitation (but see more in 9:1–6).

Verse 3 continues the identification of her location, and here we see that she is placed at the gate (or as the second colon puts it, at the entrances) of the city. The gate, like the crossroads, is a busy place, a public place. The gate of the city is also the border between the city and the countryside. Her address is to all men. Furthermore, the gate is the place of important decision making.

> 4I cry out to you, O men;
>   my voice goes out to the sons of humanity.
> 5Understand prudence, you who are simpleminded;
>   you fools, take this to heart.
> 6Listen, for I speak noble things,
>   opening virtuous lips.
> 7For my mouth utters the truth,
>   and my lips despise wickedness.
> 8All the speeches of my mouth are righteous.
>   Nothing in them is twisted or perverse.

> ⁹All of them are straightforward to those who understand
>   and virtuous for those who seek knowledge.
> ¹⁰Take discipline and not silver,
>   and knowledge more than choice gold.
> ¹¹For Wisdom is better than pearls,
>   and nothing is more delightful than she.

8:4–11. This section may be called the preamble of Woman Wisdom's speech. A new section begins in v. 12, signaled by a typical ancient Near Eastern autobiographical introduction. Her first words, though, are intended to garner the attention of the men that she addresses, so they will listen to her words.

She begins in a way that permits us to identify her implied audience. In colon 1 of v. 4, she addresses them simply as "men," and in colon 2, she calls them "sons of humanity." After her autobiography, as she again implores her audience to hear her, she refers to them as "sons." Thus, the audience presumed up to this point in Proverbs continues: young men who are at the beginning of their professional and marital lives. They are at an impressionable crossroads.

Verse 5 provides yet another nuance to their identification. They are "simpleminded" and "fools." Obviously, as is clear with the first term, these are not hardened fools or "mockers." They are naive, immature, those who are capable of responding to the message appropriately. Thus, she urgently tells them to listen to her. She wants them to understand "prudence." As explained more fully at 1:4, prudence describes one's ability to use reason, in context and under the fear of God, to navigate the problems of life. Prudence carefully considers a situation before rushing in. It implies coolheadedness. Prudence is closely associated with wisdom and is the cure for simplemindedness.

In the next few verses, particularly vv. 6–9, we are struck by the ethical quality of Wisdom. In the description of her speech, she uses words like "truth," "righteous," "straightforward," and "virtuous." She distances her speech from things that are "twisted" or "perverse." She despises "wickedness." Many proverbs to follow in chaps. 10–31 will concern speech, and we will see that the wise person emulates Woman Wisdom in this regard. Concretely, that means that they avoid speech characterized as gossip, rumor, slander, and lies.

Furthermore, by describing her speech in such a way, Wisdom prepares the reader to receive the words that will follow in the rest of the chapter.

The last two verses of this section (vv. 10–11) utilize a trope that is frequently encountered here and elsewhere.[2] Wisdom and her associates,

---

2. It is most fully developed in Job 28.

"discipline" and "knowledge," are to be preferred over precious metals and jewels.[3] Here gold, silver, and pearls are specified. Of course, riches are highly desired. Since wisdom is even more to be desired, this statement places great value on it.

> [12]I, Wisdom, dwell with prudence.
> I have found knowledge and discretion.
> [13]Those who fear Yahweh hate evil,
> pride and arrogance, and the path of evil.
> I hate a perverse mouth.
> [14]Advice and resourcefulness belong to me,
> as do understanding and strength.
> [15]By me kings reign,
> and nobles issue just decrees.
> [16]By me rulers rule,
> and princes, all righteous judgments.
> [17]I love those who love me,
> and those who seek me will find me.
> [18]Wealth and honor are with me,
> enduring riches and righteousness.
> [19]My fruit is better than gold, even fine gold,
> my yield than choice silver.
> [20]I walk on the way of righteousness,
> in the midst of the trials of justice,
> [21]to cause those who love me to inherit substance,
> and I will fill their treasuries.

8:12–21. With the preceding introduction, the reader is ready to listen to Wisdom's autobiography. Thus, we are not surprised to observe that v. 12 has the form typical to an introduction in an ancient Near Eastern autobiography.[4] After the first-person speaker identifies herself as Wisdom, she begins by telling the reader about those traits with which she is associated. Indeed, it may be that these traits—prudence, knowledge, and discretion[5]—are themselves personified and considered her colleagues. In a sense, we may consider these three characteristics her best friends. Where you find Wisdom, there you will also find these three qualities.

3. Compare the similar trope used to accentuate the value of God's reign in Matt. 13:45–46: "Again, the kingdom of heaven is like a merchant in search of fine pearls; on finding one pearl of great value, he went and sold all he had and bought it" (NRSV).

4. For which see A. Poebel, *Das appositionell bestimmte Pronomen der 1. Pers. Sing. in den westsemitischen Inschriften und im Alten Testament* (Chicago: Oriental Institute, University of Chicago Press, 1932); and T. Longman III, *Fictional Akkadian Autobiography* (Winona Lake, IN: Eisenbrauns, 1991). The form is similar to that found in Eccles. 1:12.

5. For detailed discussions, see 1:4 for the first occurrence of all three words.

Verse 13 introduces "those who fear Yahweh," a phrase which, beginning with 1:7 (for the meaning of the phrase, see commentary there), we recognize as an alternative description of those who are wise. The wise are defined not only by their positive qualities but also by those characteristics that do not typify them. They are not evil; indeed, they "hate evil." Once again, we note the ethical quality of wisdom in the book. The verse also distances the wise from pride and arrogance as well as from a perverse mouth. In the latter, the wise simply emulate Woman Wisdom (see 8:8).

Verse 14 associates advice (for which, see 1:25), resourcefulness (see 2:7; 3:21), understanding (first occurrence at 1:2), and strength with Woman Wisdom. The not-so-implicit message is that if the readers want such things, then they have to go to Wisdom to get them. These abilities are needed to navigate through life's pitfalls, and so they would be highly desired. Of this list, "strength" (*gĕbûrâ*) is the one characteristic that is somewhat surprising. Another word by which the Hebrew term could be rendered is "power," the ability to affect change. God himself combines wisdom and power (Job 12:13; Isa. 11:2), and so in the light of our understanding of the relationship of God and Woman Wisdom, we are not surprised to hear that both qualities characterize Wisdom as well.

The most powerful humans on earth are generally rulers, so it makes sense that Wisdom continues by describing her relationship to this group. In a word, those who rule well do so by virtue of their relationship with wisdom. A successful ruler is an ethical ruler, one who is characterized by justice and righteousness.

In 8:17 we are informed that Wisdom is not hard to find, not hard to attain.[6] But one must pursue her. She loves those who love her and allows those who search for her to find her. The same theme is found in chap. 2, and there we learn of the paradox that those who search and find do so because of the gift of God. As motivation for the pursuit, again Wisdom reminds the readers of the rewards that follow a relationship with her. Those who are wise get wealth and honor and righteousness. Solomon himself is a real-life illustration, at least early in his career. He asks God for wisdom, and God is so pleased that he gives him wealth and power (1 Kings 3:1–15). And yet for the second time in the chapter (see 8:10–12), wisdom—or, better here, the consequences of being wise ("my fruit," v. 19)—is better than precious silver. After all, those who pursue wisdom get wealth (8:21).

---

6. As Jesus instructs his followers, "Ask, and it will be given you; search, and you will find; knock, and the door will be opened for you. For everyone who asks receives, and everyone who searches finds, and for everyone who knocks, the door will be opened!" (Matt. 7:7–8 NRSV).

²²Yahweh begot me at the beginning of his paths,
   before his works of antiquity.
²³From of old I was formed,
   from the beginning, from before the earth.
²⁴When there were no deeps, I was brought forth,
   when there were no springs, heavy with water.
²⁵Before the mountains were settled,
   before the hills, I was brought forth.
²⁶At that time the earth and the open country were not made,
   and the beginning of the clods of the world,
²⁷when he established the heavens, I was there,
   when he decreed the horizon on the face of the deep,
²⁸when he strengthened the clouds above;
   when he intensified the fountains of the deep,
²⁹when he set for the sea its decree,
   wherein the water could not pass where he said.
³⁰I was beside him as a craftsman.
   I was playing daily,
   laughing before him all the time.
³¹Laughing with the inhabitants of his earth
   and playing with the human race.

8:22–31. A typical ancient Near Eastern autobiography begins with a self-introduction like what we have seen in vv. 12–21. After the introduction comes a narration concerning accomplishments, and that is what we have in vv. 22–31, a narration of the great deeds of Woman Wisdom. The first five verses of this passage (vv. 22–26) emphasize the creation of Wisdom at the beginning, before the earth was created, and the second five verses (vv. 27–31) focus on Wisdom's presence during the creation process. The entire section describes the interrelationship between Wisdom and creation. The implied subtext informs the reader that one must know Wisdom in order to get around in God's creation. No one knows creation better than she does!

This section is among the most controversial of the entire book of Proverbs because of the description of Wisdom's relationship with Yahweh in the joint work of creation[7] and because of the use of this material in the NT in connection with Jesus Christ. We will delay our full discussion of these issues until the section on theological implications that follows. For now, we will lay the groundwork by describing the content of the passage. As we see both in what follows and in the translation footnotes,

---

7. Whybray ("Proverbs viii 22–31," 510) compares this passage to other ancient Near Eastern creation accounts from Mesopotamia and Egypt and concludes that "none of these non-biblical texts resembles Prov. viii 22–31 in form or purpose."

however, there is interplay between exegesis and theology since some scholars want to avoid renditions suggesting that Wisdom is a created being. Thus, we will be unable to completely separate theology from exegesis in our exposition of the passage.

The controversy begins in v. 22, which in our translation describes the begetting of Wisdom by Yahweh. Murphy is clearly correct when he suggests that the following description intends to evoke a sense of mystery.[8]

The Hebrew verb behind "begot" is *qnh* and is the source of some controversy. In most instances in the OT, the verb means to "acquire" or "purchase" (Gen. 25:10; 33:19; 2 Sam. 24:21). However, in Ugaritic (where Asherah is called the "begetter of the gods" [*qnytilm*]) and on the basis of poetic parallelism (Gen. 14:19, 22; Deut. 32:6; Ps. 139:13), biblical Hebrew also attests the meaning "create" or "beget." The meanings "acquire" and "create" are connected and are the same Hebrew root; we are not dealing with homonyms here.[9] "Semantically, the range of *qnh* is similar to that of 'get' and 'beget' in Eng. (both mean 'acquire' and 'procreate'; see OED s.v.)."[10] In many appearances in the OT, the verb *qnh* seems to be a "dead metaphor" for creation. Yet the connection with human procreation is still active, as indicated by the later use of the verb *ḥyl*, "brought forth" (vv. 24, 25), which has to do with pregnancy and labor (so *NIDOTTE* 3:941). Theologically, the use of female imagery for God is attested elsewhere (Deut. 32:18; Ps. 131; Isa. 66:10–13). Virtually all translations today agree that this verb ought to be translated "create" or "beget" (NIV, NLT, NRSV, NJB), but some still put the alternative translation in a footnote (NIV).[11]

---

8. Murphy, *Proverbs*, 52.

9. Or note the statement by Fox (*Proverbs 1–9*, 279) in reference to the issue of whether the root means to "create" or "acquire": "In my view, the question is moot. The word's lexical meaning, the semantic content it brings to context, is 'acquire,' no more than that. But one way something can be acquired is by creation. English 'acquire' implies that the object was already in existence, but this is not the case with *qānāh*. To avoid misunderstanding, the better translation is 'created.'" This seems to be a compelling reply to Vawter ("Prov. 8:22," 205), who argues that the root always means "acquire" and never "create" in the Hebrew Bible.

10. *NIDOTTE* 3:941.

11. Vawter ("Prov. 8:22," 215) provides an argument in favor of taking *qnh* as "to acquire," asserting that though it is possible to translate the root elsewhere as "beget" or "create" (for instance Gen. 4:1; 14:19, 22; etc.), there is no place where such a translation is absolutely necessary. He argues that wisdom is not created but found by Yahweh. In his words, it refers to "a wisdom which is not a native attribute of God but a reality accessible to him alone and acquired by him." Thus, wisdom literature felt that wisdom was autonomous alongside God, he claims, in the same way that *ma'at* was an autonomous concept to Egyptian religion. If this is so, one among many questions might be: Why then for humans does wisdom begin with the fear of God (1:7)?

The verse also situates the birth of Wisdom in time, indeed, at the start of time. This is signaled by the reference to the "beginning of his [God's] path." It also indicates the timing of this act in relationship to the rest of creation, here referred to as "his works of antiquity."

Verse 23 underlines the idea that Wisdom was brought into being at the beginning, before other acts of creation. The verb used here is rare; its root is *nsk*. The root *nsk* I is a common verb that means to "pour out" and does not seem to apply in this context. Thus, most scholars, present company included, suggest that it comes from a rare root *nsk* II, associated with *skk* II, and both mean "to weave, form" (see *NIDOTTE* 3:253–54). "Weave/form" (*nsk*) occurs only once in the qal, in Isa. 25:7, and once in the niphal, in the present context.

There is an alternative to this understanding, and that is to take the verb as the only occurrence of the verbal root behind *nāsîk*, "prince" (or perhaps as a secondary verbal derivative from the noun). In this case, the verb could be rendered something like "to appoint."

The English versions vary widely in their translation of this verb. Most take it as "appoint" (NIV, NLT, NRSV), while some (see REB, also given in footnotes of the previous versions) take it as "form," and one intrepid translation (NAB) actually does take it from "pour forth."

Verses 24–26 form a subunit of sorts. Clifford put it well: these verses "portray precreation chaos or nothingness concretely, i.e., by listing specific cosmic elements not in existence rather than through the abstract concept of nothingness."[12]

Verse 24 is understandable when it is realized that ancient Near Eastern creation stories almost all presume a primordial watery mass from which the dry land is separated. In Egypt, creation is thought to emanate from the Nun, or watery abyss. In Mesopotamia and Canaan, the creator god (Marduk and Baal respectively) must defeat the god of the sea (Tiamat and Yam), and by bounding their waters, they create the dry land. In Gen. 1, while it is unclear whether the text explicitly or implicitly affirms creation from nothing, we do not doubt that the original mass, described as formless and void (*tōhû wābōhû*), is a watery mass from which the dry ground is separated on the second day. Poetical conceptions of creation will sometimes mimic the broader ancient Near Eastern idea of conflict with the sea (in my opinion, for polemical purposes, see Ps. 74). In any case, here Wisdom claims temporal precedence even over the deeps.

If the deeps represent the primordial unformed earth and come to stand also for the forces of chaos, then the mountains represent age-

---

12. R. J. Clifford, *Creation Accounts in the Ancient Near East and in the Bible* (Washington, DC: Catholic Biblical Association of America, 1994), 183.

old stability. Even today, we have the expression "old as the hills," and Wisdom here claims this level of antiquity. We have already anticipated the use of the verb here in v. 24 (*hyl,* "brought forth") in our discussion of *qnh* (above). It is a verb that means to "writhe in pain" and is often associated with labor pains. In essence, Wisdom claims to have been born at this primordial moment.

One more time, in v. 26 Wisdom claims to have come into being before the rest of God's creation. The crop-producing land was not yet made when she came into being.

Verses 27–29 each begin with a temporal clause that registers Wisdom's presence during specific acts of creation. Indeed, the second colon of vv. 27–28 also are temporal clauses, and v. 29b expands the thought of v. 29a.

The five specific acts are as follows:

1. The establishment of the heavens
2. The decree that constructs the horizon on the deep
3. The strengthening of the clouds
4. The intensification of the fountains
5. The decree that sets the boundary of the sea

The first concerns the making of the heavens, while the last four describe elements of the construction of earth. In terms of the latter, all four describe manipulation of water. By constructing the horizon on the deep and decreeing the boundary of the sea, we are likely to think of pushing back primordial waters to construct dry land. Genesis 1 narrates the process of creation that begins with the "formless and void" earth, where darkness was over the deep. Creation involves a series of separations, including the separation of the water from water (day 2). The waters below would include the "fountains," while the waters above would emanate from the "clouds." Day 3 then goes on to talk about the "gathering" of the waters (Gen. 1:9), which may also be described as a bounding of the waters. The language of pushing the waters back is also reminiscent of the Babylonian creation myth, the *Enuma Elish.* After defeating Tiamat, his mother and the goddess of the deeps, Marduk creates the heavens and the earth. No one passage captures this theme in its entirety, but a couple of quotations illustrate the point:

> He split her [Tiamat] in two, like a fish for drying,
> Half of her he set up and made as a cover, heaven.
> He stretched out the hide and assigned watchmen,
> And ordered them not to let her waters escape. (tablet 4.137–140)

He opened underground springs, a flood was let flow(?).
From her eyes he undimmed the Euph[rates] and Tigris,

. . . .

He drilled through her waterholes to carry off the catchwater. (tablet
5:54–55, 58)[13]

In this highly poetic passage of Prov. 8, we are not reading a technical description of the process of creation. Rather, by allusion to Gen. 1 as well as the broader ancient Near Eastern tradition of creation, we are being told of Wisdom's presence during these primordial events.

Verses 30 goes further, when it refers to Wisdom as a "craftsman" beside him. This word (ʾāmôn), a *hapax legomenon*, has occasioned much controversy (see translation footnote), and so our comments are tempered by the recognition that our translation is only probable. However, it certainly is appropriate to the context and implies that Wisdom was not only present but also involved in creation as a guiding force. Verses 30b–31 describes Wisdom like a child sporting in a new environment. The description certainly evokes a mood of celebration concerning creation. Indeed, "wisdom serves [here] as a metaphor for the goodness and playfulness of creation. Wisdom in her play pronounces creation 'good,' just as surely as the divine pronouncement 'it was good.'"[14] It also reveals the twofold direction of Wisdom's interests.[15] She laughs before him (God) and laughs and plays with the human race. Here Wisdom is seen as a mediating figure between the human and the divine, which will be important for the later theological development of this figure (see "Theological Implications" below).

> [32]And now, sons, listen to me;
>   happy are those who guard my path!
> [33]Listen to discipline, and be wise,
>   and don't avoid it.
> [34]Happy are those who listen to me,
>   watching daily at my doors,
>   guarding my doorposts.
> [35]For those who find me find life,
>   and they gain favor from Yahweh.
> [36]Those who offend me do violence to their lives;
>   all those who hate me love death.

13. The translations are by B. R. Foster, in *COS* 1:398–99.

14. The final reference is to the repeated refrain in Gen. 1. The quote is from Matlack, "Play of Wisdom," 429.

15. As Mack ("Wisdom Myth and Mythology," 50) puts it: Wisdom "lives with God and seeks to dwell among men."

8:32–36. We began the study of Wisdom's speech by noting its similarity to the genre of autobiography in the ancient Near East. The typical autobiography begins with an introduction and then continues with a selective narration of the life of the first-person speaker. However, the third concluding section is variable. In my earlier study of this tradition in Akkadian literature, I observed four possibilities.[16] Some end with blessings and curses, similar to first-person royal inscriptions (Sargon Birth Legend; Idrimi). Others end with a donation to the religious cult (Kurigalzu; Cruciform Monument to Manishtushu); and still others with prophetic predictions (Text A; Marduk Prophecy; Uruk Prophecy; Shulgi Prophecy; Dynastic Prophecy). Last and most similar to our present text are those that end with advice (Cuthaean Legend of Naram-Sin; Adad-guppi autobiography; and Sin of Sargon text).

It is in vv. 32–36 that Woman Wisdom now turns to her audience of young men (here called "sons," in good wisdom fashion) and imparts advice. She first urges her audience to "listen to" her, and then she bolsters the appeal by hinting at the positive consequences of doing what she says: "Happy are those who guard my path" (v. 32).

This pattern is repeated in vv. 33–34, but this time she specifies that they must heed rather than avoid discipline and thus grow in wisdom. Again, she pronounces the blessing of happiness on people who are attentive to her message.

Finally, the ultimate consequences of obedience or disobedience are specified. Those who seek for her, for Wisdom, will find life and God's favor, but those who do not will have difficult lives and then finally death.

This chapter, important in itself, also provides background for the choice the reader must make in chap. 9. The first part of 9 continues a description of Wisdom and a report of her call to the men who pass by her, but in that chapter we also hear a rival voice.

Theological Implications

Woman Wisdom's autobiography tells us a lot about her, which means that we learn much about wisdom itself. In the first place, her speech takes place in public space (high places above the path, crossroads, gates, entrances). Not only that, she does not speak in whispers but instead cries out; she gives forth her voice. Wisdom is not a secret matter, only for a select few. She calls out to all the men who are walking on the path of life. The fact that only men are mentioned here is a function of the

---

16. Longman, *Fictional Akkadian Autobiography*.

development of the metaphor of a female personification of Wisdom. It does not mean to exclude women; after all, Israel knew of wise women (the wise woman of Tekoa [2 Sam. 14] and the Queen of Sheba [1 Kings 10], for example).

Her speech is largely a self-revelation, and one of the major themes is the integrity of her speech (vv. 6–9). Wisdom is not simply concerned with the intellect but also with character. Words like "noble," "virtue," "righteous," "truth" are positively associated with her speech, but she distances herself from words that are twisted and perverse.

What Wisdom presents is herself, and she is more precious than valuable gold and rare pearls (vv. 10–11). Solomon's early career incarnates this hierarchy of values and helps explain it. Being given a choice of a gift from God at the beginning of his reign, he chooses wisdom (see 1 Kings 3:1–15). God is so pleased that he grants him not only wisdom but also wealth and power. In 8:17–21, Wisdom promises such rewards to those men who obey her admonition to seek her.

As Wisdom's speech continues, we see that her ethical qualities extend beyond her speech. She distances herself from such things as pride and arrogance and evil. As she describes her positive qualities and names those things that repulse her, she serves as a role model for her followers, those who seek wisdom.

Here we see a close connection between Wisdom and good rule. In other words, there is a political aspect to Wisdom. The best rulers order things according to wisdom, and in doing so they conform their actions to the way things are supposed to work (see below on the relationship between Wisdom and creation). The historical books associate good leaders and kings with the endowment of God's wisdom, as exampled by Joshua (Deut. 34:9), Solomon (1 Kings 3), and Ezra (Ezra 7:25).

The most tantalizing part of Wisdom's self-revelation is the section where she describes her association with God at the time of creation (vv. 22–31). As the section on exegesis pointed out, Wisdom was, in sum, the first act of God's creation, the firstborn, so to speak. She was there before anything else was created and then witnessed the creation process itself. Indeed, the implication is not only that she was present but that she also participated in the creation. Her reference to herself as a "craftsman" (8:30) may indicate that she helped in the project. The result of her participation is that she had an intimate, joyful relationship both with God and with the human race.

Before exploring further the intriguing relationship between Wisdom and God, it is necessary first to say the obvious. If one wants to know how the world works and therefore how to navigate life with its problems and pitfalls, then Wisdom is the one to get to know. Who would know better how to act in the world than the one through whom it was made?

However, who is Woman Wisdom anyway? The debate over her identity goes back to the beginning of the history of interpreting this chapter. One of the earliest clues we have for how Woman Wisdom was understood comes from the intertestamental books of Sirach and Wisdom of Solomon.[17]

Sirach, also known as Ecclesiasticus, is a book from the second century BC, and it begins by alluding to Prov. 8:

> Wisdom was created before all other things,
>   and prudent understanding from eternity.
>
> . . . .
>
> It is he [God] who created her [Wisdom];
>   he saw her and took her measure;
>   he poured her out upon all his works. (Sir. 1:4, 9 NRSV)

Then Sir. 24 really reflects and expands on Prov. 8. Indeed, it is largely modeled on that chapter. Here too we have a self-revelation of Woman Wisdom. But rather than making a public address, she speaks to the heavenly hosts. She recounts how God guided her to take up residence in Israel among all the nations of the earth. Among other differences, we see how Wisdom identifies herself with the Torah.[18]

> All this [Wisdom] is the book of the covenant of the Most High God,
>   the law that Moses commanded us
>   as an inheritance for the congregations of Jacob. (Sir. 24:23 NRSV)

Thus, those who study Torah are those who imbibe God's wisdom. This tradition is found in other intertestamental Wisdom books as well, as in the Wisdom of Solomon, for instance.

The NT describes Jesus Christ as the one in whom many OT themes find their ultimate expression (Luke 24:25–27, 44–48). Jesus is described as wise from the time of his youth (Luke 2:39–52) through his earthly ministry (Mark 6:2). Jesus recognized himself as wise and condemned those who rejected his wisdom. In Luke 11:31, he tells the crowd: "The queen of Sheba will rise up against this generation on judgment day and condemn it, because she came from a distant land to hear the wisdom of Solomon. And now someone greater than Solomon is here—and you refuse to listen to him" (NLT).

Although the Gospels demonstrate that Jesus was wise—indeed, wiser than Solomon—Paul asserts that Jesus is not simply wise; he is the very

---

17. See comments by Scott, "Study of the Wisdom Literature."
18. See Enns (*Exodus Retold*, 152), who cites Schnabel, *Law and Wisdom*; Blenkinsopp, *Wisdom and Law in the Old Testament*.

incarnation of God's wisdom. Twice Paul identifies Jesus with God's wisdom. First, in 1 Cor. 1:30, a passage that will occupy our attention later, he says, "God made Christ to be wisdom itself" (NLT). Second, in Col. 2:3 Paul proclaims that in Christ "lie hidden all the treasures of wisdom and knowledge" (NLT). With this as background, it is not surprising that the NT subtly associates Jesus with Woman Wisdom, particularly as she is presented in Prov. 8.

In Matt. 11, Jesus addresses opponents who argued that John the Baptist was ascetic in his lifestyle, while Jesus was too celebratory. Notice his final assertion in reply:

> For John came neither eating nor drinking, and they say, "He has a demon." The Son of Man came eating and drinking, and they say, "Here is a glutton and a drunkard, a friend of tax collectors and 'sinners.'" But wisdom is proved right by her actions. (Matt. 11:18–19 NIV)

By saying "Wisdom is proved right by her actions," Jesus claims that his behavior represents that of Woman Wisdom herself.

The association of Jesus and Wisdom may be found elsewhere in the NT as well when Jesus is described in language that is reminiscent of Prov. 8. We turn first to Col. 1:15–17 (NLT, 2nd ed.):

> Christ is the visible image of the invisible God.
>> He existed before anything was created and is supreme over all
>>> creation,
> for through him God created everything
>> in the heavenly realms and on earth.
> He made the things we can see
>> and the things we can't see—
> such as thrones, kingdoms, rulers, and authorities in the unseen world.
>> Everything was created through him and for him.
> He existed before anything else,
>> and he holds all creation together.

While this is clearly not a quotation from Proverbs, it is hard to imagine someone well versed in the OT like Paul not recognizing that Jesus occupies the place of Wisdom in this poem. Indeed, in the literal rendition of the Greek of the sentence that ends ". . . is supreme over all creation" (1:15 NLT; cf. 1:18), Paul declares: "He is the firstborn of all creation."[19] Wisdom was firstborn in Prov. 8; Jesus is firstborn in Colossians; Paul is inviting a comparison. Wisdom is the agency of divine creation in Proverbs, Christ in Colossians. In Prov. 8:

19. See the NLT footnote.

> Because of me, kings reign,
>> and rulers make just laws.
> Rulers lead with my help,
>> and nobles make righteous judgments. (8:15–16 NLT)

And in Col. 1:16, Christ made "kings, kingdoms, rulers, and authorities" (NLT). The message is clear: Jesus is Wisdom herself.

The author of Revelation is a further witness to the connection between Wisdom and Jesus. The allusion is subtle but clear. In the introduction to the letter to the church at Laodicea, we read: "This is the message from the one who is the Amen—the faithful and true witness, the ruler of God's new creation" (Rev. 3:14 NLT). The last phrase (*hē archē tēs ktiseōs tou theou*) resonates with the ideas behind Prov. 8:22–30. In particular, the phrase may represent the meaning of that difficult word in 8:30, the "craftsman" (*ʾāmôn*) of creation. In any case, once again Jesus stands in the place of Woman Wisdom.

Even more subtly, we recognize that the great preface to the Gospel of John resonates with language reminiscent of the poem of Woman Wisdom in Prov. 8. The Word of God (the Logos), who is God himself (1:1), "was in the beginning with God. He created everything there is" (1:2–3 NLT). Indeed, the "world was made through him" (1:10 NLT). Jesus, of course, is the Word and again is being associated with language reminiscent of Woman Wisdom.

So far, then, we have established the following. Woman Wisdom is a personification of Yahweh's wisdom. The chapter thus informs the reader that Yahweh created the world through his wisdom. Later Jewish interpretation of the chapter tends to identify wisdom with Torah, while Christian interpretation connects Wisdom with Jesus.

It is possible to overread these connections by not taking account of the genre of Prov. 8. One clear example of misapplying the passage comes from an early theologian named Arius (AD 260–336), commonly recognized as heretical by the orthodox church. Arius and his followers note the connection between Jesus and Wisdom and then apply all the characteristics of Wisdom to Jesus. They press literally the language that Wisdom (Jesus) was created or brought forth as the first of creation. Then they reason that since God is "unbegotten," and Wisdom, who stands for Jesus, is "begotten," Jesus cannot be God.

In response, we simply point out that Prov. 8 is not a prophecy of Jesus or any kind of literal description of him. We must remember that the text is poetry and is using metaphor to make important points about the nature of God's wisdom. Indeed, even in its OT setting where Wisdom stands for Yahweh's wisdom, we would be wrong to press the language of creation literally as if at some point God were not wise and only later became wise just in time to create the world.

We must remember all this when in the NT we see that Jesus associates himself with Wisdom. Woman Wisdom is not a preincarnate form of the second person of the Trinity. Jesus is not to be identified with Wisdom. The language about Jesus being the "firstborn of creation" is not to be pressed literally, as if Jesus were a created being. But—and this is crucial—the association between Jesus and Woman Wisdom in the NT is a powerful way of saying that Jesus is the embodiment of God's Wisdom.

However, we have not yet heard the last from Woman Wisdom. As we turn to chap. 9, we hear her voice again in a way that will help us to more closely identify her. In addition, we will be introduced to another woman: Folly, Wisdom's rival.

Chapter 9

Translation

¹Wisdom built her house;
  she erected her seven pillars.
²She slaughtered her slaughter, mixed her wine.
  She also arranged her tables.
³She sends her maidens; she issues[a] an invitation
  from the pinnacle of the heights of the city:
⁴"Whoever is simpleminded—turn aside here,"
  she says to those who lack heart.
⁵"Come, eat my food,
  and drink the wine I mixed.
⁶Abandon simplemindedness and live.
  March on the path of understanding."

⁷Those who discipline a mocker receive an insult;
  those who correct the wicked—they are blemished.[b]
⁸Don't correct mockers, or else they will hate you,
  but correct the wise, and they will love you.
⁹Give to the wise, and they will be still wiser;
  inform the righteous, and they will add to their teaching.
¹⁰The beginning of wisdom is the fear of Yahweh,

a. The breakup of the poetic line differs from the MT since the ʾatnāḥ occurs under the verb "issues." Combined with the question of the significance of the ʾatnāḥ is the question of who is the subject of the verb "issues." We understand the subject to be Woman Wisdom and not the young maidens who are sent out. See McKinlay, *Gendering Wisdom*, 46.

b. The Hebrew term *mûm* "refers predominantly to the physical nature, especially to the imperfection of animals," typically in a cultic setting (*NIDOTTE* 2:870). But here it is used in a metaphorical way parallel to "insult."

and the knowledge of the Holy One[c] is understanding.
¹¹For through me your days will be many;
    years of life will be added to you.
¹²If you are wise, you will make yourself wiser;
    if you are a mocker, you will bear it alone.

¹³Woman Folly is boisterous;
    she is simpleminded but does not even know it.
¹⁴She sits at the doorway of her house,
    on a seat at the heights of the city.
¹⁵She invites those who pass by on the path,
    those going straight on their way.
¹⁶"Whoever is simpleminded—turn aside here,"
    she says to those who lack heart.
¹⁷"Stolen water is sweet;
    food eaten in secret is pleasant."
¹⁸But they do not know that the departed are there,
    that those invited by her are in the depths of Sheol.

Interpretation

We come now to the climax of the first nine chapters. The previous discourses have spoken of a path on which the son walks. The path represents life's journey. The son has received instruction to stay on the right path and not go astray on the crooked path. The previous chapters have warned of violent ambushes from evil men and amorous advances by flattering women. These instructions have come to him from his parents, voiced by the father, and from Woman Wisdom. In chap. 9, a choice presents itself to him. Will he side with wisdom or folly? Or stated in the language of the chapter: Will he embrace Woman Wisdom or Woman Folly?

The choice is clearly stated since both women call out to the men going by on their paths with the same invitation to dine with them. The symmetry of vv. 1–6 and vv. 13–18 makes it clear that these Women issue rival invitations. The difficulty of the chapter is the relationship of the middle verses (vv. 7–12) to the rest.

¹Wisdom built her house;
    she erected her seven pillars.
²She slaughtered her slaughter, mixed her wine.
    She also arranged her tables.

c. Or "holy ones" (if the plural is not a plural of majesty) or "holy things"; see also Prov. 30:3.

> [3]She sends her maidens; she issues an invitation
>   from the pinnacle of the heights of the city:
> [4]"Whoever is simpleminded—turn aside here,"
>   she says to those who lack heart.
> [5]"Come, eat my food,
>   and drink the wine I mixed.
> [6]Abandon simplemindedness and live.
>   March on the path of understanding."

9:1–6. *Wisdom's invitation.* Before Wisdom speaks, her actions are described. These verses also have as their immediate background Wisdom's autobiography in chap. 8. We already know much about this woman.

Here we learn first that Woman Wisdom has built a magnificent house. This reminds us of a later proverb to the effect that the wise woman builds her house (14:1). In the latter case, we are to think not of actual construction of the physical edifice, but rather of the support that the wise woman gives to her household. However, here v. 1b helps us recognize that actual construction is meant. The fact that the house has seven pillars indicates that it is a magnificent and solid construction.[1] The number seven indicates perfection and/or completeness. Thus, we are to picture the scene as a large mansion; it demonstrates that Wisdom's house was "an indication of wealth and social status."[2]

Few scholars follow P. Skehan in seeing a literary reference here. Skehan argues that the seven-pillared house is actually looking back to seven poems that are each twenty-two verses long.[3] McKinlay, citing Lang, reminds us that archaeological investigation has discovered that Israelite houses were pillared, and sometimes even nonroyal residences had seven pillars.[4]

Verse 2 describes Woman Wisdom's preparations for a huge feast. The slaughter of the slaughter refers to the preparation of the meat for the meal. It indicates that this feast will be a sumptuous banquet, because in antiquity "meat was a luxury."[5] The mixed wine promises a celebra-

---

1. G. Boström (*Proverbiastudien*) offered the suggestion that the seven pillars are associated with the seven planets known at that time period, and through this he connected the imagery to Ishtar.

2. Whybray, *Proverbs*, 143.

3. Skehan, "Seven Columns"; idem, "Wisdom's House," *Catholic Biblical Quarterly* 29 (1967): 162–80 (reprinted in Skehan, *Studies in Israelite Poetry and Wisdom*, 27–45).

4. McKinlay, *Gendering Wisdom*, 51; citing Lang, *Wisdom and the Book of Proverbs*, 91–93; who is himself citing L. E. Stager, "The Archaeology of the Family in Ancient Israel," *Bulletin of the American Schools of Oriental Research* 260 (1985): 1–36. Ahlstöm, "House of Wisdom," points to seven-pillar houses in Byblos and suggests that real architecture was behind the reference, though he also believed that the number seven pointed to the "perfection" of the house.

5. Whybray, *Proverbs*, 144.

tory mood. Such wine adds either honey or spices for taste.[6] Finally, she arranges the tables for her guests to enjoy this fine, luxurious meal.

In v. 3 we hear her issue the invitation. She does so in apparently two ways. In the first place, she sends out her women servants with her message, but she also speaks from the pinnacle of the heights of the city. We assume that this is from her house. The fact that her home is built on the highest point of the city has profound theological implications; in the ancient Near East, the temple occupied such a lofty location. We will have more to say about this in the section on theological implications.

We hear Woman Wisdom speaking in the last three verses (4–6) of the unit. Specifically, she addresses the simpleminded, who are also called "those who lack heart." This reference is neither to the wise nor to the foolish, but to the naive or immature. These are people who are not yet committed to either side of the polarity, and it is the goal of the one named Wisdom to turn them to her side. She wants to instruct them in Wisdom.

She thus invites them to come to her home and share a meal with her. In the ancient Near East, for a woman to invite a man to a meal has erotic overtones. What Woman Wisdom wants is an intimate relationship with the man.[7]

Woman Wisdom issues the invitation to turn from simplemindedness and gain understanding. We do not hear what response the man makes, but before the end of the chapter we hear the voice of another woman, Folly.

9:7–12. *Wisdom sayings to the counselor.* The biggest question concerning these six verses has to do with their status in relationship to the rest of the chapter. It is clear that 9:1–6 is in contrastive parallelism to 9:13–18; the speech of Woman Folly at the end is the rival to the speech of Woman Wisdom in the beginning of the chapter. However, how these six middle verses relate to the ends is seemingly impossible to discern.

The six verses are observations and advice concerning wisdom over against folly, the latter often referred to by the extreme term "mocker"

---

6. So *NIDOTTE* 2:999.

7. This reminds us of the erotic language used earlier, in the father's admonition to the son to grow wise:

She is a tree of life to those who embrace her,
and those who hold her tight are blessed. (3:18)

Say to Wisdom, "You are my sister."
Call Understanding "Friend." (7:4)

McKinlay (*Gendering Wisdom*, 57) notes the following places where eating and drinking suggest an intimate sexual relationship: Prov. 5:15; 30:20; Song 4:13–15; Sir. 23:17.

(vv. 7, 8, 12). This section shows wisdom in a positive light and folly in a negative light. Perhaps this teaching could be seen as the teaching of Woman Wisdom or at least an argument in favor of siding with Woman Wisdom over Folly. Of special interest is the content of v. 11 that speaks in the first person. It sounds as if Woman Wisdom is speaking again as she did in vv. 1–6. In addition, the contrastive parallelism between vv. 1–6 and vv. 13–18 would be intensified if Woman's Wisdom's speech ended with a comment like v. 11, to the effect that life comes through union with her. These considerations have led many scholars to emend the text so that v. 11 follows v. 6.[8]

As Fox points out,[9] these verses seem to be advice given to those who themselves give advice. It tells them where to direct their energies and the consequences that they will reap if they try to advise a mocker.

Byargeon provides perhaps the most persuasive argument for the connection between these verses and the invitations that begin and end the chapter. As those two invitations provide a contrast and choice for the young son, so this section also sharply divides and describes the way of wisdom and the way of the fool (or mocker). In his opinion, vv. 1–6 and 13–18 are "illustrative," while here we have the "indicative" contrast. In other words, "each type of individual mentioned in 9:7–12 corresponds with the two women in Proverbs 9."[10]

Brown provocatively suggests that there is a connection between this material and parts of the prologue, particularly 1:5–7, in talking about the relevance of the material that follows for those who are already wise (1:5; 9:9) and giving another reminder that the fear of Yahweh is the beginning of wisdom/knowledge (1:7; 9:10). That this may provide a sense of closure is only muted by the fact that it appears in the middle of the chapter rather than at the end.[11]

---

[7]Those who discipline a mocker receive an insult;
    those who correct the wicked—they are blemished.
[8]Don't correct mockers, or else they will hate you,
    but correct the wise, and they will love you.
[9]Give to the wise, and they will be still wiser;
    inform the righteous, and they will add to their teaching.
[10]The beginning of wisdom is the fear of Yahweh,
    and the knowledge of the Holy One is understanding.
[11]For through me your days will be many;
    years of life will be added to you.

---

8. For instance, Clifford, *Proverbs*, 101–2.

9. Fox's rubric for these verses is "Advice to the Adviser," in *Proverbs 1–9*, 306.

10. Byargeon, "Structure and Significance of Proverbs 9:7–12," 373, though I do not think his literary arguments for the coherence of vv. 7–12 are that strong.

11. Brown, *Character in Crisis*, 42–43.

¹²If you are wise, you will make yourself wiser;
if you are a mocker, you will bear it alone.

While the connection between these six verses and the rest of the chapter is unclear, we can see themes that run throughout the six verses themselves. The first three verses (vv. 7–9) concern the danger of instructing a fool and the glory of instructing the wise. The first three cola warn people of the danger of trying to teach mockers, in particular trying to criticize (discipline or correct) them. Mockers respond to criticism with an attack; that, after all, is what mocking is—making fun of others, putting them down. The NT also warns us not to "give what is holy to dogs; and do not throw your pearls before swine, or they will trample them under foot and turn and maul you" (Matt. 7:6 NRSV).

As is taught in many places in the book (3:11–12; 10:17; 12:1; 15:10, 12; etc.), the ability to hear and respond in an honest way to criticism is crucial to positive personal growth. In a word, there is no growth in wisdom without acknowledgment of one's errors. If one does not listen to criticism and change, then one is doomed to perpetually repeat the same mistake.

Wise persons are humble enough to know that they are not perfect, and so they are willing to hear criticism. Indeed, they will love a person for the correction they receive because they know that it may keep them from making the same mistake again. Verse 9 underlines this fact and tells us that advice is not only for the naive and simpleminded but also for the wise. No one has reached the final plateau of wisdom. There is always more to learn.

Verse 10a nearly repeats the motto of the book, found in the preamble at 1:7. However, instead of "knowledge," this verse says that the "beginning of wisdom" is the fear of Yahweh. Though no two words are exactly synonymous, the meanings of "knowledge" and "wisdom" are essentially the same. For a fuller explanation, the commentary at 1:7a should be consulted. Briefly, fear is neither mere respect nor utter terror. It is something between the two. One fears a superior power, so to fear Yahweh means to acknowledge that Yahweh is vastly more powerful than oneself. It is to put oneself in a position that will elicit obedience. It is the beginning of wisdom, which suggests that there is no wisdom apart from Yahweh.

As mentioned in the introduction to this passage, v. 11 is unusual in its reversion to first-person speech. Who is speaking here? Up to this point the text refers to Yahweh in the third person. It could be the sage, but some,[12] and they have a point, connect the first-person speaker here

12. Clifford, *Proverbs*, 101–2; Waltke, *Proverbs*, 1:428, argues for a text-critical solution. On the basis of the Greek, Syriac, and Targum, he emends *bî* (through/by me) to *bāh*

with that heard in vv. 1–6. If so, then this is Woman Wisdom asserting that through herself long life comes. It is debatable whether this means that v. 11 has been misplaced and should be emended to occur right after v. 6 or whether this indicates that the whole section should be seen as a continuation of the teaching of Woman Wisdom.

Verse 12 concludes the section by coming back to an antithetical parallelism concerning wise people and mockers. Wisdom is the better route to take because things can only get better, whereas the mocker ends up alone. Mocking, after all, drives people away.

> ¹³Woman Folly is boisterous;
>   she is simpleminded but does not even know it.
> ¹⁴She sits at the doorway of her house,
>   on a seat at the heights of the city.
> ¹⁵She invites those who pass by on the path,
>   those going straight on their way.
> ¹⁶"Whoever is simpleminded—turn aside here,"
>   she says to those who lack heart.
> ¹⁷"Stolen water is sweet;
>   food eaten in secret is pleasant."
> ¹⁸But they do not know that the departed are there,
>   that those invited by her are in the depths of Sheol.

9:13–18. *Folly's invitation.* Earlier in the chapter, the actual reader, who must place him- or herself in the position of the son who is the implied reader, heard an invitation from a woman whose name is Wisdom. However, the last words of the book's first part, which encompass chaps. 1–9, are from a rival whose name is Folly.

While the introduction of Woman Wisdom included the fact that she is orderly and constructive, the narrator begins his description of Folly with the term "boisterous" (or "noisy," *hōmîyâ*). In a context like the present one, the word refers to a chaotic and disturbing noise (see Ps. 42:11 [12 MT]; 43:5; 46:6 [7 MT]). Earlier in Proverbs, the root was used to describe the promiscuous woman who desired to lure the young man off the proper path (7:11). In this, the latter might be considered the disciple of Woman Folly.

Her noise, or speaking, might be considered boisterous because she is, according to v. 13b, simpleminded or ignorant. She is so ignorant that she is not even aware of her ignorance. This means that when she does

---

(by it/her), which he understands and actually translates as "by wisdom." While this is possible—and he tries to explain the corruption by noting all the *yôd*'s in the context—it seems that the more difficult reading, the one hardest to explain, would be the more likely original reading. In other words, the versions may be emending *bî* to make the text read more smoothly.

speak, meaningless or even potentially harmful utterances will issue from her mouth. And indeed, this is the case in the invitation that she is quoted as speaking to the men passing by (vv. 16–17).

But first her location is revealed. It says that she is sitting at the doorway to her house. As opposed to Wisdom, whose ornate house is given some description, Folly's gets no real depiction. The fact that she is sitting while speaking may point to the fact that she is lazy. Interestingly and importantly, as we will discuss in the theological implications section, Woman Folly nevertheless also speaks from the "heights of the city," where a temple might be built (see vv. 3, 14).

Verse 15 names the location of those whom she invites to her home. They are those who are passing by her high habitation on the path/way. Frequently in Prov. 1–9 we have encountered the metaphor of the path as a reference to one's life journey. So her invitation comes to those who are living life; she speaks specifically to the "simpleminded." Verse 16, describing the addressees of her invitation, is identical to v. 4. In other words, Woman Folly appeals to the same immature group as Woman Wisdom. They are rivals for the attention of the same group of people, thus creating the need for a decision.

The last two verses, though, reveal the sham of Folly's invitation. Her meal appeals to the baser instincts of humans. The water is stolen, and the food is eaten in secret. The latter implies that there is something to hide, exactly what is not clear. Indeed, Judith McKinlay, quoting Lang, provides analogies supporting the idea that "stealthy savouring and delight of stolen food have long been 'part of the coded language of prostitutes.'"[13]

The very last verse of the section, though, shows the horrid consequences that will result from choosing the perhaps more appealing food of Folly. Those who accept Folly's invitation go expecting food that normally brings life and renewed energy but find death. Her other guests are "departed" ancestors (see discussion of *rěpā'îm* at 2:18 and 21:16). They are in Sheol, which minimally refers to the grave but likely implies the netherworld. In either case, the references to the departed ancestors (*rephaim*) and Sheol connect Folly's associates with death.

Theological Implications

The final chapter of the first part of Proverbs brings to culmination several major themes and demands that the reader make a fundamental

---

13. In this regard, she goes on to cite the Gilgamesh epic. See McKinlay, "To Eat or Not To Eat," especially 79.

life decision. Here and there in the first eight chapters, we have encountered the idea that there is a path on which we walk and that this path stands for one's life journey. Second, we have heard the voice of Woman Wisdom in 1:20–33. While Woman Folly is a new character in the drama of the book, her human counterpart, the "strange" and "foreign" woman, has anticipated her.

In spite of these precursors, however, in chap. 9 these themes come together in a way that presents the need for a decision. Both Woman Wisdom and Woman Folly issue invitations to the reader, who is supposed to identify with the son. With whom will the son/reader dine, Wisdom or Folly? Dining with a woman implies an intimate relationship, so we might ask more pointedly: Will Wisdom or Folly become an integral part of life?

Who is Wisdom? Wisdom is clearly a personification of Yahweh's attribute of wisdom. Perhaps the feminine nature of the verb *ḥokmâ* suggested the feminine metaphor of wisdom. More likely, wisdom was associated with women in the way that power was associated with men. After all, we hear about the wise woman of Tekoa (2 Sam. 14) and the Queen of Sheba (1 Kings 10). But we should also pay attention to the detail that Wisdom's house is built on the highest point of the city. In the ancient Near East, only one house is built on the high place of a city, and that is the temple. It is not a stretch, therefore, to suggest that Wisdom is not only the personification of Yahweh's wisdom but also of Yahweh himself.

If Wisdom is Yahweh, then who is Folly, who also has a house on the high point of the city? It is only consistent to start by saying that she is the personification of foolish thought and behavior, but more. She too represents deity, but in her case she stands for all the pagan gods and goddesses who desire to lure Israel away from the true God. She stands for Marduk, Baal, Ishtar, Anat, Asherah, Chemosh, Molech—and the list can go on and on.[14]

Again, the reader/son must make a choice, and this choice is fundamental for the exercise of wisdom. In the final analysis, there is no wisdom apart from a relationship with Woman Wisdom, meaning Yahweh. In this regard, this metaphor reinforces the point of the "motto" of the book: "The fear of Yahweh is the beginning of knowledge" (1:7).

There also is no middle road. One is either wise or foolish, associated with one or the other of the two women. Furthermore, as we move into

---

14. McKinlay's approach (*Gendering Wisdom*, 57) comes close or is similar to this idea, and she adds a provocative intrabiblical connection: "She [Folly] too calls from the heights of the town, where she has a seat. Again we see the possibility of connection with a temple cult, remembering that the women of Moab invited the Israelites to a cultic sacrifice and feast in Num. 25:1–22 [*sic*] and there was a sexual context to that invitation."

the second part of the book, chaps. 10–31, the very terms "wisdom" and "folly" and their numerous related terms are potent with theological meaning.

For instance, the first proverb of the following collection states:

> A wise son makes a father glad,
> and a foolish son is the sorrow of his mother.

We now recognize the theological meaning of a verse like this. It states that a son who makes a father (who stands for both parents) glad is wise. To be wise means that one acts like one who is in relationship with Yahweh. On the contrary, those who bring sorrow to the mother (again standing for both parents) show themselves to be fools, and that means they are acting like worshippers of pagan deities. In this way, the proverbs have important theological significance even when they do not explicitly name Yahweh or some well-known theological concept. Wisdom and folly themselves are such theological concepts.

Stallman is correct to think that the two houses of Wisdom and Folly stand behind Jesus's teaching that contrasts the house built by a wise person and the one built by a fool (Matt. 7:24–27//Luke 6:47–49).[15] The house built by wisdom withstands assault, while that by folly leads to destruction. In the introduction (see "Reading Proverbs in the Light of the New Testament"), we further explored the parallels between Jesus and Woman Wisdom.

---

15. Stallman, "Divine Hospitality," 128.

Part 2

Proverbs of Solomon: Collection I

(10:1–22:16)

Most of the rest of the book of Proverbs is composed of warnings, prohibitions, observations, and encouragements that are proverbs, strictly speaking. As explained in the introduction (see "The Structure of Proverbs"), it is my contention that these proverbs have no overarching arrangement but are rather random. Thus, I comment on these verses individually with only occasional reference to the immediately surrounding context. A synthesis of the various topics treated by these proverbs may be found in the appendix at the end of the commentary.

Chapter 10

Translation

[1]The proverbs of Solomon[a]—
A wise son makes a father glad,
    and a foolish son is the sorrow of his mother.
[2]The treasures of the wicked do not profit,
    but righteousness extricates from death.
[3]Yahweh will not let the righteous[b] starve,
    but he will push away the desire of the wicked.
[4]A slack palm makes poverty;
    a determined hand makes rich.
[5]An insightful son harvests in the summer;
    a disgraceful son sleeps during harvest.
[6]Blessings are on the head of the righteous,
    but the mouth of the wicked conceals violence.
[7]The memory of the righteous is a blessing,
    but the name of the wicked rots.
[8]The wise of heart grasps commands,
    but a dupe's lips are ruined.
[9]Those who walk in innocence walk confidently,[c]
    but those who twist their path are known.

a. The title "proverbs of Solomon" is missing in the LXX, Syriac, and some manuscripts of the Vulgate.

b. In colon 1 it is literally "the appetite of the righteous," though the English does not require appetite to be explicit in the translation. The Hebrew term *nepeš*, which literally means "throat," comes to mean the more intangible "appetite." Since the throat is also the means by which breath, necessary to life, passes, the word also carries the meaning of "soul/life," for which it is better known.

c. Or "safely." The Hebrew text of colon 1 is alliterative: *hôlēk batōm yēlek beṭaḥ*.

[10]A winking eye brings trouble,
  but those who reprimand with boldness bring peace.[d]
[11]A fountain of life is the mouth of the righteous,
  but the mouth of the wicked conceals violence.
[12]Hate arouses conflict,
  but love covers all offenses.
[13]Wisdom is found on understanding lips,
  but a rod is for the backs of those lacking heart.
[14]The wise store up knowledge,
  but the mouth of the dupe is imminent ruin.
[15]The riches of the wealthy are their strong city;
  the ruin of the poor is their poverty.
[16]The wages of the righteous tend toward life;
  the yield of the wicked tend toward sin.
[17]Those who guard discipline are on the way to life,
  and those who abandon correction wander aimlessly.
[18]Lying lips conceal hate,
  and those who spread slander are fools.
[19]In an abundance of words, wickedness does not cease;
  those who restrain their lips are insightful.
[20]Choice silver is the tongue of the righteous;
  the heart of the wicked is of little value.
[21]The lips of the righteous nourish many,
  but stupid people who lack heart will die.
[22]The blessing of Yahweh makes rich,
  and he adds no trouble with it.
[23]It is like sport for a fool to do a foul deed,
  so it is with wisdom to a competent person.
[24]The horrors of the wicked will come on them,
  but he grants the longings of the righteous.
[25]When a whirlwind passes by, the wicked are no more,
  but the righteous always have a firm foundation.
[26]Like vinegar to the teeth and smoke to the eyes,
  so are lazy people to those who send them.
[27]The fear of Yahweh increases days,
  but the years of the wicked will be cut short.
[28]The expectation of the righteous brings joy,
  but the hope of the wicked will perish.
[29]The path of Yahweh is a refuge for the innocent
  and ruin for the doers of evil.
[30]The righteous will never be shaken,
  but the wicked will not dwell in the land.
[31]The mouth of the wise grows wisdom,
  but the tongue of the perverse will be cut off.

d. The Hebrew text of the second colon is identical to 10:8b: "but a dupe's lips are ruined."
This in itself provides grounds for questioning its authenticity, but in addition it is hard to
see how such a text relates to the first colon. The LXX may preserve the original text.

³²The lips of the wise know what is acceptable,
   but the mouth of the wicked, perversities.

Interpretation

---

¹The proverbs of Solomon—
A wise son makes a father glad,
   and a foolish son is the sorrow of his mother.

10:1. The verse begins the second major section of the book, as is signaled by the opening topic heading (see 1:1). The topic heading is the same as the opening two words of the entire book. It makes one wonder whether the reader is supposed to understand that 1–9 were non-Solomonic. In any case, 10:1 clearly introduces a collection different from those chapters. No longer are there relatively long discourses of a father or Woman Wisdom to a son, but now we have an anthology of proverbs, for the most part randomly arranged. Even though chaps. 1–9 are of a different literary type and constitute a section separate from what follows in chaps. 10–31, we are to understand the theological message of those chapters as casting their long shadow across the individual proverbs in the second part of the book (see "The Structure of Proverbs" and "Theology of the Book" in the introduction). After those chapters, wisdom is associated with a relationship with the true God, and folly with rival deities.

The proverb in 10:1 is an observation that helps clarify who is wise and who is a fool. The statement calls for self-observation on the part of the son. The son must reflect on the type of response he elicits from his father and mother. What kinds of emotions do his actions, his speech, and his character evoke from his parents? This proverb illustrates the circumstantial nature of the proverbial truth. It clearly assumes that the parents are wise themselves. If the parents were fools, then their joy would be elicited by their child's evil, unrighteous behavior. Wise parents, in contrast, would be encouraged by the righteous behavior of their son but chagrined at his folly. This observation could also serve as motivation. Those who love their parents would be motivated to embrace wisdom in hopes of bringing joy to their parents' lives.

This proverb is a good illustration of an antithetical proverb, constructed in the main from antonyms (wise/foolish; glad/sorrow; father/mother). The same point is made by approaching it from its opposite sides. Interest is generated by a variation in morphology in the use of a verb in v. 1a ("makes glad"), which is paralleled by a noun ("sorrow") in v. 1b.

> ²The treasures of the wicked do not profit,
> but righteousness extricates from death.

10:2. At first glance, the connection between cola 1 and 2 seems tenuous. While "wicked" and "righteousness" are opposites and provide a kind of contrast between the two, the first colon appears to be about wealth, whereas the second does not. However, a closer look shows that the two parts of the verse are related and combine to say that there is something more valuable than wealth.

The first colon surprises because we would not expect the wicked to have treasures in the first place. Earlier and throughout, Proverbs teaches that the righteous are more likely than the wicked to have the good things of this world (as in 3:15–16; 10:22). Indeed, wealth is held out as a motivation for the pursuit of wisdom and its associated righteousness (14:24). But here we learn that wealth in the possession of the wicked provides them with no real benefit anyway. It is kind of a paradox, but treasures do not profit (see also 11:4). The second colon claims that righteousness, a quality of the wise, extricates from death; it may indicate precisely how the treasures of the wicked do not profit. They cannot save from death.

This leads to the question, How does the proverb understand how the righteous are extricated from death? The proverb could be read to say only that righteousness, associated with wisdom, keeps people out of situations that may lead to an untimely death; but, as Qoheleth pointed out, that is rather cold comfort since the wicked and the righteous both die, even the latter at an early age (Eccles. 7:15–18). It is not wise to be dogmatic on this matter, but unless we are willing to attribute to the proverb writer and its users an incredible blindness, it is hard to resist thinking in terms of a richer understanding of life (see "Afterlife" in the introduction).

> ³Yahweh will not let the righteous starve,
> but he will push away the desire of the wicked.

10:3. What the verse says is clear enough, almost too clear. This is a proverb that differentiates the righteous from the wicked in terms of their treatment from God. He protects the righteous; he does not care for the needs of the wicked. The first colon specifies care for the righteous in the area of sustenance, whereas the desire (*hawwâ*) that Yahweh pushed away from the wicked is a more general term for longing.

However, though the meaning of the proverb is clear, the urgent question is, What connection does it have with reality? Is it really true that the righteous are well cared for by God and the wicked are ignored? Can this proverb be used as a barometer for our relationship with God, so that if we starve, we must not really be true believers? Of course not. That viewpoint is totally undermined by the books of Job and Ecclesiastes (see "Reading within the Context of Ecclesiastes and Job" in the introduction). Proverbs are not promises; they are generally true principles, all other things being equal.

> 4A slack palm makes poverty;
> a determined hand makes rich.

10:4. This is the first of a number of proverbs in chaps. 10–31 that describe the contrast between laziness and hard work (among other places, see 6:6–11; 10:26; 12:11, 24; 24:30–34). In typical proverbial fashion, the point is made by reference to a specific body part, though two different Hebrew words are used to refer to it ("palm" and "hand"). This is a typical antithetical proverb with an observation on the consequences of laziness followed by an observation on the consequences of hard work. The former leads to poverty and the latter to wealth. This is a consistent message throughout the book of Proverbs.

> 5An insightful son harvests in the summer;
> a disgraceful son sleeps during harvest.

10:5. This proverb is a specific application of the more general principle of the previous verse and may well be placed in this context with the intention of having both read together. Insight is a quality of the wise; disgrace is a moral evaluation of the fool. The contrast is between an industrious son and a slacker. The diligent one works hard and presumably thrives, whereas the lazy son's actions will certainly lead to poverty and ultimately to hunger. Reflecting on 10:3, we may generally say that righteous persons would be diligent workers and would therefore not starve because of their work. Yahweh is the agent because it is Yahweh who invests a person with wisdom and the drive to succeed. Again, this works well, all things being equal.

> 6Blessings are on the head of the righteous,
> but the mouth of the wicked conceals violence.

10:6. On first reading, this proverb seems a bit unbalanced. The first colon talks about the rewards of the righteous, while the second colon warns of the dangers of the wicked. The connection between the two colons might be seen in the antithesis of righteous/wicked, and the mention of body parts (head/mouth).

The first colon associates blessings (*bĕrākôt*) with the righteous. In particular, the proverb places blessings, perhaps like a crown, on the head of the righteous. The word "blessing" is associated with the covenant in the book of Deuteronomy. Indeed, one aspect of being righteous is being in covenant relationship with God (see "Theology of the Book" and "Covenant and Wisdom" in the introduction), and that book, particularly Deut. 28, may aid us in understanding the nature of the good things that the proverb believes come as a reward to the righteous. Deuteronomy 28:2 announces that "all these blessings will come upon you and accompany you if you obey the LORD your God" (NIV). These include the gifts of children, agricultural plenty, and military victory (see 28:3–14).

One might expect that the second colon would speak of the curses upon the wicked, but instead it identifies a vice of the wicked. Perhaps by naming the vice it implies why the wicked do not share in the blessings of the righteous. It may serve as a warning to the righteous to beware of the deception of the wicked. The statement about the wicked claims that the speech of the wicked produces harmful effects. Again, the wisdom teachers of Israel fully understand that language is more than mere words but has real effects in the world. Equally important is the warning that the violent intentions of the wicked are not on the surface but rather are hidden and thus are even more dangerous. Notice that Prov. 10:6b is repeated in v. 11b (see also v. 18a).

---

⁷The memory of the righteous is a blessing,
but the name of the wicked rots.

10:7. That there is a clear association of this proverb with the previous one is obvious. We observe the same antithesis between righteous and wicked as well as the recurrence of the root "blessing," this time in the singular. However, in this case there is a much clearer sense of balance between the two cola. Here, "memory" balances "name" as near synonyms, and "righteous" and "wicked" as antonyms. "Blessing" and "rots" play off each other as well, though one is a noun and the other a verb.

This proverb may specify the type of blessing that the previous proverb has in mind, though it would be a mistake to understand the blessings of v. 6 to be exhausted by the idea of remembrance. That remembrance was important to the wisdom teachers is underlined when one reads Ecclesiastes, where his conclusion that the wise are not remembered leads him to such depressing conclusions (Eccles. 1:11; 2:16; 9:5, 15).

But it is not just remembrance that is at issue. The second colon implies that the wicked are also remembered but that their memory stinks. "Name" implies more than identity, and the Hebrew term *šēm* could just as easily be translated "reputation."

> 8The wise of heart grasps commands,
> but a dupe's lips are ruined.

10:8. As in 10:6, we have antonyms in the types of people (wise/dupe) and body parts (heart/lip), but here the connection between the first and second cola is more obvious. The wise person heeds the call of Prov. 2 and receives God's commands (see 2:1). Why are the lips of the dupe (*ĕwîl*) ruined? The implication is that they, unlike the wise, have not grasped the commands, and therefore what they say will rebound negatively on them.

> 9Those who walk in innocence walk confidently,
> but those who twist their path are known.

10:9. The first part of Proverbs has many allusions to the metaphor of life as a path (beginning with the discourse in 1:8–19). This proverb is an observation on the difference between those who live openly and honestly and those who live deceptively. "Innocence" (*tōm*, see 2:7) is a relative term in the OT. The point of the verse seems to be that an easy conscience allows one to live life openly and with boldness. The second colon issues a warning to those who live deceptive, evil lives that they pass off as innocent. The warning is that, though they try to hide it, their evil will be found out. They do not have the moral foundation to live with openness and confidence. The proverb does not specify how those who are deceptive will be discovered; it assumes that evil behavior cannot be hidden forever.

> 10A winking eye brings trouble,
> but those who reprimand with boldness bring peace.

10:10. This translation follows the Septuagint in the second colon (see translation footnote). The verse contrasts something that brings trouble with something that brings peace. The expression "winking eye" is obscure to us because such a gesture probably had a meaning embedded in the culture and thus lost. Perhaps a clue may be gained by the contrast with something that happens "with boldness." A winking eye may simply refer to a secret signal rather than an open rebuke (see also 6:13; 16:30). Some have further suggested that the gesture has a magical significance,[1] like putting a hex on someone. Both cola presume that someone is doing something that is displeasing or wrong, and then present a wrong strategy and a right strategy to deal with the situation. The verse thus encourages straightforwardness in dealing with a problem rather than secretive responses. The proverb may be a reminder to people who try to solve problems by avoiding conflicts that often it is better to approach a difficult situation head on.

> [11]A fountain of life is the mouth of the righteous,
> but the mouth of the wicked conceals violence.

10:11. As a fountain spews forth refreshing water (for this image, see also Ps. 36:9 [10 MT]; Prov. 13:14; 14:27; 16:22), so the mouth of the righteous person utters life-giving words. These might be words of encouragement or of rebuke to correct the errors of another. The life-giving words of the righteous are contrasted with the words of the wicked, which are associated with violence, a word suggesting death. As in the previous verse, where winking suggests deception, here is the idea that the violence in the words of the wicked are concealed, and therefore in that sense they are deceptive. Note that 10:11b repeats 10:6b.

> [12]Hate arouses conflict,
> but love covers all offenses.

10:12. This proverb contrasts the effects of hate and love. Whereas hate leads to social estrangement, love overcomes even the things that might separate people ("offenses"). Offenses are actions associated with the fool in Proverbs (12:13). The related verbal form of "offense" is found in 18:19 and in parallel with conflict, showing that the two are in the same semantic realm, as two ways in which social division takes place.

The word "conflict" (*mādôn*) occurs almost exclusively in the book of Proverbs. God hates conflict (6:16–19). It is associated with unsavory characters like the mocker (22:10) or those who are characterized by hate, as here. The word is used a number of times for the cantankerous wife (19:13; 21:9, 19; 25:24; 27:15). Here love is presented as an antidote to conflict. This proverb is an observation that both explains behavior and implicitly recommends the way of love. Readers of the NT are reminded of the statement on love in 1 Cor. 13.

---

1. For instance, see the argument of Bryce, "Omen-Wisdom." However, in our opinion, it is just as plausible to understand the action of the eye to be a secret signal, a gesture, rather than an omen.

> ¹³Wisdom is found on understanding lips,
>   but a rod is for the backs of those lacking heart.

10:13. The proverb contrasts those who have understanding lips with those who lack heart. Understanding lips belong to those who speak wisdom. On the other hand, the "heart" in Hebrew is connected to character, sometimes with an emphasis on cognitive abilities. While wisdom helps those who have it avoid some of life's pitfalls, the folly of those who lack heart will lead to pain. The reference to the rod may also indicate the kind of physical punishment that was doled out to those who did not get the lesson (see 13:24; 14:3; 22:8, 15; 23:13, 14; 29:15; and the closely related 26:3).

The "heart" in Hebrew conception was similar to what today we would call character. It is true that sometimes "heart" emphasizes the cognitive and is properly rendered "mind." But in this expression, to lack heart does not mean to be unintelligent, but rather to lack character.

> ¹⁴The wise store up knowledge,
>   but the mouth of the dupe is imminent ruin.

10:14. Through the instructional process, the wise accumulate wisdom. It is stored up for future use, when the need arises. They do not learn for the moment but in preparation for the future. That this knowledge will lead to the preservation of the wise person is implied by the contrast of the ruin that will come to the dupe (*ĕwîl*, one of a number of words used to refer to the fool). The source of this ruin is the mouth. In other words, the speech of the dupe gets them into trouble. Perhaps they say the wrong thing at the wrong time. This observation helps one know a dupe from a wise person and also encourages the hearer to cultivate wisdom rather than folly. According to Clifford, there is also a contrast here between the storing up of wisdom and the spewing out of folly. The wise person tends to use words sparingly, while the fool babbles on and on.[2]

> ¹⁵The riches of the wealthy are their strong city;
>   the ruin of the poor is their poverty.

10:15. As wealth and poverty are contrasted, this proverb shows that wealth is to be preferred to poverty. The point of comparing wealth to a strong city is to highlight how wealth can protect one against the dangers of life. A strong city can keep an invader out, so wealth can keep problems at bay. To give modern examples, we might begin with a plumbing

2. Clifford, *Proverbs*, 114.

emergency. If a pipe bursts, no problem. Just pay a plumber to fix it. If a lawsuit threatens, no problem. Just hire a better lawyer than the plaintiff, and if one loses, there is more money to pay the person anyway! On the other hand, if a pipe bursts in the home of the poor, what are they to do? Wealth means having shelter and plenty of food, but not so for the poor; they could starve to death. Clifford points out that the word "ruin" in colon 2 is used of a ruined city in Ps. 89:40 (41 MT) and provides a neat contrast with "strong city" in colon 1.[3]

This proverb is positive about wealth and fits in with others like 10:22, which says that it comes from Yahweh's blessing; and 3:15–16, which makes it clear that it is the wise to whom God grants such blessings. Indeed, 14:24 suggests that not only is wealth associated with the wise, but also fools should expect only more foolishness, not wealth.

As we proceed through the book of Proverbs, we will note that this is not the only perspective that the book has on wealth and poverty. Proverbs 11:18; 13:11; and 21:6 suggest that the wicked may get rich as well, but it will only be temporary and will not be the strong defense that our present proverb contemplates. The circumstantial nature of the truth of this proverb is pointed out by comparing 18:11: "The riches of the wealthy are their strong city and like a high wall in their imagination." In 18:10 the name of Yahweh is a strong tower; in comparison, one's wealth is an imaginary defense. Wealth does not always provide the help that one imagines it to have. Perhaps the lawsuit takes away all the money and leaves the person impoverished.

16The wages of the righteous tend toward life;
the yield of the wicked tend toward sin.

10:16. The contrast in this proverb is between the consequences of the gain of the righteous and the wicked respectively. The righteous and the wicked are the wise and the fool, described by their ethics. The term "wages" is a noun form of the verb *pʿl*, "to act, do, make, accomplish"; but in its nominal forms (here *pĕʿullâ*) it can mean wages or payment (so *NIDOTTE* 3:646–47). This verse assumes that both the righteous and the wicked may gain some material substance, but contrasts the value that it has for them. Money in the hand of the righteous person is a positive thing, but money in the hand of a wicked person is a negative thing. The contrast in consequences is interesting and somewhat unexpected. The natural contrast would be between life and death, but here it is between

---

3. Ibid., 114–15.

life and sin,[4] the latter certainly associated with the forces of death, a point that will not escape Paul much later (see below).

The idea is that the righteous will use it for things that enhance life, whereas the wicked will apply their wealth toward things that harm life. One can think of many examples of the latter, including obsessive gambling, overeating, using prostitutes, or drinking too much. However, there is a purpose why the proverb remains unspecified. It can be any of a number of things. The same is true for the way the wages of the righteous lead toward life. The principle could be illustrated by acts of philanthropy, paying for education that broadens the mind, enrichment programs for one's children, or, again, any number of things.

One wonders whether this verse lies behind Paul's famous saying: "The wages of sin is death, but the free gift of God is eternal life in Christ Jesus our Lord" (Rom. 6:23 NRSV).[5]

> [17]Those who guard discipline are on the way to life,
>   and those who abandon correction wander aimlessly.

10:17. As translated above, the proverb teaches that learning from one's mistakes is a key to gaining wisdom. One must heed the discipline/correction administered by one's teachers in order to mature (see "Learning from Mistakes" under "The Sources of Wisdom" in the introduction). This proverb contrasts those who do the right thing and learn from their mistakes with those who try to live oblivious to constructive criticism. The path/way image is used here for one's life, and those who guard discipline enhance their lives; those who reject correction wander about as if they have no goal.

Recognizing that the main verb of colon 2 is hiphil, it is possible[6] to translate this proverb in a slightly different way, which leads to another understanding of its meaning:

> Those who guard discipline are the way to life,
>   and those who abandon correction lead astray.

In this case, rather than understanding the verse as saying that a lack of discipline harms that individual, it goes further and says that such people also lead others astray.[7]

---

4. Though Clifford (*Proverbs*, 114) argues that *ḥaṭṭāʾt* here means not "sin" but "want."

5. See comments by Van Leeuwen, "Proverbs," 111.

6. Waltke (*Proverbs*, 1:465) recognizes that the hiphil may be taken either as "wanders aimlessly" or "leads astray," but he prefers the latter.

7. So McKane, *Proverbs*, 419.

> [18]Lying lips conceal hate,
> and those who spread slander are fools.

10:18. The proverb begins by implicitly criticizing those who keep their hatred of another from that person. Such people by definition are liars since they do not express their dislike for the other person. Colon 2, however, intensifies the offense since slanderers may continue to conceal their hate from the object of their hate, but they say negative things about that person to others. Proverbs understands that it is important to be open and honest with one's words. If there is a legitimate gripe about something, the wise person will rebuke the other, with the purpose of helping and restoring relationship. Here, however, there is no intention other than to hurt, belittle, or demean the other person. Through such actions, relationships are destroyed.

The Septuagint reads the first colon more positively: "He who conceals hatred has righteous lips." It would then teach the value of repression of anger in order to retain relationship. A further argument in support is that it seems to present a stronger antithetical parallelism in keeping with the majority of forms in the immediate context. However, in the final analysis, it is safer to retain the MT and consider the Greek text (and the Hebrew text behind it) as the less difficult reading, which arose as a scribe tried to "fix" the parallelism.

> [19]In an abundance of words, wickedness does not cease;
> those who restrain their lips are insightful.

10:19. Proverbs consistently teaches that fewer words are better than many words (see also 13:3; 17:28). Words are powerful and should be uttered circumspectly. The more one says, the more problems may arise. The wise person, here called insightful, is one who chooses words very carefully. The time and situation must be right for the words that are spoken. In addition, Proverbs teaches that speech must follow reflection about the impact of one's words; blurting out an answer is considered total folly (15:28).

> [20]Choice silver is the tongue of the righteous;
> the heart of the wicked is of little value.

10:20. The proverb comments on the respective value of the speech/character of the righteous and the wicked. The verse has a chiastic structure in that the references to body parts (tongue and heart) are in the middle of the verse and connected to the contrasted pair righteous/ wicked. The verse is then framed by evaluative phrases.

In Proverbs, "tongue" (or some other word for speech) is often paired with "heart" (see 16:23; 26:23, 24–26). The idea seems to be that words can reflect what is going on inside, and here the heart stands for one's core personality or character (see 3:1).

The tongue of the righteous person is like choice silver because it expresses wisdom. The speech of the righteous helps people out and leads them toward life. On the other hand, the heart of the wicked is worthless, which implies that their speech is also without value.

> ²¹The lips of the righteous nourish many,
> but stupid people who lack heart will die.

10:21. Again the contrast is between the wise/righteous, whose behavior leads to enriched life, and the fools (stupid people)/wicked, whose behavior leads to death. And again, the contrast is drawn by contrasting two body parts, here lips and heart. The lips stand for the speech, or words, of the righteous. What the righteous say to others encourages, edifies, builds them up. The verb "nourish" is often translated "to shepherd" in other contexts. The picture the proverb draws is of the righteous person guiding listeners to refreshing pastures. They do this not just for themselves or even for one other person, but for many. The righteous, thus, build community.

On the other hand, the "dupe" (*ʾĕwîl*)—another term for the fool who is associated with wickedness—not only does not help others but actually will die. Why? Because of "lack of heart." As mentioned in reference to v. 20, the heart is the core personality (see 3:1); dupes have nothing inside to share with others or even to sustain themselves. They lack character; see also 10:13.

The Septuagint (*epistatai*) and the Vulgate (*erudiunt*) suggest that some form of *ydʿ* stood in the place of the verb "to nourish." The evidence is not strong, though it is supported by some Hebrew manuscripts, but would produce: "The lips of the righteous grant knowledge to many."

> ²²The blessing of Yahweh makes rich,
> and he adds no trouble with it.

10:22. Taken alone, this proverb is amazing indeed. It says that the blessing of Yahweh comes with wealth and no trouble. Perhaps it is taking the proverbs that associate wealth with God's blessing (other proverbs are 3:9–10, 15–16; 10:15, 16; 14:24) literally and absolutely that led to the existential struggles of the psalmist in Ps. 73 and raised the issues of retribution that needed to be dealt with in the books of Job and Ecclesiastes. But as Ray Van Leeuwen had pointed out so well, Proverbs does not speak monolithically on the subject of wealth and God's blessing.[8] A number of proverbs imply that one may have to chose between wisdom and wealth (15:16, 17; 16:8, 16; 17:1; 22:1; 28:6), and the fool can have riches, even if only temporarily (11:18; 13:11; 21:6). The present proverb is an aspect of the truth, not the whole truth. All things being equal, those who are blessed by God, and presumably associated with wisdom, will be rich. After all, the wise are hard workers, not lazy. They do not fritter their wealth away on meaningless luxuries. However, things are not always equal, and injustice (13:23), among other things, can enter the picture. In any case, it is better to be wise, and it is more likely that people will succeed in life if they live in conformity with the way God created the world. The proverb also should lead the godly rich to look not at their own efforts but rather to God for the reason for their well-being.

Some commentators and translations take the word translated "trouble" as "toil" and render the colon as "and toil adds nothing to it" (see NRSV footnote; and Murphy, *Proverbs*, 70, 75). However, this would seem an odd thought in a book that encourages hard work.

> [23]It is like sport for a fool to do a foul deed,
> so it is with wisdom to a competent person.

10:23. The proverb contrasts what brings pleasure to a fool and to a wise person, here referred to by a closely related word, "competence" (see 2:2). The word "sport" may also be translated "pleasure" or "laughter." The idea is that doing evil is something that fools actually relish, not something that circumstances force on them. The noun "foul deed" (*zimmâ*), like *mĕzimmâ*, is formed from the verb *zmm*, "to plan, purpose, devise." Although *mĕzimmâ* can have a positive connotation, *zimmâ* rarely does (according to *NIDOTTE* 3:1113, only at Job 17:11). An evil deed is something that disrupts community.

The proverb suggests that there is something in fools that makes evil a natural outflow of their character,[9] and then it compares this with wisdom in the lives of competent persons. As Murphy (*Proverbs*, 75) points out, things like justice bring "joy" (*simḥâ*) to a righteous person (21:15).

> [24]The horrors of the wicked will come on them,
> but he grants the longings of the righteous.

8. Van Leeuwen, "Wealth and Poverty."

9. As Clifford (*Proverbs*, 116) puts it, "What gives pleasure is a good indication of character."

10:24. This proverb contrasts the wicked and the righteous in terms of what they will get out of life. Everyone has fears and desires, but this verse intends to motivate toward righteous behavior and away from wicked behavior by saying that the wicked will get what they fear and not what they desire, and vice versa for the righteous.

Colon 2 implies that it is Yahweh who grants the longings of the righteous,[10] but no agent is specified for how the horrible things the wicked fear will happen to them. Perhaps this intends to remove God from being the source of such horrible things, or perhaps we are to read the divine agent back into the first colon. In either case, there appears to be no doubt that ultimately both the wicked and the righteous get what they deserve.

It is safe to presume that the longings of the righteous conform to the divine will. People who had other longings would not be themselves righteous. The horrors (*mĕgôrâ*) of the wicked are not the same as the fear (*yirʾat*) of Yahweh held by the righteous (1:7). The horror of the wicked could be their fear of punishment as the other two uses of this noun seem to suggest (Ps. 34:4 [5 MT]; Isa. 66:4).

---

²⁵When a whirlwind passes by, the wicked are no more,
but the righteous always have a firm foundation.

10:25. Like the previous proverbs, this one contrasts the wicked and the righteous. It would be hard to imagine that the whirlwind would be understood to be only literal. Certainly, it would be a ridiculous observation to state that after a heavy storm only the wicked were harmed. Only those who have never experienced such a storm could imagine that. The idea must be that the wicked will not weather trouble of any sort ("the storms of life"),[11] while the righteous have roots that help them survive catastrophes. Most commentators[12] rightly point out the similarity in thought with Matt. 7:24–27:

> Therefore everyone who hears these words of mine and puts them into practice is like a wise man who built his house on the rock. The rain came down, the streams rose, and the winds blew and beat against that house; yet it did not fall, because it had its foundations on the rock. But everyone who hears these words of mine and does not put them into practice is like a foolish man who built his house on sand. The rain came down, the

---

10. Van Leeuwen ("Proverbs," 112) reads the passive "will be granted" rather than the active and thus removes the divine agency. Such a move would depend on the LXX and imply a revocalization of the verb, which seems unnecessary to me.
11. Ibid., 112.
12. See also Beardslee, "Uses of the Proverb," 65.

streams rose, and the winds blew and beat against that house, and it fell with a great crash. (NIV)

See also Prov. 12:7: "The wicked are overturned and are no more, but the house of the righteous will endure."

---

[26]Like vinegar to the teeth and smoke to the eyes,
so are lazy people to those who send them.

10:26. This proverb is an observation built on a simile. The key to its interpretation is to unpack the two analogies to lazy people sent on a task. Most people have had smoke in their eyes at some point in their lives and know the experience to be irritating and painful[13] as well as debilitating. The experience of vinegar on the teeth is a bit harder to describe particularly since we are not certain exactly what vinegar was like in ancient Israel. However, since the noun is constructed from a verb (*ḥmṣ*) that means "to be sour," we get the general idea.

The sages were particularly rough on lazy persons as the epitome of foolish behavior (6:6–11; 10:4; 12:11, 24; 24:30–34; etc.). They are at their most vivid and sarcastic best as they ridicule them. Of course, those who employ lazy persons or ask them to do a task are going to be bitterly disappointed. Their laziness will certainly delay them if not keep them from doing the task at all.

---

[27]The fear of Yahweh increases days,
but the years of the wicked will be cut short.

10:27. The fear of Yahweh is at the foundation of wisdom, according to 1:7 (see also 14:26–27; 15:16, 33; 16:6; 19:23; 22:4), so again, this proverb contrasts the fate of the wise, who are righteous, with that of fools who are wicked. One who fears Yahweh will act in a way that conforms to his will, but those who do not (the wicked) will ignore his commands. Everything being equal, living in a way that conforms to God's will results in a longer life. After all, such a one lives in conformity with the way God set the world up at creation. To take one example, the law and wisdom in Proverbs insist that it is God's desire that sex be enjoyed within the commitment of marriage. The fools who ignore this command bring great danger on their lives, whether from sexually transmitted diseases (known in antiquity) or from the revenge of the other woman's husband (6:30–35). Though not specified by the proverb, it is also possible that Yahweh himself will cut short the days of the wicked, either through

---

13. Van Leeuwen ("Proverbs," 112) suggests that vinegar on teeth that have not been treated by modern dentistry and are thus broken would cause significant pain.

human means or by direct intervention. The purpose of this proverb is to motivate people toward fear of Yahweh. Since all things are not equal and therefore sometimes God-fearers die young, Van Leeuwen perceptively states: "The problem's ultimate resolution requires a developed view of life after death."[14]

> **28**The expectation of the righteous brings joy,
> but the hope of the wicked will perish.

10:28. The fate of the righteous and the wicked are again contrasted. Both the righteous and the wicked have hope for the future, but when the future comes, the wicked's hope is dashed, while the righteous experience joy because what they expected comes to pass. This may be seen as a general statement, with the previous verse as an illustration. Both righteous and wicked hope for long lives, but the years of the wicked are cut short, and thus their hope is destroyed. On the other hand, the days of those who fear Yahweh, who are righteous, are lengthened, and therefore their hope leads to happiness. Again, the purpose of the book is to motivate toward righteous behavior and away from wicked actions. See a similar idea in 10:24.

> **29**The path of Yahweh is a refuge for the innocent
> and ruin for the doers of evil.

10:29. This proverb picks up on the path metaphor that is frequently encountered in the first part of the book.[15] Typically, there is a contrast drawn between two paths: the straight path, provided by Yahweh, leads to life; and the other, a crooked path, leads to death. Reading the proverb in the light of previous descriptions of the path, we would have to say that the reason the path of Yahweh is a ruin for those who do evil is that they are not on it. On the other hand, the "innocent," here used as yet another term to refer to the godly wise, find that they are protected, presumably from life's problems, including those perpetrated by doers of evil. See Ps. 27:1 for God as refuge. The path refers to life's path, and the proverb comments on the fate of those who follow Yahweh, in contrast to those who do not, and thus relates to the previous two verses.

> **30**The righteous will never be shaken,
> but the wicked will not dwell in the land.

14. Ibid., 113.

15. Less likely is the idea that the path of Yahweh is a reference to "Yahweh's way of acting"; see Clifford, *Proverbs*, 117.

10:30. This is the fourth and last proverb in a row that contemplates the fate of the righteous and the wicked, though at times different related terms are used to refer to these two diametrically opposed groups. Here the question is relative stability. While the righteous will never be shaken, the wicked will be expelled from the land. When negated, the verb "to be shaken" (from *môṭ*) indicates tremendous security. When one is shaken, it is the result of great trouble. On the other hand, the wicked will live lives of instability. In particular, they will not be allowed to grow roots in the land. The land implied by this statement is, of course, the promised land, Israel. We have seen this threat leveled against the wicked already in 2:21–22 (see also the related thought in 10:25). This proverb draws a relatively rare explicit connection between proverbial wisdom and land theology.[16] The principle behind this proverb is developed at greater length in Ps. 37.

> [31]The mouth of the wise grows wisdom,
> but the tongue of the perverse will be cut off.

10:31. A contrast is drawn between the wise and the foolish (here called the perverse [*tahpukôt*], for which see comments on 2:12, 14). The focus of attention is on their respective speech, here represented by the organs of speech, mouth and tongue (paired also in 15:2; 21:23; 26:28; 31:26). The wise are praised because their speech is wise and thus has the effect of wisdom in general—promoting life and avoiding death. The verb (*nûb*) used is relatively rare, occurring only three times in the Hebrew Bible, and creates an interesting metaphor. According to *NIDOTTE* 3:52, it is related to an Aramaic noun for "fruit" (as well as a Hebrew noun, *nîb*, as in Isa. 57:19) and means "grow" or "prosper" (Ps 62:10 [11 MT] and here) in the qal, and "prosper" or "thrive" in the polel (Zech. 9:17).

As for the tongue of the perverse, it meets an appropriate fate when it is cut off (see also Ps. 12:3 [4 MT]). Of course, the literal meaning of the verb makes perfect and vivid sense, though it should be added that nowhere does OT law allow for this in practice.[17] "To be cut off" is used throughout the Hebrew Bible to refer to punishment for unethical and uncovenantal behavior.

> [32]The lips of the wise know what is acceptable,
> but the mouth of the wicked, perversities.

---

16. It is tenuous, in my opinion, to connect the land in this proverb with the concept of the "land of the living," a phrase not found in the book of Proverbs; but see Murphy, *Proverbs*, 76.

17. Garrett, *Proverbs*, 123.

10:32. As in the previous verse, we have the contrast between wisdom and perversity associated with speech, again represented by organs of speech (in this case the lips and the mouth). The verb "know" does double duty by means of ellipsis, so that the lips of the wise know what is acceptable and the mouths of the wicked know perversities. This is the use of "know" (*ydᶜ*) in the sense of experience. Through practice comes experience. The speech of the wise is practiced in wisdom, and thus it comes naturally from them; the mouths of the wicked are practiced in perversities. For perversities, see 2:12, 14.

The noun *rāṣôn* is here translated by the phrase "what is acceptable." In reference to God, the noun means "divine favor," but the idea here is that what the wise say is appropriate for the circumstances and will win the approval of God and other wise people.[18]

It appears that the versions struggled with the idea of lips "knowing" and sometimes suggest alternative understandings. The Septuagint translates *apostazei* (to drip, flow) for the verb here and for *nwb* in the previous verse. Other Greek versions have *gnōsontai*, which affirms the MT.

---

18. Clifford (*Proverbs*, 118) takes his cue from the use of *rāṣôn* elsewhere in Proverbs to suggest that not the approval of other people is meant but rather the approval of God and king. I find it dubious to import the meaning of other proverbs back into this particular occurrence. It unhelpfully restricts the application of this proverb.

Chapter 11

Translation

¹Fraudulent scales are an abomination to Yahweh,
   but an accurate weight brings his favor.
²When insolence comes, then shame will come,
   but wisdom with modesty.
³The innocence of those with integrity guides them,
   but the duplicity of the faithless devastates them.
⁴Riches do not profit on the day of fury,
   but righteousness will extricate from death.
⁵The righteousness of the innocent will make their path straight,
   but the wicked will fall in their wickedness.
⁶The righteousness of those with integrity will extricate them,
   but those who are faithless will be caught by their desires.
⁷When a wicked person dies, hope perishes;
   yes, expectation based on money perishes.
⁸The righteous person is delivered from distress,
   but the wicked will take his place.
⁹By their mouth, the godless destroy their neighbors,
   but by the knowledge of the righteous, they are delivered.
¹⁰When the righteous flourish, a city rejoices,
   and when the wicked perish, there is shouting for joy.
¹¹By the blessing of those with integrity a city is exalted,
   and by the mouth of the wicked, it is demolished.
¹²He who despises his neighbor lacks heart,
   but a competent person stays silent.
¹³A slanderer goes about revealing secrets;[a]
   a reliable spirit covers up a word.

a. The first colon is similar to 20:19a.

¹⁴In the absence of guidance, a people will fall,
  but there is victory in an abundance of counselors.
¹⁵It will be big trouble for anyone who puts up security for a stranger;
  the one who hates making financial agreements is secure.
¹⁶A graceful woman takes hold of honor,
  but violent men take hold of wealth.
¹⁷People characterized by covenant love benefit themselves,
  but cruel people harm their own bodies.
¹⁸Those who do wicked deeds get false wages;
  those who sow righteous deeds get a reliable payment.
¹⁹Indeed, righteousness heads toward life,
  and those who pursue evil head toward death.
²⁰Those with a crooked heart are an abomination to Yahweh,
  but those who are innocent on the path bring his favor.
²¹Surely the evil person will not go unpunished,
  but the seed of the righteous will escape.
²²A gold ring in the nose of a pig;
  a beautiful woman who eschews discretion.
²³The longings of the righteous, surely good;
  the hope of the wicked, fury.[b]
²⁴There is one who gives freely yet gains more,
  but one who withholds what is due will surely become needy.
²⁵Those who bless will themselves be refreshed,[c]
  and those who satisfy others will themselves be satisfied.[d]
²⁶People will curse those who withhold grain,
  but blessing on the head of those who sell it.
²⁷Those who strive for good find favor;
  those who seek evil, it will come to them.
²⁸Those who trust in their wealth will fall,
  but the righteous will blossom like foliage.
²⁹Those who harm their house inherit wind,
  and a dupe is a servant to the wise of heart.
³⁰The fruit of the righteous is the tree of life,
  and the wise[e] gather[f] lives.[g]

b. "Fury" is based on the LXX, which, influenced by the parallel in 10:28, reads ʿābādâ. Some emend to "perished," but this seems to be a harmonizing gloss.

c. The verb dšn literally means "to be fat," but often can mean "to refresh."

d. The verb "to be satisfied" is from rwh, "to be saturated" or "to be sated." The first use is a participial form, while the second occurrence is that of an "Aramaicized biform of hophal imperfect" (*NIDOTTE* 3:1069).

e. The Greek and the Syriac may suggest ḥāmās (violence) instead of ḥākām (wise).

f. This meaning of lqḥ is to be preferred to others on the basis of its consistency with the metaphor of the tree of life in colon 1. See W. H. Irwin, "Metaphor in Prov 11,30." Snell ("'Taking Souls'") argues an old position of Qimḥi that the verb lqḥ can mean "comprehend," so "one who comprehends souls is wise."

g. Codex Leningradensis reads něpāśôt rather than něpāšôt (with śîn rather than šîn), but the latter must surely be right, as is attested by many other Hebrew manuscripts and the editions.

³¹If the righteous are paid back on earth,
how much more the wicked and sinners?

Interpretation

¹Fraudulent scales are an abomination to Yahweh,
but an accurate weight brings his favor.

11:1. This proverb applies the book's teaching on honesty and deception to business practices. The point is concrete and clear: Yahweh hates
cheats and loves those who charge what is fair. The term translated
"fraudulent" here (*mirmâ*) is used elsewhere in Proverbs (12:5, 17, 20;
14:8, 25; 20:23; 26:18–19, 24) to indicate deceit. That God hates any
kind of dissimulation may be seen in the strong teaching against lying
(6:16–19; 13:5; 14:5, 25; 25:18). The phrase "abomination to Yahweh"
(*tô'ăbat Yhwh*) is used a number of times in the book (3:32; 11:20; 12:22;
15:8, 9, 26; 16:5; 17:15; 20:10, 23) to indicate the utmost divine censure
against something. It offends Yahweh's "ritual or moral order."[1] The list
of abominable things includes "perversity, misrepresentation, deceit,
hypocrisy, wickedness, and pride."[2] As Van Leeuwen points out, the
language of the phrase "echoes Israel's legal codes (Lev. 19:35–37; Deut.
25:13–15) and the prophetic condemnation of commercial greed and
deception (Ezek. 45:10; Hos. 12:7–8; Amos 8:5; Mic. 6:11)."[3]

The scale here described had two plates suspended from a bar of
some sort. On one was a premeasured "weight" (the word *'eben* literally means "stone"), over against which the product would be balanced.
Such a system could be fraudulently manipulated in a variety of ways,
one imagines, including falsely labeling the weight.

The term here translated "favor" (*rāṣôn*) was rendered as "acceptable" in 10:32. In this verse "favor" is called for by its clear connection
with Yahweh.

See the related proverb in 16:11.

Commentators point out that Egyptian wisdom also registers the
distaste of the gods for crooked business practices. An example includes
the following from Amenemope:

Do not move the scales nor alter the weights,
Nor diminish the fractions of the measure;

1. *NIDOTTE* 4:314.
2. Ibid., 4:317.
3. Van Leeuwen, "Proverbs," 117.

Do not desire a measure of the fields,
Nor neglect those of the treasury.
The Ape sits by the balance,
His heart is in the plummet;
Where is a god as great as Thoth,
Who invented these things and made them?
Do not make for yourself deficient weights;
They are rich in grief through the might of god.
If you see someone who cheats,
Keep your distance from him.
Do not covet copper,
Disdain beautiful linen;
What good is one dressed in finery,
If he cheats before the god?
Faience disguised as gold,
Comes day, it turns to lead. (chaps. 16–17)[4]

---

²When insolence comes, then shame will come,
but wisdom with modesty.

11:2. In a number of places in Proverbs (3:5, 7; 6:17; 11:14; 25:6–7; etc.), fools are associated with pride and the wise with humility. This proverb fits that pattern. "Insolence" (*zādôn*) results in shame. For one thing, pride does not allow fools to listen to advice or learn from their mistakes. The consequence is, thus, unavoidable. They are doomed to repeat their foolish behavior, and this brings shame on them. In 13:10 we learn that those showing *zādôn* get into quarrels, probably because they would rather fight than listen to those who would criticize them. In that verse, the insolent are contrasted with those who listen to advice (see also 21:24). The term "shame" (*qālôn*) is used elsewhere in Proverbs as here to describe the "fool" (3:35; 22:10).

Those who are modest do not put up defenses and thus allow themselves to hear criticism and change their behavior in life-affirming directions. The Hebrew root of the word translated "with modesty" is used elsewhere in the Bible only at Mic. 6:8, in a passage that is often translated "walk humbly." It, along with "acting justly" and "loving mercy," is a characteristic of a person who does what God requires.

The whole principle is paradoxical. When people hold themselves in high estimation, they will be denigrated; but the more they are aware of their weaknesses, the more they will achieve a success that will bring them glory.

---

4. Translation by M. Lichtheim, *Ancient Egyptian Literature*, 2:156–57.

> ³The innocence of those with integrity guides them,
>   but the duplicity of the faithless devastates them.

11:3. The basic contrast is between those characterized by integrity and those characterized by faithlessness. Again, this is another permutation on the contrast drawn between the wise and the foolish. In particular, the proverb highlights innocence and duplicity as their respective traits. Innocence implies a kind of transparency that is completely missing from the duplicitous. It is used of Job in Job 1:1 and 9:21–24 and has nothing to do with the sense of innocence that implies naïveté. What one sees and hears honestly reflects those with integrity. After all, they have nothing to hide. On the other hand, the faithless dissimulate. Part of this strategy may be self-protective. If people really knew what was in the minds of the faithless, they would be threatened. But according to this proverb, it is their deceit that actually leads to their destruction.

The word "duplicity" (*selep*) is rare, occurring only here and in Prov. 15:4. The verbal form ("to distort, mislead") occurs more often both in Proverbs (13:6; 19:3; 22:12) as well as outside it (Exod. 23:8; Deut. 16:19). The latter two passages prohibit the giving of bribes because of their effect in distorting justice. Perhaps this is the type of activity that the present proverb also has in mind.

> ⁴Riches do not profit on the day of fury,
>   but righteousness will extricate from death.

11:4. Proverbs has nothing against riches. In a number of places, the book suggests that wealth can be a blessing from God for wise behavior (3:9–10, 15–16; 10:22). Indeed, 10:15 suggests that the wealth of the rich can protect someone against this world's troubles. The present proverb, however, makes it clear that such protection is limited and certainly not as helpful as righteousness.

The meaning of the "day of fury" is a bit difficult to define. Christian readers of the proverb may be tempted to move too quickly toward an eschatological understanding, with the proverb saying that it is only righteousness, not wealth, that protects a person from death because righteousness rather than wealth assures one of eternal life. This interpretation is not assured in its OT context, and the phrase's other occurrences in Job 21:30; Ezek. 7:19; and Zeph. 1:15 suggest that it primarily refers to "any life-threatening disaster."[5] We are uncertain about the level of knowledge of the afterlife among the faithful during this time period.

5. Clifford, *Proverbs*, 122.

The only passage that indisputably teaches about the afterlife in the OT is Dan. 12:1–3. Our passage may simply refer to moments of crisis in life that may bring death, such as a serious illness or accident. Righteousness may be thought to induce God's protection from the ravages of life, or perhaps righteousness, associated with wisdom, leads to a lifestyle that promotes rather than endangers life. The fact that it is called the "day of fury," the latter an emotion, leads one to ask who expresses such fury that could threaten well-being and life. It could be the fury of God or perhaps of a human being like a cuckolded husband, who because of his jealousy will try to kill the one who has invaded his marriage. The righteous wise will escape the wrath of both of these. However, though we should not move too quickly to a full-blown eschatological interpretation of this proverb, it would be difficult and incorrect to completely ignore such a perspective (see also comments on 10:2). The passage fits in well with the pervasive teaching in the book that the righteous tend to escape difficulties, while the wicked seem to invite them.

> ⁵The righteousness of the innocent will make their path straight,
> but the wicked will fall in their wickedness.

11:5. This proverb is based on the two-path theology that we so frequently encountered in the first nine chapters. The righteous are on the straight path that leads to life, and the wicked are on a crooked path. Typically, the book teaches that God makes the path of the righteous easy (3:6), but here we learn that it is a synergistic effort because the behavior of the wise (here referred to as "the innocent") apparently makes one's life easier. That human effort does not nullify divine sovereignty may be seen in a passage like Phil. 2:12–13, as well as in holy-war theology, where God wins the battle but demands human participation.[6]

> ⁶The righteousness of those with integrity will extricate them,
> but those who are faithless will be caught by their desires.

11:6. There is an obvious connection with the preceding proverb, but the association may simply be the result of a redactor noticing a similar beginning and topic. The two should still be interpreted separately, and looking at them together really adds no new meaning (see comments under "The Structure of Proverbs" in the introduction).

Here righteousness and integrity (in the previous verse it was innocence) are contrasted with faithlessness. Again, the point has to do with consequences of behavior. Those with positive behavior will pre-

6. T. Longman III and D. Reid, *God Is a Warrior* (Grand Rapids: Zondervan, 1995).

sumably be extricated from the troubles of life that threaten, perhaps even death (10:2), but those who have negative behavior will be caught by the same. Again, this observation would have as its purpose not just explanation of how the world works but also encouragement toward positive behavior.

The desires of the faithless must be understood as desires for evil things, and the NIV's interpretation makes that explicit. This understanding may be supported by the fact that *hawwâ*, "desire" (as opposed to its related term ʿ*awwâ*), occurs only in negative contexts (see also 10:3 and 11:6). Desires for evil things (ill-gotten gain, another man's wife) will prove to be the undoing of the faithless. Thus, in this proverb it is evil itself that comes back to haunt the evil person.

> [7]When a wicked person dies, hope perishes;
> yes, expectation based on money perishes.

11:7. This verse has more than its share of textual and philological issues, so we must not be too dogmatic about its meaning. In the first line, the expression "wicked person" (ʿ*ādām rāšāʾ*) seems odd for proverbs. Typically, Proverbs speaks simply of "the wicked," with "person" being unnecessary. This fact has led some commentators[7] to speculate that the original simply had "person" and that a later concerned scribe added "wicked" to make sure readers would understand that it is only the death of the wicked that brings hope to a close. However, as mentioned in the introduction (see "Afterlife"), the status of knowledge of the afterlife in Proverbs is debatable. The proverb could be a general warning to all people, especially as the thought is sharpened in the second colon, not to build hope on money that does not survive death.

The other textual/philological issue surrounds the phrase that has been rendered "based on money," which is a single word in the Hebrew (ʾ*ônîm*). This takes the word as coming from ʾ*ôn*, which can be translated "generative power, sexual virility, physical strength, wealth."[8] If taken as "wealth," the expression fits in with other proverbs that suggest the limited value of riches (as recently as 11:4). However, the passage also makes sense if the phrase is translated "based on strength."

However, this is not the only way the verse has been understood. For one thing, there is another noun in Hebrew (ʾ*āwen*) that looks similar. It means "evil," and in the present context could be taken with the noun "expectation" as referring to "evil expectations." Indeed, the struggle with this proverb goes back at least to the time of the Septuagint, which takes

7. Clifford, *Proverbs*, 122.
8. So *NIDOTTE* 1:315.

252

the verse as "When the righteous man dies, his hope does not perish, but the boasting of the wicked perishes." However, this involves some rather radical textual adjustments that have no support outside the Septuagint.[9] It just seems to provide a more natural contrast along the lines of the antithetical parallelisms that are concentrated in this section.

In the final analysis, it seems best, though not certain, to stay with the Hebrew text and take the root from ʾôn rather than ʾāwen. Rather than an antithetical parallelism, it is a good example of a parallelism where the second colon specifies the thought of the first colon. The teaching of the proverb serves as a warning against putting hope in the power of money.

> [8]The righteous person is delivered from distress,
> but the wicked will take his place.

11:8. This optimistic proverb suggests that in the end people get what they deserve. It implies that the righteous sometimes find themselves in distress, trouble of some sort that arouses anxiety. However, eventually they will be delivered from that distress. Even more encouraging to those who desire to see things work out so that the righteous get their reward and the wicked get their just punishment, the wicked will eventually get what they deserve: distress!

Such teaching would help the righteous get through their struggles. We see this developed in Ps. 73. The psalmist confesses that at one point he was confused and even angry as he struggled in life but saw his wicked neighbors living what seemed to be carefree lives. Finally, through what seems to amount to a divine revelation of sorts, he recognized that present realities obscured the real nature of things. Ultimately, everyone gets what they deserve.

If this proverb does not assume a concept of the afterlife, serious reflection would have led to the conclusion that it could only really be true if there were an afterlife. After all, experience teaches us that some godly people go to the grave steeped in trouble, whereas some wicked people prosper till the bitter end.

How the deliverance of the righteous takes place is unspecified and could conceivably happen in a number of ways. That is not as important to the proverb as the end result.

Van Leeuwen perceptively provides two biblical examples of this proverb: Haman is hanged on the gallows he built to hang his enemy Mordecai, and Daniel's enemies are eaten by the lions that were intended to kill him.[10]

9. Indeed, in a new study on 6Q30, H. Eshel ("6Q30") argues that this text is an excerpt from Prov. 11, including v. 7, and that it confirms the MT and not the Greek rendition. He proposes that the fragment be renamed 6QpapProv.

10. Van Leeuwen, "Proverbs," 118.

> ⁹By their mouth, the godless destroy their neighbors,
>   but by the knowledge of the righteous, they are delivered.

11:9. This proverb contrasts the effects of fools (here described as "godless") and the wise (here named the "righteous"). The contrasting effects of the "godless" (defined by Van Leeuwen[11] as "one who goes through life ignoring God") and the "righteous" are also clear. The first is negative and the second is positive. The third contrast in the antithetical proverb is the most interesting. It is between the "mouth" (of the godless) and the "knowledge" (of the righteous). We are likely to understand this to mean that the speech (advice, counsel) of the godless leads to harm for those who are close to them because it lacks knowledge. And then in the second colon, the knowledge of the righteous when spoken allows not only the righteous but also those around them (their neighbors) to navigate life's difficulties. This theme will continue in the next few proverbs.

The second colon is grammatically ambiguous, and some (NRSV, NIV) understand it to read, "But by knowledge, the righteous are delivered." This does not provide as clear a contrast with the first colon, and so I have not followed this understanding of the verse. Rather, I understand the neighbors as those who benefit.

> ¹⁰When the righteous flourish, a city rejoices,
>   and when the wicked perish, there is shouting for joy.

11:10. While it is individuals who are righteous or wicked, the influence of their character goes far beyond themselves. This proverb makes this observation by saying that the presence and prosperity of the righteous and the languishing of the wicked are good for a city. With Clifford, we observe "the prosperity of the righteous and the destruction of the wicked elicit the same emotional reaction in the citizenry—joyous expressions."[12]

We can imagine concrete realizations of this principle. The flourishing of the righteous entails that they are in positions of influence. They may thus occupy government positions where their righteous behavior would lead to social justice and the alleviation of oppression. On the other hand, the wicked are defined by their practice of such things as injustice and oppression. Therefore, their absence would be beneficial to the community as a whole.

11. Ibid., citing Job 8:13 and Isa. 32:6.
12. Clifford, *Proverbs*, 123.

Proverbs 29:2 expresses a similar thought, and the following verse is also related and clearly placed here in the collection because of that similarity.

> **11**By the blessing of those with integrity a city is exalted,
> and by the mouth of the wicked, it is demolished.

11:11. We can see the obvious relationship between vv. 10 and 11. However, as argued in the introduction, caution should be exercised in using these proverbs as interpretive contexts. They may simply have come together because of their similarity, with no intention to create a context (see "The Structure of Proverbs" in the introduction).

The first colon is particularly close to the first colon of v. 10. However, here the positive elements of society are referred to as "those with integrity," that is, those whose sterling character expresses itself in good actions. We rightly understand this word as simply a variant way to refer to the righteous. As these individuals are blessed, the whole city is benefited. That blessing may come through an increase in material prosperity, through health, through a good reputation, through advancement to positions of influence. The blessing is unspecified, allowing us to fill in all of these and other possible concrete expressions.

On the other hand, the wicked harm a city. The specific origin of their harm is identified as the mouth, but even that is not concrete and does allow for a variety of possible scenarios. Perhaps they demolish the city through bad advice or by counseling against following the advice of the righteous. The wicked are elsewhere characterized as those who gossip (11:13; 17:4; 18:8), argue (26:21), and so on. All of these negative ways of speaking demolish the city by creating social rifts.

> **12**He who despises his neighbor lacks heart,
> but a competent person stays silent.

11:12. The contrast drawn in this proverb is between one who despises his neighbor and one who stays silent. Reading the second colon in the light of the first leads us to believe that the silence is precisely in the area of despising the neighbor. In other words, the fool (here described as one who lacks heart) verbally abuses the neighbor while the wise (here referred to as the competent person) does not.

The characterization of the fool as the one who "lacks heart" is interesting. The heart is the core personality (see 3:1); fools have nothing inside to share with others or even to sustain themselves. In this context, the expression may more specifically point to a lack of discernment or judgment. We have already seen this phrase in 6:32; 10:13, 21. For a competent person, see 2:2. Elsewhere too, the wise are characterized as sparing in their use of words (13:3; 15:4; 17:28).

> ¹³A slanderer goes about revealing secrets;
> a reliable spirit covers up a word.

11:13. Again, we can see a connection with the previous proverb. One way of despising a neighbor is through slander and revealing a secret. The wise person, though, knows better and keeps silent.

Slander is connected with foolish behavior also in 10:18. Slander would involve speaking to third parties about a person with the intention of harm, not help. The wise person, here called a reliable spirit (which implies someone who is true to his or her word), does not engage in such activity. The wise person might rebuke someone, but it would be done with the intention of helping that person (24:25; 25:12; 27:5).

> ¹⁴In the absence of guidance, a people will fall,
> but there is victory in an abundance of counselors.

11:14. The point of this observation is clear. Planning is pivotal for the survival of a city. In this, we seem to be getting back to the topic of vv. 10 and 11, where it is the wise who are good for society. Without guidance a city falls, but with counsel the city will have victory. The language suggests a military situation and reminds us of Qoheleth's anecdote in Eccles. 9:13–15a:

> Moreover I observed this example of wisdom under the sun, and it made a big impression on me. There was a small city and there were a few people in it. A great king invaded and surrounded it. He built huge siege works against it. A poor but wise man was found in it, and he rescued the city by means of his wisdom. . . .¹³

Guidance (*taḥbulôt*) and counsel (*yʿṣ*) come only from those with wisdom, after all.¹⁴ So it is the wise who are needed at times of crisis. Guidance may have the specific sense of military strategy here and in 20:18 as well as 24:6 (the latter is very close to 11:14 in thought as well as wording). Qoheleth's anecdote goes on to show the limitations of wisdom, at least for the one who possesses it:

13. This and the following translation of Ecclesiastes come from Longman, *Ecclesiastes*, 233–34.
14. For "guidance," see Prov. 1:5.

. . . but no one remembered that poor wise man. And I said, "Wisdom is
better than power." But the wisdom of the poor man was despised! His
words were not heeded. (Eccles. 9:15b–16)

Proverbs, though, is not concerned about the ultimate value of wisdom
in and of itself. It simply makes the point that military planning by those
who possess wisdom is a valuable, indeed lifesaving commodity.

> ¹⁵It will be big trouble for anyone who puts up security for a stranger;
> the one who hates making financial agreements is secure.

11:15. The book of Proverbs calls on people of means to be generous
toward those in need (29:7, 14). However, it frequently warns against
helping others make loans. In the first place, the Torah is against loans
with interest to fellow Israelites (Exod. 22:25–27). Apparently, the Hebrew
Bible does not have the same scruples when it comes to outsiders. The
tenor of this proverb seems to be that a person could lose money from
securing a loan for a non-Israelite. The potential downside erases any
possible upside. See also 6:1–5; 17:18; 20:16; 22:26; 27:13.

> ¹⁶A graceful woman takes hold of honor,
> but violent men take hold of wealth.

11:16. This antithetical proverb swivels around the verb "take hold of"
(*tmk*), which occurs in a number of contexts in the book (see also 3:18;
4:4; 5:5, 22; 28:17; 31:19). The basic meaning of this verb is to "seize,
grasp, take hold of" (*NIDOTTE* 4:305–6). The first contrast between
the two cola is found in the subject of the verb: "graceful" is clearly
contrasted with "violent." Someone who is characterized by grace, thus
making that one graceful (*ḥēn*), is someone who acts for the benefit of
others, not expecting a return. The reward that comes to such a woman
is honor. She is respected and loved by others for her actions. On the
other hand, "violence" implies a willingness to take what is wanted, by
force if necessary. The ending on the participle of the verb for "violent"
(*ʿrṣ*) is masculine plural, thus providing a contrast with the singular
woman of the first colon. The reward of such violence is wealth, which
sounds good on the surface, but to make sense of the contrast, I think
we must understand "only wealth." That is, wealth without honor. To
be sure, Proverbs does not regard wealth as bad in and of itself, and in
the right context it indeed signifies a blessing of God (3:9–10; 8:17–21).
But Proverbs also recognizes that evil people can get wealth (13:11)
and that such wealth often will harm those who have it (21:6). Indeed,
when riches are said to be a blessing, it is often said to be accompanied

by honor (3:16). It is, after all, much better to be poor with honor (and wisdom) than rich without it (15:16, 17; 16:8, 16; 17:1; 22:1; 28:6).

The phrase that we translate "graceful woman" (ʾēšet-ḥēn) can be understood as parallel with the "virtuous woman," (ʾēšet-ḥayîl) of 12:4 and, more famously, of 31:10, but this is not certain. If the parallel is pressed, however, the argument could be made that we have here not just any woman but a "wife."

The versions show confusion on this verse, probably because the idea of these violent (and therefore evil) men gaining wealth does not seem immediately negative. The Septuagint deals with the issue by changes in the first colon and an addition. A translation of the whole verse from Greek reads:

> A graceful woman brings honor to her husband,
>> but the seat of shame is a woman who hates integrity,
> The lazy lack riches,
>> but hardworking men get riches.

There is, however, another possible interpretation of this difficult verse. As Van Leeuwen suggests, the adjective *ḥēn* often signifies beauty when associated with a woman (5:19; 31:30; Nah. 3:4).[15] If so, then a proper translation might be:

> A beautiful woman grasps honor;
>> violent men grasp wealth.

The proverb then would be understood not as advice but rather as an observation on how things go in the world.

---

[17]People characterized by covenant love benefit themselves,
    but cruel people harm their own bodies.

11:17. Two classes of people are contrasted in this proverb. It offers itself as an observation, but as such it also clearly intends to give implicit advice. After all, one course of action leads to benefit, while the other to harm. The observation, then, is how certain actions lead to certain benefits.[16]

The first class is composed of people whose lives are characterized by "covenant love" (*ḥesed*). This is the kind of love that God shows to people who are bound in a covenant relationship with him. It is a love where the interests of the other party are paramount. A person who loves

---

15. Van Leeuwen, "Proverbs," 118–19. See the rendition of Prov. 11:16 in the NLT.
16. As pointed out by Clifford, *Proverbs*, 124.

another in such a way protects and does not harm the other (so other translations interpret this word as "kind" or "merciful"). This would be contrasted to cruel people, who harm others for their own gain.

The paradox of the proverb is that those who look out for others because of covenant love find that their lives are better in some unspecified way. On the other hand, those who are cruel to others end up hurting themselves.

As McKane rightly points out, this proverb shows that "there is a harmony between enlightened self-interest and the common good."[17] In other words, community and the individual are not always pitted against each other.

> **18**Those who do wicked deeds get false wages;
>   those who sow righteous deeds get a reliable payment.

11:18. Here we have another observation on how different actions lead to different consequences. By making this observation, the sage is interested in influencing people's behavior. After all, it is clear which is preferable: false or reliable wages. The point of the proverb is to encourage righteous deeds.

What constitutes wicked and righteous deeds is left unspecified here and is made concrete throughout the book of Proverbs as it describes the actions of the wise/righteous over against those of the fools/wicked. What is a false as opposed to a reliable wage/payment is also left unspecified. However, it may well be that a false wage is one that will not last long. After all, Proverbs is aware that the wicked may have wealth, but either it will not last (13:11), or else it will actually harm the one who has it (21:6).

The idea of sowing implies reaping and is a powerful metaphor for the action-consequence nexus. Hosea 10:12 may be cited for "sowing righteousness" and Prov. 22:8 for sowing evil (injustice).

> **19**Indeed, righteousness heads toward life,
>   and those who pursue evil head toward death.

11:19. This proverb is terse, literally:

Indeed, righteousness to life,
    and those who pursue evil to death.

This observation, like the previous two, clearly describes opposite actions that lead to opposite conclusions. Once again, the consequences

---

17. McKane, *Proverbs*, 433.

are such that they are intended to influence behavior. The nature of righteousness and the pursuit of evil are not specified, but the rest of the book fills out the picture.

The opening participle "indeed" (*kēn*) is often emended to the verb *tik-kōn* (a niphal of *kwn*), indicating a "permanent state" and thus providing a sharper contrast with colon 1.[18] However, we have seen throughout that proverbs are not always neatly balanced either semantically or grammatically. In any case, there is not much, if any, difference in terms of meaning whether one accepts the emendation or not.

> **20**Those with a crooked heart are an abomination to Yahweh,
> but those who are innocent on the path bring his favor.

11:20. For the expressions "abomination to Yahweh" and "bring his favor," see 11:1. The proverb obviously contrasts something that Yahweh likes with something that he detests. The contrast is between a "crooked heart" and "innocence." The heart is the core of one's personality, and to characterize it as "crooked" is to say that it is evil (for "crooked," *ʿqš*, see also 2:15; 4:24; 6:12; 8:8; 17:20; 19:1; 22:5; 28:6). On the other hand, "innocence" (*tāmîm/tōm*) implies clarity and straightforwardness (see 2:7, 21; 11:3, 5; etc.). The "path" is the often-used metaphor for one's life in Proverbs (see "Imagery" in the introduction).

> **21**Surely the evil person will not go unpunished,
> but the seed of the righteous will escape.

11:21. The opening Hebrew phrase (*yād lĕyād*, literally, "hand to hand") is not certain in meaning, but from the context (see also 16:5b) most scholars take it to indicate the certainty of what follows. McKane may well be right that the phrase reflects the shaking of hands in order to finalize a deal.[19] We thus translate "surely." The proverb is again an observation that comments on the consequences of evil and righteous actions.

In the first line, the punishment of the wicked is stated, though not specified. Van Leeuwen has rightly asserted, based on the fact that this phrase occurs in "the great revelation of the name of Yahweh in Exod. 34:6–7 (see also Exod. 20:7),"[20] that the verse implies that God stands behind the proper punishment of the wicked.

The MT of the verse balances the evil person not with the righteous person but with the seed of the righteous. If the MT is right, this is an

18. See Clifford, *Proverbs*, 19–20.

19. McKane, *Proverbs*, 437, points out that Anbar ("Proverbes 11,21; 16:5") has argued that the expression indicates "le rapidité d'une action."

20. Van Leeuwen, "Proverbs," 119, who also cites 6:29; 16:5; 17:5; 19:5, 9; 28:20.

interesting intensification of the thought of the first phrase and shows the benefits of righteousness over evil. After all, the benefits go not only to the righteous (assumed) but are also extended to their children. The versions, however, emend "seed" to "the one who sows righteousness." While this provides a tighter parallelism, it is not necessarily to be expected and is more likely done under the influence of 11:18b. The benefit that the righteous seed enjoy is escape. Though not specified, the verse implies that in the first place they would escape from the punishment meant for the evil person.

> ²²A gold ring in the nose of a pig;
> a beautiful woman who eschews discretion.

11:22. By placing these two cola together, the sage invites a comparison. The force of the parallelism justifies understanding the verse in the following way:

> Like a gold ring in the nose of a pig
> is a beautiful woman who eschews discretion.[21]

The picture the proverb conjures in our minds is striking, memorable, and powerful. The ring is small, but expensive and attractive to look at. The pig is ugly and dirty, but there may be more here for the original audience. The pig was considered unclean, according to Lev. 11:7 and Deut. 14:8. Later Jewish thought elevated the pig to the apex of all animals and foods that are unclean. This perspective indicates to modern readers just how repulsive the pig was to the original audience. However, the emphasis may be on the pig as the epitome of indiscretion. After all, this animal rolls in the mud and feces, eats swill, and is generally a mess.

The sage, though, is writing from the perspective of the man. As one looks at a pig and sees only the gold ring, so is a man who is so enamored by a woman's physical beauty[22] that he does not recognize her lack of discretion. The sage is warning those who will listen that the beauty is not worth all the problems that a woman's indiscretion will bring to him. Later, in the poem concerning the virtuous woman, the sage will affirm that what is really important is not charm or beauty, but rather

---

21. The word *ṭāʿam* means in the first instance "taste," but one of its derived meanings is "discernment" or "sense" (see *NIDOTTE* 2:379).

22. Perhaps the proverb takes additional force from the fact that ancient Israelite women themselves wore nose rings (Gen. 24:47; Isa. 3:21).

a woman's fear of Yahweh. "Beauty without wisdom is the height of incongruity."[23]

> [23]The longings of the righteous, surely good;
> the hope of the wicked, fury.

11:23. Earlier proverbs have spoken of the "longings of the righteous" (10:24) as well as the "hope of the wicked" (10:28). In the first, the longings of the righteous are granted as are the horrors of the wicked. In 10:28 the hope of the wicked is said to perish while the expectation of the righteous leads to joy. All three of these proverbs talk about the consequences of righteous and wicked behavior; consequences for the first type are consistently positive and the second negative, as would be expected.

Isolated from the other proverbs, though, the present verse has a measure of ambiguity. Are the longings of the righteous themselves good, or do they lead to good consequences? As for the second colon, the question is, When their hopes are dashed, does the hope of the wicked lead to God's fury or to the fury of the wicked? It seems most consistent to follow the interpretation of the preceding colon and take the evaluative comment at the end of each half-verse as a commentary on the divine consequences of righteous and wicked behavior. In any case, the first line is true whether the good qualifies the longings or else is a comment on the consequences. In either case, this observation should lead the hearer to proper behavior.

> [24]There is one who gives freely yet gains more,
> but one who withholds what is due will surely become needy.

11:24. The contrast of this verse has to do with generosity or the lack thereof. Contrasting the consequences between philanthropy and miserliness highlights the advantage of generosity. The former gets richer; the latter gets poorer. Thus, the contrast is paradoxical, since common sense might lead one to believe that holding on to one's possessions is a more certain way to wealth. This verse thus fits in with the extensive teaching in the book that promotes generosity as the actions of the wise. Since the latter is a major theme within the book of Proverbs, we do not consider it an option to understand the verse as an admonition to invest in business ventures rather than keeping one's wherewithal on deposit.[24]

23. Murphy, *Proverbs*, 83.
24. McKane (*Proverbs*, 434–35) puts forward this idea.

Paul expresses the same idea as he encourages the Corinthians to give to the needy: "The one who sows sparingly will also reap sparingly, and the one who sows bountifully will also reap bountifully" (2 Cor. 9:6 NRSV).

> [25]Those who bless will themselves be refreshed,
> and those who satisfy others will themselves be satisfied.

11:25. This verse continues the previous verse's theme of the good consequences that flow from generosity. The teaching contains a paradox: the more one gives, the more one receives. Here the expression is general. It does not specify what it is that is given (money, help, advice), so it may be that all these things are in mind.

The naming of positive consequences for generosity shows that Proverbs is not above naming self-interest for the motivation of good behavior. Both individual and community interest are encompassed in this teaching, since both the self and the other are said to derive good from a person's giving nature.

Clifford treats the verbs more literally (see translation footnotes to this verse) and translates the verse more concretely:

> A generous soul will have food aplenty,
> and one who gives drink will be given drink.[25]

In my opinion, the verbs are better taken in a metaphorical sense.

> [26]People will curse those who withhold grain,
> but blessing on the head of those who sell it.

11:26. As with the previous two verses, the teaching encourages generosity or at least distribution over against hoarding. The principle again is that good benefits accrue to those who have the interests of the community in mind. However, it is not a matter of self-sacrifice since generosity leads to positive results for the one who practices it.

The concreteness of this verse is provided by an agrarian example, though this does not mean that the society as a whole is an agrarian rather than an urban one. As a matter of fact, it may show the latter since nonfarmers would stand to be harmed by the withholding of grain to drive up the prices.

The verse does not state why grain is being withheld, but the idea of getting a higher price for a scarce commodity seems a reasonable supposition.

25. See Clifford, *Proverbs*, 120, 125–26.

McKane[26] chides previous commentators for citing as parallel lines 110–14 from the Shamash Hymn, but this section actually bears comparison at least in a broad sense as dealing with a merchant who thinks only of himself as opposed to the one who is fair to his market:

> The honest merchant who holds the balances [and gives] good weight—
> Everything is presented to him in good measure [. . .]
> The merchant who practices trickery as he holds the corn measure,
> Who weighs out loans (or corn) by the minimum standard, but requires
>   a large quantity in repayment,
> The curse of the people will overtake him before his time.[27]

> **27**Those who strive for good find favor;
>   those who seek evil, it will come to them.

11:27. This verse also refers to consequences, but no longer are they the consequences of a generous or giving behavior. Here it has to do with the object of one's energies. The objects are stated in general moral terms. "Good" and "evil" are undefined in this proverb, but since the book of Proverbs provides the context, "good" should be understood to entail wisdom, and "evil" those things that pertain to folly. The second part of the verse repeats the truth that those who seek evil, such as the harm of others, will have that intention redound on themselves. That is, they will be harmed.

We have seen the noun "favor" ($r\bar{a}s\hat{o}n$), also translated "what is acceptable," in 10:32; 11:1, 20. As may be seen by reading the comment on the first-cited passage, the word may specifically imply *divine* favor. It certainly also implies community acceptance. In any case, the verse, though a simple observation, certainly attempts to influence behavior toward the "good."

> **28**Those who trust in their wealth will fall,
>   but the righteous will blossom like foliage.

11:28. The sage presents another paradoxical statement. One might expect wealth to lead to prosperity and success, but this proverb states that wealth cannot be relied upon to come through in dire circumstances (cf. 11:4). The two parts of the proverb are stated in such a way that it pits wealth with righteousness, not with poverty. In this way, righteousness is seen to be the more valuable asset.

26. McKane, *Proverbs*, 434.
27. Cited from Lambert, *Babylonian Wisdom Literature*, 133.

The problem is not with wealth; indeed, Proverbs recognizes the value of wealth and the fact that it often can be a blessing of God (as in 3:9–10). The issue is one's attitude toward it. Trust is something that should only be placed in God; wealth is a poor substitute. Righteousness implies godliness, in that one cannot be righteous without being godly. Thus, it is one's relationship with God that leads to prosperity. The metaphor of the righteous blossoming like foliage naturally reminds one of the description of the righteous person in Ps. 1:2–3 (see also Jer. 17:7–8):

> But his delight is in the law of the LORD,
>   and on his law he meditates day and night.
> He is like a tree planted by streams of water,
>   which yields its fruit in season
> and whose leaf does not wither.
>   Whatever he does prospers. (NIV)

Such a thought likely lies behind Jesus's shocking statement to his disciples recorded in Mark 10:23 (//Luke 18:24): "How hard it will be for those who have wealth to enter the kingdom of God!" (NRSV).

> **29**Those who harm their house inherit wind,
>   and a dupe is a servant to the wise of heart.

11:29. The most pressing difficulty of interpreting this proverb has to do with the relationship between the two parts. The first part is clear enough and fits in with the teaching that anyone who harms the family is a fool. "House" here clearly means family or household and not the physical building. The idea of inheriting wind is equivalent to saying that one receives nothing of substance. Perhaps this is because parents have cut off the troublesome child, or perhaps the harm means that the family loses whatever of value they have because of the child's foolish actions.

The connection with the second colon of the verse may simply be that those who harm their households are dupes, who have subservient positions to the wise. As Murphy puts it so well, "Incompetency of any kind leads to slavery."[28]

> **30**The fruit of the righteous is the tree of life,
>   and the wise gather lives.

11:30. As attested partially by the translation footnotes, the translation of the second line and, therefore, its meaning is difficult and obscure.

---

28. Murphy, *Proverbs*, 84.

The first colon uses the tree of life (Gen. 2:9; 3:22; Prov. 3:18; 12:12; 15:4) as a metaphor and considers the righteous to be its fruit. Fruit here also carries the connotation of consequences. Righteousness results in life.

According to the MT, the second line is also about the wise. The real question surrounds the meaning of the phrase here translated tentatively "gather lives" (*lōqēaḥ nĕpāśôt*). If this is the correct translation, there are at least two possible understandings. First, it may be that those who receive people are those who make friends easily. If so, then this verse fits in with the theme of friendship in the book. The second interpretation suggests that the actions and advice of the wise preserve and enhance the lives of others.[29] This interpretation is the one that I lean toward. The third interpretation is that presented by the NIV, which spiritualizes the text, perhaps understanding *nepeš* in the sense of "soul." It seems to be misled by the modern expression "winning souls," but this interpretation seems quite foreign to the OT. The difficulty with the phrase does lead many to adopt the emendation (changing "wise" [*ḥākām*] to "violence" [*ḥāmās*]) suggested in part by the versions and render something like the NRSV (supported by the Septuagint):

> The fruit of the righteous is a tree of life,
>   but violence takes lives away.

31If the righteous are paid back on earth,
    how much more the wicked and sinners?

11:31. The verse addresses the issue of retribution. The rhetorical question format of the verse may assume that there was some question about this, as surely there must have been and as books like Ecclesiastes (7:15–18) and Job seem to confirm. Proverbs suggests that if all things are equal, retribution will happen on earth.

However, one might misunderstand this verse to say that the righteous are paid back with blessing and the wicked with punishment. The verse may actually suggest that even the righteous are paid back for their less heinous offenses (see Eccles. 7:20 for the acknowledgment that the righteous also commit offenses).[30] If so, how much more will those who are worse get what is coming to them?

This seems to be the understanding of 1 Pet. 4:18, which quotes the Greek version:

> If it is hard for the righteous to be saved,
>   what will become of the ungodly and the sinner? (NRSV)

29. And perhaps also their own lives.
30. See Whybray, *Proverbs*, 189.

Chapter 12

Translation

¹Those who love discipline love knowledge;
    and those who hate correction are dullards.
²The good person obtains favor from Yahweh,
    but he will condemn the scheming person.
³No one will stand fast by wicked acts,
    but the root of the righteous cannot be disturbed.
⁴A noble woman is a crown for her husband,
    but like rot in his bones is a disgraceful woman.
⁵The plans of the righteous are just,
    but the guidance of the wicked is fraudulent.
⁶The words of the wicked are a murderous ambush,ᵃ
    but the mouth of those with integrity extricates them.
⁷The wicked are overturned and are no more,
    but the house of the righteous will endure.
⁸Because of his insight, a person is praised,
    but a distressed mind leads to shame.
⁹Better to be not well regarded and have a servantᵇ
    than to be thought honorableᶜ and lack food.
¹⁰The righteous know the desires of their livestock,
    but the compassion of the wicked is cruel.

a. Literally, an "ambush of blood."
b. The Greek and Latin versions vocalize ʿbd differently than the MT and end up with the meaning "to work for oneself." If correct, the verse is talking about those able to sustain themselves through their own labor.
c. Waltke-O'Connor 26.2f refers to this use of the hitpael as the "estimative-declarative reflexive" and cites other examples: 2 Sam. 13:5; Esther 8:17; Ps. 78:21; Prov. 13:7; and Ezek. 38:23.

¹¹Those who work the land will have plenty to eat,
  but those who pursue emptiness lack heart.
¹²Those who covet wickedness hunt evil,ᵈ
  but the root of the righteous endures.ᵉ
¹³In an offense of the lips is an evil trap,
  but the righteous escape from distress.ᶠ
¹⁴From the fruit of the mouth a person is satisfied with good,
  and the works of a person's hands return to him.
¹⁵The path of dupes is virtuousᵍ in their eyes,
  but those who listen to advice are wise.
¹⁶A dupe's anger is known right away,ʰ
  but those who conceal contempt are prudent.
¹⁷He who proclaims truth speaksⁱ justly,
  but a false witness is fraudulent.
¹⁸There are those who chatter on like a stabbing sword,ʲ
  but a wise tongue heals.
¹⁹Truthful lips endure forever,
  but a lying tongue lasts only for a moment.ᵏ
²⁰Fraud is in the heart of those who plan evil,
  but for those who advise peace there is joy.ˡ
²¹No calamity will come onᵐ the righteous person,
  but the wicked get filled with evil.
²²False lips are an abomination to Yahweh;
  his favor is on those who do what is true.

d. *BHS* suggests a rather significant emendation of colon 1, which produces a Hebrew line (*yiššāmēd yĕsôd rāʿîm*) that may be translated, "The foundation of evil men is destroyed" (so McKane, *Proverbs*, 450).

e. The MT has *yittēn* ("gives forth"), which makes no sense. We have accepted an emendation suggested by the LXX, which may indicate an original Hebrew *bĕʾêtān*. McKane (*Proverbs*, 450) arrives at the same meaning by revocalizing the verb to *yîtān* and associating it with an Arabic root *watana*, "to be permanent."

f. The LXX has an extra proverb at this point (marked 13a). Clifford (*Proverbs*, 128) translates, "Whose looks are gentle will win mercy, / but he that contends in the gate will oppress souls."

g. Or perhaps in a more literal sense "straight," but a "straight path" would imply a "virtuous life."

h. Literally, "on the day."

i. The verb here is the relatively rare *pwḥ* (biform is *yph*), which is used "always in a moral sense and found only in Proverbs (6:19; 12:17; 14:5, 25; 19:5, 9)" (*NIDOTTE* 3:585).

j. "The syntax of colon *a*, *yēš* + participle, occurs also in 11:24; 13:7, 23; and 18:24, and connotes a type who does such and such" (Clifford, *Proverbs*, 132).

k. The verse is chiastic in that "truthful lips" and "lying tongue" frame the rest of the line. There is also a sound play between the last phrase in the Hebrew of the first colon (*lāʿad*) and the first phrase of the second colon (*wĕʿad*).

l. The translation tries to preserve the chiasm that structures this verse.

m. The verb (*ʾnh* III) is relatively rare and occurs four times in the piel and twice in the pual (here and Ps. 91:10). It has the meaning "to come on, to befall." It also occurs once in the hitpael in 2 Kings 5:7.

²³A prudent person conceals knowledge,
   but the heart of fools proclaims stupidity.
²⁴A determined hand dominates;
   a slack one will be put to forced labor.
²⁵Anxiety makes the heart of a person depressed,ⁿ
   but a good word encourages it.ᵒ
²⁶A righteous person shows the way to his neighbor,
   but the path of the wicked makes them wander.
²⁷Slack people do not roastᵖ their prey;
   determined people, precious riches.
²⁸In the way of the righteous is life,
   and the path of abomination�q leads to death.ʳ

Interpretation

¹Those who love discipline love knowledge;
   and those who hate correction are dullards.

12:1. The sages felt that mistakes provided opportunities for learning. They also apparently assumed that everyone would make mistakes along the way. What they could not tolerate, however, was an attitude of defensiveness that refuses to admit mistakes. True learners, truely wise persons, are those who desire to know when they have done wrong so that they can change their behavior. Thus, the wise person loves "discipline" (*mûsār*, see 1:2) and "correction" (*tôkaḥat*, see 1:23). It is stupid to resist criticism because it means that a person will perpetuate wrong behavior. The word "dullard" (*bāʿar*) is strong and refers to a person "who does not have the rationality that differentiates men from animals (Ps. 73:22)."[1]

The principle expressed here reminds us why the book of Proverbs so prizes humility over pride (see "Pride/Humility" in the appendix).

n. Or "weighs the heart of a person down."

o. Or "cheers it up"; the form is a piel of *šmḥ*.

p. The verb *ḥrk* occurs only once in Hebrew and thus is of uncertain meaning, but it does occur in Aramaic. However, outside of a cooking context, it has the meaning of "burn." Dahood ("Hapax *ḥārak*") argues that the appearance of the verb *ḥrk* in a Ras Ibn Hani tablet "removes the uncertainty surrounding biblical *yaharok*." The LXX has "catch."

q. The MT has "the path of the trail" (*nětîbâ*), but this makes no good sense. Even the early versions took the colon another way, and here we follow the LXX and suppose that the noun *tôʿēbâ*, "abomination," originally stood in this place.

r. The MT has what appears to be "no death," but the negative particle ʿal occurs nowhere else with nouns, only verbs. Again, we suspect a corruption and, with many Hebrew manuscripts and early versions, emend to ʿel.

1. *NIDOTTE* 1:691.

Humility allows one to hear words of criticism and creates an openness to change, whereas pride does the opposite. Humility and the ability to hear correction thus provide the road to success and life; pride leads to failure and ultimately death.

> [2]The good person obtains favor from Yahweh,
> but he will condemn the scheming person.

12:2. The verse is an antithetical parallelism based on the contrast between two types of people. On the one hand are good people, whom Yahweh favors; and on the other are schemers, whom God will condemn. The category "good" is very broad, and one might expect the equally broad "wicked" or "evil" person to provide the contrast. However, here the negative person is a schemer. The word "scheming" is from *mězimmâ*. This word can have either a positive or negative meaning. In 2:11 we saw that it has the positive sense of discretion, but here it is the negative idea of scheming. The basic idea is, as Fox has pointed out, "private, unrevealed thought, often but not always used in scheming. As the ability to think for oneself and keep one's own counsel, it is especially valuable in withstanding temptation."[2] For "favor" (*rāṣôn*), see comments at 10:32; 11:1, 20, 27.

> [3]No one will stand fast by wicked acts,
> but the root of the righteous cannot be disturbed.

12:3. This verse contrasts the stability of the wicked and the righteous. Those who act wickedly will not have stable lives, but those who are righteous will. What constitutes stability is not clearly stated, but we may presume that the lives of the righteous are not rocked by troubles and setbacks as envisioned for the wicked. There may be a paradox involved here. People perform wicked acts to get ahead in life (steal money, cheat others, lie to cover their tracks), but according to the sages, these acts do not lead to stability but to trouble. Wickedness complicates life by making it tumultuous. The proverb is an observation that serves to motivate its hearers toward righteousness. Whybray is of the opinion, and is probably correct, that "root" (*šōreš*) is not intended to invoke a plant metaphor here.[3] The verb *môṭ* is here translated "disturbed" rather than "shaken" (as in 10:30 and elsewhere), since the latter rendering does not seem to work well with the subject "root."

2. Fox, *Proverbs 1–9*, 116.
3. Whybray, *Proverbs*, 191.

> ⁴A noble woman is a crown for her husband,
> but like rot in his bones is a disgraceful woman.

12:4. For the fullest description of the "noble woman" (*ʿēšet-ḥayîl*), see Prov. 31:10–31), the poem with which the entire book ends. See also the description of Ruth in the book that follows Proverbs in the Hebrew canon, for she is called a "noble woman" as well (Ruth 3:11). The contrast between the right and the wrong woman is a major theme in the book of Proverbs, because the subject is of such monumental importance to the young males to whom the book is primarily addressed in its ancient setting.

This proverb makes an observation, presumably based on experience, and we may speculate that its purpose was to motivate its hearers to avoid a bad marital choice. A noble woman enhances the godly man's life and is a reward for his wise behavior, whereas a disgraceful wife brings suffering to his life. Such a wife brings shame to the husband. The fact that such a wife is likened to rot in the bones shows just how deeply a bad marital choice affects a husband's life.

Precisely how a woman acts to bring the label "disgraceful" on herself is not made explicit because it may happen in a variety of ways. Perhaps she acts in a sexually promiscuous fashion or mismanages the household or the children; whatever the cause, it brings the husband pain, and such a choice should be avoided at all costs.

Van Leeuwen suggests that Paul reflects the teaching of this proverb in 1 Cor. 11:7 when he calls the woman the "glory" of the man, since "'crown' and 'glory' are closely associated (Prov. 4:9; 16:31; Isa. 28:1, 5; Jer. 13:18)."[4]

> ⁵The plans of the righteous are just,
> but the guidance of the wicked is fraudulent.

12:5. Again, this proverb contains a general observation, in this case to serve as a warning when listening to the advice of others and perhaps to motivate sages to be just in their own giving of advice. The righteous help people navigate life not just for their own benefit but also for the benefit of others. On the other hand, there are hidden motives behind the advice that the wicked give a person about the future. For the word "guidance," see also 11:14. The term translated "fraudulent" here (*mirmâ*) is also used elsewhere in Proverbs (11:1; 12:20; 14:8; etc.) to indicate deceit.

4. Van Leeuwen, "Proverbs," 125.

271

---

⁶The words of the wicked are a murderous ambush,
  but the mouth of those with integrity extricates them.

12:6. The proverb is an observation on the consequences that flow from the speech of the "wicked" and from those "with integrity," two words used to indicate the realms of fools and the wise. As we might expect, the words of the wicked lead to a negative end, even a violent death. It is a little unclear, perhaps intentionally, whether the ambush comes on those who listen to the advice of the wicked, whose guidance is fraudulent (see the previous verse), or on the wicked themselves. Certainly, the teaching of Proverbs affirms both results (11:9).

In the same way, it is not clear whether the words (indicated by the mouth from which the words flow) of those with integrity saves them from jams or saves those who listen to their advice. But again, the sage would affirm both results. Like the previous verse, this proverb serves to warn its hearers to be discerning as they listen to the speech of others (12:13).

Some scholars[5] suggest a legal setting for this proverb; although a legal situation could certainly be envisioned that would illustrate the truth of this proverb, it does not seem to be specifically tied to the court.

---

⁷The wicked are overturned and are no more,
  but the house of the righteous will endure.

12:7. This proverb expresses a similar sentiment to that of 10:25 and 12:3. The wicked lack stability, but the righteous have it in spades. Indeed, their whole household is stable and will endure the vicissitudes of life. Again, in typical proverbial fashion, the details are left unspecified. How are the wicked overturned, and who assures their downfall? It could happen in a variety of ways, and it could be accomplished by any number of people, or perhaps even by God himself.[6]

---

⁸Because of his insight, a person is praised,
  but a distressed mind leads to shame.

12:8. As Van Leeuwen has pointed out, Israel was an honor-and-shame culture. With regard to this particular proverb, he states, "Such praise and blame express the speaker's delight or dismay in the other person

---

5. Whybray, *Proverbs*, 192; Murphy, *Proverbs*, 98.
6. See also the parallel with Jesus's teaching in Matt. 7:24–27//Luke 6:47–49; so Beardslee, "Uses of the Proverb," 65.

and powerfully enforce the community's standards of good and evil upon the recipient of praise or blame."[7]

Here honor, in the form of praise, accompanies insight. The word "insight" (*śēkel*) is closely connected to "wisdom" (see 1:3) and refers to the ability to recognize the true nature of a situation or circumstance. Such recognition allows one to act in a way that allows one to navigate the difficulties of life. Indeed, the root also carries overtones of success. Such ability, whether practiced for oneself and even more for others, would bring admiration.

On the other hand, the proverb speaks of the "distressed mind." Here the word "mind" translates *lēb*, literally, "heart," a term that points to one's core personality (see 3:1) but at times will emphasize one's cognitive abilities. The modifier "distressed" (*na'ăwēh*) is a niphal from the root '*wh*, which in the qal means "to be wrong" but in the niphal has the meaning "to be distressed, disturbed."[8] A distressed mind would not think clearly and thus would not arrive at the same helpful insight expected to come from the individual in the first colon. Thus, instead of praise, this person would receive shame.

> [9]Better to be not well regarded and have a servant
> than to be thought honorable and lack food.

12:9. According to the sage, reality is more important than appearances. The form is a better-than proverb, giving relative values. In this case, actually having wealth is more important than the illusion of wealth. As is the case with better-than proverbs, it is not that reputation is unimportant to the sage; it just is not as important as reality. Indeed, better still, the sage would say, would be to have wealth and also to be known to be rich.

> [10]The righteous know the desires of their livestock,
> but the compassion of the wicked is cruel.

12:10. The contrast is between the opposite sensibilities of the righteous and the wicked. Righteous persons are so sensitive to others that they are sensitive even to their animals. One can imagine just how carefully they would treat their fellow human beings. On the other hand, even the compassion of the wicked is cruel. That is, even their best efforts are dangerous. That cruelty (*'akzārî*) can lead to violence is seen in 11:17. We are not to restrict the statement about the cruelty of the wicked only to their actions toward animals.

7. Van Leeuwen, "Proverbs," 125.
8. According to *NIDOTTE* 3:340–41.

> ¹¹Those who work the land will have plenty to eat,
> but those who pursue emptiness lack heart.

12:11. This verse fits in with others that blast laziness and promote hard work (6:6–11; 10:4, 26; etc.). Proverbs 10:5 is a particularly closely related proverb in that it situates its comments in an agrarian setting, as at least colon 1 does here.

A difference, however, may be noted in the fact that the emphasis here is not so much on lack of exertion, but rather that energy is misdirected. Fools, here characterized by lack of heart, exert energy ("pursue"), but what they pursue lacks substance. Perhaps it may be said that those who lack substance (heart) pursue that which lacks substance ("emptiness"). That emptiness is not specified is intentional and can be concretized to fit the situation. A similar proverb appears in 28:19.

> ¹²Those who covet wickedness hunt evil,
> but the root of the righteous endures.

12:12. This verse is extremely difficult from a text-critical and philological point of view (see translation footnotes). Rather than speculating on a significantly different text, our translation is based at least loosely on the Hebrew as it has come down to us. We take "wickedness" as the object of the verb in the relative clause rather than the subject, as many do. Probably the weakest point of the above translation is our treatment of *měṣôd* as a verb rather than a noun. As a noun, it is best understood as "net," derived from the verb *ṣwd*, which means "to hunt." The second colon is very similar to the Hebrew of 12:3, but here we do accept an emendation that is supported by the Greek (see translation footnote).

If this approach to the translation of the text is accepted, its meaning is not obscure. It is the idea that those who love wickedness are going to find evil or trouble and thus their lives will be unstable. This is contrasted to the lives of the righteous, whose lifestyle leads to stability. However, every interpreter, including the present one, must fully acknowledge the tenuousness of one's proposed understanding because of the difficulties with the text.

> ¹³In an offense of the lips is an evil trap,
> but the righteous escape from distress.

12:13. The first colon situates the saying in the topic of speech. If one offends with the lips in one's speech, then it will be like a trap. The word "trap" (*môqēš*) is a fowler's term and signifies the kind of trap in which a bird is caught, to its harm. While some[9] allow that this proverb may speak of the words themselves being an evil trap for others, it is more likely that the trap brings evil or trouble on the speaker. The offense is not specified, but the situation will make it concrete. Perhaps the offense is gossip or slander (10:18; 11:13; 18:8; 20:19) or simply saying the wrong thing at the wrong time. In any case, saying something offensive will bring harm on the speaker.

While the second colon does not specifically mention a speech situation, the first colon has already provided the context. In other words, we are to understand this proverb as saying that the righteous can use their power of speech to get themselves out of tough situations.

> [14]From the fruit of the mouth a person is satisfied with good,
> and the works of a person's hands return to him.

12:14. This verse deals with consequences or retribution in both speech and action. With its reference to mouth, the first colon is concerned with speech. The fruit of the mouth is the consequence that flows from the words one utters. Since the words are wise, they bring good and satisfying results to the situation as well as to the one who utters them.

The second colon says the same is true in the realm of actions. In other words, this proverb is not in an antithetic form, but in a form that furthers the thought of the first colon by applying the principle to another realm of meaning.

Whatever one does will have consequences for that person. Presumably, if the actions are good, then the consequences will be good. The same reciprocal action is true if the works are bad. If they are, then the consequences will also be bad.

The Qere reading of the second colon suggests that it is God who returns the works of persons to them. This simply makes explicit what is already implicit in the saying.

> [15]The path of dupes is virtuous in their eyes,
> but those who listen to advice are wise.

12:15. The dupe (*ʾĕwîl*) is closely connected to the fool. The way of dupes, then, would be the wayward path of fools, which leads to death. Unfortunately, the dupes are not sensitive enough to realize the problem with their lives. Wisdom teachers were suspicious of those who thought themselves wise ("in their own eyes") and thus not open to outside criti-

9. For instance, Murphy, *Proverbs*, 90.

cism (3:7; 26:12, 16). Such dupes, thus, cannot learn from their mistakes and just keep marching forward to their own destruction.

In the second colon, however, the wise are not convinced that their way is invariably correct, so they are willing to pay attention to advice that they gather along the way. The proverb is about remaining open to hearing the counsel of other people, which involves humility and the lack of pride. See 12:1 for a similar thought.

> ¹⁶A dupe's anger is known right away,
>   but those who conceal contempt are prudent.

12:16. This proverb values repression over impulsive display of emotion. It thus is similar in principle to those proverbs that value silence over much speech (10:14; 13:3, 16; 17:27, 28). In other words, there is benefit for those who do not let their rivals know how upset they are. If one's intent is to hurt another person, then the victim's immediate display of negative emotion will be received and celebrated as a victory. Prudence is the ability to regulate one's emotional display for one's own advantage.

> ¹⁷He who proclaims truth speaks justly,
>   but a false witness is fraudulent.

12:17. The setting seems most natural in a law court, as is most strongly underlined by the word "witness" (ʿēd). Though the principle may be applied outside of the courtroom, the consequences of lying in a legal setting make the contrast even more dramatic. This theme is so important that it is repeated often in the book (6:19; 14:5, 25; 19:5, 9; 21:28).

The point may be summarized by saying, on the one hand, that wise persons speak words that reflect reality and therefore their speech is just. On the other hand, false witnesses are fraudulent because their words skew the actual situation.

> ¹⁸There are those who chatter on like a stabbing sword,
>   but a wise tongue heals.

12:18. The wisdom teachers felt that the fewer words the better. To speak mindlessly about a matter is to invite great harm—thus the image of the stabbing sword. Over against these harmful words stands a wise tongue. What makes a tongue wise is not spelled out here, but we are likely to assume a contrast with chattering. Since a number of proverbs in the book encourage silence or at least a minimum of words (10:14;

13:3, 16; 17:27, 28), we should at least consider that as a characteristic of wise speech. This definition can easily be expanded by reading other proverbs that help draw the parameters of wise speech. The consequence of wise speech, just like the consequence of wisdom itself, is life, so the metaphor of healing is certainly appropriate.

> ¹⁹Truthful lips endure forever,
> but a lying tongue lasts only for a moment.

12:19. Here the proverb reverts to the contrast found in v. 17 between a lie and the truth in speech. However, here the contrast has to do with how long each lasts. A lie might last for a moment in the sense that a lie may be thought to be true at first, but the idea is that a lie will eventually be found out. On the other hand, truth endures; that is, time will side with the truth.

> ²⁰Fraud is in the heart of those who plan evil,
> but for those who advise peace there is joy.

12:20. The "fraud" (or "deceit," *mirmâ*) that is in the hearts of those who plan evil is also the topic of 11:1; 12:5, 17. Those who plan evil do not care for the truth; they are happy to deceive others or even themselves. On the other hand, joy comes to people who advise peace. The difference between planning evil and advising peace seems to be that the former leads to social disintegration but the latter to social cohesion.

> ²¹No calamity will come on the righteous person,
> but the wicked get filled with evil.

12:21. This statement taken alone is quite bold. It says quite simply that a righteous person will avoid the pitfalls of life, but the wicked person will not escape trouble. However, anyone with a modicum of life experience realizes that this cannot be taken as an ironclad promise, nor can it be used as a kind of barometer of righteousness of other people in the way that the three friends of Job so used it. In other words, this verse begs discussion of the issue of retribution, and for that the introduction should be consulted (see "Retribution" there).

The proverb form does not lay claim to universal truth. This statement of v. 21 is true if all other things are equal. And the rewards and penalties that accompany the actions of the wise and righteous on the one hand and the fool and wicked on the other are not to be understood as promises, but rather as generally true principles by which to live. It is more likely that life will be easy for the righteous than it is for the wicked. The intention behind stating this principle so boldly is to encourage righteous rather than wicked behavior.

> ²²False lips are an abomination to Yahweh;
> his favor is on those who do what is true.

12:22. Many times in the book of Proverbs we hear that lies are evil and the truth is good (see most recently 12:19). It is a fundamental precept of the book that words ought to reflect reality, the reality of the heart (16:23; 18:4) as well as the reality of what is out there in the world. Here the principle is articulated with great force by stating it in a proverb that uses the phrase "abomination to Yahweh" (*tôʿăbat YHWH*), for which also see 11:1. The opposite of this is "his favor" (again, see 11:1).

> ²³A prudent person conceals knowledge,
> but the heart of fools proclaims stupidity.

12:23. The proverb draws a contrast between the prudent person and a fool (*kĕsîl*). "Prudence" (*ʿārûm*) is a word associated with wisdom. The first is characterized by having knowledge, while the second is dull of mind. The Hebrew word "stupidity" is associated with the trait of dullness and is related to the noun "stupid person" (*ʾĕwîl*), which is often encountered in the book and is one of a number of words associated with the fool. The final contrast may be the one that is most surprising. The prudent person "conceals" knowledge, while the fool "proclaims" stupidity. We would expect the opposite! But the idea fits in with the pride/humility theme in the book (3:5, 7; 21:4; 25:6–7; etc.). It is not that prudent people do not act on their knowledge; they just do not make a big deal about it. However, by proclaiming their stupidity, fools let everyone realize just how stupid they are. The idea expressed by this proverb is similar to yet another important theme in the book, the contrast between the silence of the wise person and the chattiness of the fool (10:14; 12:18; etc.).

> ²⁴A determined hand dominates;
> a slack one will be put to forced labor.

12:24. Already in 10:4 we learned that a determined hand makes a person rich, but a slack hand leads to poverty. The contrasts in these two verses support the larger teaching in Proverbs that pits a negative view of laziness over a positive picture of diligence (see 6:6–11; etc.). Here, one who is determined, who will work hard, will be in charge, while the slack or lazy person will be forced to work.

> 25Anxiety makes the heart of a person depressed,
> but a good word encourages it.

12:25. The Hebrew word "anxiety" (*dě'āgâ*) refers to one's emotional response to a threat to one's well-being. Anxiety arises because of uncertainty about the future. Persistent anxiety leads to depression. This proverb provides an observation on life that suggests an antidote to depression: encouraging words. The "truth" expressed in this proverb is rather self-evident, but its statement reminds the hearer of it.

A "good word" is a rather general category that can be filled out in a variety of ways, depending on the situation. Perhaps it is a statement that points out strengths of a person, or perhaps it is simply a bit of positive news. This proverb fits in with the general teaching of the book about the impact that speech has on people. It also registers the sages' concern for people's psychological state.

> 26A righteous person shows the way to his neighbor,
> but the path of the wicked makes them wander.

12:26. As translated, many people suggest that the two parts of the proverb do not obviously go together except by way of contrast between something positive for the righteous person and something negative for the wicked person. Thus, there have been attempts to emend this text along the lines J. A. Emerton proposed.[10] However, there is actually a contrast between knowing where one is going (with the ability to lead others in the right direction) and being lost. Even so, there are other ways of understanding this verb, which we understand to mean "shows the way,"[11] as well as alternative possible translations of the noun we take as "neighbor."[12]

We understand the verb of the first colon to be from the verb *twr*, "to explore." If correct, the colon shows that righteous people benefit not only themselves but also other people. They lead their neighbors on the right path.

On the other hand, while righteous people and those they influence move in the right direction, the wicked have no certain guide and thus

10. Emerton ("Note on Proverbs xii.26") emends the first two words from *yātēr mērē'ēhû* to *yuttar mērā'â* and renders the whole verse:

> The righteous is delivered from harm,
> but the way of the wicked leads them astray.

11. Rather than from *twr*, the root could be *ytr*, "to be superior to," thus, "the righteous person is better than his neighbor/evil person" (see the following footnote).

12. The same consonants could be understood as "evil" or possibly even "pasture."

wander aimlessly. This observation has as its purpose the promotion of righteous behavior.

> [27]Slack people do not roast their prey;
> determined people, precious riches.

12:27. This verse is widely recognized as enigmatic. We find it hard to place the second colon in a smooth grammatical form, so we keep it abrupt. The contrast is certainly between the lazy and the diligent, here called "slack" (*rĕmîyâ*) and "determined" (*ḥārûṣ*). The former are pilloried by saying that they do not even cook the prey that they catch. On the other hand, the second colon associates determination with riches. Perhaps, with the NRSV, we should supply a verb with the second colon to achieve the translation "but the diligent obtain precious wealth."

The obvious intention of this proverb is to encourage determination and diligence and discourage laziness. This proverb shares this goal with a number of others.

> [28]In the way of the righteous is life,
> and the path of abomination leads to death.

12:28. As the translation footnotes to the verse indicate, this proverb has a number of textual issues. At first glance, the verse seems to say something like this:

> In the way of the righteous is life,
> and in the path of the trail there is no death.

It is tempting to try to make this rendition work since it would seem to be one of the clearer passages affirming a belief in the afterlife in the book (a position that is adopted in the NIV and the NRSV).[13] However, the philological and textual issues overwhelm confidence.

The verse understood in the way translated here is another example of the contrast between the two paths, the path of wisdom (here connected with righteousness) and the path of folly (here called a path of abomination). By naming the positive ultimate consequences of the former and the negative consequences of the latter, the proverb intends to guide people toward proper behavior.

---

13. Dahood ("Immortality in Proverbs 12,28"; and idem, "Hebrew-Ugaritic Lexicography VII," *Biblica* 50 [1969]: 340) argues for such an understanding of the text and offers Ugaritic support (*CTA* 17 [2 Aqht].6.25–32), but in the final analysis this seems to be yet another example of Dahood overreaching the evidence.

Chapter 13

Translation

¹A wise son,^a the discipline of a father;
   but a mocker does not hear a rebuke.
²From the fruit of the mouth a person eats well,
   but the appetite of the faithless is violence.
³People who keep a watch on their mouths guard their lives;
   those who spread their lips wide^b ruin^c it.
⁴The desire of lazy people is strong,^d but they get nothing;
   the desire of people who are determined is fully satisfied.^e
⁵The righteous hate a false word,
   but the wicked create disgrace^f and scorn.

a. This literally renders the MT, which simply associates "wise son" and "discipline of the father." From reading the second colon, the connection becomes clear: the wise son is open to the discipline of his father. The LXX supplies "listens" or perhaps simply draws the verb of colon 2 back into the first colon. Others speculate that the verb "loves" (*ʾāhab*) has collapsed into "father" (*ʾāb*), thus producing, "A wise son loves the discipline of (his) father." In any case, the sense is clear.

b. "Spread wide" (from *pśq*) is used only once elsewhere, in Ezek. 16:25, where it refers to Jerusalem as a whore who "spreads her legs wide" to everyone who passes by. See D. I. Block, *Ezekiel 1–24*, New International Commentary on the Old Testament (Grand Rapids: Eerdmans, 1997), 495.

c. For this term *mĕhittâ* in Proverbs, see 10:14, 15, 29; 14:28; 18:7; 21:15.

d. Literally, "the desire of lazy people crave" (from *ʾāwâ*).

e. The verb "fully satisfied" is a contextual translation of *dšn*, elsewhere rendered "grow fat" or "is fully refreshed."

f. As represented in the Hebrew text, this word is from the hiphil of *bāʾaš*, "to stink," though many would emend it to *yābîš*, the hiphil of *bôš*, "to create shame." As Whybray (*Proverbs*, 202) points out, there is really no difference between the two.

281

[6]Righteousness protects the innocent on the path,
   but wickedness misleads sinners.
[7]There are those who pretend to be rich, yet have nothing,
   and those who pretend to be poor,[g] but have great riches.
[8]Wealth can provide a ransom for a person's life,[h]
   but a poor person does not hear a threat.[i]
[9]The light of the righteous rejoices,[j]
   but the lamp of the wicked is extinguished.
[10]Only[k] in insolence are there quarrels,
   but there is wisdom in taking advice.
[11]Riches diminish because of haste,[l]
   but the one who gathers by hand will increase.
[12]Expectation delayed makes the heart sick;
   longing fulfilled is the tree of life.
[13]The person who despises a word, it will go badly for him,
   but the person who respects the commandment, he will be rewarded.
[14]The instruction of the wise is a spring of life;
   turning aside from death traps.
[15]Good insight gives favor,
   but the way of the faithless persists.[m]

g. The verb in the first colon is a hitpael participle, and the verb in the second is a hitpolel participle, the latter a simple variant of the former. Waltke-O'Connor 26.2f refers to this function of the root as "estimative-declarative reflexive."

h. The literal rendition of the Hebrew in colon 1 is awkward in English: "Ransom, the life of a man, his wealth."

i. The last three words repeat the last three words of 13:1b, though in this context "threat" is a better English translation than "rebuke."

j. There is early evidence of unease over the connection between the subject and the verb of this colon, and thus there are alternative understandings. One Hebrew manuscript takes the verb from ṣmḥ rather than śmḥ, but that verb is connected to the plant world ("to bloom"). The LXX appears to take it from the prepositional phrase lāneṣaḥ, rendering it dia pantos ("forever"). BHS suggests a form of the verb zrḥ, "to shine." J. C. (C. Y.) Greenfield ("Lexicographical Notes II," Hebrew Union College Annual 30 [1959]: 144) and G. A. Anderson (A Time to Dance and a Time to Mourn: The Expression of Grief and Joy in Israelite Religion [University Park: Pennsylvania State University Press, 1991], 51–53) suggest that there is a second root śmḥ that means "to shine."

k. McKane (Proverbs, 230, 453–54) represents one strand of interpretation when he repoints raq ("only") as rēq ("empty-head") and translates the colon: "An empty-head produces strife by his arrogance." Clifford (Proverbs, 135), on the other hand, omits the phrase as a dittography from dᶜk, based on Aquila, Symmachus, Theodotion, and the Vulgate.

l. The MT has hebel, "meaninglessness" or "emptiness" or even "transience," but none of these make sense here. Thus, we follow BHS, suggested by the Greek and Vulgate and followed by many modern commentators and translations, and read a form of bhl (haste) here, thus positing a metathesis of the first two consonants. It provides a much stronger contrast with the second colon.

m. Or, with the versions (Greek, Syriac, Vulgate, Targum), "is their ruin," from ʾêydām. See Murphy, Proverbs, 95, among others.

[16]Every prudent person acts knowledgeably,
    but fools spread stupidity.
[17]A wicked messenger will fall into evil,[n]
    but a reliable envoy brings healing.
[18]Poverty and shame belong to those who neglect discipline,
    but those who guard correction will be honored.
[19]A realized longing is pleasant to a person,[o]
    but eschewing evil is an abomination to fools.
[20]Walk[p] with wise people and be wise,
    but be friends with fools and get into trouble.
[21]Evil pursues sinners,
    but the righteous get a good reward.
[22]A good person causes grandchildren to receive an inheritance,
    but the wherewithal of a sinner is stored up for the righteous.
[23]Much food comes from the arable soil of the poor,[q]
    but it is[r] swept away because of a lack of justice.
[24]Those who withhold the rod hate their son,
    but the one who loves him seeks[s] discipline.
[25]The righteous eat to the point of satisfying their appetite,
    but the stomachs of the wicked will be empty.

Interpretation

[1]A wise son, the discipline of a father;
    but a mocker does not hear a rebuke.

13:1. This proverb provides an antithesis between wisdom and folly, here represented by one of its more extreme forms, the "mocker" (*lēṣ*). There is no verb in the first colon, but the idea is certainly that the wise

n. Or more idiomatically, "stumbles into trouble."

o. Traditionally, *nepeš* is translated "soul" here, and it would be appropriate here as long as soul is taken not as a separate part of a human being but rather as a way of speaking of internal processes that are really not distinct from the body in a metaphysical sense.

p. This follows the Kethib (*hōlēk*), while the Qere (*hālôk*) has "those who walk."

q. The LXX understands "poor" (*rāʾšîm*) to be a form of *yĕšārîm* (*dikaioi*), but Vulgate and other versions do not follow the Greek here. McKane (*Proverbs*, 463) takes the word as the plural of *rōʾš* in the sense of "notables" or "grandees" and translates, "The tilth [tillage, cultivated land] of grandees produces an abundance of food, but it is swept away for lack of equity." However, he does this only so it will fit into one of his categories.

r. "It is" translates *yēš*, but Clifford (*Proverbs*, 140) takes it as "substance, assets, riches," which strikes me as unnecessary.

s. The precise meaning of this verb is uncertain in this context. *Šḥr* II means "to seek, to inquire" (*NIDOTTE* 4:84–85), though some would also connect its meaning with the noun *šaḥar* ("immediately before daylight, break of day") and understand that it implies starting discipline early in a child's life (Whybray, *Proverbs*, 210).

son is wise because he is open to his father's "discipline" (*mûsār*; see 1:2). Discipline entails verbal and physical corrections. The wise son is one who pays attention when his father corrects him, and thus is not apt to repeat the same wrong behavior. A mocker is someone who resists correction. Indeed, the act of mocking is a way of attacking those who might offer advice. The mocker refuses to admit wrongdoing and so cannot tolerate a rebuke that points out mistakes. Accordingly, the mocker cannot improve behavior.

> ²From the fruit of the mouth a person eats well,
> but the appetite of the faithless is violence.

13:2. The proverb begins by commenting on the consequences of speech (see a similar statement at 12:14). The assumption is that the speech is wise and helpful, and as a result the speaker eats well. Good advice brings its rewards to the one who gives it. The second colon contrasts negative with positive, but they are not exactly parallel. We might expect a comment on how foolish words lead to hunger. But the contrast is drawn in a different and more interesting fashion. The faithless prefer violence to satisfy their appetite. They would prefer to hurt others with their words.

> ³People who keep a watch on their mouths guard their lives;
> those who spread their lips wide ruin it.

13:3. This proverb fits in with the teaching on using words sparingly (10:14; 12:18; 13:16; 17:27, 28). It employs antithetical parallelism to contrast the consequences of infrequent speech with verbosity. Talking too much leads to all kinds of problems. It is not that wise persons never speak, but they choose their words very carefully. As Van Leeuwen astutely states, "Verse 3 follows logically upon verse 2. Since speech bears good or bad fruit, the organs of speech must be carefully controlled."[1]

> ⁴The desire of lazy people is strong, but they get nothing;
> the desire of people who are determined is fully satisfied.

13:4. The contrast drawn between laziness and hard work is one of the best attested in the book of Proverbs (see "Laziness and Hard Work" in the appendix). Both have desires, but the cravings of the lazy go unrequited, presumably because they are unwilling to work toward their goals. On the other hand, hardworking people, here identified as "determined," have their desires met. The sage would certainly be thinking

---

1. Van Leeuwen, "Proverbs," 131.

of legitimate, godly desires since hardworking people are those who are wise, while laziness is the epitome of folly. Though the surface meaning of "desire" may be connected with food, the intention is to use this to state a principle that goes well beyond that of appetite.

> ⁵The righteous hate a false word,
> but the wicked create disgrace and scorn.

13:5. The second colon does not specify how the wicked create disgrace and scorn, but we should take our cue from the first colon. The first colon states that the righteous cannot abide a false word, which would be a word that misrepresents reality in some fashion. For instance, a false word could misreport a past event, or it could make a promise that was never intended to be kept. The wicked, then, would create disgrace and scorn, and thus destroy their reputations by uttering such "false words."

> ⁶Righteousness protects the innocent on the path,
> but wickedness misleads sinners.

13:6. Again we have an antithetical proverb that contrasts righteousness and wickedness. Here is a further contrast between two groups of people: the innocent, obviously on the side of the wise, and the sinners, obviously connected to fools. The verbs contrast the consequences in store for the two groups. The righteous are protected, and the sinners are misled. The verse utilizes the two-path theology of the book to make its point. The proverb thus expresses a general principle that needs to be filled out, based on the broader teaching of the book. Murphy believes that the abstract principles of righteousness and wickedness are here personified.[2]

> ⁷There are those who pretend to be rich, yet have nothing,
> and those who pretend to be poor, but have great riches.

13:7. The principle of this verse is to be careful not to allow appearances to deceive. One may look at a person and be amazed at how well-off that person is. If that person is a wicked fool, questions concerning God's fairness might arise. On the other hand, the reverse is true as well. One may observe a person who, perhaps through the quality of possessions, seems poor but really is rich. The wise need to be aware of this so they can see through appearances to reality. I do not believe that this proverb

---

2. Murphy, *Proverbs*, 96.

is a comment on the relative value of material versus spiritual wealth, saying that some are materially rich but spiritually poor.[3]

> ⁸Wealth can provide a ransom for a person's life,
> but a poor person does not hear a threat.

13:8. The proverb is about the relative but limited value of wealth. The scenario is a kidnapping. If a rich person is kidnapped (or perhaps blackmailed),[4] his or her family can probably pay the ransom and perhaps free the captive. While this seems an argument in favor of the power of riches, the second colon undermines it. If the person were poor, there would be no chance of kidnapping in the first place. What would be the use? In the final analysis, wealth is not really the protection that it purports to be.

> ⁹The light of the righteous rejoices,
> but the lamp of the wicked is extinguished.

13:9. An antithetical proverb expressing the contrary consequences of righteousness and wickedness (the ethical reflex of the bipolar contrast between wisdom and folly). "Light" here appears to be a metaphor for life energy, and when the lamp of the wicked is extinguished, it signifies at least removal of well-being if not death itself. This metaphor is used elsewhere (Job 18:6; 21:17; Prov. 20:20; 24:20 [where colon 2 is verbatim what we have here]). As in many other proverbs, this one is stated quite generally, but it serves to encourage ethical behavior.

> ¹⁰Only in insolence are there quarrels,
> but there is wisdom in taking advice.

13:10. "Insolence" (*zādôn*) is here contrasted with taking advice. Insolence is a pride that will not listen to other people, especially criticism of behavior or thought. On the other side are those who are open to correction and new ideas. The latter is the way of wisdom, and the implication is that the way of wisdom avoids "quarrels" (*māṣṣâ*). Compare 12:15.

> ¹¹Riches diminish because of haste,
> but the one who gathers by hand will increase.

---

3. Suggested as a possibility in ibid.
4. So McKane, *Proverbs*, 458. Murphy (*Proverbs*, 96) suggests that the situation is "census enrollment" for a tax, citing Exod. 30:13.

13:11. The verse has a philological/textual problem (see translation footnote). It appears to be a contrast between two different ways to accumulate wealth, one right and one wrong. The wrong way is by a get-rich-quick scheme (see also 20:21): easy come, easy go. The second colon suggests that a methodical accumulation of capital will last the test of time. Perhaps haste also suggests a "kind of disreputable action."[5]

> ¹²Expectation delayed makes the heart sick;
> longing fulfilled is the tree of life.

13:12. This proverb, better known from its traditional rendering "hope deferred makes a heart sick," illustrates how the sages were indeed interested in what today we would call psychology. It is an observation with no explicit admonition or prohibition, but as an observation it provides insight into how the human spirit typically functions. This knowledge will help the wise read others as well as themselves.

The idea is that anticipation or delay in the fulfillment of a desire leads to frustration, disappointment, or depression. The "heart" stands for the core personality of a person and here seems to connect specifically with one's emotions (see 3:1). The fulfillment of a desire is compared to the tree of life, a very positive metaphor that points not just to physical life but also to the enjoyment of it. For the metaphor of the tree of life, based as it is on the Garden of Eden story in Gen. 2–3, see also Prov. 3:18; 11:30; 15:4, as well as Rev. 2:7; 22:2, 14, 19. For a similar proverb about the fulfillment of longings, see Prov. 10:28. Some scholars[6] have seen a contrast with the previous verse, which promotes the slow acquisition of wealth, but in that case the proverb implies some success along the way. Here there is no gradual accumulation, just frustration.

> ¹³The person who despises a word, it will go badly for him,
> but the person who respects the commandment, he will be rewarded.

13:13. The proverb fits into the general theme of openness to instruction. Fools do not listen to advice, while the wise pay attention to those who guide and offer correction (3:11–12; 9:7–9; 12:1, 15; 27:5–6; etc.). The "word" of the first colon is unspecified, but it should be read in light of the more specific "commandment" in the second. The "commandment" is itself ambiguous as used here and elsewhere in Proverbs (2:1; 3:1; 4:4; etc.). Is the "commandment" the authoritative word of the father, or is there a further reference to the Torah? The statement would seem to

5. Murphy, *Proverbs*, 97.
6. See Van Leeuwen, "Proverbs," 132.

be true in either case. McKane[7] draws a large gap between the "word" and "commandment" of Yahweh, as found in the book of Deuteronomy, and the word/commandment of the father's instruction in Proverbs; but my guess is that from the perspective of the book of Proverbs, they are not all that different. The authoritative utterances of the father would be extensions of Yahweh's commands.

How things go badly or what the reward will be for the one who respects the commandment (presumably by obeying it) is also not made concrete because good and bad consequences can come in a variety of forms.

> [14]The instruction of the wise is a fountain of life;
> turning aside from death traps.

13:14. This observation is an implicit admonition to pay close attention to the instruction of the wise, including that offered in the present book. By listening and putting this advice into effect, the recipient finds life. The metaphor of a "spring of life" (see also 10:11) is apt because water provides life, and flowing, bubbling water, compared to a stagnant pool, illustrates vitality. Colon 2 provides the negative statement supporting the idea of colon 1. Wise instruction is a source of life because it avoids situations that may lead to one's death. A specific example of this proverbial truth might be the teaching found earlier in the book (see chaps. 5–7) concerning loving the right woman. Following that wise advice leads to life, but going after the strange, foreign woman results in death. See the closely related 14:27.

> [15]Good insight gives favor,
> but the way of the faithless persists.

13:15. The proverb contrasts good insight (for "insight" [*śēkel*], see 1:3) with faithlessness (see 2:22). Those with the former are rewarded with favor in life. The MT does not actually specify a negative contrast with favor but just speaks of the permanence of the way of wisdom. It may be that by now the "way of the faithless" would be known to be negative: it ends with death rather than life. Either that, or the textual alternatives are correct (see translation footnote).

> [16]Every prudent person acts knowledgeably,
> but fools spread stupidity.

---

7. McKane, *Proverbs*, 454.

13:16. The prudent are those who act with a cool head. They take into consideration the situation (compare 1:4; 12:16, 23). It is a tautology to say that the prudent act with knowledge, since otherwise they would not be prudent; but the statement places emphasis on the connection. It is true that the prudent conceal their knowledge (12:23), that is, they do not talk about it, but at the same time their actions show that they are knowledgeable. Knowledge and prudence are close associates of wisdom.

On the other hand, fools spread "stupidity" (*ʾiwwelet*), a synonym of "folly" or "foolishness" (see 12:23). While the prudent and wise back up their words with actions, fools spread stupidity by their own actions and also their words.

This observation has the intention of encouraging prudent actions and discouraging foolish behavior. It does so by contrasting "the thoughtfulness that characterizes the actions of the clever with the impetuousness of the fool who blurts out folly."[8]

> [17]A wicked messenger will fall into evil,
> but a reliable envoy brings healing.

13:17. Messengers played an important role in human relationships in an age long before email. They might be given a letter or perhaps an oral message to deliver. A reliable envoy would be one who delivered the message in a timely and accurate fashion. A wicked messenger could fail to deliver the message, delay it, or garble its content. In any case, according to the proverb, these wicked messengers could bring trouble on themselves by their actions, even conceivably as a direct result of their bad actions. On the other hand, the reliable envoy becomes a vehicle of healing, presumably for both the sender and the recipient of the message.

> [18]Poverty and shame belong to those who neglect discipline,
> but those who guard correction will be honored.

13:18. "Discipline" (1:2) and its close synonym "correction" (3:11) refer to the ability to control oneself and focus on the important tasks at hand, even if other behaviors would be more pleasurable. Those who stay focused get the reward of honor, while those who let things go will end up poor and dishonored. As its purpose, this observation encourages discipline by pointing out the consequences of pursuing or neglecting it. See also 12:1; 13:1.

8. Murphy, *Proverbs*, 97.

> ¹⁹A realized longing is pleasant to a person,
>   but eschewing evil is an abomination to fools.

13:19. In 13:12, the sage observed that a longing fulfilled is like the tree of life, and colon 1 in v. 19 expresses a similar sentiment. Colon 2, though, is of a different type than in v. 12. The most direct contrast in the verse is between the pleasure of the fulfilled longing and the disdain felt by fools at the idea of forgoing an evil act or thought. Perhaps the implication is that evil is pleasant to fools or, rather, that "fools cannot experience such satisfaction [as expressed on colon 1], for they will not turn from evil."[9]

> ²⁰Walk with wise people and be wise,
>   but be friends with fools and get into trouble.

13:20. This proverb observes that one will be like the company that he or she keeps. Those who associate with the wise will be wise, and those who associate with fools will be fools and have a hard time of it.

The most natural way of understanding this verse is that the virtues or vices of those with whom one associates will rub off on the person. But perhaps people are attracted to those who are like them, so then this observation is simply on the natural order of things. Like attracts like. Woman Wisdom herself keeps company with virtues like prudence, knowledge, and discretion; she avoids contact with pride, arrogance, evil behavior, and perverse speech (8:12–13).

> ²¹Evil pursues sinners,
>   but the righteous get a good reward.

13:21. In the final analysis, the proverb is about consequences. Evil (trouble)[10] pursues sinners. On the other hand, the righteous get a good reward. They do not have to pursue a good reward; it comes naturally to them as a result of their righteousness.

> ²²A good person causes grandchildren to receive an inheritance,
>   but the wherewithal of a sinner is stored up for the righteous.

13:22. This is one way in which the sage understands how the bad person, whether characterized as fool or wicked, could have any ma-

---

9. Clifford, *Proverbs*, 139.

10. As a matter of fact, the word "evil" could be (and was in the previous verse) translated "trouble."

terial wealth. After all, it is the wise who should have wealth, and the fool should be poor (14:24), though there are proverbs that show an awareness of the fool having substance (11:18). One way of resolving the tension was by understanding that the wealth of the fool was only temporary. Here, the idea is that good persons' wealth lasts not only for their lifetime but into future generations. On the other hand, sinners' wealth will also get handed down, not in the family line but from sinners to the righteous. Though the Teacher at Eccles. 2:26 seems to share this perspective, he also admits that a person's wealth may get passed down to a stranger (6:1–2).

> ²³Much food comes from the arable soil of the poor,
> but it is swept away because of a lack of justice.

13:23. The translation of this verse and thus its meaning are disputed (see the translation footnotes). However, granted the approach taken here, the meaning shows great sympathy toward the poor. Typically, Proverbs attributes poverty to some form of folly. While according to Proverbs the foolish behavior most commonly resulting in poverty is laziness (6:6–11; 10:4, 5; 19:15; 22:13; etc.), other reasons for poverty are also given, including indulgence (21:17). However, here folly is not in mind at all, but rather, poverty is the result of some form of injustice perpetrated toward the poor. The assumption is that some persons have worked hard and done everything within their power to gain material prosperity, but forces beyond their control have robbed them of it. The result is called a "lack of justice." The wording makes it unlikely that a natural disaster (e.g., flooding) is in mind here, but rather some type of human malice. However, the verse gets no more specific than this because injustice can come in many different forms, for example, an exploitative landlord or unfair government taxation. This verse is significant because it acknowledges that it is not only the godless fool who can be poor.

> ²⁴Those who withhold the rod hate their son,
> but the one who loves him seeks discipline.

13:24. Discipline was critically important to the sages, and people who did not want discipline for themselves were immediately suspected of being fools. The wise want to be corrected no matter what the cost. The alternative would be to live in ignorance and perpetuate wrong behavior and mistaken beliefs. Yet one can imagine how a person who understood the importance of discipline for oneself might yet hesitate to apply it to a son. After all, it is difficult to inflict discomfort of any kind on a child that one loves. However, this admonition points out that more harm is done to a child by withholding discipline than by applying it. The sage would understand reluctance to apply discipline, whether physical or verbal, to be child neglect and child abuse.

In this case, since the rod is mentioned, the discipline in mind here is physical. One should not think of severe beatings, however. As the sages' words were kind and merciful, so were the blows they administered. In this day of appropriate concern for destructive and hateful physical abuse of children, there is an understandable hesitation about proverbs like this one that advocate physical discipline (for others, see "Physical Discipline" in the appendix). Nonetheless, as is typical in such instances, there has been an equally harmful countertendency to refrain from any kind of verbal or physical correction to behavior, which is arguably not helping children either. Clifford, in my opinion, is quite unreasonable to state, "It goes without saying that this paradoxical language cannot be used as an argument for the corporal punishment of children."[11] It would be more reasonable to add the modifier "harsh" or "excessive" before corporal.

It was not only the wise of Israel who encouraged physical discipline to inculcate wise behavior, but of the rest of the ancient Near East as well. Van Leeuwen points out that the Egyptian word for education "was accompanied by the hieroglyph of a striking man or arm."[12]

25The righteous eat to the point of satisfying their appetite,
but the stomachs of the wicked will be empty.

13:25. This proverb has some similarity with the bold statement in 10:3: "Yahweh will not let the righteous starve, but he will push away the desire of the wicked." All things being equal, God will satisfy the hunger of the "righteous," but the "wicked" (a common variant of "fool," emphasizing its ethical nature) will go hungry. The fool is lazy (6:6–11 etc.) or indulgent (21:17) and so lacks the wherewithal necessary to grow or to acquire food.

However, as we have just seen, all things are not always equal. One may be poor and not have anything to eat not because of being wicked, but because of someone else's wicked actions (13:23).

---

11. Clifford, *Proverbs*, 140.
12. Van Leeuwen, "Proverbs," 134.

Chapter 14

Translation

¹Wise women[a] build their houses,
   but dupes demolish theirs with their own hands.
²Those who walk in virtue fear Yahweh,
   but those who go the wrong way on his[b] path despise him.
³In the mouth of a dupe is a sprig[c] of pride,[d]
   but the lips of the wise guard them.
⁴There are no oxen where the stall is clean,[e]
   but an abundance of yield comes by the strength of a bull.
⁵A truthful witness does not lie,
   but a false witness proclaims lies.

a. Literally, "wisdom of women," taken as a "genitive of genus" by Van Leeuwen, "Proverbs," 138, who cites Waltke-O'Connor 9.5.3i. However, Waltke himself (*Proverbs*, 1:576) takes it as a genitive of relation, involving social structure (cf. Waltke-O'Connor 9.5.1g), and translates "wise among women." Both yield the same basic meaning.

b. It is unclear whether the pronominal suffix ("his") on "path" refers to God or to the person who goes on the wrong path.

c. The only other use of this noun (*ḥōṭer*) is in Isa. 11:1, a well-known prophecy often taken as messianic, where it refers to new growth (a sprig or shoot) that springs up from a stump. Some (Clifford, *Proverbs*, 143) appeal to Aramaic use of this word to justify seeing it as a punishing "rod." Thus instead of seeing colon 1 as referring to pride's incipient growth, he understands, in my opinion wrongly, pride as a weapon that inflicts harm on the dupe.

d. Some emend *ga'ăwâ* (pride) to *gēwōh* (back) to conform to 10:13, but the MT as it stands makes sense, and there is no textual support for such an emendation.

e. Or "empty" if taken as a noun from *brr* I. It is also true that *bār* might come from *bār* III, "grain." If so, according to Van Leeuwen ("Proverbs," 139), the idea is that "you either have oxen who constantly eat up the grain in the crib, or you have a crib full of grain, but no oxen whose work in the field both fills the crib and feeds the household." In either case, the meaning seems essentially the same and, as Van Leeuwen also points out, roughly equivalent to the modern English proverb "You can't have your cake and eat it too." However, it should be pointed out that the NRSV represents a view that does further emendation, taking *'ēbûs*, "stall," as *'epes*, "there is no," but this has no evidence to support it.

[6]A mocker searches for wisdom, yet nothing happens,[f]
   but knowledge comes quickly to a person of understanding.
[7]Stay away from a foolish person,
   for you will not know[g] knowledgeable lips.[h]
[8]The wisdom of the prudent makes them understand their path,
   but the stupidity of fools is a fraud.
[9]The stupid person mocks a guilt offering,[i]
   but favor is toward the virtuous.
[10]A heart knows emotional distress,[j]
   and in its joy another person[k] cannot share.
[11]The house of the wicked will be annihilated,
   but the tent of the virtuous will blossom.[l]
[12]There is a path that is straight[m] before a person,
   but in the end it is the path of death.
[13]Even in laughter the heart may feel[n] pain,
   and in the end joy may turn to[o] sorrow.
[14]Rebellious hearts are satisfied with the consequences of their path,
   good people with the consequences of their deeds.[p]
[15]The simpleminded believe anything,
   but the prudent understand their steps.
[16]The wise fear and eschew evil,
   but the fool gets infuriated[q] and feels safe.

f. Literally, "and nothing."

g. Or "experience." In other words, the lips of a foolish person will not speak wisely.

h. This is a difficult verse, and the LXX seems to go far afield: "Everything is contrary to a foolish man, but wise lips are discerning weapons" (translation by McKane, *Proverbs*, 464).

i. This translation is given in spite of the fact that there is not number concord between the proposed subject and the verb. "Guilt mocks dullards" does not make sense.

j. Literally, "a heart knowing bitterness of its soul."

k. According to A. H. Konkel (*NIDOTTE* 1:1142), *zār* can "have a neutral sense of simply another or belonging to another," though typically it has the meaning of "strange" or "foreign."

l. The LXX suggests a form of ʿmd (stand) rather than prḥ, perhaps on the basis of a similar thought in 12:6 as well as the unusual use of a floral term here in relationship to a tent. However, the metaphorical use of "blossom" seems perfectly appropriate to the idea of the verse.

m. Or "seems right."

n. Understanding the verb here to be an example of a "potential use of the imperfect," with Whybray, *Proverbs*, 216. However, it is possible to translate it as pure indicative ("feels") and just understand that a proverb expresses observations quite baldly that need to be nuanced or provided with exceptions.

o. The Hebrew lacks a verb, reading "in its end joy sorrow."

p. The MT has "from on him," but a simple emendation from *mēʿālāyw* to *maʿălālāyw* gets the sense reflected in the above translation.

q. The Greek, followed by the Syriac and Targum, reads *meignytai*, which supposes Hebrew *mitʿārēb*, created by a metathesis of the last two consonants. Thus, the LXX takes the colon to say, "The fool gets involved (with evil) and feels safe."

¹⁷The short-tempered act stupidly,ʳ
    and people who scheme are hated.ˢ
¹⁸The simpleminded inheritᵗ stupidity,
    but the prudent wear knowledge as an ornament.ᵘ
¹⁹Evil people bow down before good people,
    and wicked people are at the gatesᵛ of the righteous.
²⁰The poor are hated by their neighbors,ʷ
    but many are those who love the wealthy.
²¹Those who despise their neighbors are sinners,
    but blessed are those who are gracious to the needy.
²²Do those who plan evil wander aimlessly?
    Those who plan good things receive covenant love and faithfulness.
²³There is an advantage to all hard work,
    but the word of the lips leads only to lack.
²⁴The crown of the wise is their wealth;ˣ
    the stupidity of fools is stupidity.ʸ
²⁵A truthful witness saves lives,
    but a fraudulent person proclaimsᶻ lies.
²⁶In the fear of Yahweh there is strong safety,
    and refuge for their children.
²⁷The fear of Yahweh is a fountain of life,
    turning aside from death traps.
²⁸In an abundance of people is the splendor of a king,
    and in the absence of a population is the ruin of a ruler.

r. This noun (ʾiwwelet) is elsewhere translated "dullness," but "stupidity," having roughly the same sense, fits the context better.

s. Those who expect an antithetical parallelism here will resort to emendation, as does the LXX, which reads yiśśāʾ rather than yiśśānēʾ, the result being something like "the discreet man (taking mĕzimmôt in the positive sense) endures much."

t. *BHS* suggests an emendation of the verb "inherit" (nāḥălû) to the noun ḥălî (ornament) based on 25:12 and a stronger parallelism, but this seems an unnecessary conjecture and is not accepted by most modern commentators. However, Clifford (*Proverbs*, 144) traces the suggestion back to Driver, "Problems in the Hebrew Text of Proverbs," 181.

u. "Wear as an ornament" is the proper rendering of the hiphil of ktr, as opposed to the NIV, which takes it as a niphal: "are crowned with." *NIDOTTE* 2:745 suggests that the verb could come from ktr II, which in the hiphil means "to surround."

v. Clifford (*Proverbs*, 146) notes the interesting alliteration in "wicked people at the gates": rĕšāʿîm ʿal šaʿărê.

w. Or "friends"; the noun is formed from the verbal root rʿh, which means "to associate with."

x. The LXX has panourgos ("prudence," implying Hebrew ʿormâ), though it should be pointed out that the Greek word often has a negative connotation not appropriate here. However, the text as it stands fits in with a theme connecting wisdom and wealth found throughout Proverbs (in passages like 3:9–10), and thus a meaning connected with prudence does not fit well.

y. *BHS* suggests liwyat (wreath), which provides better parallelism, but the tautology has its own effectiveness.

z. For the verb pwḥ, see 14:5.

²⁹Patience brings much competence,
   but impatience promotes stupidity.
³⁰The life of the body is a healthy heart,
   but jealousy is a rot of the bones.
³¹Those who oppress the poor insult their Maker,
   but those who show grace to the destitute honor him.
³²In their evil the wicked are thrown down,
   but the righteous find refuge in their death.[a]
³³Wisdom resides in an understanding heart,
   but it is not[b] known in the innards of fools.
³⁴Righteousness lifts a nation up,
   but sin diminishes[c] a people.
³⁵The king finds an insightful servant acceptable,
   but his fury will be directed toward a shameful one.

Interpretation

¹Wise women build their houses,
   but dupes demolish theirs with their own hands.

14:1. This proverb contrasts wise and foolish (here "dupe" is used [*ʾiwwelet*]) women. The intention of this observation is to warn young men (the implied reader of these proverbs) from associating and marrying foolish women. The contrast between wise and foolish women runs throughout the book (see especially chaps. 5–7) and constitutes one of the most important teachings of the book. After all, there is no more important decision that a young man has to make than his lifelong partner. In this verse, we are to understand house as household, including not just the physical shelter but also the relationships within a family.

Commentators like Murphy[1] argue that Wisdom and Folly (his translation of "dupes") are here personified. After all, compare 14:1a with 9:1a. To be sure, there is a moving back and forth between Woman Wisdom

---

a. Greek and Syriac suggest that a metathesis occurred during textual transmission (from *běmôtô* to *betûmô*, "in his innocence"). While this makes sense, so does the MT.

b. With the Greek and Syriac; Hebrew lacks "not."

c. The MT is difficult, if not impossible. Literally, the second colon could be rendered "the covenant love [*ḥesed*] of a people is sin." The above translation posits a simple emendation based on the idea that the scribe confused a *rêš* and a *dālet*, and the word should instead be *ḥeser*. Yet perhaps Clifford is right when he looks to the Targum's translation to argue that here we have another root meaning of *ḥsd*, as "shame" (Clifford, *Proverbs*, 148). See the occurrence of this root in Lev. 20:17 (also some people see it in Prov. 19:22). In either case, the basic meaning of the verse is the same.

1. Murphy, *Proverbs*, 103.

and wise women, and Woman Folly and foolish women. After all, they are reflections of one another. Nonetheless, in this particular verse the emphasis falls on human women.

> ²Those who walk in virtue fear Yahweh,
>   but those who go the wrong way on his path despise him.

14:2. The fear of Yahweh is a basic concept in the book of Proverbs (see 1:7; also 9:10; 10:27; 31:30; etc.). From these passages, we see that there is an intimate connection between one's basic religious attitude (fear of Yahweh), ethics (walking in virtue), and wisdom. Walking in virtue indicates a moral lifestyle. The verb "walk" implies a path that becomes explicit in the second colon. As is typical in this part of Proverbs, the second colon creates an antithetical parallelism. The word "virtue" in colon 1 can have the meaning "straight," so the opposite would be wandering off the path, taking a crooked route. Those who do this, implying unethical behavior, show that they despise Yahweh.

> ³In the mouth of a dupe is a sprig of pride,
>   but the lips of the wise guard them.

14:3. The syntax of the first part of the proverb is a bit odd, but the meaning is relatively clear. The shoot of pride is a metaphor for the beginnings of pride in one's personality, and the first colon claims that for "dupes" (a synonym of "fools"), pride begins with their speech. However, while the speech of dupes leads to their downfall, the speech (here represented by lips) of the wise protects them. Through their verbal skill, the wise can keep themselves out of trouble.

> ⁴There are no oxen where the stall is clean,
>   but an abundance of yield comes by the strength of a bull.

14:4. The meaning of this verse is that a productive life is messy. One desires a neat and tidy life, just as the ideal stall would be clean. However, a clean stall by the nature of things would mean an empty stall since oxen do not have to be in a stall long before it is messy. However, without oxen there is no productivity. After all, as colon 2 points out, crops do not appear magically out of thin air but rather as a result of much work. For instance, animals are typically used to plow the ground in order to plant the seed that produces crops. Another related way of construing the meaning of the line is to take it to mean that one must spend (acquire oxen) in order to get ahead (produce crops).

> **5**A truthful witness does not lie,
>   but a false witness proclaims lies.

14:5. As in 12:17 the primary setting seems to be a court of law (*ʿēd*, "witness"), but the observation has implications beyond this. The statement is simple enough. Who lies? False, not truthful witnesses. The verb "proclaims" (*pwḥ*)[2] means more specifically "blow" or "blast"; to use an anachronism, the meaning is well expressed by "broadcasts." The false witness is not subtle. A number of proverbs concern the "witness" (19:28; 21:28; 24:28–29; 25:7c–8, 18; 29:24; etc.).

> **6**A mocker searches for wisdom, yet nothing happens,
>   but knowledge comes quickly to a person of understanding.

14:6. How mockers search for wisdom is left unspecified, but since they apparently remain mockers, they must be doing it on their own terms. Mockers reject advice and correction of mistakes (12:2). They are proud (6:16–19) and certainly do not have the fear of Yahweh. If they search for wisdom on these terms, it is no wonder that they are left empty at the end of the process.

On the other hand, persons of understanding by definition are open to correction, display humility, and fear Yahweh. Again, it is no wonder that knowledge comes easily and quickly to them. This proverb therefore teaches that one's ability to learn wisdom is related to one's predisposition.

> **7**Stay away from a foolish person,
>   for you will not know knowledgeable lips.

14:7. In 13:20 we learn that those who associate with fools will become foolish themselves, and those who associate with wise people will be wise. This verse may be understood as an admonition based on the observation found in 13:20. The idea is that one who searches for knowledge will not find it with a foolish person, so don't associate with such a one.

> **8**The wisdom of the prudent makes them understand their path,
>   but the stupidity of fools is a fraud.

14:8. The first colon informs readers that if they care to know how to live their lives (the "path"), then wisdom is the answer. For "wisdom,"

---

2. Note its use also in 6:19; 12:17; 14:25; 19:5, 9.

see 1:2; for the "prudent," see 1:4. And for "path" as life, see 1:15. The opposite of the wisdom of the prudent is the stupidity of fools. In what sense is the stupidity of fools a fraud? The answer is probably to be gained by comparing the second colon with the first. Folly may hold out the promise to be the solution to life's issues, but in reality folly fails people and thus is a fraud. Rather than guiding people, it misleads them. For "fraud" (*mirmâ*), see 11:1; 12:5, 17, 20; 14:8, 25; 20:23; 26:24.

> ⁹The stupid person mocks a guilt offering,
> but favor is toward the virtuous.

14:9. This is a rare but not exceptional reference to the religious cult, specifically sacrificial ritual, and shows the sage's positive attitude toward it. Fools are those who disdain guilt offerings. After all, fools will not admit fault and therefore would never agree that a guilt offering is necessary. For guilt offering, see Lev. 5:14–6:7. In this case, the virtuous is pitted against the stupid person. The proverb therefore implies that virtue includes the acknowledgment of transgression and the necessity of a guilt offering. "Favor" here and elsewhere (see 8:35; 10:32; 11:1, 20, 27; 12:2, 22; 14:35; 16:7, 13, 15; 18:22; 19:12) may well imply divine favor, and thus the NRSV renders this colon, "but the upright enjoy God's favor."

> ¹⁰A heart knows emotional distress,
> and in its joy another person cannot share.

14:10. The proverb makes the observation that no one can really know what is going on emotionally inside another person. It looks at this from the opposing perspectives of distress and joy. Whether depressed or happy, only the person knows his or her own state of mind. The person may choose to describe this to another, either verbally or by acting it out, but unless expressed, other people may be left in the dark. This proverb is another that illustrates the interest of the sages in what today is called "psychology." As to the intention of the observation, we cannot be certain. Perhaps it is presented as an important insight about human nature. It helps the sage read other people in order to take care in presenting the right word or the right action at the right time. The fact that other persons cannot know one's heart may be compared with 15:11, which acknowledges that Yahweh knows the human heart.

> ¹¹The house of the wicked will be annihilated,
> but the tent of the virtuous will blossom.

14:11. This proverb is another (see also 1:32–33; 3:2; 4:10–19; etc.) that comments on the opposite consequences of wise behavior (here noted by the related term "virtuous") and foolish behavior (here designated by "wicked"). It is not just the person who will be affected but also the shelter. The paradox of the verse is that the house, a stable structure, will be annihilated, while the tent, an inherently less stable structure, will prosper.[3] See also the closely related 14:1.

> ¹²There is a path that is straight before a person,
> but in the end it is the path of death.

14:12. The proverb deals with human perception versus reality. What seems the right path of life may well turn out to lead to dire consequences. The proverb calls on the wise to constantly question and evaluate their life path.

The path image frequently denotes one's life course, particularly in chaps. 1–9. The path that appears easy is not the right path, because it ends in death (see the identical proverb in 16:25). Those who know the NT cannot help but think of Jesus's words in Matt. 7:13–14:

> Enter through the narrow gate. For wide is the gate and broad is the road that leads to destruction, and many enter through it. But small is the gate and narrow the road that leads to life, and only few find it. (NIV)

This is not contradictory to the wicked path elsewhere being described as "crooked" (2:15), not straight or right. In this proverb (and also 2:15), the idea is that the path leading to death is not actually straight but just perceived by the fool to be so. This observation encourages the wise person to look beneath the surface of appearances, particularly if the right way seems easy.

> ¹³Even in laughter the heart may feel pain,
> and in the end joy may turn to sorrow.

14:13. This is another psychological observation (as in 12:25; 13:12; 15:4; etc.) that probably has the intention of helping the sage understand people in order to speak the right word and perform the right action at the right time. It certainly also throws light on one's own experience and emotions. The insight is that surface realities, in this case what appear to be positive emotions, are not the whole story and may hide more dif-

---

3. I thus disagree with those like McKane (*Proverbs*, 474) who believe that "house" and "tent" are simply two different words indicating structure.

ficult and painful feelings. According to Qoheleth, sorrow better reflects reality than joy (Eccles. 7:2, 3, 4, 6).[4]

> **14**Rebellious hearts are satisfied with the consequences of their path,
> good people with the consequences of their deeds.

14:14. This is a difficult verse. The verb serves double duty in both cola. The verb *śbʾ* with the *min* preposition has the sense of being satisfied with the consequences of something. Both the good and the rebellious[5] are satisfied with what they get, but what the sage is supposed to learn from this observation is that the rebellious are happy to get something negative, since the consequences of their path, or life course, is ultimately death.

> **15**The simpleminded believe anything,
> but the prudent understand their steps.

14:15. The "simpleminded" or "naive" (*petî*) are characterized by their lack of critical thinking. By not reflecting on a matter, they may well speak or act on the basis of a misunderstanding and thus say or do the wrong thing, with horrible consequences. On the other hand, the prudent think ahead. This proverb basically defines the simpleminded over against the prudent, with the intention of encouraging the attentive reader/hearer to be prudent. Woman Wisdom herself advocates for this line of action in 9:6.

> **16**The wise fear and eschew evil,
> but the fool gets infuriated and feels safe.

14:16. Here the wise are again compared favorably with fools. The verse begins by stating that the wise fear, but it does not explain the object of their fear. In any case, their fear keeps them from committing evil acts. Evil is tempting, and it takes an emotion as strong as fear to keep them from succumbing to its lure.[6] Perhaps the fear is of the consequences. The wise know that though evil is tempting, the consequences are ultimately harmful, and thus they avoid evil. More likely, in my opinion, is that "fear" is shorthand for "fear Yahweh." After all,

---

4. For commentary, see Longman, *Ecclesiastes*, 180–86.

5. The word *sûg* here modifies "heart" and may be understood as "faithless, perverse, disloyal, or rebellious." The basic meaning of the verbal root seems to be "to deviate or diverge."

6. The NLT seems to follow this line of thinking when it translates v. 16a: "The wise are cautious and avoid danger."

the reader of the book has already heard that it is the "fear of Yahweh" that is the beginning of knowledge (1:7) and causes one to avoid evil (3:7; 8:13). Those who fear Yahweh will avoid doing what God does not want them to do—evil acts. In this verse, we again observe how wisdom is an ethical category.

The second colon marks fools as hotheads. Hotheaded persons will not avoid evil; they act impulsively. Fools are also ignorant of their situation. They feel confident or safe, but in reality they are in grave danger.

> [17]The short-tempered act stupidly,
> and people who scheme are hated.

14:17. Perhaps there is a connection with the previous verse in the fact that the fool is one who gets easily angered. In any case, those who are quick to throw a temper tantrum also act impulsively and then do stupid, thoughtless things, which get them into trouble. However, the second colon intensifies the thought of the first line. It is one thing to be short-tempered and do stupid things; it is even worse if one commits evil acts after long reflection and planning. That is the meaning of "scheme" (*mĕzimmôt*) here. The word "scheming" is from *mĕzimmâ*. This word can have either a positive or negative meaning. In 2:11 we saw that it has the positive sense of "discretion," but here it is the negative idea of "scheming." The basic idea is, as Fox has pointed out, "private, unrevealed thought, often but not always used in scheming. As the ability to think for oneself and keep one's own counsel, it is especially valuable in withstanding temptation."[7] Here it is negative, as in 12:2, where the schemer is contrasted with the good person. The latter obtains God's favor, while God condemns the schemer.

> [18]The simpleminded inherit stupidity,
> but the prudent wear knowledge as an ornament.

14:18. This proverb is descriptive, which helps the learner better understand different types of people. Here the contrast is between the simpleminded and the prudent. The verse begins by claiming that the former inherits stupidity. The statement is somewhat ambiguous in terms of the origin of the stupidity that the simpleminded inherits. The parallel colon does not really help. I think the best understanding is to recognize that stupidity is an inheritance derived from simplemindedness. Simplemindedness produces stupidity. On the other hand, the prudent wear knowledge as an ornament: the prudent are clearly rec-

7. Fox, *Proverbs 1–9*, 116.

ognized and honored for their knowledge. Stupidity and prudence are often contrasted in Proverbs.

> ¹⁹Evil people bow down before good people,
> and wicked people are at the gates of the righteous.

14:19. This optimistic proverb states that good/righteous people are much better off than evil/wicked people. Indeed, the latter find themselves in a subservient position to the former. One would have to believe the sages were bereft of real-life experience and ignorant of life in general to think that they meant this as an absolute principle and always true. They must have thought it as a generally true principle, true "in the long run." Many biblical stories support this idea. For instance, Joseph was godly but was actually abused by his brothers and thrown into prison for his righteous behavior. However, by the end of the story, Joseph is in a position of influence so that he can save the family of the covenant promise. At the beginning of the book of Esther, Mordecai finds himself persecuted by Haman, which seems the exact opposite of the claim of this proverb. However, by the end a reversal takes place so that wicked Haman finds himself at the mercy of godly Mordecai. Christians reading this would be wrong to apply this principle rigidly to their earthly existence; they also need to think in the "long run." Van Leeuwen rightly points to the parable of Lazarus and the rich man as an illustration of this principle (see Luke 16:19–31).[8]

> ²⁰The poor are hated by their neighbors,
> but many are those who love the wealthy.

14:20. The sage makes an observation on human nature. In this proverb he neither condemns nor condones this attitude (though a negative reading may be elicited by reading this proverb in the light of the next one in v. 21), but rather states it, imparting an insight to the disciple. It is a principle of human nature that most people would rather be in the company of wealthy persons than of poor persons. The latter typically have needs that require attention, while the former have resources that may prove a benefit to others. Thus, the poor are avoided and the rich have many friends. These friends and the love they seem to have toward the wealthy may be inauthentic, but even so, the statement is true. Qoheleth expresses the inauthentic nature of love directed toward the wealthy because they are rich:

8. Van Leeuwen, "Proverbs," 142.

When prosperity increases, those who consume it increase. So what success is there for its owner, except to admire it? (Eccles. 5:11).[9]

> **21**Those who despise their neighbors are sinners,
> but blessed are those who are gracious to the needy.

14:21. This verse puts a negative spin on the observation of the previous verse. Those who despise their neighbors, whether rich or poor, sin. Indeed, the second colon encourages good actions toward those neighbors and friends who are needy, a group that is related to the poor.

> **22**Do those who plan evil wander aimlessly?
> Those who plan good things receive covenant love and faithfulness.

14:22. This is a proverb about consequences. It contrasts the end result of planning evil and planning good. Evil planners are not rooted in anything but, rather, wander aimlessly. The verb "wander aimlessly" (*tʿh*) may have been chosen in order to allude to the "path theology" that runs throughout the book, especially the first part. The rhetorical question presupposes a positive answer. On the other hand, those who plan good things receive good things. "Covenant love and faithfulness" (*ḥesed weʾĕmet*) is a frequent word pair. In many contexts, they describe the quality of God's relationship toward his creatures. He is faithful to protect them and love them. But they are also characteristics of the community of God's people. Those who plan good things receive the benefits and goodwill of others of like attitude.

> **23**There is an advantage to all hard work,
> but the word of the lips leads only to lack.

14:23. This proverb contrasts hard work with loquaciousness. Talk is cheap, but actions bring a profit.[10] Certainly, there are words that bring benefit, but this proverb presupposes empty words. If someone talks all the time and does not work, it will lead to deprivation.

> **24**The crown of the wise is their wealth;
> the stupidity of fools is stupidity.

14:24. The verse contrasts wisdom and folly by pitting the reward of the former with the emptiness of the latter. The metaphor of the crown

---

9. Translation from Longman, *Ecclesiastes*, 160.

10. For *môtār*, a form related to *yitrôn*; see Eccles. 3:19 and Prov. 21:5, and also comments at Longman, *Ecclesiastes*, 129.

is apt for the material reward that comes to the wise. On the other hand, stupidity only yields stupidity, nothing more. This observation serves the purpose of motivating the hearer toward the acquisition of wisdom. The young king Solomon illustrates the truth of the first part of this proverb. He asked for wisdom, and God was so pleased that he also gave him power and wealth (1 Kings 3:1–15).

> ²⁵A truthful witness saves lives,
> but a fraudulent person proclaims lies.

14:25. This is one of many proverbs that contrast those who tell the truth in legal situations with those who tell lies. Here we can see how the contrast is a matter of life and death. See also 14:5 and other passages listed there. The veracity of witnesses is a major concern not only in Proverbs; it is also a significant issue in the Torah (Exod. 20:16; 23:1–2; Deut. 5:20; 17:6; 19:15–19).

> ²⁶In the fear of Yahweh there is strong safety,
> and refuge for their children.

14:26. For fear of Yahweh, see 1:7; 10:27; 14:26–27; 15:16, 33; 16:6; 19:23; 22:4. This proverb announces the benefits that come to those who fear Yahweh. By placing themselves in their proper subservient position to Yahweh, such people are under his protection. In the second colon, the promises of protection extend to their children. If one fears Yahweh, then they do not need to fear anything or anyone else.[11] Van Leeuwen rightly points out that the language of refuge and safety in connection with relationship with Yahweh is a significant theme in the Psalter (see especially Ps. 25).[12]

> ²⁷The fear of Yahweh is a fountain of life,
> turning aside from death traps.

14:27. The fear-of-Yahweh theme continues from the previous verse. Here it is compared to a fountain of life (see also 10:11; 13:14; 16:22). A fountain is an apt metaphor for life since it contrasts with a stagnant pool of water. It also gives the idea of an abundance of life that flows from the fear of Yahweh (for which see references given for v. 26). The life associated with fear of Yahweh is contrasted with the death traps

---

11. For theological and psychological reflections on fear, see Dan Allender and Tremper Longman III, *Cry of the Soul: How Our Emotions Reveal Our Deepest Questions about God* (Colorado Springs: NavPress, 1994), 79–105.

12. Van Leeuwen, "Proverbs," 143.

of the second colon. The identity of the latter is not made specific, but throughout the book folly is associated with death (see the description of Woman Folly in 9:13–18). See the closely related 13:14, where "instruction of the wise" replaces "fear of Yahweh."[13] Clifford suggests that the fear of God in the ancient Near East was a ritual action rather than an emotion,[14] but one wants to ask why it could not best be seen as both.

> [28]In an abundance of people is the splendor of a king,
>   and in the absence of a population is the ruin of a ruler.

14:28. A king without much of a nation is not much of a king. That seems to be the gist of the observation presented by this proverb. Perhaps the intention of this proverb is to encourage the king to implement life-promoting measures in his kingdom. Too often kings attack their own people out of insecurity or simply in the interests of their own power. Kings with large populations are able to amass more powerful armies and achieve more influence in their world. Here a royal proverb follows two Yahweh proverbs, an association that occurs elsewhere and may reflect some intentional structuring ideas (see "The Structure of Proverbs" in the introduction).[15]

> [29]Patience brings much competence,
>   but impatience promotes stupidity.

14:29. The sage knows that a coolheaded person will get further ahead in life than a hothead. The ability to control one's emotions and express them at the right time and to the appropriate degree is an important aspect of wisdom. To act impulsively, without reflection, leads to "stupidity," a close associate of "folly." Fox defines "competence" (*tĕbûnâ*, a nominal formed from *byn*; see also 2:2) as "the pragmatic, applied aspect of thought, operating in the realm of action; it aims at efficacy and accomplishment."[16]

> [30]The life of the body is a healthy heart,
>   but jealousy is a rot of the bones.

13. Whybray (*Proverbs*, 222) claims that 13:14 has temporal priority to 14:27 and that the latter represents a theological reinterpretation. Such a scheme is purely speculative and rests on the dubious idea that early wisdom was secular and only later Yahwehized.
14. Clifford, *Proverbs*, 147.
15. Note Whybray's comment (*Proverbs*, 221) and his citation of 14:34–15:3; 15:33–16:15; 20:26–21:3; 21:1–4; 22:11–12; 25:2–7; 29:12–14.
16. Fox, *Proverbs 1–9*, 37.

14:30. The translation of the proverb offered here is rather literal, awkward, and hard to understand. To provide a thought-for-thought translation, though, would require a rendition hard to track with the Hebrew, so for the purposes of this commentary, I have chosen to stay with a word-for-word translation.

There is a kind of semantic chiasm here: the "life of the body" is contrasted with "rot of the bones," and "healthy heart" is contrasted with "rot of the bones." The result is a rather striking psychological insight that shows an early awareness of what today is called "psychosomatic disease."

The first colon states that an emotionally healthy person enjoys physical well-being; the second colon observes that psychological turmoil results in physical illness. The "heart," after all, is roughly equivalent to one's core personality, including emotions (see 3:1).[17] A coolheaded person, an emotionally intelligent person, enjoys "life in the body." The latter term (from *bāśār*) focuses on the physical aspect of human existence. On the other hand, jealousy is an emotion that can destroy one's inner peace and have a physical effect. Murphy rightly points out that the association of jealousy with rot in the bones well indicates the nature of jealousy, which "eats away at a person."[18] Not all jealousy is wrongminded. It can be an emotion that moves a person to restore a threatened exclusive relationship. Even God may be described as a jealous God (Nah. 1:2), and Paul talks about his jealousy toward the exclusive religious devotion of the Corinthians as reflecting the "jealousy of God" (2 Cor. 11:1–4 NLT). However, often jealousy is wrongly directed and can lead to violent behavior, which is always inappropriate. In any case, jealousy can destroy one's mental, emotional, and physical health.[19]

> [31]Those who oppress the poor insult their Maker,
> but those who show grace to the destitute honor him.

14:31. Proverbs teaches that God blesses the wise with riches and afflicts the foolish with poverty (14:24). If one isolates this strand of teaching, one could falsely characterize the book of Proverbs as callous toward the needs of the poor. However, such a view does not take into account the sensitivity and protections offered to the poor through the compassionate teaching of the sage (see also 11:24; 28:27; 29:7, 14). After all, Proverbs also shows awareness that there are other reasons besides

17. Many commentators believe that "heart" focuses on the "mind," in seeming contrast to the emotions. I think this needlessly limits our understanding of this Hebrew word, which more generally refers to one's "inner life."
18. Murphy, *Proverbs*, 107.
19. See Allender and Longman, *Cry of the Soul*, 107–32.

foolish behavior, including laziness and indulgence, that lead to poverty. One notable proverb suggests that poverty can come about through social oppression (13:23). Here the point is made that to oppress the poor is not just an attack on them but also on God, who made them (see also 22:2). On the positive side, to honor the poor is to honor God.

The NT shares this viewpoint, as illustrated by Jesus's comments that to feed and clothe a needy stranger is, in effect, to do so for the divine king (Matt. 25:31–46), and not to do so is to offend him.

> [32]In their evil the wicked are thrown down,
> but the righteous find refuge in their death.

14:32. Although evil is occasionally on top, in the long run, so the sages suggest, the righteous are victorious and the wicked defeated. This is a proverb about ultimate consequences. Though there is a textual issue (see translation footnote), the MT indicates that even at the end of life, the righteous find support, implicitly from God. If this verse was not understood in its ancient context as pointing to the afterlife, one could certainly understand how it might lead to such a conclusion. In this regard, it strikes me that Van Leeuwen[20] and Murphy[21] both opt for the variant reading based on the presupposition that Proverbs could not possibly have eternal life in mind. This kind of reasoning is circular. Whybray, though he does not consider it an impossibility, asserts that it is "extremely improbable."[22]

> [33]Wisdom resides in an understanding heart,
> but it is not known in the innards of fools.

14:33. Wisdom is an interior quality. Those who are wise are wise from the core ("heart"). Not so the fools, who are the opposite of wise persons.

> [34]Righteousness lifts a nation up,
> but sin diminishes a people.

14:34. Righteousness, the behavior associated with wisdom, helps a nation. The proverb is ambiguous and could be applied equally to the righteous acts of an individual or to societal righteousness. As defined throughout Proverbs, this quality entails promoting the interests of others, particularly the vulnerable, and so one can naturally see how it would

20. Van Leeuwen, "Proverbs," 144.
21. Murphy, *Proverbs*, 107.
22. Whybray, *Proverbs*, 223.

help the broader society. On the other hand, sin harms others and causes alienation. Thus, it is easy to see how it could lessen a people.

> [35]The king finds an insightful servant acceptable,
>   but his fury will be directed toward a shameful one.

14:35. This proverb promotes wisdom over folly. Insight (see 1:3) is a quality of the wise, and shame is the consequence of being a fool. To say that the king finds the former acceptable indicates his favorable attitude toward insight. After all, a person with insight will be helpful to the king as he tries to resolve complex issues. A servant who is a fool and therefore shameful will be the object of his wrath since the servant will not be able to help resolve the problems of the realm, and indeed he might deepen them.

This proverb may be addressed in the first place to potential servants in the royal court, encouraging them to pursue wisdom. On the other hand, it may simply be using the king as an authority figure whose favor toward insight is being used to encourage everyone to pursue wisdom. The proverb implies a righteous king. There are plenty of examples from biblical history (such as Ahab listening to Jezebel, in 1 Kings 16:29–33) where kings have, to their own harm, found shameful advice acceptable.

Chapter 15

Translation

¹A tender answer turns back wrath,
    but a painful statement raises anger.
²The tongue of the wise improves[a] knowledge,
    but the mouth of fools bubbles forth with stupidity.
³The eyes of Yahweh are everywhere,
    keeping watch on evil and good people.
⁴A healthy[b] tongue is a tree of life,
    but one with duplicity produces a broken spirit.
⁵Stupid people disdain the discipline of their fathers,
    but those who guard correction are prudent.
⁶In[c] the house of the righteous is great treasure,
    but in the yield of the wicked is harm.
⁷The lips of the wise scatter knowledge,
    but the hearts of fools have none.[d]
⁸The sacrifice of wicked people is an abomination to Yahweh,
    but the prayer of the virtuous brings his favor.
⁹The path of the wicked is an abomination to Yahweh,
    but he loves those who pursue righteousness.
¹⁰Discipline is evil to those who abandon the way;
    those who hate correction will die.

a. The verb (from *yṭb*) makes perfectly good sense here; there is no reason to adopt the conjectural emendation proposed by *BHS*, which interprets the verb as deriving from *nṭp*, "to drip."

b. For *marpēʾ* with *lēb* (heart), see 14:30. Here the NIV renders the phrase as "the tongue that brings healing," but this is inconsistent with its treatment of the word in 14:30.

c. The prefixed preposition *bě* (in) is missing in the Hebrew and may have dropped out due to haplography.

d. Understanding *lōʾ-kēn* as "not thus."

¹¹Sheol and Abaddon are before Yahweh;
   how much more the hearts of human beings.
¹²Mockers do not love those who correct them;
   they do not go to the wise.
¹³A joyful heart brightens one's face,
   but in a troubled heart, a broken spirit.
¹⁴An understanding heart seeks knowledge,
   but the face^e of fools feeds on^f stupidity.
¹⁵All days of the needy are evil,
   but a happy heart is a continual feast.
¹⁶Better a little with fear of Yahweh
   than a great treasure and turmoil with it.
¹⁷Better a daily portion of vegetables and love there
   than a fatted calf^g and hate with it.
¹⁸Hotheads^h stir up conflict,
   but patient people quell accusations.
¹⁹The path of lazy people is like a hedge^i of thorns,
   but the way of the virtuous is a clear highway.
²⁰A wise son brings joy to a father,
   but a foolish person^j despises his mother.
²¹Stupidity is joyful to those who lack heart,
   but the competent make their going straight.
²²Plans are hindered by an absence of counsel,
   but in a multitude of advisers they will succeed.
²³It is a joy to a person to give an answer!^k
   How good a word at the right time!
²⁴For one with insight, the way of life is upward,
   to turn aside from Sheol below.
²⁵Yahweh uproots the house of the arrogant,
   but he establishes the border of the widow.
²⁶Evil plans are an abomination to Yahweh,
   but pure is pleasing speech.¹

e. With the Kethib (*pĕnê*). Qere reads "mouth" (*pî*).

f. The verb is from *rʿh*, a shepherding term.

g. Literally, the expression is "ox of a stall" (see 14:4), but it implies an ox fed and thus fattened for people to eat.

h. Alternatively, "angry people" (*ʾîš ḥēmâ*).

i. The noun is *mĕśūkâ*, an alternative spelling of *mĕsūkâ*. The above translation follows the syntax of the Hebrew, which modern translations often smooth out. See NIV: "The way of the sluggard is blocked with thorns."

j. In an attempt to sharpen the parallelism, the LXX emends "person" to "son."

k. A literal rendition of the Hebrew into English sounds awkward: "Joy to a person in the answer of his mouth." NRSV translates "answer" with the modifier "apt," which is not explicit in the Hebrew but is certainly appropriate to the context (see also "apt reply" in the NIV).

l. The NIV translates the Greek, not the Hebrew, in v. 26b: "but those of the pure are pleasing to him."

[27]Those who get unjust gain[m] harm their houses,
   but those who hate gifts will live.
[28]The heart of the righteous meditates before answering,
   but the mouth of the wicked blurts out evil.
[29]Yahweh is far from the wicked,
   but he hears the prayers of the righteous.
[30]The light of the eyes gives joy to the heart;
   a good report refreshes to the bone.
[31]The ear that listens to life-giving correction
   lodges among the wise.
[32]Those who neglect discipline disdain their lives,
   but those who listen to correction acquire heart.
[33]The fear of Yahweh is wise discipline,
   and humility comes before glory.

Interpretation

[1]A tender answer turns back wrath,
   but a painful statement raises anger.

15:1. The proverb speaks to the most effective way to interact during a disagreement or argument. Though the sage does not shirk from receiving a rebuke when necessary (17:10), it is more typically the case that a soft or tender response will create the conditions that allow for a fruitful conversation. On the other hand, if a person responds with a comment that evokes pain in the other person, then that other person will respond defensively and angrily, so no dialogue can continue. The sage is well aware that there are some who will respond angrily or defensively no matter what, and for cases like this, the recommendation is not to engage those persons at all (26:4). This proverb fits in with the general teaching in Proverbs that coolheadedness is superior to hotheadedness. This proverb also illustrates the book's concern for social cohesion. The proper response is one that maintains and promotes relationship.

[2]The tongue of the wise improves knowledge,
   but the mouth of fools bubbles forth with stupidity.

15:2. The proverb is an observation that has unspoken consequences. It seems almost tautological to say that when the wise speak, those who listen to them will grow smarter about life but that those who listen to

---

m. See Harland (*"Bṣᶜ"*), who shows that the root *bṣᶜ* implies negative, usually violent, means of gaining material substance.

the babbling (another possible rendition of the verb *nbᶜ*) of fools will hear only stupid things. But it alerts hearers that in an actual situation, they will have to judge whether they are listening to a wise person or a fool and respond accordingly. For other references to those who bubble forth stupidly, compare Ps. 59:7; 94:4; Prov. 15:28; Eccles. 10:14. Again, this proverb contributes to the idea that the wise are good for society and fools are detrimental.

> ³The eyes of Yahweh are everywhere,
> keeping watch on evil and good people.

15:3. The proverb is clear enough, but perhaps somewhat unexpected in a wisdom context. There are other religious proverbs (16:1–7, 9, 33), but this one implies God's moral governance. Many other proverbs that mention consequences do not specify who does the ultimate judgment or how that judgment is assured; this proverb helps the hearer understand that God is in control. The idea that God watches evil and good people implies that he is the one who distinguishes between these two classes of people. As Van Leeuwen observes, "This verse states a fundamental precept of biblical thought, that the Lord knows all things, including the human heart."[1] This verse supports the idea that God is omnipresent and omniscient.

> ⁴A healthy tongue is a tree of life,
> but one with duplicity produces a broken spirit.

15:4. This verse is about the consequences of one's speech. A healthy tongue is one that speaks the straightforward truth. Not that it blurts out the truth without concern for the circumstances or without the requisite tenderness (15:1), but it does speak what is right and thus promotes life. For the metaphor of the tree of life, see 3:18; 11:30; 13:12; the point is that a healthy tongue encourages life. On the other hand, a duplicitous tongue is one that lies and misleads (see 11:3; 13:6; 19:3; 21:12; 22:12 for other occurrences of *slp*). Far from positive effects, it breaks the spirits of those who listen to it. This proverb illustrates the book's sensitivity and concern for the psychological consequences of speech and actions.

> ⁵Stupid people disdain the discipline of their fathers,
> but those who guard correction are prudent.

15:5. This proverb comments on the importance of being open to discipline as a route to wisdom. If one cannot bear to hear about one's mistakes

---

1. Van Leeuwen, "Proverbs," 148.

and take steps to correct them, then one is doomed to be perpetually wrong. Thus, it is stupid not to hear those in authority give advice. For first occurrences of "discipline" (*mûsar*) and "correction" (*tôkaḥat*), see 1:3 and 1:23 respectively. For "prudence" (from *ʿrm*), see 1:4.

> ⁶In the house of the righteous is great treasure,
> but in the yield of the wicked is harm.

15:6. The proverb describes the effects of the efforts of the righteous and the wicked, the first being positive and the second being negative. The initial colon speaks to the fact that righteousness has effects beyond the individual. The great treasure does not have to be understood exclusively in terms of material goods; it may be joy of living, with psychological and social benefits. However, due to the frequent connection drawn between wisdom and material benefits, this would not be excluded either. On the other hand, these positive effects of righteousness are contrasted with the harm that comes from the efforts of the wicked person.

> ⁷The lips of the wise scatter knowledge,
> but the hearts of fools have none.

15:7. The parallel between lips or tongue and heart is found elsewhere in proverbs and indicates the sage's belief that the lips normally reveal what is going on inside a person. Since the wise are wise, when they speak, it is worth listening to. However, there is nothing inside fools, so when they speak, one expects stupidity. See 15:2.

> ⁸The sacrifice of wicked people is an abomination to Yahweh,
> but the prayer of the virtuous brings his favor.

15:8. As 11:1 (for detailed description of the phrase *tôʿăbat Yhwh*, see this verse) illustrates, abomination is often contrasted with God's favor. The purpose of such observations is to indicate behavior that pleases the Deity.

The contrast in this chapter is between wicked people and virtuous people. "It is the sacrificer, not the sacrifice, that is the issue."[2] The first colon really underlines God's dislike of wickedness because it can ruin something as otherwise God-pleasing as sacrifice. On the other hand, even the prayers (arguably a lesser act than sacrifice in terms of energy and resources expended) of the virtuous win his favor.

2. Murphy, *Proverbs*, 112.

This proverb demonstrates the sage's concern for the formal religious institutions of Israel. Other places in Proverbs where sacrifice/feasting and/or prayer are treated are 15:29; 17:1; 21:3, 27; 28:9.[3]

> [9]The path of the wicked is an abomination to Yahweh,
>   but he loves those who pursue righteousness.

15:9. This verse is connected to the previous by the phrase "abomination to Yahweh" (*tôʿăbat Yhwh*, for which see comments on v. 8). However, unlike there and elsewhere, this phrase is not contrasted with something that "brings his favor" (*rĕṣônô*, v. 8), but a comparable expression fills that function. God hates the path of the wicked, but he loves those who pursue righteousness. Thus, the contrast in the verse is between the life-styles of the wicked and the righteous. This is a quite general statement that needs to be understood in the light of the whole book's teaching on folly/wickedness and wisdom/righteousness. This verse and the following one remind the reader of the two-path metaphor that is particularly prominent in chaps. 1–9.

> [10]Discipline is evil to those who abandon the way;
>   those who hate correction will die.

15:10. This verse fits in with the extensive teaching that hearing criticism and changing wrong behavior is integral to wisdom (3:1–11; 9:7–12; etc.). It is stupid to put up defenses against legitimate criticism since that will just perpetuate wrong behavior and the negative consequences that follow. The proverb puts it in the strongest possible terms: death is the ultimate consequence for those who do not listen to negative comments. Like the preceding verse, this one also evokes the two-path theology of the book. The NRSV, the NIV, and some commentators understand the meaning in a slightly different way:

> Stern discipline awaits him who leaves the path;
>   he who hates correction will die. (NIV)

My translation takes *rāʿ* in its moral sense and also as a predicate; the NIV rather understands the word as a modifier of "discipline" (*mûsār*) and as "stern." It is debatable whether *rāʿ* can have the sense of "stern." This seems to be an extension of "harm" or "hurt," which are attested meanings. Waltke agrees with the NIV on the syntax but more persuasively takes the meaning of *rāʿ* as "painful" and translates the colon: "Painful

---

3. See the discussion of this verse in Perdue, *Wisdom and Cult*, 155–58.

discipline awaits the one who abandons the path [of life]."[4] While this translation is possible, it seems best to go with the more common moral sense of the word.[5]

> [11]Sheol and Abaddon are before Yahweh;
> how much more the hearts of human beings.

15:11. The expression in colon 1 suggests that even Sheol and Abaddon are in the purview of Yahweh, which implies his control and sovereignty. Sheol stands for the grave and, on occasion, implies the netherworld. Since the grave is dark and dank, so is the realm of the dead. While the etymology of "Sheol" is obscure, "Abaddon" is clearly a derivative of the verb *ʾābad* (to destroy), in parallel with "Sheol" standing for the place of destruction, and it is another name for the grave and the netherworld.

Since Yahweh is the God of life, one could question whether there was any connection between the two, but as Ps. 139 reminds the reader:

> Where can I go from your Spirit?
> Where can I flee from your presence?
> If I go up to the heavens, you are there;
> If I make my bed in the depths, you are there. (vv. 7–8 NIV)

Here Sheol and Abaddon are personified, and the point of the colon is that these destructive forces do not operate apart from God. The implication drawn in the second colon is that neither are human beings autonomous or superior to Yahweh. Sheol, Abaddon, and the hearts of human beings seem hidden, but they are not so to God. This verse is conceptually related to 15:3, which also comments on God's omniscience.

> [12]Mockers do not love those who correct them;
> they do not go to the wise.

15:12. See 15:10 and citations there for the theme that fools do not appreciate criticism. The term "mocker" (*lēṣ*) is a strong term describing the fool as one who mocks those who try to point out a weakness. By being self-defensive, mockers ultimately undermine themselves. One way to avoid correction is by not associating with the wise, who can see the mistakes that others make and are willing to offer advice. On the other hand, the wise really appreciate insightful criticism because it helps them to live life better and more productively.

4. Waltke, *Proverbs*, 1:616.
5. See also Murphy, *Proverbs*, 112.

> ¹³A joyful heart brightens one's face,
> but in a troubled heart, a broken spirit.

15:13. This proverb provides another insightful psychological comment (see also "Psychological Insight" in the appendix). The point of the first colon is that one's internal well-being is reflected in one's appearance. Our emotions affect our demeanor. The second colon seems to go deeper in that it is not an internal influence on the external, but an internal influence on the internal. In other words, standing behind a pained or troubled heart is a broken spirit.

One wonders whether Qoheleth was playing on the idea of colon 1 when he says:

Anger is better than laughter,
for in a troubled face the heart is made well. (Eccles. 7:3)[6]

Qoheleth believes that a happy heart and the resultant bright face are out of keeping with the harsh reality of life.

> ¹⁴An understanding heart seeks knowledge,
> but the face of fools feeds on stupidity.

15:14. This proverb talks about basic motivations of those who are "understanding" (*nābôn* is a word associated with "wisdom") and of those who are fools. As might be expected, the former pursue what will make them wiser, and the latter what will make them more foolish. The contrast between "heart" and "face" may contrast the depth of the wise over against the superficiality of fools. The contrast between "seeks" and "feeds" may imply that knowledge requires effort, while foolishness just partakes of whatever is there before a person.

> ¹⁵All days of the needy are evil,
> but a happy heart is a continual feast.

15:15. This proverb observes the difficulties encountered by the poor, since we are to understand "needy" (*'ānî*) that way rather than as spiritually or psychologically needy. On the other hand, the second colon suggests that one's state of mind may make one's circumstances irrelevant.

---

6. The verb "makes well" is from *yṭb*, which is behind the translation "brightens" in Prov. 15:13, strengthening our idea that there is a connection between these two texts. For a translation of the Ecclesiastes text and an explanation of the context, see Longman, *Ecclesiastes*, 180–84.

Life may be hard, but try to adopt a cheery attitude. The metaphor of the feast is a sensual one. The word is for a "drinking party" (*mišteh*), not a religious festival (*ḥāg*). This makes one wonder whether the thought here may be related to Qoheleth's idea that, though life is meaningless, a person can find some satisfaction in "eating and drinking."[7] Additionally, this proverb can be related to 31:6–7:

> Give strong drink to those who are perishing,
> and wine to the bitter of heart.
> Let them drink and forget their poverty
> and no longer remember their hard work.

However, Clifford suggests, without substantiation, that "good heart" signifies a "wise heart" and thus understands the verse in a more noble sense.[8]

> [16]Better a little with fear of Yahweh
> than a great treasure and turmoil with it.

15:16. The better-than proverbs express relative values. In other words, Proverbs affirms both the value of the fear of Yahweh and the value of wealth (cf. 1:7 and 10:22), but if a choice must be made, then there is no question but that the fear of Yahweh is much more valuable (see "The Fear of Yahweh" in the introduction). In other words, though the book often suggests that wealth is the reward of the wise, it also makes it clear that sometimes one must choose between fear of Yahweh and wealth.[9] The verse also implies a contrast between fear of Yahweh and turmoil. The assumption is that the fear of Yahweh brings calmness of mind as well.

> [17]Better a daily portion of vegetables and love there
> than a fatted calf and hate with it.

15:17. Again, an expression of relative values through the use of a better-than proverb (see v. 16), and the proverb again seeks to place material possessions in their proper place. Vegetables are a basic fare, but they surpass even the most expensive and desired meal ("fatted calf" represents succulent meat) if one finds oneself the object of hate rather than love. A good relationship with people rather than things is preferred.

---

7. For the carpe diem passages in Ecclesiastes (2:24–26; 3:12–14, 22; 5:18–20; 8:15; 9:7–10), see the comments offered by Longman, *Ecclesiastes*, 106–10, 121–22, 131, 160, 168, 172, 182–84, 216, 221, 224, 250.
8. Clifford, *Proverbs*, 153.
9. See Van Leeuwen, "Wealth and Poverty."

> ¹⁸Hotheads stir up conflict,
> but patient people quell accusations.

15:18. This verse speaks of the emotional intelligence of the wise. Fools respond to an attack by attacking back, only making things much worse. On the other hand, the wise are coolheaded and patient, thus in the end subduing accusations that may be directed toward them. The word "accusation" (*rîb*) is a legal one, but its application should probably not be limited to the courtroom. Egyptian wisdom often draws a contrast between hotheads and calm people. Amenemope's chap. 9 begins:

> Do not befriend the heated man,
> Nor approach him for conversation. (11.13–14)[10]

> ¹⁹The path of lazy people is like a hedge of thorns,
> but the way of the virtuous is a clear highway.

15:19. This proverb uses the two-path theology of the book to talk about the hazards accompanying one form of foolish behavior, laziness, and contrasting it with wisdom, here marked by one of its ethical synonyms, "virtue" (*yāšār*). The pair "path" (*derek*)/"way" (*ʾōraḥ*) is common in the book. The path/way represents the course of one's life and implies a destination. For lazy people, that course is hard to navigate and filled with pain, while the virtuous find their way unimpeded. The observation is a subtle encouragement to avoid laziness and pursue virtue.

> ²⁰A wise son brings joy to a father,
> but a foolish person despises his mother.

15:20. Not only is the first colon identical to 10:1a; the thought of the two proverbs is also very close to one another. Thus, the commentary at that verse should be consulted. The difference in the second colon has to do with the fact that it comments here on the son's sorry attitude toward his mother, as demonstrated through his foolishness. In 10:1b the emphasis is on the grief that such a son brings to the mother.

> ²¹Stupidity is joyful to those who lack heart,
> but the competent make their going straight.

15:21. The emotions of the fool are out of kilter with what is right. They rejoice not in wisdom but in their stupidity. Why? Because they

10. *COS* 1:118.

"lack heart": they lack any internal substance. While the heart points more generally at what today we might call core personality (see 3:1), there is sometimes an emphasis on cognitive abilities. On the other hand, as the opposite of stupid people, the competent have a clear road ahead (a subtle allusion to the two-path theology and thus a thought similar to 15:19).

> 22Plans are hindered by an absence of counsel,
> but in a multitude of advisers they will succeed.

15:22. The sage puts a premium on seeking advice. After all, the book is training its recipients to be wise, to have the ability to read circumstances and people, and thus to do the right act at the right time. Such advisers are invaluable to people as they make crucial decisions, whether for themselves or for their community, as for war strategy.[11] If one wise person is helpful, then a multitude of them would be even more beneficial.

Yet no matter how many advisers there are, they must be truly wise in order to be helpful and prove this proverb right. All we have to do is think of 1 Kings 12, where two groups are advising Rehoboam right after his ascension to the throne. There is nothing to make us think that "the elders" numbered more than the "young men," but certainly the former were more discerning of the situation than the latter. Again, this proverb is true "generally speaking."

> 23It is a joy to a person to give an answer!
> How good a word at the right time!

15:23. This proverb is important in establishing the nature of the "truth" of proverbs. There is not a single right answer that is always appropriate. It is a joy to give a helpful answer to a problem, but it must be spoken in a timely manner. The importance of the right time in wisdom in general and Proverbs in particular is discussed in the introduction (see "Genre").

> 24For one with insight, the way of life is upward,
> to turn aside from Sheol below.

15:24. With the mention of "way" (ʾōraḥ), the proverb suggests the two-path theology of the book. Here the contrast is between a way that leads upward to life and is known by the one with "insight" (for the root śkl, see 1:3), and the way that leads downward to Sheol (see 1:12),

---

11. However, 11:14 is more clearly shaped to speak of national interests.

a place to be avoided. That Sheol, meaning the grave with overtones of the netherworld, is downward is not surprising. The unstated opposite must be heaven, the very dwelling place of God. Whether "upward" and "downward" may be read in an eschatological sense in its original setting is debated,[12] but later Christian readers, heirs to a fuller revelation of the afterlife, may read them in this way now by virtue of this proverb's setting in the broader canon.

> ²⁵Yahweh uproots the house of the arrogant,
> but he establishes the border of the widow.

15:25. This proverb exploits an architectural metaphor to comment on what Yahweh approves. Yahweh will undermine the arrogant. The arrogant are those who place themselves first, above God and other humans, so God will see to their downfall. On the other hand, the widow is the epitome of social vulnerability in ancient Near Eastern culture. In a predominantly patriarchal society, a widow had no one to represent her in society or in court, so she was often the victim of malicious people. If anyone can be certain of a dismal future, it is the widow. God will step in to protect and support such people.

> ²⁶Evil plans are an abomination to Yahweh,
> but pure is pleasing speech.

15:26. For "abomination to Yahweh," see comments at 11:1, where the phrase is explained as indicating something that offends God's sense of moral or ritual order. Thus, it is not surprising that here it is in antithetical parallelism with "pure" (from *ṭhr*), a word indicating what is appropriate to those orders. The proverb thus provides a strong condemnation of evil plans, which presumably refers to those who strategize concerning the downfall of others.

> ²⁷Those who get unjust gain harm their houses,
> but those who hate gifts will live.

15:27. One may be tempted to cut or ignore morality in order to support one's household, but this proverb is a reminder that such shortcuts normally do not end well. The second colon specifies the first by naming an example of a strategy that is unjust in obtaining profit: to give bribes (in this context the "gift" is a bribe; see "Bribes/Gifts" in the appendix for other places in Proverbs where bribes are described). A bribe is an

---

12. See the broad contours of the debate as they are described in Whybray, *Proverbs*, 234.

illegitimate gift to encourage a person to act in a way that the situation does not merit. Recent business scandals in the United States provide vivid examples of the truth of this proverb, and elsewhere in the Bible we find condemnations of gifts that blind justice (Exod. 23:8; Deut. 16:19; 27:25; Isa. 1:23; 5:23; Ezek. 22:12; Ps. 15:5; Eccles. 7:7).

> [28]The heart of the righteous meditates before answering,
> but the mouth of the wicked blurts out evil.

15:28. This proverb points to the reflective nature of the wise, while fools are impulsive in all that they do, including giving advice. The proverb is a call to think before speaking and also serves as a warning against listening to those who are too quick to give their opinion. Other proverbs that advocate reflection before speaking include 19:2; 20:18, 25; 21:5; 29:20.

> [29]Yahweh is far from the wicked,
> but he hears the prayers of the righteous.

15:29. This proverb is a rare but not unique statement about prayer (see also 15:8; 28:9). It is incorrect to say that the sages had nothing to do with the cultic rituals of ancient Israel.[13] The question is, Who can approach God in prayer? The answer is, The righteous but not the wicked. Compare Pss. 1; 15; and 24.

It is not that Yahweh is unaware of the prayers of the wicked. The verse does not mean that God listens only to the prayers of the righteous and does not even hear those of the wicked. The verb "hear" in Hebrew often implies the response. God does something about the prayers of the righteous. To say that God is far from the wicked does not imply that he is merely local in his presence, but rather that he does not act on their behalf. In the light of the second colon, the first may be paraphrased: Yahweh does not respond to the prayers of the wicked. As Waltke puts it, "Assertions about the LORD's presence or distance are not theological statements that restrict his omnipresence but religious statements about the availability of his favor."[14]

> [30]The light of the eyes gives joy to the heart;
> a good report refreshes to the bone.

15:30. This proverb imparts a psychological insight. Both move from external to internal. The first observes that one can tell from others' bright

13. As is argued by Perdue, *Wisdom and Cult*.
14. Waltke, *Proverbs*, 1:639.

eyes (though it is difficult to be certain about the exact force of "light of the eyes") the positive state of the core of their being. The "eyes" in question are probably the eyes of persons whose good demeanor encourages those with whom they come into contact. Here "heart," which in general refers to the core of one's personality, clearly is connected with emotions and gives pause to those who suggest that the heart emphasizes internal cognitive processes.

The second colon also begins with something external, a good report or good news, in this case a matter of hearing rather than seeing. The effects of this news are also felt internally. A good report makes people feel good to their very bones.

> [31]The ear that listens to life-giving correction
> lodges among the wise.

15:31. The proverb observes that the wise are those who listen to "correction" (for which see 3:11–12; 9:7–9; etc.). Only the wise are willing to admit mistakes, change behavior, and improve their lives. In this way, correction enhances life. Wise persons are much less likely to make the same mistake twice. The proverb, in effect, suggests that wisdom is defined by one's willingness to listen to correction.

> [32]Those who neglect discipline disdain their lives,
> but those who listen to correction acquire heart.

15:32. The subject is similar to the previous proverb, but here the teaching is achieved by contrasting those who ignore discipline with those who pay attention to it. In other words, again the advice is to listen to criticism in order to improve one's character. Those who reject discipline disdain their lives because they run the risk of getting into trouble over and over again since they don't allow themselves to be aware of their mistakes. On the other hand, those who do listen "acquire heart," where heart points to one's core personality (see 3:1). In other words, they become people of substance. There is something to their internal makeup.

> [33]The fear of Yahweh is wise discipline,
> and humility comes before glory.

15:33. This proverb begins by conjoining two important concepts in Proverbs: "fear of Yahweh" (for which see 1:7) and "discipline," which is modified by "wise." "Discipline" relates this proverb to the previous two and refers to recognizing the importance of identifying mistakes one has made and making corrections. The second colon appropriately relates to the first colon by taking humility to be open to listening to discipline/correction. If one does this, then one's ability to navigate life will improve and in this way will lead to "glory." Humility is often contrasted with pride precisely in the area of being open to correction (3:5, 7; 6:17; 11:2, 14; etc.).

The repetition of these key concepts may signal that this proverb has been placed here in order to end the first "sub-collection" of Solomonic proverbs.[15]

15. So Van Leeuwen, "Proverbs," 152.

Chapter 16

Translation

¹To humans belong the plans of the heart,
   but from Yahweh comes a responding tongue.
²All paths of people are pure in their eyes,
   but Yahweh measures the motives.ᵃ
³Commitᵇ your acts to Yahweh,
   and your plans will be established.
⁴Yahweh makes everything for a purpose,ᶜ
   even the wicked for an evil day.
⁵All the haughtyᵈ are an abomination to Yahweh;ᵉ
   they will surelyᶠ not go unpunished.
⁶With covenant love and faithfulness guilt is atoned for,
   and with the fear of Yahweh there is turning away from evil.
⁷When a person's path draws Yahweh's favor,
   even his enemies are at peace with him.
⁸Better a little bit with righteousness

a. Or "spirits." The term "spirits" (from *rûaḥ*) seems to indicate the internal aspect of human beings. Here the closest concept that we have is "motives." See 21:2, where the related idiom is to measure one's heart.

b. This is an imperative form from the root *gll* (to cast), not—as suggested in the Syriac, Targum, and Vulgate—from *glh* (to reveal).

c. Literally, "to its answer." According to Murphy (*Proverbs*, 120), "'Answer' can mean a reaction to God, and in the context of v 4b, it is the reaction of human beings, even the wicked that is meant."

d. Literally, "the high of heart." This phrase indicates that pride was thought to reside in the core of one's personality.

e. For "abomination to Yahweh," see 6:16 (also 3:32; 11:20; 12:22; 15:8, 9, 26; 17:15).

f. For *yād lĕyād*, "surely," see 11:21. The verb *nqh* (to go unpunished) is also used there.

than a large yield without justice.

⁹Human hearts plan their path,
but Yahweh establishes their step.

¹⁰An oracular decision on the lips of a king:
he does not betray justice with his mouth.

¹¹The balance[g] and scales must be just according to Yahweh;
he concerns himself[h] with the weights of the pouch.

¹²Doing wicked deeds is an abomination of kings,
for in righteousness a throne is established.

¹³Righteous lips draw the favor of kings;
they love those who speak with virtue.

¹⁴The anger of a king is a messenger[i] of death;
the wise will appease it.

¹⁵In the light of the face of the king there is life,[j]
and his favor[k] is like a cloud that brings late rain.

¹⁶Getting wisdom is much better than gold,
and getting understanding is to be preferred over silver.

¹⁷The highway of the virtuous turns away from evil;
those who protect their path guard their lives.

¹⁸Pride comes before a disaster,
and before stumbling comes an arrogant attitude.

¹⁹Better to be a humble spirit with the needy
than dividing plunder with the proud.

²⁰Those with insight into a matter find prosperity;
blessed are those who trust Yahweh.

²¹The wise of heart will be called understanding,
and sweet lips increase teaching.

²²One who possesses insight[l] is a fountain of life,
but the discipline[m] of stupid people is stupidity.

²³The heart of the wise provides insight to their mouth
and increases teaching on their lips.

²⁴Pleasant words are liquid honey,
sweet to the taste[n] and healing to the bones.

g. According to *NIDOTTE* 3:630, the word *peles* refers to the "pointer of balance" and occurs elsewhere only at Isa. 40:12.

h. Literally, "his work," but the context suggests "his concern," which I translate in a verbal form. However, calling it "his work" reflects the fact that God was thought to stand behind both natural and social orders.

i. Hebrew has plural, "messengers."

j. Hebrew has plural, "lives."

k. For "favor," see 16:7 and passages cited there.

l. An idiomatic translation of "insight, the one who possesses it."

m. Some (NRSV) take *mûsār* here as "punishment," but it is better and just as understandable to take it as "discipline," its common use in Proverbs.

n. The word is *nepeš*, a common word often translated "person." The basic meaning, though, is "throat," and as the conduit of breath, it comes to indicate a "living being" or "person" but, as the conduit of food, refers to "appetite," "desire," or, in this case, "taste."

25There is a path that is straight[o] before a person,
but in the end it is the path of death.
26The appetite of laborers labors for them,
for their mouths press them on.[p]
27Worthless people dig up[q] evil,
and it is like a scorching fire on their lips.
28The perverse produce conflict,
and gossips separate intimate friends.
29The violent entice their neighbors
and make them walk on a path that is not good.
30Those who wink[r] the eye plot perverse things;
those who purse their lips conceal evil.
31Gray hair is a crown of glory;
it is found on the path of righteousness.
32A patient person is better than a warrior,
and those who control their emotions[s] than those who can capture a city.
33Into the lap the lot is cast,
and from Yahweh are all decisions.

Interpretation

1To humans belong the plans of the heart,
but from Yahweh comes a responding tongue.

16:1. Proverbs here, as often, parallels "heart" and a part of the body (tongue, lips, or the like) to signify internal processes and speech (see also 10:20; 16:23). This proverb makes it clear that, though humans can legitimately make plans, God's will is definitive as to what will actually happen. One can strategize about the future, to be sure, but this wise observation would lead one to acknowledge that the future can only be determined by God. Such recognition would engender a proper humility and open one up to changes. As commentators frequently point out, this

o. Or "seems right."

p. The verb "to press on" (*ʾkp*) is a *hapax legomenon*, though a noun form appears in Job 33:7.

q. The image seems strange to some, so they propose emending the text from the verb *kārâ* to the noun *kûr* (furnace), but this seems unnecessary. See Scott, *Proverbs*, 105, and the NAB.

r. The meaning of this verbal root *ʿṣh* seems difficult. On the basis of 10:10, one would expect the verb to be *qrṣ* (wink), but that verb is used in the second colon here in regard to the lips. *NIDOTTE* 3:485 suggests that the verb here "appears to have a meaning related to an Arab. cognate *gdw*, wrinkle the eyelids."

s. Literally, "spirit" (*rûaḥ*), in the sense of one's inner life. The context suggests "emotions."

proverb is often understood to mean: "Man proposes, but God disposes."[1] Whether or not "the response of the tongue" is referring to God's ultimate disposal of a thing or to the need for God's help to articulate the "plans of the heart" (so Whybray), the purpose of this proverb is not to discourage human planning, but rather to keep people aware that their plans will come to nothing without God's concurrence.

> [2]All paths of people are pure in their eyes,
> but Yahweh measures the motives.

16:2. Here human self-perception is judged in the light of Yahweh's perception. The proverb speaks to our ability to deceive ourselves concerning our righteousness. Proverbs often denigrates those who are wise (or clean) "in their own eyes" (3:7; 12:15; 26:5, 12; 30:12). The observation invites profound reflection on our motives, since God is the final arbiter of whether a path is right or wrong. This is not a function of human beings. See the similar teaching in 14:12. Murphy notes an analogy between Yahweh measuring (or weighing) the "spirits" and "the Egyptian god of the scribes, Thoth, weighing the heart of the dead person against the balance of *Ma'at*, justice."[2]

> [3]Commit your acts to Yahweh,
> and your plans will be established.

16:3. This proverb fits in with the teaching of the previous two verses. It reminds the sage that, as important as human planning is, the ultimate outcome (as in this verse) and the morality of it (as in 16:2) depend on Yahweh. All planning thus should be done in recognition that God can indeed overturn it. The thought is not that we simply pray for God to honor our plans and to establish them. Rather, it is the idea that we submit our entire life's action to God, so that even if our human plans are subverted, we can recognize an even deeper plan at work in our lives. If the "acts" are already accomplished, then the idea is that even when a plan has reached fruition, we must still trust God for its success.

In 2 Sam. 7 David approached Nathan the prophet with his plan to build the temple. While Nathan gave a quick approval, that evening God intervened and told the prophet to tell David that he did not want David to build a temple for him. At this time, God established David's line as a permanent dynasty in Judah, and his son would build a temple to honor Yahweh's name. David responded to this by spending much of the rest of his life preparing for the building of the temple.

---

1. See, for instance, Whybray, *Proverbs*, 239.
2. Murphy, *Proverbs*, 120.

> ⁴Yahweh makes everything for a purpose,
> even the wicked for an evil day.

16:4. Most commentators (Murphy, Clifford, Whybray) take this verse to mean that the wicked are made for the day of their own judgment (evil day). This is not taken as a deterministic statement, but rather as an assertion that the wicked will not escape their appropriate judgment. The text may mean this, but I would like to suggest an alternative explanation that is more in keeping with the previous verse: God is in control of the wicked acts of human beings and uses their evil for good.

Again (see comment on 14:19), the Joseph story may illustrate this principle. God overrules the evil actions of the brothers and Potiphar's wife to place Joseph in a position within the Egyptian hierarchy so he could provide haven and life to the people of God during a horrible famine. There are many other examples, and the Christian reader may also think of that ultimate good, the spiritual redemption provided by Christ, brought about through an act of horrifying evil, the crucifixion.

Another example of this proverb may also be found in the events that led to the downfall of the southern kingdom. As a specific illustration of this general time period, we may think of the early intrusion of Nebuchadnezzar into Judah, as described in the first few verses of Daniel. From the perspective of Judah, this was an "evil day," resulting in the loss of sacred objects from the temple and some of the "noble young men" of the society. From the Babylonian perspective, this victory was a gift of their gods. However, the narrator of the story tells us the divine truth: "The Lord delivered Jehoiakim king of Judah into his [Nebuchadnezzar's] hands" (Dan. 1:2 NIV).

God uses all things for his good purposes, even evil people and their wicked acts. In the NT, Peter proclaims that, though Jesus was put to death by wicked people, this was done by "God's set purpose and foreknowledge" (Acts 2:22–24; quote is from 2:23 NIV). And the idea of this proverb also lies behind Paul's reassurance that "in all things God works for the good of those who love him, who have been called according to his purpose" (Rom. 8:28 NIV).

The verse is not a statement that God authors evil. The teaching of the verse fits well with the general biblical idea that humans author their own wickedness. It is a statement of God's control. God can use the very act of human rebellion and autonomy for his purposes.

> ⁵All the haughty are an abomination to Yahweh;
> they will surely not go unpunished.

16:5. Proverbs is consistent in its condemnation of pride. Pride, after all, promotes the self and also leads to a self-defensiveness that does not allow one to hear criticism, an indispensable part of the path to wisdom. The haughty will be punished, but how is not specified. Perhaps their punishment will be effected through their own foolish behavior, or perhaps God will intervene. In any case, they will not escape. If the first, traditional understanding of v. 4 is the right one, then this proverb may be seen as a specific application to one type of wicked person.

> 6With covenant love and faithfulness guilt is atoned for,
>   and with the fear of Yahweh there is turning away from evil.

16:6. This proverb describes the positive qualities that will remove accumulated guilt and help a person turn away from evil behaviors in the future. Leviticus describes the atonement for guilt and sin taking place through the sacrificial ritual (Lev. 1–7), and this verse should not be taken as a rival to the teaching of the priests.[3] However, not even the priests believed that atonement was a matter of pure ritual. The ritual had to be enacted with the proper motives and mind-set. These might be described as covenant love, faithfulness, and fear of Yahweh (for the latter, see 1:7). Through words like "covenant love" (*ḥesed*) and "faithfulness" (*ʾemet*), Proverbs connects with the covenantal theology that permeates the OT.

> 7When a person's path draws Yahweh's favor,
>   even his enemies are at peace with him.

16:7. By now in this book, the path is a well-known metaphor for the course of a person's life. The path that is favorable with Yahweh (for "favor," often found in contrast with "abomination" [16:5], see also 8:35; 10:32; 11:1, 20, 27; 12:2, 22; 14:35; 15:8; 16:13, 15; 18:22; 19:12) is one in conformity with the principles of wisdom delineated throughout the book. The consequence of such a life pleasing to God is a lessening of problems. To make this point, the proverb draws on the metaphor of life as battle.

> 8Better a little bit with righteousness
>   than a large yield without justice.

16:8. This is yet another comparative (better-than) proverb (see also 16:19, 32; 17:1; 19:22; 22:1; 24:5; 27:5; 28:6, 23), expressing relative value.

3. Contra McKane, *Proverbs*, 498.

According to Proverbs there is nothing wrong with a large yield, but if one must make a choice, then there is no question: righteousness is more important than material possessions.

> ⁹Human hearts plan their path,
> but Yahweh establishes their step.

16:9. This proverb is closest to 16:1. Van Leeuwen, representing the majority of commentators, states that vv. 1 and 9 thus "form an envelope around the theological themes of divine sovereignty and freedom in this passage."[4] The idea is that human beings can plan, but plans do not get put into operation and do not find success unless Yahweh so decrees it. Understanding this diminishes human pride. The path indicates the course of a person's life. Taking a "step" on the path refers to various life events.

> ¹⁰An oracular decision on the lips of a king:
> he does not betray justice with his mouth.

16:10. The proverb is hard to understand because of the apparently positive reference to "oracular decision" (*qesem*) on the lips of the king. *Qesem* is frequently condemned in the other parts of the OT (Deut. 18:10; 1 Sam. 6:2; 28:8; 2 Kings 17:17; Isa. 44:24–25) because it is associated with practices of pagan divination. Nonetheless, there are positive instances of divination (though, admittedly, *qesem* is not found in these contexts) elsewhere in the OT, most notably in the use of the Urim and Thummim (Exod. 28:30). Without a fuller context, it is difficult to determine precisely how *qesem* is used here. The priests, for instance, manipulated the Urim and Thummim, but perhaps the king was the one who was responsible for announcing the decision (1 Sam. 23:1–8). If so, then perhaps the issue of justice concerns a proper presentation of the oracular decision that would have come from God. It could further point to a legal context for such an oracular decision. The temptation might be for the king to hedge the decision in the interests of his own policies, and thus the statement of colon 2 could also be understood as a kind of warning or prohibition. The wise king will not pervert the legal verdict rendered by the divinely inspired lot.[5]

> ¹¹The balance and scales must be just according to Yahweh;
> he concerns himself with the weights of the pouch.

---

4. Van Leeuwen, "Proverbs," 159.
5. See the excellent discussion of this verse in Davies, "Meaning of *qesem*."

16:11. This proverb speaks to just commercial transactions (see also 11:1; 20:10, 23). Cheating must have been known if not rampant in ancient Israel. Scales were used during purchases. It was possible to manipulate the scales to give a reading for the benefit of the seller. The weights of the pouch refer to weights placed on one side of the balance, and if they were falsely represented, then the seller could defraud the customer. God hates all fraud and deception, including that taking place in business ventures. This proverb parallels the law found in Deut. 25:13–16.

> [12]Doing wicked deeds is an abomination to kings,
> for in righteousness a throne is established.

16:12. There is a modicum of ambiguity in the proverb as to whether the wicked deeds are those of the king or those of people in the kingdom. If the former (the position implied by the NRSV), then the king is the one who produces the abomination. This seems to make more sense with the second colon, and the proverb would then be advice to the king to act righteously in order to establish his throne. However, if the latter interpretation is correct (the view supported by the majority of modern commentators; see Murphy, Clifford, Whybray), then the wicked deeds would be those of his subjects, and the king would be the one whose sense of justice would be violated. The argument in favor of this interpretation comes by analogy with the expression "abomination to Yahweh" (see discussion at 6:16; also 3:32; 11:1, 20; 12:22; 15:8, 9, 26; 16:5; 17:15). Further, the next proverb, speaking of what the king "favors" (*rāṣôn*, the word often used in conjunction with "abomination"; see 11:20; 12:22), supports this interpretation. I lean toward the latter interpretation as well. In any case, the contrast between wickedness and righteousness is frequent in Proverbs.

> [13]Righteous lips draw the favor of kings;
> they love those who speak with virtue.

16:13. This proverb does not share the ambiguity of the previous one, and indeed, as the discussion above indicates, may help us resolve the issues there. Here, as the second colon makes abundantly clear, it is the righteous lips of others that draw the king's "favor" (*rāṣôn*, often found with "abomination"; see texts cited on v. 12). "Righteous lips"/"those who speak with virtue" are those speaking the truth. They do not distort reality. This helps the king create policy that will succeed, since there may be special reference to those who speak to him in court.

> ¹⁴The anger of a king is a messenger of death;
>   the wise will appease it.

16:14. This proverb appears to be addressed to those who have contact with the king. Obviously, ancient monarchs were powerful individuals, often making life-or-death decisions. If people anger a king, they run the risk of ending their own lives. The wise know how to anticipate the reaction of the king and say the right word and do the right thing to avoid bringing his anger onto them. Qoheleth offers similar cautionary advice:

I say: Observe the king's command, and do not rush into a vow to God. You should leave his presence and not persist in an evil matter, for he will do whatever he wants. For the word of the king is supreme, so who will tell him, "What are you doing?" (Eccles. 8:2–4)[6]

Moreover, do not curse the king even in your thoughts; do not curse the
     rich even in your sleeping chamber,
For a bird may carry the message
Or some winged creature may tell the matter. (10:20)[7]

> ¹⁵In the light of the face of the king there is life,
>   and his favor is like a cloud that brings late rain.

16:15. This proverb forms a contrasting pair with the previous. Verse 14 dealt with the king's anger, and this one with his delight. The "light of his face" indicates a demeanor that reflects inner happiness. This royal disposition leads to life, which implies something more than existence: reward. The second colon provides a metaphor that illustrates the first statement. A cloud brings refreshing late rains. These rains are late in the agricultural cycle, coming in March and April and causing a growth spurt of the crops before harvest. Again, the metaphor not only indicates existence but also prosperity.

> ¹⁶Getting wisdom is much better than gold,
>   and getting understanding is to be preferred over silver.

16:16. It is hard to see how the parallelism here does more than emphasize the central point, often repeated through Proverbs, that wisdom is better than material possessions (3:14; 8:10, 19). Such relative values are expressed in the book through the use of better-than proverbs (see others cited at 16:8).

6. Longman, *Ecclesiastes*, 209–10.
7. Ibid., 252.

This verse is the middle of the book and may intentionally remind us of the foundational lesson of Prov. 1–9 ("Get wisdom!").

> ¹⁷The highway of the virtuous turns away from evil;
>   those who protect their path guard their lives.

16:17. As with the previous verse, this proverb fits in with the major themes of Prov. 1–9. There too we find the idea of the path. In the first colon, the word "highway" is used, perhaps suggesting the smooth road for those on the side of wisdom, here identified by the moral term "virtuous." The road is smooth because it bypasses evil that would bog life travelers down. The second line intensifies the thought of the first by commenting on those who take care with the quality of their life course. The results are much more favorable.

> ¹⁸Pride comes before a disaster,
>   and before stumbling comes an arrogant attitude.

16:18. This proverb has entered the lexicon of common English sayings in the form "Pride goes before a fall." This might be understood as saying that pride brings judgment on itself, but is better taken in a causal sense: Pride leads to significant problems. Throughout Proverbs, caution is directed toward pride, and humility is encouraged as a virtue characteristic of the sage (3:5, 7; 6:17; 11:2; 15:25; etc.). After all, pride does not allow one to listen to criticism and thereby correct misperceptions and harmful patterns of behavior, whereas humility does. In this proverb the "disaster" or "stumbling" is not specified and could come in a variety of forms. See also Prov. 18:12a.

> ¹⁹Better to be a humble spirit with the needy
>   than dividing plunder with the proud.

16:19. This verse is in the form of a better-than proverb, giving relative rather than absolute values (for others, see list at 16:8). Here the two items being compared are humility, on the one hand, and riches, on the other. While riches are not negative, they are not to be gotten at the expense of humility. Humility is valued because it is not the road to pride. Further, read in conjunction with the previous proverb, if wealth comes to the wise, it is likely to be short-lived or a prelude to disaster anyway. The "needy" are contrasted with those who "divide plunder," a warfare term for the victorious dividing the spoils among themselves. Perhaps having won the victory breeds pride, if the victory is thought to come because of human skill or strength.

> ²⁰Those with insight into a matter find prosperity;
> blessed are those who trust Yahweh.

16:20. This proverb is a variation on the theme that those who follow the way of wisdom will have a better life than those who do not.
After all, "insight" (for the root *śkl*, see 1:3) is a word closely associated
with wisdom and speaks of one's ability to discern a situation in order
to do or say the right thing. Since the fear of Yahweh is the beginning
of knowledge/wisdom, the second colon may be seen as the theological
expression of the first. That the reward mentioned in the proverb was
likely understood as material may be seen by the use of "prosperity"
(*ṭôb*) in the first colon. Since the second colon of a parallelism may
heighten the thought of the first colon, it may imply more than material
prosperity, but it is hard to be certain.

There is some ambiguity in the first colon. "Matter" may also be
"word," and if so, could refer either to the word of God or the teaching
of the sages. All three meanings make sense, and the idea suggested by
all three would be supported by the sages. In any of these readings, the
proverb in the first colon suggests that reward comes from human effort,
and in the second by placing oneself in a submissive position to God.
The two were obviously not thought to contradict each other.

> ²¹The wise of heart will be called understanding,
> and sweet lips increase teaching.

16:21. It is a bit hard to see a precise connection between the two
cola here. The first observes that those in whom wisdom has sunk deep
roots will be recognized and acclaimed as those who possess "understanding" (a word associated with "wisdom" and hard to distinguish
from "wisdom" and "knowledge"). The second line suggests that one's
teaching is better received or enhanced in some other way by "sweet
lips." This may refer to eloquence or to the kindly attitude by which the
sage presents material.

> ²²One who possesses insight is a fountain of life,
> but the discipline of stupid people is stupidity.

16:22. Verse 20 also speaks of "insight," an ability to assess a situation
or statement and respond to it appropriately. As one can imagine, such
ability would lead to positive results, ability, for instance, to solve difficult
problems, including those that bring people into conflict. Thus, it is a

"fountain of life," a relatively frequent metaphor (10:11; 13:14; 14:27) for the people and things that enhance life and its enjoyment.

This is contrasted with the discipline of stupid people. As one might imagine, such discipline, if it really may be spoken of as discipline, would simply reinforce unhelpful living strategies.

> 23The heart of the wise provides insight to their mouth
> and increases teaching on their lips.

16:23. This proverb is based on the sages' understanding that one's words are a reflection of one's heart. One who is wise at heart will say intelligent and helpful things to enhance another's learning. Notice the close parallel between 16:21b and the second colon of this verse.

> 24Pleasant words are liquid honey,
> sweet to the taste and healing to the bones.

16:24. Words are critically important to the sages. They never would have understood the modern idea that "sticks and stones may break your bones, but words will never hurt you." Indeed, words can hurt, and they can also heal. The latter is the message of the present proverb, and the point is communicated by a metaphor. Pleasant words are compared to *ṣûp-dĕbaš*, a phrase that is here taken as "liquid honey" but in some translations is rendered "honeycomb" (NRSV, REB, NAB, NJB). According to *NIDOTTE* 3:784, however, the phrase refers to "natural honey in its natural form" and here alludes to its "palatable taste and medicinal virtue."

Exactly what constitutes pleasant words is left unstated; however, other proverbs indicate that they are words spoken at the right time (15:23; 26:6, 9). Though the sage typically speaks with tenderness (15:1; 25:15), the right word on certain occasions may be a rebuke (25:12).

The second colon indicates that pleasant words have deep effects on a person. One's bones are the core of a person.

> 25There is a path that is straight before a person,
> but in the end it is the path of death.

16:25. See commentary at 14:12, of which this verse is a doublet.

> 26The appetite of laborers labors for them,
> for their mouths press them on.

16:26. This proverb observes that people work hard in order to meet their desires. In parallel with "appetite" in the first colon, we are surely to understand "mouth" as a reference to eating, not speaking.

It is hard to determine the attitude of the sages toward the situation. It may be that they are simply stating the nature of the case so that hearers might understand people, including themselves. However, sometimes "labor" has a negative connotation. Certainly, that is the case in Ecclesiastes, where it is a frequent subject, beginning in 1:3, where we encounter the rhetorical question "What profit is there to people in all their labor?" And 6:7 is particularly close in terminology: "All labor of humans is for their mouths, but the appetite is never filled."[8]

> ²⁷Worthless people dig up evil,
>   and it is like a scorching fire on their lips.

16:27. The expression "worthless people" (*bĕlîyaʿal*) is a particularly negative assessment of them (see also 6:12). There is a debate over the etymology of the terms. The first colon describes such people as those who work hard to do evil. The second colon further characterizes them as those who speak in a way that harms others.

> ²⁸The perverse produce conflict,
>   and gossips separate intimate friends.

16:28. Evil folly produces social divisions. The perverse are those who turn things upside down and around, and so produce conflict. The gossips of the second colon should be understood as a subcategory or specification of the perverse, and through their loose and misleading tongues, they end up even separating those who beforehand were "intimate associates" (for ʿallûp, see 2:17).

> ²⁹The violent entice their neighbors
>   and make them walk on a path that is not good.

16:29. Violence characterizes fools because of the harm that they bring on others. However, this proverb specifies a different type of harm; they influence others near them (neighbors) to act like them. Through their association and influence, they cause others to walk on the same wrong path. The seductive appeal of the violent is dramatized in the wisdom discourse found at 1:8–19. The neighbors would do well to listen to the advice found in 20:19 and 22:24 not to associate with fools.

8. Longman, *Ecclesiastes*, 164.

> [30]Those who wink the eye plot perverse things;
> those who purse their lips conceal evil.

16:30. Since we are at a considerable chronological and cultural remove from the original setting of Proverbs, matters like the significance of facial gestures are not crystal clear to us. From the context, we surmise that the gestures of winking eyes and pursing lips communicate some secret or subtle signal that indicates a person's evil intent.[9] Perhaps this observation has the intent of helping people read another person's face, to get behind the words.

> [31]Gray hair is a crown of glory;
> it is found on the path of righteousness.

16:31. Experience informs wisdom; the aged are more likely to be mature than the young. These are suppositions of wisdom literature of the OT. As Job will point out, age does not determine wisdom, but all things being equal, an older person will be more likely to be wise than a younger person. Thus, gray hair is a crown.

The idea of age as reward may also be seen in the light of the teaching that wisdom allows one to grow old, while fools will die prematurely. This is presupposed in the constantly offered enticement that wisdom leads to life, while folly leads to death. Again, this is not an absolute principle in Proverbs, but a generally true one. It is more likely, for instance, that a man will grow old if he does not sleep with another man's wife (6:20–35).

> [32]A patient person is better than a warrior,
> and those who control their emotions than those who can capture a city.

16:32. As is typical, this better-than proverb (see also 16:8 and passages cited there) expresses relative rather than absolute value. The skills of a warrior are good and necessary at the right time, but preference is given to a patient person. "Conquest of self is better than conquest of others."[10] Those who are patient can control their emotions and thus can see things clearly. Proverbs often contrasts the coolheaded person favorably over against the hothead (Prov. 12:16; 14:29, 30; 17:27; etc.). The comparison between controlling emotions and taking a city may suggest that it is harder to do the former.

9. I am unconvinced by Bryce's attempt ("Omen-Wisdom") to see the influence of Babylonian omen literature here; see comment at 16:10 as well.
10. Clifford, *Proverbs*, 162.

> ³³Into the lap the lot is cast,
>   and from Yahweh are all decisions.

16:33. The last proverb of the chapter returns to a theme from the beginning of the chapter, cf. 16:1–3, 9. The point is that God is the final arbiter of the future. Human beings may try to find out what the future holds, but they should know that God determines it. The OT approved at least one type of divination, the Urim and Thummim, and the principle behind this proverb certainly applied to it. The reason the determinations of the Urim and Thummim were followed by leaders like David (1 Sam. 23:1–6; for a description, see Exod. 28:30–31) is that it was known that God determined what they would indicate. See also the NT use of lots in Acts 1:26.

Chapter 17

Translation

[1]Better a dry crust with peace and quiet
   than a house full of contentious feasting.[a]
[2]An insightful servant is superior to[b] a disgraceful son,
   and he will divide an inheritance with brothers.
[3]A crucible for silver and a furnace for gold,
   and Yahweh is the one who refines hearts.
[4]An evildoer pays attention to guilty lips;
   a liar,[c] one who listens[d] to a destructive tongue.
[5]Those who ridicule the poor insult their Maker;
   those who rejoice in disaster will not go unpunished.
[6]Grandchildren are the crown of the elderly,
   and the glory of children is their parents.
[7]It is not right for a fool to have eloquent lips,
   even more for an honorable person to have lying lips.
[8]A bribe is a magic stone[e] in the opinion of[f] those who give it;

a. Literally "sacrifices," but in the context it probably refers to eating the meat after offering a sacrifice.

b. A context-driven translation of the verb *mšl*, which often means "to rule, dominate, control."

c. Literally, a "lie," but here "an abstract is used for the concrete" (Murphy, *Proverbs*, 127).

d. The verb has elided an *ʾālep*.

e. Literally, "stone of favor," probably a reference to some kind of magical talisman.

f. Literally, "in the eyes of." In support of the interpretation adopted in the commentary, Montgomery ("Bribe Is a Charm," 139) points out that on "at least eight occasions in Proverbs the phrase *běʿênê(w)* reflects a state of self-delusion."

it grants success to all who use[g] it.

[9]One who seeks love conceals an offense,
but one who repeats a thing divides an intimate relationship.

[10]A rebuke goes deeper[h] to an understanding person
than a hundred lashes to a fool.

[11]Evil people seek only rebellion;[i]
a cruel messenger will be sent to them.

[12]Encounter a bear bereft of her cubs,[j]
but not fools in their stupidity.[k]

[13]Those who return evil for good—
evil will never depart from their houses.

[14]The beginning of a conflict is[l] letting out water,
so abandon the accusation before the outburst.[m]

[15]Judging the righteous wicked and the wicked righteous—
Yahweh detests both of these.

[16]Why is it that the price is in the hand of the fool
to acquire wisdom with an empty heart?

[17]A friend[n] loves all the time,
and a brother is born for adversity.

[18]A person who clasps hands in agreement[o] lacks heart—
that is, one who puts up security for[p] a friend.[q]

g. The verb is from *pnh*, literally, "turn to the side, pay attention to." In this context, paying attention to something implies use, though most translations understand it to refer to areas in which the one who uses a bribe finds success (cf. "wherever they turn they prosper," NRSV).

h. The verb is from *nāḥet* (qal third-person singular), "to go down, descend" (Clifford, *Proverbs*, 165).

i. Or possibly "rebellious people seek only evil." The point remains virtually the same, however, that rebellion and evil go hand in hand.

j. S. E. Loewenstamm, "Remarks on Proverbs xvii 12 and xx 27," *Vetus Testamentum* 37 (1987): 221–22, suggests reading the *bĕʾîš* at the end of the first line as "in her desperation," based on a Mishnaic Hebrew verb. That the hypothetical root is Mishnaic Hebrew rather than Biblical Hebrew, coupled with Loewenstamm's own admission that adopting this rendition "does not affect the overall meaning of the proverb," makes us hesitate to adopt his suggestion.

k. Some translations make this verse sound as though it has the form of a better-than proverb (NIV, NLT), which it does not, but the effect is basically the same.

l. Many translations (NIV, NRSV) add "like" here, making explicit the comparison by turning it into a simile.

m. The word "outburst" (from *glʿ*) is used three times in Proverbs in conjunction with arguments (also 18:1; 20:3); cf. *NIDOTTE* 1:870.

n. Or "neighbor," since the Hebrew word can refer to either, but "friend" makes more sense in the context.

o. Literally, *tqʿ* in the qal simply means "to clasp or clap hands." However, in some contexts the gesture of bringing the hands together seals a legal agreement of some sort (Job 17:3; Prov. 6:1).

p. Literally, "in the presence of," but it likely has the sense of "on behalf of."

q. Or "neighbor."

¹⁹Those who love an offense love a quarrel;
    those who build a high doorway are seeking a collapse.
²⁰Those who have crooked hearts do not find good,
    and those who twist matters with their tongues[r] fall into evil.
²¹The one who gives birth to a fool has sorrow;
    the father of a blunderhead does not rejoice.
²²A joyful heart enhances healing,[s]
    but a broken spirit dries up bone.
²³The wicked take a bribe from the bosom
    to stretch the way of justice.
²⁴Wisdom is in front of understanding people,
    but the eyes of fools are at the ends of the earth.
²⁵A foolish son is irritating to his father
    and bitter to her who gave birth to him.
²⁶It is not good to punish[t] the righteous,
    and it is against the right to strike[u] an honorable person.
²⁷Those who hold back their speech know wisdom,
    and those who are coolheaded[v] are people of understanding.
²⁸Even a dupe who keeps silent seems wise;
    those who keep their lips shut are smart.

Interpretation

¹Better a dry crust with peace and quiet
    than a house full of contentious feasting.

17:1. Again, this better-than proverb presents a relative assessment. Feasting is better than a dry crust, to be sure, but peace and quiet are better than feasting, so much more so that it would be better to eat a dry crust than to put up with the social problems implied in the second colon. Since only the rich could have a house "full" of feasting, this proverb also assesses the relative value of wealth and good social relationships.

r. Literally, the phrase *nehpāk bilšônô* would be rendered "overturned of tongue."

s. While some want to emend to "face" on the basis of parallelism (Clifford, *Proverbs*, 167), it is better to understand *gēhâ* as a *hapax legomenon* with the meaning "healing," based on a variant form *kēhâ* in Nah. 3:19. Both *gēhâ* and *kēhâ* are difficult to define, but in the Nahum occurrence the LXX helps with the translation *iasis* ("healing"). In both contexts, "healing" works extremely well. The meaning "healing" in Proverbs 18:22 may also be supported by the occurrence of a possibly related verbal form in Hosea 5:13.

t. In some contexts, the verb *'nš* means "to fine," but here the more general meaning is probably intended.

u. In a legal context, the verb *nkh* may indicate "to flog."

v. This translation follows the Kethib (*qar-rûaḥ*); the Qere (*yĕqar*) suggests a form of *yqr*, "the precious of spirit."

> ²An insightful servant is superior to a disgraceful son,
> and he will divide an inheritance with brothers.

17:2. The form of this proverb provides relative values in a way similar to the better-than proverbs. The assumption of the proverb provided by culture is that a son is prized far above a servant in the father's eyes. However, here the insight of the servant is enough to tip the balance in his favor, especially in the light of the disgraceful reputation of the son. In other words, ability outweighs birthright, at least in extreme cases.

The consequence of insight over disgrace (which implies a lack of insight) is that the servant will be treated like a son when it comes to inheritance. The purpose of this proverb may be to warn sons to pay close attention to their filial duties and to act in such a way that their reputations bring honor and not shame on the family.

> ³A crucible for silver and a furnace for gold,
> and Yahweh is the one who refines hearts.

17:3. The proverb sets up a comparison between God, who refines hearts, and the refining of two precious materials. Metalworkers separate silver and gold from impurities by a process of heating the metal until the dross can be poured off. In the same way, God puts his people into difficult situations that will reveal their sin (the impurity of their hearts). Since the crucible does not only expose but also gets rid of dross, the implication may be that he not only evaluates hearts in this way but also helps people get rid of their sin. For other texts that use the refining metaphor, see Ps. 12:6; Isa. 1:24–26; Jer. 9:7 [6 MT]; Zech. 13:8–9.

> ⁴An evildoer pays attention to guilty lips;
> a liar, one who listens to a destructive tongue.

17:4. This proverb provides an observation that allows one to evaluate oneself and others. Guilty lips, more closely defined in the second colon, heed people who talk in a way that harms others. This may be done through lies, slander, gossip, rumors, false accusations, and the list can go on. Often in Proverbs this foolish type of talk is condemned; here we see that listening to such talk is equally condemned.

> ⁵Those who ridicule the poor insult their Maker;
> those who rejoice in disaster will not go unpunished.

17:5. This proverb is an interesting one especially in the light of the numerous proverbs that ridicule the poor (6:6–11; 10:4, 5). Close examination shows that it is not their poverty that is being ridiculed, but the foolish, lazy behavior that got them there. The sages recognized other causes of poverty beyond the control of the poor, such as injustice (13:23). This is why it is so dangerous to ridicule the poor; they may be poor through no fault of their own. The poor, after all, were also created in the image of God, and thus to insult the poor is to insult God himself (see also 22:2). No wonder such people will not go unpunished. The second colon may enlarge the idea to include any type of disaster, not just what results from poverty.

Ruffle cites similar proverbs from Egypt and Mesopotamia that frown on those who are cruel to the less fortunate:

> Do not laugh at a blind man nor scorn a dwarf
> Nor spoil the plan of a lame man.
> Do not scorn a man who is in the hand of God
> Nor be fierce of countenance towards him when he has erred. (Amen-
>   emope 24.9–12)

> Do not insult the downtrodden and . . .
> Do not sneer at them autocratically.
> With this a man's god is angry.
> It is not pleasing to Shamash, who will repay him with evil. (Babylonian
>   Counsels of Wisdom 57–60)[1]

6Grandchildren are the crown of the elderly,
and the glory of children is their parents.

17:6. This remarkable statement shows the importance of family. It is also an observation on how families are interconnected. The assumption is that all the family members are wise and not doing things that bring shame on themselves and the family (10:1). The actions of family members reflect either glory or shame on others who are connected to them. That the elderly have grandchildren at all is testimony to their long lives and their fertility and thus the rewards ("crown") of godliness. Parents may be the glory of their children since godly parents help their children by directing them in the right path.

The Instructions of Any express a similar idea: "Happy is the man whose people are many; he is saluted on account of his progeny."[2]

7It is not right for a fool to have eloquent lips,
even more for an honorable person to have lying lips.

---

1. See Ruffle, "Teaching of Amenemope," 39.
2. Translated by M. Lichtheim, in *COS* 1:111.

17:7. The sages had a sense of what is right and proper, and this proverb presents two situations where matters are out of kilter. In the first place, a fool has nothing worthwhile to say. Indeed, a fool's speech is often destructive. For a fool to have an eloquent manner of speaking would only increase the possibility of harm. The term for "fool" here (*nābāl*) is not used often in Proverbs (see also 17:21; 30:22), though it is impossible to differentiate it from the other words for "fool" used in the book, such as *kĕsîl* or *ĕwîl*. Nabal in the David story may be taken as an illustration of the type of person implied (see 1 Sam. 25). On the other hand, it is an oxymoron for a person who is honorable to lie. Lies do not befit the mouths of the wise.

> ⁸A bribe is a magic stone in the opinion of those who give it;
>   it grants success to all who use it.

17:8. On the surface of it, the proverb seems positive toward bribes, and indeed bribes have been known to open doors. However, the key to understanding the tone is the fact that the evaluation presented is that of the one who bribes. The opinion of the briber is not to be relied upon as a key to the opinion of the sages. The fact that a bribe is also compared to a "magic stone" may also be pejorative. Furthermore, a bribe's purpose is to get a person to act in a way contrary to justice or the real situation, a purpose that is clearly out of keeping with the perspective of wisdom literature. Other statements in the book of Proverbs are even more clearly negative about bribes (see "Bribes/Gifts" in the appendix; see also Exod. 23:8; Deut. 16:19; 27:25; Isa. 1:23; 5:23; Ezek. 22:12; Ps. 15:5; Eccles. 7:7).

> ⁹One who seeks love conceals an offense,
>   but one who repeats a thing divides an intimate relationship.

17:9. Love covers many transgressions. Friendship thinks the best of others and overlooks offenses. On the other hand, a person who harps on problems will drive another away, robbing both people of the opportunity to develop a relationship. Christian readers will be reminded of 1 Cor. 13, which describes love as "not self-seeking, . . . not easily angered, . . . keeps no record of wrongs" (v. 5 NIV). This proverb probably is not intended to promote the idea that friends will never divide over an offense. It is an observation that can serve as a warning. Don't keep bringing up the faults of others if you want to enjoy an intimate relationship with that person. The repeating of a transgression may also involve gossip if the story is told to third parties.

> ¹⁰A rebuke goes deeper to an understanding person
> than a hundred lashes to a fool.

17:10. The wise listen to criticism, even if it is harsh. This contrasts with the hardheadedness of fools, who mock rather than pay attention to negative comments. Indeed, fools are so hardheaded that even a hundred lashes could not break through and get them to listen and change their wrongminded behavior. This exaggerated language[3] serves the purpose of making fun of fools.

> ¹¹Evil people seek only rebellion;
> a cruel messenger will be sent to them.

17:11. On the basis of the context-sensitive nature of the proverb, it would be wrong to take this statement as condemning all rebellion against authority. The assumption would be that the authority in question is wise and godly. The second colon does make clear that the rebellion envisioned is directed toward an established institution; it assumes that someone can send a messenger to take care of the "problem." Qoheleth also warns his hearers about the dangers of rebelling against the king (Eccles. 8:2–9).[4]

Both Whybray and Van Leeuwen argue that the root *mārâ* (to rebel) and the specific form of the word here, *mĕrî* (rebellion), refer only to an assault on divine authority.[5] However, I remain uncertain, finding the second colon more naturally referring to the type of revenge sent by a human institution.

> ¹²Encounter a bear bereft of her cubs,
> but not fools in their stupidity.

17:12. The point of the comparison is fairly obvious. A bear is dangerous enough, but one that has suffered loss of cubs would be furious and especially dangerous (see also Hosea 13:8, where the angered bear represents Yahweh himself). But more dangerous than this is a fool whose stupid decisions will create great harm. The sages often used humorous exaggeration to make a point. This verse would certainly serve as a warning not to associate with foolish people.

> ¹³Those who return evil for good—
> evil will never depart from their houses.

---

3. After all, the law limited whippings to no more than forty lashes (Deut. 25:3).
4. For comment, see Longman, *Ecclesiastes*, 209–15.
5. Whybray, *Proverbs*, 257; Van Leeuwen, "Proverbs," 167.

17:13. It is never right to say evil words or do evil actions, and to respond to kind words or deeds with evil ones is particularly egregious. But what goes around comes around. Those who treat other people with malevolence will find that they and their households will never be far from trouble. Paul takes this more than a step further when he counsels: "Never pay back evil for evil to anyone" (Rom. 12:17 NLT).

> ¹⁴The beginning of a conflict is letting out water,
> so abandon the accusation before the outburst.

17:14. The first colon presents a metaphor that implicitly compares the start of a fight to allowing water to escape. Once it starts, it is hard to control and bring to an end. The second colon provides advice based on this observation: Don't even begin a conflict by making an accusation. At the very least the one who confronts another person ought to be willing to pay the price of the trouble that it will initiate.

> ¹⁵Judging the righteous wicked and the wicked righteous—
> Yahweh detests both of these.

17:15. It is so wrong to misjudge people at the fundamental level of righteousness and wickedness. God hates seeing the righteous considered or treated as if they are wicked and vice versa. Judging correctly would be especially important in a legal context, and perhaps that background is specifically in mind. Deuteronomy 25:1 directs judges to judge the righteous as righteous and the wicked as wicked. If the legal context is primary, then the verse could be rendered:

> Acquitting the guilty and condemning the innocent—
> the Lord detests them both. (NIV)

For the formula "Yahweh detests," see comments on 3:32; 11:1; and 20:23.

> ¹⁶Why is it that the price is in the hand of the fool
> to acquire wisdom with an empty heart?

17:16. We do not know whether the "price" for wisdom is literal or metaphorical, but the general principle is still clear: fools cannot buy wisdom with money when they have no real desire or capacity for it ("empty heart"). If literal, the "price" may refer to tuition money that a student would pay to the teacher, but we are not certain about the social background of wisdom literature (see "Social Setting" in the introduction). If metaphorical, the saying simply questions any pursuit of wisdom on the part of a fool, who by virtue of being a fool is constitutionally unable to acquire it. After all, fools say in their hearts that there is no God (Ps. 14:1; 53:1); how in the world could they affirm that the "beginning of wisdom is the fear of God" (see Prov. 9:10)?

> [17]A friend loves all the time,
> and a brother is born for adversity.

17:17. The proverb comments on one's foundational relationships, particularly those one can count on during trying times. The relationship between the two cola is ambiguous; it is not perfectly clear whether the intention of the proverb is to highlight the brother over the friend. I think not. The relationship between the cola seems to be one of intensifying and particularizing, but not contrasting. That a friend loves all the time would include moments of adversity. That a brother is born for adversity does not mean that he is the one who is causing friction, but a brother is there through thick and thin in order to provide help during adversity.[6]

> [18]A person who clasps hands in agreement lacks heart—
> that is, one who puts up security for a friend.

17:18. The parallelism of this proverb moves from general to specific. Colon 1 demeans a person who shakes hands with another to confirm a legal agreement, but the exact nature of that agreement is not identified until the second colon. There it is specified as putting up security for some kind of loan or other transaction for a friend. Proverbs is consistent in its advice not to put up security, whether for friend or stranger (cf. 6:1–5; 11:15; 20:16; 22:26; 27:13). It is indeed good to help another, but when a situation of need arises, then be generous (11:24; 28:27; 29:7, 14). However, people must avoid giving something that they need to get back. The expression "lacks heart" is used elsewhere in Proverbs and indicates a lack of character. It may emphasize faulty judgment, an absence of intelligence, or perhaps a lack of courage.

> [19]Those who love an offense love a quarrel;
> those who build a high doorway are seeking a collapse.

17:19. This proverb is one of the most difficult in the book. Both cola are enigmatic.

6. McKane (*Proverbs*, 505–6) discusses both possibilities.

The first colon obviously criticizes those who like to fight. However, what does it mean to "love an offense"? It could mean to love the offense of another person and just pick away at it until the other person cannot stand it any longer and responds angrily. Or perhaps it is simply saying that those who love to fight just like to offend people.

Whatever the difficulties of the first colon, the second is harder to understand. What does it mean to build a high doorway? And how does it relate to colon 1? Some people understand the word translated as "high" (*gābah*) to mean "arrogant"[7] and to fit in with the idea that arrogance leads to a fall. That seems unlikely. More likely it refers to an architectural problem. Just as people who love to pick away at an offense or to offend others will naturally lead to the chaos of a fight, so those who build a doorway that is too high will certainly have that doorway collapse.[8]

> [20]Those who have crooked hearts do not find good,
> and those who twist matters with their tongues fall into evil.

17:20. This proverb parallels "hearts" with "tongues," not untypical of the book, which recognizes that people's speech reflects their core personality (16:23 and especially 3:1). The proverb simply observes that the wicked will experience dire consequences.

> [21]The one who gives birth to a fool has sorrow;
> the father of a blunderhead does not rejoice.

17:21. This proverb expresses a sentiment often found in the book, beginning with the first proverb of this collection (10:1). Proverbs has a varied vocabulary for the fool and here uses both "fool" (*kĕsîl*) and "blunderhead" (*nābāl*). Our understanding of the nuances, however, is limited. Elsewhere we have translated both words simply "fool." However, for a historical illustration of a *nābāl*, the reader can read the story of a character with that name in 1 Sam. 25.

> [22]A joyful heart enhances healing,
> but a broken spirit dries up bone.

17:22. Again, the sages show their insight into what we today would call a person's psychology (see also "Psychological Insight" in the ap-

---

7. Suggested by Whybray, *Proverbs*, 260.
8. The interpretation offered here is close to that presented by Clifford (*Proverbs*, 166), where he cites Isa. 30:13 and suggests that "the point of the saying is that harping on a fault risks an eruption like that from a poorly constructed wall."

pendix). The proverb states that one's emotional well-being has physical effects.

> ²³The wicked take a bribe from the bosom
> to stretch the way of justice.

17:23. This proverb clearly speaks negatively about bribes (see "Bribes/ Gifts" in the appendix as well as Exod. 23:8; Deut. 16:19; 27:25; Ps. 15:5; Eccles. 7:7; Isa. 1:23; 5:23; Ezek. 22:12), at least toward bribes that are given with the clear intention of perverting justice. The giving of a bribe to pervert justice is a great crime. The reference to the bribe coming from the bosom likely indicates that bribes are given secretly. It is not absolutely clear that the bosom is that of the wicked, who may be taking it from the bosom of another person. In other words, we are not certain whether the wicked in this proverb are the givers or recipients of the bribe. In either case, it is wrong. The reference to "way" (*ʾōraḥ*) is reminiscent of the two-path theology particularly prevalent in the first nine chapters, with *ʾōraḥ* as a frequently used alternate to "path" (*derek*). The reference to "justice" (*mišpāṭ*) may indicate a specifically legal context for this proverb.

> ²⁴Wisdom is in front of understanding people,
> but the eyes of fools are at the ends of the earth.

17:24. This proverb may speak of concentration on a goal. Wisdom is the focus of people with understanding, and that is why they have understanding. On the other hand, fools are distracted. Their focus is too broad and scattered. Qoheleth, the Teacher in Ecclesiastes, may be responding to the idea behind this proverb when he states: "'I will be wise!' But it was far from me. Far away is that which is, and deep, deep, who can find it?" (7:23–24)[9]

> ²⁵A foolish son is irritating to his father
> and bitter to her who gave birth to him.

17:25. This is another in a series of proverbs describing parental disappointment if a child turns out to be a fool (see also 10:1; most recently 17:21). The object of these proverbs may be in part to motivate parents to work hard at inculcating wisdom into their children. But such a proverb could also be addressed to children, to motivate them not to live in a way that would anger their parents.

9. See translation and commentary in Longman, *Ecclesiastes*, 200.

> ²⁶It is not good to punish the righteous,
>   and it is against the right to strike an honorable person.

17:26. This proverb presents two situations where consequences do not rightly match a person's character. The righteous deserve reward, not punishment, and so does an honorable person. Once again, it is likely that the primary setting of this proverb is legal and condemns those who would render an improper verdict in a court case.

> ²⁷Those who hold back their speech know wisdom,
>   and those who are coolheaded are people of understanding.

17:27. The idea of wisdom suggests a person who is sparing in words (see "Appropriate Use of Words" in the appendix) and also careful in emotional expression (see "Appropriate Expression of Emotions" in the appendix). In other words, the wise are in control of themselves. In this way, they regulate how other people will perceive them. By speaking with restraint, the wise are able to reflect on what they are going to say.

> ²⁸Even a dupe who keeps silent seems wise;
>   those who keep their lips shut are smart.

17:28. Connected in theme to the previous proverb, this verse reiterates the value of speaking only when it counts. Using humor in the first colon, the sages suggest that the best chance a fool has for being thought intelligent is to avoid speaking.

Chapter 18

Translation

¹The antisocial seek their own longings;^a
 they break out^b against all resourcefulness.
²Fools do not delight in competence
 but only in disclosing their hearts.
³When the wicked^c arrive, so arrives contempt,
 and with shame, insult.
⁴The words of a person's mouth are deep waters,
 a bubbling wadi, a fountain of wisdom.
⁵Showing the wicked favor^d is not good,
 by subverting the righteous in justice.
⁶The lips of a fool lead to accusation;
 his mouth invites blows.
⁷The mouth of fools is their ruin;
 their lips are a trap for their lives.

a. The LXX has *prophaseis* (pretext), which suggests *tōʾănâ* in place of "longings" (*taʾăwâ*), but there is no good reason to reject the MT. The LXX assumes a connection with a similar expression found in Judg. 14:4.

b. See 17:14 for this verb (*glʿ*).

c. This is the concrete form, not the abstract "wickedness" as some translations suggest.

d. Literally, the Hebrew phrase means "raising the face of the wicked."

⁸The words of gossips are like choice morsels;
    they go down to their inmost parts.ᵉ
⁹Those who are slack in their work
    are brothers to a destroyer.
¹⁰The name of Yahweh is a strong tower;
    the righteous run to it and find refuge.
¹¹The riches of the wealthy are their strong city
    and like a high wall in their imagination.ᶠ
¹²Before disaster a person's heart is proud,
    but before glory comes humility.
¹³Those who respond before they listen
    are stupid and a disgrace.
¹⁴The human spirit can sustain a person when sick,
    but who can bear a broken spirit?
¹⁵An understanding heart acquires knowledge;
    the ear of the wise seeks knowledge.
¹⁶A gift widens the way for people;
    it leads them to important people.
¹⁷The first person to speak in a court case seems innocent
    until his neighbor comes and cross-examines him.
¹⁸The lot settles conflicts
    and is decisive among powerful people.
¹⁹An offended brother is stronger than a city,
    and conflicts are like the bar of a castle.
²⁰From the fruit of the mouth of a person is their stomach satisfied;ᵍ
    the yield of their lips satisfies.
²¹Death and life are in the powerʰ of the tongue,
    and those who love it will eat its fruit.
²²The one who finds a wife finds a good thing,
    and he obtains favor from Yahweh.
²³The poor speak supplications,
    but the wealthy respond with strength.
²⁴There areⁱ friends who want to associate,ʲ
    and there are those who love and cling closer than a brother.

e. *Ḥadrê-bāṭen* is literally "inner room of the stomach." The word *ḥeder* refers to an inner private room; in the Song of Songs it implies "bedroom" (1:4; 3:4).

f. With Murphy (*Proverbs*, 184) we stay with the MT, taking the phrase to mean, literally, "'in his/its image,'" and the term is used metaphorically to indicate 'imagination.'"

g. Similar expressions are found in 12:14a and 13:2a.

h. Literally, "hand."

i. Here I emend *ʾîš* as *yēš* along with several early versions and bring the first colon into conformity with the second.

j. Another understanding of the hitpael of *rʿh* II is "to pretend to be friends" (see NRSV). If so, the contrast between the two cola would be between false friends and true friends rather than between casual acquaintances and true friends. Other versions (REB, NAB, NJB) repoint the verb as a form of *rʿʿ* ("to be bad, harmful"). Here the contrast is between people who harm and people who help.

Interpretation

> ¹The antisocial seek their own longings;
>   they break out against all resourcefulness.

18:1. The term "antisocial" (*niprād*) comes from the verb *prd*, which suggests "someone who is divided, either internally or externally." Our translation opts for the former since the verse describes those who are internally focused on their own desires, but such a focus would naturally separate them from the community. In the second colon, they are defined by their stance against wisdom, since "resourcefulness" is related to wisdom. In 2:7, we observed that God gives resourcefulness, which Fox defines as "an inner power that helps one escape a fix."[1]

> ²Fools do not delight in competence
>   but only in disclosing their hearts.

18:2. The verse suggests that fools are again (see previous verse) only interested in their own desires and ideas. They do not have the patience to achieve the goals associated with wisdom (for competence, see 2:2), nor do they want to listen to people with competence. They only want to blurt out what is on their minds, thus "disclosing their hearts." As Van Leeuwen points out, however, the thought is ironic since elsewhere we learn that the fool "lacks heart" (see 11:12).[2]

> ³When the wicked arrive, so arrives contempt,
>   and with shame, insult.

18:3. The verse displays a progression set in motion by wickedness. Wickedness leads to contempt. The second colon substitutes "shame," a close synonym of "contempt," and takes the thought further by suggesting that insults will follow.

> ⁴The words of a person's mouth are deep waters,
>   a bubbling wadi, a fountain of wisdom.

18:4. The proverb would not apply to all people and their speech, but to the speech of the sages. What they say reflects thoughts that are profound and sometimes mysterious, requiring reflection and interpretation. The water image suggests that the sage's words are life-giving.

1. Fox, *Proverbs 1–9*, 114.
2. Van Leeuwen, "Proverbs," 172.

The second colon in particular depicts this. The sage's words are like a wadi bubbling or flowing with water. Such an observation implies that listeners attend to the sage's speech.

This reading of the proverb suggests that colon 2 is continuous and supportive, not in contrast, to colon 1. Another reading interprets the "deep waters" of colon 1 as inaccessible and confusing, in contrast to the words of the wise in colon 2.

> ⁵Showing the wicked favor is not good,
> by subverting the righteous in justice.

18:5. This proverb supports others that condemn improper judgments in a legal context (16:10; 17:23; 19:28; etc.). "Lifting the suppliant's bowed head [the literal sense of colon 1; see translation footnote] is a gesture of pardon; thrusting an accused person away is a gesture of rejection or finding guilty."[3] As recently as 17:23, we observed a proverb that mentions one motive for showing the wicked favor and stretching justice: a bribe. Proverbs is interested in proper outcomes for wicked and righteous actions. The law forbids subverting justice in Lev. 19:15 and Deut. 10:17. For other sayings that determine an action "not good," see 16:29; 17:26.

> ⁶The lips of a fool lead to accusation;
> his mouth invites blows.

18:6. Quarrels, conflicts, rebukes, accusations are at best a last resort for the wise, who try to turn away anger with a gentle or kind word (15:1). Fools are those who are primed for an argument. The term "accusation" (*rîb*) is a legal word and may suggest such a context, but the principle is much broader. In any case, their words will bring on a fight; the word "blows" suggests a physical confrontation. What fools say triggers punches.

> ⁷The mouth of fools is their ruin;
> their lips are a trap for their lives.

18:7. The moral of this observation is clear: The speech (represented by the concrete body parts "mouth" and "lips") of fools brings them great harm. They say things that get them into trouble or into fights. Wise speech helps people get out of trouble; foolish speech plunges them into harm. This proverb is similar to the previous one, though

3. Clifford, *Proverbs*, 170.

more general. Connected to the previous verse, there is a chiasmus: lips, mouth, mouth, lips.

> [8]The words of gossips are like choice morsels;
> they go down to their inmost parts.

18:8. The sages often speak against gossip and rumors (see also 11:13; 17:4; as well as the identical 26:22). Rumors are negative reports about other people that are based on uncertain evidence. They are spread to injure people, not to help them. Gossip may ultimately turn out to be true, but that does not exonerate those who speak it to others. If true, then the report is being given to inappropriate people at an inappropriate time. Even though so harmful, people often find the words of gossips irresistible, and this proverb likens gossip to fine food that is hard not to eat, but once eaten, it penetrates deeply into a person.

> [9]Those who are slack in their work
> are brothers to a destroyer.

18:9. This proverb lacks some of the satirical punch of the group that criticizes laziness, yet it certainly agrees with the sentiment (see "Laziness and Hard Work" in the appendix). Those who are lazy harm themselves and others. The observation is an implicit admonition to work hard. The lazy are ultimately detrimental to society.

> [10]The name of Yahweh is a strong tower;
> the righteous run to it and find refuge.

18:10. This verse sounds like it comes from the Psalms, with its assertion of the protective power of Yahweh's name, and thus of Yahweh himself. The second colon may describe the behavior of the righteous person as a way of determining whether one is righteous. The use of military imagery in the next proverb invites us to read them together.

> [11]The riches of the wealthy are their strong city
> and like a high wall in their imagination.

18:11. This verse also talks about trust, but it is in contrast with the previous verse. As the righteous trust in God for protection, so the wealthy trust in their own riches. With possessions comes a sense that one can buy anything needed, but this is not true. Only God can protect anyone from dangers.

This verse should also be read in conjunction with 10:15, where it is said:

The riches of the wealthy are their strong city;
the ruin of the poor is their poverty.

It is true that wealth can help us navigate some problems in life, but it lets us down in the area of life's ultimate issues.

> ¹²Before disaster a person's heart is proud,
> but before glory comes humility.

18:12. Pride resists correction, and therefore the proud do not change destructive behaviors and attitudes. Though people with pride think themselves great, they will be cast down by life. On the other hand, the humble are open to correction and are more likely to achieve the kind of success that leads to honor. For similar teaching in Proverbs, see 16:18 and 15:33b for repetitions of cola 1 and 2 respectively. For the teaching that humility is the proper course, see also 11:2 and 29:23.

> ¹³Those who respond before they listen
> are stupid and a disgrace.

18:13. Fools speak impulsively, without really listening and reflecting on what they hear (see also 15:28; 19:2; 20:18, 25; 21:5; 29:20). They say whatever comes to mind, and what comes to their empty minds is particularly vacuous. Fools babble all sorts of things that get them into trouble and earn them the reputation of being stupid, and in this way they are humiliated. Some commentators believe that this statement finds its primary setting in the courtroom,[4] but this is not clear from the language.

> ¹⁴The human spirit can sustain a person when sick,
> but who can bear a broken spirit?

18:14. This proverb again (see 15:13 and 17:22) makes an observation about the relationship between one's psychological state of mind and the health of the body. There is no strong body-soul dualism in the OT, to be sure. The idea that a positive attitude can have a positive effect on a person's health is widely recognized even today, as well as the reverse idea that depression or anxiety (among the states of mind that could be signaled by "broken spirit") can worsen a physical condition.

> ¹⁵An understanding heart acquires knowledge;
> the ear of the wise seeks knowledge.

4. Van Leeuwen, "Proverbs," 173.

18:15. It is the wise who grow in knowledge. One must have a predisposition to learn in order to actually learn; there is nothing magical about it. The proverb assumes that teaching will come through listening to the wisdom of a teacher. See also 15:14a.

> ¹⁶A gift widens the way for people;
> it leads them to important people.

18:16. This proverb comments on the benefits of a gift given at the right time and at the right place. Such gifts can indeed make important people accessible in order to make a deal. Elsewhere a "bribe" (*šōḥad*) is discouraged, but here the "gift" (*mattān*) seems to garner a positive comment, at least at first sight. It is possible that the subtext of the proverb is critical of this way of gaining access to people not on merit but on the strength of a gift, which in the final analysis is a bribe. See also "Bribes/Gifts" in the appendix.

> ¹⁷The first person to speak in a court case seems innocent
> until his neighbor comes and cross-examines him.

18:17. This observation seeks to discourage hasty judgments, particularly in a legal proceeding. Appearances can be misleading, and so critical questions need to be raised to establish the truth or falsehood of testimony. Though the primary setting seems to be the courtroom, the principle applies more broadly.

> ¹⁸The lot settles conflicts
> and is decisive among powerful people.

18:18. According to the wisdom of the sages, conflicts and fights create disorder and are to be avoided. Perhaps surprisingly, the lot is mentioned as a way of suppressing conflict. However, it must be remembered that in 16:33, the lot expresses a divine decision and is not simply the result of chance. It would be particularly important to resolve conflicts between powerful people because their disagreements could lead to the most widespread damage, not only to themselves as individuals but also to society at large. In narrative, the only example of God's people using the lot is in a context, typically with the Urim and Thummim (Exod. 28:30), where God is explicitly said to be involved. However, most commentators believe that the preceding context of this saying implies that the lot is thought to resolve tough court cases, though there is no evidence of this happening outside of this context.[5]

5. See ibid., 174.

> ¹⁹An offended brother is stronger than a city,
> and conflicts are like the bar of a castle.

18:19. This observation is an implicit warning to avoid conflict because of the intractable problems that will arise. "Brother" may refer to a biological relationship or to some other kind of close relationship. If a breach occurs in that relationship, it will be hard to break through to resolution because of hard feelings. An offended brother may close down any opening to relationship like a strong city, raising a barrier that is resistant to approach, like a city fortress whose gate has been reinforced by a bar.

Psalm 55 (see especially vv. 12–14, 20–21) records the psalmist's deep distress, and the psalm reflects his desire for the betrayer's destruction. Psalm 133 provides the same sort of observation but from a positive perspective. If conflict between brothers is bad, then unity between brothers is unbelievably rewarding.

> ²⁰From the fruit of the mouth of a person is their stomach satisfied;
> the yield of their lips satisfies.

18:20. The proverb observes that a person finds satisfaction in speech, presumably edifying, righteous speech. The proverb is probably to be understood figuratively. Just as food satisfies one's physical hunger, so also words satisfy one's intellectual and spiritual hunger. The verse, however, may also be understood literally as suggesting that the ability to speak well and benefit others will help one earn a living. It is not totally clear whether the person who is satisfied is the recipient of good advice or its dispenser.

> ²¹Death and life are in the power of the tongue,
> and those who love it will eat its fruit.

18:21. The first colon is relatively clear. What a person says will have serious and even life-and-death consequences for the person.[6] The second colon is a bit more ambiguous. The "it" must refer to "the tongue," but what does it mean to love the tongue? Perhaps it refers to those who love to hear themselves speak. Proverbs has much negative to say about those who talk too much (10:14; 13:3). They will suffer the consequences ("fruit") of their verbosity.

6. It is possible that this verse also has in mind life-and-death consequences that result from the quality of speech that one hears.

> ²²The one who finds a wife finds a good thing,
> and he obtains favor from Yahweh.

18:22. The book of Proverbs as a whole has much to say about the right woman, though much of the teaching is about avoiding the wrong woman and is found in chaps. 1–9 (see chaps. 5–7). This verse underlines the importance of a good wife by claiming that she is a divine gift. In the introduction, we observed that Proverbs' teaching on the difference between a good wife and the strange woman reflects the difference between a relationship with personified Wisdom and Folly, figurative language that ultimately points to the conflict between true and false religion. Indeed, Whybray points out that the language of finding a wife reflects the language of 8:35b, which refers to finding Woman Wisdom.[7]

The language of finding a wife also anticipates the final portion of the book, the so-called "poem of the valiant woman" (31:10–31). In the context of the book, we can turn to that poem to understand the substance behind the phrase "good wife."

Clifford rightly points out that colon 1 emphasizes human effort in that a man has to find the wife, while colon 2 underlines divine grace.[8]

> ²³The poor speak supplications,
> but the wealthy respond with strength.

18:23. The verse makes an observation that the poor ask for help, and the wealthy answer their supplications "with strength." However, the exact force of some of the language and the attitude that the proverb desires to convey are not clear.

The observation could take a positive approach toward the poor and a negative one toward the wealthy. The poor ask for help, but the wealthy respond "with strength," roughly or callously.[9] It is possible that the opposite is the stance of the proverb: the poor may be seen negatively and the wealthy positively. The poor have their hands out, but the wealthy do not cave in to their pitiful requests. After all, poverty is often, but not always, seen to be the result of foolish behavior.[10] Perhaps the best understanding of this proverb, though, is in keeping with the attitude expressed in 30:5–9, which recognizes problems with riches and poverty.

7. Whybray, *Proverbs*, 274.

8. Clifford, *Proverbs*, 174.

9. This is the view of Van Leeuwen, "Proverbs," 175, who speaks of the "arrogance" of the wealthy over against the poor.

10. It is also conceivable that the proverb means that the wealthy respond "in strength" in the sense of boldly meeting the needs of the poor.

Thus, poverty and riches put people in conflict with one another, and the best state is for everyone to have just enough.

> ²⁴There are friends who want to associate,
>   and there are those who love and cling closer than a brother.

18:24. This proverb observes different gradations of friendship. The first speaks of those who want to spend time with a person, while the second describes a relationship of greater intimacy and intensity. Those friends are so close that their relationship even surpasses the biological relationship of brothers.

Chapter 19

Translation

[1]Better to be poor and walking in innocence
    than have crooked lips and be a fool.[a]
[2]Indeed, ignorant desire[b] is not good,
    and rushing feet make mistakes.
[3]People's stupidity frustrates their path;
    their hearts rage against Yahweh.
[4]Riches add up to many friends,
    but the poor are separated from their friends.
[5]False witnesses will not escape punishment,
    and those who proclaim lies will not escape.
[6]Many people seek the face of rulers,
    and everyone is the friend of a person who bears gifts.
[7]All the brothers of the poor hate them;
    how much more their friends keep far from them.
    When they pursue them to speak, they are not there.
[8]Those who acquire "heart" love themselves;
    those who guard competence find good.[c]
[9]False witnesses will not escape punishment,
    and those who proclaim lies will perish.

a. Some scholars try to achieve a better parallelism by comparing the closely related 28:6 and the versions to produce a translation like that of Clifford (*Proverbs*, 175): "Better a poor person walking in his integrity than one walking on a crooked way though he is rich." However, it is easier to explain this rendition as arising out of a desire to harmonize and make stronger parallelism than to explain how it is derived from the **MT**.

b. "Ignorant desire" translates *bĕlōʾ-daʿat nepeš*, which is more literally rendered "in no knowledge desire."

c. The final phrase is actually an infinitive form, and the colon could be rendered literally, "those who guard competence, to find good."

¹⁰Luxury is not right[d] for a fool,
  even more for a servant to rule over people.
¹¹Insightful people hold in[e] their anger,
  and their glory is to ignore[f] an offense.
¹²The rage of the king growls like a lion;
  his favor is like the dew on the grass.
¹³A foolish son is a disaster to his father,
  and a contentious wife is a constant dripping.
¹⁴House and riches, the inheritance from fathers,
  but an insightful wife is from Yahweh.
¹⁵Lazy people fall into a deep sleep,
  and the appetite of a slacker stays famished.
¹⁶Those who guard the commandment guard their lives;
  those who despise their way[g] will die.[h]
¹⁷Those who are gracious to the poor lend to Yahweh,
  and he will fully repay[i] them.
¹⁸Discipline your son while[j] there is hope;
  don't be intent[k] to kill him.
¹⁹People of great[l] wrath carry around punishment;
  if you rescue them, then you will have to do so again.
²⁰Listen to advice and receive discipline,
  so you might grow wise in your future days.[m]
²¹Many plans are in people's hearts,
  but the advice of Yahweh, that is what will succeed.
²²The longing[n] of people is for their covenant love.[o]
  It is better to be poor than a liar.

d. See colon 1 of 17:7.

e. The verb is a hiphil of ʾrk, "to lengthen." The idea seems to be that insightful people do not act immediately on their anger.

f. Literally, "to pass by."

g. Some emend to "his words," but this seems unnecessary.

h. This follows the Qere. The Kethib is "put to death."

i. I understand the verbs here to form a hendiadys. Literally, "he will benefit and repay them."

j. The kî may be understood as temporal, as translated here, or causal.

k. The idiom "nśʾ nepeš ʾel/lě ('lift one's soul to') occurs 9x in the OT, 7x in q[al] and 2x in pi[el]. In six of these nine the object is a thing and the basic meaning of the phrase is 'direct one's desire toward, long for' (Deut. 24:15; Ps. 24:4; Prov. 19:18; Jer. 22:27; 44:14; Hos. 4:8)" (NIDOTTE 3:161).

l. The MT here makes no sense, so I emend gěrāl to gědāl, following the Qere. The versions have the equivalent of gěbar-ḥēmâ, "man of wrath," which is also a possibility.

m. Murphy (Proverbs, 145) translates this phrase "finally" and considers it a reference to the end of the educational period.

n. The LXX has karpos (fruit), which may suggest Hebrew těbûʾâ (income), but the MT makes sense as it stands.

o. Murphy (Proverbs, 141) and others take ḥesed here not as the well-attested "covenant love" but rather as a rare homonym meaning "disgrace," attested in Lev. 20:17 and (it is claimed) Prov. 14:34.

[23]The fear of Yahweh leads[p] to life,
    and those who spend the night are contented; they don't pay attention to
    evil.[q]
[24]Lazy people bury their hand into the bowl,
    but they do not return it to their mouth.
[25]Hit a mocker, and a simpleminded person will become prudent;
    and correct those who understand, and they will understand knowledge.
[26]Those who devastate their father and drive out their mother
    are disgraceful children, worthy of reproach.
[27]Cease, my son, from listening[r] to discipline,
    and you will wander from knowledgeable speeches.[s]
[28]A worthless witness mocks justice,
    and the mouth of the wicked conveys[t] guilt.
[29]Punishments[u] were made for mockers,
    and blows for the backs of fools.

Interpretation

---

[1]Better to be poor and walking in innocence
than have crooked lips and be a fool.

19:1. Better-than proverbs impart relative values. The sages would certainly say that it was better to have some wealth, if not be rich, than to be poor. However, ethical qualities are more important than material possessions. This proverb affirms the principle that folly is an ethical concept. Fools are not only dull of mind and do stupid things; they also are evil people. In particular, according to this proverb, they speak in a way that does not faithfully reflect reality ("crooked lips"). The "walking" metaphor in colon 1 is an allusion to the metaphor of

p. "Leads" is not in the Hebrew but has been provided to make the translation smoother.

q. The difficulty of this verse explains why there is a rather divergent version in the LXX. Clifford (*Proverbs*, 176) provides the following translation of the Greek: "but the person without fear [of the Lord] will spend the night in places where knowledge (*dēaᶜ* for Hebrew *rāᶜ*, from *d/r* confusion) is not observed."

r. The LXX has "guard," probably reflecting Hebrew *šmr*.

s. The grammar of this verse is difficult. Here we follow the NIV in understanding the syntax to suggest a kind of conditional sentence.

t. *NIDOTTE* 1:667 discusses the root *blᶜ* and notes that most philologists are in agreement that here (as well as in 2 Sam. 17:16 and Job 37:20) we encounter a root described as *blᶜ* II, with the meaning "convey, report, slander or reach, affect, assault, injure" and an etymology that connects it with Arabic *balaga*. The alternative would be to take the verb as *blᶜ* I, "to swallow."

u. Or "judgments."

life as a path, which is strongly developed in the first nine chapters of the book.

> [2]Indeed, ignorant desire is not good,
> and rushing feet make mistakes.

19:2. This proverb may be close to the well-known English aphorism "Haste makes waste." If one is impulsive, not thinking before acting, then one is going to commit errors. Desire propels one toward acting in a way that fulfills those desires, but this proverb warns the hearer to think before doing anything.

> [3]People's stupidity frustrates their path;
> their hearts rage against Yahweh.

19:3. This proverb first observes that it is people's stupidity that keeps them from getting ahead in life. The metaphor of the path is well known throughout Proverbs, particularly in the first nine chapters, as a metaphor of the course of one's life. Stupidity keeps people from making progress.

Even so, such people do not blame themselves and then try to correct their errors by learning right strategies for living. Rather, they rage against God, whom they blame for all their troubles. Since they do not put the blame for their problems in the right place, they cannot possibly improve their lives. As Whybray rightly comments, "Folly and blasphemy are closely linked here."[1]

> [4]Riches add up to many friends,
> but the poor are separated from their friends.

19:4. Everyone wants to be the friend of the rich, but no one wants to associate with the poor. The poor, after all, have problems and may need help or even generous gifts to survive, whereas the wealthy at least give the appearance of being able to help.

This proverb is an observation that everyone who knows rich and poor can understand. However, it is harder to determine the attitude behind the statement, if there is one. In other words, does the proverb understand the friends of the rich to be true friends or hangers-on? If the latter, it may be appropriate to put "friends" in quotation marks. Indeed, Qoheleth understood that wealth attracts people, but also made it clear that they were leeches: "When prosperity increases, those who

---

1. Whybray, *Proverbs*, 276.

consume it increase. So what success is there for its owner, except to admire it?" (Eccles. 5:11 [10 MT]).[2]

> [5]False witnesses will not escape punishment,
> and those who proclaim lies will not escape.

19:5. The teaching in Proverbs on lying in court is pervasive[3] (see especially 6:19; 12:17; 14:5, 25; 19:9; 21:28) and clear. This particular verse emphasizes the certain negative fate of those who engage in such speech. Though the primary setting is clearly legal, the principle applies to all speech.

> [6]Many people seek the face of rulers,
> and everyone is the friend of a person who bears gifts.

19:6. The proverb is in the form of an observation. People present themselves positively to those from whom they expect to gain favors. Rulers are usually wealthy and have positions of influence, and thus people are nice to them, at least to their faces, hoping to gain advantages. The same is true with anyone else known to bring gifts.

The purpose of the proverb, if there is one, is harder to ferret out. Is this advice on how to gain favor with the rich and influential? Is it making fun of people who act positively toward others out of self-interest? Is it critical? At least it informs those who read it of the reality of the situation so that they can act accordingly. This verse makes a point similar to 19:4.

> [7]All the brothers of the poor hate them;
> how much more their friends keep far from them.
> When they pursue them to speak, they are not there.

19:7. The first two cola are quite clear in meaning and in keeping with the message of 19:4. No one likes to be around poor people, not their relatives ("brothers") and not their friends. The poor are too much trouble, and they are no help to others.

The difficulty in this verse is in the third colon. It may be, as many commentators suggest,[4] that this third colon is the corrupted remnant of another bicolon. Along with versions like the NIV and NRSV, we try to make it fit as a third colon, though the connection is tenuous. The

---

2. For translation and commentary, see Longman, *Ecclesiastes*, 160, 165.

3. Whybray (*Proverbs*, 277) suggests that this is because lying was pervasive in law courts of the day.

4. Murphy, *Proverbs*, 141.

idea is that neither brothers nor friends are there when the poor try to speak to them about their problems.

---

[8]Those who acquire "heart" love themselves;
those who guard competence find good.

19:8. This observation serves as motivation to work at acquiring wisdom. "Heart" connotes character, in my opinion. Many scholars believe that "heart" points specifically to one's mind,[5] and certainly the parallel with "competence," a word formed from the verb "to understand" (*tĕbûnâ* from *bîn*) would help support this idea. However, the second colon does not provide an exact parallel to the first colon but, rather, more carefully specifies the meaning. Thus, I understand the first colon as saying that those who want to improve their character want the best for themselves, and the second colon as more specifically talking about one aspect of character: competence, practical knowledge.

In this last line, self-interest is used as a motivation. Why should people work at character development? Because it is in their best interest.

---

[9]False witnesses will not escape punishment,
and those who proclaim lies will perish.

19:9. This verse is almost identical to 19:5 (see comments there). The only variation is in the final verb, which is not much different in meaning.

---

[10]Luxury is not right for a fool,
even more for a servant to rule over people.

19:10. The sages had a definite sense of what was appropriate in terms of social arrangements. From the perspective of wisdom, the first colon is obviously true. It is not in keeping with what is right for fools to have material ease. That such a comment must be made, however, alerts us to the fact that the sages knew that sometimes fools do have luxury. The second line seems to indicate a certain rigid idea of social stratification. Servants serve. They do not rule, and when they do, it is not good. This teaching is similar to that found in Eccles. 10:5–7, which also comments negatively on the reverse situation—kings, nobles, and the wealthy having low social positions.[6]

---

5. Ibid., 143: "'Heart' stands here for intelligence."

6. The idea of the "world upside down" is a frequent theme in ancient Near Eastern wisdom. Besides Proverbs (see also 30:21–22) and Ecclesiastes in Hebrew tradition, the

> [11]Insightful people hold in their anger,
> and their glory is to ignore an offense.

19:11. Those with wisdom ("insight" is associated with *ḥokmâ*) avoid conflict. Here they do so by controlling their emotions. Sometimes when responding to an annoying offense, people make more trouble and annoyance for themselves. Thus, the wise are not quick to respond angrily to someone. God himself is slow to take offense (Exod. 34:6; Mic. 7:18).

> [12]The rage of the king growls like a lion;
> his favor is like the dew on the grass.

19:12. Kings hold power over others, even the power of life and death. This proverb's observation helps remind the wise that it is foolish to arouse a ruler's anger. Anger makes him like a destroying lion, but saying or doing things that bring his favor will bring a person refreshment that is like the dew on the grass. The dew in dry, arid Palestine brought life to vegetation. For other teaching on the king in Proverbs, see 8:15–16; 14:28, 35; 16:10, 12, 13, 14, 15; 19:12; 20:8, 26, 28; 21:1; 22:11; etc., especially 20:2.

> [13]A foolish son is a disaster to his father,
> and a contentious wife is a constant dripping.

19:13. This proverb combines two concerns individually addressed in other proverbs. The perspective is that of the senior male of the household and deals with two important relationships. On the one hand, a son who makes foolish life decisions is a disaster to a father (see 10:1; etc.). After all, a foolish son ends up in all kinds of trouble that the father feels intently because of his love for the child. The second intimate relationship that can be a source of annoyance is his wife (21:9, 19; 25:24). Nagging is here likened to the torture of dripping water. It is not an overwhelming force, but it wears one down.

The elder male perspective is a function of the original recipients of the proverb. Women need to simply substitute "husband" for "wife" (see "Gender and Theology" in the introduction).

> [14]House and riches, the inheritance from fathers,
> but an insightful wife is from Yahweh.

---

same theme may also be found in the Egyptian Admonitions of Ipu-Wer. This theme is also found in apocalyptic literature (see Isa. 24:2; as well as the Akkadian Marduk and Shulgi Prophecies). See Van Leeuwen, "Proverbs 30:21–23."

19:14. Good things ("house and riches") come from the previous generation, but this is nothing compared to the gift that can only come from Yahweh: a wise wife. This proverb balances the previous one, which speaks of a contentious wife. Proverbs does not pick on women as women, only on those who disrupt social harmony in the family. Proverbs reserves its highest praise for virtuous women (31:10–31). See also 18:22.

> [15]Lazy people fall into a deep sleep,
>   and the appetite of a slacker stays famished.

19:15. This proverb is one of a series of sarcastic statements about laziness (see "Laziness and Hard Work" in the appendix). The sage believes that the lazy have adopted a foolish strategy for living, which will lead to their own self-destruction. Here, the lazy would rather sleep than work. Not even their appetites will motivate them to go out and work. They would rather starve to death.

> [16]Those who guard the commandment guard their lives;
>   those who despise their way will die.

19:16. For the significance of the "commandment," see 2:1, where it was argued that the word points to the law and provides a bridge to the Torah.[7] Keeping God's law as well as following the advice of the father allows one to live life in a way that minimizes the possibilities of premature death. However, death will come to those who ignore the strategy of proper living (and thus despise their lives ["way"]).

> [17]Those who are gracious to the poor lend to Yahweh,
>   and he will fully repay them.

19:17. This proverb uses the metaphor of credit to commend generous behavior toward the poor. To give to the poor is like a loan to God himself, who will reward those who do it. It suggests that the main type of gracious or generous behavior in mind is in terms of material goods. Those who give sustenance to the poor will find their own material possessions increase, though it is possible that other nonmaterial rewards are meant or included. Compare Deut. 15:1–11.

> [18]Discipline your son while there is hope;
>   don't be intent to kill him.

---

7. So also Van Leeuwen, "Proverbs," 180; but contra Murphy, *Proverbs*, 144.

19:18. Discipline, a term that has implications of physical punishment, is the key to wisdom. Children are not naturally wise but must be trained in wisdom. The sages put a lot of emphasis on the urgency of instructing the young in the ways of wisdom. If they are allowed to grow old without being influenced toward the way of wisdom, then they will be locked into a foolish mind-set, and folly leads to death. Thus, withholding instruction from children is regarded as an atttempt on their lives.

An alternative understanding of the relationship of the two cola is represented by Murphy's translation:

> Discipline your son while there is hope,
> but no death! Don't get overwrought![8]

In this interpretation, the second colon puts restrictions on the first colon. Discipline your son, but don't get carried away and beat him so much that he dies. In my opinion, this understanding, while possible, is not the most natural reading, since we know from elsewhere (23:13–14) that the idea of disciplining a child has as its purpose keeping that child from the death that comes to those who follow the way of folly.

> [19]People of great wrath carry around punishment;
> if you rescue them, then you will have to do so again.

19:19. This proverb makes an observation about people who are characteristically angry. They contain the seeds of their own punishment. They grow angry and bring people's resentment on them. The observation is actually addressed not to people who cannot control their anger, but to those who help them get out of scrapes. It is a reminder that the problem is habitual. Perhaps the implicit message is not to try to rescue such people; like the fool who does not deserve a response (26:4), the angry person should not be helped.

> [20]Listen to advice and receive discipline,
> so you might grow wise in your future days.

19:20. Becoming wise is not an overnight or an automatic thing. One must listen to other wise people and accept their correcting instruction. Over time, then, a person grows in wisdom. This proverb may seem most naturally addressed to young persons at the beginning of their journey, but it can be heeded by even the most experienced (see the admonition that the wise listen so they may become even wiser in 1:5).

8. Murphy, *Proverbs*, 145.

> ²¹Many plans are in people's hearts,
>   but the advice of Yahweh, that is what will succeed.

19:21. This thought is similar to that expressed in 16:1 and 9, and similar to vv. 2, 3, and 33 of the same chapter. People have many strategies, but unless they follow the advice of God, they will not come to fruition. This observation discourages the idea that human strategy can lead to success. We must depend on God.

> ²²The longing of people is for their covenant love.
>   It is better to be poor than a liar.

19:22. This proverb is not easy to penetrate, thus explaining differences in translations. The interpretation tentatively adopted here is as follows. The first colon states that people desire *ḥesed*, a term that describes the heart of the covenant relationship. *Ḥesed* can refer to either the divine-human or human-human relationship, and it is likely that the latter is meant here. The second colon gives a better-than proverb that privileges integrity over wealth. Again, it does not demean wealth but just presents relative values. The connection with the first colon would then be a matter of sharpening the focus of "covenant love." *Ḥesed* entails many virtues, one of which is integrity, faithfulness in the area of relationships. Those in a covenant relationship must stay true to their word. Lying is a fundamental breach of trust, often spoken against in Proverbs (6:16–19; 13:5; 14:5; 25:18).

> ²³The fear of Yahweh leads to life,
>   and those who spend the night are contented; they don't pay attention to evil.

19:23. The fear of Yahweh (for which see 1:7 in the commentary and "Fear of Yahweh" in the introduction) drives out all other fears and leads to life (see also colon 1 of 14:27) and not death. The specific fear in view in colon 2 seems odd but may be illustrated by a couple of well-known stories in the OT. In Gen. 19 and in Judg. 19, we have stories of travelers who lodge for the evening in a strange town and face incredible evil, even though they have sought refuge in someone's home. These stories inform us that travel in the ancient world was not a secure matter, and the only sure recourse was Yahweh.

> ²⁴Lazy people bury their hand into the bowl,
>   but they do not return it to their mouth.

19:24. The sages are at their sarcastic best when describing the lazy. They may be able to muster enough energy to send their hand into a bowl to eat, but not even hunger can motivate them to finish the job by lifting it to their mouth. For other proverbs on laziness, see "Laziness and Hard Work" in the appendix.

---

²⁵Hit a mocker, and a simpleminded person will become prudent;
and correct those who understand, and they will understand knowledge.

19:25. The vocabulary of this proverb is reminiscent of the instructions of chaps. 1–9 ("mocker," *lēṣ*; "simpleminded," *petî*; etc.). This proverb gives inspiration for the difficult work of education. "Mockers" (*lēṣ*) cannot learn because they become defensive concerning their mistakes. They will make fun of those who try to instruct them. However, this proverb points out that the effort to educate them through the kind of physical punishment often associated with learning in Proverbs (see "Physical Discipline" in the appendix) may not help them (because they can be beaten silly with no effect; cf. 17:10); yet such punishment will teach a lesson to an immature person, whose defenses are not so high (for "simpleminded," see 1:4). The second colon reminds us that those who already are on the side of wisdom can continue to learn, and so correction directed toward them will lead to an increase in their knowledge. For a closely related proverb, see 21:11.

---

²⁶Those who devastate their father and drive out their mother
are disgraceful children, worthy of reproach.

19:26. Children are to honor their parents (Exod. 20:12); when they not only do not honor but also positively shame them, they are worthy of utter contempt. The proverb is an observation that serves as a warning against improper behavior toward one's parents.

---

²⁷Cease, my son, from listening to discipline,
and you will wander from knowledgeable speeches.

19:27. It is not enough to heed wise advice one time: it is a continual process. The sage warns the son not to think that he will reach a point where no more instruction is necessary. Gathering wisdom is a lifelong process. The father ironically (a dynamic common in chaps. 1–9 but attested only here in 10–31) instructs the son to stop listening to instruction. The negative consequences expressed in the second colon make it clear that he really does not want his son to follow through on this particular instruction.

> ²⁸A worthless witness mocks justice,
> and the mouth of the wicked conveys guilt.

19:28. Yet another proverb that condemns false witness, particularly in a court of law (14:5, 25; etc.), but the principle was surely understood more broadly than that. The second line may be taken to specifically mean that the wicked attribute guilt where it is not justified. For "worthless," see 16:27; see also 1 Sam. 2:12.

> ²⁹Punishments were made for mockers,
> and blows for the backs of fools.

19:29. There is a natural fit between punishment and fools. They deserve it. This observation could serve as motivation for avoiding such behavior. The verse may be an answer to the immediately preceding one, which suggests that mockers make fun of "justice" (the same Hebrew word, which we here translate "punishments").

Chapter 20

Translation

¹Wine is a mocker; strong drinkᵃ a carouser.
　　Those it leads astray will not become wise.
²The dread of a king growls like a lion;
　　those who infuriate him lose their lives.
³The glory of a person is to back awayᵇ from an accusation,
　　but every stupid person lets it break out.
⁴During winter, the lazy do not plow;
　　at harvest, they will ask, but nothing!
⁵Advice is deep waters in the heart of a person,
　　but those who understand draw it out.
⁶Many people will tell a person they are loyal,
　　but who can findᶜ a reliable person?
⁷The righteous walk about in their innocence;
　　blessed are their children after them.
⁸A king who sits on his judgment throne
　　scattersᵈ all evil with his eyes.
⁹Who can say, "I am innocent to the core;ᵉ
　　I am cleansed from my sin"?

a. According to the article in *NIDOTTE* 4:113–14, *škr* may represent all nongrape wine alcoholic drinks. This would include "wine from dates, figs, or promegranates, and beer from barley. . . . Distillation techniques were unknown in ancient Palestine."

b. Taking the verb from *šbt*, "to cease."

c. As Murphy points out, the phrase "who can find" in wisdom literature "is used . . . to indicate either rarity, as here, or even impossibility of occurrence" (Murphy, *Proverbs*, 150).

d. Or "winnows." The metaphor may reflect the practice of winnowing the chaff from the wheat. For the king's winnowing action, see also 20:26.

e. Literally, "I have made my heart pure."

374

¹⁰Stone and stone, ephah[f] and ephah—
    Yahweh detests both of these.
¹¹Even young people feign by their deeds,
    though their conduct seems pure and upright.
¹²An ear to hear and an eye to see—
    Yahweh made both of them.
¹³Don't love sleep lest you are dispossessed.
    Keep your eyes open; be satisfied with bread.
¹⁴The buyer says, "Bad, bad,"
    but he disappears and then brags.
¹⁵There is gold and many pearls,[g]
    but the most precious jewels[h] are knowledgeable lips.
¹⁶Take his garment, for he puts up surety for a stranger;
    take his pledge for a foreigner.[i]
¹⁷False bread is pleasant to a person,
    but afterward his mouth is full of gravel.
¹⁸Plans are firmed up by advice;
    wage war with guidance.
¹⁹Slanderers go about revealing secrets,
    so do not associate with those who are foolish[j] with their lips.
²⁰Those who curse their father and their mother—
    their lamp will be extinguished in the middle[k] of the dark.
²¹Inheritance quickly gained[l] at the start
    does not bless in the future.
²²Don't say, "I will repay the evildoer!"
    Wait for Yahweh, and he will save you.
²³Yahweh detests stone and stone,
    and fraudulent scales are not good.
²⁴From Yahweh are the steps of a person;[m]
    how can people understand their path?

f. The exact meaning of this dry measure is uncertain, but its uncertainty is irrelevant for the meaning of this proverb. The interested reader may refer to the discussion in *NIDOTTE* 1:382–88.

g. Following *NIDOTTE* 3:640–41. Other renditions are "rubies" or "coral." The point remains the same.

h. The word *kĕlî* means "instrument" or the like. However, in this context it means "ornament" or even "jewel" (with many modern translations). See Gen. 24:53; Exod. 3:22; Isa. 61:10; Clifford, *Proverbs*, 184.

i. The NIV follows the Qere (*nokrîyâ*), which reads "wayward woman," as opposed to the Kethib (*nokrîm*), which suggests a foreigner.

j. From *pth*, though some take it as a variant of *ptḥ*, "to open," which makes sense in the context and is attested in Mishnaic Hebrew (see Whybray, *Proverbs*, 298).

k. Reading the Kethib (*ʾîšôn*) with the majority of modern commentators. The Qere, however, is *ʾešûn* (time), thus "in the time of the dark."

l. Translating the Qere *mĕbōhelet* rather than the enigmatic Kethib *mĕbūḥelet*. Clifford takes a stab at the meaning of the Kethib by citing an Arabic cognate and translating "an inheritance greedily guarded at the beginning." However, referring to Arabic is something of an argument of last resort.

m. See the parallel between colon 1 of 20:24 and Ps. 37:23.

²⁵It is a trap for someone to speak rashly about holy things
    and after vows to investigate.
²⁶A wise king scatters wicked people,
    and he rolls[n] the wheel over them.
²⁷The lamp of Yahweh is the breath of a person;
    he is the one who searches all the inner parts.[o]
²⁸Covenant love and faithfulness protect the king;
    he supports his throne by covenant love.
²⁹Strength is the glory of young men;
    gray hair is the splendor of old age.
³⁰Blows and bruises cleanse away[p] evil,
    and beatings the inner parts.[q]

Interpretation

¹Wine is a mocker; strong drink a carouser.
    Those it leads astray will not become wise.

20:1. Wisdom requires clear thinking, an ability to make decisions.
Wine clouds judgment and thus may end up causing a person a lot of
trouble. This proverb is not necessarily advocating abstinence from alcoholic drinks. If it did, it would be out of kilter with the rest of the OT.
In any case, the description that is associated with personified wine and
strong drink (as a mocker and carouser, respectively) suggests overindulgence. However, wine must be consumed in moderation and only at certain times. Later in Proverbs (31:4–7) as well as Ecclesiastes (10:16–17),
it is especially leaders who are warned against the use of alcohol since
it clouds their judgment. After all, leaders' judgments affect more than
their own well-being. Often, if one drinks too much wine, it leads them
to harass or mock others, but the reference here is ambiguous and may
well refer to wine mocking the person who drinks too much.

²The dread of a king growls like a lion;
    those who infuriate him lose their lives.

---

n. Literally, "he causes the wheel to return on them."

o. "Inner parts" may be rendered literally "chambers of the belly."

p. Following the Kethib (*tamrîq*), which is a verb rather than the Qere (*tamrûq*), which
suggests a noun. It is true that the verb is difficult, being a hiphil feminine singular, but
the meaning is clear and fits in with a relatively frequently attested principle (that physical
punishment is a needed part of the discipline of youth).

q. For "inner parts," literally, "chambers of the belly," see 20:27.

20:2. The first colon is very similar to 19:12. The king is a powerful person in an ancient Near Eastern society. His dread can be destructive since he holds the power of life and death, as explicated in the second colon. The image of a lion makes the danger particularly clear.

It is not wise to anger such a powerful individual, so great care should be taken around him. This proverb would have most use to those who actually were in the presence of a king (contra Whybray), even if it may be rightly said that the principle is applicable to other instances of power relationships.[1]

> ³The glory of a person is to back away from an accusation,
>   but every stupid person lets it break out.

20:3. Proverbs is a book that frequently advocates conflict avoidance. Often fights, even if based on a real offense, create more trouble than they are worth. The wise person lets things lie, while the stupid person doesn't hesitate to enter the fray. It is the pride of the stupid person and the humility of the wise person that motivate their respective behaviors.

> ⁴During winter, the lazy do not plow;
>   at harvest, they will ask, but nothing!

20:4. Winter (October to March) was the time for plowing in Palestine. The lazy cannot get themselves to do such an onerous task. However, actions—or in this case a lack of actions—have consequences. If one does not do the work at the beginning of the agricultural season, then how can one expect to reap (literally) the benefits? In colon 2 the context indicates that what they ask after is the crop, and the answer is "nothing"; there is nothing in the field. Lazy persons do not do the work necessary to have adequate food when they need it. For other proverbs on laziness, a major theme in the book, see "Laziness and Hard Work" in the appendix.

> ⁵Advice is deep waters in the heart of a person,
>   but those who understand draw it out.

20:5. Advice is what the sages offer to others in order to give them guidance to navigate the troubles of life. The metaphor of "deep waters" was used in 18:4 to indicate thoughts that are profound and sometimes mysterious, requiring reflection and interpretation. Colon 2 indicates that it sometimes takes a sage to understand a sage.

---

1. So Van Leeuwen, "Proverbs," 185.

> ⁶Many people will tell a person they are loyal,
> but who can find a reliable person?

20:6. The proverb may be roughly understood as saying "talk is cheap." People are willing to claim they are loyal, but when the chips are down, will these same people actually come through? The word translated "tell" (*qārāʾ*) is more literally "call out," pointing to a kind of public assertion. The term "loyal" (*ḥesed*) denotes the kind of love that flows between covenant partners. In other words, these people will say that they are bound by love, with the implication that they will assist when threats emerge, but the question of the second colon implies that these are often false claims. The proverb will put the wise on warning not to accept all claims of friendship at face value.

> ⁷The righteous walk about in their innocence;
> blessed are their children after them.

20:7. The first colon defines righteousness in moral terms: they are innocent. Perhaps we should go to Job to get an example of an innocent man (Job 1:1). Too quickly Christian readers balk at the idea of someone who is "innocent." Paul, after all, makes it very clear, even quoting OT passages, that there is no one who is righteous (Rom. 3:9–20). However, an innocent person is not someone who never sins (see Job 9:1–2), but rather a person who strives to be obedient and pleasing to Yahweh.

The point of the proverb seems to be found in the second colon, which expresses the influence of the righteous on those who observe them closely, particularly the children (which may imply not just one but many generations—descendants). And this is the most natural way of understanding their influence; the righteous are good role models to those who watch their lifestyle.

> ⁸A king who sits on his judgment throne
> scatters all evil with his eyes.

20:8. This is the picture of the just and wise king, who dissipates evil through his deliberate application of law in his kingdom. Because of his just determination of law, criminal elements are fragmented and unable to coalesce into a substantial threat to order. The reference to the king's eyes may reflect the idea that nothing escapes his notice. Wisdom is a quality especially required for the exercise of proper legal judgment. The history of the monarchy gives us few concrete examples of this proverb, but Van Leeuwen suggests that David in 2 Sam. 8–9 demonstrates this kind of justice, both in terms of external enemies as well as in the practice of judgments internal to the kingdom.[2]

> 9Who can say, "I am innocent to the core;
> I am cleansed from my sin"?

20:9. This proverb seeks to bring self-awareness to the wise, who are also the righteous and may sometimes be tempted to self-righteousness. Even the wise must be aware that they are not perfect. They too need to grapple with sin. Even the "innocent" Job (see comments on 20:7) recognized that he too had faults (Job 9:2). Not to know this would lead to a wrong self-assessment and then to errors in behavior and speech. Even so, a number of Proverbs implicitly recognize that some people are "righteous" and others are "wicked." This proverb relativizes this otherwise fairly strict dichotomy.

> 10Stone and stone, ephah and ephah—
> Yahweh detests both of these.

20:10. The "stone" was a means of measuring weight, and the "ephah" a means of measuring dry capacity, of wheat or the like. These were used for commercial transactions. The literal rendition makes little sense on a surface reading. The idea seems to be that two different measures are being used. The buyer understands an "ephah" one way, but the seller another, false way. The proverb fits with others (see especially 11:1; 16:11; 20:23) that condemn[3] false commercial transactions. McKane captures this sense in his paraphrastic rendering of the verse:

> Variations in weights and measures,
> both are loathed by Yahweh.[4]

> 11Even young people feign by their deeds,
> though their conduct seems pure and upright.

20:11. The debate in this proverb surrounds the first verb, which can mean either "to disguise" or "to make known" in the hitpael. The versions go both ways, as do modern commentators,[5] though most contemporary translations opt for the second meaning, as illustrated by the NRSV:

2. Ibid., 186.
3. The phrase "Yahweh detests" (*tôʿăbat Yhwh*) registers a strong condemnation. See comments on 3:32; 11:1; 20:23.
4. McKane, *Proverbs*, 241.
5. This commentary sides with Clifford (*Proverbs*, 183–84) over against Murphy (*Proverbs*, 151), for instance.

> Even children make themselves known by their acts,
>   by whether what they do is pure and right.

If the NRSV interpretation is the right one, then the idea is that children, like adults (the force of "even"), demonstrate their integrity by their actions. This may well be right, but it seems tautologous even for a proverb.

The alternate interpretation at least has interest going for it. If it is correct, then the intention is to warn people that appearances can be deceiving and to encourage them to keep their eyes open in dealing with children as well as with adults. Perhaps further, as Clifford comments, "If a child can fake virtuous actions, an adult can do so even more."[6]

> ¹²An ear to hear and an eye to see—
>   Yahweh made both of them.

20:12. So much of the wisdom of proverbs is based on experience that arises out of observation. This is what makes wisdom seem so practical and, to some, even secular. This latter view ignores the explicitly theological teaching of the book that connects the acquisition of wisdom to the "fear of Yahweh" (1:7) or the metaphor that rules the first nine chapters of the book, describing a relationship with Woman Wisdom. But this simple proverb brings additional insight: even observation only happens because of Yahweh. There is no seeing or hearing apart from his good gift.

> ¹³Don't love sleep lest you are dispossessed.
>   Keep your eyes open; be satisfied with bread.

20:13. This proverb is yet another that warns about the negative consequences of laziness (see "Laziness and Hard Work" in the appendix). The implication seems to be that whoever prefers sleep to work may anger the father enough to be cut out of the family inheritance. The converse expressed in the second colon is that an alert person will not lack for sustenance.

> ¹⁴The buyer says, "Bad, bad,"
>   but he disappears and then brags.

20:14. Here we have the case of "seller beware." Ancient Near Eastern commercial transactions, as in some quarters even today, were done by barter and negotiation. Here the shrewd buyer makes it seem as if there is something wrong with the merchandise; when the seller parts with it at a low price, the buyer goes to his friends and brags about his

---

6. Clifford, *Proverbs*, 184.

good fortune. The function of this proverb seems again to be a warning against the deception of appearances. Proverbs is often concerned that commercial transactions are fair. Typically (11:1; 16:11; 20:10), the warning is directed at the shrewd seller, but here it is the shrewd buyer.

> ¹⁵There is gold and many pearls,
>> but the most precious jewels are knowledgeable lips.

20:15. This verse is a variant of the teaching that wisdom is better than precious jewels and expensive metals. If a choice must be made, then wisdom is better than these desired objects. The proverb is intended to teach a proper perspective. After all, wealth often comes through wisdom, so better to get that, so, like Solomon, one can be wise and rich!

> ¹⁶Take his garment, for he puts up surety for a stranger;
>> take his pledge for a foreigner.

20:16. This proverb is another warning against providing loans or supporting loans for another person, particularly for a stranger (see also 6:1–5; 11:15; 17:18; 22:26; 27:13). This proverb is addressed to those who have made the loan, and it says that no mercy should be shown to foolish people who stick their necks out in such a way. Better to be generous to someone in need (11:24; 28:27; 29:7, 14) than to expect to get paid back for such a loan.[7]

> ¹⁷False bread is pleasant to a person,
>> but afterward his mouth is full of gravel.

20:17. We begin with the question: In what way is bread false? Bread, considered the staple of food, may stand for any kind of material possession. Such may be false by virtue of how it was gained. The principle of the proverb is that material gained by false pretenses or in an illegitimate way may at first seem enjoyable and beneficial, but in the end shows itself harmful. What appears to be bread in the mouth is actually gravel to be spit out. Illustrative of this is the stolen water that Woman Folly offers to the young men and proclaims "sweet" (9:17). In reality, though, consuming these waters leads to death. The proverb is thus a warning against pursuing gain through false means.

---

7. As Scherer points out ("Is the Selfish Man Wise?" 64), the command to take a garment appears to be prohibited by Deut. 24:17 (but cf. Deut. 24:10–13) and Amos 2:8. Scherer goes on to argue persuasively that when read in the light of the law, this proverb "gains an ironical connotation: the one who puts up security for a stranger is so foolish that even the loss of his garment causes no further trouble to him."

> [18]Plans are firmed up by advice;
> wage war with guidance.

20:18. The wise person does not act on impulse but only after careful reflection (15:28; 19:2; 20:18, 25; 21:5; 29:20). This proverb encourages thoughtful preparation for action and then applies this principle particularly to battle. Bad things will happen if one enters battle rashly. The thought is similar to 24:6. This proverb is an excellent example of the sharpening effect of parallelism. The general principle is given first, but then it is applied to one particular area, warfare. The general principle, though, allows the reader to apply the idea to other aspects of life. On the other hand, it seems odd to conclude that the second colon is only metaphorical and does not have reference to actual warfare.[8] Since the proverb applies the principle to warfare, this may well be a proverb that finds its primary setting in the royal court.

> [19]Slanderers go about revealing secrets,
> so do not associate with those who are foolish with their lips.

20:19. A slanderer takes private information and makes it public so as to embarrass people. Thus follows the advice given in the second colon: the wise should not get near to such people for fear that they will reveal something unwanted about them. For other teaching about slander, see the closely related 11:13 and 10:18. See also Lev. 19:16.

> [20]Those who curse their father and their mother—
> their lamp will be extinguished in the middle of the dark.

20:20. Cursing father and mother was a serious offense in ancient Israel, even calling the death penalty upon the perpetrator (Exod. 21:17). Indeed, according to the fifth commandment, children had the positive duty to honor their parents (20:12). In Proverbs, fathers and mothers were the source of sound and wise advice, so to curse them would mark their children as fools.

This proverb essentially applies a curse to those who curse their parents. "Lamp" here may stand for one's life energy, but whether or not the penalty implied here is death, horrible consequences are in store for those who treat their parents with disdain. The metaphor of the extinguished lamp appears as a curse in Prov. 13:9 and 24:20 as well as outside of Proverbs (Job 18:6; 21:17). As to how the penalty will come about, this is not named in the proverb.

8. So Whybray, *Proverbs*, 297.

²¹Inheritance quickly gained at the start
does not bless in the future.

20:21. This proverb may well fit in with the extensive teaching on the dangers of "quick wealth" (11:18; 13:11). It may envision a young, immature person coming into an inheritance because of the untimely early death of parents. Without the wisdom needed to manage well, the material goods are not a blessing but rather quickly evaporate. I do not think that this proverb intends to speak of those who come into possessions in an illegitimate way (Van Leeuwen cites the way Ahab takes over the possessions of Naboth; 1 Kings 21),[9] though one might legitimately extend the principle of the proverb to include such instances.

²²Don't say, "I will repay the evildoer!"
Wait for Yahweh, and he will save you.

20:22. The wise do not look for revenge. They rather can expect their God to act on their behalf. Christian readers will recognize the same idea behind Paul's teaching in Rom. 12:17–20: "Do not take revenge, my dear friends, but leave room for God's wrath, for it is written: 'It is mine to avenge; I will repay,' says the Lord" (TNIV).[10]

The wisdom in this advice is that it is often frustrating to try to get back at the person who has harmed you. In the end, revenge provides the occasion for the perpetrator to harm even further. Solace is taken in the idea that God will work out the revenge and take care of the victim. How this works out is not specified in the proverb.

This proverb should not be understood as applying to sins punishable by the law found in the Torah. These are the purview of the community and the court, not the individual, as presumed here by the first-person speaker. These are rather offenses for which there are no prescribed punishments or where the perpetrator is somehow beyond the power of the law.

²³Yahweh detests stone and stone,
and fraudulent scales are not good.

20:23. This is yet another in a list of proverbs that condemn deceptive business transactions (see 11:1; 16:11; 20:10). The formula "Yahweh detests" (literally, "abomination of Yahweh"; see 3:32; 11:1) judges the stated action in the strongest possible terms. The phrase to "stone and stone" is a reference to weighing a product that is being sold and must

9. Van Leeuwen, "Proverbs," 187.
10. The quotation is from Deut. 32:35.

indicate some irregularity in the transaction. Perhaps an equivalent would be a shopkeeper who puts his foot on the scale to make the portion seem larger and thus charge accordingly. This teaching in the area of business ethics fits in with the even larger teaching informing the reader that Yahweh is against all deceit.

> [24]From Yahweh are the steps of a person;
> how can people understand their path?

20:24. The teaching of this proverb is similar to that found in 16:1, 9. The path of a person, representing one's life journey, is enigmatic. Indeed, to claim to know where one is heading is presumptuous and dangerous. The book of Proverbs certainly does not denigrate planning; just the opposite is true (16:1, 3). Yet planning must be done with the awareness that God can intervene and change one's future. This proverb is a call to recognize God's sovereignty over one's life.

> [25]It is a trap for someone to speak rashly about holy things
> and after vows to investigate.

20:25. This proverb, whose syntax seems a bit awkward, fits in with others that warn concerning the danger of speaking before thinking. Here the stakes are particularly high since impetuous commitments are being made in terms of one's relationship to God. A vow (Lev. 7:16–17; 22:18–23) is a commitment made to God if God sees fit to answer one's request. This commitment could take the form of money or some other possession that would be turned over to the sanctuary upon the answer to the prayer. Jephthah, for instance, made a rash vow without thinking of the consequences, which turned out to be tragic for him and his daughter (Judg. 11:29–40). Ecclesiastes 5:1–7 issues a similar warning in what might be a more estranged relationship with God, who is considered distant.[11] Proverbs does not reflect Qoheleth's sense of alienation from God but knows that God is powerful and therefore dangerous. One should not speak mindlessly about holy matters.

> [26]A wise king scatters wicked people,
> and he rolls the wheel over them.

20:26. A wise king is set against evildoers, and he will use his considerable power to destroy them. Evil in the kingdom will destroy it, so before that happens the king should destroy them. The image of scattering or winnowing evokes the idea of separating the wheat from the chaff. The metaphor of the second colon is perhaps that of the chariot or even of

---

11. See the discussion in Longman, *Ecclesiastes*, 148–56.

an instrument of torture,[12] but may be that of a wheel that he used to winnow grain and thus be consistent with the first colon.[13] For a similar thought about the wise use of royal power, see 20:8.

> ²⁷The lamp of Yahweh is the breath of a person;
> he is the one who searches all the inner parts.

20:27. Though the metaphor is a bit hard to penetrate, the idea is certainly clear. In other words, though the specification of the "lamp of Yahweh" as the breath of the person is a bit unclear, the point of the saying is that the person lives only because of Yahweh. The use of *nišmâ* for "breath" here clearly invites us to recall the very creation of the first human in Gen. 2:7. The lamp image makes more sense in connection with the second colon. In essence, nothing is hidden from the lamplike illumination of Yahweh, who knows us inside and out (Prov. 15:11; Ps. 139). If so, as Murphy suggests, this proverb could either be "a consolation or also a warning," though he also wonders whether the "lamp" may be a way of referring to the conscience.[14]

> ²⁸Covenant love and faithfulness protect the king;
> he supports his throne by covenant love.

20:28. "Covenant love and faithfulness" form a frequent word pair (see 3:3; 14:22; 16:6; etc.) and refer to God's disposition toward those he loves. It is not clear that the love and faithfulness mentioned here in the first colon refer specifically to that divine attitude toward the king, but it might. However, it may refer to the king's own attitude toward his subjects or to the covenant love the king directs toward his subjects, or to both. The second colon makes more sense if the covenant love is what he expresses, but the whole saying may refer to "covenant love" all around. It is through that kind of constant faithfulness between all the parties involved that productive governance can take place and the king himself can avoid usurpation or even assassination.

> ²⁹Strength is the glory of young men;
> gray hair is the splendor of old age.

12. Snell ("Wheel in Proverbs xx 26") argues that the "wheel" is a royal instrument of torture on the basis of the fact that such an instrument is known from ancient Hittite texts. Franzmann ("Wheel in Proverbs xx 26") argues against Snell's suggestion and supports the agricultural interpretation of the wheel by an appeal to the *Odes of Solomon* (23.11–16), a pseudepigraphic text (around AD 100) that he suggests provides a closer parallel than the Hittite texts to which Snell appeals.

13. So Whybray, *Proverbs*, 302.

14. Murphy, *Proverbs*, 154.

20:29. This proverb is an observation on what brings glory to young and old men and, in essence, compares them. The observation may serve as motivation for young men to grow in wisdom and for older men not to commiserate for their loss of youthful energy. Vigor has been replaced with something that, certainly within the context of the book of Proverbs, is considered more important: wisdom. The latter is indicated by the reference to gray hair. Here modern Western society is out of odds with ancient Near Eastern and specifically biblical ideas. Today gray hair is almost something to be ashamed of. Youth now is venerated, but in antiquity gray hair, indicating advanced age, was a sign of distinction. The reason age was respected was that, all things being equal, it meant that a person had matured and was wiser than a youth. Experience would have led to advanced knowledge, and the very fact of surviving to old age meant that life strategies were successful. That all things are not always equal was certainly known in biblical times, as demonstrated by the three friends of Job. They are advanced in years and indeed often bolster their arguments by reference to the authority of age (Job 15:7–10), proffering foolish arguments. Indeed, on the basis of the fact that according to our understanding of biblical parallelism, the second colon intensifies the first, it is likely correct to understand the proverb as saying something good ("strength") is being replaced by something better ("gray hair" = wisdom). For a similar sentiment, see Prov. 16:31:

> Gray hair is a crown of glory;
>> it is found on the path of righteousness.

---

[30]Blows and bruises cleanse away evil,
and beatings the inner parts.

20:30. Proverbs does not shrink from physical punishment to support the acquisition of wisdom and the concomitant avoidance of evil (10:13; 13:24; 19:18, 25; 20:30; 22:15; 23:13–14; 26:3; 29:15, 17, 19). Though the proverb may be considered harsh, it does not imply that a person would be hurt seriously. Indeed, the obvious fact that evil flourishes among a generation raised on the advice not to inflict physical punishments like spanking calls into serious question whether modern child-rearing strategies are more beneficial than biblical wisdom. The proverb claims that physical punishment does more than produce outward conformity; it also helps transform the heart. As the translation footnote indicates, there are some issues with the verb in colon 1, but this is not sufficient reason to obscure the general sense of the proverb as represented in our translation.[15]

---

15. As is evidenced by Perdue (*Proverbs*, 181), who translates "Blows and wounds come upon the wicked, beatings, into their inmost beings." He suggests that the meaning, "Outer blows destroy the inner person," is the very opposite of what the proverb seems to teach and what other proverbs clearly teach.

Chapter 21

Translation

¹The heart of a king is a canal of water in the hand of Yahweh;ᵃ
    he inclines it wherever he wants.
²Every path of a person is straight in one's own eyes,
    but Yahweh weighs the heart.
³Practicing righteousness and justice
    is more preferable to Yahweh than sacrifice.ᵇ
⁴Haughty eyes and arrogant heart,ᶜ
    the lamp of the wicked, are sin.
⁵The plans of the determinedᵈ end up in profit,
    but all those who hurry end up with loss.ᵉ
⁶Those who workᶠ for treasures with a lying tongue
    are pursuers of meaninglessness and seekersᵍ of death.
⁷The violence of the wicked will sweepʰ them away,
    for they refuse to act with justice.
⁸Twisty the way of a person, and strange,
    but pure, virtuous in action.

a. The Masoretic accentuation breaks the parallel line at this point, though it produces a long first colon.

b. See also Prov. 15:8; 21:27; and Isa. 1:11–17.

c. Literally, "uplifted eyes and broad heart."

d. For *ḥārûṣ* in the sense of "determined," see Prov. 10:4.

e. Literally, the phrases that end the two cola are translated "surely/only [*ʾak*] for profit" and "surely/only for loss."

f. Emending *pōʿal* to *pōʿēl* (the participle), with the Greek and Vulgate.

g. A few Hebrew manuscripts as well as Greek and Latin versions understand *môqšê* (snares) here, but this seems an unnecessary emendation.

h. From *grr*; see also Hab. 1:15 for the use of this verb in a similar context.

[9]It is better to live in the corner of a roof
　　than with a contentious woman in a shared house.[i]
[10]Wicked people[j] crave evil,
　　so their neighbors find no favor in their eyes.
[11]When a mocker is punished, a simpleminded person grows in wisdom.
　　When insight comes to a wise person, knowledge increases.
[12]The righteous observes[k] the house[l] of the wicked,
　　turning the wicked toward trouble.
[13]Those who stop up their ears to the cry for help from the poor—
　　they also will call out but not be answered.
[14]A gift in secret calms[m] anger,
　　and a hidden bribe, passionate wrath.
[15]Acting justly is a joy to the righteous,
　　but it is a ruin to those who do evil.
[16]People who wander from the path of insight
　　will reside in the congregation of the departed.
[17]Those who love pleasure end up lacking;
　　those who love wine and oil will not grow rich.
[18]The wicked are a ransom for the righteous,
　　and the faithless in place of the virtuous.
[19]It is better to live in a desolate land
　　than with a contentious and angry woman.
[20]Precious treasure and oil are in the abode of the wise,
　　but fools will swallow them up.
[21]Those who pursue righteousness and covenant love
　　will find life, righteousness,[n] and honor.
[22]A wise person went up against a city of warriors
　　and brought down the stronghold in which they felt safe.
[23]Those who guard their mouth and tongue
　　are those who guard themselves from trouble.
[24]Incredibly presumptuous[o]—mockers are their name,
　　those who do excessively insolent things.

i. This prepositional phrase is difficult; literally, the second colon reads "than a contentious woman and a house of an associate." The above translation is suggested by the LXX: *en oikō koinō*, "in a common house." The footnote in *BHS* suggests an emendation based on a metathesis of the letters, changing *ḥāber* to *rāḥāb*, a "spacious" house.

j. The Hebrew phrase *nepeš rāšā* can be understood as either "wicked person" or "the desire of the wicked." In either case, the meaning remains much the same.

k. Though it has a different nuance here, this word has the same root (*śkl*) as the one translated "has insight" in v. 11.

l. The LXX has "the hearts of the wicked," but the MT makes sense as it stands.

m. This verb (*kph*) occurs only in this place in the Hebrew Bible. Its translation is based on context and its meaning in postbiblical Hebrew as well as Aramaic and Syriac (see Clifford, *Proverbs*, 188).

n. Some (e.g., Murphy, *Proverbs*, 157) find the repetition of "righteousness" in the second colon difficult and do not translate it, citing the LXX.

o. This is an hendiadys of two nouns: "presumptuous arrogant" (*zēd yāhîr*).

388

²⁵The longings of the lazy will kill them,
    for their hands refuse to do anything.
²⁶Longings pull at us^p all day long,
    but the righteous give without holding back.
²⁷Yahweh detests the sacrifice of the wicked,
    because they bring it, scheming.
²⁸A lying witness will perish,
    but one who listens^q will keep speaking.
²⁹The wicked put on an impudent face,
    but the virtuous establish their path.
³⁰There is no wisdom and no competence,
    and no advice against Yahweh.
³¹A horse is prepared for the day of battle,
    but victory belongs to Yahweh.

Interpretation

> ¹The heart of a king is a canal of water in the hand of Yahweh;
>   he inclines it wherever he wants.

21:1. The king was a powerful person in ancient Israelite society, but this proverb instructs that even this powerful figure is subservient to the will of Yahweh. The modern equivalent to the image of a "canal of water" in the hand of Yahweh would be to say that the king is like "putty" in his hands. That God does not always incline the king in the direction of righteousness may be illustrated by the case of Pharaoh in the book of Exodus. Here God "hardens his heart." This is not to be understood as making the pharaoh do evil, but rather in confirming an inclination already there. Yet since water brought fertility, this image may mean that God inclines the king in good directions. Also in support of this is the idea that chaotic waters are representative of chaos and hostility, so channeled water means bringing these contrary forces under control.

> ²Every path of a person is straight in one's own eyes,
>   but Yahweh weighs the heart.

p. The grammatical form is that of a cognate accusative used with an impersonal subject: "he longs with longings."

q. Emerton ("Interpretation of Proverbs 21,28," 161) recognizes a "connexion between listening and wisdom" in Egyptian and biblical texts, and he also cites 1 Kings 3:9, where Solomon requests a "listening heart" (*lēb šōmēaᶜ*). Eaton ("Memory and Encounter," 181) describes the "hearing heart" as a "wonderful educational ideal," which "implies a teachable and open mind, the gift of sympathetic attention, the power of observation, and above all an ear for truth, a listening to the divine voice and a readiness to follow it."

21:2. This proverb is a variant of 16:2. The point is that human beings can misperceive their integrity or falsely claim to have integrity. Humans are not the final judges of the rightness of their own actions: God is. Humans do not define standards of virtue: God does. The path metaphor stands for one's life direction here and is pervasive throughout the book.

> ³Practicing righteousness and justice
> is more preferable to Yahweh than sacrifice.

21:3. Like better-than proverbs (see, among others, 16:19, 32; 17:1; 19:22; 22:1; 24:5; 27:5; 28:6, 23), this proverb presents relative values. To be sure, Yahweh loves sacrifice, but more so righteousness and justice. Indeed, it might be argued from this proverb and elsewhere (Isa. 1:11–17; Hosea 6:6; Mic. 6:6–8; 1 Sam. 15:22) that sacrifice without righteousness and justice is worthless.

The proverb does not define "righteousness" and "justice," but since these categories are closely connected to wisdom and all these are associated with certain behaviors and attitudes, the book may be said to define it. Also, reading Proverbs within the context of the canon would also lead the reader to the rest of the canon, perhaps particularly to the Law. If so, then the practice of righteousness and justice would include, but not be defined by, the offering of sacrifices.

> ⁴Haughty eyes and arrogant heart,
> the lamp of the wicked, are sin.

21:4. This verse, while clear in its main point, has its complications and, with other commentators, we must ultimately admit that it remains enigmatic, particularly in terms of the image. Certainly, there is nothing obscure about the connection between pride, on the one hand, and wickedness and sin, on the other. Pride, putting oneself first, leads to sin and, as Calvin would state, is the ground of all other sins. In contrast to the description of the wicked as those with prideful eyes and arrogant heart, we think of the psalmist's exclamation:

> [O Yahweh], my heart is not proud;
> my eyes are not haughty. (Ps. 131:1 NLT)

The enigma comes with the metaphor of the "lamp." Perhaps the idea is that the eyes and heart (standing for the outer and inner person) are the lamp of the individual, which in the case of the wicked are perverted.

In this understanding, there may be an intentional contrast with the "lamp of Yahweh" in 20:27.

It has been suggested that the Hebrew word *nir* means "tillage" here, but I take it as a variant of *nēr* (many manuscripts have this latter form, as do the versions), which usually means "lamp." Rendering it as "tillage" seems to overreach the evidence, and in any case the metaphor is not made more clear.[1]

> [5]The plans of the determined end up in profit,
> but all those who hurry end up with loss.

21:5. Those who are determined have their eye on the goal; they are able to make decisions and devise plans. This is to be contrasted with those who hurry, which in this context must mean something like being "impulsive." Proverbs frequently denigrates those who make quick, non-reflective decisions. The consequences of these two courses of action are contrasted in terms of profit and loss.

> [6]Those who work for treasures with a lying tongue
> are pursuers of meaninglessness and seekers of death.

21:6. Proverbs is not against the acquisition of wealth, but it must be done with honesty and industry. Fraudulent pursuit of wealth is consistently condemned (22:16) along with any form of lying (6:16–19; 25:18). Here the proverb cuts to the reality of the situation. These people think they are going after material possessions, but what they will gain is a meaningless[2] life and ultimately death.

> [7]The violence of the wicked will sweep them away,
> for they refuse to act with justice.

21:7. Wicked people do not act with justice and thus harm those who are innocent. They act this way to get the advantage over others, but this proverb points out that they themselves will meet a tragic end. "Violence begets violence."[3] The proverb can serve as a warning against violent behavior without cause or provide comfort to those who are the victims of their violence.

---

1. See the suggestion of Murphy, *Proverbs*, 157.
2. "Meaningless" (*hebel*) is the word used by the Teacher (Qoheleth) in the book of Ecclesiastes to indicate life's ultimate lack of worth. For the use of the term, see Longman, *Ecclesiastes*, 61–65.
3. So Van Leeuwen, "Proverbs," 193.

> [8]Twisty the way of a person, and strange,
> but pure, virtuous in action.

21:8. Appearances can be deceiving. Here the path of a person may appear "windy" or "twisty" (from *hpk*), but this does not appear to have the moral sense of "crooked" (from *ʿqš*; 2:15; 11:20). "Strange" (*zār*) can also have a moral sense, but here I think it is used in the sense of "enigmatic." This reading seems correct in the light of the second colon, which describes the person's actual behavior in strong positive terms: "pure" and "virtuous" are used to indicate wise behavior in Proverbs.

> [9]It is better to live in the corner of a roof
> than with a contentious woman in a shared house.

21:9. The proverb has a better-than form, which gives relative, not absolute values. While marriage and companionship are positive things in Proverbs, it is better to be alone than with a person who makes life unbearable. Though the roof of an ancient Israelite home was a living space, unlike most modern homes, the location would be an uncomfortable place to live and sleep. Van Leeuwen states well the point of the proverb: "One is better exposed to nature than to a wife's 'storms.'"[4] In its primary setting, this proverb, consistent with the whole book, is directly addressed to a male audience. Women who read it today must simply substitute "man/husband" into the proverb; it can apply with equal force in that direction. The principle is that it is difficult to live with those who are constantly looking for a fight. Similar proverbs may be found at 21:19; 25:24; 27:15–16.

> [10]Wicked people crave evil,
> so their neighbors find no favor in their eyes.

21:10. This proverb helps us understand the psychology of the wicked. These are not people who occasionally do bad things; they habitually act in bad ways. Thus, the second colon is not surprising. They do not give their neighbors any slack. If their neighbors stand in the way of the fulfillment of their wickedness, to which they are addicted, then the neighbors will suffer. Clifford comments on the wordplay in the Hebrew: "The wicked (*rāšāʿ*) are so obsessed by their desire for evil (*rāʿ*) that (colon *b*) they totally neglect their neighbor (*rēʿēhû*). In other words, the wicked are so absorbed by *rāʿ* that they forget *rēʿ*."[5]

---

4. Ibid., 193.
5. Clifford, *Proverbs*, 190.

> ¹¹When a mocker is punished, a simpleminded person grows in wisdom.
> When insight comes to a wise person, knowledge increases.

21:11. This verse is grammatically more complex than most proverbs and is hard to represent in a pithy manner in English, though it is not inordinately long in the Hebrew. The point is both clear and interesting. It basically makes the point that the punishment of a mocker—though it will do no good for the mocker, who by definition does not respond to criticism or punishment—may help a third party, the immature or simpleminded, who sees it and responds. In the second colon, it is a bit unclear exactly whose knowledge increases, whether other wise people, the simpleminded, or both. See also 19:25.

> ¹²The righteous observes the house of the wicked,
> turning the wicked toward trouble.

21:12. One of the leading questions to ask concerning this proverb is the identity of the "righteous." Most commentators believe that the reference is to God, who is the "Righteous One," and this may well be true. However, there is nothing in the proverb that makes this interpretation certain, and it could refer to a righteous person. After all, both God and righteous people might keep an eye on the wicked and do their best to turn the plans of the wicked toward a bad end. However, it is true that such a picture of the righteous as scheming busybodies is not too complimentary, and so perhaps it is best to think of the actor here as God himself.

> ¹³Those who stop up their ears to the cry for help from the poor—
> they also will call out but not be answered.

21:13. "Others will do unto you as you do unto them." If people do not respond to calls for help, then when they are in trouble, no one will help them. This proverb is a call to be sensitive to requests from the needy. It fits in with others that show a concern for those in need (22:2; 28:27; 29:7, 14).

> ¹⁴A gift in secret calms anger,
> and a hidden bribe, passionate wrath.

21:14. The teaching on bribes/gifts is hard to synthesize in the book of Proverbs. Here both "gift" (*mattān*) and "bribe" (*šōḥad*) are most naturally understood in a positive manner; elsewhere the idea of a bribe is frowned upon as skewing justice (see "Bribes/Gifts" in the appendix;

see also Exod. 23:8; Deut. 16:19; 27:25; Ps. 15:5; Eccles. 7:7; Isa. 1:23; 5:23; Ezek. 22:12). It may be a matter of the right time and right place for a bribe. Perhaps if the motive is good and it does not pervert justice, a bribe was considered the right thing to do. Indeed, one can imagine scenarios where a bribe might actually allow justice to prevail. One other strategy of interpretation would consider this proverb to be sarcastic,[6] but this seems to be a reach, since the calming of anger appears to be a positive outcome.

> [15]Acting justly is a joy to the righteous,
> but it is a ruin to those who do evil.

21:15. Justice brings joy to the righteous, but ruin on those who do evil. After all, justice implies reward for the righteous and punishment as the consequence of evil deeds. Clifford believes that this nullifies what he calls a psychological interpretation, which interprets the joy as a good conscience,[7] but I would raise the possibility that the reward/punishment interpretation does not rule out the idea of a good conscience. My translation (contra the NIV and NRSV) implies an active justice; it may also include not only doing justice but also the joy that comes when the righteous observe justice being worked out.

> [16]People who wander from the path of insight
> will reside in the congregation of the departed.

21:16. Throughout Proverbs, but particularly in the first nine chapters, the metaphor of the path as life journey is pervasive. There are essentially two paths. The path of wisdom is straight and protected by God. Here that path is associated with a synonym of "wisdom" (ḥokmâ), "insight" (haśkēl). The crooked and dark path ends up in death. The simple observation is that those who leave the straight path that leads to life will find death. The term used for "departed" here (rĕpāʾîm) refers to the departed ancestors (see comments at 9:18).

One might respond by saying that everyone, wise and foolish, ends up at death. At a minimum, this proverb suggests that fools are more likely to die early as a result of their foolish decisions. However, the proverb may imply more, though a doctrine of the afterlife is not fully developed here (see "Afterlife" in the introduction).

6. This appears to be Murphy's (*Proverbs*, 160) intent: "Instead of being an explicit condemnation, it registers a fact that the naïve person should be aware of: bribery works, even if it is not to be imitated."

7. Clifford, *Proverbs*, 191.

---

¹⁷Those who love pleasure end up lacking;
those who love wine and oil will not grow rich.

21:17. Proverbs identifies a number of causes of poverty. Certainly, the most common cause is laziness (see "Laziness and Hard Work" in the appendix), but here another reason is given: overindulgence or spending above one's ability to pay. The first colon is a general statement about the pursuit of pleasure leading to a diminishment of resources. The second line refers to celebrations or feasts, what today we might call "parties." The oil would be used to refresh the skin of the guests, while the wine would be used to lubricate their throats. The Bible is not opppposed to alcohol, but consumption should be reasonable.

An interesting contrast may be drawn between Proverbs' teaching that the pursuit of wisdom involves the avoidance of overindulgence and the Teacher's (Qoheleth's) advocacy of it after he gives up on finding meaning in wisdom:

Go, eat your food with pleasure, and drink your wine with a merry heart, for God has already approved your deeds. Let your clothes be white at all times, and do not spare oil on your head. (Eccles. 9:7–8)

One makes a feast for laughter;
wine makes life even merrier;
and money answers everything. (10:19)[8]

---

¹⁸The wicked are a ransom for the righteous,
and the faithless in place of the virtuous.

21:18. No matter how one cuts it, this proverb is difficult. The idea is clear enough. The wicked/treacherous are a ransom for the righteous/virtuous. That must mean that the first pays the penalty for the second. But if the punishment deserved by the righteous is paid by the wicked, where is the justice in that? Further, if the righteous need a ransom, are they really righteous? Perhaps the proverb is being sarcastic. The wicked will ultimately get all the punishment. In any case, Murphy[9] is surely right in asserting against other interpreters[10] that this verse is not saying the same thing as 11:8:

8. See Longman, *Ecclesiastes*, for the translation and proper understanding of these verses in their broader context.
9. Murphy, *Proverbs*, 160–61.
10. For instance, Van Leeuwen ("Proverbs," 194), who also cites Isa. 43:3.

The righteous person is delivered from distress,
but the wicked will take his place.

Contra 11:8, the present proverb through the use of the term "ransom" implies some kind of guilt or fault (on the part of the righteous) that 11:8 does not. This verse ultimately remains difficult.

> ¹⁹It is better to live in a desolate land
> than with a contentious and angry woman.

21:19. This verse is another in a series of proverbs that warn against entering a relationship with a difficult woman (see comments and other text citations at 21:9). Here the analogy is with a desolate land; the term *midbār* used here is best known as referring to the wilderness region through which Israel journeyed to get from Egypt to the promised land.

> ²⁰Precious treasure and oil are in the abode of the wise,
> but fools will swallow them up.

21:20. This verse seems to follow along the lines of 21:17. The wise, through their hard work and stewardship of their resources, have many material blessings. The poor consume them, so they are gone. The "oil" mentioned here, as in v. 17, refers to oil used to freshen the skin in a dry climate; it is an indication of wealth and luxury.

> ²¹Those who pursue righteousness and covenant love
> will find life, righteousness, and honor.

21:21. The pursuit of righteousness and love will be successful. Proverbs are not guarantees or promises, but they present the best strategy for achieving desired ends. All things being equal, those who pursue righteousness will find it (see "Genre" in the introduction). Righteousness and covenant love are closely related to wisdom, so the pursuit of these qualities are at least in part bound up with following the path of wisdom as it is laid out in this book. The verb "pursue" connotes a passionate quest for something.

> ²²A wise person went up against a city of warriors
> and brought down the stronghold in which they felt safe.

21:22. Wisdom is better than strength. How could this be? Most likely this proverb is thinking of strategies devised by advisers who brilliantly lead to the defeat of a strong city. All the brute force in the world is fruitless unless it is guided in the right direction by wisdom.

The Teacher (Qoheleth) undermines the optimism of this idea by telling a story:

> Moreover I observed this example of wisdom under the sun, and it made a big impression on me. There was a small city and there were a few people in it. A great king invaded and surrounded it. He built huge siege works against it. A poor but wise man was found in it, and he rescued the city by means of his wisdom, but no one remembered that poor wise man. And I said, "Wisdom is better than power." But the wisdom of the poor man was despised! His words were not heeded. (Eccles. 9:13–16)[11]

> ²³Those who guard their mouth and tongue
> are those who guard themselves from trouble.

21:23. The sage would laugh at the statement "Sticks and stones may break my bones, but words will never hurt me." Ridiculous. The wrong word can kill and can lead to one's own death. The wise are very careful with their words and will not say things that get them into trouble. This proverb is particularly brief in the Hebrew and may well try to represent linguistically what it is communicating semantically.

> ²⁴Incredibly presumptuous—mockers are their name,
> those who do excessively insolent things.

21:24. This proverb defines what makes a mocker a mocker: pride. Pride causes people to look at others and make fun of them. Specifically, when they themselves are criticized, rather than taking an inward look and transforming for the better, they defend themselves by ridiculing those who are pointing out their weaknesses. For wisdom's distaste for pride and affirmation of humility, see "Pride/Humility" in the appendix.

> ²⁵The longings of the lazy will kill them,
> for their hands refuse to do anything.

21:25. The longings of the lazy do not include work. But without work there is no income, no crops, nothing to eat. Therefore, the desire of the lazy will kill them. This proverb is true, all things being equal. But all things are not always equal. Sometimes people will help out the lazy, so that they survive, but according to Paul's advice to the Thessalonians: "Whoever does not work should not eat" (2 Thess. 3:10 NLT). For the extensive teaching of Proverbs on laziness, see "Laziness and Hard Work" in the appendix.

11. See Longman, *Ecclesiastes*, 233–35.

> ²⁶Longings pull at us all day long,
> but the righteous give without holding back.

21:26. The point of the proverb seems to be that everyone has cravings for things for themselves. We want more and more food, luxuries, and possessions. However, what distinguishes the righteous person from others is that these longings can be redirected, and a self-centered person may become an other-centered person. The righteous do not hesitate to share their wealth. It is not a matter of meeting one's own desires (which never end) and then becoming generous. That generosity is a trait of the wise may be seen also at 22:2; 29:7, 14.

It is interesting to read vv. 25 and 26 together, while not allowing the one to obscure the other. Verse 25 points out that longings are necessary for survival; v. 26 warns that uncontrolled longings are harmful.

> ²⁷Yahweh detests the sacrifice of the wicked,
> because they bring it, scheming.

21:27. Sacrifice does not work *ex opere operato*: it is not a magical ceremony. Using modern theological language, we might call it sacramental in the sense that it is an outward sign of an inward act, such as repentance. The wicked are not repentant; they bring sacrifices for other, hidden motives (the sense of "scheming," *zimmâ*).[12] This false type of sacrifice may be connected to the Teacher's idea of a "sacrifice of fools," though in that context the Teacher may be referring to all sacrifice (see Eccles. 5:1).[13]

Murphy, Clifford, and others translate the particles at the beginning of the second colon to provide a worse practice than the first:

> The sacrifice of the wicked is an abomination;
> how much more when one offers it with calculation.[14]

This is indeed a possible interpretation. However, can one imagine a wicked person offering a sacrifice without duplicitous motives? For this reason, I translate the second colon as giving the definition of a wicked sacrifice. See also 15:8.

> ²⁸A lying witness will perish,
> but one who listens will keep speaking.

---

12. See the discussion of the root meaning of the word (built on the root *zmm*) in 1:4.
13. Longman, *Ecclesiastes*, 140–51.
14. So Clifford, *Proverbs*, 188; see also Murphy, *Proverbs*, 27.

21:28. This proverb fits in with a pervasive theme in the book of Proverbs that damns the false witness and promotes truth in legal proceedings (19:28; 24:28–29; 25:8, 18; 29:24; etc.). The difficult issue of interpretation focuses on the second colon and the phrase *lāneṣ aḥ*, which is typically rendered "forever." Literally, the phrase might be construed something along the lines of "the one who listens will speak forever," but that seems odd. The contrast seems to be between the silencing of the false witness and the continuance of the one who listens, pays attention, and reports the truth. Emerton (see translation footnote) has argued that the verb *dbr* in the second colon should be understood as "destroy," based on Pss. 18:48; 47:3 (4 MT); and 2 Chron. 22:10, while *lāneṣaḥ* should be taken as "completely" rather than "forever," with the result that it should be translated "and one who listens will subdue (or, destroy) (him) completely." He then explains the meaning of the verse as "by listening carefully to a lying witness, his opponent will detect weaknesses and inconsistencies in his testimony, and will defeat him."[15] Emerton's argument has plausibility but is built on rare meanings for both *dbr* and *neṣaḥ* and should be considered only a possibility. One might also suggest that in a context like the present one, where listening and speaking are at issue, the far more frequent use of the verb *dbr* (to speak) would be more likely to provide its meaning.

> [29]The wicked put on an impudent face,
>   but the virtuous establish their path.

21:29. The phrase "impudent face" is also used in 7:13 for the promiscuous woman when she seduces a man who is not her husband, even in the context of performing a religious ritual. It is also used in Dan. 8:23 in reference to a future king, usually identified with Antiochus Epiphanes,[16] who does great damage against the people of God. It is clear that this phrase is associated with horrible evil. In contrast to this, the virtuous have a clear "path," the "way," a pervasive metaphor in Proverbs, standing for the journey of life.

Garrett reads the Qere of the verb of the second colon as "understands" and takes the reference to "their" path as referring not to the path of the virtuous, though this seems the most likely because the closest antecedent, but to the wicked. In other words, the virtuous can "see through" the hard face of the wicked. While not impossible, this seems a less likely

---

15. Emerton, "Interpretation of Proverbs 21,28," 170.

16. For my interpretation of this passage, see T. Longman III, *Daniel*, NIV Application Commentary (Grand Rapids: Zondervan, 1999), 199–215.

reading of the antecedent to "their" and depends on taking the Qere (*yābîn*) rather than the Kethib (*yākîn*).[17]

---

³⁰There is no wisdom and no competence,
and no advice against Yahweh.

21:30. This proverb seems to be saying essentially the same thing, but from a negative point of view, as in 1:7. Wisdom flows from Yahweh, and therefore "wisdom" that speaks contra Yahweh is not really wisdom. This point seems in tension with the well-known international setting of wisdom and Proverbs' own apparent use of ancient Near Eastern proverbs. On this issue, see "Ancient Near Eastern Background" in the introduction.

---

³¹A horse is prepared for the day of battle,
but victory belongs to Yahweh.

21:31. This proverb is in keeping with holy-war theology. Human preparation and strategy is called for, but one must keep in mind that these only succeed if Yahweh so wills.[18] The sentiment seems the same as that expressed in Ps. 33:16–17:

> The best-equipped army cannot save a king,
> nor is great strength enough to save a warrior.
> Don't count on your warhorse to give you victory—
> for all its strength, it cannot save you. (NLT)

This verse in Proverbs may be read in conjunction with the previous proverb to illustrate one area where human wisdom cannot succeed apart from the wisdom of God.

---

17. See Garrett, "Votive Prostitution Again."
18. See T. Longman III and D. Reid, *God Is a Warrior* (Grand Rapids: Zondervan, 1995).

Chapter 22A

Translation

¹A reputation is preferable to much wealth,
   and graciousness is better than silver and gold.
²The wealthy and poor meet together.
   Yahweh made both of them.
³Prudent people see evil and hide,
   but the simpleminded transgress and are punished.
⁴The reward of humility, the fear of Yahweh,
   is wealth, honor, and life.
⁵Thorns[a] and[b] nets are in the path of the crooked person;
   those who guard their lives stay far away from them.
⁶Train up[c] youths[d] in his path;
   then when they age, they will not depart from it.

a. This word is notoriously difficult, but the context suggests that it is some kind of obstacle in the path of the crooked person. Whybray (*Proverbs*, 319) says that the second word, "snares" (here translated "nets"), may be a gloss attempting to define the meaning of an already obscure word, though the LXX also has two words here, which it joins by "and."

b. There is no connective "and" in the Hebrew, but it should be supplied by context, and the LXX does so.

c. This verb (*ḥnk*) is used most frequently to refer to the dedication of a religious object, such as the temple (Deut. 20:5; 1 Kings 8:63). Indeed, the name of the festival of Hanukkah, the celebration of the rededication of the temple after its cleansing in the period of the Hasmoneans, derives from this verbal root.

d. The term is *naʿar*, which Hildebrandt ("Proverbs 22:6a") argues is not a reference to young age but to the social status of someone who serves another: "a squire." This is unlikely; *naʿar* often simply means a "youthful person." As V. Hamilton states (*NIDOTTE* 3:124–27), "The word is used to cover a wide range of age-groups, from an unborn child (Judg. 13:5, 7, 8, 12), to a child not yet weaned (1 Sam. 1:22), to a child recently weaned

401

⁷The wealthy rule over the poor,
  and a borrower is a slave to a lender.
⁸Those who sow injustice will reap evil;
  the rod of their fury will fail.
⁹Generous peopleᵉ he will bless,
  for they give someᶠ of their food to the poor.
¹⁰Banish the mocker, and conflict will go out;
  judgment and shame will cease.
¹¹Those who love a pure heart—
  their lips are gracious; the king is their friend.
¹²The eyes of Yahweh protect knowledge,
  but he frustrates the words of the faithless.
¹³A lazy person says, "There is a lion in the street!
  I will be killed in the middle of the public square!"
¹⁴The mouth of strange women is a deep pit;
  the recipients of Yahweh's wrathᵍ fall into it.
¹⁵Stupidity is bound up in a youth's heart;
  the rod of discipline drives it far from him.
¹⁶Those who oppress the poor in order to multiply
  and those who give to the wealthy—will certainly lack.

Interpretation

> ¹A reputation is preferable to much wealth,
>   and graciousness is better than silver and gold.

22:1. This proverb is in the form of a better-than parallelism that imparts relative values. Wealth is indeed a good thing, but something even better is a sterling reputation. The second colon specifies this as a reputation of graciousness. People who show grace to others are indeed those who have a wonderful reputation with those with whom they come into contact. The Teacher in Eccles. 7:1 also records the value of a good reputation. It is better to be in a healthy relationship with other human

---

(1 Sam. 1:24), to a seventeen-year-old (Gen. 37:2), to a thirty-year-old (Gen. 41:12). There seems to be no case where a *naʿar* was married." Hildebrandt himself believes that this verse refers not to a young person but rather to a young adult and that the verse advocates treating such a person with great respect as he embarks on his career.

  e. The expression is literally "the good of eye," which is widely taken as "generous" in contrast to the "evil eye" (see 23:6; 28:22). The eye is the window into one's inner character, and so whether the eye is good or bad tells us something about the quality of the person.

  f. Taking the *min* prefix in a partitive sense.

  g. This seems to be the best translation of *zĕʿûm*, which is the qal passive participle of *zʿm*, "to be angry, curse."

beings than it is to have an abundance of impersonal material possessions. If one has to choose between the two, and that is not always the
case, it is better to choose the things that bring us into more intimate
relationship with other people.

> ²The wealthy and poor meet together.
> Yahweh made both of them.

22:2. On the surface, those who are rich and those who are poor
have plenty of differences. In most societies, ancient Israelite as well as
modern, the two keep a healthy distance between themselves. Even in
Proverbs, the two social classes are discussed separately, and, all things
being equal, the wise devise living strategies that will bring them material
blessings, while the poor often, but not always (13:23), are poor because
of poor life choices (particularly laziness: 6:6–11; etc.). However, this
proverb reminds all, probably particularly the rich, that the poor are
human beings, fashioned by the same Creator. This observation should
lead the rich to avoid oppressing those who have less than they do. The
idea of these two classes meeting together should likely be understood
more in the sense of "have (the following) in common" rather than the
idea of mixing in the real world, though that happens to a limited extent.
See also 14:31; 17:5; 29:13.

> ³Prudent people see evil and hide,
> but the simpleminded transgress and are punished.

22:3. This is an observation on a basic principle of living that separates
the "wise" (here "prudent"; see 1:4) from the "fool" (here "simpleminded"
in the sense of immature; see 1:4).[1] One recoils from evil and its possibility, while the other goes out of his way to get involved with evil. In Prov.
7, we get a picture of a simpleminded man who, seeing the promiscuous
woman, does not withdraw but rather goes to her house. The result is
punishment for the transgression. See the virtually identical proverb in
27:12; also 14:15 and 18.

> ⁴The reward of humility, the fear of Yahweh,
> is wealth, honor, and life.

22:4. It seems best to take "fear of Yahweh," for which see 1:7, to be
in apposition to "humility." Those who fear Yahweh and thus know their
place in the cosmos are by definition humble. They know they are not

---

1. Indeed, the preface defines the purpose of Proverbs in part as that of making the
simpleminded prudent (1:4).

the center of the universe. The proverb describes the rewards to such persons, who are truly wise, as wealth, honor, and life.

> ⁵Thorns and nets are in the path of the crooked person;
>   those who guard their lives stay far away from them.

22:5. Though the exact wording of the first colon is difficult (see translation footnotes), the idea behind the proverb is fairly clear. It is simply that the lives (represented by the path) of crooked people are beset by all kinds of obstacles. Therefore, those who care about the course of their lives ought to stay far removed from such people. This proverb fits in with those that encourage people to associate only with the wise and to avoid connections with fools.

> ⁶Train up youths in his path;
>   then when they age, they will not depart from it.

22:6. This well-known proverb has been misappropriated in a number of ways.[2] It has some built-in ambiguities, and these should be acknowledged to prevent too dogmatic an application of the principle enunciated here. It is also absolutely essential to remember the nature of this saying as a proverb, rather than a law (see "Genre" in the introduction), as we consider the consequences of colon 2.

The proverb is clearly an admonition to train children. The program for the training is simply stated as "their [his] path." Some have argued that this simply means that children are to be raised according to their natural tendencies. Yet this clearly would not be supported by the understanding of the rest of the book that it takes work, discipline, and even physical coercion to encourage a person to take the right direction in life. Most modern translations understand the verse correctly and communicate the verse's teaching by adding some kind of adjectival qualifier to the path (marked here by italics):

> Teach your children to choose the *right* path,
>   and when they are older, they will remain upon it. (NLT)
>
> Train children in the *right* way,
>   and when they are old, they will not stray. (NRSV)
>
> Train a child in the way *he should go*,
>   and when he is old he will not turn from it. (NIV)

2. For a perceptive analysis of this verse in the midst of a number of different options, see Hildebrandt, "Proverbs 22:6a."

The book of Proverbs is consistent in teaching that there is one and only one right way. It also acknowledges that there is a wrong path, to be avoided. The idea is to train a child in the way of wisdom as explicated in the book of Proverbs. And this is none other than God's ("his") path.

Additionally problematic is the way that people understand the second colon. It sounds like a promise, but a proverb does not give a promise.[3] The book of Proverbs advises its hearers in ways that are most likely to lead them to desired consequences if all things are equal. It is much more likely that a child will be a responsible adult if trained in the right path. However, there is also the possibility that the child might come under the negative influence of peers or be led astray in some other way. The point is that this proverb encourages parents to train their children, but does not guarantee that if they do so their children will never stray. This insight into the form of the proverb is particularly important for parents to grasp when their adult children have not turned out well; otherwise, the verse becomes a sledgehammer of guilt—a purpose that it was not intended to carry. On the other side, the proverb should not become a reason for pride if one's children turn out well either. The proverb is simply an encouragement to do the right thing when it comes to raising one's children.

Clifford represents the interpretive tradition that takes the proverb in an ironic sense. That is, "train up children in *their* way," the way they want to go, and they will never leave that dastardly way!

> [7]The wealthy rule over the poor,
> and a borrower is a slave to a lender.

22:7. The proverb begins with an observation that is hard to gainsay. Those with material means usually call the shots in a society. The wealthy are those who hire the poor and therefore can tell them what to do. The wealthy are typically in positions of government that dictate societal rules. It is not necessarily the case that the proverb is approving of this, but it is a good guess to suggest that this proverb implies that it is better to be a wealthy person ruling over the poor than vice versa.

This preferential reading is certainly supported by the second colon, though typically the sages discourage lending rather than borrowing (6:1–5; 11:15; etc.). However, there is no question who in the borrower/lender relationship has the bulk of the power. Thus, there is no doubt but that this proverb discourages borrowing.

---

3. See "Genre" in the introduction.

> [8]Those who sow injustice will reap evil;
> the rod of their fury will fail.

22:8. This proverb expresses the simple idea of retribution. Those who do bad things will suffer bad things themselves. They may try to hurt others with "the rod of their fury," but their efforts will be thwarted.[4] The proverb does not say how this will come about, and indeed sometimes, if not often, it appears that this simple idea of retribution does not work out in actual life (see "Retribution" in the introduction). However, understood as a general principle and not as a guarantee, one can recognize the truth of this "live by the sword, die by the sword" principle (cf. Matt. 26:52). Indeed, in the light of the NT's fuller teaching about the fate of the righteous and the wicked in the afterlife, it may be correct to speak of this as an "ultimately true principle."

> [9]Generous people he will bless,
> for they give some of their food to the poor.

22:9. The proverb observes that those who are generous will be blessed. It thus fits in with a broad teaching in the book that encourages generosity (11:24; 29:7, 14). This proverb does not specify the nature of the blessing or even who will do the blessing. In terms of the latter, we may be right to understand that this is an unspoken reference to God. It seems less likely that it is a reference to the thanks of the poor, who have not even been named yet.[5] In terms of the latter, other proverbs specify that the blessing may even include material prosperity that rebounds on the giver (28:27).

> [10]Banish the mocker, and conflict will go out;
> judgment and shame will cease.

22:10. Fights are not abstract entities; they arise from specific individuals. Mockers are those who pick fights. They respond to criticism in a defensive manner. In general, they are self-protective people who

---

4. Whybray (*Proverbs*, 320) is typical of other interpreters in his struggle to understand the relationship between the two cola. He points out that some (and we would add Murphy, *Proverbs*, 163) prefer to read "rod of pride" rather than "rod of fury," but Whybray insists that it still does not solve the problem. I believe that the "rod of their fury" refers to the instrument by which the wicked manifest their "injustice," and the failure of such is one way in which they harvest evil.

5. Even less likely, but asserted by some modern commentators, is that the "he" is pleonastic and refers to "generous people." Murphy (*Proverbs*, 163), for instance, translates, "The generous one, he will be blessed."

respond to any perceived assault with a counterattack. Thus, the solution to a situation of conflict may be to get rid of the troublemaker. In other words, this proverb says that it is often not the situation but rather the people involved in a situation who cause problems. Sometimes it is necessary to remove a difficult individual to preserve the harmony of a community.

> [11]Those who love a pure heart—
> their lips are gracious; the king is their friend.

22:11. It all begins with a pure heart. If one's core personality is not oriented in the proper way, then the rest will not follow. But those who do have a pure heart will speak gracious words, because words are the reflection of the heart (16:23). The result is positive. Such people have the king as a friend, and it is always good to have friends in high places.

> [12]The eyes of Yahweh protect knowledge,
> but he frustrates the words of the faithless.

22:12. The proverb is an antithetical one that contrasts Yahweh's stance toward knowledge with his attitude toward the words of the faithless. Yahweh's protection of "knowledge" is likely shorthand for those who seek or possess "knowledge,"[6] a common synonym for "wisdom." On the other hand, he thwarts the intention behind the speech of those without faith, who are on the side of folly. That God can do this is principally expressed in 16:5 (etc.).

> [13]A lazy person says, "There is a lion in the street!
> I will be killed in the middle of the public square!"

22:13. The lazy person is the butt of satirical jokes throughout the book of Proverbs (see "Laziness and Hard Work" in the appendix). Making fun of the sloth does not have ridicule as its ultimate purpose but, rather, warning and motivation. If the hearer understands just how ridiculous and, in the case of other proverbs, just how dangerous lazy behavior is, then the idea is that it will be avoided.

In this case, the lazy person is imagined as using fear of lions as an excuse for not venturing into the public domain. Indeed, we know from various historical narratives (Judg. 14:5; 1 Kings 13:24) that there were

---

6. Though Clifford (*Proverbs*, 198) may be correct in suggesting a different meaning: Colon 1 "states that Yahweh scrutinizes and safeguards the knowledge that comes to expression in words."

lions in Palestine at this time, but the chance of being mauled by one in a city was probably slight or nonexistent.

> ¹⁴The mouth of strange women is a deep pit;
>   the recipients of Yahweh's wrath fall into it.

22:14. This passage goes back to the extensive teaching in the discourses in the first part of the book (cf. chaps. 5–7) that warns the young son about the dangers of the "strange" and "foreign" woman. The woman is strange in that she acts outside of the bounds of traditional social and religious mores restricting intimate sexual relationships to the commitment of marriage. The woman's mouth is particularly attractive to young men, not simply because of her kisses but even more because of the flattery that appeals to the man's vanity (5:3; 6:24; 7:5). But though attractive on the surface, her mouth is a source of great danger, into which those who succumb to temptation will fall. Here the latter are described not as fools, but rather as those with whom God is angry, though the two are not ultimately separate groups.

> ¹⁵Stupidity is bound up in a youth's heart;
>   the rod of discipline drives it far from him.

22:15. The first colon states the sorry condition of youth, and the second gives the prescription for rectifying the problem. The sages had no question about the state of the untended human heart. The "heart," roughly equivalent to what we would call character, of the young is bad. The term "stupidity" (*ʾiwwelet*) is closely associated with folly. It takes the application of discipline to remove their stupidity, which is so integrally and naturally a part of a person. Indeed, physical discipline is necessary (for other proverbs that talk about the rod as an agent of instruction, see "Physical Discipline" in the appendix).

> ¹⁶Those who oppress the poor in order to multiply
>   and those who give to the wealthy—will certainly lack.

22:16. The syntax and understanding of this proverb are very difficult. It is clear that the subject of the first colon is the oppressor of the poor. This is followed by an infinitive clause "to multiply for himself," and we understand this phrase as referring to the intention of the oppressor to get rich off the poor. The second colon mentions another class of people, those who give, probably gifts or maybe bribes, to the rich, likely with the intention of getting more in return. The final phrase seems to indicate that these two strategies will fail. After all, if someone tries to multiply their riches on the backs of the poor, it is like trying to squeeze water from a stone. And those who give to the wealthy to get back more will also fail. The right way to proceed is to give generously to the poor; these are the ones who will get a good return for their money (28:27).

Part 3

Sayings of the Wise

(22:17–24:34)

Proverbs 22:17–21 provides an introduction to the next main division of the book. The speaker exhorts hearers to listen to the "words of the wise" (22:17), comprising thirty (22:20) sayings (through 24:22) supplemented by additional sayings from the "wise" (24:23–34). Since early in the twentieth century, this portion of Proverbs has been regarded as having an interesting special relationship to ancient Egyptian literature, particularly the Instruction of Amenemope.

Chapter 22B

Translation

[17]Incline your ear and hear the words of the wise;
   set your heart toward my knowledge,
[18]for they are pleasant if you guard them in your innermost being
   and have all of them ready on your lips.
[19]So your trust will be in Yahweh,
   I will inform you, even you, today.
[20]Have I not written for you thirty[a] sayings
   with advice and knowledge?
[21]Their purpose is[b] to inform you of true,[c] reliable speeches,
   so you can return reliable speeches to those who sent you.[d]

a. The translation "thirty" is based on an emendation (first proposed by Gressmann, "Neugefundene Lehre des Amen-em-ope") of the Hebrew (Kethib) šilšôm, which means "formerly" or "in three days time," to šĕlōšîm (thirty). The emendation is based on the recognition of similarities between some of the proverbs in this section and sayings in the Egyptian Instruction of Amenemope, which is composed of thirty chapters. In Amenemope, however, the explicit mention of the thirty chapters is reserved to the end rather than mentioned at the beginning, as here. It is also possible (but admittedly not necessary) to divide Prov. 22:22–24:22 into thirty separate sayings. The ancient scribes also had trouble with the original Hebrew, but they understood the text to be read (Qere) as šalîšîm (officers), which makes no sense. The Greek and Vulgate took it to be "three times." See Emerton ("Teaching of Amenemope," 441) for the sentiment that the change to "thirty" involves only a minor change.

b. "Their purpose is to" is not in the Hebrew, but it is a way of smoothing out the Hebrew, which simply presents a purpose clause "to inform you. . . ."

c. This word, qōšĕṭ, "true," occurs only here in Hebrew, but it may be related to the Aramaic word that occurs in Dan. 2:47 and 4:37 [34 MT]. It is often argued that qōšĕṭ is a gloss on the Hebrew ʾimrê ʾĕmet (reliable speeches), but this seems unlikely because probably unnecessary.

d. Cody ("Notes on Proverbs 22,21 and 22,23b," 422) notes the similarity of this verse to Amenemope 1.5–6:

> To know how to return an answer to him who said it,
> And to direct a report to one who has sent him.

²²Don't steal from the poor, because they are poor,
  and don't oppress the needy in the gate.
²³For Yahweh will accuse their accusers,
  and he will press the life out of those who oppress them.ᵉ
²⁴Don't befriend people controlled by anger;
  don't associate with wrathful people,
²⁵lest you learn their ways
  and you get yourself trapped.
²⁶Don't shake handsᶠ
  to pledge security for a loan.
²⁷If you are not able to repay,
  why should they be able to take your bed away from you?
²⁸Don't remove an ancient boundary marker,
  which your ancestors established.
²⁹Do you see people who do their work with diligence?ᵍ
  They will stand before kings;
  they will not stand before the obscure.ʰ

Interpretation

¹⁷Incline your ear and hear the words of the wise;
  set your heart toward my knowledge,
¹⁸for they are pleasant if you guard them in your innermost being
  and have all of them ready on your lips.
¹⁹So your trust will be in Yahweh,
  I will inform you, even you, today.
²⁰Have I not written for you thirty sayings
  with advice and knowledge?
²¹Their purpose is to inform you of true, reliable speeches,
  so you can return reliable speeches to those who sent you.

22:17–21. This passage serves as an introduction to a new section in the book entitled "the words of the wise," which concludes with 24:22.

e. The translation of this colon is that suggested by Cody, "Notes on Proverbs 22,21 and 22,23b," 425–26. He takes his cue for the meaning of the verb *qbᶜ* (occurring only here and in Mal. 3:8–9) from a cognate in Arabic, *qabada*.

f. Literally, "strike hands," referring to some ritual that signifies the sealing of a deal and thus not too far from the modern gesture of shaking hands to show agreement.

g. Or "skill," as typically translated. The verb, however, means "to be in a hurry" and may imply speed and accuracy at work. Since this adjective is used twice to describe a scribe (Ezra 7:6; Ps. 45:1 [2 MT]), it may be the scribe that is especially in mind here, but the principle would apply to other tasks as well.

h. The word is literally "the darknesses," so it is something of a guess that this refers to unknown people, but the key is the contrast drawn with kings.

If our emendation to "thirty" in v. 20 is correct, then this section may
be called the "thirty sayings of the wise." This emendation is based on
a supposed connection with the Egyptian Instruction of Amenemope
(see "Ancient Near Eastern Background" in the introduction). In any
case, reading the two texts together demonstrates some kind of association between the two, and as a result, we are predisposed to structure
this section as thirty sayings. As an introduction to a major section of
the book of Proverbs, these verses serve essentially the same function
as the introduction to the whole book (1:2–7), giving us insight into the
intentions of the composer/compilers of the material.

The introduction begins with an exhortation to pay attention to the
material that follows. The exhortation is addressed to an unspecified
"you," but we may be confident that it is directed from a wisdom teacher
to a pupil. Any readers of this material (including us) find themselves
in the position of the addressees.

The content of the teaching is first called the "words of the wise."
There is some disagreement about exactly where this expression occurs
in the passage. Many scholars and modern versions follow the Greek
translation by placing this phrase as a heading for the whole section,
and then understand the object of the verb "hear" as "my words" (*emon
logon* = *dibrê*). We prefer to follow the MT and include it within the poetic introduction. The reference to the "wise" attributes the following
sayings to a group of unnamed wisdom teachers. Proverbs often are
passed down anonymously, and so it is not likely that the writer of the
introduction had specific people in mind. It is a way of saying that the
following teaching has its origin in the wisdom tradition. If some proverbs happen to come to Israel by way of Egypt, then we are not even to
restrict the "wise" to a collection of Israelite wisdom teachers. However,
even if their origin is foreign, their content is perfectly in keeping with
native Israelite wisdom.

In the second colon, the phrase "words of the wise" is parallel with
"my knowledge." The specific teacher appropriates the accumulated
wisdom of the tradition as his own in order to pass it on to his disciple.
The student is encouraged to approach the teacher's instruction with a
receptive attitude: "set your heart toward." One must be predisposed to
wisdom in order to benefit from it.

Verse 18 begins to give a motive for why students should be receptive
to the teaching. They will have good consequences if these sayings are
internalized. The term rendered "innermost being" in v. 18 is literally
"stomach." To guard them in your stomach is a picture of integrating
them into the inmost part of a person's being. The integration of the
teacher's wisdom is prerequisite to its use in the student's own life. In
other words, appropriation into students' character is then followed

415

by their own ability to express the wisdom: "Have them ready on your lips." Amenemope 3.13 says: "Let them [the sayings] rest in the casket of your belly."

Verse 19 gives the theological motivation for the teaching of wisdom, the increase in trust in Yahweh. This gives the teacher the urgency to impart instruction to the pupil. It is not made explicit how the teaching will increase trust, and so we are left to speculate. Perhaps the idea is that as the advice works in life, then it breeds confidence in its ultimate author. Or perhaps it is calling on trust in Yahweh as the first step toward implementing the advice found here. As one practices trust by following the advice, which may direct one in a not so obvious way (for instance, to be generous in order to grow more wealthy [11:24]), then one grows in trust as the unexpected consequences come.

It is then (v. 20) that the following teaching is specified as "thirty sayings," and the second colon characterizes these thirty sayings as imparting advice and knowledge. This verse also makes a rare mention of the written character of the instruction that follows.

In v. 21, a final purpose is specified, yet it is a bit enigmatic. The teacher is imparting advice and knowledge so the student might go and speak them (give answer?) to the ones who sent the student. It is not quite clear who the latter are, but perhaps the situation implies that the pupil is being trained for a specific task or career. Another possibility suggested by others[1] is that the pupil is a messenger, a role considered extremely important in Proverbs (10:26; 13:17; 25:13), though it is a little odd to think that the subject of the messenger would be inserted precisely at this place. However, a positive argument may be made in that the prologue to Amenemope includes as a purpose for its wisdom "To reply to one who sends a message."[2]

> **22**Don't steal from the poor, because they are poor,
>   and don't oppress the needy in the gate.
> **23**For Yahweh will accuse their accusers,
>   and he will press the life out of those who oppress them.

22:22–23. To rob anyone is a crime, but to rob the poor, who are already in difficult straits, is particularly heinous (see also Exod. 22:21–23; 23:6; Deut. 24:14–15). The same is true about the oppression of those who are already afflicted. To do so publicly is a particularly bad thing to do. The reference to "the gate" at the least points toward a public setting, and probably more specifically to a legal setting. Amenemope expresses a similar idea in 4.4–5:

1. See Whybray, *Proverbs*, 328.
2. Amenemope 1.6, from the translation by M. Lichtheim, in *COS* 1:116.

> Beware of robbing a wretch,
> Of attacking a cripple.[3]

The Hebrew text continues with a motive clause for avoiding this shameful behavior. Yahweh will avenge those who are unable to defend themselves. The parallelism between the two verses seems to be abb'a', since the first and last phrases have to do with robbery of one sort or another (though different Hebrew words are used), and the middle two cola are reflecting on the oppression of the afflicted.

> [24]Don't befriend people controlled by anger;
>   don't associate with wrathful people,
> [25]lest you learn their ways
>   and you get yourself trapped.

22:24–25. The book of Proverbs teaches that we must associate with people of wisdom and avoid those who practice foolish behavior (1:8–19). Otherwise, as this passage states, their bad behavior will rub off on us and so will the negative consequences due them. In this case, angry behavior is specifically named as something to be avoided. This passage is talking not just about an occasional outburst of anger but rather about people characterized by their anger. This shows a lack of self-discipline and an absence of emotional intelligence (see "Appropriate Expression of Emotions" in the appendix).

Amenemope 5.10–19 speaks about the hotheaded man and how it is necessary to avoid him:

> Don't start a quarrel with a hot-mouthed man,
> Nor needle him with words.
> Pause before a foe, bend before an attacker,
> Sleep (on it) before speaking.
> A storm that bursts like fire in straw,
> Such is the heated man in his hour.
> Withdraw from him, leave him alone,
> The god knows how to answer him.
> If you make your life with these (words) in your heart,
> Your children will observe them.

> [26]Don't shake hands
>   to pledge security for a loan.
> [27]If you are not able to repay,
>   why should they be able to take your bed away from you?

---

3. Ibid.

22:26–27. Proverbs makes it clear that the wise are generous. However, to be generous means giving money to the poor without the expectation of return, though that may well happen. Here and elsewhere, however, we have a different situation. Instead of generosity through giving freely, there is an expectation of return. It is not even clear that the person is in need; the situation may be that of a business loan of some sort. Whatever the circumstance, giving a loan is a mistake, because a loan expects a return of the money.[4] And if giving a loan is a mistake, it is even more of a mistake to be a guarantor of a loan. Such people may find their very bed repossessed. This proverb not only gives good advice; it also provides an "out" if a friend should press us for such an arrangement. See also 6:1–5; 11:15; 17:18; 20:16; 27:13.

> [28]Don't remove an ancient boundary marker,
> which your ancestors established.

22:28. Land was absolutely necessary for ancient Israelites. After all, their society was predominately agricultural for much of their history. The importance of land was felt throughout the ancient Near East, as demonstrated by the similar admonition in Amenemope:

> Do not move the markers on the borders of fields,
> Nor shift the position of the measuring-cord.
> Do not be greedy for a cubit of land,
> Nor encroach on the boundaries of a widow.
> The trodden furrow worn down by time,
> He who disguises it in the fields,
> When he has snared (it) by false oaths,
> He will be caught by the might of the Moon. (7.11–19)[5]

Though important throughout the ancient Near East, there is reason to think that the connection between the land and the people of Israel was an even more critical issue. After all, the land was distributed by divine choice to the tribes and then to individual families after settlement. The land was God's gift in fulfillment of his promise to Abraham (Gen. 12:1–3). Indeed, if for any reason a family was separated from its ancestral lands (perhaps for reasons of debt), their property would be returned to them during the Jubilee Year, which occurred every fifty years (Lev. 25:24–34).

---

4. It is unlikely that these loans are given with the hope of making money from interest, since Exod. 22:25 forbids such loans to fellow Hebrews, and here it is not specified that only non-Hebrews are meant.

5. Translation from M. Lichtheim, in *COS* 1:117.

The removal of a boundary stone would be an attempt to encroach on or even totally possess the land of another person. Not even a king should take the land of another (the Naboth incident in 1 Kings 21). We don't know what Israelite boundary stones looked like, but they may have been similar in function to the Babylonian *kudurru*, a stone marker that included a description of the property. Other passages that have to do with the prohibition of the removal of a boundary stone include Deut. 19:14; 27:17; Job 24:2; Prov. 23:10; Hosea 5:10.

> [29]Do you see people who do their work with diligence?
>   They will stand before kings;
>   they will not stand before the obscure.

22:29. This proverb states that those who work hard and with skill will succeed in their careers. They will work for the most powerful and influential people in the society, while those who are not diligent will spend their careers working for people on the lower end of the social stratum. We might compare a statement found in the final chapter of Amenemope:

> The scribe who is skilled in his office,
> He is found worthy to be a courtier. (27.16–17)[6]

6. Ibid., *COS* 1:122.

Chapter 23

Translation

¹When you sit down to dine with a ruler,
  carefully consider what[a] is in front of you.
²Place a knife at your gullet[b]
  to control your appetite.[c]
³Don't long for his delicacies,
  for they are false food.
⁴Don't wear yourself out trying to get wealthy.
  Stop, because of your understanding.
⁵You will let your eyes fly[d] to it, but it will be no more.
  For it will surely grow wings
  like an eagle and fly heavenward.
⁶Do not eat food with stingy people;[e]
  don't long for their delicacies.
⁷For it is like a hair in the throat.[f]
  "Eat and drink," they say to you.

a. Or "who is in front of you." The effect is similar.

b. Both the word "knife" (*śakkîn*) as well as the word "gullet" (*lōaʿ*) are *hapax legomena* with possible Aramaic cognates and may point to an Aramaic origin for the proverb.

c. See Kobert, "Zu Prov 23,1–2."

d. Reading with the Qere. It is the same verb (*ʿûp*) as in the last colon of the verse and stands behind other common translations, such as "cast a glance" (NIV) and "light upon it" (NRSV).

e. Literally, "evil eye." See 22:9, where the "good eye" refers to the generous person. The eye is the window into one's inner character, and so whether the eye is good or bad tells us something about the quality of the person.

f. This phrase is difficult. The MT reads *šāʿar* (with *šîn*), but the above translation follows the LXX (*tricha*) and many modern interpreters (Murphy, *Proverbs*, 172–73) as well as versions like the NRSV in making a small emendation to *śaʿar* (with *śîn*) and read-

But their heart is not with you.
⁸You will eat your crust and vomit it out
and waste your pleasant words.
⁹Don't speak in the ears of a fool,
for he will despise the insight of your utterance.
¹⁰Don't remove an ancient boundary marker,
and don't invade the fields of orphans.
¹¹For their redeemer is strong and will make
accusations against you.
¹²Bring your heart to discipline,
your ear to knowledgeable speeches.
¹³Don't withhold discipline from young people.
If you strike them with the rod, they will not die.
¹⁴Strike them with a rod,
and you will extricate their lives from Sheol.^g
¹⁵My son, if your heart is wise,
my heart will also be happy.
¹⁶My inmost being^h will rejoice
when your lips speak with integrity.
¹⁷Don't allow your heart to envy sinners,
rather those who fear Yahweh all day long.
¹⁸For thenⁱ you will have a future,
and your hope will not be cut off.
¹⁹Listen, my son, and be wise!
March in the way of your heart.
²⁰Don't be inebriated with wine;
don't be glutted with meat.
²¹For those who are inebriated and glutted will be dispossessed,
and stupor clothes with rags.
²²Listen to your father, the one who begot you,
and don't despise your elderly mother!
²³Acquire truth, and don't sell
wisdom and discipline and understanding.^j
²⁴The father of the righteous will enthusiastically exult;
the one who begets a wise person will rejoice in him.
²⁵Your father and your mother will rejoice;
she who bore you will exult.

---

ing "hair." The MT would produce a *hapax legomenon*, which, on the basis of Ugaritic and Arabic cognates as well as postbiblical Hebrew, has the meaning "to calculate" (see *NIDOTTE* 4:208), and use *nepeš*, not in its meaning of "throat," but as a reference to the inner person. The MT would be rendered, "who has calculated in his mind."

g. For a discussion of Sheol and the afterlife, see "Afterlife" in the introduction.

h. Literally, "my kidneys" (*kilyôtāy*).

i. This is not the typical meaning of *kî ʾim* ("for if" or "except"), but these meanings make no sense in the context.

j. This seems to be another case of enjambment (see also translation footnote for 2:9).

²⁶My son, give your heart to me,
and let your eyes observe my path.
²⁷For a prostitute is a deep pit,ᵏ
and a foreign woman is a narrow well.
²⁸Indeed, she ambushes like a robber
and increases the number of unfaithful men.
²⁹Who cries "Woe!"? Who cries "Alas!"?
Who has conflicts? Who has complaints?
Who has unnecessary bruises? Who has glazed eyes?—
³⁰those who linger over wine,
those who go in search of the mixing vessel.
³¹Don't look at wine when it is red,
when it gives its eye in the cup,
going down smoothly.
³²Afterward, it bites like a snake
and poisons like a viper.
³³Your eyes will see strange things,
and your heart will utter perversities.
³⁴And you will be like one who lies down in the heart of the sea,
and one who lies on top of the mast.
³⁵"Though hit, I feel no pain;
though pummeled, I do not know it.
When I wake up,
I will again look for it!"

Interpretation

¹When you sit down to dine with a ruler,
carefully consider what is in front of you.
²Place a knife at your gullet
to control your appetite.
³Don't long for his delicacies,
for they are false food.

23:1–3. This proverbial saying is composed of three related admonitions and seems to be most relevant for those who are in service, or at least have access, to a powerful ruler. Nonetheless, broader application may be derived from this teaching.

This particular proverb gives advice to a courtier for table manners. It may seem a banal thing, but dining is actually an opportunity for people to manifest the type of self-control that demonstrates wisdom. Just as the wise are to control their emotional expressions and the frequency

k. See 22:14a.

and content of their speech, so also they must not let their appetites get control of them. Nowhere would this be a larger temptation than at the sumptuous table of a ruler. If the ruler sees a potential adviser's appetite carry him away, then how could the ruler trust him? In this way, the food is "false": it is a potential trap that would cause the prospective courtier to lose an opportunity.

The image of the knife at the gullet is vivid, suggesting that it would be better to slice one's throat than to fall into the trap of overeating in the presence of the ruler.

Though not exactly alike, Amenemope also gives warning to the dangers of dining in the presence of a powerful superior:

> Do not eat in the presence of an official
> And then set your mouth before (him);
> If you are sated pretend to chew,
> Content yourself with your saliva.
> Look at the bowl that is before you,
> And let it serve your needs.
> An official is great in his office,
> As a well is rich in drawings of water. (23.13–20)[1]

This type of teaching is also found in other Egyptian texts, as demonstrated by the following quote from the very early Kagemni:

> When you sit with company,
> Shun the food you love;
> Restraint is a brief moment,
> Gluttony is base and is reproved.
> A cup of water quenches thirst,
> A mouthful of herbs strengthens the heart;
> One good thing stands for goodness,
> A little something stands for much.
> Vile is he whose belly covets when (meal)-time has passed,
> He forgets those in whose house his belly roams.[2]

And then finally also Ptahhotep:

> If you are one among guests
> At the table of one greater than you,
> Take what he gives as it is set before you;
> Look at what is before you,

---

1. Translation by M. Lichtheim, *COS* 1:121.
2. Translation by M. Lichtheim, *Ancient Egyptian Literature*, 1:59–60, who dates this text to the Sixth Dynasty, ca. 2360–2205 BC.

> Don't shoot many glances at him,
> Molesting him offends the *ka*. (119–26)[3]

---

⁴Don't wear yourself out trying to get wealthy.
   Stop, because of your understanding.
⁵You will let your eyes fly to it, but it will be no more.
   For it will surely grow wings
   like an eagle and fly heavenward.

23:4–5. This proverb is often cited as one that has a rather specific parallel in Amenemope:

> Do not strain to seek increase,
> What you have, let it suffice you.
> If riches come to you by theft,
> They will not stay the night with you.
> Comes day they are not in your house
> Their place is seen but they're not there;
> Earth opened its mouth. Leveled them, swallowed them,
> And made them sink into *dat*.
> They made a hole as big as their size,
> And sank into the netherworld;
> They made themselves wings like geese,
> And flew away to the sky. (9.14–10.5)[4]

The Egyptian text is more extensive; one is struck by the similar sentiment and also the image of the flying bird to capture the idea of the transience of wealth. Even with these parallels, it is certainly not definite that any kind of direct borrowing is involved here, since one could certainly imagine that the proverbs developed independently or that both texts are dependent on another yet unknown text or texts.[5]

In any case, the proverb, within the context of the book of Proverbs, is rather striking. After all, there are a considerable number of proverbs that advocate hard work (see "Laziness and Hard Work" in the appendix) and imply that wealth will come to those who are wise (3:9–10; 10:22; 14:24). But these proverbs are not giving the whole truth, since proverbs do not intend to do so. There are times and circumstances where people can work their fingers raw and still have insufficient return on their labor. There comes a time when enough is enough, according to

---

3. Ibid., 65, also from the Sixth Dynasty.
4. From chap. 7; translation by M. Lichtheim, in *COS* 1:118.
5. This idea may be supported by the appearance of a Sumerian proverb from the early second millennium BC, quoted by Whybray, *Proverbs*, 333: "Possessions are sparrows in flight which can find no place to alight."

our present saying. And in any case, wealth, when it does come, often does not stay. In sum, this proverb helps people put riches in a proper perspective. As with poverty, there are dangers that are also a part of being rich (30:7–9; see also Eccles. 5:13–17). Christian readers will note a similar sentiment toward the transience of riches in Matt. 6:19, which talks of "treasures on earth, where moth and rust consume and where thieves break in and steal" (NRSV).

> 6Do not eat food with stingy people;
>   don't long for their delicacies.
> 7For it is like a hair in the throat.
>   "Eat and drink," they say to you.
>   But their heart is not with you.
> 8You will eat your crust and vomit it out
>   and waste your pleasant words.

23:6–8. Whereas 23:2–3 gave advice about table manners with a king, here we have advice about dining with a stingy person. A specific connection can be seen in the warning in both passages not to desire their delicacies. In both cases, though the food is tempting on the surface, it should be resisted. Stingy (lit., "evil eye") people are those who may seem to encourage your partaking of the meal, but in reality they are not interested in your well-being or enjoyment. The interpretation that we advocate here is that the delicacies are really sham. The hosts are, after all, stingy, and so they will be cheap in the provisions. The food (it) really tastes horrible, "like a hair in the throat," so it will be vomited. The guest would waste words on such a cheapskate, who serves such revolting food.

> 9Don't speak in the ears of a fool,
>   for he will despise the insight of your utterance.

23:9. The wisest advice will bounce off the ears of fools. Even worse, it will bring on their hostility. Fools are set against wisdom, particularly if that wisdom involves any kind of criticism of their behavior. Jesus makes a similar comment in the Gospels when he admonishes his disciples: "Don't give what is holy to unholy people. Don't give pearls to swine! They will trample the pearls, then turn and attack you" (Matt. 7:6 NLT).

> 10Don't remove an ancient boundary marker,
>   and don't invade the fields of orphans.
> 11For their redeemer is strong and will make
>   accusations against you.

23:10-11. This proverb has to do with social justice. The first colon is identical to that of 22:28, and the discussion of land and boundaries there should be consulted. The second colon applies the prohibition against raiding the property of others to a specific group: orphans. Along with widows, orphans are a group that is socially powerless, not having parents to advocate for them. This proverb lends the authority of wisdom teaching behind the charge not to take advantage of the weakness of orphans.

This prohibition is backed up by a strong sanction. The word for "redeemer" is *gōʾēl* and is found in pentateuchal laws (Lev. 25:25–30, 47–55; cf. Ruth 3; Jer. 32:1–15). It is most likely that the obligations of the *gōʾēl* extend beyond that specified in the pentateuchal laws and "encompassed a variety of duties in support of weakened relatives."[6] In this case, the unnamed redeemer is surely Yahweh himself, and the weakened party is a reference to those whose boundaries are tampered with, particularly orphans.

> [12]Bring your heart to discipline,
>   your ear to knowledgeable speeches.
> [13]Don't withhold discipline from young people.
>   If you strike them with the rod, they will not die.
> [14]Strike them with a rod,
>   and you will extricate their lives from Sheol.

23:12-14. This passage fits with others that also speak of the need to instruct young people. The fact that the rod is mentioned indicates that the sages had no illusions about young people. It is not a matter of trying to bring the best out of children. Wisdom had to be drummed into them, sometimes literally.

After an initial admonition to put oneself in a posture of learning by subjecting oneself to discipline and instruction, the text turns to the topic of young people. To withhold discipline, even physical discipline, is a matter of neglect. Coercing them to instruction is a lifesaving act. Again, the teaching is based on a paradox. If one doesn't hit a youth, then that youth will die because he or she will not grow in wisdom but will become a fool. Hit children in the context of instruction, and they will live. The sage is not talking about a rigorous beating, but rather something equivalent to a spanking. This may be surmised from the matter-of-fact statement "They will not die" as well as this book's general emphasis on moderation, kindness, and gentleness.

6. R. L. Hubbard Jr., *The Book of Ruth*, New International Commentary on the Old Testament (Grand Rapids: Eerdmans, 1988), 52.

While this teaching is not found in Amenemope, it is interestingly discovered in the Aramaic Tale of Ahiqar:[7] "Spare not your son from the rod; otherwise, can you save him (from wickedness)?" (saying 3).

> ¹⁵My son, if your heart is wise,
>   my heart will also be happy.
> ¹⁶My inmost being will rejoice
>   when your lips speak with integrity.

23:15–16. The teacher's joy is contingent on the student's demonstration of wisdom. After all, that is the purpose behind the teacher's efforts at instruction. These two verses demonstrate again (see 16:23 as well) the connection between the inner person and speech. A wise heart will lead to words of integrity, and from the words of integrity, the hearer can deduce a wise heart. Perhaps this passage is to be taken as words of inspiration to students who can make their teacher happy by pursuing wisdom and speaking with integrity. As Van Leeuwen points out, the desire is that the son speaks like Woman Wisdom (8:6).[8]

> ¹⁷Don't allow your heart to envy sinners,
>   rather those who fear Yahweh all day long.
> ¹⁸For then you will have a future,
>   and your hope will not be cut off.

23:17–18. Psalm 73 (see also Ps. 37) is a classic instance of a person who struggled with envy toward sinners and may serve to give a solid example to the principle expressed here. The psalmist looked at the wicked and saw that they seemed to live a much more pleasant life than he, a godly person, enjoyed. He "saw them prosper despite their wickedness" (Ps. 73:3 NLT). They seemed rich, healthy, and happy, while he was struggling. As a result, he began questioning God. The psalm was written, though, after the struggle. He had come to see that the prosperity of sinners was only apparent and short-lived. They really are "on a slippery path, . . . sliding over the cliff to destruction" (v. 18 NLT). He saw that his reasoning up to this point would have led to his own destruction. In other words, it would have taken away his hope for the future. He came to realize that "my health may fail, and my spirit may grow weak, but God remains the strength of my heart; he is mine forever" (v. 26 NLT). Thus, he can begin his poem with "Truly God is good to Israel, to those whose hearts are pure" (v. 1 NLT). Thus, this proverbial passage encourages those to adopt the final perspective of the psalmist.

7. For which, see "Ancient Near Eastern Background" in the introduction.
8. Van Leeuwen, "Proverbs," 206.

It is not superficially apparent that it is true that those who fear God (for which see Prov. 1:7) have a future, but that is ultimate reality. See also 24:1–2, 19–20.

> [19]Listen, my son, and be wise!
>   March in the way of your heart.
> [20]Don't be inebriated with wine;
>   don't be glutted with meat.
> [21]For those who are inebriated and glutted will be dispossessed,
>   and stupor clothes with rags.

23:19–21. This passage begins with an exhortation to be wise. It is followed by another imperative admonishing the son to march in the way of his heart. What is surprising about this is that elsewhere it is assumed that the natural inclination of a person, particularly a youth, is negative. I think the best understanding of the dynamics of this verse is that it assumes that the son is on the path of wisdom through making a commitment to pursuing the right path. Once the decision to be wise is made, then the exhortation becomes one to continue in that way.[9]

At this point the passage turns into a prohibition of overindulgence in terms of alcohol and food.[10] Drunkenness and gluttony are here castigated. Elsewhere the rationale for criticizing getting drunk has to do with clouding one's ability to think and make decisions. In other words, it disrupts one's wisdom. The same can apply to overeating, which would lead to lethargic behavior, not the kind of diligent work so frequently encouraged in the book. However, the explicit motive given here against overdrinking and eating is that such overindulgence would lead to poverty. Spending too much money on too much food and too much drink would be foolish, not wise. For other teaching against overdrinking, see 20:1; 23:29–35; 31:1–9.

> [22]Listen to your father, the one who begot you,
>   and don't despise your elderly mother!
> [23]Acquire truth, and don't sell
>   wisdom and discipline and understanding.
> [24]The father of the righteous will enthusiastically exult;
>   the one who begets a wise person will rejoice in him.
> [25]Your father and your mother will rejoice;
>   she who bore you will exult.

---

9. In this I am agreeing with Murphy (*Proverbs*, 176) that "it is best to interpret the 'way' (a significant symbol in chaps. 1–9) as the way of wisdom, thus implementing the imperative of v 19a."

10. The language of drunkenness and gluttony is used of the rebellious child in Deut. 21:20; see Callaway, "Deut. 21:18–21."

23:22–25. This passage reminds us of the admonitions of the first part of Proverbs, and the connection between the emotional well-being of parents and the wisdom quotient of children reminds us of a number of proverbs (e.g., 10:1). It all begins with one's willingness to pay attention to the instruction that wise parents impart to their children. The emphasis in the text on "begot"/"bore" underlines the basis for the accountability that children have toward those who want to instruct them. After all, the very life of the child is the result of the union between father and mother. Besides appeal to birth, v. 22 also specifies the advanced age of the mother. This reference to age is not an appeal to pity but rather fits in with the wisdom idea that advanced age has the consequence of additional experience, and therefore the mother is a source of great wisdom. This is a resource that should not be ignored, not to speak of despised.

Verse 23 adopts a commercial metaphor to emphasize the importance of wisdom and its associated qualities of truth, discipline, and understanding. The son should buy (acquire) wisdom but not sell it. After all, as we have seen in many places in Proverbs, there is no amount of wealth that would be worth parting company with wisdom.

Finally (vv. 24 and 25), if the son listens to the parents and pursues wisdom, then the parents will rejoice. This seems to be presented as a motive to the son. It assumes that the son would want the parents to be happy. The connection between the student/child's pursuit of wisdom and the joy of the parent/teacher is also the subject of 23:15–16.

> 26My son, give your heart to me,
>   and let your eyes observe my path.
> 27For a prostitute is a deep pit,
>   and a foreign woman is a narrow well.
> 28Indeed, she ambushes like a robber
>   and increases the number of unfaithful men.

23:26–28. Again, the father appeals to his son to pay attention to his teaching. He desires that his son follow his instruction and thus stay on the right path.[11] The path is a metaphor for the course of one's life and derives from the idea that life is a journey, with a beginning, middle, and end. This metaphor is rather extensively used throughout Proverbs, but particularly in chaps. 1–9.

The passage continues with another theme that is pervasive in chaps. 1–9 (particularly 5–7), though it is also found in 10–31: The father warns the son concerning the dangers surrounding seductive and promiscu-

---

11. According to Whybray, *Proverbs*, 339, "The father is demanding that his son should submit his will to his [the father's]."

ous women. For the description of the woman as "foreign," see 5:10, 20; 6:24; 7:5. What is interesting here is the metaphor of the "deep pit" and "narrow well." On the surface, these are metaphors of danger. If one falls into a deep pit or a narrow well, then injury or even death would be the result. In reference to sexual danger, however, one cannot miss the likely allusion to a vagina. It may have multiple allusions, also reminding us of "the underworld (Sheol), to which the strange woman's house leads (2:19; 5:5; 7:27)."[12]

In the last verse of the passage, the promiscuous woman is described as the initiator. She ambushes like a robber. It's not that the man who falls for her seductions is guiltless, but it is a bit disconcerting to think that the sage only thinks of the woman making the advance. The proverb provides only a snapshot. The description is a warning not to just any male but to males who are on the right path, not to predatory males, who would be described as fools. The passage then may recognize that illicit sexual relations are a particularly difficult temptation even for those who have their eyes set on the right path.

> [29]Who cries "Woe!"? Who cries "Alas!"?
>> Who has conflicts? Who has complaints?
> Who has unnecessary bruises?
>> Who has glazed eyes?—
> [30]those who linger over wine,
>> those who go in search of the mixing vessel.
> [31]Don't look at wine when it is red,
>> when it gives its eye in the cup,
>> going down smoothly.
> [32]Afterward, it bites like a snake
>> and poisons like a viper.
> [33]Your eyes will see strange things,
>> and your heart will utter perversities.
> [34]And you will be like one who lies down in the heart of the sea,
>> and one who lies on top of the mast.
> [35]"Though hit, I feel no pain;
>>> though pummeled, I do not know it.
>> When I wake up,
>>> I will again look for it!"

23:29–35. This proverb warns against the dangers of alcoholism by providing a frightening picture of the grip of addiction. The passage begins with a series of questions that are easily answered by reading

12. Van Leeuwen, "Proverbs," 207.

the remainder of the text, particularly v. 30.[13] Alcoholics cry "woe" and "alas" because of the pain and distress the compulsion brings to their lives. Alcoholics get into conflicts and fights that produce bruises because under the influence of drink they lose all sense of propriety. They say the wrong thing and do the wrong thing at the wrong time, and this gets them into trouble. Alcohol brings a literal glaze to their eyes, but this may also speak metaphorically to an inability to properly see circumstances correctly. They do not see clearly, think clearly, and act rightly under the influence.

It would be a mistake to see this as a passage that condemns any use of alcoholic beverages. Earlier in the book, vats bursting with wine were mentioned as a consequence of honoring Yahweh (3:10). Indeed, Woman Wisdom's banquet presents mixed wine (9:2, 5). As with many good things, however, there is a danger for addiction, and the warnings in Proverbs must be seen as highlighting the danger of alcoholism, here identified as lingering over wine and going in search of the mixing vessel. For other passages that warn against alcoholism, see also 20:1; 21:17; 31:4, 6.

The warning comes in v. 31 as the sage tells alcoholics to stay far away from drink: Don't even look at it! Like a promiscuous woman (see chaps. 5–7), it looks so enticing, and the drink goes down the throat so smoothly, but the consequences are disastrous. Alcohol is like the poisonous bite of a snake. It can kill.

But before it kills, it disorients. It blurs the vision, so the drunk sees things that are not there. How can one react with wisdom if one cannot know the reality of a situation? Also, the mouth starts speaking things that are offensive. Again, this goes counter to the wisdom enterprise. The metaphors of v. 34 well capture the sickening lack of balance of a drunk. In a sense, one even loses the ability to physically orient oneself. It softens pain in an unhelpful way. If one does not feel pain, then there is no motivation to remove oneself from the source of pain. In such circumstances, there will be plenty of pain once the "anesthetic" wears off.

The tragedy of addiction, however, is that despite the horrible experience of being drunk, once one sobers up, there is a frantic search for the next drink.

As a parallel Clifford cites the following passage from the Instruction of Ani (4.7–10), an Egyptian wisdom text:

> Don't indulge in drinking beer,
> Lest you utter evil speech

13. Andrews ("Variety of Expression in Proverbs xxiii 29–35") describes the dynamic of the passage as moving from a riddle (v. 29) to its answer (v. 30), then an instruction (v. 31), to direct speech that names the consequences of wrong behavior (vv. 33–34), and then closing the argument with a quote from the drunk (v. 35).

> And don't know what you're saying.
> If you fall and hurt your body,
> None holds out a hand to you:
> Your companions in the drinking
> Stand up saying: "Out with the drunk!"
> If one comes to seek you and talk with you,
> One finds you lying on the ground,
> As if you were a little child.[14]

It is in contrast with this more straightforward warning that Whybray's description of the Proverbs passage as "jocular, not to say burlesque, style" makes sense.[15]

---

14. Clifford, *Proverbs*, 214.
15. Whybray, *Proverbs*, 340.

Chapter 24

Translation

¹Don't envy evil people,ª
  and don't long to be with them.
²For their hearts are fixated on violence,
  and their lips speak trouble.
³With wisdom a house is built;
  with competence it is established.
⁴With knowledge rooms are filled
  with all precious and pleasant wealth.
⁵A wise person is better thanᵇ a strong one,
  and a knowledgeable person is better than a powerful one.
⁶For you should make war with guidance,
  and victory comes with an abundance of counselors.
⁷Wisdomᶜ is beyondᵈ stupid people;
  in the gate they don't even open their mouths.

a. In a complex (overly so, I think) analysis, Hurowitz ("Often Overlooked Alphabetic Acrostic in Proverbs 24:1–22") uncovers an alphabetic acrostic in Prov. 24. In my opinion, one has to work too hard to make it work. It involves only thirteen letters, and half of these are not at the beginning of the verse. He must account for extra cola in the *hêh* line as well as a missing *wāw* line and emend *rêš* to a *dālet* in v. 7—and this is just the beginning. An acrostic is not a subtle poetic convention. It is either clearly there or not there at all. In this case, it is not there, which better explains why it is "often overlooked."

b. Here I emend the *bêt* to a *mêm*, considering the latter an indication of a comparative and following the evidence of the Greek (*ischyrou*). See also the Syriac and Targum. The MT may be translated "a wise man is in strength."

c. The form here is *ḥokmôt*, which otherwise in Proverbs is found only in 1:20 and 9:1, in both cases referring to Woman Wisdom. Whybray (*Proverbs*, 45; and idem, *Book of Proverbs: A Survey*, 71) may well be right in claiming that "Wisdom" here is also personified, though it does not make much difference to the thought of the passage.

d. Taking the form *rāʾmôt* as a qal feminine plural participle spelled unusually with *ʾālep*, from the root *rwm*, "to be exalted." The form is occasionally taken as the noun

[8]Those who plot evil
will be called master schemers.[e]
[9]The scheming of stupid people is sin;
people despise[f] mockers.
[10]If you show yourself weak on a day of distress,
your strength is distressed.[g]
[11]Rescue those being taken to death;
don't[h] restrain yourself from those tottering to a killing.
[12]If you say, "But we didn't know about it,"
the one who weighs hearts[i]—doesn't he understand?
The one who protects your life—he knows.
He will make people pay for their deeds.
[13]My son, eat honey, for it is good.
The honeycomb is sweet on your palette.
[14]Know wisdom is that way for your soul.[j]
If you find it, there is a future.
Your hope will not be cut off.[k]
[15]Don't ambush, O wicked,[l] at the home of the righteous;
don't destroy their dwelling.
[16]For the righteous may fall seven times, but get up,
but the wicked will stumble in evil.
[17]When your enemy falls, don't rejoice.
When he stumbles, don't let your heart be glad.[m]
[18]Otherwise, Yahweh will see, and it will be evil in his eyes,
and he will turn his anger from him.

"coral" and literally understood to be "Wisdom is coral to a stupid person," meaning that wisdom is much too precious for a stupid person to possess. The sense is basically the same in either translation.

e. The noun and its root verb can have a positive (discretion) or a negative (scheme) sense; see 1:4. Here the sense is clearly negative, since it is connected with the stupid person.

f. Literally, "an abomination [tôʿăbat] to a person is a mocker." The formula "X is an abomination to Yahweh" is found frequently as a strong condemnation in Proverbs (see 3:22; 11:1; 20:23; and references cited).

g. Or "narrow," or like many translations, "small." I stay with "distressed" to show the repetition of the word (ṣār) from the first colon.

h. The verb "restrain" (ḥśk) is preceded by the particle ʾim (normally indicating a conditional sentence, "if"), which does not make sense here. Either this is an abbreviated oath form, or it has a negative sense. See Whybray, Proverbs, 347, for a fuller discussion.

i. For this reference to God, see 16:2; 21:2.

j. Many find the poetic structure awkward here and suggest that a colon has been lost in the transmission of the text. Even if this is so, we can still make sense of the verse.

k. The last two cola are a repetition of 23:18.

l. Murphy (Proverbs, 180) omits the reference to the wicked person on the grounds that he believes the whole section is addressed to the young student. However, there is no textual support for this. He admits this and suggests, as an alternative, taking it as an appositive, "like a wicked person."

m. The verbs "fall" and "stumble" are repeated from the previous passage and may explain why these two texts are placed next to each other.

[19]Don't get fighting mad at evil people;
   don't be envious of the wicked.
[20]For there will be no future for evil;
   the lamp of the wicked will be extinguished.[n]
[21]Fear Yahweh, my son, as well as the king.
   Don't associate with those who rebel.[o]
[22]For disaster will rise up suddenly from them.
   Ruin from both of them—who can experience?[p]
[23]These are also according to the wise.
   Those who show favoritism[q] in judgment are not good.
[24]Those who say to the wicked person, "You are righteous,"
   the people will curse them;
   the population will be angry with them.
[25]It will go well for those who establish what is right,
   and a blessing of prosperity will come on them.
[26]They kiss lips
   who utter truthful words.
[27]Establish your affairs in public;
   prepare them in the field;
   afterward you can build your house.
[28]Don't be witness against your neighbor without a reason;
   do you want to deceive with your lips?
[29]Don't say "As they did to me, so I will do to them.
   I will repay people according to their deeds."
[30]I happened upon the field of a lazy person,
   by the vineyard of one who lacks heart.
[31]Thorns grew up over all of it;
   weeds covered its surface,
   and the stone wall was dilapidated.
[32]I observed this and took it to heart;[r]
   I saw it and learned a lesson.[s]
[33]A little sleep, a little slumber,
   a little folding of the arms to lie down,
[34]and poverty will come creeping up on you,
   your deprivation like a person with a shield.

n. The last colon is identical to 13:9 and similar to 20:20.

o. This is a difficult word to translate. I am taking it from *šnh* (to change) but in the sense of "change attitude toward." Admittedly, this is not a strong argument, and an emendation may be necessary, but exactly what to emend it to is not certain. The NRSV follows the LXX and translates: "Do not disobey either of them."

p. The LXX has a different order here. Between 24:22 and 24:23, there are five additional verses, as well as 30:1–14 MT.

q. Literally, "those who recognize the face," an idiom for showing partiality (see also Deut. 1:17; 16:19; Prov. 28:21).

r. Literally, "I set my heart" (*ʾāšît libbî*).

s. Literally, "received instruction" (*laqaḥtî mûsār*).

Interpretation

> ¹Don't envy evil people,
>   and don't long to be with them.
> ²For their hearts are fixated on violence,
>   and their lips speak trouble.

24:1–2. This passage is similar to 23:17–18 and 24:19–20, and the comments about envy of the wicked as explicated particularly in Ps. 73 should be examined. We might add that Ps. 37 is also relevant to this issue with its theme expressed in its first two verses:

> Don't worry about the wicked.
>   Don't envy those who do wrong.
> For like grass, they will soon fade away.
>   Like springtime flowers, they will soon wither. (NLT)

In the present passage, association with the wicked is prohibited because the sages understood the power of influence. If one envies and associates with evil people, then it is more than likely that they will become evil themselves. The second verse reminds the reader of the nature of evil people, once again showing the connection between the heart and lips. Their heart, representing their inner character, desires destruction, so their lips speak trouble that will lead to their ultimate goal.

> ³With wisdom a house is built;
>   with competence it is established.
> ⁴With knowledge rooms are filled
>   with all precious and pleasant wealth.

24:3–4. Elsewhere the sage has made a similar connection between wisdom and house building. Here the house is not just the physical structure but would include it. Wise living would bring the resources and smooth the way for the construction of a fine house building. However, the deeper meaning is more relevant, and that has to do with family relationships. Wisdom implies the ability to say the right thing and act the right way to build up community and not destroy it. We should also remember that Yahweh constructed the cosmos by means of his wisdom (3:19–20; 8:22–31). We also think of Prov. 31:10–31, where the noble woman builds her house through wisdom.

> ⁵A wise person is better than a strong one,
>   and a knowledgeable person is better than a powerful one.

⁶For you should make war with guidance,
and victory comes with an abundance of counselors.

24:5–6. In this better-than proverb, we learn that wisdom is more important than strength. Again, as is the case with better-than proverbs, it is not a matter of strength being wrong or bad, but that wisdom is better. Indeed, the value of wisdom is not that it necessarily avoids war, but that it can provide the strategy through which strength can find its most efficient expression and thus lead to victory. Ecclesiastes provides statements and anecdotes that back this up and yet also acknowledge that ultimately even wisdom itself has its limits (7:19; 9:13–16).

⁷Wisdom is beyond stupid people;
in the gate they don't even open their mouths.
⁸Those who plot evil
will be called master schemers.
⁹The scheming of stupid people is sin;
people despise mockers.

24:7–9. This unit is bound together by the repetition of the term "stupid people" (ʾĕwîl/ʾiwwelet) in vv. 7–9. In vv. 8 and 9 is also the repetition of nouns built on the verbal stem *zmm*, meaning "scheming." The purpose is to negatively characterize stupid people as those who in the final colon are identified as mockers, the most extreme form of fools.

Stupid people cannot be wise because it is beyond them, with the result that they are quiet in a key place of community leadership: "the gate." They may not plan beneficial community strategy in a public place like the gate, but they do plot and secretly scheme in a way that is destructive to the community. The latter we can derive from the fact that it is called "evil" and "sin." The final colon reveals that the community despises such people. As Clifford puts it, "Folly . . . alienates one from the community."[1]

¹⁰If you show yourself weak on a day of distress,
your strength is distressed.
¹¹Rescue those being taken to death;
don't restrain yourself from those tottering to a killing.
¹²If you say, "But we didn't know about it,"
the one who weighs hearts—doesn't he understand?
The one who protects your life—he knows.
He will make people pay for their deeds.

1. Clifford, *Proverbs*, 214.

24:10–12. These verses are difficult to understand and raise a number of questions. Ultimately, to achieve any kind of concreteness, the passage should be understood in the light of the rest of the book of Proverbs and ultimately the canon as a whole. In the first place, this passage cannot be quoted in all instances where one is to be killed. This may not be used to argue that the Bible, for instance, is against capital punishment in principle or against all killing in war. It would not have been understood in that way in the context of a canon that includes narrative and law supporting by divine sanction capital punishment in certain instances as well as killing in warfare under certain conditions. Thus, at most, this proverb would only be true in the circumstances where it may be shown that killing is unjustified.

However, perhaps even more persuasive is the idea that the death is not the result of an actual killing, but rather of foolish behavior that leads to death. For instance, Prov. 7 pictures a young man who goes to a promiscuous woman, and the sage likens him to an ox going off to the slaughter. If this type of situation is implied, then the passage is a call to courage for trying to stop people from their foolish behavior, with its consequences of death.

However, in any reading v. 12 is difficult to understand. What does the student not know in this hypothetical situation: that the person's behavior has death as its consequence, or that the person was even behaving in a way that would lead to death? Then, is the appeal to God knowing hearts a comforting assurance? But who are the people who will pay for their deeds? It does seem to be a passage making the point that "cowardice in the face of injustice is reprehensible,"[2] but nonetheless, much of this passage remains difficult.

> [13]My son, eat honey, for it is good.
>   The honeycomb is sweet on your palette.
> [14]Know wisdom is that way for your soul.
>   If you find it, there is a future.
>   Your hope will not be cut off.

24:13–14. The proverb is yet another encouragement to pursue the acquisition of wisdom. It draws an analogy between eating honey and knowing wisdom. As honey is to the taste buds, so wisdom is to one's inner life. Eating honey is a pleasurable experience and can have beneficial results, as in 16:24, where honey is likened to wise words, both having medicinal quality. Furthermore, honey has sexual undertones in a context like Song 4:11.[3] The analogy can only be pressed so far

2. Murphy, *Proverbs*, 181.
3. See Yee, "'I Have Perfumed My Bed,'" 53.

since, as the sage warns in Prov. 25:16, 27, eating too much honey can make a person sick. Surely the sage would not issue the same warning concerning wisdom.[4]

The benefit of wisdom is that it provides a future for a person. It gives that person hope. At the simplest level, this would refer to the fact that living by the principles of wisdom as enunciated by Proverbs would provide the strategy to avoid problems that might lead to an early death. On the other hand, and certainly read from a canonical perspective, the pursuit of wisdom that entails a relationship with divine Wisdom would lead to life even beyond death. Clifford notes a similarity of this passage with Sir. 24:19–20: "Come to me, you who desire me, and eat your fill of my fruits. For the memory of me is sweeter than honey, and the possession of me sweeter than the honeycomb" (NRSV).[5]

> [15]Don't ambush, O wicked, at the home of the righteous;
>   don't destroy their dwelling.
> [16]For the righteous may fall seven times, but get up,
>   but the wicked will stumble in evil.

24:15–16. As it is in the MT, the passage is most naturally understood as addressed to the wicked. If so, then the proverb serves as a warning against trying to undermine the righteous on the basis of its futility. However, it might be that this is a fictional address and that the actual hearer of the proverb is the student of the sage, in which case the proverb would serve as an encouragement in the light of the attacks of the wicked.

In any case, the principle is clear. From the proverb, the sages understood that the righteous wise would suffer in life, but they also have the endurance to withstand the attacks of life. Life may beat them down, but they have hope (previous passage) because of wisdom. They see beyond the present misfortune. The number "seven" is to be understood not literally but rather as a symbolic number for completeness, meaning that the righteous will always get up. On the other hand, the wicked will fall easily.

> [17]When your enemy falls, don't rejoice.
>   When he stumbles, don't let your heart be glad.
> [18]Otherwise, Yahweh will see, and it will be evil in his eyes,
>   and he will turn his anger from him.

4. See "Honey," in *Dictionary of Biblical Imagery*, ed. L. Ryken, J. Wilhoit, and T. Longman III (Downers Grove: InterVarsity, 1998), 396–97.

5. Clifford, *Proverbs*, 215.

24:17–18. The warning is clear enough. When something bad happens to an enemy, don't be happy lest God should be upset (see similar ideas expressed in Ps. 35:15–16; Job 31:29). But what type of enemy are we talking about here? Certainly, God does not get upset with Moses and the Israelites as they celebrate the destruction of the Egyptian troops at the Red Sea (Exod. 15) or with Deborah as she sings of the victory over Midian (Judg. 5).

We may be speaking of personal enemies, fellow Israelites. This proverb would be true only if spoken in the right circumstance and hence is not universally true, but exactly what that circumstance would be is not clear.

In any case, the motive clause is at first rather shocking. It appears that the fall of the enemy envisioned in v. 17 is the result of divine anger against the enemy, and the fear is that if Yahweh grows angry at one's joy at the enemy's defeat, then God will leave him alone. What is clear is that vengeance is the work of God and not of human beings (see Deut. 32:35 and the further development of this idea in Rom. 12:17–21).

> [19]Don't get fighting mad at evil people;
>   don't be envious of the wicked.
> [20]For there will be no future for evil;
>   the lamp of the wicked will be extinguished.

24:19–20. This passage is the third time within the "sayings of the wise" where the sage warns against envy toward wicked people (see also 23:17–18; 24:1–2). It must have been a common temptation for the wise to get their blood boiling as they saw godless people do well in life. In the present passage, appeal is made to the lack of "future" for the wicked, which certainly implies that the godly have a future. In regard to the nature of the future envisioned here, it certainly is true that this passage and ones like them could not be used to proof-text a belief in the afterlife. On the other hand, it seems banal to the extreme to think that the sages were thinking only of this life. After all, if the passage is alluding to physical death in v. 20, the sages were smart enough to know that the wise too died, and some of them even died at a young age. At the least, this passage is suggestive of the idea that life lasted beyond the grave.

> [21]Fear Yahweh, my son, as well as the king.
>   Don't associate with those who rebel.
> [22]For disaster will rise up suddenly from them.
>   Ruin from both of them—who can experience?

24:21-22. Sages knew that successful living came from knowing one's right place in the power structure of the universe and their culture. They understood that it was important to respect the powers above them, both divine and human. This is particularly the case when those powers have the ability to destroy them. The latter is certainly the case with both God and king.

Here is an unusual collocation of "God" and "king." We might consider the fact that the proverb likely presumes a godly king who would reflect God's kingship. To see an abuse of this provision, see 1 Kings 21, where the trumped-up charge against Naboth is that he cursed God and king.

Further Sayings of the Wise

> ²³These are also according to the wise.
>   Those who show favoritism in judgment are not good.
> ²⁴Those who say to the wicked person, "You are righteous,"
>   the people will curse them;
>   the population will be angry with them.
> ²⁵It will go well for those who establish what is right,
>   and a blessing of prosperity will come on them.

24:23-25. In the addendum to the sayings of the wise, the first proverbial passage has to do with judging fairly, and its primary setting is in the law court. The passage begins with a monocolon that rather clearly states the principle behind the rest and condemns favoritism in judgments. Verse 24 spells this out by citing an instance where the guilty party is declared innocent and presumably let go. No reasons are given for this faulty judgment, but since it probably presumes that the judges know better, it may envision a bribe and the possibility that the defendant is a crony of those making judgments.

Such perversion of justice will have a devastating effect on the society. Besides being grossly unfair to the victims, the lack of a competent or just judicial system encourages malfeasance in the community. While v. 24 provides negative motivation for judges to observe strict rules of justice, v. 25 describes the carrot. Those who judge with equity will be rewarded. Again, it is not explicated how, but we see the contrast between the curse on those who twist justice and the blessing on those who render fair judgment.

While the primary focus of this passage is the courtroom, the principle could be applied to honesty in all areas of life.

> [26]They kiss lips
> who utter truthful words.

24:26. This stand-alone proverb repeats a thought commonly heard in proverbs, that truth is not only right but also beneficial (12:17, 19; 14:25). Kissing and truth-telling are two positive and pleasurable acts one can perform or receive from lips. Telling the truth is a kind act.

We reject the claim of J. M. Cohen that the verse "can yield no satisfactory meaning" if the verb *nšq* is taken in its by-far typical meaning, "to kiss." He argues for an obscure meaning here (and also in Gen. 41:40 and Job 31:27): "to bind, seal up the lips." He thus translates, "He that gives forthright judgement will silence all hostile lips."[6]

> [27]Establish your affairs in public;
> prepare them in the field;
> afterward you can build your house.

24:27. This proverb warns against establishing one's internal needs before getting things in order in public. The reference to "field" may be a reference to getting one's source of income in order first, presuming, that is, an agrarian setting of the proverb. The general principle is well expressed by Whybray: "Don't undertake anything hastily without due preparation."[7]

> [28]Don't be witness against your neighbor without a reason;
> do you want to deceive with your lips?
> [29]Don't say "As they did to me, so I will do to them.
> I will repay people according to their deeds."

24:28–29. It is hard to determine whether these are two separate proverbs. The first one is a variant of the common warning against bearing false witness (14:5, 25). In this case, the focus is on false testimony about a neighbor. Though the language of "witness" (*ʿēd*) suggests a formal legal setting, the principle certainly applies also to gossip and rumor. To speak against a neighbor, there needs to be a reason; otherwise, the speaker is deceptive and creating discord in the community. The force of the motive clause in v. 28b seems dependent on the fact that the hearer is an honorable person. Certainly, those who are not honorable may be perfectly willing to engage in deception in order to achieve some kind of advantage over a neighbor.

6. See J. Cohen, "Unrecognized Connotation," 422.
7. Whybray, *Proverbs*, 354.

The second proverb warns against seeking revenge. If connected with the previous verse, then the idea would be that persons would feel justified in giving false witness against a neighbor on the basis of the fact that the neighbor had harmed them earlier. It is possible that the entire verse is to be enclosed in quotation marks and thereby understood to be a warning against seeking revenge pure and simple; yet it is also possible that the last colon is to be taken as a comment from God, who says, in the spirit of Rom. 12:19–21 (citing Prov. 25:21–22), that human beings do not need to seek revenge because God himself will take care of the situation. Against this understanding is the fact that in these proverbs the sage typically is speaking, not God directly.[8]

> ³⁰I happened upon the field of a lazy person,
>   by the vineyard of one who lacks heart.
> ³¹Thorns grew up over all of it;
>   weeds covered its surface,
>   and the stone wall was dilapidated.
> ³²I observed this and took it to heart;
>   I saw it and learned a lesson.
> ³³A little sleep, a little slumber,
>   a little folding of the arms to lie down,
> ³⁴and poverty will come creeping up on you,
>   your deprivation like a person with a shield.

24:30–34. This passage is an extended satire on lazy people. This topic is one of the most extensively commented upon throughout the book of Proverbs (see "Laziness and Hard Work" in the appendix; see especially 6:10–11, which is similar to 24:33–34). Laziness is the height of foolish behavior and deserves to be parodied. After all, it leads to difficult consequences for both the individual and the community, and it is easily remedied. The latter is the case for true laziness, not lack of work for other reasons such as disability. If one is simply lazy, then the antidote is hard work.

This passage narrates an anecdote, which is reminiscent of Prov. 7, where an anecdote also warns about foolish behavior. Both these anecdotes are narrated from the point of view of the sage who observes foolish behavior. In this case, the lazy person is a farmer whose fields are in sad shape due to neglect. Thorns and weeds are there in abundance, presumably crowding out the crop. Not only that, but the walls that delimit the field are also crumbling. The lesson is simple and obvious.

---

8. Nevertheless, the principle of divine retribution is mentioned in these "words of the wise," in 24:12; see also 20:22. Perhaps the connection is to "show a human arrogating a prerogative that is God's" (see Van Leeuwen, "Proverbs," 214).

Neglect caused by laziness leads to unproductive fields, which signify poverty.

In v. 34 the description of the consequences of laziness is the most difficult part of the passage, and the above translation and following explanation are offered tentatively. A literal translation of the first colon might be something like this:

> It comes creeping your poverty.

The second colon:

> Your deprivation like a person of shield.

My translation takes "poverty" as the subject of the sentence, with "comes" as the main verb. "Creeping" then is descriptive of how poverty comes on the lazy person. The second colon is more straightforward, understanding the main verb as "creeping," elided but understood from the first colon. Some commentators, however, point out that "person of shield," whom we take as "person with a shield," is sometimes taken as a synecdoche (part for the whole) and translated "armed person." Other times a more radical approach is taken, so that *māgēn* is not taken as the relatively common noun "shield," but rather as "beggar," based on another Hebrew noun: *megen*, "gift." This translation is usually paired with an understanding of "creeping" as "wandering," and pointing to a vagrant.[9] Clifford's translation follows this route:

> And the poverty of a vagabond will come upon you,
>   the destitution of a beggar.[10]

While one cannot definitely determine the exact force of this final verse, it is clear that the warning is intended to inform people that poverty can creep up unexpectedly on the lazy person.

---

9. Translations such as "robber" (NRSV) and "bandit" (NIV) are based on the parallel with "person with a shield."

10. Clifford, *Proverbs*, 217–18, and his fuller discussion at 6:10–12 (ibid., p. 74). See also Murphy, *Proverbs*, 184.

Part 4

Proverbs of Solomon: Collection II

(25:1–29:27)

The fifth superscription in the book (25:1) introduces yet another collection of Solomonic proverbs. However, there is a twist in that the collection is said to have been transcribed by the "men of Hezekiah." It would be interesting to know the sociological and theological reasons for why these proverbs found their way into the collection in this way, but such speculation would be futile.

Chapter 25

Translation

¹These are also proverbs of Solomon, which the men of Hezekiah, king of
  Judah, transposed.
²It is the glory of God to hide a matter
  and the glory of kings to examine a matter.
³The heavens so high and the earth so deep,
  and there is no examining the heart of a king.
⁴Separate^a the dross from the silver,
  and a vessel will come out for refining.
⁵Separate the wicked from the presence of the king,
  and his throne will be established in righteousness.
⁶Don't honor yourself in the presence of a king;
  in the place of important people, don't stand.
⁷For it is better that he say to you, "Come up here,"
  than to lower yourself before a ruler.
That which your eyes see,^b
  ⁸don't be quick to bring out^c an accusation,
lest what will you do in the future,
  when your neighbor humiliates you?
⁹Make your accusation against your neighbor,
  but do not reveal your secret to another,

a. The verb here and at the beginning of v. 5 is an infinitive absolute that has the force
of an imperative.
b. The formal verse division seems clearly wrong, since v. 7c works well as the first
colon of a parallelism associated with v. 8a.
c. Repointing the qal form (*tēṣēʾ*) as a hiphil (*tōṣēʾ*).

[10]lest the one who hears it denigrate you,
and the slander against you never stops.
[11]Apples[d] of gold in a silver setting
is a word spoken in its right timing.[e]
[12]A gold earring and an ornament of fine gold
is a wise correction on a listening ear.
[13]Like the coolness of snow on the day of harvest
are envoys who are reliable to those who send them.
They restore the soul of their master.
[14]Clouds and wind, but no rain—
people who brag about a false gift.
[15]A military commander is persuaded by patience,
and a tender tongue breaks bone.
[16]If you find honey, eat just the right amount.
Otherwise, you have your fill and vomit it up.
[17]Let your feet rarely step in the house of your neighbors.
Otherwise, they will have their fill and hate you.
[18]Hammer and sword and sharpened arrow—
people who testify against their neighbors with false witness.
[19]A bad tooth and a wobbly foot—
trusting an unreliable person on a day of distress.
[20]Removing a garment on a cold day,[f]
vinegar on soda,[g]
singing a song to a troubled heart.
[21]If those you hate are starving, feed them bread,
and if they are thirsty, give them water to drink.
[22]For you will heap burning coals on their heads,
and Yahweh will reward you.
[23]The north wind stirs up rain,
and a hidden tongue angry faces.
[24]Better to dwell in the corner of a roof
than with a contentious woman in a shared house.
[25]Cold water for a person who is weary;
a good report from a distant land.
[26]A foul well and a ruined fountain,
a righteous person who staggers before a wicked person.

d. The identification of *tappûaḥ* is uncertain, since it is possible that the apple was not introduced into Palestine until a later time. In a discussion of the appearance of this word in the Song of Songs, M. Falk (*Love Lyrics from the Bible: A Translation and Literary Study of the Song of Songs* [Sheffield: Almond, 1982], 174) argues that it is the quince. In any case, the word denotes a fruit of some sort.

e. This word is a *hapax legomenon*, which, according to *NIDOTTE* 1:491, is related to the Arabic *iffan* (time).

f. Some commentators believe that the first colon is a dittography of v. 19b, but this is an unnecessary hypothesis. See Clifford, *Proverbs*, 222.

g. Murphy (*Proverbs*, 189) follows the LXX: "wound." The idea again would be that vinegar would just increase the pain.

[27]Eating too much honey is not good,
    nor[h] is it honorable to investigate honor.
[28]A city breached without a wall,
    a person who is unrestrained in spirit.

Interpretation

> [1]These are also proverbs of Solomon,
>   which the men of Hezekiah,
>   king of Judah, transposed.

25:1. This is the fifth superscription (see also 1:1; 10:1; 22:17–21; 24:23) of the book. It begins another section of Solomonic proverbs (which implies that what comes before is not Solomonic) that will continue through the end of chap. 29, but this time, others are said to be involved. The mystery of the verse has to do with the nature of the involvement of the men of Hezekiah.

However, first of all, we should mention that Hezekiah was king of Judah from 715 to 687 BC. Though he had lapses in good judgment, he was essentially a king known for his devotion to God (2 Kings 18–20; 2 Chron. 29–32; Isa. 36–39). It is likely that along with other acts of reform and renewal of worship following the destruction of the northern kingdom in 722, he also initiated more care in the transmission of sacred literature.

The tradition represented here, that people associated with him had something to do with the composition and transmission of Proverbs, certainly is in keeping with what we know about this king from these other sources. However, the rather general reference to "men of Hezekiah" does not allow us to be more specific in identifying who exactly they are: sages employed by the court? priests charged with the transmission of the text, which may already have been considered sacred and authoritative? We cannot tell for sure.

h. This translation assumes that the negative of the first colon serves double-duty with the second colon as well. Macintosh ("Note on Proverbs xxv 27," 112–14), on the other hand, understands the force of the root *kbd* to refer here not to "glory" or "honor" but rather to "distress" (with the Vulgate as supporting evidence). He thus translates, "It is not good to eat too much honey: and he who searches for glory will be distressed." Van Leeuwen ("Proverbs xxv 27 Once Again") argues for yet another interpretation, based on his understanding of the redactional intention of 25:2–27, a subunit of chaps. 25–27: "To eat too much honey is not good and to seek difficult things is (no) glory." This interpretation understands the repeated root *kbd* to be exploiting two different nuances in the verse, a view I find difficult to affirm.

But the biggest mystery has to do with what they were doing with the text. The verb is ʿātaq in the hiphil.[1] The basic meaning of the verb (qal) is "to move; to become old." In the hiphil, it may mean "to cause something to move." It appears that the verb indicates that the men of Hezekiah moved these proverbs from one source to another (thus "transpose"). Perhaps we should surmise that it was recognized that these Solomonic proverbs were also authoritative and needed to be added to the growing collection that up to this point was being transmitted separately.[2] Whybray, however, suggests that the verb may indicate "editing," though not composing, and throughout his writings he vigorously maintains that this does not prove the existence of a guild of professional wisdom teachers.[3]

I remain unpersuaded by G. Bryce's attempt to locate a "wisdom book" analogous to the "thirty sayings of the wise" (22:17–24:22) in 25:2–27. He also proposes an analogy with short Egyptian wisdom texts, the Instruction of Sehetepibre and the Kemit. This analysis requires that the "men of Hezekiah" misunderstood what they were doing and obscured the structure. The main problem with his viewpoint is that he insists that vv. 6–15 deal with the ruler and vv. 16–26 discuss the wicked, but a reading of these verses does not consistently demonstrate this fact.[4] Even so, along with Bryce we do note a number of legitimate connections between proverbs in the chapter that can be seen in content and/or structure and wordplay. While he believes chap. 27 has to do with the training of young courtiers, Malchow argues for taking chaps. 28–29 as a unit for the guidance of future monarchs.[5]

---

²It is the glory of God to hide a matter
   and the glory of kings to examine a matter.
³The heavens so high and the earth so deep,
   and there is no examining the heart of a king.

25:2–3. These two proverbs are linked by their common reference to the "king" as well as the repetition of the verb "examine" (ḥqr). The

---

1. *NIDOTTE* 3:569–70 has a lengthy discussion of this verb, but, inexplicably, there is no consideration of this particular reference.

2. I agree with M. Carasik ("Who Were the 'Men of Hezekiah' [Proverbs xxv 1]?" *Vetus Testamentum* 44 [1994]: 289) in his criticism of Whybray's argument that the verb refers to "editing."

3. R. N. Whybray, "The Sage in the Israelite Royal Court," in *The Sage in Israel and the Ancient Near East*, ed. J. G. Gammie and L. G. Perdue (Winona Lake, IN: Eisenbrauns, 1990), 138.

4. Nevertheless, his insistence on the theological foundation of the wisdom of Prov. 25 is very helpful. See Bryce, "Another Wisdom-'Book.'"

5. Malchow, "Manual for Future Monarchs."

first proverb sounds like a case of hide-and-seek. God hides something (Deut. 29:29), and kings try to search it out. Clifford puts it well: "God's world is full of conundrums and puzzles beyond the capacity of ordinary people, but the king is there to unravel them and lead people to serve the gods."[6]

In both cases, God and king are honored and held in high respect, though clearly the hierarchy is God first, next the king, then the rest of humanity. The second proverb teaches about the inscrutability of the king's heart, presumably his thinking, motives, and emotions—his whole inner life. This is compared with other grand matters like the heavens and earth.

The proverb is addressed primarily to the sages who would work with the king, perhaps instilling within them proper respect. It may also warn them about trying to psychoanalyze (using a modern term) the monarch.

> [4]Separate the dross from the silver,
>   and a vessel will come out for refining.
> [5]Separate the wicked from the presence of the king,
>   and his throne will be established in righteousness.

25:4–5. This proverb fits in with those that speak to the dangers of associating with evil. Proverbs operates with the concern that people will become like those with whom they associate (1:8–19). Here the stakes are high because the person in view is the king, the most influential person in the kingdom.

An analogy is drawn between the two verses of the passage. In the first, the process for refining silver is described in general terms. Lead ore contained some silver, and to get it in a pure form, it was necessary to heat it and to melt off the lead oxide (dross).[7] To get the good metal, one had to separate it from the worthless metal. In the same way, one should remove wicked people from the presence of the king, which is probably a reference to the king's associates and advisers. If this is done correctly, then the king's reign (symbolized by his throne) will be characterized by righteousness.

We wonder to whom the imperatives are addressed. Perhaps it is to the king's righteous advisers, who must be on the lookout to keep their master from bad influences. Or perhaps it just has the force of a general principle to explain why one king is bad and another good.

---

6. Clifford, *Proverbs*, 222.

7. The process is more complicated than this and is described at greater length in the article on *ṣîg* found in *NIDOTTE* 3:244–45.

> 6Don't honor yourself in the presence of a king;
>   in the place of important people, don't stand.
> 7For it is better that he say to you, "Come up here,"
>   than to lower yourself before a ruler.

25:6–7b. Proverbs is consistently teaching against self-aggrandizement as well as boasting. In general, the book warns against pride and promotes humility (see "Pride/Humility" in the appendix). How much more important these principles are when in the presence of nobility. After all, these are individuals who are due honor themselves, and they will find it difficult to tolerate people who try to confer honor on themselves.

Verse 7 makes it clear that it is not the honor itself that is bad. Rather, it is self-honor. The hope is that the king will on his own initiative confer honor on a person. The most natural primary audience for this warning is the sage who serves in the court, though the principle may have wide application.[8]

The warning delivered by these verses is similar and perhaps even the background to the advice given by Jesus in Luke 14:7–11.[9]

> 7cThat which your eyes see,
>   8don't be quick to bring out an accusation,
> lest what will you do in the future,
>   when your neighbor humiliates you?

25:7c–8. This proverb warns against an overhasty accusation of some kind of wrongdoing. The language makes it sound like a legal "accusation" (*rîb*), but again, the principle is relevant for an informal accusation toward a neighbor or even toward a third party (thus making the situation a form of gossip, also roundly condemned by Proverbs).

Eyes can be deceptive, so one must reflect on a situation before making an accusation. It could also be that one saw truly but can't prove it, and so one's accusation looks like a trumped-up charge. If the charge is false or unproved, then the neighbor can cast aspersions on one who makes charges.

> 9Make your accusation against your neighbor,
>   but do not reveal your secret to another,
> 10lest the one who hears it denigrate you,
>   and the slander against you never stops.

8. Though Whybray, *Proverbs*, 362, registers his objection to a primary court setting.
9. Beardslee, "Uses of the Proverb," 65.

25:9–10. This proverbial warning follows nicely on the heels of the immediately preceding one. They both inform about wise protocol for dealing with perceived problems with a neighbor.

Here the advice is to criticize one's neighbor directly and make the charge without going public. The secret is the criticism that one has of a neighbor. The fear is that the criticism may be overheard by a third party, perhaps sympathetic to the neighbor, and then the accuser will have the reputation of being a gossip, something roundly condemned by the book of Proverbs (11:13; 17:4; 18:8). As Clifford points out, this advice has similarities with the Gospel teaching found in Matt. 18:15 as well as 5:22–26.

> ¹¹Apples of gold in a silver setting
>   is a word spoken in its right timing.
> ¹²A gold earring and an ornament of fine gold
>   is a wise correction on a listening ear.

25:11–12. These proverbs emphasize the circumstantial nature of speaking wise words. It is simply not the case that proverbs are effectively or even truly spoken in every situation. Sometimes the wise person needs to remain silent (12:23; 17:27–28; 23:9). It is only fools who speak all the time, without regard for the circumstance and to their own detriment (26:7, 9). The wisdom formula is to speak the right word to the right person at the right time (15:23). For instance, the circumstance and the nature of the fool determine whether the wise person should respond to a foolish argument (26:4, 5).

The first proverb (24:11) specifically mentions speaking the right word at the right time. It draws an analogy to make its point. The "word" (probably a proverb or a point of advice) is like an "apple of gold"; it does have inherent worth, but when spoken at the right time, it is as if the gold apple is given a setting of silver. It enhances its value.

The second proverb (v. 12) addresses the need for a receptive listener for a bit of advice. In particular, it refers to a word of correction, likely some word that confronts faulty behavior in another person. The wise will listen to such correctives, but not the fool. In any case, when a listening ear pays attention to a wise correction, it has great value for the person and is likened to golden jewelry.

> ¹³Like the coolness of snow on the day of harvest
>   are envoys who are reliable to those who send them.
>   They restore the soul of their master.

25:13. Effective communication over distances in the ancient Near East typically depended on human messengers. Business transactions, political decisions, not to speak of personal communication—all depended on the reliability of those who were commissioned to carry the message. Proverbs' commendation of faithful messengers, as well as its negative comments on messengers who let their masters down (13:17), may well indicate that there were some problems in this area. Thus, a reliable messenger is like snow on the day of harvest. Harvest would be difficult work and on a hot day could be unbearable. Snow would bring cool relief.[10] In this proverb, we have a third colon, which makes the meaning of the metaphor even more explicit as it talks about restoring the soul of the master.

> ¹⁴Clouds and wind, but no rain—
> people who brag about a false gift.

25:14. Like the previous proverb, this one also contains a metaphor that begins with the comparison. Where there are clouds and wind, rain is expected. Not to get rain is a disappointment, especially in an area like Palestine, where rainfall is not abundant and is desperately needed for agriculture. In other words, colon 1 is a way of saying that something is "all show and no results."

This helps us understand the "false" or "deceptive" gift of the second colon. In what way is it deceptive? It likely refers to those who say they will give a gift, and indeed brag about it, but then never give it. They may preannounce a gift in order to get in the good graces of the supposed recipient and then never actually give the gift. If this interpretation is correct, then the proverb serves as a warning to watch out for these false claims and not give favors based on the promise of a gift.

> ¹⁵A military commander is persuaded by patience,
> and a tender tongue breaks bone.

25:15. This proverb tells the reader that tough things are won over not by force or a show of force, but by patience and tenderness. This is the exact opposite of what might be expected. A military commander is presumably a tough individual, one who is accustomed to dealing with confrontation. The unexpected, "patience," wins him over. In the second

---

10. As Murphy (*Proverbs*, 192) points out, it is unlikely that snow would actually appear during the harvest season (April–May) in Israel, but that is not the point. Metaphors call on the imagination to make their point. Clifford (*Proverbs*, 224) wonders whether the reference is to snow actually brought down from the mountains. However, the nearest snow-covered mountain would be Hermon, far to the north.

colon, one might expect the best results from a harsh word, but here it is the tender word.

> ¹⁶If you find honey, eat just the right amount.
>   Otherwise, you have your fill and vomit it up.
> ¹⁷Let your feet rarely step in the house of your neighbors.
>   Otherwise, they will have their fill and hate you.

25:16–17. These two proverbs are joined by their second cola, each warning against overdoing good things and the bad consequences that follow from such behavior.

The first warning has to do with eating too much of a good thing. Honey tastes deliciously sweet, to be sure, but those who eat too much of it will find that their stomachs can't keep it down. It will make them sick. This principle is not tied just to honey but also applies to any food. Overeating or overdrinking will sicken rather than energize.

The second colon has to do with relationship with one's neighbors. Again, it is not that the sage recommends having nothing to do with one's neighbors. It is a matter of overdoing it and, as our own expression states it, "overstaying your welcome." A person who does so will become a nuisance rather than a friend or a help.

While both of these proverbs have their applications in a particular aspect of life (eating and social relationships), they still raise the question of application even more broadly. Too much of virtually any good thing will have negative consequences.

> ¹⁸Hammer and sword and sharpened arrow—
>   people who testify against their neighbors with false witness.
> ¹⁹A bad tooth and a wobbly foot—
>   trusting an unreliable person on a day of distress.

25:18–19. These two proverbs are united by their form more than their content. They both begin with a list of items that will be implicitly compared, thus forming a metaphor, with something in their second cola. It is the item in the second colon that is the object of the teaching.

Verse 18 lists three weapons: "hammer," "sword," and "arrow." These may be used to hurt or even kill another person. They are compared to someone who gives false witness against a neighbor. The language in v. 18b is similar to that in the ninth commandment (Exod. 20:16). The teaching against false witness is pervasive throughout Proverbs (14:5, 25; etc.). It is likely that the primary setting of the teaching is in the courtroom. False witness could result in penalties against the neighbors that would really hurt them. In an extreme case, where capital punishment might be called for, it is conceivable that it could even result in someone's death. The story of the trumped-up case against Naboth in 1 Kings 21 is a good example of the latter, not to speak of the witnesses brought to testify falsely against Jesus.

Verse 19 presents a list of two items, body parts, that are disabled and producing pain, certainly in the case of the first one. The proverb points out that an unreliable or unfaithful person is just like that when trouble arises. Just as a bad tooth will let you down and hurt when you are trying to eat, or a wobbly foot lets you down and hurts when you try to walk, so also will such a person. The comparison invites the hearer to think about the character of one's associates and assess whether they will help or hurt when trouble starts up.

> ²⁰Removing a garment on a cold day,
>   vinegar on soda,
>   singing a song to a troubled heart.

25:20. The proverb sets up a comparison that functions as a metaphor. The intention is to explain the effects of trying to be happy in the midst of trouble. It makes things worse to sing a happy song when someone is down. Removing a garment certainly does not help warm a cold person. Vinegar also reacts violently when mixed with soda (mixing an acid with an alkali). Happiness just aggravates a troubled heart. This would instruct a sage as to how to approach a depressed individual. The NRSV here follows the Greek by omitting the first colon of the Hebrew, translating "soda" as "wound," and including the additional comparison:

> Like a moth in clothing or a worm in wood,
>   sorrow gnaws at the human heart.

> ²¹If those you hate are starving, feed them bread,
>   and if they are thirsty, give them water to drink.
> ²²For you will heap burning coals on their heads,
>   and Yahweh will reward you.

25:21–22. Our natural inclination is to want to hurt those who hurt us. We want revenge against our enemies. Ancient tribal society tended to be extreme in its methods of revenge. Indeed, institutions like the "cities of refuge" (Josh. 20) and even the principle of an "eye for an eye" (Exod. 21:23–24) were attempts to curb excessive vengeance.

But this proverb presents a remarkable statement of compassion toward enemies that works against this natural inclination. Instead of harming opponents when their weakness presents an opportunity, we are to help them!

The motivation to do this does not appeal to many modern readers, who may prefer a more lofty reasoning. Such behavior, it is said, will actually be a form of vengeance. One's enemies will be exasperated by the acts of compassion. Furthermore, God will reward the one who acts in such a way.

Other proverbs suggest kindness toward enemies (14:29; 19:11; 20:22; 24:17, 29), but this one takes the idea the furthest. In the OT, similar sentiments are also expressed in Exod. 23:4 and Lev. 19:17–18. This proverb is quoted by Paul in Rom. 12:20 to discourage the taking of revenge against enemies. The broader context includes vv. 19–21:

> Dear friends, never avenge yourselves. Leave that to God. For it is written,
>
>> "I will take vengeance;
>>> I will repay those who deserve it,"
>> says the Lord.
>
> Instead, do what the Scriptures say:
>
>> "If your enemies are hungry, feed them.
>> If they are thirsty, give them something to drink,
>>> and they will be ashamed of what they have done to you."
>
> Don't let evil get the best of you, but conquer evil by doing good. (NLT)

Jesus cites the "eye for an eye" teaching of the OT and presents an even more radical idea about retaliation: "Love your enemies" (Matt. 5:38–48).

Clifford cites a series of teachings from other ancient Near Eastern wisdom literature that expresses the same type of idea:

> Steer, we will ferry the wicked,
> We do not act like his kind;
> Lift him up, give him your hand,
> That he may be sated and weep. (Amenemope 5.1–6)

> It is better to bless someone than to do harm to one who has insulted you. (Papyrus Insinger 23.6)

> Do not return evil to the man who disputes with you; requite with kindness your evildoer. (Babylonian Counsels of Wisdom 1.35–36)[11]

11. Clifford, *Proverbs*, 226.

There have been many explanations of the difficult phrase about heaping burning coals on the head. Some see a connection with an Egyptian ritual of penitence, where a person bears a pan of coals on the head, while others see it as referring to the red face of shame. Still others translate in a way that reverses the meaning and suggests that burning coals are removed from the enemy. None of these are completely convincing, but I include myself in the vast majority who have no doubt that it refers to some kind of punishment or pain inflicted on the enemy.

Whybray is surely right in stating, "Like many other passages in Proverbs, these verses are concerned with the harmony and well-being of the local community, which ought to override the selfish interests and feuds of individuals."[12]

25:23–28. *Assorted analogies.* With the exception of v. 24, which is a virtual repeat of 21:9, the remaining proverbs in chap. 25 present analogies. The second cola present the focus of the teaching, while the opening cola present a striking and illuminating comparison to something from everyday life. However, beyond that formal similarity, there is not much relationship in terms of the teaching, and so we will treat each verse separately.

> [23]The north wind stirs up rain,
>   and a hidden tongue angry faces.

This proverb instructs about the effects of a certain type of a speech, which comes under the name "hidden tongue." Whatever it is, it produces angry faces, just as the north winds brought rain to Palestine.[13] A "hidden tongue" may refer to speech that remains hidden, perhaps whispering or speaking behind someone's back. In other words, here we may be dealing with a statement about gossip. Once gossip is discovered, it produces anger in those toward whom it is directed. The implicit warning of the proverb, then, is to inform people that gossip may well result in the gossiper being the object of some rather intense anger.

> [24]Better to dwell in the corner of a roof
>   than with a contentious woman in a shared house.

---

12. Whybray, *Proverbs*, 367.

13. It is widely recognized as a problem that the west winds and not the north winds bring rain to Palestine. It may be, as is often argued (see Murphy, *Proverbs*, 192, plus his references), that the connection is suggested by the verbal root *ṣpn* (to conceal) related to "north" (*ṣāphôn*).

With a minor syntactical variation,[14] this proverb is identical to 21:9. Commentary on that verse should be consulted.

> 25Cold water for a person who is weary;
> a good report from a distant land.

If one is far from family and friends ("distant land"), the desire for news about their well-being grows intense. To receive news, particularly good news, satisfies a fundamental craving. The metaphor that begins the proverb indicates that the intensity of the desire for news and the feeling of relief upon hearing good news are the object of the proverb. After all, weariness from extreme exertion generates a tremendous thirst. Cold water not only meets the need of hydration, but cool water is also particularly satisfying.

The proverb could be stated to express the desire for news or to explain the satisfaction that comes to one when receiving welcome news. It could also be used as a motivation to send good news to a loved one far away.

> 26A foul well and a ruined fountain,
> a righteous person who staggers before a wicked person.

According to 10:30:

> The righteous will never be shaken [from *môṭ*],
> but the wicked will not dwell in the land.

And 12:3:

> No one will stand fast by wicked acts,
> but the root of the righteous cannot be disturbed [from *môṭ*].

But this verse envisions "a righteous person who staggers [from *môṭ*] before a wicked person"! This is not the way it is supposed to be, but this proverb acknowledges that sometimes it does happen that the righteous will be ill-treated in favor of the godless. But such a situation is not right. It is like a poisoned water source.

> 27Eating too much honey is not good,
> nor is it honorable to investigate honor.

14. The verb "dwell" is missing the prefix *lĕ* in this occurrence.

Earlier (25:16), we learned that seeking too much of a good thing, such as eating too much honey, can lead to adverse consequences (vomiting). Here we are reminded that eating honey (a good thing) is not good if done in excess, and this is compared to trying to gain too much honor for oneself. The investigation of honor is best understood as an attempt to look into honor to gain it for oneself. The lesson is not to be overly concerned at the acquisition of great glory for oneself. In other words, the wise person should not be proud.

> ²⁸A city breached without a wall,
> a person who is unrestrained in spirit.

Self-discipline and self-control are necessary. Otherwise, one might run rampant. This lesson is taught by comparison to a city without a wall, which would leave it open to attack. Such a city and such a person have no focus, which leaves them without strength.

Chapter 26

Translation

¹Like snow in the summer and like rain at harvest,
    so it is not appropriate for a fool to have honor.
²Like a bird for darting, like a swallow for flying—
    so a curse without reason never comes.
³A whip to a horse, a bridle for a donkey,
    and a rod for the backs of fools.
⁴Don't answer fools according to their stupidity;
    otherwise, you will become like them yourself.
⁵Answer fools according to their stupidity;
    otherwise, they will become wise in their own eyes.
⁶Cutting off one's feet; drinking violence—
    sending messages via a fool.
⁷The legs of a lame person dangle,ᵃ
    and a proverb in the mouth of fools.
⁸Like a bag of stone in a sling,
    so are those who give honor to a fool.
⁹A thornbush in the hand of a drunk,
    and a proverb in the mouth of fools.
¹⁰An archer who wounds all,
    and those who hire a fool and those who hire a passerby.
¹¹Like a dog returning to its vomit
    are fools who repeat their stupidity.

a. There is general agreement on the meaning and significance of the verb here translated "dangle," but much disagreement about its etymology and syntax, as evidenced by its discussion in *NIDOTTE* under three different roots: *dlh* I, *dlh* II, and *dll* II.

¹²Do you see people who are wise in their own eyes?
  There is more hope for a fool than for them.
¹³Lazy people say, "There is a lion cub on the path,
  a lion in the public square!"
¹⁴The door turns on its hinge,
  and lazy people on their beds.
¹⁵Lazy people bury their hand into the bowl,
  but they are not able[b] to return it to their mouth.
¹⁶Lazy people are wise in their own eyes,
  even more than seven who respond with discernment.
¹⁷Those who yank the ears of a dog,
  those who grow infuriated[c] in a quarrel not their own.
¹⁸Like a madman[d] shooting
  flaming arrows and death,
¹⁹so people who deceive their neighbors
  and say, "Wasn't I joking?"
²⁰Without wood, a fire is extinguished.
  When there are no gossips, conflict calms down.
²¹Adding charcoal to burning charcoal, and wood to a fire,
  so contentious people to kindle accusation.
²²The words of gossips are like choice morsels;
  they go down to their inmost parts.
²³Silver dross[e] overlying clay,
  smooth[f] lips and an evil heart.
²⁴Those who hate dissimulate with their lips,
  but they set deception inside.

b. Or "too tired," from *l'h*.

c. There is an issue of stichometry in this verse. The Masoretes accented the verse in such a way as to lead us to put the verbal phrase here translated "grow infuriated" (*'ōbēr mit'abbēr*) in the second colon. However, this makes for an extremely long second colon, where typically the first colon is longer than the second, according to the tenets of biblical parallelism. This causes some commentators, as well as versions, to ignore the Masoretic accentuation and also to understand the verb to come from two different roots—*'ābar* (to pass by) and then (with a slight emendation) *'ārab* (to associate with or to meddle), resulting in the rendering "Like somebody who takes a passing dog by the ears is one who meddles in the quarrel of another" (NRSV). I take the two verbal forms together and derive them from *'ābar* II, "to infuriate." Commentators who take this position include Murphy, *Proverbs*, 197, 201–2; and Clifford, *Proverbs*, 230, 233.

d. This word occurs only here, and its translation is therefore uncertain.

e. Ever since an Ugaritic text was found that has a phrase thought to have the consonants *kspsgym*, meaning "like glaze" (*k-spsgym*), it has been suggested that what we have in the Hebrew, "silver dross" (*ksp sygym*), represents a misdivision of the phrase by the Masoretes (first proposed by H. L. Ginsberg, "The North-Canaanite Myth of Anat and Aqht," *Bulletin of the American Schools of Oriental Research* 98 [1945]: 21). However, this seems unlikely and also does not really affect the meaning of the verse.

f. The MT has "burning [*dōlĕqîm*] lips," but this does not fit the context well. The LXX (*leia*) suggests that the original text may have had "smooth [*hălāqîm*] lips." I follow the latter.

²⁵Though their voice is gracious, don't believe them,
   for seven abominations are in their heart.
²⁶Hatred is covered^g with guile,
   but they reveal their evil in the assembly.
²⁷Those who dig a pit will fall into it;
   those who roll a stone will have it turn back on them.
²⁸A lying tongue hates those crushed^h by it,
   and a flattering mouth causes destruction.ⁱ

Interpretation

¹Like snow in the summer and like rain at harvest,
   so it is not appropriate for a fool to have honor.
²Like a bird for darting, like a swallow for flying—
   so a curse without reason never comes.

26:1–2. These two proverbs are unrelated in terms of content, but they are likely put together because of their form. As is obvious from the translation, they both begin with two points of comparison in the first colon and then continue with the object of instruction in the second colon.

The first verse offers "snow in the summer" and "rain at harvest" as comparisons to a fool with honor. In other words, a fool with honor is impossible. The summers in Palestine are hot and dry. Harvest is a time of no rain. Fools have no honor, or at least no honor that they deserve. Indeed, the comparison may imply that on the off chance that snow came in the summer or rain at harvest, it would do great damage. After all, the only time in the Bible that rain came during harvest was through divine intervention, and when it came, it threatened great harm to the harvest (1 Sam. 12:17–25).

The second verse presents "darting birds" and "flying swallows." To be sure, these descriptions are a bit more ambiguous than those in the first colon, more difficult to understand without appeal to the second colon. The second colon speaks of a "curse without reason." This must mean an undeserved curse. The ancient Near East knew curses that took on formal and ritualistic patterns. Some even in Israel may have been convinced that a curse worked just by the power of the words, regardless

g. With Murphy (*Proverbs*, 197), I understand this to be a "hithpael, with assimilation of the *t*," citing GKC §54c.

h. *Dakkāyw* is here taken as a form derived from *dkʾ*, "to crush."

i. The noun *midḥeh* is derived from the verb *dḥh*, "to push, overthrow"; see *NIDOTTE* 1:932–33.

of their deserts. This proverb would have been reassuring to a person that undeserved curses would really have no affect.

> ³A whip to a horse, a bridle for a donkey,
>   and a rod for the backs of fools.

26:3. This verse is similar, though not identical, in syntax to the previous two. Whereas vv. 1 and 2 provided explicit similes in the first colon, which then were compared to the object of teaching in the second colon, here the points of comparison are simply listed. The object of teaching in the present verse is the rod on the backs of fools. In comparison with a whip for the horse and a bridle for the donkey, the idea is surely that the only hope for getting fools to go in the right direction is the use of a rod. "By implication a fool is a stupid animal."[1] Elsewhere, however, even the rod of discipline is seen to be fruitless when applied to fools. They just simply are hell-bent on going in the wrong direction.

> ⁴Don't answer fools according to their stupidity;
>   otherwise, you will become like them yourself.
> ⁵Answer fools according to their stupidity;
>   otherwise, they will become wise in their own eyes.

26:4–5. The Talmud notes what appears to be a contradiction here, and these verses provided evidence for an essential problem that casts doubt on the canonical authority of the book of Proverbs.[2] The question may be pointedly put: Does Proverbs advise that the sage should answer the fool or not?

This proverb pair is prime evidence leading toward the proper understanding of the proverb genre. Proverbs are not universally true laws but circumstantially relevant principles (see "Genre" in the introduction). In short, the answer depends on the nature of the fool with whom one is engaged in conversation. In other words, the wise person must assess whether this is a fool who will simply drain one's energy with no positive results or whether an answer will prove fruitful to the fool or perhaps to those who overhear. The wise not only know the proverb but also can read the circumstances and the people with whom they dialogue.

---

1. Clifford, *Proverbs*, 231.

2. So Beckwith, *Old Testament Canon in the New Testament Church*, 284. However, according to Hoglund ("Fool and the Wise in Dialogue," 162), the Babylonian Talmud tractate Šabbat states that "in cases dealing with Torah, one should correct the fool's error, but in most other cases it is better not to answer the fool." Hoglund's article argues for the view that these two verses "give a condensed expression to a profound ambivalence." In my opinion, as argued in the commentary, the "truth" of the proverb depends on the situation. Hoglund rejects this idea, but his rejection flies in the face of what a proverb is.

> ⁶Cutting off one's feet; drinking violence—
> sending messages via a fool.
> ⁷The legs of a lame person dangle,
> and a proverb in the mouth of fools.

26:6–7. These two proverbs provide metaphors for the speech of fools. The proverb in v. 6 parodies the stupidity of sending a message via a fool. This is compared in the first instance to "cutting off one's feet." Perhaps this suggests that the message will never be delivered. In the second place, it is compared to "drinking violence," which may suggest that the one who sent the message will be harmed due to the incompetence of the one who carries his message. Precisely how harm will come is not specified, but it could come in a number of ways. Perhaps a lost message, the garbled nature of the message as delivered, or even the disrespectful way in which a fool might deliver a message—any of these may lead the intended recipient to seek revenge. Perhaps simply the fact that the message is not delivered or is delivered in a negative way will lead to some bad response or no response, which may harm the sender financially. One can compare this warning about the foolish messenger to 10:26, which lampoons the lazy messenger, a type of foolish messenger.

The second proverb speaks of a different type of speech act. Rather than a message, this proverb speaks of a proverb in the mouth of a fool. Such a person may know the proverb, but since proverbs are only true or helpful if uttered in the right context to the right person, then its knowledge and use will prove as ineffective as the legs of a paralyzed person. For instance, one may know the proverbs expressed in Prov. 26:4–5, but if one can't tell which kind of fool one is speaking with, then the knowledge of those proverbs will not help the person.

> ⁸Like a bag of stone in a sling,
> so are those who give honor to a fool.

26:8. The first colon of this proverb is extremely difficult to translate. The only certain word is "stone," so there is not a lot on which to base a certain interpretation. The first word is *ṣĕrôr*, which we here take from *ṣĕrôr* I, similar to Prov. 7:20. However, we note the possibility that it could be *ṣĕrôr* II, "pebble." The third word is *margēmâ*, which apparently is derived from *rgm*, "to stone, to throw stones." We here follow the Greek and modern translations like the NIV and take it as "sling."

Since numerous possibilities of interpretation are plausible, it is not surprising that various commentaries offer other understandings of the verse. Murphy, for instance, translates, "Like tying a stone in a sling, so the one who gives honor to a fool." If one ties a stone in a sling, it can't be thrown.[3] The Jerusalem Bible translates, "Like a bag of [precious] stones on a heap of rocks"—but *'eben* only means precious stones in Zech. 3:9, where the context makes that meaning clear.

In any case, it is difficult to be dogmatic about the point of comparison with giving honor to a fool. However, the main point of the verse is clear: giving such honor is a stupid thing to do (26:1). It is little more than a guess, but I understand the verse to talk about putting a whole bag of stones in the sling, rather than one. In such a situation, the stones would go everywhere rather than in the intended path and thus be ineffective or perhaps even harmful.[4]

> [9]A thornbush in the hand of a drunk,
> and a proverb in the mouth of fools.

26:9. Though it does not have the same grammatical form as the previous verse, this proverb too invites us to compare colon 1 to colon 2. We are to ask how a thornbush in the hand of a drunk is like a proverb in the mouth of a fool, and as we contemplate the comparison, we conclude that it is saying something similar to 26:7. Thus, a fool may be able to learn a proverb but won't be able to apply it to the right circumstance. While v. 7 suggested that such a situation renders the proverb ineffective, this one points out that it can actually be dangerous. A thornbush in the hand of a drunk can cut that hand and maybe even hurt someone nearby. The same is true with a proverb misapplied. Timing is everything when it comes to the truth of a proverb (see "Genre" in the introduction).

> [10]An archer who wounds all,
> and those who hire a fool and those who hire a passerby.

26:10. There are some uncertainties with this proverb, but it seems to me that too many commentators resort to rather uncertain emendations to achieve at best an equally uncertain translation. For instance, the NRSV, supported by Van Leeuwen,[5] emends the second "hire" (*śōkēr*) to "drunkard" (*śikkōr*), thus rendering: "Like an archer who wounds everybody is one who hires a passing fool or drunkard." Since this is

---

3. Murphy, *Proverbs*, 200. This is essentially the view of Whybray, *Proverbs*, 374, and the NRSV and NIV.

4. This seems to be the position of Clifford (*Proverbs*, 231–32), but his translation ("One puts a stone in a sling who gives honor to a fool") does not seem to support it.

5. Van Leeuwen, "Proverbs," 225.

equally as speculative, if not more so, than the Hebrew as we have it, I stick with the Masoretic text.[6]

The comparison here has the same grammatical structure as the preceding verse, the two items simply being placed next to each other. In this case, the objects of the teaching are those who hire a fool or someone who is simply passing by. We are already well acquainted with the fool and understand why someone who hires such a person may be spreading harm (the point of the archer comparison). Fools will not do the job, or if they do, they will do it in an incorrect fashion. The problem with hiring a passerby is that one does not know the nature of the person employed and thus also runs the great danger of causing havoc.

> [11]Like a dog returning to its vomit
> are fools who repeat their stupidity.

26:11. One of the characteristics of fools is their unwillingness to listen to correction. They make mistakes, but since they will not listen to criticism, they are doomed to repeat those mistakes (see also "Openness to Listening to Advice" in the appendix). For this reason, they are compared to a dog that throws up and then eats its vomit. The presumption is that the dog throws up because the food does not agree with it. In spite of that, it eats it again! Second Peter 2:22 makes use of the first colon to refer to false teachers within the Christian community. They knew "the right way to live" (2:21 NLT) but then rejected it, thus returning to their old lifestyle.

> [12]Do you see people who are wise in their own eyes?
> There is more hope for a fool than for them.

26:12. Proverbs makes it clear from the start (1:7) that the only true wisdom is wisdom from God (see "Embracing Woman Wisdom" in the introduction). Human beings are not inherently wise, so it is the ultimate hubris to think oneself wise (3:5, 7; 27:1; 28:11, 26). Humility, not pride, is a quality of the wise (see "Pride/Humility" in the appendix).

The sad nature of this self-wisdom is that there is less hope for such persons than for a fool. Now, one may well respond that those who are wise in their own eyes are fools, but here the proverb is saying they are even worse than fools. See the similar structure in the proverb found in 29:20.

---

6. I commend Snell's treatment of this verse ("Most Obscure Verse in Proverbs"), which I think has nearly equal plausibility with the one that I argue for in the commentary. With a minimum of emendation and a different understanding of some of the roots, he ends up with the translation "A great one makes a fool of everyone, but a drunkard is a fool (even of) passers-by."

> ¹³Lazy people say, "There is a lion cub on the path,
>   a lion in the public square!"
> ¹⁴The door turns on its hinge,
>   and lazy people on their beds.
> ¹⁵Lazy people bury their hand into the bowl,
>   but they are not able to return it to their mouth.
> ¹⁶Lazy people are wise in their own eyes,
>   even more than seven who respond with discernment.

26:13–16. Proverbs parodies laziness more than any other form of foolishness (see "Laziness and Hard Work" in the appendix). This behavior bothers the hard-working sages to the extreme. Here we have a collection of four separate proverbs, some of which virtually repeat previous examples, that form an intense criticism of sloth.

Verse 13 is identical to 22:13 in content and very close in actual wording. The proverb ridicules lazy people for using thin excuses for avoiding work. While it is true that lions could be found in Palestine at this time, they were not so numerous that they could be a legitimate excuse for not leaving one's house. In this case, the "lion" of 22:13 is replaced by "lion cub," a less formidable threat, in colon 1. The second colon does mention the fully grown lion.

The second proverb (v. 14) makes fun of the propensity of lazy people to spend too much time in bed. They are fixed in bed like a door in a socket, and they turn in bed like a door swiveling on a socket. They may move, but they go nowhere; they make no progress. By making fun of lazy people in this way, the sage is trying to motivate the young people whom he instructs to avoid this inappropriate behavior.

The third in the list (v. 15) is a near repetition of 19:24; there is simply a slight change in grammar and syntax. See commentary there.

The problem with lazy people, and probably the reason they perpetuate their self-destructive behavior, is that they are "wise in their own eyes" (see also 3:7; 26:12). As such, they are unwilling to hear the criticism of other people. Indeed, here they claim a sevenfold wisdom, that they are wiser than even seven (the symbolic number for "never-ending" or "many") discerning people.

> ¹⁷Those who yank the ears of a dog,
>   those who grow infuriated in a quarrel not their own.
> ¹⁸Like a madman shooting
>   flaming arrows and death,
> ¹⁹so people who deceive their neighbors
>   and say, "Wasn't I joking?"

26:17-19. These two proverbs (vv. 18–19 constitute a single saying) both provide analogies for foolish behavior that needlessly angers people. The first proverb simply places the two parts of the analogy side by side, but the second uses the comparative particle (*kě*) in order to create a simile. In the latter, v. 18 provides the comparison while v. 19 gives the object of the comparison.

The first proverb (v. 17) ridicules those who would get involved in a fight in which they have no part. It is obviously stupid to pull the ears of a dog. To make sense of the proverb, however, the dog must be understood to be mean, so that such behavior would certainly cause it to bite. The comparison suggests that those who butt into a fight that they have no part in are asking for the same consequence. Both parties may well turn against the person who tries to step in to help or take one of the two sides. The comparison is an observation, but it certainly functions as a warning.

The second proverb (vv. 18–19) considers yet another situation: when people deceive those who are close to them and then claim that it was a joke. From the context it is unclear whether the claim that they were kidding comes before or after the deception is discovered. Certainly, if the admission comes afterward, the claim to be joking would be even weaker. In this case, their speech starts a war. One may as well shoot at neighbors with deadly flaming arrows. Certainly, it will result in the death of any kind of relationship they may have with their neighbors.

> ²⁰Without wood, a fire is extinguished.
>   When there are no gossips, conflict calms down.
> ²¹Adding charcoal to burning charcoal, and wood to a fire,
>   so contentious people to kindle accusation.
> ²²The words of gossips are like choice morsels;
>   they go down to their inmost parts.

26:20-22. These three proverbs are loosely related. The first and the third proverbs are united by speaking of the gossip (*nirgān*). The first and the second make the point that it is the people who make the fights: they don't happen spontaneously. The first makes the point negatively, the second positively. These two proverbs are also united by the repetition of the noun *mādôn*, translated "conflict" in v. 20 and "contentious" in v. 21.

Verse 20 presents an analogy. In the first colon, it makes the obvious point that one cannot have a fire without wood. The second colon claims that conflict is absent when gossips are not present. Gossips create conflict because they are secretly telling negative stories about people.

When those people or their friends discover that they are the brunt of people's negative talk, they will get mad.

This point is told in a positive way in v. 21. Some people just like to pick fights; the proverb refers to them as contentious people. If they are present, it is like piling new charcoal on top of a fire. It will only fan the flames.

The last verse of the section also speaks of gossips, but since this verse is a repetition of 18:8, the reader may refer to the commentary at that point.

> [23]Silver dross overlying clay,
>   smooth lips and an evil heart.
> [24]Those who hate dissimulate with their lips,
>   but they set deception inside.
> [25]Though their voice is gracious, don't believe them,
>   for seven abominations are in their heart.
> [26]Hatred is covered with guile,
>   but they reveal their evil in the assembly.

26:23–26. All four[7] of these proverbs speak of dissimulating speech. The wicked say nice things, but really mean harm. These proverbs serve as warnings not to take what people say at face value.

The first proverb presents its teaching in an imaginative way. It begins by describing how silver can cover clay in order to produce a beautiful jar. However, the silver is only paper thin, and once one penetrates to the inside, one sees that the silver gives way to ordinary clay. The surface gives the illusion of a completely silver vessel, but that is not the reality. The same is true of the smooth speech of someone with evil intentions. The translation footnote to v. 23 indicates that I have emended the text from "burning" to "smooth," in accord with the Greek version, which seems to make more sense. However, I should acknowledge that "burning" might mean "fervent." The reference might thus be to someone who is fervently expressing affection but feeling hate underneath. If so, however, the saying is rather ambiguous since "fervent" would not necessarily be positive.

The second proverb (v. 24) moves in the same direction as the first but does so with a more direct statement. It characterizes those who hate as often hiding their emotions. They dissimulate, probably by saying nice things, while inside their hatred burns. This kind of dissimulation

7. A number of commentators believe that only the first three proverbs are part of this group, but in the latter half of the chapter, they are driven more by the desire to see a symmetry in groups of three than by the content of the verses. The content of v. 26 certainly belongs in this group, and there are problems anyway in treating vv. 26–28 as a group.

is dangerous because one will find an attack coming out of nowhere, perhaps from someone thought to be an ally or friend.

The third proverb (v. 25) moves from observation to advice. It is a call to be skeptical or critical of the speech of others. Always be looking for signs that others are not honestly reflecting their true feelings. This lack of trust is based on what they really are like on the inside. Here, the strong statement concerning "seven abominations" is used. In the first place, "seven" is a symbolic number representing "completion or abundance." Hence, they are totally abominable. The term "abomination" has been used frequently so far in the expression "abomination to Yahweh" (*tôʿăbat Yhwh*: 3:32; 11:20; 12:22; 15:8, 9, 26; 16:5; 17:15; 20:10, 23). It indicates the utmost divine censure against something. It offends Yahweh's "ritual or moral order."[8] The list of abominable things includes "perversity, misrepresentation, deceit, hypocrisy, wickedness, and pride."[9] As Van Leeuwen points out, the language of the phrase "echoes Israel's legal codes (Lev. 19:35–37; Deut. 25:13–15) and the prophetic condemnation of commercial greed and deception (Ezek. 45:10; Hos. 12:7–8; Amos 8:5; Mic. 6:11)."[10]

The last proverb (v. 26) indicates that though people can hide their true thoughts for a while, they will eventually come out in public. There is some ambiguity in the proverb, however. Is this proverb saying that the truth will come out to the detriment of the deceiver? Actually, it seems most likely that the proverb warns that though such people may successfully hide their harmful intentions in private, they are just waiting to go public in order to turn their speech against others to harm them.

> [27]Those who dig a pit will fall into it;
>   those who roll a stone will have it turn back on them.

26:27. This proverb does not seem related to what occurs before or after it. It expresses the idea that those who try to hurt others will be hurt themselves and by their own harmful actions. The idea that the wicked will be hurt by their own actions aimed at others appears with some regularity in the book (see 1:18–19; also Ps. 7:4–5 [5–6 MT]; Eccles. 10:8). The thought of the first colon is clear enough: falling into a pit dug as a trap for another person. The second colon only makes sense if provided with a bit of narrative. We might imagine the wicked rolling a stone to the top of a hill, planning to drop it on the head of a passerby. Instead, as they roll it up the height, its weight proves too much, and it rolls back, crushing the wicked.

8. *NIDOTTE* 4:314.
9. Ibid., 4:317.
10. Van Leeuwen, "Proverbs," 117.

> ²⁸A lying tongue hates those crushed by it,
> and a flattering mouth causes destruction.

26:28. The first colon simply states that people who lie about others hate those people that they are trying to harm. The second colon makes the point that a flattering tongue also causes destruction. Flattery may be taken as a specific type of lying. Without conviction, it exaggerates the positive points of another person. Flattery may be used to set a person up to be taken advantage of. Flattery may also cause those who are flattered to think too highly of themselves and so act in a way that is detrimental.

Chapter 27

Translation

¹Don't brag about tomorrow,
    for you don't know what the day will bear.
²Let a stranger brag about you and not your own mouth,
    someone you don't know and not your own lips.
³Heavy stone and weighty sand—
    a stupid person's irritation is heavier than both.
⁴Wrath is cruel, and anger is a flood,
    and who can stand up in the face of jealousy?
⁵A public correction is better
    than love that is hidden.
⁶Trustworthy are the bruises of a friend,
    and dangerousª are the kisses of the hater.
⁷A sated person tramplesᵇ on honey,
    but to a famished person anything bitter is sweet.
⁸Like a bird wandering from its nest,
    so are people who wander from their place.
⁹Oil and incense make a heart glad;
    the sweetness of a friend more than one's own advice.

a. The meaning of this word is unclear. It comes from a well-attested root ʿātar, "to plead" or "to pray." Here I am following the speculation of Clifford (*Proverbs*, 236), who is guessing based on context (i.e., it should be something that contrasts with "trustworthy" in the first colon) and points out that the versions seem to be guessing as well, with "voluntary" in the Greek and "deceptive" in the Vulgate.

b. I take the verb as coming from *bûs* (to trample) rather than emending to *bûz* (to despise) as some do.

[10]Don't abandon your friend or the friend of your father,
and don't go to the house of your brother when you experience disaster.[c]
Better someone who lives near than a brother far away.
[11]Be wise, my son, and make my heart glad
that I might answer back those who insult me.
[12]Prudent people see evil and hide,
but the simpleminded transgress and are punished.
[13]Take his garment, for he puts up surety for a stranger;
take his pledge for a foreign woman.
[14]Those who bless[d] their neighbors with a loud voice[e] in the early morning—
it will be considered a curse to them.
[15]The constant dripping on a day of heavy rain[f]
is similar to a contentious wife.[g]
[16]Whoever hides her hides the wind,
and oil on his right hand announces.
[17]As iron sharpens[h] iron,
so people sharpen the edge[i] of their friend.
[18]Those who protect the fig tree will eat its fruit,
and those who guard their master will be honored.
[19]As water reflects the face,[j]
so the heart reflects a person.[k]
[20]Sheol and Abaddon are not satisfied,
and the eyes of people are not satisfied.
[21]A crucible for silver and a furnace for gold,
so people in the presence of those who praise them.
[22]Though you grind stupid people with a mortar,
with a pestle among the grains,[l]
their stupidity will not turn aside from them.
[23]Know well the face of your flock;
set your heart on[m] your herds.
[24]For no treasure lasts forever,
nor a diadem for ever and ever.

c. Literally, "on the day of your disaster."
d. Perhaps simply meaning a greeting (see 1 Sam. 13:10; 2 Kings 4:29).
e. I see no reason to take the "loud voice" as implying insincerity, as some commentators suggest (see Murphy, *Proverbs*, 208).
f. The word "heavy rain" (*sagrîd*) occurs only here in Hebrew, but it is connected to Arabic *sagara* (to fill with rain), according to *NIDOTTE* 3:226.
g. Or "woman."
h. I am revocalizing *yāḥad* as *yaḥîd* (hiphil from *ḥdd*) in both cola, though the first is often revocalized as a hophal (is sharpened). The alternative would be to take the verb from *ḥādâ* (to be joyful).
i. Or "face."
j. Literally, "like water, the face to face."
k. Literally, "so the heart of a person to a person."
l. There is no persuasive reason to treat this translated colon as a later addition to the proverb.
m. Or, more idiomatically, "pay attention to."

²⁵The dry grass goes away, and new growth is seen,
  and the vegetation of the mountains is gathered together.
²⁶Lambs, for your clothes,
  and he-goats, for the price of fields,
²⁷and enough goats' milk for your food,
  for the food of your house,ⁿ
  and life for your young girls.

Interpretation

¹Don't brag about tomorrow,
  for you don't know what the day will bear.
²Let a stranger brag about you and not your own mouth,
  someone you don't know and not your own lips.

27:1–2. Warning against bragging unites these two proverbs. The first proverb warns against overconfidence concerning the future.¹ One may think of the bragging done by Ben-hadad, king of Aram, that he would defeat Samaria. At this point the unnamed king of Israel (probably Ahab) responds with what looks like a proverb: "One who puts on armor should not brag like one who takes it off" (1 Kings 20:11 NRSV). Indeed, thanks to divine intervention, the Israelite army repulsed the army of Aram. Of course, our present proverb extends beyond a simply military context. Boasting in the future would entail a claim of one's control over the future, and as we already learned in Proverbs, though one can plan the future, the future is ultimately in the hands of God (16:1, 3, 9, 33).

The second proverb also warns against improper boasting, but here it does not concern certainty about the future, but rather one's character or accomplishments. The sages direct their students not to take it upon themselves to boast, but rather to let others do it. Such teaching shows that the praise of others is something that can be desired. In the NT Paul has extensive teaching about boasting, and the most important point that he makes is that God's people should boast in the Lord. He redirects toward God any praise that might come his way (1 Cor. 1:31; 2 Cor. 10:17), just as Jeremiah does (Jer. 9:23–24).

³Heavy stone and weighty sand—
  a stupid person's irritation is heavier than both.

n. The fact that this translated colon is missing in the LXX may be a sign that it is a later expansion.

1. This proverb may be seen as a variant of those that warn against thinking too much of one's wisdom; see 3:5, 7; 26:12; 28:11, 26.

> [4]Wrath is cruel, and anger is a flood,
>   and who can stand up in the face of jealousy?

27:3–4. These proverbs are united by their common comments on anger, though the vocabulary differs between them. While v. 3 refers to "irritation" (*ka'as*), v. 4 utilizes "wrath" (*hēmâ*), "anger" (*'ap*), and then finally "jealousy" (*qin'â*).

In v. 3 the heaviness of the irritation of a "stupid person" (a term in the semantic range of "folly") outstrips that of stone and sand. Even today, we talk about a "heavy mood" when feeling oppressed. We even can talk about how a mood "weighs heavily" on people and those around them.

The proverb in v. 4 presents a series of growing intensity. It acknowledges the harm caused by wrath and anger but suggests that they pale in light of jealousy. Jealousy is the angry desire to keep what we possess and are afraid someone else wants. The Hebrew word may also imply envy, which is the angry desire for what someone else possesses. It can also be used in a positive sense of "passion" or "zeal" applied to some positive object (like God), but the context makes it clear that the sense here is negative. The rhetorical question implies the answer "No one." Jealousy/envy creates a destructive energy decimating all who fall into its path.[2] See also the comments at 14:30.

> [5]A public correction is better
>   than love that is hidden.
> [6]Trustworthy are the bruises of a friend,
>   and dangerous are the kisses of the hater.

27:5–6. Sages do not fear correction; indeed, they hope for it. After all, how else can they improve? Otherwise, they would be doomed to repeat their past mistakes. In any case, the openness of the correction is helpful; an unexpressed correction would not be. One might expect that kind of parallelism, something along the lines of "a public correction is better than discipline that is hidden," but the contrast is even stronger with the introduction of "love." Love would bring discipline, so that is included here, but the repression of love would serve the object of affection no good purpose.

---

2. Though it is clear that negative jealousy is meant here (see also Ps. 73), there is also such a thing as positive jealousy, for instance, the jealousy God displays toward his people (cf. Exod. 34:14), that also can be reflected in some human relationships. Anger, too, has a positive and a negative side. For more, see D. Allender and T. Longman III, *The Cry of the Soul: How Our Emotions Reveal Our Deepest Questions about God* (Colorado Springs: NavPress, 1994).

That the bruises are those of a friend and are declared trustworthy means that they are inflicted with the good purpose of correction. In other words, the bruises must be the result of constructive criticism brought to bear by a friend. On the other hand, this is contrasted with the pleasant speech and actions of someone who is really an enemy ("the hater") but acts as if they like others and want to affirm them. One must look behind the surface of actions to see what the motives are. Kisses are not always what they seem to be. The paradigmatic example of this is Judas's kiss of betrayal in Matt. 26:48–50.

> ⁷A sated person tramples on honey,
> but to a famished person anything bitter is sweet.

27:7. In the book of Proverbs, the right course of action or saying the right thing depends on circumstances, or timing (see "Genre" in the introduction). Honey is a delicacy, sweet to the taste and providing all kinds of energy. However, for those who are full, it may cause vomiting (25:16). Thus, this proverb says that they trample on it: they reject it out of hand.

On the other hand, anything tastes good to someone who is hungry. Something naturally sweet like honey is spurned by someone with a full stomach; yet even something sour tastes sweet (like honey) to someone whose stomach is empty. The message articulated by this proverb is that it is important to know the situation. In Murphy's words, "Circumstances can make things relative." He also goes on to say that the proverb teaches, "One also loses appetite or zest for certain things precisely because they are so easily attainable."[3]

> ⁸Like a bird wandering from its nest,
> so are people who wander from their place.

27:8. People have a place, most notably a home with family members. To leave that place is as dangerous and foolhardy as a bird leaving its nest. Perhaps this proverb is a warning to those who might think that the "grass is greener on the other side of the hill."

In private correspondence, Andrew Savage, who engaged in a large study comparing biblical proverbs with Tuareg ones, compares this proverb to the Tuareg "The protection of the horse is its stable." As he interviewed contemporary users of this proverb, they understood the idea to emphasize the protection people enjoy in their own place. When people leave home (or birds their nest or a horse its stable), they become

---

3. Both quotes are from Murphy, *Proverbs*, 207.

vulnerable. The proverbs serve as a warning against wandering from one's familiar area.

> ⁹Oil and incense make a heart glad;
>   the sweetness of a friend more than one's own advice.
> ¹⁰Don't abandon your friend or the friend of your father,
>   and don't go to the house of your brother when you experience disaster.
> Better someone who lives near than a brother far away.

27:9–10. Both these proverbs praise friendship and encourage the cultivation of deep and loyal friendships. The first proverb begins by talking about two expensive luxuries that make people very happy, but the second colon (in a "from minor to major" poetic structure) celebrates the sweetness of friendship over one's own advice. That advice, mentioned in the second part of the second colon, may well imply that the "sweetness" refers specifically to the effect of the advice that a friend gives.

The second proverb is quite complex structurally. It is a tricolon, where the initial two cola impart advice about how to relate to friend and relative, and then the third colon proclaims a principle in the form of a better-than proverb.

The first colon advises the hearer not to burn any bridges with friends. Interestingly, this proverb mentions not only one's own friends but also those of one's father. The implication is that when trouble comes or help is needed, one can gain it not only from one's immediate circle of friends but also from one's family's friends, so all these relationships need to be maintained.

The second colon is more puzzling. It advises that one not go to, not appeal to, a brother when trouble comes. For some reason, a brother is seen as less likely to provide assistance in trouble. One can speculate about why friends are privileged over brothers in this proverb. Friends are associated with a person by choice and affection, whereas a brother has no say. However, one might still think that, particularly in an ancient society, relatives would help even if they did not like the person. Perhaps the key to understanding is the last colon, where the brother is thought to live at a distance. Maybe the friend is someone close and the brother far away. But again, ancient society was not as mobile as modern society, so one wonders how often brothers would be split by such great distance.

> ¹¹Be wise, my son, and make my heart glad
>   that I might answer back those who insult me.

27:11. The discourse of the father giving advice to the son reminds us of the dynamic of chaps. 1–9. The same is true for the nature of the advice, which is a general call to seek wisdom. The motivation given for the son to seek wisdom is the benefit that comes to the parents. They are happy because they can respond to the insults of others. Perhaps the insults attack the reputation of the son. If the son pursues wisdom rather than folly, then the father's enemies won't have any fodder for their verbal attacks on the family. That the wisdom of children positively affects their parents may be seen in 10:1.

> ¹²Prudent people see evil and hide,
> but the simpleminded transgress and are punished.

27:12. Here the "prudent" (*ʿārûm*, a word associated with "wisdom") and the "naive" (*pĕtî*, a word associated with "folly") are differentiated based on their ability to navigate life, really the heart of the wisdom enterprise. It is easy to avoid problems if one sees them coming. The prudent have that sense, and this allows them to work around the problems. On the other hand, the naive just plunge ahead and suffer the consequences of their foolish actions. This statement could serve as motivation for working at the acquisition of wisdom. See the identical proverb at 22:3.

> ¹³Take his garment, for he puts up surety for a stranger;
> take his pledge for a foreign woman.

27:13. This verse is substantially the same[4] as in 20:16, for which see the commentary there.

> ¹⁴Those who bless their neighbors with a loud voice in the early morning—
> it will be considered a curse to them.

27:14. This proverb is a specific application of the principle that the sage must learn to say the right thing at the right time (15:23; see also 26:7, 9). In this case, people are just slowly getting up in the early morning; their minds are still groggy. If they in this condition are greeted by someone with a loud, cheerful voice, it can be disturbing. The second colon is a bit ambiguous as to whether the curse refers to the effect of the greeting on the hearer or is what the hearer wants to send back to the speaker. In any case, what is meant as a blessing turns out to be a curse.

---

4. There are some relatively minor grammatical differences, one of which is that "foreigner" is here in the feminine form, which is only the case for the Qere in 20:16.

---

¹⁵The constant dripping on a day of heavy rain
  is similar to a contentious wife.
¹⁶Whoever hides her hides the wind,
  and oil on his right hand announces.

27:15–16. The language of v. 15 is similar to 19:13b, which proclaims that "a contentious wife is a constant dripping." Here the language of 19:13b is broken into two parts and distributed in the two cola of the verse, and the dripping is placed into the context of a heavy rain. The metaphor highlights just how annoying and depressing a contentious wife can be. It seems clear that 27:15 is connected to v. 16 in that the opening verb of v. 16 has a third-person feminine object suffix that must refer to the contentious woman, although the proverb can apply to any contentious person. However, the meaning of the verse is difficult. In terms of 16a, it may be making the point that a contentious woman is hard to hide. The wind cannot be controlled and, though invisible, has noticeable and sometimes chaotic effects. One may try to hide the fact that his wife is contentious, but it is her very contentiousness that will not allow him to control her.

However, if v. 16a is enigmatic, v. 16b is downright obscure. In its original historical setting, what oil on the hand signified was probably well known, but we have lost touch with what it means. Some suggestions include the following. Murphy translates, "And his right hand meets oil." He argues that, like the wind metaphor, it speaks of the inability to control the contentious woman. Trying to grab and control her is like trying to grab something when oil is on your hand. To get this interpretation, Murphy must emend the verb.[5] Clifford translates, "The oil on her hand announces her presence," and suggests that the oil is her perfume, which gives her presence away. He does not address the fact that the possessive pronominal suffix on "hand" is masculine and not feminine.[6] In the final analysis, we simply have to declare that the Hebrew is difficult.

---

¹⁷As iron sharpens iron,
  so people sharpen the edge of their friend.

27:17. This proverb is one of the best-known and often-quoted verses in the book. It is often exclusively cited in connection with male friendship, but there is really no reason to think it does not apply to women.

---

5. From a form of *qrʾ* to a form of *qrh* (or else treat it as a biform); see Murphy, *Proverbs*, 205, 208.
6. Clifford, *Proverbs*, 239.

The rubbing of iron against iron produces a sharp edge, so the only real question has to do with what sharpening a person implies. It is usually understood, and there is no argument against this interpretation, to mean that friends help each other prepare for the ups and downs of life. In the context of the book of Proverbs, this in the first place likely means mutual instruction in matters of wisdom, which would help a person navigate life successfully. It would certainly include receiving and giving correction to foolish behavior and speech. In this way, the friends could avoid making the same mistake in the future. The wisdom enterprise is a community effort.

> [18]Those who protect the fig tree will eat its fruit,
>   and those who guard their master will be honored.

27:18. The proverb encourages the wise to take good care of those who employ them for their professional services. The proverb pivots on the use of "fruit" for consequences or rewards. Just as those who "protect" (or perhaps simply "take care of") a fig tree will have the benefit of the fruit, so those who guard (again perhaps "take care of") their employer will have good reward, here "honor," but the word may also imply beneficial material reward.

> [19]As water reflects the face,
>   so the heart reflects a person.

27:19. This concisely worded proverb (see the translation footnotes) has some ambiguity in interpretation. The translation supports the idea that the image is that of water functioning as a kind of mirror, reflecting one's face back to oneself. In this way, the point of colon 2 is that the heart tells the story of the person. The heart is a general reference to one's character. Thus, character defines who and what a person is.

On the other hand, perhaps the second line is saying that the heart reflects the person to another person. So it is not so much self-revelation, but rather revelation of another.

In any case, the idea, taught elsewhere in Proverbs, is that the heart of a person is what counts. Other proverbs mention that one's words reflect the heart of a person (12:23; 16:23; 18:4).

> [20]Sheol and Abaddon are not satisfied,
>   and the eyes of people are not satisfied.

27:20. This proverb is about the impossibility of fulfilling desires. Sheol and Abaddon, at a minimum, represent the grave and therefore death. Even if they imply some kind of conscious existence after death, they still here personify death, which is never satisfied. There is always room for one more dead person; they cannot get enough. Like death, human craving can never be satisfied. One can never have enough money, power, pleasure, relationship, love, and on and on. The proverb helps people become self-aware and also aware of what makes other people tick. If we know that desires are never truly satisfied, then perhaps this may help to slow our pursuit of needless things. Ecclesiastes is well aware of this endless cycle of desire, and it comes to a pessimistic conclusion concerning the meaning of life (2:10–11; 5:10; etc.). Pursuing ultimate satisfaction is like chasing the wind.

> [21]A crucible for silver and a furnace for gold,
> so people in the presence of those who praise them.

27:21. This proverb invokes a refining metaphor again. Indeed, the first colon is identical to the first colon of 17:3, where the refinement is done by God. Metalworkers separate silver and gold from impurities by a process of heating the metal until the dross can be poured off. The result of the process is pure silver and pure gold. So the second colon presents a circumstance that can lead to moral refinement of a person. The circumstance is receiving praise. Precisely how this leads to positive results is not explicitly stated. We speculate that receiving praise from another provides a tremendous temptation for self-boasting. Refusing to let that produce pride is not an easy task. However, if one resists, then the person will be better off for the effort.[7]

> [22]Though you grind stupid people with a mortar,
> with a pestle among the grains,
> their stupidity will not turn aside from them.

27:22. There is not much you can do with stupid people. This proverb and others like it may explain why some people just do not respond to wisdom instruction. The metaphor of grinding in a mortar may very well imply physical punishment and would fit in with other proverbs that

---

7. Clifford (ibid., 240) rejects this interpretation because he believes it "obscures the parallelism," though I don't see how it does. In its place, he offers an interpretation that is certainly possible, given the ambiguity of the language. He suggests that a person's character is tested (refined) by the quality of the people who praise him or her. To arrive at this position, he first of all notes that refining will determine the quality of the ore. He then says that a person's character is determined by the character of those who praise him or her. If wise people offer the praise, then that indicates that the person is indeed good.

talk about the ineffectiveness of even such tactics in the case of fools (17:10). However, some fools are teachable (22:15).

> ²³Know well the face of your flock;
>   set your heart on your herds.
> ²⁴For no treasure lasts forever,
>   nor a diadem for ever and ever.
> ²⁵The dry grass goes away, and new growth is seen,
>   and the vegetation of the mountains is gathered together.
> ²⁶Lambs, for your clothes,
>   and he-goats, for the price of fields,
> ²⁷and enough goats' milk for your food,
>   for the food of your house,
>   and life for your young girls.

27:23–27. This section has its most immediate setting in an agricultural scene. The sage encourages the farmer-shepherd to take care of his flocks and crops for the well-being of his household. The motive clause in v. 24 suggests that such care is necessary even if the farmer has some "money in the bank." If one lives off past surplus ("treasure"/"diadem"), the proverb warns, and neglects one's day-to-day work, the surplus will run out, and then the crops and animals will not be there to provide for sustenance. This proverb unit seems to advocate a fundamental dependence on renewable resources, such as letting fresh grass replace dried grass and gathering vegetation from the mountains as crops for food. Lambs and goats provide food, milk, and clothes. All that is really necessary for life are associated with the things that are part of a farmer's daily life. Dreaming of treasures and diadems may distract people from what is really important over the long haul.

That wisdom is concerned about the right strategy to sustain life may be seen in the book of Ecclesiastes, where a lengthy passage gives advice to work hard in the light of the risks of life:

> Send your bread upon the surface of the waters, for after many days you may find it. Give a portion to seven, even to eight, for you do not know what evil may occur in the land. If the clouds are full, they will empty rain on the earth; and whether a tree falls south or north, the place where the tree falls, there it is. Those who watch the wind do not sow, and those who observe the clouds do not harvest. In the same way that you do not know what is the way of the wind or how the bones are formed in the mother's womb, so you do not know the work of God, who does all things. In the morning plant your seed, and do not let your hand rest at evening. For you do not know which will succeed, whether this or that, or whether both will do equally well. (11:1–6)[8]

8. For the translation and commentary, see Longman, *Ecclesiastes*, 254–58.

Though farming and shepherding are the surface meaning of the text, Van Leeuwen and others suggest that this passage is really emanating from and directed toward the royal court. The hint of this is supposedly the reference to "diadem" in v. 24. This hardly seems sufficient to make his argument. However, since "shepherd" is a metaphor for "king" elsewhere in the Bible (e.g., Ezek. 34) and the ancient Near East, it certainly could apply in principle to the court. Indeed, the passage may very well, as with many proverbs, be taken as a general principle that applies in many areas of life: Take care of the necessities of life.[9]

9. See R. C. Van Leeuwen, *Context and Meaning in Proverbs 25–27*, Society of Biblical Literature Dissertation Series 96 (Atlanta: Scholars Press, 1988), 131–43; idem., "Proverbs," 233; and Malchow, "Manual for Future Monarchs."

Chapter 28

Translation

¹The wicked flee,[a] though no one pursues,
  but the righteous are confident like a lion.
²When a land commits an offense, many are its leaders,
  but with people of understanding knowing thus, they last a long time.
³Poor people who oppress the destitute
  are rain that washes away so there is no food.
⁴Those who abandon instruction praise the wicked,
  but those who guard instruction battle them.
⁵Evil people do not understand justice,
  but those who seek Yahweh understand everything.
⁶It is better to be a poor person and walk blamelessly,
  than one with crooked paths[b] and wealthy.
⁷A child who understands protects instruction,
  but those who associate with gluttons humiliate their father.
⁸Those who increase their wealth by interest and surcharge
  will have it accumulated for those who give relief to the poor.
⁹Those who turn their ear from hearing instruction,
  even their prayers will be an abomination.
¹⁰Whoever causes those with integrity to go astray on an evil path
  will fall into his own pit,
  but the blameless will inherit good things.

a. Clifford (*Proverbs*, 242, quoting GKC §145) explains that the plural verb is appropriate when, as here, the subject is a collective singular.

b. The Masoretes have vocalized this as a dual, which may be an allusion to the "two paths," but since here the paths are called "crooked" and elsewhere the good path is said to be straight, it would be an odd way of referring to the two paths.

[11]The wealthy are wise in their own eyes,
 but a poor person of understanding examines him closely.
[12]When the righteous rejoice, there is much glory,
 but when the wicked rise up, people hide.[c]
[13]Those who simply conceal their wickedness will not succeed,
 but those who confess and abandon it will receive compassion.
[14]Blessed are those who are continually fearful,
 but may those whose hearts are hard fall into harm.
[15]A growling lion and a prowling bear—
 a wicked ruler over a poor people.
[16]A prince who lacks understanding is a cruel oppressor,
 but one who hates unjust profit[d] will live long.
[17]A person oppressed by the murder of another—
 don't hold him from flight to the pit.
[18]Those who walk in innocence will be saved,
 but those who twist paths will fall in one.
[19]Those who work the land will have plenty to eat,
 but those who pursue emptiness will have poverty.
[20]Reliable people have abundant blessings,
 but those who rush to make themselves rich will not remain unpunished.
[21]Those who show favoritism are not good;
 people transgress even for a crust of bread.
[22]The stingy make haste to riches,
 but they do not know that deprivation will come to them.
[23]Those who reprove find favor afterward[e]
 more than a flattering tongue.
[24]Those who steal from their father and their mother and say,
 "I did nothing wrong!"
 Such people are the friend of a destroyer.
[25]The greedy[f] stir up conflict,
 but those who trust Yahweh are refreshed.
[26]Those who trust in their own heart are fools,
 but those who walk in wisdom will escape.
[27]Those who give to the poor will lack nothing,
 but those who avert their eyes will have numerous curses.
[28]When the wicked rise up, people hide,
 but when they are destroyed, the righteous increase.

c. There is some dispute over the verb here (*yĕḥūppaś*), which is in the pual but translated according to its hitpael meaning. A hint that we have the proper meaning here may come from the near parallel in 28:28, though there the verb is from *str* rather than *ḥpś*.

d. The word *bṣ*[c] often connotes material gain achieved by violence (so Harland, "*Bṣ*[c]").

e. I make here a minor textual correction by ignoring the first person suffix, literally "after me," which does not communicate meaning in the context.

f. Literally, "wide of appetite." Such persons are greedily trying to fill their gigantic desire.

Interpretation

Malchow ("Manual for Future Monarchs") argues that chaps. 28 and 29 are a manual for future monarchs. However, as is typical of such attempts to find deep structure, the effort fails on close analysis. Take, for instance, the first grouping within these chapters. Malchow argues that 28:2–11 "centers on law and justice to the poor" (p. 240), a topic certainly appropriate for future rulers. However, once one reads this section, we see that (1) most of the proverbs have nothing to do with this subject (vv. 2, 4, 7, 9, 10), and (2) even those proverbs that have to do with the poor are not addressed to the king (v. 3, though Malchow conveniently agrees with an emendation that has little in favor of it on strictly text-critical grounds). We therefore reject his overarching approach to chaps. 28 and 29. However, it is certainly true that kings (and others) should read and observe the wisdom of these proverbs.

> ¹The wicked flee, though no one pursues,
> but the righteous are confident like a lion.

28:1. The contrast between the wicked and the righteous could not be stated more clearly or in more contrastive terms. The wicked are afraid and thus run away from conflict, so much so that they even run before there is a fight. This may indicate their bad conscience. As many other commentators point out, the language of flight even without pursuit is found also in the covenant curses of Lev. 26:17, 36. They know they don't have a leg to stand on. On the other hand, the confidence of the righteous is likened to a lion. The comparison implies that they are well prepared to take care of any assault that comes their way. They do not fear any person, only Yahweh (Prov. 1:7).

> ²When a land commits an offense, many are its leaders,
> but with people of understanding knowing thus, they last a long time.

28:2. The translation of the first colon is relatively clear, and its point is almost as transparent. Basically, the point is that the offense of a land will lead to a proliferation of leaders, which is not a good thing. Long-lived benevolent rulers are the best circumstance for a nation, providing security. The offense may well be a rebellion, which itself could inject instability into a country. The many leaders may point to the fragmentation of a previously united land or perhaps to a succession of leaders as they violently jockey for power.

The second colon provides the most difficulty in this proverb. While all the words in the colon are easily recognized, the syntax is difficult. In particular, the difficulty is to know the relationship between "understanding" (*mēbîn*) and "knowing" (*yōdēaʿ*). Murphy adopts a different understanding of the syntax: "but with a person intelligent, knowing—stability will endure." However, this translation also entails understanding *kēn* (we translate "thus") as a word that means "stability," which Murphy himself calls "doubtful."[1]

According to our translation, the second colon is simply asserting that people of understanding know that an "offense" will lead to trouble, and they avoid giving offense (or rebelling) and thereby avoid the destructive consequences.

> [3]Poor people who oppress the destitute
> are rain that washes away so there is no food.

28:3. Those who try to get something out of the poor are trying to get "blood out of a rock," as the modern saying goes. This proverb envisions a particularly pitiful scene as poor people oppress poor people, leading to devastating results. People who have nothing try to get something from people who have nothing, which leads to nothing. The rains that wash away food may refer to crop-destroying rains that ruin a harvest (see 26:1). Murphy believes that the phrase "poor people" needs to be understood as referring to the "formerly poor" who have come into some money but nonetheless show no mercy to those who are in the same circumstances they formerly experienced. This seems unnecessary since it is very possible to imagine a circumstance where one poor person might oppress another.[2]

> [4]Those who abandon instruction praise the wicked,
> but those who guard instruction battle them.

28:4. The contrast is between those who reject instruction and those who affirm it. One group caves in to wickedness, while the other not only resists it but also fights it. The exact referent of "instruction" (*tôrâ*) is not clear. At a minimum, instruction points to the teaching of the sages in the book of Proverbs. However, we need to be open to the possibility, especially as the book is now situated in a larger canon, that the word may refer to the law of God in the Torah.

> [5]Evil people do not understand justice,
> but those who seek Yahweh understand everything.

---

1. Murphy, *Proverbs*, 212.
2. Clifford (*Proverbs*, 243) recognizes this, but he seems to be stretching it to suggest that something as particular as "tax-farming" lies behind this proverb.

28:5. The first colon is clearly true. Understanding involves more than mere awareness of a concept of justice. It implies that they appreciate it. Evil people don't want to understand justice because they live lives that are at odds with justice. On the other hand, those who desire to be in relationship with Yahweh do understand. One question we may ask is, What does the proverb mean by "everything"? It would seem a strange arrogance to claim complete understanding of anything in the universe. It probably is best to delimit the "everything" to matters of justice. Those who seek Yahweh, after all, are wise, and they want to know what Yahweh's will is. Yahweh defines the nature of justice, so by pursuing Yahweh, they come to know what justice entails. Clifford rightly captures the sense of this proverb: "People bent on evil are not wise; they do not know judgment in the sense that they do not see the divine justice that eventually will catch up with them. On the other hand, those seeking Yahweh understand 'all things,' including Yahweh's rewarding them and punishing the wicked."[3]

> [6]It is better to be a poor person and walk blamelessly,
> than one with crooked paths and wealthy.

28:6. This better-than proverb provides a relative judgment between integrity and wealth. Nothing is wrong with wealth in and of itself, but if a decision must be made, it is clear that integrity is more important, and riches should be sacrificed. The metaphor of walking on a path, so familiar from chaps. 1–9, underlies this proverb. There are two paths, one good (here described as "blameless") and one bad (here "crooked/ twisted"). Proverbs 19:1 provides a similar idea.

> [7]A child who understands protects instruction,
> but those who associate with gluttons humiliate their father.

28:7. The proverb, presuming a wise father, gauges the child's wisdom by whether the parent is shamed by his or her actions. As in 28:4, the term "instruction" (*tôrâ*) could hypothetically refer either to the commands of God in the Torah or to the father's advice. Elsewhere in Proverbs, the father encourages moderation, and a lack of control in one's diet is criticized (23:1–3). It is possible that instruction here refers to the advice that we find represented in Proverbs itself, but we should also refer to Deut. 21:18–21, where a stubborn and rebellious son is further described as a "glutton and drunkard." There the Torah allows for the stoning of

3. Ibid., 244.

the child. In the present proverb, even associating with gluttons is condemned, though association may presume participation.

> [8]Those who increase their wealth by interest and surcharge
> will have it accumulated for those who give relief to the poor.

28:8. Wealth is good and often considered a sign of wisdom and the blessing of God (3:9–10; 10:15, 22), but not always. Proverbs recognizes that some people amass wealth illegitimately (11:18; 21:6; 22:16), and one such illegitimate way is through charging interest. Charging interest to fellow Israelites was against the law (Exod. 22:25 [24 MT]; Deut. 23:20). Here the consequence is that wealth would be taken away and given to someone who would be kind to the poor. Proverbs often encourages generosity to the poor (11:24; 28:27; 29:7, 14). In the present verse, the implicit assumption may be that that these people are gouging the poor by charging them interest but that whatever material is gained by this strategy will be returned to the poor. The mechanism of the "gathering up" of this inappropriately gained wealth is not specified, but the assumption may be that God will see that it happens.

> [9]Those who turn their ear from hearing instruction,
> even their prayers will be an abomination.

28:9. This proverb again speaks of the importance of "instruction" (see also 28:4, 7). Here even more than in the previous contexts, the question of the referent of "instruction" is unclear. However, since we found it likely that vv. 4 and 7 included both the wisdom instructions of the book of Proverbs and the commandments of the Torah, we may rightly assume the same is true here. Not hearing an instruction implies disobedience, and the point of the proverb is God will not listen to the prayers of those who do not listen to his instructions. Abomination is a strong negative; for an explanation see 3:22; 11:1; 20:23.

> [10]Whoever causes those with integrity to go astray on an evil path
> will fall into his own pit,
> but the blameless will inherit good things.

28:10. It is bad enough being wicked, but it is doubly bad to make those who are walking on the straight path go astray. Those who might be tempted to influence the righteous to act wickedly are warned that they are the ones who will suffer.[4] Here and elsewhere in Proverbs, the

---

4. Van Leeuwen ("Proverbs," 238) points out the similar teaching in the New Testament (Matt. 5:19; Luke 17:1–2).

wicked are told they will experience the pain that they want to inflict on others. On the other hand and in contrast, the blameless, those who do act with integrity and wisdom, will inherit good things. The good things are not specified, but one might imagine things like wealth, health, spiritual vitality, and a good family life.

> ¹¹The wealthy are wise in their own eyes,
>   but a poor person of understanding examines him closely.

28:11. This proverb strikes out at pretense. The contrast between the wealthy and the poor is just to make the contrast between those who pretend and those who can see through the pretense all the more dramatic. In Proverbs, wealth is better than poverty, but as people use wealth to self-delude and delude others, then wealth is worse than poverty. The expression "in their own eyes" is used in a number of places in Proverbs (3:7; 12:15; 26:5; 30:12) to refer to self-presumption. Wealth can sometimes cloud the mind so that the rich think they have more resources than they do. It can breed conceit and a feeling of self-reliance. On the other hand, a person of understanding, even if poor, can see through this pretense.

> ¹²When the righteous rejoice, there is much glory,
>   but when the wicked rise up, people hide.

28:12. Righteousness is the ethical side of wisdom, and wickedness the ethical side of folly. The proverb comments on community benefits of wisdom versus the disadvantage of folly. The righteous rejoice when wisdom prevails, and when wisdom prevails there is success, not just for the individual but also for the society as a whole. Much glory accrues to the community where wisdom makes its influence felt. This wisdom influence is probably gained by the presence of wise leaders. The second colon describes the reaction of the people when wicked fools "rise up" and take control. They hide for fear that bad consequences will fall on them, through either abuse or neglect.

> ¹³Those who simply conceal their wickedness will not succeed,
>   but those who confess and abandon it will receive compassion.

28:13. Wickedness, the ethical side of folly, does not lead to success in relationships, work, and life in general. This is true whether wickedness is blatant or acted on clandestinely. In order to reverse their fate, the wicked must confess their wickedness and then demonstrate their commitment by desisting from wicked actions. At that time, they will receive mercy or compassion. This compassion may come from fellow human beings, but the unspoken agent of mercy is God himself.[5] At bottom, this verse (like 28:11) is against pretense and for openness and mercy. Murphy is helpful pointing out that this is the only verse in Proverbs calling for confession. He also observes that in Proverbs "one can 'cover' the faults of another (Prov. 10:12), but not one's own sins."[6] Improvement only comes when people listen to criticism and are open to acknowledging their faults and changing their lifestyle.

> [14]Blessed are those who are continually fearful,
> but may those whose hearts are hard fall into harm.

28:14. This is an interesting proverb in the light of present-day desires to rid life of all stress. The sages here apparently are commending fear over insensitivity. It does not seem that the fear meant here is specifically "fear of Yahweh," which typically uses the verb *yr'* (1:7) rather than *phd*, as we have here.[7] Fear has a way of keeping people alert to potential problems. If one does not experience a certain level of stress, then it is likely that complacency will set in, and sooner or later negative consequences will result. After all, it is a fear of not being able to pay bills that helps motivate most of us today to get up early and go to jobs. In antiquity, if there were not the fear of starvation, it would likely have been just as tempting to stay in bed rather than rise early and tend the crops and animals. In short, worry has a redemptive value. On the other hand, those whose hearts are hard, in the sense of unfeeling, will suffer for the opposite reasons.

> [15]A growling lion and a prowling bear—
> a wicked ruler over a poor people.

28:15. This proverb presents an image of comparison by simply listing the objects. The first colon presents two animals, the lion and the bear, both known as dangerous. The danger is intensified by the addition of the modifiers "growling" and "prowling." These are animals in search for prey that they can consume. In the second colon, the wicked ruler is mentioned, and we are to understand the ruler as the third violent and vicious animal. This ruler's prey is his own poor people. Tyrants in the past, even as today, were known to suck the lifeblood of their people,

---

5. See Crenshaw, "Concept of God."
6. Murphy, *Proverbs*, 216.
7. The idea of this verse is similar to that of 14:16, where I suggest that the unspecified "fear" might be shorthand for "fear of Yahweh." However, the earlier verse uses the verb *yr'* rather than *phd*. But, again, it is not impossible that this verse also implies "fear of Yahweh."

making themselves affluent while their people were impoverished. This comparison is an observation, but an observation that serves as a warning about wicked rulers. Subjects of a wicked ruler could generally do little about the circumstance, but it would warn them to walk carefully when they lived under a wicked ruler.

> [16]A prince who lacks understanding is a cruel oppressor,
>   but one who hates unjust profit will live long.

28:16. This proverb does not appear to be perfectly balanced in its two parts, but it still makes sense without resorting to emendation.[8] The proverb is associated with the previous one according to the theme of the "evil ruler." In any case, the two cola contrast bad and good rulers. The first colon describes a cruel oppressive ruler as one who is without "understanding," a word that is closely related with wisdom. In the second colon, we read about "one," that is, a prince, who hates an unjust profit. Though the term is not specifically used, this prince is obviously one who has "understanding," that is, wisdom. Wisdom is an ethical category, and by not exploiting people in economic ways, this prince is showing himself to be wise. As is well known in Proverbs, wisdom leads to life.

> [17]A person oppressed by the murder of another—
>   don't hold him from flight to the pit.

28:17. This proverb upholds the dignity of human life. If people take a life, their own lives are forfeit (Gen. 9:5–6). Here the first colon describes someone who has taken the life of another person and feels oppressed or tormented by that act. Indeed, the second colon, admittedly difficult to understand with certainty, seems to suggest that the person is suicidal. That is likely what is suggested by the statement that such a person is on a flight to the pit, with "pit" standing for the underworld.[9]

The proverb offers no comfort to such a person—indeed, just the opposite. The sages advise the hearer that they offer the tormented person no help. It does not encourage a person to hurry the murderer's dash to death, but it does prohibit hindering it.

> [18]Those who walk in innocence will be saved,
>   but those who twist paths will fall in one.

---

8. Murphy (*Proverbs*, 213), for instance, takes his cue from the Greek and translates: "A prince, lacking in revenues, increases oppressions—whoever hates unjust gain will prolong his days."

9. Johnston, *Shades of Sheol*.

28:18. The metaphor that drives this proverb is that of the path, so pervasive in the first part of the book but also found sporadically in chaps. 10–31 as well. There are two paths: straight and twisted. The first colon presupposes the former. Those who walk in innocence will be saved. This raises the question "From what?" At least, the person will be saved from trouble and an early death. The opposite of those who walk on the (impliedly) straight paths of innocence are those who walk on the twisted paths. Twisted paths presume evil. In any case, such will fall. Stumbling on the path means encountering problems that are not overcome. The difficulty attendant on the second colon is the meaning of the prepositional phrase "in one." Commentators handle this in different ways,[10] but in the final analysis we cannot be dogmatic.

> [19]Those who work the land will have plenty to eat,
> but those who pursue emptiness will have poverty.

28:19. This proverb is another version of the warning against the dangers of laziness. Hard workers get rich; lazy people are soon poor (see "Laziness and Hard Work" in the appendix). Here, as elsewhere (10:5), this truth is expressed in agricultural terms. The point is obvious. If people go out and do the work of planting, caring for their crops, and harvesting, they will have plenty of food for themselves and their families. But if, instead of concentrating on the important work of crop maintenance, they fritter their time away on nonessential matters, then they will have nothing at harvesttime. Like all proverbs, this one is true if all things are equal. It does not intend to take into account all the possibilities. A storm or a drought may undermine even the hardest efforts, but if one does not do the labor, then there is no chance for a good crop. See 12:11 for a nearly similar proverb.

> [20]Reliable people have abundant blessings,
> but those who rush to make themselves rich will not remain unpunished.

28:20. Proverbs worries about those who rush to get rich (13:11). Experience showed that it led to shortcuts that were ethically dubious. In contrast to the overhasty, this proverb presents those who are "reliable." This word indicates people who are ethical and trustworthy. The conse-

---

10. Murphy (*Proverbs*, 213) argues that the phrase means "quickly" or "suddenly." On 216, however, he seems to take a different approach, suggesting that "paths" is a dual in Hebrew and thus refers to double-mindedness. To fall into one means that double-dealing will eventually catch up with people, and they will fall into one of the two ways. Clifford (*Proverbs*, 243) simply omits it as a gloss, using a dubious argument built on syllable counting.

quences of reliable behavior are the rather vague "blessings." According to the parallel, these blessings were probably thought to include riches, and certainly a number of other proverbs also associate material gain with wisdom (as in 3:15–16). However, it is also likely that the blessings could have been understood even more broadly to include things like relational happiness or long life. The punishment of those who rush to riches also goes unspecified. Such could include the deep disappointment of the sudden loss of those riches, since other proverbs understand the gain of get-rich-quick schemes as short-lived.

> ²¹Those who show favoritism are not good;
>   people transgress even for a crust of bread.

28:21. The first colon is similar, though not identical, to what is found in 24:23, where the idiom "recognize the face," translated "show favoritism," is explained. There the context is more explicitly the courtroom since the expression "in justice" is added, but the courtroom setting is the most natural primary context for this proverb as well. However, the principle is broader and would certainly cover other areas such as showing favoritism in business practices. The second colon provides the motivation for those who do show favoritism: personal gain. It parodies those who are willing to show favoritism by pointing out that they engage in such an unethical practice for the slightest kind of bribe.

> ²²The stingy make haste to riches,
>   but they do not know that deprivation will come to them.

28:22. The expression "stingy" is a translation of "evil eye,"[11] for which see the translation footnote for 23:6. This proverb, like 28:20 and other passages (21:6), displays the sages' contempt for those who try to find shortcuts to riches. Those who are stingy with their time and money would not to any great extent want to invest either into the acquisition of more. However, the proverb informs them that they have a surprise waiting for them: not more, but less.

> ²³Those who reprove find favor afterward
>   more than a flattering tongue.

28:23. We have already been introduced to the idea that constructive criticism is better than superficial and misleading praise (13:1; 17:10). It

---

11. An argument based on this context, however, suggests that "greedy" might be a good translation of this difficult expression; for which, see Whybray (*Proverbs*, 395) and Murphy (*Proverbs*, 217).

is also the subject of this proverb, with its encouragement of reproof over flattery. Although it is true that initially people are likely to get a bad reaction from those whose faults they are highlighting, this proverb indicates that favor, gratitude for the advice, will come not immediately but "afterward." Proverbs is interested in cutting through pretense and getting to the truth of a matter. This proverb motivates honest assessment of others.

> [24]Those who steal from their father and their mother and say,
>   "I did nothing wrong!"
> Such people are the friend of a destroyer.

28:24. Proverbs insists that children show proper respect for their parents (20:20; 30:11–14, 17). A number of these passages presuppose that the parents are godly, and probably this proverb does as well. However, the principle of not stealing would apply to anyone, and those who stoop low enough to rob their parents, no matter what their parents were like, would earn the sages' contempt. Their actions destroy relationships of the most intimate type. What is particularly horrible about their behavior is that they do not feel remorse. Perhaps they feel a sense of ownership of their parents. The "destroyer" may refer to a particularly dangerous criminal type (see also 18:9). Such children may think that they are simply taking what belongs to them by virtue of being members of the family, but in reality they are no better than a criminal from outside the family. Such a proverb may be seen to derive from the commandment to honor one's parents (Exod. 20:12). If one is stealing from them, one is certainly dishonoring them.

> [25]The greedy stir up conflict,
>   but those who trust Yahweh are refreshed.

28:25. The contrast here is between those who are greedy and those who trust Yahweh. Those who trust Yahweh do not have to grasp after things to find satisfaction with their lot in life. As the greedy push for more, they annoy and even anger others from whom they are trying to grasp the things they need to feed their overweening desire. Thus, fights break out. On the other hand, those who put their trust in Yahweh are content with life.

> [26]Those who trust in their own heart are fools,
>   but those who walk in wisdom will escape.

28:26. Wisdom entails fear of Yahweh (1:7) and an aversion to self-reliance (3:5, 7; 26:12; 27:1; 28:11). To trust in one's own heart (note the linkage by contrast to the second colon of the previous proverb) is the epitome of folly because the heart is limited in its knowledge and also, apart from relationship with God, wicked. The sage would have agreed with Jeremiah, who in 17:9 states: "The human heart is most deceitful and desperately wicked. Who really knows how bad it is?" (NLT). As is taught in numerous places in Proverbs, fools are on the road to death (1:19, 32; 2:18; 8:36; 9:18; etc.), which may be implied here by the explicit statement in the second colon that those who walk (a metaphor suggestive of the path theology of the book) in wisdom will be rescued. The proverbs typically leave general the danger from which the wise are rescued, but they would at least include things like relational entanglements and early death. Reading the text from a NT perspective would allow an even richer understanding of this rescue.

> ²⁷Those who give to the poor will lack nothing,
>   but those who avert their eyes will have numerous curses.

28:27. Proverbs consistently teaches that those with means must be generous toward the poor. This proverb motivates such generosity with the promise that the giver will lack nothing. This would imply that God would take care of such a person and would undercut the primary fear behind not giving. Not to give is a form of control and a human attempt to grasp at security. To give requires the giver to trust more. Those who don't give, according to the second colon, will only increase their troubles. It remains unspecified who or what is the driving force behind the curses, but one might think of God as the ultimate referent. Van Leeuwen comments in regard to this verse, "The paradox of giving to the poor and having no lack is characteristic of one whose trust is in God."[12]

Proverbs is not in favor of wholesale charity, however. In the light of the extensive teaching on laziness (see "Laziness and Hard Work" in the appendix), it is unlikely that the sages would encourage giving help to those who themselves are simply unwilling to work. Furthermore, Proverbs would say that one either should give the money away or not help at all. Loans that were expected to be repaid are strongly discouraged at a number of points in the book (6:1–5; 11:15; 17:18; etc.).

> ²⁸When the wicked rise up, people hide,
>   but when they are destroyed, the righteous increase.

28:28. The first colon is a close variant of 28:12b, and the thought is essentially the same. When wicked people are in positions of power and

---

12. Van Leeuwen, "Proverbs," 240.

influence, the harm that results is such that people "head for the hills," if they can. People go underground because if their rulers are wicked, then it is likely that they will abuse those under their power. On the other hand, when these abusive leaders or influence peddlers are destroyed, then the righteous can increase. Such a situation bodes well for the public good. This proverb, among many others, points out that wisdom benefits not just the individual but also the community.

Chapter 29

Translation

[1]A person who often receives reproof[a] is stiff-necked;[b]
he will be suddenly broken, with no healing.
[2]When the righteous increase, the people rejoice,
but when the wicked dominate, the people moan.
[3]Those who love wisdom make their father rejoice,
but those who associate with prostitutes destroy riches.
[4]A king with justice causes the land to endure,
but the tax man tears it down.
[5]People who pour out flattery on their friends
are spreading out a net for their feet.
[6]In the offense of the evil man is a trap,
but the righteous sing[c] and rejoice.
[7]The righteous know the just cause of the poor,
but the wicked do not understand knowledge.
[8]Mockers blast[d] a city,
but the wise turn back anger.

a. Literally, the phrase is "man of reproof," which seems in context to indicate those whose lives are characterized by reproof and implies that they do not respond to correction.

b. For the expression "stiff-necked," see Exod. 32:9 and Deut. 31:27. It is an idiom that means "extremely stubborn."

c. Clifford (*Proverbs*, 249) works too hard to achieve a closer parallelism by emending the verb to a form of *rûṣ*: "but a righteous person runs rejoicing."

d. Or "inflame" (so Clifford, *Proverbs*, 251). The verb is *pûaḥ*, "to blow."

⁹The wise debate the stupid,
   and there is agitation and scoffing and no rest.
¹⁰Murderous people hate the innocent,
   and the virtuous seek their lives.
¹¹A fool lets nothing go unexpressed,ᵉ
   and the wise quiet things down afterward.
¹²A ruler who pays attention to a false word—
   all those who serve him are wicked.
¹³The poor and the exploiters have a common bond—
   Yahweh gave light to the eyes of both of them.
¹⁴A king who judges the poor reliably—
   his throne will be established forever.
¹⁵The rod and correction impart wisdom,
   but youths who are unsupervised shame their mothers.
¹⁶When the wicked increase, offense increases.
   As for the righteous, they will see to their downfall.
¹⁷Instructᶠ your son, and he will grant you ease
   and give you delight in your life.
¹⁸When there is no vision, the people cast off restraint,
   and whoever guards the law—blessed.
¹⁹By words servants are not instructed.
   Though they understand, there is no response.
²⁰Do you see people who are hasty with their words?
   There is more hope for a fool than for them.
²¹Pamper one's servants from youth,
   and later on they will be trouble.
²²Angry people stir up conflict,
   the wrathful much offense.
²³The arrogance of people causes them to fall;
   but a lowly spirit holds glory tight.
²⁴Those who divide plunder with a thief hate their own lives.
   They hear an imprecation, and don't say anything.
²⁵Anxiety about peopleᵍ is a trap,
   but those who trust Yahweh are protected.
²⁶Many are those who seek the face of the ruler,
   but justice for humanity is from Yahweh.
²⁷The unjust are an abomination to the righteous,
   and the straight path is the abomination of the wicked.

e. Literally, "a fool lets out all his spirit." I do not see how "spirit" signifies specifically "anger," as in NIV and NRSV, but see it rather as referring to all emotions.

f. Or, perhaps, "discipline." The verb is *ysr*, the verbal root of the noun *mûsār*, which we have been translating "discipline."

g. Conceivably, the genitive relationship can be understood as subjective ("people's anxieties") rather than objective ("anxiety about people"). In that case, the anxiety would be more generalized and not specifically toward people.

Interpretation

> ¹A person who often receives reproof is stiff-necked;
> he will be suddenly broken, with no healing.

29:1. The proverb addresses the danger of not listening to those who constructively criticize. Those who are repeatedly warned about behavior that has potentially dangerous consequences but do not listen (are stiff-necked) will find all of a sudden that the consequences have caught up with them, and they will have moved beyond the point where an easy fix is possible. The purpose of the proverb is not just to explain why some people reach a bad end but also to encourage the wise not to reject criticism. For similar teaching about listening and not ignoring criticism elsewhere, see "Openness to Listening to Advice" in the appendix.

> ²When the righteous increase, the people rejoice,
> but when the wicked dominate, the people moan.

29:2. This proverb is similar in thought to 28:28 as well as 28:12. The contrast is between a situation in which the righteous are dominant and in control and one in which the wicked are the major influence in society. In these circumstances, the well-being of the people is at stake. They rejoice when the righteous are in control because they will lead the community with wisdom and with justice. As a result, the community will prosper. However, they moan if the wicked are in control, because, at best, they will make foolish decisions, and, at worst, they will exploit the people.

> ³Those who love wisdom make their father rejoice,
> but those who associate with prostitutes destroy riches.

29:3. The first colon is a general statement. A wise child makes a father rejoice. Here we may clearly see that the father himself is understood in the proverb to be a wise man. After all, what other kind of father would rejoice at the wisdom of a child? The contrast between colon 1 and 2 has to do with "wisdom" and "folly." Though the latter word is not used in the second colon, we know well that consorting with prostitutes is an act of fools (see chaps. 5–7). Here the trouble caused by sleeping with prostitutes is financial. That does not mean that this is the only problem with associating with prostitutes; after all, proverbs are not nuanced or exhaustive statements. And it is true that prostitutes are expensive women. It is unclear whether the riches are those of the father or the son, but especially if the former (unless the latter is gained by inheritance), we can see why such foolish behavior would lead to the sadness of the father.

> [4]A king with justice causes the land to endure,
> but the tax man tears it down.

29:4. This proverb likely cannot be used to argue against all taxes as detrimental to a nation. The tax man (literally, "man of tribute") is a person whose influence and motivation are defined by "taxes."[1] Likely, this person's taxes are to be understood as unjust since the contrast is with the just king of the first colon. Unjust taxation takes all the energy out of the land. Samuel also warned Israel that the king they wanted could well turn out to be an exploiter and detrimental to the people (1 Sam. 8:10–18).

On the other hand, the first colon describes the king who rules justly. Such a strategy leads to the long-term health of the land.

> [5]People who pour out flattery on their friends
> are spreading out a net for their feet.

29:5. Proverbs speaks consistently against flattery (5:3; 6:24; 7:5, 21; 26:28; 28:23). Flattery is different from encouragement because the latter is based on the truth. As the proverb indicates, flattery hypes people but does not help them; rather, it harms them. The harm is communicated here by the image of the net that is spread out. Just as a net is set out in secret and camouflaged from the prey, so flattery sets up people for a fall.[2] Flattery might, for instance, convince people that their abilities are superior to what they really are. Thus, when they try to act on their supposed abilities, they fall flat. Closer to the intention of the proverb, however, is the idea that the flatterer is buttering up the recipients in order to gain an advantage over them or a favor from them. In any case, the sages warn their listeners to beware of such a tempting thing as flattery, since it will lead to trouble. In Prov. 5–7, we see that the strange woman uses flattery to lure the man into her bed, causing him much harm.

> [6]In the offense of the evil man is a trap,
> but the righteous sing and rejoice.

---

1. In many contexts this word (*tĕrûmâ*) refers to contributions to the cult (Lev. 10:12–13; Num. 18:8–19; cf. *NIDOTTE* 4:335), but the context here is clearly political and not cultic.

2. Some commentators note what they think is an ambiguity in the suffix on "feet." They say it may refer not to the one flattered but to the flatterer. See Whybray, *Proverbs*, 399. I find this possible but unlikely.

29:6. To the wicked and sometimes even to the righteous (see Ps. 73), it seems as if sin is the way to get ahead in life. The wicked often seem to prosper, while the righteous suffer. But as this proverb points out, that is only true from a superficial look. Sin complicates life, setting traps for the sinner. On the other hand, righteous behavior leads to rejoicing. The Christian takes the long view on retribution. Although in the short run the righteous may suffer for their righteousness, the future brings rejoicing.

> 7The righteous know the just cause of the poor,
> but the wicked do not understand knowledge.

29:7. The sages are often stereotyped as callous rich who believe that God blesses them with their wealth and that poverty is a sign of God's displeasure with folly. It is true that some proverbs hold out the reward of riches for the acquisition of wisdom (3:9–10, 15–16), and the fear of poverty for the lack of it. However, the proverb is a generally true proposition, not a promise. It is true if all things are equal, but often all things aren't equal. Sometimes the wise are poor because of an injustice or a natural disaster. Thus, the wisdom of Proverbs also calls for compassion and action in favor of the poor.

The second colon is a bit awkward in terms of its relationship with the first; it seems to imply that by their lack of compassion for the poor, the wicked show they are not on the side of the wise, who would "understand knowledge." As most commentators point out, this knowledge, like wisdom in general, refers to "an active, caring concern."[3]

> 8Mockers blast a city,
> but the wise turn back anger.

29:8. Mockers are radical fools. They not only lack wisdom; they also ridicule those who do. When they have influence over a city,[4] whether officially or by their own assertions, they rock it in negative ways. They are those who would take a bad situation and intensify it into a riot. On the other hand, the wise are coolheaded. In a bad situation, they would calm tempers for the good of the community.

> 9The wise debate the stupid,
> and there is agitation and scoffing and no rest.

---

3. Van Leeuwen, "Proverbs," 243.
4. Thus, I agree with Van Leeuwen (ibid., 243) that this proverb is fundamentally a "political observation." Murphy (*Proverbs*, 221) points out that in Isa. 28:14, the word "mockers" is used for "arrogant politicians."

29:9. When the wise and fools get into a debate, this proverbs asserts, there is not a reasoned discussion that leads dispassionately toward resolution. There is chaos. The fool (here called "stupid") will not listen to correction (see references at 29:1) and will just cause trouble. For this reason, 26:4 allows for the possibility of not entering into a debate with a fool to begin with.

> ¹⁰Murderous people hate the innocent,
> and the virtuous seek their lives.

29:10. Commentators are thrown into a tizzy with this verse.[5] The first colon is clear and easy to understand. Murderers don't care for the innocent. They are evil and care only for themselves. They prey on the innocent. It is the second colon that is problematic because the idiom "seek their lives" is commonly recognized as an expression meaning that they desire to kill them. But why is this problematic? It certainly is not unethical, at least in the OT world, to desire to put murderers to death (Gen. 9:5–6 NLT: "And murder is forbidden. Animals that kill people must die, and any person who murders must be killed. Yes, you must execute anyone who murders another person, for to kill a person is to kill a living being made in God's image"). The proverb observes a conflict between criminals and those on whom they prey, a conflict that has continued to the present day.

> ¹¹A fool lets nothing go unexpressed,
> and the wise quiet things down afterward.

29:11. Fools may not listen well, but they certainly talk a lot. Their talk gets them into trouble and also agitates others. They are not emotionally intelligent, and their talk will often inappropriately express emotions that will only inflame a situation.

On the other hand, the wise, who are coolheaded, speak only when necessary and helpful. They also can clean up the mess started by the speech of fools.

> ¹²A ruler who pays attention to a false word—
> all those who serve him are wicked.

29:12. According to this proverb, it all begins with the ruler's lax ethics. If the ruler shows himself open to unethical influence, then everyone will take advantage of that fact. A wicked ruler leads to wicked officials

---

5. See, for instance, Murphy (*Proverbs*, 222) and Clifford (*Proverbs*, 251–52).

serving under him. This proverb puts the ultimate blame for a troubled reign squarely with the person at the top. A psalm of David declares that the psalmist will not tolerate deception and fraud: "Only those who are above reproach will be allowed to serve me. I will not allow deceivers to serve me, and liars will not be allowed to enter my presence. My daily task will be to ferret out criminals and free the city of the LORD from their grip" (Ps. 101:6b–8 NLT).

> ¹³The poor and the exploiters have a common bond—
> Yahweh gave light to the eyes of both of them.

29:13. On the surface of things, nothing could seem to be farther apart than the rich and the poor, and particularly the rich who exploit the poor in order to get rich. The rich live lives of ease and luxury; the poor are dirty and scrape by in life. But this proverb points to a very important truth: they are both God's creatures.

We might imagine that the intention of the proverb is to bring hope to the poor. Perhaps, however, it was meant to serve as a warning to those who exploit them and treat them like the dirt under their feet. Perhaps the proverb served both purposes. In any case it fits in with a group of proverbs that urge care for those who are poor (29:7, 13). The proverb that is closest to it in concept as well as form is 22:2.

> ¹⁴A king who judges the poor reliably—
> his throne will be established forever.

29:14. This proverb bolsters the teaching that the righteous wise are characterized by compassion for the poor. This is particularly the case for the king, who is charged by Yahweh to care for all the socially vulnerable. Those in power are not to exploit those who are weak, but rather to take care of them. Here the king who does so is encouraged by the possibility of a strong reign.

> ¹⁵The rod and correction impart wisdom,
> but youths who are unsupervised shame their mothers.

29:15. The sages believed that people left to their own natural tendencies are bad and would get worse. Though there is no explicit connection, this idea certainly fits in with the rest of the biblical teaching about the inherent sinfulness of postfall humanity. Thus, "youths" are anything but innocent.

It takes energy to move from the state of folly to that of wisdom. Correction is required, and that often will have to be accompanied by the "stick." Physical punishment in the service of wisdom education is a common theme in Proverbs (see "Physical Discipline" in the appendix). With the strong emphasis on emotional moderation throughout the book, this teaching certainly does not encourage parental abuse. Indeed, this proverb raises the question whether abuse is suffered when there is no discipline in a young person's life. Parents are motivated to do the hard work of correction in order to avoid the shame that a wayward child brings on a family.

> ¹⁶When the wicked increase, offense increases.
> As for the righteous, they will see to their downfall.

29:16. The proverb begins with the observation that as the wicked increase, so do the number of offenses (see also 28:12, 28; 29:2). The verb "increase" seems most naturally to point to numerical increase but may also imply a growth in strength. Actually, as the wicked increase in number, it is natural to think that they also increase in their strength of influence. The offenses may be seen as sin against the law and crime against society, which are often intertwined.

The second colon points out that the predominance of the wicked is always temporary. In the end, the righteous will win. Clifford may well be right in how he connects the two cola: "When a wicked faction becomes numerous, it sows the seeds of its destruction through the increase in offenses against others. . . . The very increase of the wicked class will bring about its downfall, for offenses bring social unrest as well as divine retribution."[6]

This proverb could be read as a word of warning to the wicked: You may be strong now, but it won't last. The proverb is also a comfort to the righteous during a period where it appears that the lawless dominate.

> ¹⁷Instruct your son, and he will grant you ease
> and give you delight in your life.

29:17. This word of advice is directed toward parents and is another admonition to engage in the tough work of instructing children. Whereas parental neglect of instruction will lead to tremendous problems in the future (see 29:15), this proverb gives positive reinforcement to the parent. Instruct the child now, and in the future the parent will not have to deal with the problems that arise from a wicked child.

The second colon could be translated, "and give you delicacies in your throat." This could be narrowly interpreted to refer to the good

---

6. Clifford, *Proverbs*, 253.

eating that a well-employed and generous child will provide for an aged parent. But my translation prefers the more metaphorical and inclusive understanding of the phrase.

> [18]When there is no vision, the people cast off restraint,
> and whoever guards the law—blessed.

29:18. The first colon presents a bad situation. No vision leads to a lack of restraint. Though often quoted, the lack of vision is hard to define and is sometimes used today in an almost mystical sense. After all, vision (*ḥāzôn*) comes from a verb (*ḥzh*) often used to describe the revelatory experience of the prophets (Isa. 1:1; 2:1; 13:1; Amos 1:1; Mic. 1:1; Hab. 1:1), though it is also used for the simple act of seeing (Prov. 22:29; 29:20; Dan. 3:19, 25, 27; etc.).[7] Here it is unlikely to refer to the idea of prophetic revelations. Two other related possibilities present themselves, more closely related to the verb's simple meaning of "seeing." In the first place, it could be a vision of the end, a goal. In the second, it could also include the idea of the "plan" to achieve that goal. The meaning of the colon seems to warn that those who don't have a goal and/or a plan for the future have nothing to guide them onward, so they go every which way. The "vision" restrains them because it suggests a strategy to achieve that goal.

The second colon may allow us to become even more specific. This colon pronounces "happy" or "blessed" those who "guard" (keep) the law. The law or instruction[8] may be what provides the "vision" of colon 1. Pitiful are those who lose sight of the instruction that guides them into the future. I find strained the interpretation that sees this as a late addition to the book, charting the cessation of prophetic activity in the postexilic period and its replacement by the primacy of the Torah.[9] Again, such an interpretation is dependent on associating *ḥāzâ* with prophetic activity rather than its more general sense of simple "seeing."

> [19]By words servants are not instructed.
> Though they understand, there is no response.

29:19. The sages operated by the principle that wisdom is not an inherent human quality. Their teaching implies that people in their natural state are naive, or foolish. It takes work to become wise. They also thought that it is harder to educate some people than others to do

---

7. See *NIDOTTE* 2:56–61.

8. For the debate concerning the reference of *tôrâ* in Proverbs, see comments at 1:8; 3:1; 6:20, 23; 7:2; 13:14; 28:4, 7, 9; 31:26.

9. So Whybray, *Proverbs*, 403.

the wise thing. Here we see that "servants" were thought by the wise to be particularly difficult to train. Words alone won't do it. It is not that they are not intelligent enough to understand intellectually what they are being told. The second colon affirms that they do understand but that there is no response. This likely indicates a lack of desire to carry out the commands of the master. It appears that they need something more to motivate them (perhaps fear of the rod? See "Physical Discipline" in the appendix). Whybray appropriately cites Papyrus Insinger 14.11: "If the rod is far from his master, the servant will not obey him."[10] Though physical discipline of a servant may well be implied here, Murphy rightly reminds us: "Bodily injury is punishable by law" (Exod. 21:20–21, 26–27).

> [20]Do you see people who are hasty with their words?
> There is more hope for a fool than for them.

29:20. The sages frown on impulsivity in speaking or action (15:28; 19:2; 20:18, 25; 21:5). If people blurt something out, it is likely that they will say something stupid. The wise reflect on their words before they speak. Those who do not are "worse than a fool," though it is hard to imagine what that would be! See a similar structure in the proverb in 26:12.

> [21]Pamper one's servants from youth,
> and later on they will be trouble.

29:21. The punchword, *mānôn*, here translated as "trouble" based on a suggestion by Murphy,[11] is impossible to render with any degree of certainty. It only occurs here in the Hebrew Bible, and it has no clear etymology. What is clear is that pampering[12] a servant (thus, not heeding the warning of 29:19) is a mistake and will lead to unfortunate consequences.

> [22]Angry people stir up conflict,
> the wrathful much offense.

29:22. Proverbs recognizes that some people are angry. They are not angry about anything in particular, but if something arises that "sets them off," the conflict is on. Such behavior is not helpful. Conflict generated

---

10. Ibid., 403.

11. Murphy, *Proverbs*, 220.

12. Also, like *mānôn*, the word *mĕpannēq* is a *hapax legomenon*, but its meaning is made more certain by its use in postbiblical Hebrew and Aramaic (see *NIDOTTE* 3:641).

by anger hurts the social fabric and thus is an "offense." The sages promoted the coolheaded approach to difficulties and put down hotheads; nothing is more hotheaded than an angry person. For other proverbs on the detrimental effects of anger, see "Anger" in the appendix.

> ²³The arrogance of people causes them to fall;
> but a lowly spirit holds glory tight.

29:23. In a number of places, the sages warn concerning pride and promote humility (see "Pride/Humility" in the appendix). The proverb here contributes to this important theme. Humility is valuable for the wisdom enterprise because it depends on a teachable spirit. Wisdom is not a natural trait that needs to be preserved in a human. Folly is natural; wisdom must be inculcated. To do so, people need to be open to criticism of their words and behavior. They hear and change. On the other hand, because of pride fools will resist criticism, even mocking those who try to help them in this way. The results are clear. The proud are doomed to repeat their mistakes and end up falling, while the humble will gain glory. The paradox of the teaching is that a "high" spirit will come crashing down, while a "low" spirit will be lifted up.

> ²⁴Those who divide plunder with a thief hate their own lives.
> They hear an imprecation, and don't say anything.

29:24. At first this proverb is enigmatic to the modern reader, but it is understandable against the background of the law found in Lev. 5:1:

> If a person does wrong:
>   When he has heard a public imprecation (against withholding testimony)—and although he was a witness, either having seen or known (the facts)—yet does not testify, then he must bear his punishment.[13]

The situation envisioned in the proverb is of persons so closely associated (by sharing in the crime) with a robber that they will not or cannot testify against the criminal. Leviticus 5 describes a judicial circumstance when testimony against a criminal is called for on pain of curse/imprecation. However, because of the association, the person will not step forward, thus opening up the possibility of the curse resting on him, which could mean his own death.

This proverb is a specific instance of the broader proverbial warning against consorting with the ungodly (1:8–19).

13. The translation is from J. Milgrom, *Leviticus 1–16*, Anchor Bible (New York: Doubleday, 1991), 292. See also his supporting discussion on 293–96.

> 25Anxiety about people is a trap,
>   but those who trust Yahweh are protected.

29:25. At heart, when read in the context of the whole book of Proverbs, this verse is stating something akin to "perfect love casts out fear" (1 John 4:18 NRSV). Those who trust Yahweh have nothing to fear from any person. Another way of conceptualizing the thought of Proverbs on this subject is to think that one who fears God (1:7) does not fear human beings. God can protect his people from human harm. As Ps. 56:11 says:

> In God I trust; I will not be afraid.
> What can man do to me? (NIV)[14]

However, anxiety about people is a trap that even the most religious can fall into, and it is a hard one to get out of.

> 26Many are those who seek the face of the ruler,
>   but justice for humanity is from Yahweh.

29:26. When people want something done, they go to the one with the power to do it. For justice, the obvious person to go to is the political leader, and in ancient Israel that person was the ruler. To seek the face of persons is to try to get into their presence, in order to make one's request. People clamor to meet the ruler to get done what they think needs to be done.

The first colon makes this observation, but then critiques it in the second colon. The ruler is not the one who can assure justice in this world; it is Yahweh. The implication of the second colon is that people should be clamoring to get into the presence of Yahweh. One might also remember that—according to the theology of 1 Sam. 12; 2 Sam. 7; and elsewhere—whatever power the Israelite ruler has is from God, who is the true and ultimate king of Israel.

> 27The unjust are an abomination to the righteous,
>   and the straight path is the abomination of the wicked.

29:27. In the early part of the book, we grew familiar with the phrase "abomination to Yahweh" (*tôʿăbat Yhwh*: 3:32; 11:1 [see lengthy discussion at this verse], 20; 12:22; 15:9, 26; 16:5; 17:15; 20:10, 23) to indicate the utmost divine censure against something. Here the term "abomination"

14. Cited by Van Leeuwen, "Proverbs," 245.

is the same Hebrew word, but instead of something being an abomination to Yahweh, we have the "righteous" and the "wicked" specified. By structuring the verse in this way, we are able to see the relative values of these two groups, and we see precisely how much in contrast they are. On the one hand, the righteous find the unjust repulsive; on the other, the "straight path" (spoken of frequently in the first part of the book and associated with God's way) is despised by the wicked. The righteous find the straight path wonderful, and the wicked embrace the unjust path.

Part 5

Sayings of Agur and King Lemuel and Poem to the Virtuous Woman

(30:1–31:31)

The final division of the book of Proverbs contains four sections (or possibly three, if one views all of chapter 30 as constituting the sayings of Agur). The first half of chapter 30 (30:1–14) comprises sayings of an otherwise unknown man named Agur, who is identified as a Massaite, a non-Israelite. The second half of the chapter (30:15–33) contains seemingly unrelated, mostly numerical, proverbs. The final chapter of the book has two distinct sections. The first (31:1–9) is the sayings of King Lemuel, also identified as a Massaite, in which he repeats the instructions of his mother. The second section (31:10–31), which closes the book of Proverbs, is a poem celebrating the noble woman. She epitomizes and embodies the characteristics of Woman Wisdom emphasized throughout the book.

Chapter 30

Translation

¹The words of Agur, the son of Yaqeh, the Massaite.
 The utterance[a] of the man: "I am weary, O God;
 I am weary, O God, and I am exhausted.
²Actually,[b] I am a dullard more than a person,
 a man of no understanding.
³I have not learned wisdom,
 nor do I have knowledge of the Holy One.[c]
⁴Who has gone up to heaven and come down?
 Who has gathered the wind by the handful?[d]
Who has bound up water in a garment?
 Who has established all the ends of the earth?
What is his name and the name of his son,
 if you know it?"

a. The Hebrew term *nĕʾūm* is usually and often connected with a divine oracle. However, E. Strömberg Krantz ("'A Man Not Supported by God': On Some Crucial Words in Proverbs xxx 1," *Vetus Testamentum* 46 [1996]: 549) has noted three (though she lists only two!) instances where "*nĕʾūm* is not used in immediate conjunction with YHWH," Num. 24:3–4 and 2 Sam. 23:1.

b. I follow the suggestion to take the *kî* as an asseverative (see Franklyn, "Sayings of Agur," 244).

c. This is similar to Prov. 9:10, which shows this phrase in parallelism with the divine name (see Whybray, *Proverbs*, 408).

d. On the basis of an Ugaritic cognate, Cathcart ("Proverbs 30,4") has suggested that *bĕhopnāyw* here means "garment" rather than "handful." This is possible, but one cannot be dogmatic about it. Malul ("*Kappî*") ends up with the same meaning, based on his research that words meaning "hand/lap" also can often be used to refer to the garment that covers the lap. However, one must question the premise that leads them to search for an alternate reading. In Malul's case, it is because he feels he must have a closer parallel to the following colon, but this seems a rather mechanical approach to parallelism. See the more recent article by Cathcart ("*Bᵉhopnāw*") in which he continues to support his and Malul's approach, but he points out that Malul is wrong, at least in his treatment of the Ugaritic evidence, to conclude that the word means both "hand/lap" and the garment that covers that area. He believes that they represent two different words.

⁵All the speeches of God are refined;
  they are a shield with which to take refuge.
⁶Don't add to his words,
  or he will correct you and show you to be a liar.
⁷Two things I ask of you;
  don't withhold them from me before I die.
⁸Fraud and lying words—
  keep far from me!
Poverty and wealth don't give to me!
  Allow me to devour my regular allotment of bread,
⁹lest I am sated and act deceptively
  and say: "Who is Yahweh?"
Lest I don't have much and I steal,
  and I profane^e the name of my God.
¹⁰Don't slander a servant to his master,
  lest he curse you and you stand under the curse.
¹¹There is a type of person^f who curses their father
  and does not bless their mother.
¹²There is a type of person who is clean in their own eyes,
  but they have not cleaned off their own excrement.
¹³There is a type of person—how haughty their eyes!
  How raised their eyelids!
¹⁴There is a type of person whose teeth are swords;
  their jaw is a butcher's knife,
to consume the needy from the land
  and the destitute from humanity.
¹⁵The leech has two daughters: "Give, give!"
  There are three things that are never satisfied,
  four that never say "Enough!"
¹⁶Sheol and a barren womb,
  a land that is not saturated with water,
  and fire that does not say "Enough!"
¹⁷An eye that ridicules one's father
  and despises the teaching of one's mother,
may ravens of the wadi pick it out,
  and the young of the eagle eat it.
¹⁸Three things are too wonderful for me,
  and four things I cannot figure out:
¹⁹The way of an eagle in the sky,
  the way of a snake on a rock,
The way of a ship in the heart of the sea,
  and the way of a man with a young woman.

e. Literally, "to take hold of" (*tpś*), but in this context "profane" or "blaspheme" seems an appropriate and well-accepted translation.

f. Typically, this word (*dôr*) means "generation," but in this context the word seems to signify a class or type of person.

²⁰This is the way of an adulterous woman:
   she eats and wipes her mouth,
   and she says: "I have done nothing wrong!"
²¹Under three things the earth trembles,
   and under four it cannot bear up:
²²under a servant when he becomes king
   and a blunderhead when sated with food,
²³under a disdained woman when she gets a husband
   and a maidservant when she dispossesses her mistress.
²⁴There are four things among the smallest on earth,
   but they are the apex of wisdom:ᵍ
²⁵Ants as a group are not strong,
   but in the summer they ready their food.
²⁶Coneysʰ as a group are not powerful,
   but they make their homes in the crags.
²⁷Locusts do not have a king,
   but they advance together in ranks.
²⁸You can gather lizards in your hand,
   but they are in the palaces of a king.
²⁹There are three things that are excellent in gait,
   four that are excellent as they walk:
³⁰a lion, a warrior among beasts
   and does not back down before anything;
³¹the strut of a roosterⁱ or a he-goat,
   and a king accompanied by an army.ʲ
³²If you have been acting disdainfully in pride,
   or if you have been scheming—
   put your hand to mouth!ᵏ
³³For pressing milk yields curds,
   and pressing the nose yields blood,
   and pressing anger yields accusations.

Interpretation

30:1–14. *Sayings of Agur.* The "words of Agur" passage is easily the most difficult section of the book of Proverbs to translate and understand. We begin with the person of Agur. We simply have no real idea of who this individual is. He is not mentioned in biblical or extrabiblical texts.

g. "Apex of wisdom" is, literally, "they are the wise among those who are wise."

h. See Ps. 104:18; also called "rock badgers."

i. Following the versions, the Hebrew *zarzîr* is a *hapax legomenon*.

j. *ʾAlqûm* is a *hapax legomenon*, though the context suggests something like we have rendered here. Murphy (*Proverbs*, 233) believes that the problem is one of word division and suggests "the king at the head of his people" (*qm ʿl ʿmw*).

k. The Hebrew of this colon is curt, having simply "hand to mouth."

We also do not know the identity of his father, Yaqeh. We are perhaps on a bit more solid ground with the phrase "Massaite," because this seems related to the name of a tribe in Arabia related to the Ishmaelites mentioned in Gen. 25:14 and 1 Chron. 1:30. The only hesitation we have here is that the MT reads "oracle" (*maśśāʾ*), and to make the identification with the tribe work, a minor emendation is necessary (*hammaśśāʾî* or *mimmaśśāʾ*). The emendation is supported, however, by the fact that "oracle" would likely not be followed immediately in the next line by "utterance" (*nĕʾūm*).

If the identification of Agur as an Arabian wise man is correct, then that raises interesting questions as well. Why is a non-Israelite cited in the book? Certainly, this problem is not equivalent to, say, a non-Israelite prophet or priest[1] being commended in Scripture. After all, Israelite wisdom is not so much contrasted with non-Israelite wisdom as declared superior to it (1 Kings 4:29–34). Indeed, one might be tempted to say that the words attributed to Agur are so convoluted and, in what we think we understand, self-abasing, that it makes that very point! But then we have a second Massaite quoted in chap. 31, Lemuel's mother, which prevents us from making that point!

The next question has to do with the number of verses that we should attribute to this section. The answer to this question may be provided by a look at the Greek translation of Proverbs, which has a different structure. In sequence after 24:22 come 24:22a–e; 30:1–14; 24:23–34; 30:15–33; 31:1–9; chaps. 25–29; 31:10–31. This, of course, raises a whole host of issues (see "Text" in the introduction), but what is of interest to us here is the fact that 30:1–14 and 30:15–33 are clearly treated as two different sections. There still remains disagreement over the precise boundaries of Agur's passage. Murphy, for instance, takes all of vv. 1–14 as belonging, but some like Van Leeuwen point to the parallelism in vv. 11–14 as closer to what we have in vv. 15–33.[2] I wonder, however, whether that connection between the end of vv. 1–14 and the beginning of vv. 15–33 is what suggested the MT binding of these two units.

There is even some discussion of whether there is more than one voice in the first four verses. Whybray attributes vv. 1b–3 to a skeptical speaker, but then v. 4 to an orthodox response or God's own answer.[3] Our own approach is to consider vv. 1–4 as the address of Agur.

Finally, there is a question of whether to take Agur's words, using the alternatives articulated by Franklyn, as skeptical or pious affirmation. We accept his reasoning, based partly on the similarity between

1. Melchizedek is a mysterious exception!
2. See Murphy (*Proverbs*, 226–27) and Van Leeuwen ("Proverbs," 250–52).
3. Whybray, *Proverbs*, 107.

the rhetorical questions posed in v. 4 with Job 38 (see vv. 5, 6, 25, 28, 29, 36, 37, 41; see also 39:2), that we see here "strong religious affirmation on the heels of a frank confession of human frailty, ignorance, and uncertainty."[4] In a later article supportive of Franklyn's main thesis, Moore suggests the perspective that Agur's speech toward the end of the book should be read in the light of the enthusiastic comments on the acquisition of wisdom. In his words, he asks the following question: "Doesn't it seem significant that a book, which begins with exuberant invitations to young men to pursue the promise of wisdom, winds down with reverent reflections of an old man pointing toward essentials which wisdom cannot give?"[5]

The issues of translation are more detailed and will be mentioned in the verse-by-verse exposition that follows.

> ¹The words of Agur, the son of Yaqeh, the Massaite.
> The utterance of the man: "I am weary, O God;
> I am weary, O God, and I am exhausted."

The issues surrounding the introductory colon are addressed in the above paragraphs. Here we concern ourselves with the translation and meaning of the "utterance of the man." This phrase occurs in connection with a Balaam oracle in Num. 24:3–4 as well as introducing an oracle of David in 2 Sam. 23:1 (see vv. 2–7). What follows is among the most disputed lines in Biblical Hebrew. We will first give the Hebrew transliteration, followed by options, and finally some arguments that move us toward our final tentative translation (the sources for the possible translations below may be slight variants of the actual quoted version):

lĕʾîtîʾēl[6] *lĕʾîtîʾēl wĕʾūkāl*

1. Prophecy of this man for Ithiel, for Ithiel and for Ucal (traditional, NJB, NIV).[7]
2. I am not God; I am not God, that I should prevail (NAB, Murphy).
3. I am weary, O God, I am weary, O God, and I am exhausted (NLT, NRSV, REB, Clifford, Longman).

Interpretation 1 is the traditional rendering, taking the difficult words for personal names, always a choice of last resort. True, Ithiel is a name

4. Franklyn, "Sayings of Agur," 251.
5. Moore, "Home for the Alien," 104.
6. Interestingly, Murphy (*Proverbs*, 226) observes that *lĕʾîtîʾēl* forms a palindrome, a word that is spelled the same forward and backward..
7. First proposed by Torrey, "Proverbs, Chapter 30."

found in Neh. 11:7 and may mean something like "God is with me," but again, this translation is unlikely and should not be supported unless all else fails, and even then it might be better simply to put in blanks!

Interpretation 2 gets its inspiration from Aramaic, where *lā' îtay 'ēl* (a redivision and repointing of *lě'îtî'ēl*) means "I am not God." The redivision of the word is not a large problem, but the repointing is a bit more problematic, and the appeal to Aramaic makes it an even more difficult translation to defend.

Though it too has its criticisms, the third interpretation requires the least emendation and seems to fit into the context. This approach takes *lě'îtî'ēl* as a first-person verbal form from *l'h*, "to be weak, weary." It separates the *'ēl* and treats it as a vocative. The verb is repeated, and then the third verb is slightly repointed from *'ūkāl* to *'ekel* (from the root *klh*). The resultant translation fits in well with the rather depressing continuance of the speech.

> 2"Actually, I am a dullard more than a person,
>   a man of no understanding.
> 3I have not learned wisdom,
>   nor do I have knowledge of the Holy One."

We take these words as those of Agur. They are clearly self-effacing. Those who would be truly wise must first acknowledge their ignorance. Agur is obviously not someone who is "wise in his own eyes." People must first recognize their own ignorance before they can turn to God for true insight.

The language, however, is extreme. He calls himself a "dullard." The word "dullard" (*ba'ar*) is a strong one and refers to a person "who does not have the rationality that differentiates men from animals."[8] We have encountered this word already in 12:1, where it surprisingly refers to those who refuse correction. However, here we have someone who calls himself a dullard, showing self-awareness. In 12:1, that label was applied to another; by the nature of the case, the person so designated would not accept the label. Another text where someone, in retrospect in this case, calls himself a "dullard" is in Ps. 73:22. Here the psalmist, consumed by envy, questions the divine wisdom and justice as he sees the wicked prosper while the wise struggle:

> I was a dullard and I did not know;
>   I was like an animal to you. (author's translation)

8. *NIDOTTE* 1:691.

520

In Proverbs, Agur describes himself as more a dullard than a person, perhaps also implying that the status of the dullard is that of animal intelligence or even lower. He also describes himself as one who has no wisdom and no knowledge of the Holy One. If the latter is the correct translation—though "holy things" is also possible—then we can see the connection. After all, "fear of Yahweh is the beginning of knowledge" (1:7), as we have learned all along. However, I believe we are to understand the language of these two verses as hyperbolic. The truly wise know just how ignorant they are. Those who think they are wise do not think they have to put any further effort into the acquisition of insight.

> 4"Who has gone up to heaven and come down?
>   Who has gathered the wind by the handful?
> Who has bound up water in a garment?
>   Who has established all the ends of the earth?
> What is his name and the name of his son,
>   if you know it?"

This lengthy verse may be compared to a number of other passages that ask questions designed to awaken recognition of the ignorance of human knowledge and the inaccessibility of divine wisdom. In these other contexts, such an argument serves to shape a dependence on God's wisdom rather than on one's own.

We begin with the well-known divine speech in Job 38–39. Up to this point in the narrative, the suffering yet innocent Job has been appealing to God for an audience where he can present his case. Though here Job gets the audience he hopes for, he does not get to present his case; instead, God blasts him with questions that serve to put Job in his place. God begins with "Who is this who questions my wisdom with such ignorant words?" (Job 38:2 NLT). God then peppers him with questions to show him his ignorance, and Job submits before him.

Job was one who, in the words of Prov. 30:4, thought he "had gone up to heaven" to receive God's wisdom and "come down." At least that is the impression he has given to Eliphaz, who charges Job in 15:7–8:

> Were you the first person ever born?
>   Were you born before the hills were made?
> Were you listening at God's secret council?
>   Do you have a monopoly on wisdom? (NLT)

We might also see a connection between Yahweh's responses to Job and our verse in Proverbs when we recognize how God refers to his establishment of creation as something that human beings had no participation in. Here, of course, we are also reminded of Woman Wisdom's association with creation in Prov. 8:22–31.

Moreover, we find a series of rhetorical questions in Isa. 40:12–14, which have the purpose also of pointing out the incomparability of God to human beings:

> Who else has held the oceans in his hand?
>> Who has measured off the heavens with his fingers?
> Who else knows the weight of the earth
>> or has weighted out the mountains and the hills?
> Who is able to advise the Spirit of the LORD?
>> Who knows enough to be his teacher or counselor?
> Has the LORD ever needed anyone's advice?
>> Does he need instruction about what is good or what is best? (NLT)

One other related biblical passage expresses the inaccessibility of wisdom, in the Teacher's words in Eccles. 7:23–24: "All this I tested with wisdom. I said, 'I will be wise!' But it was far from me. Far away is that which is, and deep, deep, who can find it?" However, in the Teacher,[9] while there is this related recognition of inability to generate wisdom by means of human resources, there is not the same affirmation of divine wisdom and certainly no indication that God will share his wisdom with human beings as we have in Job (see chap. 28) and in the present passage in Proverbs.

Now that we have discussed the function and sense of Prov. 30:4 as a whole, we offer a few words pertinent to each of the rhetorical questions that comprise it.

Who has gone up to heaven and come down?

The question begins from earth and asks who has gone up and come down. The answer is, "No human being." God may be said to come down from heaven,[10] and certainly the angels come down and go back up, as Jacob's dream at Bethel describes (Gen. 28:10–22). But this question presupposes that wisdom and knowledge of the Holy One is in heaven, which is not the source of human beings. Those who think they can go to heaven and come back on their own power are cited in Scripture as examples of overweening pride, such as we see at the Tower of Babel (Gen. 11:1–9) and in the taunt against Babylon's king (Isa. 14:13–15).

---

9. For the translation and a fuller discussion of the passages quoted from Ecclesiastes, as well as for a more general discussion of wisdom in the book, see Longman, *Ecclesiastes*.

10. Or better yet, he is in heaven as well as on earth (Ps. 139:8).

The NT affirms the special nature of Jesus Christ in this regard: "But if you don't even believe me when I tell you about things that happen here on earth, how can you possibly believe if I tell you what is going on in heaven? For only I, the Son of Man, have come to earth and will return to heaven again" (John 3:12–13 NLT).

Who has gathered the wind by the handful?

This question demands the answer "No one, no human being." Only God could gather the wind by the handful. God is the one who controls the wind (Gen. 1:2; 8:1; Exod. 10:13; 15:10; Num. 11:31; Amos 4:13). The winds are in his storehouses (Ps. 135:7).

Who has bound up water in a garment?

Again, the answer is negative: "No human being has bound up water in a garment. Only God can do such a thing." Indeed, a reference in Job indicates this as well as presenting the clue that helps us understand the metaphor of the garment; Job himself says: "He [God] binds up the waters in his thick clouds" (Job 26:8 NRSV). It is probably best to think of the binding of water in a garment as infusing the clouds with water, which manifests itself as rain.

Who has established all the ends of the earth?

Again, this is not something that human beings have accomplished, but only God. See Prov. 8:27–29.

> What is his name and the name of his son,
>   if you know it?

Here the questioner taunts the reader because he knows there is no answer. It has been a matter of debate why this question asks for the name of the son. I believe it makes sense by making clear that the questioner is asking about human beings in the previous questions.

> ⁵All the speeches of God are refined;
>   they are a shield with which to take refuge.
> ⁶Don't add to his words,
>   or he will correct you and show you to be a liar.

In the previous verses, Agur had denied knowledge to himself and indeed any human being. Here he puts forward the "speeches of God" as something pure, using the metallurgical metaphor of refinement, and as a protection to people, using the military metaphor of the shield. By describing the speeches of God in this way, he is encouraging people to avail themselves of their help in the midst of human ignorance. He continues with the warning of not adding to God's words. Again, this entails the idea that human beings on their own have nothing to contribute to God's wisdom. By definition, adding to his words would be incorrect, and the individual who does so is a liar. God's words are true; apart from God's words, human words are not true.

As we can see, Whybray, arguing that these verses are "not directly relevant to the matter of the preceding verses," is quite wrong in claiming: "It is unlikely that they (vv. 5–6) were originally part of the same composition (as vv. 1–4)." However, he helpfully reminds the reader that the contents of these verses come from Ps. 18:30 [31 MT]; 2 Sam. 22:31; Deut. 4:2; 12:32; and other passages.[11]

Exactly what the term "speeches of God" refers to is ambiguous, at least in what it meant to the author of the passage. To us, it means all those words that we recognize as the "speeches of God," some of which were not yet in existence at the time of the book of Proverbs: the Bible as a whole. Indeed, among the final words of the Christian canon as we have them is a warning about tampering with God's words: "If anyone adds anything to what is written here, God will add to that person the plagues described in this book. And if anyone removes any of the words of this prophetic book, God will remove that person's share in the tree of life and in the holy city that are described in that book" (Rev. 22:18–19 NLT).

> [7]Two things I ask of you;
>   don't withhold them from me before I die.
> [8]Fraud and lying words—
>   keep far from me!
> Poverty and wealth don't give to me!
>   Allow me to devour my regular allotment of bread,
> [9]lest I am sated and act deceptively
>   and say: "Who is Yahweh?"
> Lest I don't have much and I steal,
>   and I profane the name of my God.

This complex proverb is still presumably to be understood as the words of Agur. It has the form of a prayer to God; at least that seems to be the most reasonable understanding of "you" in v. 7. After all, who else could grant such a request? As Clifford points out, the prayer form

---

11. Whybray, *Proverbs*, 410.

is appropriate because "Agur has rejected all wisdom except that given by God, for only God's word is reliable and gives protection."[12]

In any case, Agur requests two things[13] in his prayer, both of which concern well-known themes in the book of Proverbs. In the first place, he asks for honesty. He does this negatively by asking God to keep him from deception (see "Lies" in the appendix for other places in Proverbs where lying and other types of deception are condemned). Proverbs urges people to tell the truth.

While the second request also contributes to a major theme in the book—wealth and poverty—it speaks with a voice not yet heard in the book. Up to this point, wealth seems to be the desired goal. While recognizing that godliness does not always lead to wealth, it nonetheless is what one would expect, all things being equal. Certainly, this is the first and only time in Proverbs where the sage asks not to acquire wealth. Indeed, the same is true for poverty. In modern sociological terms, the sage asks for middle-class status rather than affluence or poverty. The sage wants his needs met: "Allow me to devour my regular allotment of bread." By so saying, he seems to reject the ambition of great luxury. Christian readers will hear an echo of this request in the Lord's Prayer ("Give us this day our daily bread" [Matt. 6:11 NRSV]; see also 1 Tim. 6:8: "If we have food and clothing, we will be content with these" [NRSV]).

Verse 9 is insightful in its description of the motives for this request. On the one hand, if one is rich (and therefore "sated"), the person has no concern for Yahweh. All needs are met. In such a situation, who needs God? On the other hand, not having enough may compel a person to steal and by stealing dishonor God's name.

Now of course, not all wealthy people disdain God, and not all poor people resort to theft. Thus, it is possible to be a godly wealthy person and a moral poor person. Nonetheless, the sage does pinpoint the temptations for the rich and the poor and opts for the middle, and by doing so he gets the reader to think through the issues.

Byargeon has pointed out the "echoes of wisdom" that may be heard when comparing this prayer with the so-called Lord's prayer in Matt. 6:9-13.[14] He does not think there is necessarily literary dependence between the two texts, but he hears echoes "not simply related to the concept of daily bread but also [to] the issue of sanctifying God's name."

12. Clifford, *Proverbs*, 262.
13. Murphy (*Proverbs*, 229) and others believe that the prayer asks three things and that there is a textual problem here. However, they wrongly, in my opinion, divide the request for neither riches nor poverty from the request for a regular allotment of food. But the latter is simply the definition of the middle way—neither too much nor too little but just the right (middle) amount.
14. Byargeon, "Echoes of Wisdom," 364.

These echoes indicate that Jesus's prayer lives in the conceptual world of OT wisdom.

> ¹⁰Don't slander a servant to his master,
>   lest he curse you and you stand under the curse.

To slander people is to speak negatively about them in a way that besmirches their reputation. It is certainly appropriate to speak negatively about people if the intention is to help them recognize their mistakes and improve. But slander is different from constructive criticism. It often implies false representation as well. Proverbs consistently condemns slander as a form of foolish speech (10:18; 20:19). Here the slander of servants is envisioned. Servants are without much power. One might mistakenly believe that servants would have no recourse against someone who slanders them. However, even servants are able to invoke curses. Curses, even uttered in secret, are not to be taken lightly. Especially if deserved, curses would present a threat to those who stand under them.

On the other hand, the Teacher advises masters not to listen too closely to the speech of their servants in such cases: "Moreover, do not pay attention to all the words they speak lest you hear your servant cursing you. For furthermore, your heart knows that you also have cursed others many times" (Eccles. 7:21–22).[15]

> ¹¹There is a type of person who curses their father
>   and does not bless their mother.
> ¹²There is a type of person who is clean in their own eyes,
>   but they have not cleaned off their own excrement.
> ¹³There is a type of person—how haughty their eyes!
>   How raised their eyelids!
> ¹⁴There is a type of person whose teeth are swords;
>   their jaw is a butcher's knife,
> to consume the needy from the land
>   and the destitute from humanity.

These four verses cohere by virtue of their common opening. They each describe a "type of person" (see translation footnote), and all four of these types of people are bad. We have heard about them before in Proverbs, but now Agur gets in his licks. All it takes is a description to indicate that these people are, as in the rest of Proverbs, fools.

Those of the first type do not respect their parents (see also 20:20; 30:17). They should bless their parents, but instead they curse them, breaking not only the strictures of wisdom but also the fifth command-

---

15. For translation and commentary, see Longman, *Ecclesiastes*, 193.

ment (Exod. 20:12), and Exod. 21:17 describes this type of behavior as a capital crime.

People of the second type think they are in good shape, but they are really filthy in the most grotesque way. Their own perception is warped. They imagine that they are clean or pure, but they are covered in their own feces!

The word "clean" (*ṭāhôr*) is often used in a ritual context to indicate that state of spiritual preparedness that allows for entry into the divine presence. But they are covered with excrement, which we know from the latrine law of Deut. 23:12–14 renders one ritually unclean. The Israelites must have a place outside the camp; there, "whenever you relieve yourself, you must dig a hole with the spade and cover the excrement" (v. 13 NLT). Such a lack of self-understanding in Prov. 30:12 is folly. If one does not understand how bad one is, one cannot improve.

Perhaps this idea of thinking more highly of oneself than is really fitting leads to the next type of people, those who are pilloried for their pride. This verse makes one think of the psalmist, who expresses the opposite state of mind:

> LORD, my heart is not proud;
>   my eyes are not haughty.
> I don't concern myself with matters too great
>   or awesome for me.
> But I have stilled and quieted myself,
>   just as a weaned child is quiet with its mother.
> Yes, like a weaned child is my soul within me.
> O Israel, put your hope in the LORD—
>   now and always. (Ps. 131 NLT)

Again, this condemnation of pride is a common theme in Proverbs (see "Pride/Humility" in the appendix).

Finally, we hear of those who use their power of speech to destroy others, particularly the vulnerable, the "needy" and "destitute." The threat of their speech is emphasized by the metaphor of weapons. Their words, like swords and a butcher's knife, cut, wound, and kill. For similar ideas elsewhere in Proverbs, see 25:18.

30:15–33. *Numerical proverbs.* While the first part of chap. 30 contains the words of Agur, the remainder gives five numerical proverbs, interrupted twice by proverbs that do not have that form (vv. 17, 20). The chapter ends with a proverb concerning the danger of anger, which also does not have the form of a numerical parallelism (vv. 32–33). Numerical proverbs are found elsewhere in the book (see 6:16–19), but there is obviously an intent to group the majority of them in one location in the collection. Numerical proverbs have more than one function in Hebrew and other ancient Near Eastern poetry, so we will discuss each separately. However, one overarching purpose seems to be that "the graded numerical sequence provides a frame within which a list of items can be given."[16]

> ¹⁵The leech has two daughters: "Give, give!"
>   There are three things that are never satisfied,
>   four that never say "Enough!"
> ¹⁶Sheol and a barren womb,
>   a land that is not saturated with water,
>   and fire that does not say "Enough!"

The first numerical proverb in the series starts with a rather interesting monocolon before the proverb itself actually begins. It describes the two daughters of the leech. Why a leech? In the first place, the leech is something that sucks the blood of its host and does so until it appears overfull. The leech does not seem to become satisfied. Even today, we use the term "leech" to refer to people who attach themselves to others in order to drain them of their resources. Why daughters? Perhaps daughters, even more than sons, were known to be consumers, so the daughter of a leech would be particularly demanding.[17] Why two daughters? The answer here might be found in the introduction to the numerical proverb, which will begin with three and go to four. Thus we see the "two" leech daughters, resulting in a two, three, four sequence.

Such a list following the introduction of a numerical proverb will not always conform to the numbers announced. Famously, the judgment oracles at the beginning of Amos have the following pattern:

> Thus says the LORD:
> For three transgressions of [x],
>   and for four, I will not revoke the punishment. (1:3 etc., NRSV)

Then the oracle may specify only two transgressions. However, in the following cases, the list is as long as the larger number of the sequence, in this case four. These are the four things that are never satisfied:

---

16. For extensive discussion and bibliography on numerical proverbs, see Watson, *Classical Hebrew Poetry*, 144–49 (quote is from 147). Whybray (*Book of Proverbs: A Survey*, 97–98) provides four possible motivations behind the numerical proverb form: (1) entertainment, (2) simple observation, (3) education, and (4) reflection.

17. Another explanation is that the daughters refer to the two suckers of a leech; so Murphy, *Proverbs*, 234. North ("Four Insatiables") also believes the two daughters refer to suckers. He admits that the leech actually has only one sucker, but from a distance it looks as if it has two.

1. *Sheol.* We have already encountered a number of proverbs about Sheol and even one that specifies the impossibility of satisfying it (27:20). Sheol is the grave, with overtones of the underworld generally.[18] Sheol is here personified as an entity that is never satisfied. There is always room for one more dead person. Death never stops, and its insatiability means that everyone inevitably will be found in the grave.

2. *The barren womb.* Perhaps we should look to some of the barren women of the OT narrative tradition to paint a picture of the insatiability of a barren woman. Having a child was of paramount importance during OT times, and women who did not become pregnant often had a mood of desperation around them.

   We can think of Rachel, about whom it is said: "When Rachel saw that she wasn't having any children, she became jealous of her sister. 'Give me children, or I'll die!' she exclaimed to Jacob" (Gen. 30:1 NLT). Or we can remember Hannah, who is described as "crying bitterly as she prayed to the LORD" for a child (1 Sam. 1:10 NLT).

3. *A land not saturated with water.* Palestine is a land where rainfall is minimal, and large areas are wilderness. Rain on parched ground soaks up the available water and never seems to get enough.

4. *Fire.* As long as there is combustible material, fire does not stop. Throw another log into a raging fire, and it burns and burns.

In this case, the four examples are perhaps to state and illustrate a principle that could be extended. When a person confronted a situation when there seems to be insatiable desire, this proverb could be cited to make the point that no matter how much is given, it will never be enough.

> **17**An eye that ridicules one's father
>   and despises the teaching of one's mother,
> may ravens of the wadi pick it out,
>   and the young of the eagle eat it.

Verse 17 is one of two exceptions to the rule of numerical proverbs found in the second part of chap. 30. Of all the proverbs that warn about punishments awaiting those who ignore or abuse their parents, this one is the most hard-hitting. The potential punishment envisioned in this proverb is that nature itself will punish such an unnatural child, who would not heed parental instruction.

18. See Johnston, *Shades of Sheol*, for a full discussion.

The obvious purpose is to motivate listening to the advice of godly parents. Throughout Proverbs, there is positive inducement to listen to one's parents as well as negative warnings to those who don't.

> ¹⁸Three things are too wonderful for me,
>   and four things I cannot figure out:
> ¹⁹The way of an eagle in the sky,
>   the way of a snake on a rock,
> The way of a ship in the heart of the sea,
>   and the way of a man with a young woman.

Here again we have a three, four numerical proverb, with a list of four that follows. The category enumerated here includes mysteries, things beyond the ken of the sage. As we look at the four, we can notice yet another similarity: each describes a motion of one thing on another. The focus of attention is likely on the fourth and final wonder.

It is a mystery how an eagle glides across the sky. It is a mystery how a snake slithers across a rock. It is a mystery how a ship cuts across the sea. What about the fourth, a young man and a young woman? Since the previous three have highlighted the motion of one body moving on another (gliding, slithering, cutting), the point of reference here might be sexual intercourse: how a man's body moves on a woman's body. That a sexual meaning is intended may explain why the sages placed the next proverb (v. 20) after this numerical proverb.

> ²⁰This is the way of an adulterous woman:
>   she eats and wipes her mouth,
>   and she says: "I have done nothing wrong!"

In the preceding numerical proverb, we have learned about the way of a "man with a young woman." That is a wondrous matter. Here we have the converse, a shocking one, the way of an adulterous woman. The adulterous woman is callous. She engages in illicit sex as casually as eating something. This proverb plays on the fact that eating is often used as a euphemism for sexual relations, as virtually any page of the Song of Songs will attest (see also the imagery associated with Woman Wisdom and Woman Folly in Prov. 9).

The woman claims to have done no wrong, but such relationships threaten the stability of marriage. This verse seems to have an abundance of consonants that can be classified as labials (sounds formed by the lips: *m, b, p*), which fit well with the subject matter.

> ²¹Under three things the earth trembles,
>   and under four it cannot bear up:

> ²²under a servant when he becomes king
>   and a blunderhead when sated with food,
> ²³under a disdained woman when she gets a husband
>   and a maidservant when she dispossesses her mistress.

With this numerical proverb (also a "three, yea four" formatted parallelism), we learn something about the sages' social values. To the sages the social world had a definite order and hierarchy; when this order is disturbed, the "earth trembles." Indeed, this is a prime example of a *māšāl* form in which the social order affects the cosmic order (see "Genre" in the introduction).[19]

To the sage, a servant is a servant and does not have what it takes to be a ruler. If someone with the mentality and background of a servant takes over, then who knows what havoc would be the result? We have already seen this sentiment expressed in 19:10, but also notice Eccles. 10:5–7: "There is an evil that I have observed under the sun, an error indeed that originates from the ruler. The fool is placed in important positions, while the rich sit in low places. I observed slaves on horses and nobles walking on foot like slaves."[20] Similar negative thoughts about a topsy-turvy world may be found in the Admonitions of Ipu-Wer and apocalyptic texts like Isa. 24:2 and the Akkadian Marduk Prophecy and Shulgi Prophecy.[21]

In the second place, "blunderheads" (*nābāl*, another word for "fool")[22] should not have an abundance of food or anything else. This is wrong, because it is the wise who should be rewarded for their wisdom. But that such anomalies happen and that they are a cause for concern on the part of the wise may be seen in the Teacher's classic statement about the failure of retribution in Eccles. 9:11:

> Then I turned and observed something else under the sun. That is, the race is not to the swift, the battle not to the mighty, nor is food for the wise, nor wealth to the clever, nor favor to the intelligent, but time and chance happen to all of them.[23]

19. So Suter, "*Māšāl*," 204–5.
20. See Longman, *Ecclesiastes*, 241–42, for this translation.
21. For Ipu-Wer, see *ANET* 441–44; and for the apocalyptic texts, see T. Longman III, *Fictional Akkadian Autobiography* (Winona Lake, IN: Eisenbrauns, 1991), 132–36, 144. See the important work by Van Leeuwen on these verses ("Proverbs 30:21–23"). Against McKane ("Functions of Language"), who takes this as a lighthearted satire, Van Leeuwen argues that this passage is "a coherent example of WUD (the theme of the world turned upside-down) used to legitimate the hierarchical status quo from a royal perspective, . . . to quash revolutionary thoughts." In other words, the purpose of this text is to quell social revolt.
22. And well known for supplying the name of the husband of Abigail, who lived up to his name in his dealings with David in 1 Sam. 25.
23. Longman, *Ecclesiastes*, 232–33.

Verse 23 presents two situations involving females that are not right, according to the sages. They are situations that will cause chaos in the social realm. In the first place, a woman who has been hated finally gets a husband, and now that she has a position of power, she can begin her work of revenge. The second case is similar to the first. It is bad for a servant to be in the position of a king, so it is bad for a maidservant to take the position of the mistress. Here perhaps we can see why Sarah was so perturbed by Hagar. Hagar was a secondary wife; once she had given birth to the required child, she began to "treat her mistress Sarai with contempt" (Gen. 16:4 NLT). Sarah did not waste time, however, in putting down this minirebellion.

> ²⁴There are four things among the smallest on earth,
>   but they are the apex of wisdom:
> ²⁵Ants as a group are not strong,
>   but in the summer they ready their food.
> ²⁶Coneys as a group are not powerful,
>   but they make their homes in the crags.
> ²⁷Locusts do not have a king,
>   but they advance together in ranks.
> ²⁸You can gather lizards in your hand,
>   but they are in the palaces of a king.

This numerical proverb has a bit of a twist. Instead of following the x, x+1 pattern like the preceding passages, this proverbial saying simply states that the following list has four members. The category so listed includes small animals that seem unpretentious but demonstrate wisdom. Here we can clearly see how wisdom is not a matter of intellectual capacity; none of these animals would score well on an IQ test. What makes them wise is their skill in living. In essence, the passage pits wisdom against strength. These are small animals that are extremely wise.

The first is the ant. Definitely small, they nonetheless have an excellent strategy for survival. They get their food ready in the summer for consumption during the winter. Their wisdom is demonstrated in their planning for the future and their hard work at the opportune time. They are like the wise youth in 10:5:

> An insightful son harvests in the summer;
>   a disgraceful son sleeps during harvest.

Such a son will live well in the nonsummer months.

The second animal marked out for its wisdom is the coney. These are small animals (technical name is hyrax) that have small hooves with soles that are suctionlike, and thus they can climb steep cliffs. By doing so, they keep themselves relatively safe from predators and thus show a skillful life-preserving strategy.

The third illustration of wisdom is locusts, who don't appear to have a leader but operate like a large army. Not even humans can organize themselves as efficiently without a leader barking orders.

Then finally, lizards can be held in the hand, but they are found living in the most opulent surroundings, even in palaces.

> ²⁹There are three things that are excellent in gait,
>   four that are excellent as they walk:
> ³⁰a lion, a warrior among beasts,
>   and does not back down before anything;
> ³¹the strut of a rooster or a he-goat,
>   and a king accompanied by an army.

The next numerical proverb concerns a stately demeanor as indicated by an excellent walk. Power breeds confidence, and confidence is reflected in the way one walks. The "three, yea four" parallelism gives us four examples of those who walk without fear. Three are from the animal world, and the fourth is the king. It is likely that the emphasis is on the king. However, it starts with the animal that even today we call the "king of beasts," the lion. The lion is afraid of nothing, as indicated by the second colon of v. 30. Roosters also have a cocky gait, as do he-goats. They all are dangerous animals in their own way. But the most dangerous is the king accompanied by an army.

> ³²If you have been acting disdainfully in pride,
>   or if you have been scheming—
>   put your hand to mouth!
> ³³For pressing milk yields curds,
>   and pressing the nose yields blood,
>   and pressing anger yields accusations.

This proverb urges the listener to be careful about mistreating others in pride and through plotting. Verse 33 gives the motivation by suggesting that pride and plotting will lead to anger, which will result in accusations (a legal term) just as naturally as churning milk will give way to curds and pinching the nose will lead to nosebleeds.

The warning to put one's hand to one's mouth may be paralleled in the context of Job's repentance before God in Job 40:4 (see also 21:5 and 29:9). It is equivalent to saying "Shut up."

Chapter 31

Translation

¹The words of Lemuel,ᵃ the king of Massa,ᵇ which his mother taught him.
²What, my son?ᶜ
    What, son of my womb?
    What, son of my vow?
³Don't give your strength to women,
    your waysᵈ to that which wipes out kings.
⁴It is not for kings, O Lemuel,
    it is not for kings to drink wine,
    for rulers to craveᵉ strong drink;
⁵lest they drink and forget the decrees
    and violate the legal rights of the needy.

    a. The LXX seems to have (mis)understood this name "Lemuel" as a phrase meaning "from God" (*lmw ʾl*). Jirku ("N. pr. Lemuʾel") has argued that the name means "Lim is god." Lim is a divine name well attested among the kings of Mari in the second millennium BC (i.e., Zimri-Lim), though Whybray (*Book of Proverbs: A Survey*, 100) says, without argumentation, that this "seems to have little to support it."

    b. The Masoretes apparently took this as "Lemuel, the king, an oracle." See the placement of the *ʾatnāḥ* accent under "king."

    c. Note that the Aramaic word for "son" (*bar*) rather than the typical Hebrew word (*bēn*) is used in this verse. Does this indicate the foreign origin of the proverb, a dialect, or a late form of Hebrew? A definitive answer to this question is not possible on the basis of our present knowledge of the Hebrew language.

    d. Thus, clearly, the MT. Murphy (*Proverbs*, 240), citing an Ugaritic cognate, takes *drk* as "strength." However, though awkward, the MT makes sense, as even Murphy admits, and fits in with a large theme in the book. I therefore stick with that translation.

    e. I am taking this form (*ʾēw*) as a form of the verb *ʾāwâ* (to crave) rather than following either the Kethib (*ʾô*, "or") or the Qere (*ʾēy*, "where"). See the discussion in Thomas, "*ʾĒw*."

[6]Give strong drink to those who are perishing,
  and wine to the bitter of heart.
[7]Let them drink and forget their poverty
  and no longer remember their hard work.[f]
[8]Open your mouth for the speechless,
  and legal rights of all fragile[g] human beings.
[9]Open your mouth; judge righteously,
  and defend the needy and destitute.
[10]A noble woman, who can find?
  Her price is far above pearls.
[11]Her husband entrusts his heart to her,
  and he does not lack plunder.[h]
[12]She brings him good and not evil
  all the days of her life.
[13]She goes out to find wool and flax,
  and she works with her hands with pleasure.
[14]She is like a trading ship;
  from a distance she brings her food.
[15]She rises up while it is still night,
  and she gives prey to her household
  and a portion to her maidens.
[16]She surveys a field, and she takes it over;
  from the fruits of her hands she plants a vineyard.
[17]Her loins are girded with strength,
  and her arms are powerful.
[18]She realizes that her trading is successful;
  she does not put her lamp out at night.
[19]She sends her hands to the doubling spindle,[i]
  and her palms hold the spindle-whorl tightly.

f. "Hard work" translates *ʿāmāl*, which could also be rendered "drudgery" or even "misery." See Num. 23:21; Isa. 59:4; Jer. 20:18; Ps. 7:14 (5 MT) as well as in many places in Ecclesiastes (see discussion in Longman, *Ecclesiastes*, 65).

g. This is my attempt to translate the difficult phrase "sons of those who pass by" or "disappear." Murphy (*Proverbs*, 240) translates "dispossessed" and rightly comments that "the context suggests something like weak, abandoned, unfortunate."

h. Kassis ("Note on *šālāl*") prefers an Arabic cognate for the word translated "plunder." That Arabic cognate might mean either "group of people" or "sheep." However, he never tells us why it is necessary to avoid the obvious, which is that *šālāl* is a perfectly good Hebrew word that means "plunder." D. Winton Thomas ("Textual and Philological Notes on Some Passages in the Book of Proverbs," in *Wisdom in Israel and in the Ancient Near East: Presented to Professor Harold Henry Rowley by the Society for Old Testament Study in Association with the Editorial Board of Vetus Testamentum, in Celebration of His Sixty-fifth Birthday, 24 March 1955*, ed. M. Noth and D. Winton Thomas, Supplements to Vetus Testamentum 3 [Leiden: Brill, 1955], 291–92) makes a similar speculative connection with the same Arabic term but translates it "wool."

i. This precise interpretation of *kîšôr*, usually rendered "distaff," is argued for by A. Wolters, "The Meaning of *Kîšôr* (Prov. 31:19)," *Hebrew Union College Annual* 65 (1994): 91–104.

²⁰She stretches her palm to the needy;
　she sends her hands to the destitute.
²¹She is not afraid of the snow for her household,
　for all her household are dressed in warm clothes.ʲ
²²She makes bed coverings for herself;
　Egyptian linen and purple are her clothing.
²³Her husband is known in the gates
　when he sits with the elders of the land.
²⁴She makes a garment and sells it;
　she gives clothing to traders.
²⁵Strength and honor are her clothing;
　she laughs at the future.
²⁶She opens her mouth in wisdom,
　and covenantal instruction is on her lips.
²⁷She is a lookout postᵏ for the doings of her household;
　she does not eat the food of laziness.
²⁸Her children rise up and bless her;
　her husband praises her:
²⁹"Many daughters act nobly,
　but you surpass all of them!"
³⁰Charm is false and beauty meaningless;
　a woman who fears Yahweh is to be praised!
³¹Give to her from the fruit of her hands,
　and praise her deeds in the gates.

Interpretation

The final chapter of the book concludes with what appears to be two separate poetic compositions: (1) the instructions that the mother of King Lemuel gives to her royal son (vv. 1–9) and (2) an acrostic poem that celebrates the noble woman (ʾēšet-ḥayîl, vv. 10–31). A cursory reading

j. With Murphy (*Proverbs*, 244) and others, I take this word (with vocalic emendation) from "double" rather than "scarlet" and thus render it "doubly thick clothes" (in line with the Greek and Vulgate).

k. According to Wolters ("Ṣôpiyyâ"), the word "lookout" is an unusual participle that is typical to heroic hymns, to which he assigns this poem as a whole. The form of the participle, however, is also unusual, and here he detects a subtle wordplay on the Greek term *sophia* (wisdom). It is a bilingual pun to be translated "watches over," but hinting at the Greek meaning of "wisdom" as well. Rendsberg ("Bilingual Wordplay") points out other bilingual wordplays in support of Wolters's suggestion.

The connection with Greek would imply a late date of composition and, therefore, a late date for the final redaction of the book as a whole, for which discussion, see "Authorship and Date" in the introduction. Note that *NIDOTTE* 3:831–32 understands the word to be a noun, "lookout post," and in either case the verb is related to the noun that means "watchtower" (*miṣpeh* I).

of the chapter does not encourage seeing any connection between the two parts that would be significant to the meaning of the text, and such a reaction is supported by the fact that the Septuagint demonstrates a different order of this latter part of Proverbs, so that these two poems are not juxtaposed.[1] Furthermore, vv. 1–9 are an instruction spoken in the second person by a mother to her son, while vv. 10–31 represent a different genre, described by Wolters as a "heroic hymn"[2] (see discussion below). Finally, the acrostic form of vv. 10–31 clearly sets that text off as a separate unit from what precedes.

Even so, a few have recently attempted to persuade readers that there is a connection between the two poems that is not obvious on the surface of the text. V. A. Hurowitz,[3] building on an earlier study of M. Lichtenstein,[4] has argued for linkage between the two poems based on a chiasmus of individual words and also of theme, though the latter does not conform to the former. The problem with such studies, in my estimation, is that they produce an unbalanced structure. The following, for instance, is Hurowitz's chiastic thematic structure of the chapter:

A warning against women (31:3a)
　　danger of woman (31:3b)
　　B warning against wine (31:4)
　　　　danger of wine (31:5)
　　B′ ideal aspects of wine (31:6–7)
　　　　[judgment] (31:8–9)
A′ the desired woman (31:10–31)[5]

But a close look at this pattern shows just how awkward and unbalanced it is with a one-verse unit (A: 31:3) paralleled with a twenty-two verse unit (A′: 31:10–31).

Thus, with the majority of scholars, I treat these two poems as separate rather than intentionally linked. In other words, I do not think that the picture of the noble woman is intended to provide an alternative choice to the women to whom the king might inappropriately give his strength (v. 3).[6]

---

1. The order is 31:1–9; 25:1–28; 26:1–28; 27:1–27; 28:1–28; 29:1–27; 31:10–31.
2. See Wolters, "Proverbs xxxi 10–31"; reprinted as chapter 1 in idem, *Song of the Valiant Woman*. The page references (below) are to the book.
3. Hurowitz, "Seventh Pillar."
4. Lichtenstein, "Chiasm and Symmetry."
5. From Hurowitz, "Seventh Pillar," 216.
6. Lichtenstein ("Chiasm and Symmetry," 211) suggests such a connection as he ends his article: "The juxtaposition of the two poems of Proverbs 31, as it now stands in the

¹The words of Lemuel, the king of Massa, which his mother taught him.
²What, my son?
    What, son of my womb?
    What, son of my vow?
³Don't give your strength to women,
    your ways to that which wipes out kings.
⁴It is not for kings, O Lemuel,
    it is not for kings to drink wine,
    for rulers to crave strong drink;
⁵lest they drink and forget the decrees
    and violate the legal rights of the needy.
⁶Give strong drink to those who are perishing,
    and wine to the bitter of heart.
⁷Let them drink and forget their poverty
    and no longer remember their hard work.
⁸Open your mouth for the speechless,
    and legal rights of all fragile human beings.
⁹Open your mouth; judge righteously,
    and defend the needy and destitute.

31:1–9. *The instruction of the mother of King Lemuel.* As at the beginning of chap. 30, here we have a short section attributed to a hitherto-unknown and rather enigmatic source. The name given to us is Lemuel, king of Massa. For "Massa" as the name of a tribe in Arabia, see the introduction and discussion of the "words of Agur" at 30:1–14. We have no clue, biblical or extrabiblical, as to this king's identity. In any case, the teaching is directed to this king and is attributed to his mother.[7] We have already noted and commented on the fact that in Hebrew proverbs, as opposed to other ancient Near Eastern proverbs, mothers are mentioned as those engaged in the instruction of their children (see comments at 1:8). However, this is the only place where we actually hear the voice of the mother independently of that of the father. The topic of her conversation is something that a wise mother, especially the wise mother of a leader, would want to drive home to her child: women and drink are two large temptations to a man with power and money.

The syntax and meaning of v. 2 is a bit difficult, and we have rendered it rather literally. Besides three vocatives that indicate the mother's intimacy

---

Hebrew text, and however it may have come about, has effected a most happy and fitting union. Indeed, Lemuel's mother has been provided with a most appropriate daughter-in-law, in more ways than one."

7. The fact that this is a royal instruction, a queen to a son, makes it similar to the Egyptian Instruction of King Amenemhet and the "Instruction for King Merikare," as well as the Akkadian "Advice to a Prince," though here the teacher is the queen mother.

with her son and therefore her right to speak to him in an authoritative manner, as few could address the king, the three cola all simply begin with "What?"[8] Perhaps it is an incredulous "What!" short for "What are you doing!" that leads her to comment on women and drink. In any case, this opening salvo leads to these two subjects in that order.

It would be a tremendous temptation for a king to use his power to amass a number of wives, concubines, and other women. But women can get even a king into trouble. Solomon is an example of that, with his multitudinous wives, who ultimately led him astray. This is also illustrated by David, whose pursuit of Bathsheba was responsible for many of the palace intrigues that plagued his later years and succession. In any case, the sages surely would argue that even the king had the same responsibility to act with integrity in sexual relationships as their teaching required for other young men (see chaps. 5–7). In light of the parallelism, the "ways" that wipe out kings certainly refers to the wrong way of relating to women.

Lemuel's mother also warns him about the danger of alcoholic drinks. The sages have already warned about drinking too much (20:1; 23:19–21, 29–35). The problem has to do with one's ability to make good decisions if under the influence of alcohol. A clear mind is important to the wise person. The Bible as a whole is not at all opposed to alcohol and even praises what might be understood as slight intoxication, but heavy drinking is frowned upon. It is very important for a king to know what he is doing as he makes decisions, because his decisions have important ramifications for many people.

That Lemuel's mother commends the use of alcohol to the poor may be seen in part as a strategy to discourage her royal son. In other words, she may be saying the equivalent of "Don't act like those derelicts who drink to forget their hardships. Act like the king you are." The king is the human representative of God, who protects the rights of those who lack power (the needy and the destitute).

31:10–31. *The noble woman.* The concluding passage of the book of Proverbs is a wisdom poem extolling the "noble woman."[9] Form-critically, Wolters has persuasively argued that the poem is an example of a heroic hymn, a poem that typically celebrates the victory of soldiers, but here is used to praise a "noble woman."[10] In support of this, he points out that

---

8. The NRSV takes it as a negative particle, "No." Justification for this might be gained by citing Paul Joüon, *A Grammar of Biblical Hebrew*, trans. and rev. T. Muraoka (Rome: Pontifical Biblical Institute Press, 1991), §144h.

9. For a careful and interesting description of the history of interpretation of this passage, see Wolters, *Song of the Valiant Woman*, 59–154.

10. He does this without denying the poem's connection to the genre of wisdom psalm. See Wolters, "Proverbs xxxi 10–31."

the description of the woman is permeated with allusions to her strength and also often uses explicitly military terminology to describe her (see commentary below).[11]

Furthermore, this poem reminds us of the role that women play in this book, which is explicitly addressed to young men. Most pointedly, we read here of a woman who is the human reflex of Woman Wisdom herself. She is to be contrasted with the strange and foreign woman (chaps. 5–7), who is the reflex of Woman Folly. That this poem concludes the book helps explain why, in the Hebrew canon, Proverbs is followed by Ruth (who herself is called a "noble woman" in Ruth 3:11), and then by the Song of Songs, a book in which the woman is the main speaker and initiates the relationship.

The poem describes an unbelievably energetic and competent woman. She is well off, but not from the highest stratum of society.[12] Indeed, the qualities and abilities of this woman make one wonder whether the proper answer to the opening question, "A noble woman, who can find?" is "No one, because she doesn't exist." There may be something to this intuitive response. The description is an ideal and should not be used as a standard by which to measure and critique women. As Yoder states it, "Proverbs 31:10–31 remains a portrait of the most desirable woman, an image of the ideal wife intended for a predominantly male audience. . . . She embodies no one woman, but rather the desired attributes of many."[13]

This woman is described predominantly from the perspective of others, particularly her husband. We again are reminded that the book in its original setting was written to men. This type of woman is one who makes husband, children, and household happy.

How does she make her husband happy? Much of the passage is devoted to her ability as a businesswoman. By means of military metaphors and the metaphor of shipping (see comments on particular verses) as well as straightforward description, she is said to be involved in trading that brings income to the household. Furthermore, by her purchase of land and its cultivation, she also provides food for her family. She exerts her energies to manufacture items for use in the household. She is the epitome of the hard worker, eschewing laziness, a wisdom principle that has been taught throughout the book to this point (6:6–11; 10:4, 26; 12:11, 24, 27; 13:4; etc.).

11. Lyons ("Note on Proverbs 31.10–31," 240) suggests that the picture of the "ʾēšet-ḥayîl was the wise matriarch of the household. She was the natural counterpart to the paterfamilias—she was the materfamilias."

12. As noted by Whybray (*Book of Proverbs: A Survey*, 111) on the basis of the fact that she does work that the wealthiest class of women would relegate to servants.

13. Yoder, "Woman of Substance," 446. See also Yoder's fuller work, *Wisdom as a Woman of Substance*.

But she is a woman who is defined not just by her actions but also by her attitudes. She is confident in the light of threats to security and to the future in general. Her confidence rests in her wisdom. She knows how to stay out of trouble through preparations such as making warm clothes in anticipation of winter.

Her industry frees her husband up for tasks important to his life. While she is taking care of the home front, he is in the gate, the place where town leaders gather to decide on the important matters affecting the whole community.

To top it all off, this woman is also concerned about the plight of the poor and afflicted, again in keeping with an important teaching of the book as a whole. She works for the betterment not only of her own household but also for those outside of it.

This poem is notable not only for the remarkable qualities and characteristics of the woman but also for what it leaves out or even names as unimportant. Especially taking into account the fact that this poem is written from the perspective of (and probably by) a male, physical beauty is said to be meaningless. Furthermore, the woman's sexual abilities are not commented on (though they might be alluded to in v. 22). Song of Songs provides a contrast, encouraging and promoting sexuality and sensuality. Furthermore, "charm," a superficially attractive personality trait, is also specifically denigrated as "deceptive."

The bottom line of the poem is to underline "fear of Yahweh" as the most important characteristic of a noble woman. After all, "the fear of Yahweh is the beginning of knowledge" (1:7), and the qualities already mentioned—hard work, discernment in business, generosity to the poor, and so forth—are all outworkings of this fundamental truth about the woman.

Often missed is the male counterpart to this poem in Ps. 112. This poem begins (following the NIV): "Blessed is the man who fears the Lord" (v. 1). It goes on to describe such a man as generous to the poor (v. 5) and confident in the future (vv. 7–8).

Finally, this poem has the form of an acrostic, its twenty-two verses beginning with successive letters of the Hebrew alphabet. Such a structure gives one the sense that we are reading a complete and ordered description of the "noble woman."[14]

Yoder argues that the description of the woman fits well into the Persian period, when she dates the composition of this poem and its addition, along with chaps. 1–9, to provide a frame for the book as a whole. She does a good job of showing how the socioeconomic picture

---

14. In keeping with the similarities already drawn between Prov. 31:10–31 and Ps. 112, we note that Ps. 112 is also in the form of an acrostic.

of this woman fits in with the Persian period, but most if not all of the relevant characteristics fit in with other periods, too. At least she does not show clearly that these characteristics are unique to the Persian period. Furthermore, her assumption that the Yehudite view of women would conform with the broader Persian picture from which she draws these typical characteristics is not proved by her appeal to female figurines that are similar to broader ancient Near Eastern figurines.[15]

> **10**A noble woman, who can find?
> Her price is far above pearls.

Proverbs 12:4 has already introduced the phrase "noble woman" (cf. Ruth 3:11). The word "noble" (*ḥayîl*) has military overtones but is not restricted to military use. The basic meaning of the term is "strength" and "power," and it "can be applied to a variety of people, including a warrior (powerful), a functionary (able), and a landowner (wealthy)."[16] While this indicates that "noble" here may not be military, the fact that the poem will associate military language with this woman in the following verses suggests that the composer intends the reader to recognize warrior imagery here. In what follows, we see a woman who is engaged in the battle of life, dealing with people and winning an advantage for her family.

The question (Who can find?) underlines the rarity and therefore the preciousness of such a woman. The second colon emphasizes this by asserting that her price exceeds that of precious pearls. Throughout Proverbs and elsewhere, we have seen this trope used to point out the importance of wisdom, and here it is being applied to the human embodiment of Woman Wisdom herself. The "price" or "value" of wisdom is clearly metaphorical elsewhere in the book, which thus counts against Yoder's view that this is referring to Persian period dowries.[17]

Though it is true that marriage was more of an economic transaction (dowry, bride price, etc.) than it is today, we are not to think of the "price" of the noble woman in strictly literal terms. Rather, "price" here is a metaphor of value or worth.

> **11**Her husband entrusts his heart to her,
> and he does not lack plunder.

The woman is first described by her husband's attitude toward her. He entrusts his heart to her. The heart stands for one's core personality

---

15. Yoder, "Woman of Substance," esp. 432n16.
16. *NIDOTTE* 2:116–26. For the most extensive study of the word, advocating the translation "woman of substance," see Yoder, *Wisdom as a Woman of Substance*.
17. See Yoder, "Woman of Substance," 432.

and not specifically emotions, as it tends to do in modern idiom (see 3:1). In any case, it means that the husband is confident to make himself totally vulnerable to her. He trusts her to follow through and take care of him and the household.

The second colon shows that she does not fail him. In the original Hebrew, the wording is striking. The term "plunder" (*šālāl*) refers to the spoils of warfare.[18] The idea of the verse seems to suggest that the woman is a warrior in the battle of life. She goes out and fights on behalf of her family and comes back with the victor's spoils, which allow her family to thrive in the midst of the conflict. The versions mute this interpretation by providing the following bland renditions:

> and he will have no lack of gain (NRSV)
> and children are not lacking (REB)
> has an unfailing prize (NAB)
> from her he will derive no little profit (NJB)
> and lacks nothing of value (NIV)
> and she will greatly enrich his life (NLT)

> ¹²She brings him good and not evil
> all the days of her life.

The poem continues to describe the benefits that the noble woman brings to her husband. In this case, the statement is general. As long as she lives, she will bring him good things, not evil things. Good things and evil things can encompass a wide variety of moral and material blessings, some of which will be unpacked in the verses to come.

> ¹³She goes out to find wool and flax,
> and she works with her hands with pleasure.

The woman is not stuck at home, but goes out into the public square, the market, in order to obtain the materials that she needs. We presume that she needs the wool and flax in order to make the clothes described in the following verses. The second colon informs us that she not only does the labor, but she also does it joyfully.

> ¹⁴She is like a trading ship;
> from a distance she brings her food.

A ship of trade sells and buys. It sets out from one port to deliver goods needed there and then picks up and delivers other goods needed at the

---

18. See *NIDOTTE* 4:128–29, though, regrettably, this article does not discuss the word's occurrence here in Prov. 31.

home port. The woman works with her hands to produce products she can sell in the public market, and then she buys food and brings it back to sustain her household.

> **¹⁵**She rises up while it is still night,
>   and she gives prey to her household
>   and a portion to her maidens.

To accomplish all that she does, this woman does not sleep much. She gets up early, and we will discover that she goes to bed late in v. 18. She is an energetic worker. She does this in order to provide sustenance for her household, including her maidservants. A word from the realm of hunting ("prey") is used to describe what she brings back to the house. It is almost like the modern saying "The early bird gets the worm." "Prey," though, is another word that suggests violence or struggle.

> **¹⁶**She surveys a field, and she takes it over;
>   from the fruits of her hands she plants a vineyard.

This verse pictures the woman as engaged in real estate and agricultural ventures. She is one who goes out to find land that is worth managing, and then with her own resources she plants a vineyard, again presumably as a business venture.

> **¹⁷**Her loins are girded with strength,
>   and her arms are powerful.

The phrase "loins are girded" (*motnayim*, here used with the verb *ḥgr*) is an expression of physical energy and power (see also Exod. 12:11; 2 Kings 4:29; 9:1; Dan. 10:5). The same is true for the second colon's reference to her powerful arms. In this way, the woman's strength is praised in a way that may surprise those who incorrectly believe that this quality is reserved for men in the Bible.

> **¹⁸**She realizes that her trading is successful;
>   she does not put her lamp out at night.

We have already heard of the woman's involvement in trade (*shr* is used in v. 14). Here we are told that the results are "successful" (our contextual translation of the regular word for "good" [*ṭôb*]). We have also earlier been told that she works hard and does not sleep much, getting up early in the morning (v. 15), and here the other shoe drops, since the text tells us that the woman also stays up late at night.

> ¹⁹She sends her hand to the doubling spindle,
> and her palms hold the spindle-whorl tightly.

On the surface of it, this verse returns us to the woman's abilities to manufacture clothes. The "doubling spindle," also called "distaff" (*kîšôr*), is "a wooden staff onto which the wool or flax was attached before it was spun into thread."[19] The "spindle-whorl" (*pelek/pālek*) is the flywheel of a stick used to collect the yarn or thread.

Though on the surface, this description of the woman's industry seems domestic in nature, it may have an additional nuance. Anat, the warrior goddess of Ugarit, used her distaff and whorl as a weapon. Again, this may underline the warrior imagery, which laces this description of the "noble woman."

> ²⁰She stretches her palm to the needy;
> she sends her hands to the destitute.

The sages have taught that the wise must be generous to the poor (11:24; 28:27; 29:7, 14). Here the "noble woman" shows her wisdom by being concerned about the needs of the destitute.

> ²¹She is not afraid of the snow for her household,
> for all her household are dressed in warm clothes.

As we learn at the end of the poem, this wise woman's only fear is Yahweh (v. 30). The fear of Yahweh drives out all other fears. Specifically, the woman is not afraid of the weather because she prepares for it. It is not unusual for it to snow in the central hill country of Israel, though it is not frequent. However, even though not frequent, the woman is ready, having already made warm clothes for all the members of her household. She plans ahead.

> ²²She makes bed coverings for herself;
> Egyptian linen and purple are her clothing.

The first colon may be provocatively compared to 7:16, where the promiscuous woman tells the man she is trying to seduce, "I have ornamented my bed with bed coverings." This context may indicate that the word "bed coverings" (*marbaddîm*) has sensual overtones, but if so, they are rather understated. Her clothing is made of the finest and expensive materials. Purple was so expensive, indeed, that most of its

---

19. Ibid., 2:635–36.

use took place among royalty. At least, these materials point to significant wealth.

> 23Her husband is known in the gates
> when he sits with the elders of the land.

This verse describes the important status and function of the woman's husband. He is a leader in the community. That he sits with the elders in the gate indicates that he is an elder himself. The gates of a city were the public meeting area and served as a kind of city hall. There the elders would make decisions and render judgments that affected the whole city.

The implication is that her husband can achieve such a significant status only with the support of his wife. She takes care of the household while he works in the community. Her reputation also enhances his.

> 24She makes a garment and sells it;
> she gives clothing to traders.

The poem again speaks of her dealing in garments. She is a business-woman selling clothing. The specific terms for "garment" (*sādîn*) and "clothing" (*ḥăgôr*) may suggest intimate clothing such as undergarment and girdle respectively.

> 25Strength and honor are her clothing;
> she laughs at the future.

A number of the verses of this poem describe the woman's facility at making clothes for herself, her household, and for sale. Perhaps this is what has suggested the more metaphorical use here. She conducts and carries herself as though clothed in strength and honor. Since clothing may display style and status, so her demeanor displays strength and honor. People who looked at her would recognize these qualities in her.

The second colon might then be seen as a particular feature of her "strength and honor," the confidence she has as she faces the future. The future is unknown. The one thing that everyone knows about the future is that it will bring difficulties and obstacles. Yet in spite of that knowledge, she is fearless because her wisdom (which implies a relationship with God: "The fear of Yahweh is the beginning of knowledge") will sustain her.

> 26She opens her mouth in wisdom,
> and covenantal instruction is on her lips.

Like her divine counterpart, Woman Wisdom, the noble woman's speech is qualified by wisdom (8:6–9). Wise speech is a broad category, but it would include words that are godly, righteous, and also strategic to successful living. She would impart good advice to those who would listen to her.

The second colon also praises her speech as that which is characterized as "instruction" (from *tôrâ*) of *ḥesed*. *Ḥesed* is a word amenable to a number of different English translations, none of which capture the whole range of its meaning. In my translation, I underline the connection between this word and the covenant. The word itself does not mean covenant, but it does characterize the type of relationship that exists between covenant partners. Other translations chose to highlight the fact that the word entails "kindness" or "loyalty," "faithfulness," "goodness." All of these terms could be appropriate, and I intend my translation, "covenantal," to cover all of them. It also safeguards against the idea that her words are just generally kind. They are kind by flowing from the covenant between God and his people.

> [27]She is a lookout post for the doings of her household;
> she does not eat the food of laziness.

The woman is vigilant as she looks out for the needs of her household. She may not be concerned about the future (v. 25), but that does not mean that she takes a laissez-faire attitude toward it. The term "lookout post" (*ṣôpiyyâ*) is a noun derived from the verb *ṣph* I, which implies great diligence in observation. Ezekiel understood his role as a watchman (Ezek. 33:7).[20]

By now we are far from surprised about the information provided us in the second colon. She is definitely not lazy. The specific way of stating her industry strikes us as odd and somewhat difficult to understand. What is the "food of laziness"? Is this simply a metaphor, or does it mean that she works hard in food preparation? Certainly, the former would imply the latter.

> [28]Her children rise up and bless her;
> her husband praises her:
> [29]"Many daughters act nobly,
> but you surpass all of them!"

Such a woman elicits praise from those closest to her and those who most benefit from her abilities and competence. Her children and husband praise her. The latter is then quoted in v. 29. Here he acknowledges

20. So ibid., 3:831–32.

that she is not the only noble woman, but she stands out among all of them. She is the noblest of the noble.

---

³⁰Charm is false and beauty meaningless;
a woman who fears Yahweh is to be praised!

It is possible that this verse continues the husband's praise, and if so, it would appropriately be put in quotation marks. However, it does not affect the meaning of the verse, whether it is the husband or the poet who states it.

Basically, this verse puts things in perspective. People, and men in particular, are typically attracted to superficial attributes like charm and beauty. However, charm may hide a nasty personality, and beauty is meaningless unless it is also accompanied by godliness (11:22). The word "meaningless" (*hebel*) in some contexts may mean transient, though I think that is a nuance. In any case, common experience shows that the meaninglessness of physical beauty derives in large part from its relative brevity.

The verse does not mean that a noble woman is abrasive and ugly; it simply contrasts these relatively worthless traits (charm, beauty) with what is truly important: fear of Yahweh. This is true of all people, male and female, but here there is a reminder that a woman who deserves to be called noble is motivated by a proper relationship with her God.

---

³¹Give to her from the fruit of her hands,
and praise her deeds in the gates.

Such a woman deserves reward, and the final verse of the poem calls for it. She should benefit from her hard work. She should also be praised not just at home but also publicly.

Appendix
Topical Studies

As we argued in the introduction to the commentary (see "The Structure of Proverbs"), I do not believe that there is an overarching structure to the book beyond the macrostructural observation that differentiates the discourses of chaps. 1–9 from the proverbs per se in 10–31. Discourses and proverbs on various topics are scattered throughout; there is no systematic organization to various topics. By their nature, individual proverbs do not pretend to give a full-orbed comment on any topic, but are more or less a snapshot, stating a truth in the form of an observation, admonition, prohibition, or advice. Thus, there is some advantage to taking a number of proverbs on a particular topic and studying them together to gain a fuller perspective on the book's understanding of the topic. That is what I do in this appendix. As far as I am aware, only Derek Kidner's Tyndale commentary does this and on a more limited scale.[1] The present rage for finding deep structures in the book works against this approach, and that is at least one reason we don't find such essays in other commentaries.

The following essays are intended to be suggestive rather than exhaustive in both the selection of topics and the extent of the discussion of each topic. Passages are cited here illustratively; full treatments of their meaning may be found in the commentary proper. The topics are arranged alphabetically for ease of reference.

1. Kidner, *Proverbs*.

Alcohol (20:1; 21:17; 23:19–21, 29–35; 31:1–9)

According to the sages, an excess of alcohol is dangerous in that it leads to foolish behavior, especially fighting (23:29–35). In the first place, it clouds judgment, thus destroying the possibility of wise thinking and decisions (20:1). Thus, it is particularly wrong for a king to drink a lot of alcohol, presumably because the king's decisions will affect a large number of people (31:4–5). On the other hand, in the speech directed to King Lemuel by his mother, she allows for heavy drinking by those who suffer pain in their lives. The same numbing effect of alcohol that makes drinking threatening to a leader is what is attractive for those who are down on their luck. However, it is not altogether clear whether the words of Lemuel's mother should be taken as a prescription for heavy drinking by those who live in unmitigated difficulty, or whether she is trying to goad her royal son into abstinence by saying that only the lower classes drink. While 20:1 and 30:1–9 try to preserve one's power of clear thinking from the effects of too much drinking, it appears that the concern of 23:19–21 is the way heavy drinking and gluttony can lead to poverty. Such a luxurious lifestyle can cost a lot, and it can also sap some of the energy people need for more productive activity. Thus, luxury and extreme pleasure can lead to destitution. Finally, 23:29–35 gives a particularly insightful description of addiction in spite of the shame and pain involved in alcoholism.

Anger (15:18; 16:14; 19:11, 12, 19; 21:19; 25:23; 27:3–4; 29:8, 22)

Proverbs overall advocates a temperate expression of emotion. We thus are not surprised that anger is identified as a destructive emotion when it is out of control.

> Wrath is cruel, and anger is a flood,
>   and who can stand up in the face of jealousy? (27:4)

Anger destroys familial and community relationships. It is better to live in a desolate wilderness, for instance, than with an angry woman (21:19). The wise will not only control this emotion in themselves but will also seek to minimize it in others. In terms of the latter, the king is specifically mentioned because his anger can cause the greatest harm:

> The anger of a king is a messenger of death;
>   the wise will appease it. (16:14)

Appropriate Expression of Emotions (12:16; 14:29, 30; 16:32; 17:27; 19:11; 25:28; 29:11)

The wise person is coolheaded, the fool an impetuous hothead. In the same way that the wise are sparing in speech (see "Speaking and Listening" below), so they are sparing in emotional expression. It is not that the wise are emotionless or that they don't express anger or disappointment, but they do so in a way that is appropriate to the context. They don't blow up in anger, though they may get angry. Moderate expressions of emotions allow the wise to think and strategize. Emotions don't cloud their thinking. They are still able to navigate life. Another way to put this is that the wise are patient, whereas fools are impatient.

> Patience brings much competence,
>> but impatience promotes stupidity. (14:29)

> A patient person is better than a warrior,
>> and those who control their emotions than those who can capture a
>> city. (16:32)

> Those who hold back their speech know wisdom,
>> and those who are coolheaded are people of understanding. (17:27)

Appropriate Use of Words (10:14; 11:12, 13; 12:18; 13:3, 16; 15:28; 17:27, 28; 19:1; 20:18, 25; 26:4)

Another characteristic of wise speech is that the speaker is reticent, sparing in the use of words. Fools are those who run off at the mouth and hoist themselves on their own petard. The wise are careful and speak only when necessary:

> People who keep a watch on their mouths guard their lives;
>> those who spread their lips wide ruin it. (13:3)

> Those who hold back their speech know wisdom,
>> and those who are coolheaded are people of understanding. (17:27)

Perhaps most cutting of all toward the fool is 17:28:

> Even a dupe who keeps silent seems wise;
>> those who keep their lips shut are smart.

Related to this is the idea that wise people are those who think before they talk (and act), while fools are impetuous:

> The heart of the righteous meditates before answering,
>> but the mouth of the wicked blurts out evil. (15:28)

To speak without thinking usually creates more harm than help, both for others and for oneself:

> Do you see people who are hasty with their words?
>> There is more hope for a fool than for them. (29:20)

Bribes/Gifts (15:27; 17:8, 23; 18:16; 19:6; 21:14; 25:14; 28:21)

At first, the teaching on bribes/gifts seems contradictory. Taken as absolute statements, they are. Most often a bribe is negative, something that perverts justice:

> The wicked take a bribe from the bosom
>> to stretch the way of justice. (17:23)

But at other times, it seems to be evaluated positively, as something that makes the achievement of a desirable goal possible:

> A gift widens the way for people;
>> it leads them to important people. (18:16)

Although it is possible to take texts like the latter in a sarcastic way, this seems unnecessary. It is better to understand the circumstance of a gift to be the issue. If one gives a gift to circumvent justice, then it is wrong. But there are situations where a bribe can open doors to good ends. In other words, the purpose of the bribe is the issue here.

There are two words used for a bribe here: one we translate by "bribe" (*šōḥad*), and a second that we translate "gift" (*mattān*). They are not used to differentiate a good bribe from a bad one. Indeed, they are used as roughly synonymous and both in a positive sense in 21:14:

> A gift in secret calms anger,
>> and a hidden bribe, passionate wrath.

One verse even berates those who offer a "false gift," which is probably best understood as the promise of a gift never delivered (25:14).

Business Ethics (6:1–5; 10:2; 11:1, 15, 18, 24–26; 13:11; 14:23; 15:27; 16:8, 11, 13, 26; 17:18; 20:10, 14, 16, 23; 21:5; 22:7, 26–27; 26:10; 27:13, 18; 28:8, 16)

The relevant proverbs are much more extensive than those listed here. Indeed, if we approach the question of what Proverbs teaches about proper business practices in general, the entire book is relevant. For instance, the wise businessperson operates with integrity (10:9; 11:3), works very hard, and avoids laziness (see "Laziness and Hard Work" below). Here, however, we will concentrate on passages that refer specifically to business practices.

According to Proverbs, the preeminent principle for business is honesty. When a merchant sells something to customers, they should get what they pay for:

> Fraudulent scales are an abomination to Yahweh,
> but an accurate weight brings his favor. (11:1)

According to 16:11 and 20:10, Yahweh himself keeps an eye on the accurate measurement of goods. Even so, Proverbs warns the wise person to cast a wary eye on the merchant:

> The buyer says, "Bad, bad,"
> but he disappears and then brags. (20:14)

Proverbs devotes a considerable amount of teaching to warn the wise against securing loans for other people (6:1–5; 11:15; 17:18; 20:16; 22:26–27; 27:13; 28:8). Charging interest was forbidden except to non-Israelites, but securing loans was thought to be a bad risk even in the case of the latter. If a person needed help and one had the ability, one should simply give a gift out of generosity, without the hope of ever getting it back (11:24–26).

Even so, it is important to note that the Torah on occasion encourages lending to those in need (Deut. 15:1–7), and though no interest may be taken, a reasonable pledge may be secured for the repayment of the loan (Exod. 22:25–27). In light of this, Proverbs may be seen not as prohibiting such loans but as warning of the dangers. If one lends to the poor, one had better be ready to sacrifice the loan.

Finally, any kind of ill-gotten profit would never ultimately be beneficial and would typically be a temporary gain (10:2; 11:18).

Family Relationships (6:16–19; 10:1; 15:20; 17:2, 6, 17, 21; 19:13, 18, 26; 20:7, 20; 22:6; 23:13–14, 22–25; 27:8; 28:7, 24; 29:3, 15, 17; 30:11, 17, 21–23)

Family is an important topic in Proverbs.[2] Indeed, the explicit dynamic of the teaching provided in the book is that of a father, speaking on behalf of himself and his wife, instructing his son. In one sense, then, the whole book is relevant to family, but here we simply outline the major and explicit issues relating to family in the book. In this section, we focus on the family overall and the parent-child relationship. In the next section, we will highlight the teaching concerning the husband-wife relationship. Since we are here simply giving a sense of the major teaching points, we will simply list each, along with a single illustrative verse.

1. *The sages insist on the importance of a strong cohesive family and denigrate anyone and anything that erodes the family bond.*

> Look, there are six things Yahweh hates,
>   and seven that are an abomination of his soul:
> haughty eyes, a lying tongue,
>   and hands that spill the blood of the innocent,
> a heart set on iniquitous plans;
>   feet hurrying to run to evil,
> a false witness who proclaims lies,
>   and those who cause conflicts among brothers. (6:16–19)

2. *The family is the locus for instruction.*

> For I was a son to my father,
>   tender and the only one of my mother.
> He taught me and said to me . . . (4:3–4a)

3. *Children must respect the teaching of their parents.*

> An eye that ridicules one's father
>   and despises the teaching of one's mother,
> may ravens of the wadi pick it out,
>   and the young of the eagle eat it. (30:17)

4. *Parents must discipline their children for their own good.*

> Don't withhold discipline from young people.
>   If you strike them with the rod, they will not die.

2. For a fuller discussion of this topic, incorporating all of biblical wisdom literature, see T. Longman III, "Family in the Wisdom Literature," in *Family in the Bible*, ed. R. S. Hess and M. Daniel Carroll R. (Grand Rapids: Baker, 2003), 80–99.

> Strike them with a rod,
> and you will extricate their lives from Sheol. (23:13–14)

5. *Parents must model godly behavior.*

> The righteous walk about in their innocence;
> blessed are their children after them. (20:7)

Fights and Conflicts (6:19; 10:12; 15:18; 16:28; 17:14, 19; 18:6, 19; 19:11; 20:3; 22:10; 23:29–30; 26:17, 20, 21; 28:25; 29:22)

Proverbs teaches in a way that promotes social harmony; thus, anything that causes conflict is condemned. Proverbs 6:19b tells us that Yahweh himself hates conflict between brothers. Among the things that incite conflict and fights among people are the following: hate (10:12), impatience (15:18), gossip (16:28), mocking (22:10), drunkenness (23:29–30), greed (28:25), and anger (29:22). Antidotes against conflict include love (10:12), patience (15:18), controlling one's temper (19:11), avoiding contentious people (22:10), and trusting Yahweh (29:22). Some proverbs even suggest overlooking an offense in order to avoid conflict (10:12; 15:18; 17:14). According to 26:17, the epitome of folly is getting involved in a fight that is not one's own:

> Those who yank the ears of a dog,
> those who grow infuriated in a quarrel not their own.

Friendship/Neighbors (3:27–31; 6:1–5; 11:9, 12; 14:20; 16:29; 17:9, 17, 18; 18:17, 24; 19:4, 6, 7; 20:6; 21:10; 22:11; 23:10–11; 24:28–29; 25:8, 9–10, 17, 18; 26:18–19; 27:9–10, 14, 17)

The most commonly used word for "friend" and "neighbor" is the noun *rēaʿ* II, which is formed from the verb *rʿh* II (to associate with). The noun thus refers to another person with whom one is close. The translation "friend" indicates emotional attachment, while "neighbor" fits those contexts where spatial intimacy is meant. Surely the two sometimes overlap. However, in some contexts it proves difficult to decide between "neighbor" and "friend" as the best English translation. In any case, we will treat friends and neighbors together in this short description, knowing that at times our translation "friend" might better be rendered "neighbor" and vice versa.

Friendship and good relationships with neighbors are very important to the sages. A good friend is as valuable in tough times as a close relative such as a brother (17:17).[3] Indeed, 27:9–10 suggests that friends are sometimes more valuable than relatives during hard times, especially if a friend is closer at hand. One of the most quoted proverbs today indicates that interaction with friends makes a person better:

> As iron sharpens iron
>> so people sharpen the edge of their friend. (27:17)

Thus, there is no doubt that to the sage, friends and neighbors form a community that helps a person navigate through the difficulties of life. Indeed, to sabotage a relationship with a neighbor or friend is utter stupidity (11:9, 11). After all, a truly reliable friend is rare and should be treasured (20:6). Fools, on the other hand, want their associates to join them on the path of evil (16:29).

Because of the value of friendship, most of the teaching about friends/neighbors warns against behavior that will hurt a relationship and encourages proper behavior toward a friend.

For instance, 3:27 urges the student to be helpful to a neighbor when it is in one's power to do so. One should build up a relationship of trust and goodwill with others with whom one associates. Indeed, even when offended, it is usually best not to harp on it with an associate for fear that an intimate relationship might be strained or broken (17:9; 25:8). It is not a good idea to seek revenge for a wrong (24:28–29).

There is, however, one area of life in which one should not aid friends or neighbors, and that is with a loan, a situation in which the lender expects to be repaid. Certainly, people are to be generous to needy compatriots, but in such cases they should give money outright rather than expecting something to come back to them (6:1–5; 17:18).

Indeed, money complicates relationships.[4] There are a handful of proverbs whose tone is hard to discern, but they seem to suggest, when read in context, that when money is involved, it is hard to know whether a friend is a friend for selfish reasons. A good example is 14:20:

> The poor are hated by their neighbors,
>> but many are those who love the wealthy.

At first glance this seems to be a simple statement of reality. People flock to the wealthy and avoid the poor. The tone, however, is hard to gauge. Theoretically, it could be a warning to avoid poverty and do one's

---

3. Though one must be careful not to overstay one's welcome (25:17)! Further, one should be friendly to one's neighbors but also sympathetic to their moods (27:14).

4. See the discussion in Scherer, "Is the Selfish Man Wise?" 67–69.

best to gain wealth in order to acquire a number of friends. However, when read in the light of the next verse, 14:21, it suggests that this statement of reality is being criticized. That is, those who take such a stance are acting wickedly:

> Those who despise their neighbors are sinners,
>> but blessed are those who are gracious to the needy.

Guidance/Planning/Looking to the Future (1:5; 6:18; 11:14; 12:5, 20; 14:22; 15:22, 26; 16:1, 2, 3, 9, 33; 19:21; 20:18, 24; 21:5; 24:6, 27; 27:1; 29:18; 31:25, 27)

Planning requires a goal. Once the goal is envisioned, then a strategy may be devised to reach the goal. Planning involves the imagination. To be a successful planner, one must understand what it takes to reach a goal. A good planner must anticipate obstacles on the way and devise alternatives to reach the goal or perhaps even alter the goal. In short, to plan well requires wisdom, a skill of living that knows how to navigate life.

A number of proverbs make it clear that the sages knew the value of planning. Wise planning will be successful and lead to great benefits. As 21:5a states, "The plans of the determined end up in profit." Indeed, this verse goes on to compare those who plan with those who are impulsive, and the latter end up with loss.

Wise planning leads to great confidence in the future such as that displayed by the "noble woman" (31:25). Perhaps most notably, those who plan wisely receive "covenant love" and "faithfulness," qualities that can only come from Yahweh.

What differentiates wise planning from foolish planning? For one thing, wise planning seeks advice from other wise people (11:14; 15:22; 20:18; 24:6). Yet the counsel of others is only helpful if the advice is coming from those who are wise. For a good example of advice coming from a bad source, see 2 Sam. 13:5, where the "wise man" (ḥākām) Jonadab tells Amnon how to rape Tamar, his stepsister.

Wise planning also has a virtuous goal and will only utilize strategies that are fair and honest (12:5a). And 29:18 may even suggest that planning, here evoked by the word "vision," may be defined or at least bounded by the law.

However, the most salient feature of wise planning is awareness that one's plans are ultimately at the service of God's superseding purpose. This point is most dramatically driven home in a series of proverbs found in chap. 16:

> To humans belong the plans of the heart,
> > but from Yahweh comes a responding tongue.
> All paths of people are pure in their eyes,
> > but Yahweh measures the motives.
> Commit your acts to Yahweh,
> > and your plans will be established.
>
> Human hearts plan their path,
> > but Yahweh establishes their step.
>
> In the lap the lot is cast,
> > and from Yahweh are all decisions. (16:1–3, 9, 33; see also 19:21;
> > 20:24).

Thus, humans cannot be absolutely certain that they know the way the future will pan out. In spite of their planning, they must be ready to implement changes if God so wills. Thus, while confidence is well founded in God's sovereign control, sages still say: "Don't brag about tomorrow, for you don't know what the day will bear" (27:1). As 16:3 specifically teaches, humans must plan in such a way that they "commit their acts to Yahweh."

A good example of such wise planning is Daniel, as illustrated by an episode in chap. 1. Daniel wants to eat differently than the king desires, consuming vegetables and water instead of the rich food and wine of the king. His plans lead him to request the chief official, Ashpenaz, to substitute the former for the latter, but Ashpenaz refuses out of fear of Nebuchadnezzar. Daniel does not panic but rather devises an alternate plan. He privately approaches the unnamed servant who actually brings the food to him and his three friends and asks him to make the substitution. He proposes a ten-day trial period, and if the four Israelites grow weak and tired looking—what Ashpenaz feared—they would go back on the rich-food menu. The underling agrees, and Daniel reaches his desired goal.

Proverbs, though, does not talk only about wise planning; it also contrasts it with foolish planning. God condemns such plans (6:18; 15:26). They are characterized as fraudulent (12:5b, 20a). Those who plan in such a way will not succeed but will wander aimlessly (14:22).

Illness and Health (3:7–8; 12:4; 13:12; 14:30; 15:30; 16:24; 17:22; 18:14)

The ancient sages had an understanding of the relationship between what we call mental health and bodily well-being. Difficult emotions can make the body sick, while positive ones promote health:

> A joyful heart enhances healing,
>> but a broken spirit dries up bone. (17:22)

> The human spirit can sustain a person when sick,
>> but who can bear a broken spirit? (18:14)

The purpose of these observations is both to help the sages understand themselves and other people as well as to encourage them toward attitudes and behaviors that would make them feel better. According to 3:7–8, it is especially fear of Yahweh that will lead to good health.

Kings/Authority (8:15–16; 14:28, 35; 16:10, 12, 13, 14, 15; 17:7; 19:12; 20:2, 8, 26, 28; 21:1; 22:11; 23:1–3; 24:21–22; 25:2–3, 4–5, 6–7; 27:18; 28:2, 15, 16; 29:4, 12, 14, 26; 30:21–23; 31:1–9)

Most of the passages listed above concern the king explicitly, but a handful (such as 17:7) have to do with authority in general. Today, few countries, at least in the West, have monarchies wielding substantial power, but the principles enunciated here are often appropriate for behavior and attitudes toward other powerful individuals in our lives, whether employers or political leaders. A number of the following proverbs are actually given for the benefit of the ruler himself, encouraging that ruler to godly behavior, and such advice has relevance for leaders today.

The first thing to note is the obvious. Much of the book is presented as wisdom coming from the court. Solomon is named in three superscriptions, including the main one that opens the book (1:1; 10:1; 25:1). Lemuel is also described as a king in 31:1.

Kings were supposed to govern by wisdom given to them by Yahweh. As Woman Wisdom states:

> By me kings reign,
>> and nobles issue just decrees.
> By me rulers rule,
>> and princes, all righteous judgments. (8:15–16)

Indeed, many of the proverbs about a king presuppose a godly, wise king like Solomon in his youth.

> A king who sits on his judgment throne
>> scatters all evil with his eyes. (20:8)

> A wise king scatters wicked people,
>> and he rolls the wheel over them. (20:26)

Such a godly king is implied in 22:11, a proverb urging the hearer to pursue godliness to get ahead:

> Those who love a pure heart—
> their lips are gracious; the king is their friend.

However, the proverbs also know the kind of king who does not befriend the pure of heart, but rather the wicked:

> A growling lion and a prowling bear—
> a wicked ruler over a poor people. (28:15)

The wish of the wise for such a ruler is that wickedness be removed from his realm:

> Separate the dross from the silver,
> and a vessel will come out for refining.
> Separate the wicked from the presence of the king,
> and his throne will be established in righteousness. (25:4–5)

A number of proverbs seem to encourage kings by holding out the carrot of a successful reign for godly behavior and the stick of a failed nation for wicked behavior.

> A king with justice causes the land to endure,
> but the tax man tears it down. (29:4)

> A ruler who pays attention to a false word—
> all those who serve him are wicked. (29:12)

> A king who judges the poor reliably—
> his throne will be established forever. (29:14)

Godly king or not, the wise knew that, around such a powerful human being, certain behaviors were dangerous and others were productive:

> The king finds an insightful servant acceptable,
> but his fury will be directed toward a shameful one. (14:35)

The book even contains advice about how to act at a dinner table with the king:

> When you sit down to dine with a ruler,
> carefully consider what is in front of you.
> Place a knife at your gullet
> to control your appetite.

> Don't long for his delicacies,
> for they are false food. (23:1–3)

Proverbs such as these latter two as well as others raise questions about the original setting of at least some of the sayings. After all, not many people would directly benefit from advice concerning how to eat with the king; only a small percentage of the population would ever have the opportunity. As discussed in the introduction, we should think of a variety of settings for the individual proverbs of the book, and the ones in this category are mostly from a court background.

Finally, and perhaps most important, though the power of the king is beyond that of any other human being (25:2–3), he is putty in the hands of God.

> The heart of a king is a canal of water in the hand of Yahweh;
> he inclines it wherever he wants. (21:1)

Laziness and Hard Work (6:6–11; 10:4, 5, 26; 12:11, 24, 27; 13:4; 14:23; 15:19; 18:9; 19:15, 24; 20:4, 13; 21:25; 22:13, 29; 24:30–34; 26:13–16; 27:23–27; 28:19; 31:27)

Proverbs is intolerant of lazy people; they are considered the epitome of folly. The quantity of proverbs on laziness and hard work is surprising. The sting of the images used to parody those who refuse to put in effort is also notable. Indeed, the sage is at his most sarcastically comedic when it comes to the lazy person:

> Lazy people say, "There is a lion cub on the path,
> a lion on the public square!"
> The door turns on its hinge,
> and lazy people on their beds.
> Lazy people bury their hand into the bowl,
> but they are not able to return it to their mouth.
> Lazy people are wise in their own eyes,
> even more than seven who respond with discernment. (26:13–16)

Because it takes effort to make it in this world, the wise teacher is concerned that the lazy will soon impoverish themselves. Thus, the sages admonish their disciples to work hard (6:6–11).

It is true today as in antiquity that some lazy people are rich, not because of their efforts but because of being born into a family of means. However, the fact that there are exceptions does not disprove the importance of the point that is relevant in 99 percent of the cases, that laziness leads to destitution or want.

On the other hand, according to a proverb like 22:29, those who work hard get ahead in life:

> Do you see people who do their work with diligence?
>> They will stand before kings;
>> they will not stand before the obscure.

We are not surprised to find the following description of the noble woman in 31:27: "She is a lookout post for the doings of her household; she does not eat the food of laziness."

Lies (6:16–19; 10:18; 12:17, 19, 22; 14:5, 25; 17:4; 19:5, 9, 28; 21:6, 28; 24:28–29; 25:8, 18; 30:7–9)

Lies are a specific form of foolish speech that the sages roundly condemn. Indeed, 12:22 throws the weight of Yahweh's condemnation against lying:

> False lips are an abomination to Yahweh;
>> his favor is on those who do what is true.

Lies destroy relationships. The sages believe that words can truly and authentically reflect the actual state of things as well as a person's thinking, and when fools purposely mislead by their words, they perform an act of violence: "Lying lips conceal hate, and those who spread slander are fools" (10:18). On the other hand, the truth can bring healing:

> A truthful witness saves lives,
>> but a fraudulent person proclaims lies. (14:25)

Lies may work temporarily, but ultimately the truth will come out. However, by warning about the dangers of lying, the sages not only want to dissuade those people from that behavior but also warn the righteous not to automatically take people at their word.

The law court is an especially important place for the truth to be told. People's lives depend on it. Thus, a number of proverbs specifically show contempt toward those who lie as witnesses (14:5; 19:28; 21:28; 24:28–29; 25:8, 18; 29:24), and they eventually will be found out:

> False witnesses will not escape punishment,
>> and those who proclaim lies will not escape. (19:5)

Messengers (10:26; 13:17; 25:13, 25; 26:6)

Communication is vital to human society. For a community to function as a social group, the individuals must be able to speak and hear each other. As we have seen elsewhere, it is vitally important that interpersonal communication be truthful and reliable (see "Speaking and Listening" below).

However, where distance enters the equation, it is not possible for a person to actually be present to deliver a message. In the days before phones or email or even before a widely accessible postal system, people had to rely on messengers, who would physically deliver a message—usually orally, though a large number of written letters from the ancient world are attested as well.

In any case, it was crucial that one's messenger be reliable. In a typical manner, Proverbs makes its point by contrasting good and bad messengers. Good messengers are reliable (13:17b; 25:13b), presumably meaning that they are timely and actually deliver the intended message to the recipient. Such messengers have a positive effect described by metaphors like snow on the harvest day (25:13a) or cold water for a weary person (25:25a). It is interesting to see that Woman Wisdom utilizes messengers in her dinner invitation to the simpleminded men who go by her seven-columned house (9:3).

On the other hand, we have foolish messengers. These messengers are lazy, which implies that they do not hurry to deliver the message (10:26), or evil, which may mean that they get distracted by things that keep them from getting the message to the intended recipient (13:17a). Striking metaphors used for foolish messengers also emphasize the trouble they bring to their employers: vinegar to the teeth, smoke in the eyes (10:26a). The effect of their bad work is described by the violent images of amputated feet and drinking violence (26:6).

Openness to Listening to Advice (3:11–12; 9:7–9; 12:1, 15; 13:1, 10, 13–14, 18; 15:5, 10, 12, 31, 32, 33; 17:10; 18:2, 15; 19:25, 27; 21:11; 23:9; 24:5–6; 25:12; 26:11; 27:5–6, 22; 28:13, 23; 29:1, 9)

As mentioned elsewhere and not needing further development (see "Pride/Humility" below), those who are humble are open to hearing advice and receptive to correction. Those who are proud resist. The listed verses indicate the importance of these themes to the wisdom enterprise. Since it is the wise and not the fools who will listen and change due to advice that includes correction, the sages direct their teaching toward the former and not the latter, who are considered a lost cause:

Those who discipline a mocker receive an insult;
　　those who correct the wicked—they are blemished.
Don't correct mockers, or else they will hate you,
　　but correct the wise, and they will love you.
Give to the wise, and they will be still wiser;
　　inform the righteous, and they will add to their teaching. (9:7–9)

Physical Discipline (3:11–12; 10:13; 13:24; 17:10; 19:18, 25; 20:30; 22:15; 23:13–14; 26:3; 29:15, 17, 19)

The word "discipline" (*mûsār*, sometimes translated "instruction") and its frequent word pair "correction" (*tôkaḥat*) may imply at times physical coercion in the service of education or growth in wisdom, but here we are looking at those passages that explicitly mention physical discipline. And this is most often signaled by the Hebrew word *šēbeṭ*, which we translate as "rod." The "rod" is not to be taken metaphorically in the book, but rather as a tool of physical discipline. However, there are passages that do not specifically mention the "rod" and yet also clearly have to do with physical punishment (19:18).

Two groups are mentioned as the legitimate recipients of the rod: children and fools. However, there is more hope for the former than the latter.

> Stupidity is bound up in a youth's heart;
> 　　the rod of discipline drives it far from him. (22:15)

> Wisdom is found on understanding lips,
> 　　but a rod is for the backs of those lacking heart. (10:13)

It is a sign of wisdom when a rebuke will suffice in the place of physical punishment (17:10). The use of discipline is for the positive end of teaching a person wisdom:

> The rod and correction impart wisdom,
> 　　but youths who are unsupervised shame their mothers. (29:15)

Such physical punishment was not severe, and these passages should never be used to legitimize any form of child abuse:

> Don't withhold discipline from young people.
> 　　If you strike them with the rod, they will not die.
> Strike them with a rod,
> 　　and you will extricate their lives from Sheol. (23:13–14)

And again, it must be borne in mind that the application of any proverb depends on the people involved as well as the situation. These proverbs do not imply that parents must apply physical punishment when they judge that a simple verbal reprimand will do.

Discipline is never to be done out of anger or hate or a desire to harm, but out of love and a desire that the person improve. In this way, the parent follows the model of God, who disciplines his children (3:11–12).

Positive Influence of the Righteous/Negative of the Wicked
(11:11; 14:34; 16:29; 20:7; 25:4–5; 28:10, 12, 28; 29:2, 8, 16)

Wisdom benefits not only the self but others as well. Communities are stronger if their members are wise, not fools, and this is especially true if their leaders lead with wisdom.

> By the blessing of those with integrity a city is exalted,
>> and by the mouth of the wicked, it is demolished. (11:11)

This is true of the family:

> The righteous walk about in their innocence;
>> blessed are their children after them. (20:7)

Likewise for the nation:

> Righteousness lifts a nation up,
>> but sin diminishes a people. (14:34)

For this reason the community needs to get rid of fools in its midst and in particular keep its leaders far from their influence:

> Separate the dross from the silver,
>> and a vessel will come out for refining.
> Separate the wicked from the presence of the king,
>> and his throne will be established in righteousness. (25:4–5)

The very mood of a community is determined by whether the righteous wise are in charge:

> When the righteous increase, the people rejoice,
>> but when the wicked dominate, the people moan. (29:2)

Prayer/Sacrifice/Vows (3:9; 7:14–15; 15:8, 29; 20:25; 21:3, 27; 28:9)

For years, scholars have attempted to drive a wedge between the sages and the cult.[5] Although it must be granted that explicit mention of formal worship practices is minimal in Proverbs, it is nonetheless not absent. Furthermore, what is there is read wrongly if taken as critical about certain religious actions. When read fairly, the sages are concerned that their disciples do religious acts out of heartfelt devotion.

For instance, the sages are not antisacrifice per se; they just warn against thinking that the act of sacrifice is beneficial without the involvement of one's heart. This is consistent with the teaching throughout the Bible. The prophets also made it clear that religious acts without proper heart engagement are useless (Jer. 7). The sages communicate this with diatribes against the sacrifice of wicked people as well as better-than proverbs. In terms of the latter, it must be borne in mind that the better-than form is used to present relative values, not absolute values.

> The sacrifice of wicked people is an abomination to Yahweh,
> but the prayer of the virtuous brings his favor. (15:8)

> Practicing righteousness and justice
> is more preferable to Yahweh than sacrifice. (21:3)

Prayer is typically thought to be superior to sacrifice because it more typically unites act and heart. However, even empty prayer merits Yahweh's contempt:

> Those who turn their ear from hearing instruction,
> even their prayers will be an abomination. (28:9)

The most pervasive principle connected to this topic is that one's heart had better be where one's actions indicate. The promiscuous woman's heart is perverse as she recites vows and sacrifices in the context of seducing the young man (7:14–15). But the sages suggest that a true honoring of God with one's material wealth will be viewed favorably by God (3:9–10).

Pride/Humility (3:5, 7; 6:17; 11:2; 15:25, 33; 16:5, 18, 19; 18:12; 21:4, 24; 22:4; 25:6–7, 27; 26:12; 29:23; 30:1–4, 13)

In Proverbs, there is a clear and close association between wisdom and humility and between folly and pride.

---

5. Both the history of discussion and an excellent corrective may be found in the seminal work of Perdue, *Wisdom and Cult*.

> Incredibly presumptuous—mockers are their name,
>   those who do excessively insolent things. (21:24)

> The fear of Yahweh is wise discipline,
>   and humility comes before glory. (15:33)

As the latter verse also indicates, humility comes from a healthy fear of Yahweh. Those who fear Yahweh (see commentary at 1:7) know that they are not the center of the universe. They are not "wise in their own eyes":

> Don't be wise in your own eyes.
>   Fear Yahweh and turn away from evil. (3:7)

It leads to a healthy distrust of one's own abilities and a rewarding dependence on God himself:

> Trust in Yahweh with all your heart,
>   and don't depend on your own understanding. (3:5)

Indeed, arrogance will lead to one's destruction, while humility will lead to success:

> The arrogance of people causes them to fall;
>   but a lowly spirit holds glory tight. (29:23)

Perhaps the most practical and beneficial result of humility is openness to correction. Someone who is humble will listen to criticism and take it to heart. The proud will not listen but will mock attempts at instruction (see "Openness to Listening to Advice" above).

Protection of the Socially Vulnerable (15:25; 23:10–12)

Illustrating God's special care for the humble are texts that specify God's concern for those who are socially vulnerable in ancient Israel. Most pointedly, these include the orphan and the widow.

> Yahweh uproots the house of the arrogant,
>   but he establishes the border of the widow. (15:25)

> Don't remove an ancient boundary marker,
>   and don't invade the fields of orphans.
> For their redeemer is strong and will make
>   accusations against you. (23:10–11)

Psychological Insight (12:25; 13:12; 14:10, 13, 30; 15:4, 13, 30; 17:22; 25:20; 27:19; 28:17)

Proverbs shows an uncanny sensitivity to the working of the human heart and in particular to how one's emotions affect one's mental, spiritual, and even bodily existence.

These sages know that people walk a lonely path with respect to their inner lives:

> A heart knows emotional distress,
>> and in its joy another person cannot share. (14:10)

They articulate an understanding of both anxiety and depression and recognize the debilitating effects of these states:

> Anxiety makes the heart of a person depressed,
>> but a good word encourages it. (12:25)

> Expectation delayed makes the heart sick;
>> longing fulfilled is the tree of life. (13:12)

The sages also know that one's outer demeanor does not always reflect one's inner life:

> Even in laughter the heart may feel pain,
>> and in the end joy may turn to sorrow. (14:13)

And, as 14:30 points out, one's whole being is affected by one's emotional state:

> The life of the body is a healthy heart,
>> but jealousy is a rot of the bones.

Rumors/Gossip/Slander/Insult (6:19; 9:7; 10:18; 11:13; 16:28; 18:3, 8; 20:19; 25:8–10, 23; 26:20, 22; 30:10)

The gossip is a classic example of a foolish speaker. Gossips spread information behind people's backs, not to help but rather to damage their reputations. As is typical of foolish speech, spreading rumors destroys relationships and thus community:

> The perverse produce conflict,
>> and gossips separate intimate friends. (16:28)

If a gossip is removed from a situation, then community is enhanced:

> Without wood, a fire is extinguished.
> When there are no gossips, conflict calms down. (26:20)

It does not matter whether or not what is said is true. It is the intention and timing of the speech that is reprehensible. Usually, however, gossip is based on uncertain knowledge of a matter.

Even so, the sage recognizes just how tempting it is not only to spread rumors but also to listen to them:

> The words of gossips are like choice morsels;
> they go down to their inmost parts. (18:8; repeated verbatim in 26:22)

Slander and gossip are cousins of each other, but the former may be differentiated by being a direct attack on the reputation of a person, which might be delivered to the person directly as an insult or, like gossip, spread behind the person's back.

Slanderers reveal the secrets of others (11:13a; 20:19a), while the wise do not dredge up damaging information against another (11:13b) and do not even associate with those who want to harm the reputation of another (20:19b).

Proverbs provides some information about why someone might engage in slander, and the motivations are not pretty. Thus, 9:7 suggests that slander is a tool to ward off constructive criticism. Mockers cannot stand to be corrected, so they slander those who try to help them. According to 18:3, slander is a result of the slanderer's shame, perhaps felt when an inadequacy is exposed. In 25:8–10 and 30:10, the sage provides a strategy for avoiding the slander of others.

Shame (3:35; 6:32–33; 9:7; 11:2; 12:8; 13:18; 14:35; 18:3; 22:10; 25:8; 28:7; 29:15)

Shame results when something ugly is revealed about oneself. Today the argument may be made that people are callous to public humiliation, but this was not true in ancient Israel. In Proverbs, it is the fool who is shamed, and this fact is used in order to discourage foolish behavior that might lead to shame:

> The wise possess glory,
> but fools exude shame. (3:35)

It may be not just people's own actions that lead to shame but also the actions of those for whom they are responsible, most pointedly, their children:

> The rod and correction impart wisdom,
>> but youths who are unsupervised shame their mothers. (29:15)

The opposite of shame is praise, and the latter belongs to the wise.

> Poverty and shame belong to those who neglect discipline,
>> but those who guard correction will be honored. (13:18)

The paradox is that it is the wise who show humility and therefore are not humiliated, whereas the wicked are proud and end up shamed.

> When insolence comes, then shame will come,
>> but wisdom with modesty. (11:2; see also "Pride/Humility" above)

Speaking and Listening (6:16–19; 8:6–9, 12–14; 10:6, 18, 19, 20, 21, 31, 32; 11:11, 12, 13; 12:6, 13, 14, 25; 13:2, 5, 16; 14:3, 5, 25; 15:1, 2, 4, 7, 23, 28; 16:10, 13, 24; 17:4, 7, 20, 27, 28; 18:4, 6, 7, 8, 13, 20, 21; 19:5, 9; 20:19; 21:23; 22:11; 23:15–16; 24:7–9, 26; 25:10–11, 14, 24; 26:28; 27:14; 29:5, 20; 30:5–6, 10, 14; 31:26)

Communication is a large subject in the book of Proverbs. The proper use and reception of words was critically important to the sages. Proverbs is a book that imparts advice about how to live wisely in a way that avoids problems and promotes success, and this advice comes in the form of words. The right words bring life, and the wrong words bring death. In the words of 18:21:

> Death and life are in the power of the tongue,
>> and those who love it will eat its fruit.

The tongue can kill or can bring healing both to the listener and to the one who speaks: "The lips of a fool lead to accusation; his mouth invites blows" (18:6). While on certain occasions this may refer to literal life and death, it can also refer metaphorically to the renewal or cessation of other beneficial things, such as community. Wise words promote relationships; foolish words alienate them:

> Banish the mocker, and conflict will go out;
>> judgment and shame will cease. (22:10)

To fully understand this proverb, it must be remembered that the "mocker" is the foolish speaker par excellence, the one who uses words to ridicule others and push them away. But it is not only on an individual level. Wise words promote city life, and foolish words destroy it:

> By the blessing of those with integrity a city is exalted,
> and by the mouth of the wicked, it is demolished. (11:11)

Accordingly, great care and attention should be directed to the use of speech.

As is typical in Proverbs, the sages teach by contrast, using antithetical parallelisms to highlight the differences between wise speech that leads to life and foolish speech that results in death. Wise speech reflects reality; foolish speech twists it. This point is made by a series of proverbs, some near repetitive, that contrast truth-speakers from liars, particularly in the courtroom (see "Lies" above). Wise words not only reliably reflect external reality but also authentically express one's internal reality or "heart."

> The heart of the wise provides insight to their mouth
> and increases teaching on their lips. (16:23)

Foolish words dissimulate, but the sages knew that such dissimulation would not endure:

> Truthful lips endure forever,
> but a lying tongue lasts only for a moment. (12:19)

> Those who hate dissimulate with their lips,
> but they set deception inside.
> Though their voice is gracious, don't believe them,
> for seven abominations are in their heart.
> Hatred is covered with guile,
> but they reveal their evil in the assembly. (26:24–26)

Thus, wise speech reflects reality and the heart. But there is more. A wise word is one that is spoken at the right time. Good words are not inherently good; they must be spoken at the appropriate time. This idea is taught most famously by 15:23 as well as in the metaphorically rich 25:11:

> It is a joy to a person to give an answer!
> How good a word at the right time! (15:23)

> Apples of gold in a silver setting
> is a word spoken in its right timing. (25:11)

Even cheerful greetings are foolish words if spoken too early in the morning, before the recipients can receive such warmth:

> Those who bless their neighbors with a loud voice in the early
> morning—
> it will be considered a curse to them. (27:14)

An hour later, after waking up a bit more, this greeting would be a blessing rather than a curse. Timing is everything, even when it comes to speaking and applying proverbs themselves:

> The legs of a lame person dangle,
> and a proverb in the mouth of a fool. (26:7)
>
> A thornbush in the hand of a drunk,
> and a proverb in the mouth of fools. (26:9)

Much more can be said about wise and foolish speech, but rather than continuing to discuss the subject under this essay, we will now turn our attention to various topics that illustrate both wise and foolish speech.

Before we do, however, we need to point out how these two modes of human speech reflect the diametrically opposed speech of the two metaphorical women: Wisdom and Folly. Woman Wisdom herself states:

> Listen, for I speak noble things,
> opening virtuous lips.
> For my mouth utters the truth,
> and my lips despise wickedness.
> All the speeches of my mouth are righteous.
> Nothing in them is twisted or perverse.
> All of them are straightforward to understanding
> and virtuous for those who seek knowledge. (8:6–9)

On the other hand, Woman Folly is "boisterous," loud, noisy (9:13). The word denotes not only volume but also confusion of speech. Her speech is characterized by those qualities from which Wisdom has distanced herself. In the introduction, I argue that Woman Wisdom represents Yahweh, while Woman Folly represents false gods and goddesses. Thus, those who speak wise words follow the true God, while those who speak falsely act like idolaters.

Table Manners (23:1–3, 6–8)

Wisdom teaches how to act in specific situations. In two passages, the sages instruct their students concerning proper etiquette at the table. In the first text, dining with a ruler (23:1–3) is specified, though the principle of moderation can be applied more broadly. Even though such a broader application is possible, a text like this points most strongly in favor of a court origin for at least some of the proverbs of the book. After all, not everyone gets to eat with the king. The king would have an opulent table, and therefore the temptation would be strong to indulge. However, the advice is to control oneself. It seems unlikely that the motivation would be weight control or health. Rather, it may be the broader issue of self-control or greed. Those who gorge themselves may lack control in other areas of life or be open to temptations of greed in general.

The other passage that deals specifically with table manners (23:6–8) also calls for self-control. However, here the table is not that of the king but rather of a stingy person. Such persons may seem to be offering a bountiful table, but they don't really want you to indulge. It is a false invitation. In this case, it is better not to eat with them at all.

In these passages, we can see the specific outworking of general wisdom attributes like self-control, moderation, and the right action at the right time.

Wealth and Poverty (3:9–10; 6:1–5; 8:18–19; 10:2, 3, 4, 15, 16; 11:4, 7, 15, 24, 28; 12:9; 13:7, 8, 11, 22, 23, 25; 14:20, 21, 24, 31; 15:15, 16, 17; 16:8, 19; 17:1, 5, 18; 18:11, 23; 19:4, 7, 10, 14, 17, 22; 20:17, 21; 21:6, 17, 20; 22:2, 4, 7, 9, 13, 16, 22–23; 23:4–5; 24:3–4; 27:13, 23–27; 28:3, 6, 8, 11, 16, 20, 25, 27; 29:3, 7, 13, 14; 30:7–9)

The topic of wealth and poverty is a good example of the dangers of isolating any single proverbial saying and taking it as representative of the teaching of the book as a whole. Indeed, on the basis of a text like 3:9–10, the book has been taken to promote the idea that godliness automatically leads to wealth:

> Honor Yahweh with your wealth
> and the first of your produce.
> And your barns will be filled with plenty,
> and your vats will burst with wine.

However, other proverbs acknowledge that the fool may have wealth, albeit temporarily. In addition, other proverbs make it clear that the wise person will sometimes have to decide between wealth and wisdom.

A survey of Proverbs concerning wealth and poverty suggests that it is best to describe the book's teaching as providing seven snapshots, none of which are complete in themselves. They are as follows (with a selection of illustrative verses):

1. *God blesses the righteous with wealth.* Woman Wisdom says:

> Wealth and honor are with me,
> enduring riches and righteousness.

> My fruit is better than gold, even fine gold,
> my yield than choice silver. (8:18–19)

The paradigmatic example of this is Solomon in 1 Kings 3. Given a choice of any gift from God, he chose wisdom. God was so pleased with this choice that he also gave him wealth and power.

2. *Foolish behavior leads to poverty.* As one might expect, Proverbs also teaches that foolish behavior results in poverty, often using antithesis to reinforce this point. The purpose of these observations and warnings is to keep people from acting in these self-destructive ways. Preeminent among foolish behaviors that lead to destitution is laziness (see "Laziness and Hard Work" above), as 10:4–5 states quite directly:

> A slack palm makes poverty;
> a determined hand makes rich.
> An insightful son harvests in the summer;
> a disgraceful son sleeps during harvest.

Sometimes this snapshot is taught more generally and in direct contrast to snapshot 1, as in 14:24:

> The crown of the wise is their wealth;
> the stupidity of fools is stupidity.

3. *The wealth of fools will not last.* Proverbs recognizes that fools may amass material advantage, but if so, it will be only temporary and in any case will provide no real advantage:

> Those who do wicked deeds get false wages;
> those who sow righteous deeds get a reliable payment. (11:18)

> Riches diminish because of haste,
> but the one who gathers by hand will increase. (13:11)

> Riches do not profit on the day of fury,
> but righteousness will extricate from death. (11:4)

4. *Poverty is the result of injustice and oppression.* Proverbs is often accused of a rather callous view of poverty. As we have seen, the book does make a connection between poverty and laziness, but it would be wrong to conclude that the sages thought that all struggle was the result of some foolish behavior. Though it is a comparatively minor theme, a proverb like 13:23 indicates awareness that poverty is sometimes the

result of factors beyond a person's control and may be caused by the evil intentions of another:

> Much food comes from the arable soil of the poor,
>   but it is swept away because of a lack of justice.

5. *Those with money must be generous.* As a further example of a nuanced view of wealth and poverty, we observe proverbs that urge generosity toward the poor. If poverty were thought to be always connected to foolish behavior, it is unlikely that the sages would encourage the king or others to be as helpful as the following proverbs suggest:

> Those who give to the poor will lack nothing,
>   but those who avert their eyes will have numerous curses. (28:27)

> The righteous know the just cause of the poor,
>   but the wicked do not understand knowledge. (29:7)

> A king who judges the poor reliably—
>   his throne will be established forever. (29:14)

6. *Wisdom is better than wealth.* In a series of better-than proverbs (see "Literary Style" in the introduction), we learn that wisdom and its associated qualities are more important than wealth. Such a statement of relative values implies that people will sometimes have to make a choice between wisdom and wealth; they do not always accompany each other, as a naive reading of snapshot 1 might indicate:

> Getting wisdom is much better than gold,
>   and getting understanding is to be preferred over silver. (16:16)

> It is better to be a poor person and walk blamelessly,
>   than one with crooked paths and wealthy. (28:6)

7. *Wealth has limited value.* Finally, though Proverbs never denigrates wealth as such, it does recognize that it has its limits:

> Riches do not profit on the day of fury,
>   but righteousness will extricate from death. (11:4)

Indeed, riches may bring more trouble than they prevent. It is much more likely that a rich person will be kidnapped, according to 13:8:

> Wealth can provide a ransom for a person's life,
>   but a poor person does not hear a threat.

Again, no single proverb can be taken as representing the teaching of Proverbs on wealth and poverty. While wealth is seen as positive, it is not always associated with wisdom. Indeed, though hard work is encouraged, at a certain point it is no longer worth it:

> Don't wear yourself out trying to get wealthy.
>> Stop, because of your understanding.
> You will let your eyes fly to it, but it will be no more.
>> For it will surely grow wings
>> like an eagle and fly heavenward. (23:4–5)

And in the final analysis, wealth and poverty have their pitfalls, and this realization leads to a statement that prefers the halfway point between the two:

> Two things I ask of you;
>> don't withhold them from me before I die.
> Fraud and lying words—
>> keep far from me!
> Poverty and wealth don't give to me!
>> Allow me to devour my regular allotment of bread,
> lest I am sated and act deceptively
>> and say, "Who is Yahweh?"
> Lest I don't have much and I steal,
>> and I profane the name of my God. (30:7–9)

Women/Wife (5:1–23; 6:20–35; 7:1–27; 11:22; 12:4; 14:1; 18:22; 19:13, 14; 21:9, 19; 22:14; 25:24; 27:15–16; 30:18–19, 20; 31:1–9, 10–31)

Since the husband-wife relationship is the matrix of the family, this topic is an extension of the previous "Family Relationships." However, women receive such an extensive treatment separate from the parent-child relationship that it is worth considering it separately.

As in the previous section, here we simply summarize the salient points that the book of Proverbs makes about women and illustrate each point with a single quotation. We begin with a principle that, if judged by sheer quantity of teaching, is the most important point that the book makes to the young men who are the explicit recipients:

1. *Avoid immoral women.*

> . . . to guard you from the evil woman,
>> from the flattering tongue of the foreign woman.
> Don't desire her beauty in your heart;
>> and don't let her absorb you with her eyelashes.

> For a prostitute costs a loaf of bread,
> but a married woman hunts for a man's life.
> Can a man scoop fire into his lap
> and his clothes not get burned?
> Or can a man walk on hot coals
> and his feet not get singed?
> Thus, the person who goes to the wife of his neighbor;
> all who touch her will not go unpunished. (6:24–29)

2. Cultivate a strong relationship with your wife.

> Drink water from your own well,
> gushing water from your own cistern.
> Should your fountains burst forth outside;
> streams of water in the pubic squares?
> They are yours alone
> and not for strangers who are with you.
> May your spring be blessed;
> rejoice in the wife of your youth.
> She is a deer of love and an ibex of grace.
> Let her breasts intoxicate you all the time;
> be continually inebriated by her love.
> Why, my son, should you be inebriated by a stranger
> and embrace the bosom of a foreigner? (5:15–20)

3. Appreciate the joys of a good wife.

> The one who finds a wife finds a good thing,
> and he obtains favor from Yahweh. (18:22)[6]

4. Avoid the agony of a bad choice.

> The constant dripping on a day of heavy rain
> is similar to a contentious wife. (27:15)

5. *Reflections of Woman Wisdom and Woman Folly.* According to Proverbs, there are two classes of women: the strange and foreign woman, and the wife. Descriptions of these women echo descriptions of Woman Folly and Woman Wisdom respectively. They are echoes of these personifications, which we have argued stand for idols and the true God (see "Theology of the Book" in the introduction).

---

6. At this point, the well-known poem concerning the noble woman (31:10–31) contributes to the theme.

A final word: As pointed out earlier in the commentary, Proverbs discusses women and wives and not men and husbands because in its original setting the book was addressed to young men. However, modern women can certainly read the proverbs and apply them to their relationships with men.

Bibliography

Ahlstöm, G. W. "The House of Wisdom." *Svensk exegetisk årsbok* 44 (1979): 74–76.

Aitken, K. T. *Proverbs*. Daily Study Bible—Old Testament. Philadelphia: Westminster, 1986.

Albertson, R. G. "Job and Ancient Near Eastern Wisdom Literature." In *More Essays on the Comparative Method*, edited by W. W. Hallo, J. C. Moyer, and L. G. Perdue, 213–30. Scripture in Context 2. Winona Lake, IN: Eisenbrauns, 1983.

Alden, R. L. *Proverbs: A Commentary on an Ancient Book of Timeless Advice*. Grand Rapids: Baker, 1983.

Aletti, J.-N. "Proverbes 8,22–31: Étude de structure." *Biblica* 57 (1976): 25–37.

Alster, B. *Proverbs of Ancient Sumer: The World's Earliest Proverb Collection*. 2 vols. Bethesda, MD: CDL, 1997.

Anbar, M. "Proverbes 11,21; 16,5: *yd lyd*, 'sur le champ.'" *Biblica* 53 (1972): 537–38.

Andrews, M. E. "Variety of Expression in Proverbs xxiii 29–35." *Vetus Testamentum* 28 (1978): 102–3.

Assmann, J. *Ma'at: Gerechtigkeit und Unsterblichkeit im alten Ägypten*. Munich: Beck, 1990.

Barr, J. "BᵓRṢ-MOLIS: Prov XI.31, 1 Pet IV.18." *Journal of Semitic Studies* 20 (1975): 149–64.

Barré, M. L. "'Fear of God' and the World View of Wisdom." *Biblical Theology Bulletin* 11 (1981): 41–43.

Bartholomew, C. G. *Reading Proverbs with Integrity*. Cambridge: Grove, 2001.

———. "A Time for War and a Time for Peace: Old Testament Wisdom, Creation and O'Donovan's Theological Ethics." In *A Royal Priesthood? The Use of the Bible Ethically and Politically; A Dialogue with Oliver O'Donovan*, edited by C. Bartholomew et al., 91–112. Scripture and Hermeneutics Series 3. Carlisle, UK: Paternoster; Grand Rapids: Zondervan, 2002.

Barucq, A. *Le livre des Proverbes*. Sources bibliques. Paris: Gabalda, 1964.

Baumann, G. "A Figure with Many Facets: The Literary and Theological Functions of Personified Wisdom in Proverbs 1–9." In *Wisdom and Psalms*, edited by A. Brenner and C. R. Fontaine, 44–78. Feminist Companion to the Bible 2/2. Sheffield: Sheffield Academic Press, 1998.

Beardslee, W. A. "Uses of the Proverb in the Synoptic Gospels." *Interpretation* 24 (1970): 61–73.

Beckwith, R. *The Old Testament Canon in the New Testament Church*. Grand Rapids: Eerdmans, 1985.

Bellis, A. O. "The Gender and Motives of the Wisdom Teacher in Proverbs 7." *Bulletin for Biblical Research* 6 (1996): 15–22.

Bennema, C. "The Power of Saving Wisdom: An Investigation of Spirit and Wisdom in Relation to the Soteriology of the Fourth Gospel." Ph.D. diss., London Bible College/Brunel University, 2001.

Blenkinsopp, J. "The Social Context of the 'Outsider Woman' in Proverbs 1–9." *Biblica* 72 (1991): 457–73.

———. *Wisdom and Law in the Old Testament*. Oxford: Oxford University Press, 1983.

Blocher, H. "The Fear of the Lord as the 'Principle' of Wisdom." *Tyndale Bulletin* 28 (1977): 3–28.

Boström, G. *Paronomasi i den äldre hebreiska maschallitteraturen med särskild hänsyn till proverbia*. Lund universitets årsskrift 23.8. Lund: Gleerup, 1928.

———. *Proverbiastudien: Die Weisheit und das fremde Weib in Spr. 1–9*. Lund universitets årsskrift 30.3. Lund: Gleerup, 1935.

Boström, L. *The God of the Sages: The Portrayal of God in the Book of Proverbs*. Coniectanea biblica: Old Testament Series 29. Stockholm: Almqvist & Wiksell, 1990.

Brenner, A. "Some Observations on the Figuration of Woman in Wisdom Literature." In *Of Prophets' Visions and the Wisdom of Sages: Essays in Honour of R. Norman Whybray on His Seventieth Birthday*, edited by H. A. McKay and D. J. A. Clines, 192–208. Journal for the Study of the Old Testament: Supplement Series 162. Sheffield: JSOT Press, 1993.

Brenner, A., and F. van Dijk-Hemmes. *On Gendering Texts: Female and Male Voices in the Hebrew Bible*. Leiden: Brill, 1993.

Bricker, D. P. "The Doctrine of the 'Two Ways' in Proverbs." *Journal of the Evangelical Theological Society* 38 (1995): 501–17.

Brown, J. P. "Proverb-Book, Gold-Economy, Alphabet." *Journal of Biblical Literature* 100 (1981): 169–91.

Brown, W. P. *Character in Crisis: A Fresh Approach to the Wisdom Literature of the Old Testament*. Grand Rapids: Eerdmans, 1996.

Brueggemann, W. *In Man We Trust*. Richmond: John Knox, 1972.

———. "Scripture and the Ecumenical Life-Style: A Study in Wisdom Theology." *Interpretation* 24 (1970): 3–19.

———. "The Social Significance of Solomon as a Patron of Wisdom." In *The Sage in Israel and the Ancient Near East*, edited by J. G. Gammie and L. G. Perdue, 117–32. Winona Lake, IN: Eisenbrauns, 1990.

Bryce, G. E. "Another Wisdom-'Book' in Proverbs." *Journal of Biblical Literature* 91 (1972): 145–57.

———. *A Legacy of Wisdom: The Egyptian Contribution to the Wisdom of Israel*. Lewisburg, PA: Bucknell University Press, 1979.

———. "Omen-Wisdom in Ancient Israel." *Journal of Biblical Literature* 94 (1975): 19–37.

Byargeon, R. W. "Echoes of Wisdom in the Lord's Prayer (Matt 6:9–13)." *Journal of the Evangelical Theological Society* 41 (1998): 353–65.

———. "The Structure and Significance of Proverbs 9:7–12." *Journal of the Evangelical Theological Society* 40 (1997): 367–75.

Callaway, P. R. "Deut 21:18–21: Proverbial Wisdom and Law." *Journal of Biblical Literature* 103 (1984): 341–52.

Camp, C. V. "What's So Strange about the Strange Woman?" In *The Bible and the Politics of Exegesis: Essays in Honor of Norman K. Gottwald on His Sixty-fifth Birthday*, edited by D. Jobling, P. L. Day, and G. T. Sheppard, 17–31. Cleveland: Pilgrim, 1991.

———. *Wisdom and the Feminine in the Book of Proverbs*. Sheffield: Almond, 1985.

———. *Wise, Strange, and Holy: The Strange Woman and the Making of the Bible*. Sheffield: Sheffield Academic Press, 2000.

———. "Woman Wisdom as Root Metaphor: A Theological Consideration." In *The Listening Heart: Essays in Wisdom and the Psalms in Honor of Roland E. Murphy, O. Carm.*, edited by K. G. Hoglund et al., 45–76. Journal for the Study of the Old Testament: Supplement Series 58. Sheffield: Sheffield Academic Press, 1987.

Carpenter, J. B. "Prosperity in Proverbs and Confucius: The Twain Meet." *American Journal of Theology* 13 (1999): 71–93.

Cathcart, K. J. "*Bᵉhopnāw* in Proverbs XXX 4." *Vetus Testamentum* 48 (1998): 264–65.

———. "Proverbs 30,4 and Ugaritic *ḥpn*, 'Garment.'" *Catholic Biblical Quarterly* 32 (1970): 418–20.

Clements, R. E. "The Good Neighbor in the Book of Proverbs." In *Of Prophets' Visions and the Wisdom of Sages*, edited by H. A. McKay and D. J. A. Clines, 209–28. Journal for the Study of the Old Testament: Supplement Series 162. Sheffield: JSOT Press, 1993.

Clifford, R. J. *Proverbs*. Old Testament Library. Louisville: Westminster/John Knox, 1999.

———. "Proverbs IX: A Suggested Ugaritic Parallel." *Vetus Testamentum* 25 (1975): 298–306.

———. "Woman Wisdom in the Book of Proverbs." In *Biblische Theologie und gesellschaftlicher Wandel*, edited by G. Braulik et al., 269–86. Freiburg: Herder, 1993.

Cody, A. "Notes on Proverbs 22,21 and 22,23b." *Biblica* 61 (1980): 418–26.

Cohen, A. *Proverbs*. Soncino Books of the Bible. London: Soncino, 1952.

Cohen, J. M. "An Unrecognized Connotation of *nšq peh* with Special Reference to Three Biblical Occurrences." *Vetus Testamentum* 32 (1982): 416–24.

Collins, J. J. "Proverbial Wisdom and the Yahwist Vision." *Semeia* 17 (1980): 1–17.

Cook, J. "The Dating of Septuagint Proverbs." *Ephemerides theologicae lovanienses* 69 (1993): 383–99.

———. "*ʾIshâ zārâ* (Proverbs 1–9 Septuagint): A Metaphor for Foreign Wisdom?" *Zeitschrift für die alttestamentliche Wissenschaft* 106 (1994): 548–76.

———. "The Law of Moses in Septuagint Proverbs." *Vetus Testamentum* 49 (1999): 448–61.

———. *The Septuagint of Proverbs: Jewish and/or Hellenistic Proverbs? Concerning the Hellenistic Colouring of LXX Proverbs*. Supplements to Vetus Testamentum 69. Leiden: Brill, 1997.

Cory, C. "Wisdom's Rescue: A New Reading of the Tabernacles Discourse (John 7:1–8:59)." *Journal of Biblical Literature* 116 (1997): 95–116.

Cox, D. "Fear or Conscience? *Yirʾat* YHWH in Proverbs 1–9." *Studia hierosolymitana* 3 (1982): 83–90.

———. *Proverbs with an Introduction to Sapiential Books*. Old Testament Message 17. Wilmington, DE: Michael Glazier, 1982.

Crenshaw, J. L. "The Acquisition of Knowledge in Israelite Wisdom Literature." *Word and World* 7 (1987): 245–52.

———. "The Concept of God in Old Testament Wisdom." In *In Search of Wisdom: Essays in Memory of John G. Gammie*, edited by L. G. Perdue et al., 1–18. Louisville: Westminster/John Knox, 1993.

———. "Education in Ancient Israel." *Journal of Biblical Literature* 104 (1985): 601–15.

———. "Impossible Questions, Sayings, and Tasks." *Semeia* 17 (1980): 19–34.

———. "'In Search of Divine Presence': Some Remarks Preliminary to a Theology of Wisdom." *Review and Expositor* 74 (1977): 353–69.

———. "Method in Determining Wisdom Influence upon 'Historical Literature.'" *Journal of Biblical Literature* 88 (1969): 129–42.

———. *Old Testament Wisdom*. Atlanta: John Knox, 1981.

———. "The Sage in Proverbs." In *The Sage in Israel and the Ancient Near East,* edited by J. G. Gammie and L. G. Perdue, 205–16. Winona Lake, IN: Eisenbrauns, 1990.

———. "Wisdom." In *Old Testament Form Criticism,* edited by J. H. Hayes. San Antonio: Trinity University Press, 1974.

———. "Wisdom and Authority: Sapiential Rhetoric and Its Warrants." In *Congress Volume: Vienna 1980,* 10–29. Supplements to Vetus Testamentum 32. Leiden: Brill, 1981.

———. "Wisdom Literature: Retrospect and Prospect." In *Of Prophets' Visions and the Wisdom of Sages,* edited by H. A. McKay and K. J. A. Clines, 160–87. Journal for the Study of the Old Testament: Supplement Series 162. Sheffield: JSOT Press, 1993.

Curtis, E. M. "Old Testament Wisdom: A Model for Faith-Learning Integration." *Christian Scholar's Review* 15 (1986): 213–27.

Dahood, M. J. "The Hapax *ḥārak* in Proverbs 12,27." *Biblica* 63 (1982): 60–62.

———. "Honey That Drips: Notes on Proverbs 5,2–3." *Biblica* 54 (1973): 65–66.

———. "Immortality in Proverbs 12,28." *Biblica* 41 (1960): 176–81.

———. *Proverbs and Northwest Semitic Philology*. Rome: Pontifical Biblical Institute, 1963.

———. "Proverbs 8,22–31." *Catholic Biblical Quarterly* 30 (1968): 512–21.

Davidson, R. *Wisdom and Worship*. London: SCM, 1990.

Davies, E. W. "The Meaning of *qesem* in Prv 16,10." *Biblica* 61 (1980): 554–56.

Day, J., R. P. Gordon, and H. G. M. Williamson, eds. *Wisdom in Ancient Israel: Essays in Honour of J. A. Emerton*. Cambridge: Cambridge University Press, 1995.

Delitzsch, R. *The Book of Proverbs*. Commentary on the Old Testament. 1872. Reprint, Grand Rapids: Eerdmans, 1971.

Dell, K. J. "The Use of Animal Imagery in the Psalms and Wisdom Literature of Ancient Israel." *Scottish Journal of Theology* 53 (2000): 275–91.

Dillistone, F. W. "Wisdom, Word, and Spirit: Revelation in the Wisdom Literature." *Interpretation* 2 (1948): 275–87.

Donald, T. "The Semantic Field of Rich and Poor in the Wisdom Literature of Hebrew and Accadian." *Oriens antiquus* 2 (1964): 27–41.

Driver, G. R. "Problems in 'Proverbs.'" *Zeitschrift für die alttestamentliche Wissenschaft* 9 (1932): 141–48.

———. "Problems in the Hebrew Text of Proverbs." *Biblica* 32 (1951): 173–97.

Duty, R. W., "Creation, History, and the Ethics of the Book of Proverbs." *Word and World* 7 (1987): 261–71.

Eaton, J. *The Contemplative Face of Old Testament Wisdom*. London: SCM, 1989.

———. "Memory and Encounter: An Educational Ideal." In *Of Prophets' Visions and the Wisdom of Sages: Essays in Honour of R. Norman Whybray on His Seventieth Birthday,* edited by H. A. McKay and D. J. A. Clines, 179–91. Journal for the Study of the Old Testament: Supplement Series 162. Sheffield: JSOT Press, 1993.

Emerton, J. A. "The Interpretation of Proverbs 21,28." *Zeitschrift für die alttestamentliche Wissenschaft* 100 (1988): 161–70.

———. "A Note on Proverbs 2:18." *Journal of Theological Studies* 30 (1979): 153–58.

———. "A Note on Proverbs xii.26." *Zeitschrift für die alttestamentliche Wissenschaft* 76 (1964): 191–93.

———. "The Teaching of Amenemope and Proverbs xxii 17–xxiv 22: Further Reflections on a Long-Standing Problem." *Vetus Testamentum* 41 (2001): 431–65.

———. "Wisdom." In *Tradition and Interpretation,* edited by G. W. Anderson, 214–37. Oxford: Oxford University Press, 1979.

Enns, P. *Exodus Retold: Ancient Exegesis of the Departure from Egypt in Wis 10:15–21 and 19:1–9.* Harvard Semitic Monographs 57. Atlanta: Scholars Press, 1997.

Erman, A. *Eine ägyptische Quelle der "Sprüche Salomos."* Pages 86–93, and tables 6 and 7. Sitzungsberichte der Preussischen Akademie der Wissenschafte, philosophisch-historischen Klasse 15. Berlin, 1924.

———. "Weisheitsbuch des Amen-em-ope." *Orientalistische Literaturzeitung* 27 (1924): 241–52.

Eshel, H. "6Q30, a Cursive Šîn, and Proverbs 11." *Journal of Biblical Literature* 122 (2003): 544–46.

Estes, D. J. *Hear, My Son: Teaching and Learning in Proverbs 1–9.* Grand Rapids: Baker, 1998.

Farmer, K. A. *Who Knows What Is Good? A Commentary on the Books of Proverbs and Ecclesiastes.* International Theological Commentary. Grand Rapids: Eerdmans, 1991.

Fensham, F. C. "Widow, Orphan and the Poor in the Ancient Near Eastern Legal and Wisdom Literature." *Journal of Near Eastern Studies* 21 (1962): 129–39.

Fontaine, C. R. "Brightening Up the Mindworks: Concepts of Instruction in Biblical Wisdom and Rinzai Zen." *Religious Education* 79 (1984): 590–600.

———. "Proverb Performance in the Hebrew Bible." *Journal for the Study of the Old Testament* 32 (1985): 87–103.

———. *Traditional Sayings in the Old Testament.* Sheffield: Almond Press, 1982.

———. "Wisdom in Proverbs." In *In Search of Wisdom: Essays in Memory of John G. Gammie,* edited by L. G. Perdue et al., 99–114. Louisville: John Knox/Westminster, 1993.

Foster, B. *Before the Muses: An Anthology of Akkadian Literature.* 2 vols. Bethesda, MD: CDL, 1993.

Fox, M. V. "ʾĀmôn Again." *Journal of Biblical Literature* 115 (1996): 699–702.

———. "Aspects of the Religion of the Book of Proverbs." *Hebrew Union College Annual* 39 (1968): 55–69.

———. "Egyptian Onomastica and Biblical Wisdom." *Vetus Testamentum* 36 (1986): 302–10.

———. "Ideas of Wisdom in Proverbs 1–9." *Journal of Biblical Literature* 116 (1997): 613–33.

———. "The Pedagogy of Proverbs 2." *Journal of Biblical Literature* 113 (1994): 233–43.

———. *Proverbs 1–9.* Anchor Bible. Garden City, NY: Doubleday, 2000.

———. Review of K. M. Heim, *Like Grapes of Gold Set in Silver: An Interpretation of Proverbial Clusters in Proverbs 10:1–22:16. Hebrew Studies* 44 (2003): 267–72.

———. "Wisdom in the Joseph Story." *Vetus Testamentum* 41 (2001): 26–41.

———. "Words for Wisdom." *Zeitschrift für Althebräistik* 6 (1993): 149–69.

Franklyn, P. "The Sayings of Agur in Proverbs 30: Piety or Scepticism?" *Zeitschrift für die alttestamentliche Wissenschaft* 95 (1983): 238–52.

Franzmann, M. "The Wheel in Proverbs xx 26 and Ode of Solomon xxiii 11–16." *Vetus Testamentum* 41 (1991): 121–22.

Frydrych, T. *Living under the Sun: Examination of Proverbs and Qohelet.* Supplements to Vetus Testamentum 90. Leiden: Brill, 2002.

Gammie, J. G., and L. G. Perdue, eds. *The Sage in Israel and the Ancient Near East*. Winona Lake, IN: Eisenbrauns, 1990.

Garrett, D. A. *Proverbs, Ecclesiastes, Song of Songs*. New American Commentary 14. Nashville: Broadman, 1993.

———. "Votive Prostitution Again: A Comparison of Proverbs 7:13–14 and 21:28–29." *Journal of Biblical Literature* 109 (1990): 681–82.

Gemser, B. "The Spiritual Structure of Biblical Aphoristic Literature." In *Adhuc Loquitur: Collected Essays of Dr. B. Gremser*, edited by A. van Selms and A. S. van der Woude, 138–49. Pretoria Oriental Series 7. Leiden: Brill, 1968. Reprint, in *Studies in Ancient Israelite Wisdom*, edited by J. L. Crenshaw, 208–19. New York: Ktav, 1976.

Gerleman, G. "The Septuagint Proverbs as a Hellenistic Document." *Old Testament Studies* 8 (1950): 15–27.

Giese, R. L., Jr. "Compassion for the Lowly in Septuagint Proverbs." *Journal for the Study of the Pseudepigrapha* 11 (1993): 34–43.

———. "Qualifying Wealth in the Septuagint of Proverbs." *Journal of Biblical Literature* 111 (1992): 409–25.

———. "Strength through Wisdom and the Bee in LXX—Prov 6,8a–c." *Biblica* 73 (1992): 404–11.

Gladson, J. A. "Retributive Paradoxes in Proverbs 10–29." Ph.D. diss., Vanderbilt University. Ann Arbor, MI: University Microfilms, 1978.

Goldingay, J. E. "The Arrangement of Sayings in Proverbs 10–15." *Journal for the Study of the Old Testament* 61 (1994): 75–83.

———. "The 'Salvation History' Perspective and the 'Wisdom Perspective' within the Context of Biblical Theology." *Evangelical Quarterly* 51 (1979): 194–207.

Golka, F. "Die israelitische Weisheitsschule oder 'des Kaisers neue Kleider.'" *Vetus Testamentum* 33 (1983): 257–71.

———. *The Leopard's Spots: Biblical and African Wisdom in Proverbs*. Edinburgh: Clark, 1993.

Gordon, E. I. *Sumerian Proverbs: Glimpses of Everyday Life in Ancient Mesopotamia*. Philadelphia: University Museum, 1959.

Greenfield, J. C. "The Wisdom of Ahiqar." In *Wisdom in Ancient Israel*, edited by J. Day et al., 3–53. Cambridge: Cambridge University Press, 1994.

Gressmann, H. "Die neugefundene Lehre des Amen-em-ope und die vorexilische Spruchdichtung Israels." *Zeitschrift für die alttestamentliche Wissenschaft* 42 (1924): 272–96.

Habel, N. C. "The Symbolism of Wisdom in Proverbs 1–9." *Interpretation* 26 (1972): 131–57.

Hadley, J. M. "Wisdom and the Goddess." In *Wisdom in Ancient Israel*, edited by J. Day et al., 234–43. Cambridge: Cambridge University Press, 1995.

Hallo, W. W., ed. *The Context of Scripture*. 3 vols. Leiden: Brill, 1997–2002.

Harland, P.-J. "*Bṣᶜ*: Bribe, Extortion or Profit?" *Vetus Testamentum* 50 (2000): 310–20.

Harris, S. L. "'Figure' and 'Riddle': Prov 1:8–19 and Inner-biblical Interpretation," *Biblical Research* 41 (1996): 58–76.

———. "Proverbs 1:8–19, 20–33 as 'Introduction.'" *Revue biblique* 107 (2000): 205–31.

Healey, J. F. "Models of Behavior: Matt 6:26 (//Luke 12:24) and Proverbs 6:6–8." *Journal of Biblical Literature* 108 (1989): 497–98.

———, trans. *Targum of Proverbs*. Aramaic Bible 15. Collegeville, MN: Liturgical Press, 1991.

Heim, K. M. *Like Grapes of Gold Set in Silver: An Interpretation of Proverbial Clusters in Proverbs 10:1–22:16*. Berlin: de Gruyter, 2001.

Hensell, E. "The 'Proverbial' in Proverbs." *The Bible Today* 19 (1981): 162–67.

Hermisson, H.-J. "Observations on the Creation Theology in Wisdom." In *Creation in the Old Testament*, edited by B. W. Anderson, 118–34. Philadelphia: Fortress, 1984.

———. *Studien zur israelitischen Spruchweisheit*. Wissenschaftliche Monographien zum Alten und Neuen Testament 28. Neukirchen-Vluyn: Neukirchener Verlag, 1968.

Hildebrandt, T. "Motivation and Antithetic Parallelism in Proverbs 10–15." *Journal of the Evangelical Theological Society* (1992): 433–44.

———. "Proverbial Pairs: Compositional Units in Proverbs 10–29." *Journal of Biblical Literature* 107 (1988): 207–24.

———. "Proverbs 22:6a: Train Up a Child?" *Grace Theological Journal* 9 (1988): 3–19.

Hoglund, K. G. "The Fool and the Wise in Dialogue." In *The Listening Heart: Essays in Wisdom and the Psalms in Honor of Roland E. Murphy, O. Carm.*, edited by K. G. Hoglund et al., 161–87. Journal for the Study of the Old Testament: Supplement Series 58. Sheffield: Sheffield Academic Press, 1987.

Horsley, R. A. "Wisdom of Word and Words of Wisdom in Corinth." *Catholic Biblical Quarterly* 39 (1977): 224–39.

Hubbard, D. A. *Proverbs*. Communicator's Commentary Series: Old Testament. Dallas: Word, 1989.

———. "The Wisdom Movement and Israel's Covenant Faith." *Tyndale Bulletin* 17 (1966): 3–33.

Hugenberger, G. P. *Marriage as a Covenant: Biblical Law and Ethics as Developed from Malachi*. Grand Rapids: Baker, 1998.

Hurowitz, V. "Nursling, Advisor, Architect? *ʾMwn* and the Role of Wisdom in Proverbs 8:22–31." *Biblica* 80 (1999): 391–400.

———. "An Often Overlooked Alphabetic Acrostic in Proverbs 24:1–22." *Revue biblique* 107 (2000): 526–40.

———. "The Seventh Pillar—Reconsidering the Literary Structure and Unity of Proverbs 31." *Zeitschrift für die alttestamentliche Wissenschaft* 113 (2001): 209–18.

———. "Two Terms for Wealth in Proverbs VIII in Light of Akkadian." *Vetus Testamentum* 50 (2000): 252–57.

Irwin, W. A. "Where Shall Wisdom Be Found?" *Journal of Biblical Literature* 80 (1961): 133–42.

Irwin, W. H. "The Metaphor in Prov 11,30." *Biblica* 65 (1984): 97–100.

Jenks, A. W. "Theological Presuppositions of Israel's Wisdom Literature." *Horizons in Biblical Theology* 7 (1985): 43–75.

Jirku, A. "Das n. pr. Lemuʾel (Prov 31:1) und der Gott Lim." *Zeitschrift für die alttestamentliche Wissenschaft* 66 (1954): 151.

Johnson, J. E. "An Analysis of Proverbs 1:1–7." *Bibliotheca sacra* 144 (1987): 419–32.

Johnston, P. S. *Shades of Sheol: Death and the Afterlife in the Old Testament*. Downers Grove, IL: InterVarsity, 2002.

Jones, S. C. "Wisdom's Pedagogy: A Comparison of Proverbs VII and 4Q184." *Vetus Testamentum* 53 (2003): 65–80.

Kaiser, W. C., Jr. "True Marital Love in Proverbs 5:15–23 and the Interpretation of the Song of Songs." In *The Way of Wisdom: Essays in Honor of Bruce K. Waltke*, edited by J. I. Packer and S. K. Soderlund, 106–16. Grand Rapids: Zondervan, 2000.

Kassis, R. A. *The Book of Proverbs and Arabic Proverbial Works*. Supplements to Vetus Testamentum 74. Leiden: Brill, 1999.

———. "A Note on *šālāl* (Prov. XXXI 11b)." *Vetus Testamentum* 50 (2000): 258–59.

Kayatz, C. *Studien zu Proverbien 1–9*. Neukirchen-Vluyn: Neukirchener Verlag, 1966.

Kidner, D. *The Proverbs*. Tyndale Old Testament Commentaries. Leicester, UK: Inter-Varsity; Downers Grove, IL: InterVarsity, 1984.

———. *The Wisdom of Proverbs, Job and Ecclesiastes*. Downers Grove, IL: InterVarsity, 1985.

Kirschenblatt-Gimblett, B. "Toward a Theory of Proverb Meaning." *Proverbium* 22 (1973): 821–27.

Kitchen, K. A. "Proverbs and Wisdom Books of the Ancient Near East." *Tyndale Bulletin* 28 (1977): 69–114.

Kobert, R. "Zu Prov 23,1–2." *Biblica* 63 (1982): 264–65.

Koptak, P. E. *Proverbs*. NIV Application Commentary. Grand Rapids: Zondervan, 2003.

Kovacs, B. W. "Is There a Class-Ethic in Proverbs?" In *Essays in Old Testament Ethics*, edited by J. L. Crenshaw and J. T. Willis, 171–89. New York: Ktav, 1974.

———. "Sociological-Structural Constraints upon Wisdom: The Spatial and Temporal Matrix of Proverbs 15:28–22:16." Ph.D. diss., Vanderbilt University. Ann Arbor, MI: University Microfilms, 1978.

Krispenz, J. *Spruchkompositionen im Buch Proverbia*. Frankfurt: Lang, 1989.

Kruger, T. "Komposition und Diskussion in Proverbia 10." *Zeitschrift für Theologie und Kirche* 92 (1995): 413–33.

Kugel, J. *The Idea of Biblical Poetry*. London: Longman Group, 1969; reissued, New Haven: Yale University Press, 1981.

Lambert, W. G. *Babylonian Wisdom Literature*. Oxford: Clarendon, 1960.

Lamp, J. S. "Wisdom in Col 1:15–20: Contributions and Significance." *Journal of the Evangelical Theological Society* 41 (1998): 45–54.

Lang, B. *Wisdom and the Book of Proverbs: An Israelite Goddess Redefined*. New York: Pilgrim, 1986.

Lemaire, A. "The Sage in School and Temple." In *The Sage in Israel and the Ancient Near East*, edited by J. G. Gammie and L. G. Perdue, 165–83. Winona Lake, IN: Eisenbrauns, 1990.

———. "Sagesse et écoles." *Vetus Testamentum* 34 (1984): 270–81.

Lichtenstein, M. H. "Chiasm and Symmetry in Proverbs 31." *Catholic Biblical Quarterly* 44 (1982): 202–11.

Lichtheim, M. *Ancient Egyptian Literature: A Book of Readings*. 3 vols. Berkeley: University of California Press, 1973–80.

———. *Late Egyptian Wisdom Literature in the International Context: A Study of Demotic Instructions*. Freiburg: Universitätsverlag; Göttingen: Vandenhoeck & Ruprecht, 1984.

———. *Maat in Egyptian Autobiographies and Related Studies*. Freiburg: Universitätsverlag; Göttingen: Vandenhoeck & Ruprecht, 1992.

Lindenberger, J. M. *The Aramaic Proverbs of Ahiqar*. Baltimore: Johns Hopkins University Press, 1983.

Loader, J. A. "Wisdom by (the) People for (the) People." *Zeitschrift für die alttestamentliche Wissenschaft* 111 (1999): 211–33.

Longman, T., III. *Ecclesiastes*. New International Commentary on the Old Testament. Grand Rapids: Eerdmans, 1997.

———. *How to Read Proverbs*. Downers Grove, IL: InterVarsity, 2002.

———. *How to Read the Psalms*. Downers Grove, IL: InterVarsity, 1988.

———. *Song of Songs*. New International Commentary on the Old Testament. Grand Rapids: Eerdmans, 2001.

Lyons, E. L. "A Note on Proverbs 31.10–31." In *The Listening Heart: Essays in Wisdom and the Psalms in Honor of Roland E. Murphy, O. Carm.*, edited by K. G. Hoglund et al., 237–45. Journal for the Study of the Old Testament: Supplement Series 58. Sheffield: Sheffield Academic Press, 1987.

Macintosh, A. A. "A Note on Proverbs xxv 27." *Vetus Testamentum* 20 (1970): 112–15.

Mack, B. L. "Wisdom Myth and Mythology: An Essay in Understanding a Theological Tradition." *Interpretation* 24 (1970): 46–60.

Maier, C. "Conflicting Attractions: Parental Wisdom and the 'Strange Woman' in Proverbs 1–9." In *Wisdom and Psalms*, edited by A. Brenner and C. R. Fontaine, 92–108. Feminist Companion to the Bible 2/2. Sheffield: Sheffield Academic Press, 1998.

Malchow, B. V. "A Manual for Future Monarchs." *Catholic Biblical Quarterly* 47 (1985): 238–45.

———. "Social Justice in the Wisdom Literature." *Biblical Theology Bulletin* 12 (1982): 120–24.

Malul, M. "*Kappî* (Ex 33,22) and *běhopnāw* (Prov 30,4): Hand or Skirt?" *Zeitschrift für die alttestamentliche Wissenschaft* 109 (1977): 356–68.

Matlack, H. "The Play of Wisdom." *Currents in Theology and Mission* 15 (1988): 425–30.

McCreesh, T. P. *Biblical Sound and Sense: Poetic Sound Patterns in Proverbs 10–29*. Sheffield: Sheffield Academic Press, 1991.

———. "Wisdom as Wife: Proverbs 31:10–31." *Revue biblique* 92 (1985): 25–46.

McKane, W. "Functions of Language and Objectives of Discourse according to Proverbs 10–30." In *La sagesse de l'Ancien Testament*, edited by M. Gilbert, 166–85. Bibliotheca ephemeridum theologicarum lovaniensium 51. Gembloux: Duculot, 1979.

———. *Proverbs: A New Approach*. Old Testament Library. Philadelphia: Westminster, 1970.

McKenzie, J. L. "Reflections on Wisdom." *Journal of Biblical Literature* 86 (1967): 1–9.

McKinlay, J. E. *Gendering Wisdom the Host: Biblical Invitations to Eat and Drink*. Sheffield: Sheffield Academic Press, 1996.

———. "To Eat or Not to Eat: Where Is Wisdom in This Choice?" In *Food and Drink in the Biblical Worlds*. Semeia 86 (1999): 73–84.

Meinhold, A. *Die Sprüche*. 2 vols. Zürcher Bibelkommentare: AT. Zurich: Theologischer Verlag, 1991.

Melchert, C. F. "Creation and Justice among the Sages." *Religious Education* 85 (1990): 368–81.

———. "Wisdom Is Vindicated by Her Deeds." *Religious Education* 87 (1992): 127–51.

Michel, D. "Proverbia 2—eine Dokument der Geschichte der Weisheit." In *Alttestamentlicher Glaube und biblische Theologie: Festschrift für Horst Dietrich Preuss*, edited by J. Hausmann et al., 233–43. Stuttgart: Kohlhammer, 1992.

Mieder, W. "The Essence of Literature Proverbs Study." *Proverbium* 23 (1974): 888–94.

———. *Proverbs Are Never out of Season: Popular Wisdom in the Modern Age*. New York: Oxford University Press, 1993.

Miller, J. W. *Proverbs*. Believers Church Bible Commentary. Scottdale, PA: Herald Press, 2004.

Montgomery, D. J. "'A Bribe Is a Charm': A Study of Proverbs 17:8." In *The Way of Wisdom: Essays in Honor of Bruce K. Waltke*, edited by J. I. Packer and S. K. Soderlund, 134–49. Grand Rapids: Zondervan, 2000.

Moore, R. D. "A Home for the Alien: Worldly Wisdom and Covenantal Confession in Proverbs 30,1–9." *Zeitschrift für die alttestamentliche Wissenschaft* 106 (1994): 96–107.

Morgan, D. F. "Searching for Biblical Wisdom." *Sewanee Theological Review* 37 (1994): 151–62.

Moss, A. "Wisdom as Parental Teaching in Prov 1–9." *Heythrop Journal* 38 (1997): 426–39.

Mouser, W. E. *Walking in Wisdom: Studying the Proverbs of Solomon.* Downers Grove, IL: InterVarsity, 1983.

Muller, A. *Proverbien 1–9: Der Weisheit neue Kleider.* Beihefte zur Zeitschrift für die alttestamentliche Wissenschaft 291. Berlin: de Gruyter, 2000.

Murphy, R. E. "A Brief Note on Translating Proverbs." *Catholic Biblical Quarterly* 60 (1998): 621–25.

———. "Can the Book of Proverbs Be a Player in 'Biblical Theology'?" *Biblical Theology Bulletin* 31 (2001): 4–9.

———. "The Hebrew Sage and Openness to the World." In *Christian Action and Openness to the World,* edited by J. Papin, 219–44. Villanova, PA: Villanova University Press, 1970.

———. "Hebrew Wisdom." *Journal of the American Oriental Society* 101 (1981): 21–34.

———. "The Interpretation of Old Testament Wisdom." *Interpretation* 23 (1969): 289–301.

———. "Israel's Wisdom: A Biblical Model of Salvation." *Studia missionalia* 30 (1981): 1–43.

———. "The Kerygma of the Book of Proverbs." *Interpretation* 20 (1966): 3–14.

———. *Proverbs.* Word Biblical Commentary. Dallas: Word, 1998.

———. "Religious Dimensions of Israelite Literature." In *Ancient Israelite Religion: Essays in Honor of Frank Moore Cross,* edited by P. D. Miller Jr., P. D. Hanson, and S. D. McBride, 449–58. Philadelphia: Fortress, 1987.

———. "The Theological Contributions of Israel's Wisdom Literature." *Listening* 19 (1984): 30–40.

———. *The Tree of Life.* Garden City, NY: Doubleday, 1990.

———. "Wisdom and Creation." *Journal of Biblical Literature* 104 (1985): 3–11.

———. "Wisdom and Eros in Proverbs 1–9." *Catholic Biblical Quarterly* 50 (1988): 600–603.

———. *Wisdom Literature: Job, Proverbs, Ruth, Chronicles, Ecclesiastes, and Esther.* Forms of the Old Testament Literature. Grand Rapids: Eerdmans, 1981.

———. *Wisdom Literature and Psalms.* Nashville: Abingdon, 1983.

———. "Wisdom's Song: Proverbs 1:20–33." *Catholic Biblical Quarterly* 48 (1986): 456–60.

———. "Wisdom Theses." In *Wisdom and Knowledge,* edited by J. Armenti, 187–200. Villanova, PA: Villanova University Press, 1976.

———. "Wisdom—Theses and Hypotheses." In *Israelite Wisdom: Theological and Literary Essays in Honor of Samuel Terrien,* edited by J. G. Gammie et al., 35–42. Missoula, MT: Scholars Press, 1978.

Murphy, R. E., and E. Huweiler. *Proverbs, Ecclesiastes, Song of Songs.* New International Biblical Commentary on the Old Testament. Peabody, MA: Hendrickson, 1999.

Nel, P. J. "Authority in the Wisdom Admonitions." *Zeitschrift für die alttestamentliche Wissenschaft* 93 (1981): 418–26.

———. "The Genres of Biblical Wisdom Literature." *Journal of Northwest Semitic Languages* 9 (1981): 129–42.

———. "A Proposed Method for Determining the Context of the Wisdom Admonitions." *Journal of Northwest Semitic Languages* 6 (1978): 33–40.

———. *The Structure and Ethos of the Wisdom Admonitions in Proverbs.* Berlin: de Gruyter, 1982.

Newsom, C. "Woman and the Discourse of Patriarchal Wisdom: A Study of Proverbs 1–9." In *Gender and Difference,* edited by P. L. Day, 146–49. Minneapolis: Fortress, 1989.

North, F. S. "The Four Insatiables." *Vetus Testamentum* 15 (1965): 281–82.

Noth, M., and D. W. Thomas, eds. *Wisdom in Israel and in the Ancient Near East: Presented to Professor Harold Henry Rowley by the Society for Old Testament Study in Association with the Editorial Board of Vetus Testamentum, in Celebration of His Sixty-fifth Birthday, 24 March 1955*. Supplements to Vetus Testamentum 3. Leiden: Brill, 1955.

O'Connell, R. H. "Proverbs VII 16–17: A Case of Fatal Deception in a 'Woman and the Window' Type–Scene." *Vetus Testamentum* 41 (1991): 235–41.

Oesterley, W. O. E. *The Book of Proverbs*. London: Methuen, 1929.

———. "The 'Teaching of Amen-em-ope' and the Old Testament." *Zeitschrift für die alttestamentliche Wissenschaft* 4 (1927): 9–24.

Olivier, J. P. J. "Schools and Wisdom Literature." *Journal of Northwest Semitic Languages* 4 (1975): 49–60.

Overland, P. "Did the Sage Draw from the Shema? A Study of Proverbs 3:1–12." *Catholic Biblical Quarterly* 62 (2000): 424–40.

Pardee, D. *Ugaritic and Hebrew Poetic Parallelism: A Trial Cut (ʾnt I and Proverbs 2)*. Supplements to Vetus Testamentum 39. Leiden: Brill, 1988.

Parker, S. B. "The Literatures of Canaan, Ancient Israel, and Phoenicia: An Overview." In *Civilizations of the Ancient Near East*, edited by J. M. Sasson, 4:2399–2410. New York: Charles Scribner's Sons, 1995.

Peels, H. G. L. "Passion or Justice? The Interpretation of *beyom naqam* in Proverbs vi 34." *Vetus Testamentum* 44 (1994): 270–74.

Perdue, L. G. "Liminality as a Social Setting for Wisdom Instructions." *Zeitschrift für die alttestamentliche Wissenschaft* 93 (1981): 114–26.

———. *Proverbs*. Interpretation. Louisville: John Knox, 2000.

———. *Wisdom and Creation*. Nashville: Abingdon, 1994.

———. *Wisdom and Cult*. Society of Biblical Literature Dissertation Series 30. Missoula, MT: Scholars Press, 1977.

Perry, S. C. *Structural Patterns in Proverbs 10:1–22:6: A Study in Biblical Hebrew Stylistics*. Ann Arbor, MI: University Microfilms, 1988.

Plaut, W. G. *The Book of Proverbs*. New York: Union of American Hebrew Congregations, 1961.

Pleins, J. D. "Poverty in the Social World of the Wise." *Journal for the Study of the Old Testament* 37 (1987): 61–78.

Ploger, O. "Zur Auslegung der Sentenzensammlung des Proverbienbuches." In *Probleme biblischer Theologie: Gerhard von Rad zum 70. Geburtstag*, ed. H. W. Wolff, 402–16. Munich: Kaiser, 1971.

Polk, T. "Paradigms, Parables, and *Mĕšālîm*: On Reading the *Māšāl* in Scripture." *Catholic Biblical Quarterly* 45 (1983): 564–83.

Quack, J. F. *Die Lehren des Ani: Ein neuägyptischer Weisheitstext in seinem kulturellen Umfeld*. Freiburg: Universitätsverlag; Göttingen: Vandenhoeck & Ruprecht, 1994.

Rad, G. von. *Wisdom in Israel*. Translated by James D. Marton. Nashville: Abingdon, 1972.

Ray, J. D. "Egyptian Wisdom Literature." In *Wisdom in Ancient Israel: Essays in Honour of J. A. Emerton*, edited by J. Day et al., 17–29. Cambridge: Cambridge University Press, 1995.

Rendsberg, G. A. "Bilingual Wordplay in the Bible." *Vetus Testamentum* 38 (1988): 354–57.

Richter, H.-F. "Hielt Agur sich für den Dummsten aller Menschen? (Zu Prov 30,1–4)." *Zeitschrift für die alttestamentliche Wissenschaft* 113 (2001): 419–22.

Rogers, C. L. "The Meaning and Significance of the Hebrew Word ʾāmôn in Proverbs 8:30." *Zeitschrift für die alttestamentliche Wissenschaft* 109 (1997): 208–21.

Romheld, D. *Wege der Weisheit: Die Lehren Amenemopes und Proverbien 22,17–24,22*. Beihefte zur Zeitschrift für die alttestamentliche Wissenschaft 184. Berlin: de Gruyter, 1989.

Ross, A. P. "Proverbs." In *The Expositor's Bible Commentary*, edited by F. E. Gaebelein, 5:881–1134. Grand Rapids: Zondervan, 1991.

Ruffle, J. "The Teaching of Amenemope and Its Connection with the Book of Proverbs." *Tyndale Bulletin* 28 (1977): 29–68.

Rylaarsdam, J. C. *The Proverbs, Ecclesiastes, the Song of Songs*. Richmond: John Knox, 1964.

Scherer, A. "Is the Selfish Man Wise? Considerations of Context in Proverbs 10.1–22.16 with Special Regard to Surety, Bribery and Friendship." *Journal for the Study of the Old Testament* 76 (1997): 59–70.

———. *Das weise Wort und seine Wirkung: Eine Untersuchung zur Komposition und Redaktion von Proverbia 10,1–22,16*. Neukirchen-Vluyn: Neukirchener Verlag, 1999.

Schnabel, E. J. *Law and Wisdom from Ben Sira to Paul*. Wissenschaftliche Untersuchungen zum Neuen Testament 2.16. Tubingen: Mohr Siebeck, 1985.

Scobie, C. H. H. "The Place of Wisdom in Biblical Thinking." *Biblical Theology Bulletin* 14 (1984): 43–48.

Scoralick, R. *Einzelspruch und Sammlung: Komposition im Buch der Sprichwörter Kapitel 10–15*. Beihefte zur Zeitschrift für die alttestamentliche Wissenschaft 232. Berlin: de Gruyter, 1995.

Scott, R. B. Y. "Priesthood, Prophecy, Wisdom, and the Knowledge of God." *Journal of Biblical Literature* 80 (1961): 1–15.

———. *Proverbs, Ecclesiastes*. Garden City, NY: Doubleday, 1965.

———. "Solomon and the Beginnings of Wisdom in Israel." *Vetus Testamentum* 3 (1955): 262–79.

———. "The Study of the Wisdom Literature." *Interpretation* 24 (1970): 20–40.

———. *The Way of Wisdom in the Old Testament*. New York: Macmillan, 1971.

———. "Wisdom in Creation: The ʾāmôn of Proverbs viii 30." *Vetus Testamentum* 10 (1960): 213–23.

———. "Wise and Foolish, Righteous and Wicked." *Vetus Testamentum* 23 (1972): 146–65.

Shupak, N. "The 'Sitz im Leben' of the Book of Proverbs in the Light of a Comparison of Biblical and Egyptian Wisdom Literature." *Revue biblique* 94 (1987): 98–119.

———. *Where Can Wisdom Be Found?* Freiburg: Universitätsverlag; Göttingen: Vandenhoeck & Ruprecht, 1993.

Skehan, P. W. "Proverbs 5:15–19 and 6:20–24." *Catholic Biblical Quarterly* 8 (1946): 290–97.

———. "The Seven Columns of Wisdom's House in Proverbs 1–9." *Catholic Biblical Quarterly* 9 (1947): 190–98.

———. Structures in Poems on Wisdom: Proverbs 8 and Sirach 24." *Catholic Biblical Quarterly* 41 (1979): 365–79.

———. *Studies in Israelite Poetry and Wisdom*. Catholic Biblical Quarterly Monograph Series 1. Washington, DC: Catholic Biblical Association of America, 1971.

Smith, M. *The Early History of God*. 2nd ed. Grand Rapids: Eerdmans, 2001.

Snell, D. C. "The Most Obscure Verse in Proverbs: Proverbs xxvi 10." *Vetus Testamentum* 41 (1991): 350–56.

———. "'Taking Souls' in Proverbs xi 30." *Vetus Testamentum* 33 (1983): 362–65.

———. *Twice-Told Proverbs and the Composition of the Book of Proverbs*. Winona Lake, IN: Eisenbrauns, 1993.

———. "The Wheel in Proverbs xx 26." *Vetus Testamentum* 39 (1989): 503–7.

Stallman, R. C. "Divine Hospitality and Wisdom's Banquet in Proverbs 9:1–6." In *The Way of Wisdom: Essays in Honor of Bruce K. Waltke*, edited by J. I. Packer and S. K. Soderlund, 117–33. Grand Rapids: Zondervan, 2000.

Steinmann, A. "Proverbs 1–9 as a Solomonic Composition." *Journal of the Evangelical Theological Society* 43 (2000): 659–74.

Suter, D. W. "*Māšāl* in the Similitudes of Enoch." *Journal of Biblical Literature* 100 (1981): 193–212.

Thomas, D. W. "*Beliyaʿal* in the Old Testament." In *Biblical and Patristic Studies in Memory of Robert Pierce Casey*, edited by J. N. Birdsall and R. W. Thomson, 11–19. Freiberg: Herder, 1963.

———. "*ʾĒw* in Prov. xxxi 4." *Vetus Testamentum* 12 (1962): 499–500.

———. "Notes on Some Passages in the Book of Proverbs." *Vetus Testamentum* 15 (1965): 271–79.

Toombs, L. E. "Old Testament Theology and the Wisdom Literature." *Journal of Bible and Religion* 23 (1955): 193–96.

———. "The Theology and Ethics of the Book of Proverbs." *Consensus* 14 (1988): 7–24.

Torrey, C. C. "Proverbs, Chapter 30." *Journal of Biblical Literature* 73 (1954): 93–96.

Tov, E. "Recensional Differences between the Masoretic Text and the Septuagint of Proverbs." In *Of Scribes and Scrolls: Studies on the Hebrew Bible, Intertestamental Judaism, and Christian Origins Presented to John Strugnell on the Occasion of His Sixtieth Birthday*, edited by H. W. Attridge, J. J. Collins, and T. H. Tobin, 43–56. College Theology Society Resources in Religion 5. Lanham, MD: University Press of America, 1990.

Toy, C. H. *A Critical and Exegetical Commentary on the Book of Proverbs*. International Critical Commentary. New York: Charles Scribner's Sons, 1902.

Van Leeuwen, R. C. "Building God's House: An Exploration in Wisdom." In *The Way of Wisdom: Essays in Honor of Bruce K. Waltke*, edited by J. I. Packer and S. K. Soderlund, 204–11. Grand Rapids: Zondervan, 2000.

———. "In Praise of Proverbs." In *Pledges of Jubilee: Essays on the Arts and Culture, in Honor of Calvin G. Seerveld*, edited by L. Zuidervaart and H. Luttikhuizen, 308–27. Grand Rapids: Eerdmans, 1995.

———. "Liminality and Worldview in Proverbs 1–9." *Semeia* 50 (1990): 111–44.

———. "Proverbs." In *The New Interpreter's Bible*, edited by L. E. Keck et al., 5:17–264. Nashville: Abingdon, 1997.

———. "Proverbs xxv 27 Once Again." *Vetus Testamentum* 36 (1986): 105–14.

———. "Proverbs 30:21–23 and the Biblical World Upside Down." *Journal of Biblical Literature* 105 (1986): 599–610.

———. "Wealth and Poverty: System and Contradiction in Proverbs." *Hebrew Studies* 33 (1992): 25–36.

Vawter, B. "Prov. 8:22: Wisdom and Creation." *Journal of Biblical Literature* 99 (1980): 205–16.

Waltke, B. K. "The Book of Proverbs and Ancient Wisdom Literature." *Bibliotheca sacra* 136 (1979): 221–38.

———. "The Book of Proverbs and Old Testament Theology." *Bibliotheca sacra* 136 (1979): 302–17.

———. "Does Proverbs Promise Too Much?" *Andrews University Seminary Studies* 34 (1996): 319–36.

———. "How We Got the Hebrew Bible: The Text and Canon of the Old Testament." In *The Bible at Qumran: Text, Shape, and Interpretation,* edited by P. W. Flint, 27–50. Grand Rapids: Eerdmans, 2001.

———. *Proverbs.* 2 vols. New International Commentary on the Old Testament. Grand Rapids: Eerdmans, 2004–5.

Watson, W. G. E. *Classical Hebrew Poetry: A Guide to Its Techniques.* Journal for the Study of the Old Testament: Supplement Series 26. Sheffield: JSOT Press, 1984.

Webb, B. G. *Five Festal Garments: Christian Reflections on the Song of Songs, Ruth, Lamentations, Ecclesiastes, Esther.* New Studies in Biblical Theology 10. Downers Grove, IL: InterVarsity, 2000.

Webster, J. S. "Sophia: Engendering Wisdom in Proverbs, Ben Sira and the Wisdom of Solomon." *Journal for the Study of the Old Testament* 78 (1998): 63–79.

Weeks, S. D. "Wisdom in the Old Testament." In *Where Shall Wisdom Be Found? Wisdom in the Bible, the Church and the Contemporary World,* edited by S. C. Barton, 19–30. Edinburgh: Clark, 1999.

Westermann, C. *Wurzeln der Weisheit: Die ältesten Sprüche Israels und anderer Völker.* Göttingen: Vandenhoeck & Ruprecht, 1990. ET, *Roots of Wisdom.* Louisville: Westminster/John Knox, 1995.

Whybray, R. N. *The Book of Proverbs.* Cambridge: Cambridge University Press, 1972.

———. *The Book of Proverbs: A Survey of Modern Study.* Leiden: Brill, 1995.

———. *The Composition of the Book of Proverbs.* Sheffield: JSOT Press, 1994.

———. *The Intellectual Tradition in the Old Testament.* Berlin: de Gruyter, 1974.

———. *Proverbs.* Grand Rapids: Eerdmans, 1994.

———. "Proverbs viii 22–31 and Its Supposed Prototypes." *Vetus Testamentum* 15 (1965): 504–14.

———. "Some Literary Problems in Proverbs I–IX." *Vetus Testamentum* 16 (1966): 482–96.

———. "The Structure and Composition of Proverbs 22:17–24:22." In *Crossing the Boundaries: Essays in Biblical Interpretation in Honour of Michael D. Goulder,* edited by E. E. Porter et al., 83–96. Leiden: Brill, 1994.

———. *Wealth and Poverty in the Book of Proverbs.* Sheffield: JSOT Press, 1990.

———. *Wisdom in Proverbs: The Concept of Wisdom in Proverbs 1–9.* London: SCM, 1965.

———. "Yahweh-Sayings and Their Contexts in Proverbs 10,1–22,16." In *La sagesse de l'Ancien Testament,* edited by M. Gilbert, 153–65. Bibliotheca ephemeridum theologicarum lovaniensium 51. Gembloux: Duculot, 1979.

Williams, H. H. D., III. *The Wisdom of the Wise: The Presence and Function of Scripture in 1 Cor. 1:18–3:23.* Leiden: Brill, 2001.

Williams, J. G. *Those Who Ponder Proverbs: Aphoristic Thinking and Biblical Literature.* Sheffield: Almond, 1981.

Williams, R. J. "The Sages of Ancient Egypt in the Light of Recent Scholarship." *Journal of the American Oriental Society* 101 (1981): 1–19.

Wilson, F. M. "'Sacred or Profane?' The Yahwistic Redaction of Proverbs Reconsidered." In *The Listening Heart: Essays in Wisdom and the Psalms in Honor of Roland E. Murphy, O. Carm.,* edited by K. G. Hoglund et al., 313–34. Journal for the Study of the Old Testament: Supplement Series 58. Sheffield: Sheffield Academic Press, 1987.

Witherington, B., III. *Jesus the Sage: The Pilgrimage of Wisdom.* Minneapolis: Fortress, 1994.

Wittenberg, G. H. "The Lexical Context of the Terminology for 'Poor' in the Book of Proverbs." *Scriptura: Tydskrif vir bybelkunde* (Stellenbosch) 2 (1986): 40–85.

Wolters, A. "Proverbs xxxi 10–31 as Heroic Hymn: A Form-Critical Analysis." *Vetus Testamentum* 38 (1988): 446–57.

———. *The Song of the Valiant Woman: Studies in the Interpretation of Proverbs 31.10–31*. Carlisle, UK: Paternoster, 2001.

———. "Ṣôpiyyâ (Prov 31:27) as Hymnic Participle and Play on *Sophia*." *Journal of Biblical Literature* 104 (1985): 577–87.

Yee, G. A. "An Analysis of Prov. 8:22–31 according to Style and Structure." *Zeitschrift für die alttestamentliche Wissenschaft* 94 (1980): 48–65.

———. "'I Have Perfumed My Bed with Myrrh': The Foreign Woman (ʾiššâ zārā) in Proverbs 1–9." *Journal for the Study of the Old Testament* 43 (1989): 53–68.

Yoder, C. R. *Wisdom as a Woman of Substance: A Socioeconomic Reading of Proverbs 1–9 and 31:10–31*. Beihefte zur Zeitschrift für die alttestamentliche Wissenschaft 304. Berlin: de Gruyter, 2001.

———. "The Woman of Substance (אשת־חיל): A Socioeconomic Reading of Proverbs 31:10–31." *Journal of Biblical Literature* 122 (2003): 427–47.

Zimmerli, W. "Concerning the Structure of Old Testament Wisdom." In *Studies in Ancient Israelite Wisdom*, edited by J. L. Crenshaw, 175–209. New York: Ktav, 1976.

Zornberg, A. G. *Malbim on Mishley: The Commentary of Rabbi Meir Leibush Malbim on the Book of Proverbs*. Jerusalem: Feldheim, 1982.

Zuck, R. B., ed. *Learning from the Sages: Selected Studies on the Book of Proverbs*. Grand Rapids: Baker, 1995.

Subject Index

Author Index

Index of Scripture and Other Ancient Writings